D0898813

"Whereas Mr. Roger Williams, one of the elders of the church of Salem, hath broached and divulged divers new and dangerous opinions against the authority of magistrates, has also writ letters of defamation, both of the magistrates and churches here, and that before any conviction, and yet maintaineth the same without retraction, it is therefor ordered, that the said Mr. Williams shall depart out of this jurisdiction within six weeks now next ensuing, not to return anymore without license from the Court."

—Decree of Banishment

"Roger Williams's banishment is the point where religious and civil liberty became a vital and aggressive force in American life. His trial opened the floodgates of controversy and turned public opinion in New England from mere theological questions to problems of civil society. Unwittingly the magistrates and ministers by their sentence of banishment gave the death warrant to their own theocracy by making possible the first civil experiment based on liberty of conscience—Providence Plantation."

—James Ernst

"Roger Williams was the most provocative figure thrown upon the Massachusetts shores by the upheaval in England, the one original thinker amongst a number of capable social architects. He was the 'first rebel against the divine church-order established in the wilderness.' But he was very much more than that; he was a rebel against all the stupidities that interposed a barrier betwixt men and the fellowship of their dreams."

—Vernon L. Parrington

"As the panorama of Roger Williams's life unrolls before us in its entirety, its slope and direction are constant. What was the 'root of the matter' with this man? He was a complex personality, plenteous in contradiction. Yet there was in him also a great simplicity, a great selflessness. Personal ambition was almost totally lacking. Honors were dust. Money, time, possessions, influence, position were naught. He saw what he had to do as a simple thing, and he did it simply, without a thought of the consequences to himself.

"Perhaps there is the reason that somehow his individual life seems to lie outside and beyond all that he did. There was something in him more massive than his record can catch, a sense of amplitude and of greatness, out of proportion to any listing of his services to a colony, to a cause, even to a great idea. His victory was by no means final, nor even acknowledged as a victory. The fight for freedom, by any definition, is never won. Nor will it ever be quite lost, as long as there is such a man to personify something in the human spirit that perpetually renews the battle. Over and above the symbol there was a human being, generous, warm-hearted, magnetic; 'a man lovely in his carriage,' as Governor Winslow put it, 'the sweetest soul I ever knew.'"

—Ola Winslow

THE

Complete Writings of
ROGER WILLIAMS

THE
COMPLETE WRITINGS
OF
ROGER
WILLIAMS

VOLUME FIVE

Wipf & Stock
PUBLISHERS
Eugene, Oregon

Wipf and Stock Publishers
199 W 8th Ave, Suite 3
Eugene, OR 97401

The Complete Writings of Roger Williams
By Williams, Roger
ISBN 13: 978-1-55635-607-0
Publication date 2/21/2007
Previously published by Russell & Russell, Inc., 1963

The Complete Writings of Roger Williams

In Seven Volumes

Introduction to the Series

Shortly after the U.S. Civil War, a group of men in Providence, Rhode Island, calling themselves the Narragansett Club, determined to rescue the widely scattered literary remains of Roger Williams. The happy result of their efforts was the publication in six volumes (1866–1870) of the writings of Roger Williams. These gentlemen made no effort to present a modern text, but maintained the original orthography and Williams's extravagant use of italic and parentheses. Fewer than two hundred copies of this set were published.

By the second half of the twentieth century, these volumes were long out of print. Any volumes that happened to turn up were, moreover, prohibitively expensive. Under the stimulus of Harvard's Professor Perry Miller, the decision was made to reprint these six volumes, along with a seventh that would include new material or items that the Narragansett Club chose not to reprint. Volume VII begins with an interpretive essay by Professor Miller who also provided invaluable introductions to each item in this new tome. The publishing house of Russell & Russell in 1963 published four hundred sets of this edition, entitled *The Complete Writings of Roger Williams*.

Now, in the early years of the twenty-first century this edition is likewise exhausted. The firm of Wipf & Stock, recognizing the need to keep Williams in print, has fortunately filled this vacuum. On a separate page in each book, one will find a listing of the contents of each of the seven volumes, and in Volume I a new introduction to the life and works of Roger Williams has been provided.

Edwin S. Gausted

GEORGE FOX

DIGG'D OUT OF HIS BURROWES.

EDITED BY

REV. J. LEWIS DIMAN.

INTRODUCTION.

———o———

ROGER Williams for well nigh a quarter of a century after the publication of *The Bloody Tenent yet more Bloody*, refrained from "ufing the help of printer men." In the year 1676, and when nearing the fober limit of fourfcore, he made his final appearance as a controverfial writer in the Treatife which is here reprinted for the firft time. The circumftances which led him to affume an attitude fo unlike that maintained during the earlier portion of his career, form an interefting epifode in the early hiftory of Rhode Ifland.

At the time when "the People called Quakers,"[1] were excluded by harfh enactments from the other New England Colonies, in Rhode Ifland alone they were received with fympathy and kindnefs. While the fecond party of Quaker miffionaries that had arrived in Maffachufetts were languifhing in Bofton gaol, Samuel Gorton, though dif-

---

[1]This name, which has come by ufage to be the familiar defignation of the followers of George Fox, was firft applied to them in 1650, by Gervace Bennet, a magiftrate of Derby, "who was the firft that called us Quakers, becaufe I bid them tremble at the word of the Lord." *Journal of George Fox*, 3d edit. 1765, p. 35. The explanation given by Williams on page 41, *infra*, Fox in his reply denies, (*A New-England-Fire-Brand Quenched*, Part i: p. 26 ;) repeating the account given in his *Journal*. In the following pages I have ufed, for convenience, a term that has long ceafed to convey reproach.

fering with them in principle not lefs than he differed
with Roger Williams, found the means of conveying to
them the affurance of his Chriftian fympathy. Had his
benevolent projeér been carried out, this little company
would have been the earlieft apoftles of the new faith on
the fhores of the Narraganfett. He propofed, if he could
be informed what time the fhip would fail, "to have a
veffel in readinefs," to take them in, and fet them where
they might enjoy their liberty. In their reply, they ftated
that the mafter of the veffel had been placed under fuch
heavy bonds "to fet them afhore in England," as to render the undertaking hopelefs.[1]

At their annual meeting in September, 1656, the Commiffioners of the United Colonies, refolved to "propofe to
the feveral General Courts, that all Quakers, Ranters, and
other notorious heretics, fhould be prohibited coming into
the United Colonies, and, if any fhould hereafter come or
arife, that they fhould be forthwith fecured, or removed
out of all the jurifdictions."[2] Each of the four confede-
rated colonies enaéted laws in accordance with this recommendation. After an experience of two years rendered it
plain that thefe meafures had failed of the defired effeét,
the Commiffioners, under the prefidency of Endicott,
"ferioufly commended to the feveral General Courts, to
make a law that all fuch Quakers formerly conviéted and
punifhed as fuch, fhall, (if they return again,) be imprifoned, and forthwith banifhed or expelled out of the

---

[1] This interefting correfpondence was
publifhed by Gorton in 1657, as an Appendix to his "*Antidote againft the Common Plague of the World.*" *R. I. Hift.
Coll.* ii: 16. The letter refutes the
remark of Palfrey that his motive was
to annoy Maffachufetts. *Hift. N. E.* ii:
464.

[2] Hazard's *State Papers,* ii: 349.

said jurifdiction, under pain of death ; and if afterwards they prefume to come again into that jurifdiction, then to be put to death as prefumptuoufly incorrigible, unlefs they fhall plainly and publickly renounce their curfed opinions."[1]   To Maffachufetts belongs the diftinction of being the only one of the United Colonies to carry this advice into full effect.   It was under a ftatute paffed by the General Court in compliance with the foregoing recommendation, that William Robinfon, Marmaduke Stevenfon, Mary Dyer and William Leddra were hung on Bofton Common.[2]

Almoft from the beginning Rhode Ifland became an afylum for the "curfed fect."   In the autumn of 1656 Nicholas Upfall a "weakly old man," for "reproaching the honored magiftrates, and fpeaking againft the law made and publifhed againft Quakers," was fined twenty pounds, and fentenced to "depart the jurifdiction within one month."[3] Upfall having been denied a refting place in Plymouth Colony, at laft found refuge in Rhode Ifland.[4] Although a member of the Bofton Church, Upfall had adopted Quaker principles, and feems to have been the firft of that perfuafion who fought fhelter in this Colony.[5] The number, however, foon increafed.   Little more than a year had elapfed from the landing of the firft Quakers before the Commiffioners of the United Colonies, "being

[1] Hazard ii : 399.

[2] Bifhop, *New England Judged,* 114. John Winthrop, of Conn., who fubfcribed to the vote of the Commiffioners " as a query, and not as an act " tried to fave the lives of Robinfon and Steveufon. See Letter of Wm. Coddington to J. Winthrop, Jr., June 29, 1672.

Mass. Hift. Coll. 4th feries, vol. vii : p. 287.

[3] *Mass. Rec.* iv : (1) 277, 280. Bifhop, *New Eng. Judged,* 39.

[4] Bifhop, 40, 161.   Whiting, *Truth and Innocency Defended,* 15.

[5] Bifhop, 39.   Burnyeat, *Truth Exalted,* 49.

informed that divers Quakers are arrived this fummer at
Rode Ifland, and entertained there, which may prove dangerous to the Colonies," addreffed a letter to the Governor, re-
quefting that meafures might be taken for removing thofe
Quakers who had already been received, and for prohibit-
ing their coming in the future.[1] In reply, the authorities
of Rhode Ifland declared that while defirous of maintaining a "fayre and loveing correfpondence and entercourfe
with all the collonys," and while ready at all times to return "fuch as fly from the hands of juftice, for matters of
crime," they had no law "whereby to punifh any for only
declaring by words, &c., their minds and underftandings
concerning the things and ways of God, as to falvation and
an eternal condition."[2] At the fame time they expreffed
their willingnefs to commend the confideration of any
"extravagant outgoings" on the part of the Quakers to
the next General Affembly. At the next meeting of the
Affembly, at Portfmouth, March, 1658, a letter was addreffed to Maffachufetts, affirming that freedom of confcience was "the principal ground of their Charter," and
was ftill prized by them "as the greateft hapines that men
can poffefs in this world," but that in cafe the Quakers
fhould refufe to fubject themfelves to ordinary duties, "as
members of civill focieties, for the prefervation of the
fame in juftice and peace," the matter would be laid before
the authorities in England, "humbly craving their advice
and order, how to carry ourfelves in any further refpect
towards thefe people foe that therewithall theire may be
no damadge, or infringement of that chiefe principle in
our charter concerninge freedom of confciences."[3] From

[1] Letter of Com. of the United Colonies, Sept. 12, 1657. Hazard, ii : 377.

[2] Hazard, ii : 552. *R. I. Rec.* i : 377.
[3] *R. I. Rec.* i : 378.

this "chiefe principle" nothing could force them to fwerve. Even the further threats of being excluded from trade with their fifter colonies, only led in the following year to an appeal to the Protector that they "may not be compelled to exercife any civill power over men's confciences, foe longe as humane orders in poynt of civility are not corrupted and voyalated."[1]

This confiftent liberality of the Colony of Rhode Ifland appears in a ftill more ftriking light when the fact is borne in mind that the doctrines advocated by the Quakers at this time, were far from receiving a general affent. In the Reply of the Authorities to the Commiffioners of the Colonies their diflike of the new comers is uttered in very decided terms: "We moreover find" they write, "that in thofe places where thefe people aforefaid, in this coloney, are moft of all fuffered to declare themfelves freely, and are only oppofed by arguments in difcourfe, there they leaft of all defire to come, and we are informed that they begin to loath this place, for that they are not oppofed by the civill authority, but with all patience and meeknes are fuffered to fay over their pretended revelations and admonitions, nor are they like or able to gain many here to their way; furely we find that they delight to be perfecuted by civill powers, and when they are foe, they are like to gain more adherents by the confeyte of their patient fufferings, than by confent to their pernicious fayings. And yet we conceive, that theife doctrines tend to very abfolute cutting downe and overturninge relations and civill government among men, if generally received."[2]

Notwithftanding, however, the opinion here expreffed

---

[1] *R. I. Records,* i: 398.   [2] *R. I. Records,* i: 377.

with regard to the probable growth of the sect, the facts
go to show that the number of Quakers in Rhode Island
constantly increased.   Horred Gardner, who was flogged
and imprisoned by the authorities at Boston, in May, 1658,
was "an Inhabitant of Newport in Rhode-Island."[1]   Thomas Harris, who was imprisoned and repeatedly flogged in
the following month, had moved from Barbadoes to Rhode
Island.[2]   Catherine Scot, who was imprisoned for two
weeks, and publicly flogged, in the autumn of the same
year, was wife of Richard Scot of Providence.[3]   William Robinson, the first Quaker put to death, had been
"moved of the Lord to go from Rhode Island" to bear
his testimony in Massachusetts.[4]   His companion at the
gallows, Marmaduke Stevenson, came by way of Rhode
Island from Barbadoes.[5]   Mary Dyer, the only woman put
to death, was wife of William Dyer, Secretary of Providence Plantations.

   While Rhode Island lacked the allurement of persecution it still furnished an inviting field to the Quaker mis-
sionary.   It had been settled mainly by Baptists, and it was
from among the Baptists that many, if not most of the
early converts to Quakerism had been gained.   Many of
the doctrines, and much of the discipline afterwards
adopted by the Quakers can be traced directly to a Baptist
source.   The most striking resemblance is presented by the
General Baptists, who existed as a distinct body forty years
before the founder of Quakerism began to preach.   Like
the Quakers, the Baptists had claimed that the church was

---

[1] Bishop, *New Eng. Judged,* 60.
[2] Bishop, 61.
[3] Bishop, 95.
[4] Bishop, 114.

[5] Marmaduke Stevenson's *Paper of his
Call to the Work and Service of the Lord,*
in *New England Judged,* 133.

a fociety of equals; they held that the ordinances of the
Old Teftament were abolifhed; they were inclined to lay
ftrefs on inward revelations; they faid that allegiance was
due the civil government only in temporal things. Like
the Quakers the Baptifts had permitted women to preach
in public; they had the fame fcruples about ufing the pagan names of months and days; they had protefted againft
the neceffity of a learned miniftry; they had oppofed any
regular minifterial fupport; they had expreffed the fame
repugnance to taking oaths. Both Baptifts and Quakers
held their monthly, quarterly and yearly church affemblies
and both termed them "meetings for difcipline." The
"brother confirmed" of the Baptift was but another name
for the "acknowledged minifter" of the Quaker. The
method of folemnizing marriages adopted by the early
Baptifts was nearly identical with that followed by the
Quakers. Both bodies were much exercifed by their members "marrying out of church." Many of the early Baptifts ufed the fingular pronoun "thou" and "thee" in addreffing individuals.[1] George Fox indeed added little beyond boundlefs enthufiam to the views which the Baptifts
had already advanced. He had an uncle who was a Baptift; one of his earlieft fermons was preached at "a great
meeting of the Baptifts at Broughton;" when he went
into Leicefterfhire "there were fome Baptifts in that
country" whom he defired to meet.[2] The firft perfon
in Providence who embraced the principles of George
Fox, according to tradition, was Richard Scot,[3] who

[1] On this unexplored fubject fee *George Fox, the Friends, and the Early Baptifts.*, By William Tallack, London: 1868.
[2] Fox's *Journal*, p. 3, 12, 26, 99, &c., compare Edmundfon's *Journal*, p. 34, 35.
[3] Staples' *Annals of Providence:* 420.

like Roger Williams, had been for a time connected with
the Baptifts.[1]

In a fhort time the number of Quakers muft have con-
fiderably increafed, for when the General Meeting was
"fet up" at Rhode Ifland, in the fpring of 1661, the concourfe was fo numerous, that in Maffachufetts grave apprehenfions were aroufed "that the Quakers were gathering
together to kill the People, and to fire the town of Bofton."[2]   As early as 1665 the Quakers had been reinforced
by men as prominent as Coddington and Eafton, fince in
March of that year thefe two prefented a memorial to the
Royal Commiffioners in behalf of their fellow-religionifts.
The greatly increafed influence of the Quakers in Rhode
Ifland at this time may be ftill more conclufively inferred
from the fact that when the Commiffioners required that an
"oath of allegiance" fhould be adminiftered to "to all
houfeholders inhabiting the colony," the General Affembly fubftituted "an engagement," in favor of "fuch as made
a fcruple of fwearing."[3]   According to the account of
Richard Scot, when two of the Commiffioners were at
Providence, "being in the Houfe of Thomas Olney, Senior,
of the fame Town," Roger Williams propounded to them
the following queftion: "We have a People here
amongft us, which will not act in our Government with
us;   What courfe fhall we take with them?"   "Then
George Cartwright, one of the Commiffioners afked him,
What manner of Perfons they were?   Do they live quietly and peaceably amongft you?   This they could not
deny;   Then he made them this Anfwer;   If they can

[1] Letter of R. Scot in *New-England-
Fire-Brand-Quenched*, Part ii : 247.

[2] Bifhop, *New England Judged*, 351.
[3] *R. I. Rec.* ii : 110–118.

Govern themfelves, they have no need of your Government."[1] This is the earlieſt indication of Roger Williams' attitude with reference to the Quakers.

The firſt Quaker miſſionary of eminence who viſited Rhode Iſland, was John Burnyeat, who having ſpent ſome time at New York "in the *fourth month* 1666," then "took ſhipping for *Road Iſland* in *New England,* and there ſpent ſome time in viſiting Friends, and their Meetings."[2] He next viſited Boſton and the towns in Eaſtern New England, and returning to Rhode Iſland in the winter and ſtayed for ſome time; "for there was no going off the Iſland unto the Main, the Snow was ſo deep."[3] In the latter part of March, 1667, he ſailed for Barbadoes, and in the autumn returned to England. In July, 1670, he again left England for Barbadoes and having remained there ſix months, ſailed for New York, in April, 1671. Having

---

[1] Letter of R. Scot in *New-England-Fire-Brand Quenched,* p. 248. "This was told again by a Woman of the ſame Houſe (when the Speech was ſpoken) to another Woman, whom the Complaint with the reſt was made againſt, who related it to me."

[2] *The Truth Exalted in the Writings of that Eminent and Faithful Servant of Chriſt John Burnyeat,* p. 35. Burnyeat was born about 1631, at Crabtreebeck, pariſh of Lowſwater, in the county of Cumberland, "where his Parents were of good repute, aud his Education was according to his Parentage." See *Teſtimony concerning the Life and Death of John Burnyeat* prefixed to *Truth Exalted.* He became a diſciple of George Fox in 1653. In 1657 the Lord "began to ſtir in his heart by his Spirit to

go forth in the ſtrength of his Word." After preaching for a time in England in 1658, he preached in the northern and weſtern parts of Scotland. In 1659 he viſited Ireland, where he "travelled and labored in the Goſpel for *Twelve Months.*" Early in 1662, he was "moved by the Lord to go to *London* to *George Fox,* and others of the Elders, and acquaint him with what was upon me from the Lord to go to *America.*" Circumſtances, however, delayed his going for two years. "About the *Seventh Month,* 1664," he "took ſhipping at *Galloway* in *Ireland* for the *Barbadoes.*" He then viſited Virginia and Maryland, and in June, 1666 went to New York. See *Truth Exalted;* p. 1, 16, 26, 29, 32, 35.

[3] *Truth Exalted,* p. 35.

fpent fome time on Long Ifland he "took fhipping for
Road Ifland, and was there at their Yearly Meeting in 1671,
which begins the *ninth* of the *fourth month* every Year, and
continues for much of a Week, and is a General Meeting
once a year for all Friends in *New-England.*"[1]   After
going Eaft as far as Pifcataway he "came to Road-Ifland
again, and there fpent fome time, and went up to *Providence,* and did vifit Friends there."[2]   The winter of 1671
was fpent at the South.   Returning to Long Ifland he
"then fet Sail for *Road-Ifland* the 29th of the *third Month,*
(1672) and arrived at *Road-Ifland* the *thirtieth of the fame,*
and there ftayed till the *Yearly Meeting,* which began the
eighth day of the *fourth Month,* which was the fixth day of
the next Week following; and at that *General Meeting*
there were many Friends from moft places in *New-England,* where Friends dwelt, and abundance of other People
came into our Publick Meetings.   And we had Meetings
for *eight days* together, every day a Meeting, fome publick
and others *Men*-and *Womens-Meetings* for fettling the affairs of the Churches in the Order of the Truth; that all
things might be kept fweet, clear, and well.   And when all
was over, and the Service of the Meetings finifhed, I took
my Journey *Eaftward,* to go through the Meetings in the
Eaftern Parts of *New England,* and with me went *John
Cartwright* and *George* Pattifon, and feveral other Friends
to accompany us; and we left *G. F. upon the Ifland,* and he
went to *Providence* and the *Narraganfet Country.*"[3]

   The vifit of George Fox, to which allufion is here made,
was an event that could not fail to fix the attention of the

---

[1] *Truth Exalted,* p. 40.
[2] "   "   p. 41.

[3] *Truth   Exalted,* p.   47 : compare
Fox's *Journal,* p. 443.

whole community.[1]   If Fox may not, with ſtrict truth be called the founder, he was certainly the recognized leader of the ſect.[2] He was the foremoſt repreſentative of its doctrines during the firſt period of its hiſtory. For a quarter of a century he had been laboring with tireleſs zeal to commend them to his countrymen. His name was now familiar wherever the Engliſh language was ſpoken. Thoſe who oppoſed his teachings were everywhere filled with alarm when it was announced that "the man in leathern breeches had come."[3]   Beneath an external garb of wild and coarſe fanaticiſm he poſſeſſed an unuſual ſhare of prudence, great ſhrewdneſs, and an indomitable courage that commended him highly to the fierce religioniſts who had been trained in the Civil War. In perſon he was large ; his eyes were bright and piercing, and his voice pow-

[1] "I was born in the month called July, in the year 1624, at Drayton in the Clay, in Leiceſterſhire. My father's name was Chriſtopher Fox. He was by profeſſion a weaver, an honeſt man, and there was a ſeed of God in him. The neighbors called him Righteous Chriſten. My mother was an upright woman ; her maiden name was Mary Lago, of the family of the Lago's, and of the ſtock of the martyrs." *Journal* of George Fox, p. 1. When towards nineteen, "at the command of God" he left his relations and broke off all fellowſhip with young or old. Some adviſed him to marry ; one "ancient prieſt" bade him take tobacco and ſing pſalms." The Lord ſhowed him clearly "that he did not dwell in theſe temples which men had commanded and ſet up, but in peoples hearts." After he had received the "opening from the Lord that to be bred at Oxford or Cambridge, was not ſufficient to fit a man to be a miniſter of Chriſt," he "regarded the prieſts leſs and looked more after the diſſenting people." But ſoon he "left the ſeparate preachers alſo." He began his extraordinary career as a preacher in 1647. *Journal,* p. 6.

[2] "Fox was rather the *organizer* or *completing agent,* than the founder of Quakeriſm." Tallack, *George Fox,* p. 67.

[3] "Perhaps the moſt remarkable incident in Modern Hiſtory is not the Diet of Worms, ſtill leſs the Battle of Auſterlitz, Waterloo, Peterloo, or any other Battle ; but an incident paſſed careleſſly over by moſt Hiſtorians, and treated with ſome degree of ridicule by others : namely, George Fox making to himſelf a ſuit of Leather." *Sartor Reſartus,* B. iii : Chap. I.

erful enough to command the attention of the moſt tumultuous aſſemblage.   According to the teſtimony of Thomas
Ellwood, who did not meet him till the year 1660,
but who " from that time till the time of his death knew
him well, converſed with him often, obſerved him much,
loved him dearly, and honoured him truly," he was
" graceful in countenance, manly in perſonage, grave in
geſture, courteous in converſation, weighty in communication, inſtructive in diſcourse, free from affectation in
ſpeech or carriage."[1]

In 1671 it "was upon him from the Lord to go beyond
ſea, to viſit the plantations in America."   Accordingly with
twelve companions, among whom were William Edmundson[2] and John Stubbs,[3] he ſailed from Graveſend, Aug.
13th, "in a yatch, called the Induſtry."   "The third of
the eighth month" he reached Barbadoes.   In March,
1672, he landed in Maryland.   Continuing his journey
through the Jerſeys and Long Iſland, he waited at Oyſter
Bay for a wind to take him to Rhode Iſland.   His *Journal*
thus continues :

[1] Ellwood's *Account of Fox*, prefixed
to Fox's *Journal.*

[2] William Edmundſon was born at
Little Muſgrove, in Weſtmoreland, in
1627.   His mother died when he was
four years old, his father when he was
eight.   He was brought up by an uncle
who "uſed him hardly."   As a child
he was greatly exerciſed " concerning
his Salvation, alſo about Election and
Reprobation."   He entered the army,
and in 1650 ſerved in Scotland under
Cromwell.   Returning to England the
next year he heard two Quaker women
preach, "and the more he heard of this
people the better he loved them."   In
1652 he married, and in 1654 began to
preach.   *Journal* of William Edmundſon, p. 1–15.

[3] John Stubbs was an old ſoldier of
the Commonwealth who had been diſ-
charged from the army becauſe he would
not take the oath of allegiance to Cromwell.   He became a convert to Quakeriſm in 1653.   In company with Samuel
Fiſher he preached in the Low Countries and Germany.   Afterwards he viſited Rome.   When George Fox came to
America, Stubbs, in company with Edmundſon and others came with him.
George Fox's *Journal*, p. 113, 139, 426.
William Edmundſon's *Journal*, p. 60,
Biſhop, *New-England Judged*, p. 16, 17.

"As foon as the wind ferved we fet fail, and arrived in Rhode Ifland the thirtieth of the third month; where we were gladly received by friends.   We went to Nicholas Eafton's,[1] who was governor of the Ifland; where we lay, being weary with travelling.   On firft day following we had a large meeting; to which the deputy governor[2] and feveral juftices came, and were mightily affected with the truth.   The week following the yearly meeting for friends of New England, and other colonies adjacent, was held in this ifland; to which, befides many friends who lived in thefe parts, came John Stubbs from Barbadoes, and James Lancafter and John Cartwright from another way.   This meeting lafted fix days.   The firft four were fpent in general publick meetings for worfhip; to which abundance of other people came.   For having no priefts in the ifland, and no reftriction to any particular way of worfhip; and the governor and the deputy-governor, with feveral juftices of the peace, daily frequenting meetings; it fo encouraged the people, that they flocked in from all parts of the ifland. Very good fervice we had amongft them, and the truth had good reception.   I have rarely obferved a people, in the ftate wherein they ftood, to hear with more attention, diligence, and affection, than generally they did, during the four days; which was alfo taken notice of by other friends.   Thefe publick meetings over, the men's meeting began, which was large, precious and weighty.   The day following was the women's meeting, which alfo was large

---

[1] Eafton, like Coddington, was a convert to Quakerifm from the Antinomians. More than thirty years before this Winthrop fpeaks of him as "man very bold, though ignorant." Winthrop's *Journal,* i: 338; 2: 48.

[2] John Cranfton. The degree of "Doctor of phiffick and chirrurgery" was conferred upon him by the General Affembly in 1664. Arnold, *Hift. R. I.* i: 303.

and very folemn. Thefe two meetings being for ordering
the affairs of the church, many weighty things were
opened and communicated to them, by way of advice, information and inftruction in the fervices relating thereunto; that all might be kept clear; fweet, and favoury
amongft them. In thefe, feveral men's and women's meetings for other parts were agreed and fettled, to take care of
the poor, and other affairs of the church, and to fee that all
who profefs truth walk according to the glorious gofpel of
God. When this great general meeting was ended, it was
fomewhat hard for friends to part ; for the glorious power
of the Lord, which was over all, and his bleffed truths and
life flowing amongft them, had fo knit and united them
together, that they fpent two days in taking leave one of
another, and of the friends of the Ifland ; and thefe being
mightily filled with the prefence and power of the Lord,
they went away with joyful hearts to their feveral habita-
tions, in the feveral colonies where they lived."

"When friends had taken their leave one of another,
we, who travelled amongft them, difperfed ourfelves into
our feveral fervices, as the Lord ordered us. John Burney-
eate, John Cartwright, and George Pattifon went into the
eaftern parts of New England, in company with the
friends that came from thence, to vifit the particular meetings there;[1] whom John Stubbs and James Lancafter
intended to follow a while after, in the fame fervice; but
they were not yet clear of this ifland. Robert Widders[2]
and I ftaid longer upon this ifland ; finding fervice ftill
here for the Lord, through the great opennefs, and the

---

[1] Compare *Truth Exalted*, p. 47.
[2] Cartwright, Pattifon, Lancafter and

Widders had accompanied Fox from
England. See Fox's *Journal*, p. 426.

daily coming in of frefh people from other colonies, for fome time, after the general meeting; fo that we had many large and ferviceable meetings among them."

"During this time, a marriage was celebrated amongft friends in this ifland, and we were prefent. It was at a friend's houfe, who had formerly been governor of the ifland;[1] and three juftices of the peace, with many others not in profeffion with us, and friends alfo faid, they never faw fuch a folemn affembly on fuch an occafion, fo weighty a marriage and fo comely an order. Thus truth was fet over all. This might ferve for an example to others; for there were fome prefent from many other places."

"After this I had a great travail in fpirit concerning the Ranters in thofe parts who had been rude at a meeting which I was not at. Wherefore I appointed a meeting amongft them, believing the Lord would give me power over them, which he did, to his praife and glory; bleffed be his name forever! There were at this meeting many friends, and divers other people; fome of whom were juftices of the peace, and officers, who were generally well affected with the truth. One, who had been a juftice twenty years, was convinced, fpoke highly of the truth, and more highly of me than is fit for me to mention or take notice of."

"We had a meeting at Providence, which was very

---

[1] Coddington writing to John Winthrop, Jr., under date of June 29th, apparently refers to this; "and Geo. Fox being at my howfe (who faw thee in England) fpake to me to write to thee, viz: that Samuell Winthrope, thy brother, was with him at Barbadoes, came thither to vifit him, and G. F. could wifh that thou was like him, and that thou would ftaue of perfecution in thy day, in thy Jurifdiction, that thou mayeft not be numbered amongeft perfecutours, and thee wicked, whofe names fhall rote." *Mafs. Hift. Coll.* 4th feries, vii: 288.

large, confifting of many forts of people. I had a great travail upon my fpirit, that it might be preferved quiet, and that truth might be brought over the people, and might gain entrance and have place in them ; for they ewer generally above the priefts in high notions ; and fome came on purpofe to difpute. But the Lord, whom we waited upon, was with us, his power went over them all ; and his bleffed Seed was exalted and fet above all. The difputers were filent, and the meeting quiet and ended well ; praifed be the Lord! The people went away mightily fatisfied, much defiring another meeting. This place (called Providence) was about thirty miles from Rhode Ifland ; we went to it by water. The governor of Rhode Ifland, and many others, went with me thither ; and we had the meeting in a great barn[1] which was thronged with people, fo that I was exceeding hot, and in a great fweat ; but all was well ; the glorious power of the Lord fhined over all, glory to the great God forever."

"After this we went to Narraganfett, about twenty miles from Rhode Ifland ; and the governor went with us. We had a meeting at a juftice's, where friends never had any before. The meeting was very large, for the country generally came in ; and the people from Connecticut, and other parts round about. There were four juftices of peace. Moft of thefe people were fuch as had never heard friends before ; but they were mightily affected, and a great defire there is after the truth amongft them. So that meeting was of very good fervice ; bleffed be the Lord forever ! The juftice, at whofe houfe it was, and another

---

[1] The " fair large meeting houfe " in Providence was not built till 1703 or 1704. Staples' *Annals*, p. 424. The Quakers feem to have increafed flowly, fince they are defcribed at that time as " courageous and noble being but few."

juftice of that country, invited me to come again ; but I was then clear of thefe parts, and was going towards Shelter Ifland. John Burnyeate and John Cartwright, being come out of New England into Rhode Ifland before I was gone, I laid this place before them, and they felt drawings thither, and went to vifit them.[1] At another place, I heard fome of the magiftrates faid among themfelves, ' if they had money enough, they would hire me to be their minifter.' This was, when they did not underftand us, and our principles : but when I heard of it, I faid, ' It was time for me to be gone ; for if their eye was fo much to me, or any of us, they would not come to their own teacher.' For this thing (hiring minifters) had fpoiled many, by hindering them from improving their own talents ; whereas our labour is, to bring every one to their own teacher in themfelves."[2]

From Rhode Ifland Fox returned to Shelter Ifland, where he met William Edmundfon on his way North from Virginia.[3] Burnyeat, Stubbs, and Cartwright remained

---

[1] According to Burnyeat this vifit to Narraganfett was in company with Stubbs, and after the difcuffion with Williams. " So after fome time together upon the Ifland, *John Stubbs* and I went over, with feveral Friends that did accompany us, to *Narraganfet ;* and then we had a Meeting the *four and twentieth* of the *fixth month* at one *Richard Smith's ;* and *next day* took our journey towards *Hartford*." *Truth Exalted,* 54. Compare Edmundfon's *Journal,* 76.

[2] Fox's *Journal,* pp. 442–444.

The above account of the memorable vifit of George Fox to Rhode Ifland, is taken from the third edition of his *Journal,* London : 1765. The remark of Macaulay fhould be borne in mind : " This Journal, before it was publifhed, was revifed by men of more fenfe and knowledge than himfelf, and therefore, abfurd as it is, gives us no notion of his genuine ftyle."—*Hift. Eng.* iv : p. 22. Yet Macaulay's account of Fox can hardly be regarded as any thing more than caricature. While his eccentricities are vividly depicted, the true fource of his great influence is unnoticed. The leader of fo marked a religious movement muft have been fomething more than a man " too much difordered for liberty, and not fufficiently difordered for Bedlam."

[3] " From thence (Long Ifland) I went to Shelter Ifland, where I met with

behind, and what followed is thus narrated by the former :
" J. S. and I went up to Providence, had a Meeting
there ; and as we returned, we had a meeting at *Warwick*,
where none had been before ; and feveral were Convinced
and did own the Truth.   And there we had to do with one
Gorton, and his Company, who were by other People then
called *Gortonians*, but they called themfelves *Generalifts*.
They were of Opinion, *all fhould be faved*.   But they were
in reality *Ranters :* for in our Difcourfe they would maintain, and fay, *No Creaturely actions could be Sin ;* and would
have no *Whoredom*, nor *Drunkennefs*, not the like to be *Sin*,
but what was fpiritual ; the outward action was but creaturely.   And thus in their filthy, unclean Spirit, they like
the old *Ranters*, made merry over the reproof of God's
Spirit."[1]

   " So from thence we came down again to *Road-Ifland*,

George Fox again, and feveral Friends
with him, coming from *New England*
and going to *Virginia*.   I told him of my
Travels and Service for the Lord, at the
Hearing of which he was glad, and we
praifed the Lord for his Goodnefs; I
told him I was much preft in Spirit to
haften for *Ireland :* he told me *That
Friends in* New England *had heard of
me, and they expected I would vifit them,
and befides, the Paffage of Ships from thofe
Parts were ftopped, by reafon of Wars between* Holland *and* England."—Edmundfon's *Journal*, p. 73.

[1] When Prefident Stiles was in Providence, Nov. 18, 1771, he vifited Mr.
John Angell, then eighty years of age,
and the laft furviving follower of Gorton.   " I afked him if Gorton was a
Quaker ; as he feemed to agree with
them in rejecting outward ordinances.
He faid, no ; and that when George Fox,
or one of the firft Friends, came over,
he went to Warwick to fee Gorton, but
was a mere babe to Gorton.   The Friends
had come out of the world, in fome
ways, but ftill were in darknefs or twi-
light, but that Gorton was far beyond
them, he faid, high way up to the difpenfation of light.   The Quakers were
in no wife to be compared with him.   He
faid, Gorton was a holy man; wept day
and night for the fins and blindnefs of
the world.   He was univerfally beloved
by all his neighbors, and the Indians, who
efteemed him, not only as a friend, but
one high in communion with God in
Heaven, and indeed he lived in Heaven."
R. I. Hift. Coll. ii : 20.

and there we fpent fome time, and had a long Difpute with one *Roger Williams*, that fent us a *Challenge* from *Providence*, with *fourteen Propofitions*, as he called them, but they were *Charges;* and he engaged to maintain them againſt all Comers; the firſt *Seaven* to be difputed on at *Road-Iſland*, and the latter *Seven* at *Providence.*"[1]

Roger Williams, never indifferent to novelties in religion, had watched with intereſt the rife of Quakerifm. He had "long heard of the great name of G. Fox," and "fome years" before Fox came to Rhode Iſland had "read his book in Folio."[2] He was familiar with other Quaker writers.[3] He had alſo examined "above *ſix ſcore Books* and Papers written by pious and able pens againſt them." But notwithſtanding a marked coincidence on fome minor points, he was never inclined to their more peculiar notions. In a letter to the younger Winthrop, he notes with evident fatisfaction that Catherine Scott, one of the firſt to fuffer for the new faith, had been led in part to renounce it.[4] When Burnyeat made his vifit to Newport in 1671, Williams attended the General Meeting, where was a "great *Concourfe*," and attempted to hold a difcuffion with them, but was ſtopped by "the fudden praying of the

---

[1] *Truth Exalted,* p. 53.

[2] p. 1, *infra.* The title of this work was "*The Great Myſtery of the Great Whore unfolded; and Anti-Chriſt's Kingdom revealed into Deſtruction;*" By Geo. Fox. London, 1659. cf. p. 53, *infra.* The writings of Fox were very numerous. For a full liſt fee "*A Deſcriptive Catalogue of Friends' Books,*" by Joſeph Smith. 2 vols. 4to, London: 1867, pp. 644–697.

[3] p. 277, *infra.*

[4] "Sir, my neighbor, Mrs. Scott, is come from England; and what the whip at Boſton could not do, converfe with friends in England, and their arguments, have, in a great meafure drawn her from the Quakers, and ufually from their meetings. Try the ſpirits. There are many abroad, and muſt be, but the Lord will be glorious, in plucking up whatever his holy hand hath not planted." Letter of Williams to John Winthrop, Jr.: Sept. 8, 1660.

Governour's Wife," and by the fummary action of Burnyeat in difmiffing the affembly.[1] Warned by this experience
although Fox was "feveral weeks at Rode Ifland,"[2] Williams fought no opportunity of feeing him at any of the
ordinary meetings of the Quakers. Even when Fox was
in Providence, Williams did not vifit him.[3] "Tis true G.
Fox was at *Providence* fome -few dayes before, and fpake
publickly; and it was free for me publickly to have heard
him and oppofed him; But going the laft year to one of
their general affemblyes at *New-Port*, and having begun
to prefent to them fome Confiderations about the *True
Chrift* and the *falfe*, the *True Spirit* and the *Falfe*, and being
cut of in the mideft, by the fudden *Prayer* of one, and the
Singing of another, and then by the *Prayer* of another,
and the fudden diffolving of the Affembly, I refolved to try
another way, and to offer a fair and full Difpute, according
to *Ed. Burrowes* (and therein G. *Foxes*) Offer in his large
Epiftle to Foxes Book."[4]

In accordance with this refolution, Williams drew up
the Fourteen Propofitions which gave rife to the difcuffion
narrated in the volume now reprinted.[5] But inftead of

[1] p. 12, *infra.*

[2] Fox arrived at Newport, May 30,
1672, and "was fome hours departed"
when the letter of Williams was brought
to Cranfton, July 26.

[3] "For he had not fo much *Civility,*
as to fpeak to G. F. when he was at
Providence ; but fnarling behind his back,
Bafe and Un-warlike." *New-England-
Fire-Brand-Quenched,* Pt. i: 183.

[4] The "*Epiftle to the Reader,*" prefixed to *The Great Myftery of the Great
Whore unfolded,* was written by Edward
Burrough, and contained a challenge to
"any unfatisfied ftill in the matter," to

a public difcuffion, "with the confent of
the chief in authority that have power
in this nation, who may preferve peace
and fafety among people, and thereby
ftop all jealoufies." George Fox's *Works,*
iii: 25.

Thus it appears that the courfe adopted by Williams of fending the Propofitions to Cranfton, was ftrictly in accordance with the fuggeftion of Burrough
himfelf. The "Epiftle" is dated London, the Ninth Mo., 1658.

[5] Thefe are given in full on pp. 4, 5,
infra.

being fent directly to Fox, they were inclofed in a letter to Captain Cranfton, the Deputy Governor of the Colony. Had the contents of this communication not been divulged it would doubtlefs have reached its deftination in feafon. Unfortunately, however, for his purpofe, before the boat which was to carry the letter to Cranfton had failed, Williams furnifhed a copy of the Propofitions to a neighbor whom he knew to be inclining to Quakers views.[1] This copy was read at a meeting of the Quakers, and in that way the purport of the letter became known to the mafter of the boat, who was alfo a difciple of Fox. Thus the plan of Williams was difclofed before the letter had been delivered to Cranfton, and according to Williams, "in the *Junto* of the *Foxians* at *Newport*, it was concluded for *Infallible Reafons*, that His *Holinefs G. Fox* fhould withdraw." Accordingly they arranged that the letter to Cranfton fhould not be delivered until Fox had gone. The Propofitions had been enclofed to Cranfton in order "that

[1] Williams feems to have taken confiderable pains to circulate information of the propofed difcuffion. Under date of Aug. 23, 1672, Coddington writes to J. Winthrop, Jr., "fence whofe departuer (Fox,) even that daye, in a letter incloffed to John Cranfton, our Deputie Governour, was inclofed 14 propofitions to George Fox or other of his Countriemen at Newport, on Rode Ifland, who fay they are apoftles or meffengers of Jefus Chrift, which he offered againft all comers to maintaine in publicke, the firft 7 at Newport, the other 7 at Providence. I fhall not neede to trouble thee with further relation conferneing them, (he had difperced them into the Maffachufetts,) but refere thee to thee berer herof."—4 *Mafs. Hift. Coll.* 7 : 291.

Among the archives of the State of Connecticut, is preferved a copy of the 14 Propofitions in the handwriting of Williams and bearing his fignature. It is ftyled *Mr Wms Q againft ye Quaker*, and, in addition to fome unimportant verbal differences, is dated "ye 15th" inftead of the 13 of July. Poffibly this is one of the copies which Williams "had difperced." It is printed in the *Hiftorical Mag.* ii : 56. In the courfe of the third day's difcuffion, Williams refers to "one copy" of the Propofitions that did not ftrictly agree with that fent to the Quakers; p. 137 *infra*. With regard to dates Williams was a little carelefs as appears from his Second Letter to J. T. p. 17 *infra*.

being fuch a public perfon, he might timely be informed
of fuch a publicke Affembly, and as alfo might vouchfafe
(as afterwards he carefully did) to afford his *Countenance
and Affiftance* to fuch *Peaceable* and *Pious Exercifes.*" Cranfton "did publickly teftifie" that the letter of Williams,
dated July 13th, was not delivered until the 26th of the
fame month, "and untill G. *Fox* was fome hours departed."
Williams did not hefitate to accufe Fox of complicity in
this tranfaction : "G. F. fuppofed I would be forced to be
as plain in my *Proofs* as I was in my *Pofitions.* He knew
that I was furnifhed with Artillery out of his own *Writings.* He faw what *Confequences* would roll down the
mountaines upon him from his proud and Infolent, yet
poor and bald *Writings;* and how far fome of his prefent
practices were fallen out with his *Writings,* and therefore
this old *Fox* thought it beft to run for it, and leave the
work to his *Journeymen* and *Chaplains* to perform in his abfence for him."[1]   This accufation Williams brings forward
ftill more confpicuoufly on the title page of his book.[2]

The charge, that he thus purpofely avoided Williams,
Fox denies in the moft emphatic language. Of the 14
Propofitions he declares that he "not only never received,
but never faw, nor fo much as knew of them;"[3] he "*knew
nothing* of his Accufations, or pretended proof, which *R.
W.* vainly calls his *Artillery;* nor that he ever read, much
lefs objected anything againft *G. F.'s* Book."[4]   To the
affertions of Williams that Fox "run for it;" that he arranged that the 14 Propofitions fhould not be delivered till

---

[1] p. 7, *infra.* Compare the prelimi-
nary letter " *To the People called* Quakers."

[2] (*G. Fox* flily departing.)

[3] *New-England-Fire-Brand-Quenched,*
Pt. i: 1.

[4] *New-England Fire-Brand-Quenched,*
Pt. i: 2.

after his departure; that he did this that he might fay he never faw the paper; and that he knew the fubftance of the Propofitions perfectly before his departure; Fox rejoins; "Thefe are *four great Lies*: for G. F. knew not what was in thy Papers *Roger*, neither had G. F. feen the *Copies* of thefe *Propofals*; neither did G. F. hinder their being delivered to the *Governour*. Nor did G. F. ever receive any letters from R. W., or go away for fear of him or them; nor was it a likely thing, that he fhould, when he knew nothing of them: for as I faid before, when I was at *Providence*, where this *Roger* lives, he came not at me. And if he had anything to have fpoken to me, he might eafily have done it, or have written to me, and have fent the fame copies to me, he fent to Captain Cranfton; and not have made a clamour againft me, belying of me to the world behind my back, when I was gone. But this is like the *Fruits of his Spirit*, but not the Spirt of Chrift, and his Difciples."[1]

[1] *New-England-Fire-Brand Quenched*, p. 9. To fhow that Fox was not lefs fkilled than his opponent in the amenities of religious controverfy, I fubjoin the following fpecimens of his ftyle : "a Lying, Slanderous Book :" "How dare R. W. to Dedicate fuch palpable Lies to the King :" "Oh how dareft thou *Roger* Williams, publifh fuch *falfe lyes* to the World, when thou knoweft in thy Confcience, that G. F. had never any *Writing, or Letter or Propofals* from thee: neither did he ever exchange a word with thee. The Lord God of Heaven knowes it, and the *Deputy Governour* knowes, that I received none of thy Writings or Papers of Propofals by him. Behold all fober people the foundation of this mans Attempt, the beginning of his work; and fince the foundation of thy Book is a *notorious lye*, the building upon fuch a *foundation of lyes* is not like to be otherwife: which *lyes* thou haft made thy *refuge*; as throughout thy Book may be evidently feen. For except a man had fold himfelf to work falfehood, and make lyes; he could not have done more wickedly, and have uttered felfer charges than thou haft done. But the Lord God which knows them, and fees thy evil defign in them, will *fweep them away with the Befom of Deftruction*, and clear his people from thy manifeft falfe tongue. And I doubt not but the *Deputy Governour* will teftifie for me, that I am clear of this charge; and that I never

That Williams fent the Propofitions in good faith, and
that he defired the controverfy with Fox, cannot be for a
moment doubted. The reafons that he affigns for not feeking
his opponent at any of the public meetings of the Quakers, and for not addreffing his letter to Fox directly, remove any fufpicion of intentional evafion.[1] On the other
hand it feems not lefs certain that Fox never faw the letter.   Not only do we have his own repeated denial that it
ever reached him, or that its contents ever were known
to him, but Burnyeat profeffed "that he knew nothing of
the detaining of the Letter, only he knew that *G. Fox*
never faw the Papers,"[2] and Williams concedes that "probably, as afterwards in the difpute, he fpake honeftlie not
knowing the Myftery."[3]   There feems, therefore, no
ground whatever for the charge made by Williams that
Fox " flily departed."   No characteriftic of Fox was more
marked than felf-confidence.   At no time did he ever
fhrink from meeting an adverfary; he was now in the
prime of life, and in the full flufh of his career as prophet
of a new fect.   No reafon can be conceived why he fhould
have been unwilling to meafure his ftrength with Roger
Williams, a man paffed three fcore and ten, and wield-
ing at this time, but little influence.[4] As little does it feem

---

faw, nor knew that which *R. W.* writ,
and fent to him."   *N. E. Firebrand
Quenched,* Pt. i : 2.

[1] Fox makes this charge. *N. E. Fire-
Brand Quenched,* Pt. i : 23.

[2] p. 7 *infra.*

[3] p. 35 *infra.*

[4] " And why cannot this Man be *quiet*
with his own *Liberty* in his own *Opinions* and *Imaginations,* but he muft *grudge*
at others ? but the *Governors* have not
grudged at him for *his;* but he may

preach as long as he will, if people
will go to hear him ; but I think he is
an *Old Doting Man,* and few mind
him ; for I did not hear, that he
preached to any, when I was at *Providence.*   And he may think by publifhing
this Book of *Lies* to get fome *Followers :*
Its like, he may get *fuch, as are given up
to believe Lies,* but none that fear God
and follow Chrift *Jefus." New-England-
Fire-Brand-Quenched,* Pt. i : 25.

likely that "in the Junto of the Foxians at Newport," as Williams alleged, it was arranged that Fox fhould withdraw, for not only did Burnyeat know nothing of the matter, but it is difficult to underftand why, if the difcuffion was to take place, one party fhould wifh to have their ftrongeft man out of the way. The more probable conclufion feems to be that fome perfonal enemies of Williams in Providence, detained the letters, unwilling perhaps that he fhould gain any credit from the controverfy. This feems likely from the faƈt that Throckmorton,[1] to whom a copy of the papers was furnifhed, wrote to Williams advifing him "to refrain any further publifhing thereof;" and Croffman, mafter of the boat, infulted Williams "in the open ftreet," becaufe he "durft fend 14 Lyes to fuch a man as *G. Fox.*"[2]

The departure of Fox[3] did not interfere with the propofed difcuffion. A few days after Cranfton had delivered to the Quakers the fourteen propofitions of Williams, Stubbs, Burnyeat and feveral others, went to Providence and made an agreement to meet their opponent at Newport on the ninth of Auguft.[4] As fome of the neighbors

---

[1] That his "former antient Neighbor and friend *J. T.*" to whom Williams fent a Copy of his pofitions, cf. p. 6, *infra*, was John Throckmorton, appears from the Letter of Richard Scot, *New-England-Fire-Brand Quenched,* Pt. ii : 249. Throckmorton was one of the original fettlers of Providence, and in the affignment of "home lots," his was located next fouth to that of Williams. Staples' *Annals of Providence,* 35.

[2] pp. 6–8, *infra.*

[3] The day before he left Fox addreffed a communication to two citizens of Providence, Thomas Olney, jr., and John Whipple, which makes no allufion to the difpute with Williams, but deferves notice for fome of its praƈtical fuggeftions. Among other things he recommends a "law againft drunkennefs, and them that fell liquors to make people drunk," "a market once a week, and a houfe built for that purpofe," and "in every town and place in all your colony, one to receive all your births, marriages, and them that die." The letter is printed in the *Philadelphia Friend,* vii : 55. The earlieft Regiftration Law in R. I., was enaƈted in 1708.

[4] p. 35, *infra.*

of Williams were "grieved that the *Conference* fhould be
carried away from *Providence* to *Newport*," it was further
agreed that after the firft feven propofitions had been difcuffed at Newport, fome of the Quakers fhould meet Williams at Providence. Having thus arranged the prelimi-
naries Williams promifed that he would not fail to meet
them, "and God" he fays "gracioufly affifted me in rowing all day with my old bones fo that I got to *Newport*
toward the *Midnight* before the morning appointed."

The place of difcuffion was the Quaker Meeting Houfe
at Newport, the fcruples of thofe who hefitated about enter-
ing fuch a place having been overcome by the argument
of Williams "that it was one thing to goe into a *Jews
Synagogue*, or a *Popifh Chappell* to worfhip, or countenance
their Worfhips; another thing to Profefs and Inteft againft
them." The aged Governor, Eafton, and feveral other
Magiftrates, who had adopted Quaker views, were prefent,
affording the affurance that no unfeemly difturbances would
interrupt the debate.

When Williams made his appearance at the hour appointed, he found his three opponents "fitting together on
an high Bench." The diftinctive characteriftics of thefe
whom he terms "able and noted preachers," are fketched
in a few words. He had heard that John Stubbs "was
learned in the *Hebrew* and the Greek," and found him fo.
On the fecond day, Stubbs brought with him his Hebrew
Bible, and Williams fays, "it may be he underftands the
Hebrew and the *Greek* and other Languages as well as myfelf and better too."[1] So Burnyeat he found "to be a mode-

---

[1] p. 95, *infra*. Stubbs was affociated
with Benjamin Frisby in compiling the
book called the "Battledore," "which
was written to fhow that in all languages
Thou and Thee is the proper and ufual
form of fpeech to a fingle perfon. This

rate *Spirit*, and a very able Speaker."[1] But Edmondſon ſeems to have arouſed his ſpecial diſlike. While Stubbs and Burnyeat were "civil and ingenious," Edmundſon "was nothing but a bundle of Ignorance and Boiſterouſneſs." He "would frequently and inſolently interrupt;" he was "very ignorant in the *Scripture* or any other Learning;" he "had been a ſoldier in the late warres, a ſtout, portly man of a great voice, and fit to make a *Bragadocia;*" he is termed "*a Pragmatical and Inſulting Soul.*"[2]

was ſet forth in examples or inſtances taken out of the Scriptures, and out of books of inſtruction in about thirty languages."—Fox's *Journal*, p. 328.

Fox himſelf added ſome things to the book. Cotton Mather ſays "it was afterwards found that certain Jews were hired to do that work, and had fourſcore pounds for their pains, and a dozen bottles of wine over and above."—*Magnalia*, ii: 527. But Whiting denies this: "And what if a *Jew* was hired to help in ſome part of that Work, was that any Crime? It was known, that John Stubbs, the Chief Author of it, was a very learned Man, and had thirty Languages (almoſt as many as are in that Book) as *C. M.'s* Champion, *Roger Williams*, confeſſed."—*Truth and Innocency Defended*, p. 113.

Coddington writing to J. Winthrop, jr., under date of Aug. 23, 1672, ſays of Stubbs; "he is a larned man, as witneſs the battele dore in 35 languages."—4, *Mass. Hiſt. Coll.* vii: 292.

[1] Fox ſays of Burnyeat: "He travelled and Preacht the Goſpel in Ireland, Scotland, Barbadoes, Virginia, Maryland, New Jerſeys, Long-Iſland, Road-Iſland, and up and down in New England, and had many Diſputes with many Prieſts and Profeſſors, that oppoſed the Truth; but the Lord gave him Dominion over all, and to ſtop the mouths of the Gainſayers, and he turned many to the Lord, and was a *Peacemaker;* and he preacht in his *Life* and *Converſation*, as well as his *Words*."—Fox's Teſtimony in *Truth Exalted*, p. 1. "His *Innocent Deportment* and blameleſs Converſation preached wherever he came." "And the Lord Cloathed him with *Humility* before all, as became the *Goſpel* he preached."—Teſtimony of Friends in Cumberland, do. pp. 6–7. "He was *meek* and *gentle* and of a healing *Spirit*."—Teſtimony of Friends in Ireland, do. p. 16.

[2] p. 99, *infra*. With this deſcription of Edmundſon it is intereſting to compare the ſtatements of his friends: "He was a man of uncommon Courage, and the Truth invigorating his underſtanding, made him as bold as a Lion; he was early convinced of the everlaſting Truth, and ſoon after was publickly engaged in its Service; he had a great Share of natural Parts, though not much outward Education; and he who enabled *Gideon* of old, though but of a mean Tribe and Family, and advanced him to

Taking his feat at the oppofite end of the houfe, Williams began by calling God to witnefs that he had not been prompted to the difcuffion by any perfonal or interefted motives. Like the Quakers he had acted from a "motive within," and his end was threefold;[1]

1st, to vindicate the moft holy Name of God, trodden in the dirt by Fox and his difciples.

2d, to vindicate the Colony of Rhode Ifland which on account of receiving the Quakers was liable to be reckoned among their abettors.

3d, to make a practical application of the leffon to be derived from the dying outcries, while drowning, of a well-known Quaker, Mr. Nicholas Davis.[2]

The Debate which followed confumed three days, the 9th, 10th and 12th of Auguft. On the 11th which came of a Sunday, it was fufpended, not as Williams averred, becaufe the Quakers "cordially owne that day,"[3] but

---

be a great General of the Hoft of *Ifrael,* making him a Deliverer of his chofen People when in Diftrefs, the fame Almighty Power raifed this our dear Friend, and led him from an outward to a fpiritual Warfare, in which the Lord his God was with him, covering his Head as in the Day of Battle, and *teaching* (according to the Words of the Pfalmift) his Hands to war and his Fingers to fight." A Short Teftimony concerning Wm. Edmundfon, prefixed to *Journal,* p. 12. " Indeed to me he feemed to be as a *Boanerges,* or *Son of Thunders,* his Miniftry was fo powerful in the Demonftration of the Spirit "—Teftimony of Chriftopher Wins, lxvii.

[1] p. 39, *iafva.*
[2] Davis was from Barnftable in Plymouth Colony. He joined Stevenfon

and Robinfon at Bofton, and was banifhed with them and Mary Dyer.—Bifhop, *New England Judged,* 114. Williams makes no further allufion to Davis in the courfe of the difcuffion, but enforced the leffon in his Second Pofition, that the inward Chrift of the Quakers was not the true Chrift.

[3] Fox replies to this; " But we Meet together on the *Firft Day* of the Week, as the *Primitive Chriftians* did; and fo beftow it better, than to *Hear thy Lies* and Blafphemies: any other *day* would ferve *R. W.* But we do not underftand that *R. W.* maketh any *Confcience,* or hath fuch a *Zeal* either for *God* or that *Day,* as to *Meet* to Worfhip God upon that *Day.*"—*N. E. Fire-Brand Quenched,* Pt. i: 68.

" they wifely refolved to have the whole firſt day with the People to make up their *Breaches,* ſtop *Leakes,* dreſs the wounds that might be in the foregoing *Agitations* againſt their *Conſciences* & *Credits.*" But it is more likely that when the Quakers fixed upon the 9th they did not anticipate that their opponent would conſume ſo much time in the difcuſſion. They repeatedly complained of the unreaſonable length to which his argument was extended. Each Propoſition was read aloud by the Quakers as the debate proceeded.[1]

The firſt day was devoted wholly to the Firſt of the 14 Propoſitions; *That the People called Quakers are not true Quakers according to the Scriptures.* Williams argued that the Quakers were "but a new upſtart party,"[2] and that their "horrid and monſtrous motions" were not ſuch trembling as the Scriptures enjoined, but the "workings of Sathan upon his ſervants."[3] Throughout the day Williams made conſtant reference to Fox's "book in folio," ſo that the latter, though, not preſent, was in faĉt a leading party to the controverſy. The three aĉtive participants on the Quaker ſide did little more than defend the poſitions of their leader. Notwithſtanding the precaution taken to preſerve order, ſeveral beſides the regular champions entered the liſts, "ſome in favor of, and ſome againſt the

---

[1] p. 137, *infra.*

[2] Fox comments ſharply on the contradiĉtory aſſertions of Williams, that "the Quakers were but a new upſtart party riſen up little above 20 years ſince," p. 42, *infra;* that "their ugly Child and Daughter Rantiſme roſe from their Bowels," p. 43; and that he had known the Ranters "almoſt ſixty year," p. 243,

" ſo he hath made the Child, according to his own Knowledge, nigh 40 *years* Elder than the *Mother.*"—*N. E. Fire-Brand Quenched,* Pt. i: 177.

For an account of *Theora John,* whom Williams incorreĉtly repreſents as a Quaker, ſee Burton, *Cromwellian Diary* i: cxxvi.

[3] p. 45 *infra.*

Quakers." Among the reſt, a brother of Roger Williams, "Mr. *Robert Williams*,[1] School-Maſter in *Newport*," ſubmitted a paper which the Quakers very properly declined to receive, as not included in the original propoſitions. The diſcuſſion naturally became quite diſcurſive, the uſe which the Quakers made of Scripture becoming a ſubjeċt of warm diſpute. Both Coddington and Eaſton ſpoke, the latter " ſharply," but throughout the day Williams paid chief attention to his principal antagoniſts, who were placed " on high in their Deſks againſt him."[2] "*John Stubs* and John *Burnet* were more ſober and manly, but W. *Edmundſon* (who was the junior of three) would ſpeak all like *Solomon's* fooliſh woman, loud and *clamorous*, *ſimple* and *knowing nothing*, being in truth nothing but a *ſlaſh* of wit, a *Face of Braſs* and a *Tongue* ſet on *fire* from the *Hell of Lyes and Fury*."[3] In one inſtance Edmundſon was called to order by Cranſton. When, near the cloſe of the day, he inveighed againſt Williams for ſlandering the Quakers, the latter retorted by adducing the Quaker praċtice of going ſtark naked into public aſſemblies,[4] which led to a long diſcuſſion of the doċtrine of Figures and Signs. In the

---

[1] The name of Robert Williams ſtands firſt in the liſt of thoſe to whom " home lots " were aſſigned at the ſettlement of Providence. It is alſo ſubſcribed to the agreements of 1640 and 1647. He was living in Providence as late as 1655.—Staples' *Annals*, pp. 35, 43, 112. In a letter to J. Winthrop, jr., dated Sept. 8, 1660, Roger Williams writes : " My brother runs ſtrongly to Origin's notion of univerſal mercy at laſt, againſt an eternal ſentence."— Knowles' *Life*, 314.

Beſides Robert, Roger Williams had another brother "a Turkey-Merchant," p 146, *infra*.

[2] Fox denies this, and ſays : " It was but upon a *Common Seat* as was at the other End."—*N. E. Fire-Brand Quenched*, i : 32.

[3] p. 57, *infra*.

[4] " We told thee then, we own'd no ſuch *Praċtice* in any, unleſs they were called into it by the Lord, as a *Sign* of the *Nakedneſs* of the *Profeſſors* of *Our Ages*, who want the *Covering of the Spirit*."—*N. E. Fire-Brand Quenched*, i : 28.

midſt of the debate the ſun was eclipſed, an event which Williams interpreted as betokening that the true Sun of Righteouſneſs would only be for a time obſcured by Quaker errors ; but ſo far as the arguments on either ſide were concerned, the firſt day cloſed with no deciſive reſult. Both ſides were diſappointed becauſe the whole diſcuſſion was not ended.

The ſecond day found Williams more inclined to keep his bed than to go forth to a freſh diſpute. Loud ſpeaking the day before, and wet feet, the reſult of a heavy rain that followed the eclipſe, had combined to make him very hoarſe. He chooſe a middle ſeat, nearer his three antagoniſts, ſo that he might be heard with leſs ſtraining of his voice. On the ſecond day there was again a "great Aſſembly," and as on the firſt the diſcuſſion continued until evening. The phyſical diſability of Williams gave occaſion to a ſlander, circulated in private, that he was drunk, but he ſtates that though his daughter kindly offered him a dram for his illneſs, he declined it left it might curdle the milk he had taken at breakfaſt.[1] The incident deſerves notice only as illuſtrating the bitterneſs which the controverſy had created. The day was devoted to the diſcuſſion of the Second of the 14 Propoſitions, *That the* Chriſt *they profeſs is not the* true Lord Jeſus Chriſt. The main point on which Williams inſiſted was that the Quaker doctrine of the Chriſt within tended to obſcure or deſtroy the Chriſt without.[2]

---

[1] p. 67, *infra.* Fox makes no alluſion to this report.

[2] Fox earneſtly repudiates this charge, " As for his *Ungracious, Unfavoury* words, they are not worth mentioning: let the *Reader* ſee, if *G. F.* ever denied *Chriſt* (*that died at* Jeruſalem) in any of theſe *pages,* that he hath wrought, or any of the *Quakers* Writings ?"

" *Roger,* thou addſt *Lie* with *Lie.* For that Chriſt, *that died at* Jeruſalem *bodily,* we own."—*N. E. Fire-Brand,* Pt. i : 49.

The argument turned, even more than on the day before, upon the teachings of Fox, whofe "Book in folio" was in conftant requifition. Burnyeat held a copy in his hands, and followed Williams clofely in all quotations. "Ever and anon," in the midft of this examination, Williams "made fallies out upon them, and had fome *Skirmifhings* and fometimes fharp *Difputes.*" He charged that the Quakers' notion of Chrift was "Frantick and Whimfical; Grofs and Blockifh." Although Williams defired to complete the difcuffion of the firft feven pofitions on the fecond day he was prevented by two long harangues which Edmundfon and Stubbs were moved to addrefs to thofe prefent. When they had ended Williams complained with juftice that a mutual difputation had been turned into a preaching fervice.[1] He clofed the day's debate by fhowing that the denial of the "Chrift Without" involved the denial of the vifible Church. When, at this point, Williams was taunted with "not being in Church ordinance," himfelf,[2] he briefly explained his own peculiar pofition with refpect to Church communion. After complaints on both fides about the time already confumed, the Quakers agreed to meet Williams "on the fecond Day following *at nine in the Morning*, only they would not endure any long and tedious Difcourfes."

---

[1] Fox rejoins: "And when *W. E.* did *Appeal to the People*, thou haft not fhewed, that the people was diffatisfied with *W. E.'s Appeal;* and were not *W. E.'s.* and *J. S.'s*, their *Speeches* (which thou fcoffingly call'ft Sermons) to the Matter of the *Falfe Charges*, which thou could'ft nct make Good ?"--*N. E. Fire-Brand*, Pt. i: 59.

[2] "*J. Stubs* had *Good Reafon* to ask then this *Queftion*, feeing thou liveft not in the *Practie*, nor under the *Exercife* of none thyfelf, as we underftand. And whom hath *R. W.* Fellowfhip withal ? or of what *Church* is he a *Member* of? but is not *R. W.'s* (like wild *Ifmael*) his *Hand againft* every man ?"—*N. E. Fire-Brand*, Pt. i: p. 63.

On the third day, it was agreed that Williams fhould devote but fifteen minutes to each Propofition, in order that the remaining five might be defpatched at a fingle feffion. In confequence of this he was obliged to omit the reading of many paffages from Fox, but thefe have been fupplied in his account of the debate. Before he began to fpeak a fealed letter was handed to him directed in the handwriting of his brother Robert. The letter was not read but is printed by Williams.[1] While it appears that Robert Williams did not approve of the manner in which his brother had affailed the Quakers, whom he recognizes as "fervants of the Lord," and falutes as "Loving Friends," he complains of their rudenefs in conftantly addreffing their opponent as "Old Man,"[2] and of their unfairnefs in reproaching him with wafte of time when it was their own fault that the arguments had fo much exceeded the anticipated bounds.

Putting the letter unopened into his pocket, Williams proceeded to his third Pofition; *That the Spirit by which they acted was not the true Spirit of God.* On this point he argued that the ordinary operation of the Holy Spirit was "by means," while the Quakers claimed that it was immediate.[3] Before, however, he had fpoken for the ftipulated fifteen minutes he was interrupted, as ufual, by the other fide. In the warm debate that followed, Williams

---

[1] p. 111, *infra.*

[2] "But as to our faying OLD MAN to thy Brother, it was not in *Dif-refpect* to his *Perfon*, nor to fet at nought his *Old-Age* (for we have learned better;) but it was a True Title to him, and not *Difhonorable*, nor by us given in *Derifion*, though thou and thy Brother take it fo."

N. E. Fire-Brand Quenched, Pt. i : 73.

[3] p 120, *infra.* Fox replies: "But we never denied the *means* of the *Spirit* of God to work withal; but your *Means*, which are without the *Immediate Spirit* of God, and the *Light* of Chrift *Jefus*, which thou *Blafphemoufly* calleft an Idol." *N. E. Fire-Brand*, Pt. i : 74.

was accufed by Edmundfon of uttering blafphemy, but Cranfton declared that his meaning had been miftaken. As one proof that the Quakers were not led by the true Spirit of God, Williams adduced "their monftrous way of Singing and Toning and Humming many at once, as they often do, and notorioufly did at *Portfmouth*, in *Rhode Ifland* this laft year."

"After fome few interchanges and altercations," the fourth Pofition was taken up; *That the People called Quakers did not own the Holy Scriptures.* On this point Williams argued that the doctrine of the Inner Light, as held by the Quakers, was no lefs fatal to the authority of Scripture than the Papal theory of Infallibility. He ftood ftrictly on the common Proteftant ground. There was no middle courfe between "fubfcribing to the Papifts," or with Luther and Calvin "fearching the originals alone.[1] He maintained that a pure Chriftianity had always been marked by "Love to the *Holy Scriptures.*" It was no wonder that the Quakers "cried out fo fiercely againft the Schools of Learning in *Old* and *New England*," fince "the right and regular propagation of natural, of civil, and efpecially of *Divine Knowledge* fcatters the thick Fogs of the *Quakers* affected hellifh ignorance."

The fifth Pofition was that their *Principles and Profeffions are full of Contradictions and Hypocrifies*, which Williams explained to mean not that the Quakers knowingly deceived, but that they were "*blind Guides or Followers.*"[2] On this point he claimed that the ftatements of the Quakers refpecting Chrift, the Church, the Scriptures, and the

[1] p. 142, *infra.* "*R. W.* may fub-fcribe to the Papifts. How can he fearch the Scriptures and ftudy the Originals without the *Light* of Chrift?" *N. E. Fire-Brand*, Pt. i: 92.
[2] p. 164, *infra.*

power of the Civil Magiſtrates were at variance. He
quoted Fox to prove that the Quakers owned no magiſtrates but ſuch as were godly in their ſenſe.

With regard to the ſixth Poſition, that *The Religion of
the Quakers is not only an Hereſie in the matters of Gods holy
worſhip, but alſo in the Doctrines of Repentance, Faith, &c.,*
Williams claimed that as to worſhip, they denied the Viſible
Church and its Ordinances ; and as to Repentance, a true
ſorrow for ſin and godly contrition. They were haunted
for the moſt part by "a ſoure, proud, and melancholy"[1]
ſpirit ; while they talked of Faith in Chriſt they turned him
into a "meer Fiction."

At laſt, "by God's merciful help," Williams reached the
ſeventh and final Poſition to be diſcuſſed at Newport, that
*Their Religion is but a confuſed mixture of Popery, Armine-
aniſme, Socineaniſme, Judaiſme, &c.* As Williams was pro-
poſing to return to Providence by boat the ſame night, he
was here compelled "not to exceed his quarter glaſs," but
in the printed account he gives his argument more fully.
He declared that the Quakers "were *downright Papiſts* in
many points."[2] They both agreed in denying Total Depravi-
ty ; in maintaining "that *dolefully, uncomfortable,* and *deſperate Doctrine* of falling away from *true* and *ſaving grace;*"
they "were *great Confederates* in their endeavours to raze
the *Records of Heaven;*" they "ſhake hands in the moſt *hel-*

---

[1] Compare the ſtatement of Evelyn. At
Colcheſter, July 8, 1656, he writes : "I
had the curioſity to viſit ſome Quakers
here in priſon ; a new fanatic ſect, of
dangerous principles, who ſhow no reſpect to any man, magiſtrate, or other,
and ſeem a melancholy, proud ſort of
people, and exceedingly ignorant."—

Evelyn's *Diary,* i: 315. So Henry
More ſpeaks of the "Phariſaical *Sour-
neſs*" of the Quakers, and ſays, that
they "undoubtedly are the moſt *Melancholy Sect* that ever was yet in the
world."—See *Theological Works,* 371 ;
Enthuſiasmus Triumphatus, 19.

[2] p. 196, *infra.*

lifh Doctrine of Juftification by what is within us;" they "arrogate Infallibility;" agree in the "lofty Conceit of their Perfection;" in their notion of "Revelations;" and in various other matters of belief and practice.[1] Their agreement with Arminians and other fects was alfo not lefs fully infifted upon.

Thus ended the three days' debate at Newport, and the difcuffion of the firft feven of the fourteen Pofitions which Williams had advanced. The unufual fpectacle had drawn together a great number, who had watched, with eager intereft, the fortunes of the ftrife. During the courfe of the debate, they had, from time to time, freely expreffed their views, and their judgment feems to have been divided. Even thofe who fympathifed with Williams, were not wholly fatisfied with the manner in which his felf-impofed tafk had been accomplifhed. The only full report of the proceedings is from his pen, and from the pains which he took to preferve and publifh this account it is evident that, in his own opinion, he had vanquifhed his opponents. They naturally took a very different view. The fecond day after the difcuffion at Newport clofed, John Stubbs, in a

---

[1] The coincidence of the Quaker doctrine with the Roman Catholic was early noticed. One of the firft publications of Penn, was a Reply to Clapham's *Guide to the True Religion,* in which Papifts, Socinians and Quakers had been claffed together. In a public difcuffion about the fame time, (1668) Penn was called a Jefuit.—Clarkfon's *Life,* i: 39. In his addrefs before the Houfe of Commons, during the excitement occafioned by the Popifh Plot, he fays, "for a long time I have not only been fuppofed a Papift, but a Seminary, a Jefuit, an emiffary of Rome, and in pay from the Pope," *do :* 215. An opponent of the Quakers, Leflie, declared, "The *Quaker Infallibility* was contrived on purpofe to bring men back to the Infallibility of the *Church* of *Rome.*"—*The Snake in the Grafs,* p. 188. Barclay defended the Quakers in *The Anarchy of the Ranters; the Hierarchy of the Romanifts; equally reproved and refuted.*" 1674.

letter to Margaret Fox,[1] the wife of George, gave this curious account of the proceedings.

John Stubbs to Margaret Fox, at Swathmoor Hall.[2]

Newport in Rhode Iſland, yᵉ. 14: 6: 1672.

"Since thy huſband's departure from this place we have had a diſpute with one a great linguiſt & a Scholler, an Orthodox man ſoe called, who lives at a place called providence about 30 miles from this place ; he ſent a challenge to this place to thy huſband or any of his Countreymen to Argue with him in 14 poſitions which he would maintaine ag: all commers. Wee could not avoyd it but to give him a meeting, the firſt Seaven he was to performe at this place and the others at providence. Soe yᵉ laſt ſixt day being ye 9ᵗʰ of this inſtant we gave him a meeting and yᵉ Countreys adjacent came in from all parts ſoe that there was a very great congregation of high and lowe ; and before he began we laid it upon him to prove all his charges againſt us by the Scriptures, and Soe he be-

---

[1] Margaret Fox was the widow of Judge Fell, of Swathmore Hall. "A convincement of the Lord's truth came upon her" early in Fox's miniſtry. Fell remained a Churchman, but favored the Quakers. In 1669, eleven years after his death, Margaret married Fox, ſhe being fifty-five and he ten years younger. He writes in his *Journal:* "I had ſeen from the Lord a conſiderable time before, that I ſhould take Margaret Fell to be my wife ; and when I firſt mentioned it to her ſhe felt the anſwer of Life from God thereunto." At the marriage "in the public meeting-houſe at Broad Mead in Briſtol," "living and weighty teſtimonials were borne thereunto by friends in the movings of the heavenly power." Fox's *Journal*, pp. 71, 412.

[2] Swathmoor Hall, the ſeat of Judge Fell, was near Ulverſtone, in Lancaſhire, juſt north of Morecambe Bay. After his wife had adopted the views of Fox, the Judge gave the Quakers permiſſion to hold a regular meeting at the Hall. This continued to be held until 1686, when Fox built a meeting houſe adjoining the Hall, which is ſtill uſed.—Tallack, *George Fox*, p. 110.

gan about ye Ninth houre in ye morning and continued
till about 6 in the afternoone, and could not prove ye firſt
charge, for we would not let him proceed to a ſecond till
he had proved the firſt, or if he could not, then to acknowledge the wrong to us; but nothing he could prove neither
from Scripture nor Argument nor Example. He could
give Satisfaction noe not to his owne friends wh. conſiſted
moſtly of Baptiſte and ſome other Separated people, for y^e
Baptiſts here were full of rage agt. us,[1] ſoe the night in a
manner put a period to ye firſt dayes Diſpute. And the
next day being y^e ſeaventh day of ye week, about ye 9th
houre in the Morning we begunne againe : and then wee
deſired him to be as full and as ſhort as he could in things,
and if the Scriptures of truth would not beare us out in
our principal Doctrines and practice then let us fall with
ſhame. And ſoe we deſired him to proceed to ye Second
ſeing in a whole dayes time before he had made nothing
of the firſt to to prove anything but had altogether diſat-
isfied ye Auditt. Soe then he told us he would be as
Briefe as he could. And he had the day before ſpoken of
ſuch & ſuch greevous errors and Blaſphemies &c, by Such
& Such, & in Such & Such Bookes of ye Quakers & moſt
Eſpecially in a Book of Georg ffox's in folio and this he
mentioned the day before, and ſoe the ſecond dayes diſcourſe in ye beginning of ye diſcourſe as was Said before
we deſired him to be as full and as Briefe as he could, and

---

[1] The ſtriking reſemblance between
the views of the Quakers and the early
Baptiſts which has been before referred
to, and the fact that *George* Fox and
other preachers were ſo often "moved
by the Lord" to go among them, naturally made ſuch Baptiſts as did not adopt
his views eſpecially bitter in their oppoſition. Edmundſon's *Journal* atteſts his
deſire to meet the Baptiſts, and the min-
gled favor and oppoſition with which
he was received. pp. 35, 95, 102.

whereas ye day before in ye Audience of ye people he had ſpoken much of Errors in Bookes and Eſpecially in a Book of folio of Georg ffoxes we bid him read thoſe errors to ye people y^t all ye Congregation might hear him and judg of them, and ſoe he began and read w^thout interruption and gave his own inferrences and continued reading and giving his inferrences all ye day almoſt, for he had noted (as he conceived) abundance of errors in ye Book in near 40 pages, and Soe is ſaid before he read diſtinctly to ye Auditt. ye Preiſts and ye Profeſſors principles & G F.; anſwers in thoſe heads y^t he had noted for Errors. And truly thoſe wh. he had marked wh. they came to be read proved quite contrary to his Expectations for ye people generally ſaw and were fully ſatisſied y^t thoſe places wh. he alledged out of y^t Book as great Errors and Soe to make for him ag^t us, but as I ſaid before it proved quite contrary, for indeed when that wh. he called errors were read Generally peoples Eyes and eares were opened and their hearts and minds ſatisfied[1] wh. made us greatly rejoyced w'hin ourſelves when we ſaw how the Lord vindicated his own cauſe and how the crafty was caught in his own ſnare, and ye innocent delivered; and Soe moſt of y^t Second dayes diſpute was ended in turning over from page to page in y^t prementioned Book wh. proved better ſervice for the truth than my tongue or pen can demonſtrate, and then w^n the night ended ye dayes worke, he deſired to have another day, and ſoe we told him we would give him 3 houres time upon y^e ſecond day of the ffollowing week,

[1] "And did not a *ſtranger* ſpeak aloud then, and ſaid; *I am no* Quaker; *yet I ſee, that* Mr. Williams *hath rather proved* againſt himſelf, *and not for himſelf.*"—*N. E. Fire-Brand Quenched,* i: 73.

and w^n he came he made a preamble and proceeded on
in the Book ag^n in some other pages and soe continued
some houres, and ye Book vindicated itself still ag. him and
for us.   And then the man began to be much confounded
and amazed in himself when he understood his friends
were dissatisfied[1] & every thing made ag.^{t} him soe y^t not
any one of ye first 7 propositions he could make good.
Soe W^m. Edmundson stood up and spoke a pretty while to
ye people very well, and then Jno Burnyeat, and the truth
came over all, Blessed be the Lord for it.   And now the
next Seventh day, wh. is the 7th of this instant Wm Edmundson and I are to goe to providence to give him a
meeting about ye last 7 propositions and the day following,
if ye Lord will, to have a meeting for ye Town for there
is a great openness in those parts of late."[2]

[1] All were not, for as Williams was
stepping down to the boat the Lord
"opened the mouth" of Elizabeth Williams, his brother Robert's wife, "one
of the Society of the *Baptists* in *Newport*" to declare that he had "fully
proved" what he undertook.—p. 213,
infra.

[2] The original of this letter is in the
Cabinet of the R. I. Hist. Society.

Of the proceedings at Newport, Edmundson, who as we have seen met Fox
at Shelter Island, gives the following account :

"After some Day's Travel by *Narra-
ganfet* and those Parts, I came to *Rhode-
Island*, where I met with *John Burnyeat,
John Stubbs* and *John Cartwright ;* then
one *Roger Williams* an old Priest and an
Enemy to Truth, had put forth fourteen
Propositions, as he called them, which
he would maintain against any of the
Quakers, that came from *Old-England,*

and challenged a Dispute of seven of them
at *Newport* in *Rhode-Island,* and the other
seven at *Providence.*"

"I joined with Friends in answering
the Challenge, at the Time and Place appointed for the Dispute, which was to
be in Friends' Meeting-house at *Newport ;* thither a great Concourse of People of all Sorts gathered.   When those
Propositions, as he called them, came to
be discoursed of, they were all but Slanders, and Accusations against the *Quakers;*
the bitter old Man could make Nothing
out, but on the contrary they were
turned back upon himself ; He was baf-
fled, and the People saw his Weakness,
Folly, and Envy against the Truth and
Friends."

"There were many prejudiced Baptists who would fain have helped the old
Priest against Friends ; but they durst not
undertake his Charge against us, for they
saw it was false and weak.   So the Tes-

On the feventeenth of Auguſt, the difcuffion, according to agreement was continued at Providence ; as at Newport there was a very large affeṃblage. Of the place where it was held no tradition has been preſerved.[1] Poſſibly it was the "great barn" in which Fox had ſo copiouſly perſpired. In Rhode Iſland, it muſt be remembered, the meeting houſe was not, as in Maſſachuſetts, the nucleus of each new ſettlement. Providence had been founded for more than two generations before any place of public worſhip was erected. By adhering to the fifteen minutes rule the remaining ſeven Propoſitions were diſpatched in a ſingle day.[2] On the ſide of the Quakers, only Stubbs and Edmundſon appeared ; but, as in Newport, the debate was not confined to the principal antagoniſts. At the outſet, Thomas Olney, "an able and *Leeding man* amongſt the People called *Baptiſts* at *Providence*," Captain Holden, Captain John Green, and Mr. Caverly, of Warwick, all made themſeves heard, the latter urging that a Moderator ſhould be choſen. When the firſt Poſition, *that the Quakers in Effect held no God, no Chriſt, no Spirit, &c., but what was in Man*, had been a little while debated, Samuel Gorton deſired to ſpeak. He argued that if the ſoul, as Fox held, was "a part of God," the argument of Williams was concluſive. In the application of Scripture he proved himſelf more than a match for Stubbs.[3] As the ſhort time allowed

timony of Truth in the Power of God was ſet over all his falſe charges, to the great Satisfaction of the People."—Edmundſon's *Journal*, p. 73.

[1] Staples' *Annals*, p. 422.

[2] It would ſeem from a diſpute about time, that Williams was not the owner of a watch.—p. 106, *infra*.

[3] Gorton like Williams had received a good claſſical training. His religious views at this period of his life may be found in an intereſting letter to John Winthrop, jr., dated Warwick, Oct. 21, 1674.—4 *Maſs. Hiſt. Coll.* vii : 604 He ſeems never to have inclined to the Quakers.

him did not enable Williams to bring forward all his quotations from Fox, he has commented upon them more freely in his printed account.

The remaining Pofitions difcuffed at Providence related not to doctrine fo much as to matters of perfonal opinion. Williams muft have had uncommon confidence in his own powers if he ever cherifhed the remoteft expectation that his opponents would be brought to acknowledge that their religion required no more than a reprobate might eafily attain to; that the Popes did not fwell with a greater pride; that their belief was more deftructive to falvation than moft religions extant; that their books were poor and made up of boafting and vapor. Burnyeat was right in faying that thefe were charges rather than propofitions to be debated. At length Williams clofed, with his 14th Pofition, in which the fpirit of Quakerifm was affirmed to tend to Barbarifm; to arbitrary Government; to Affaffination and to Perfecution. In point of breeding the Quakers, he declared, were worfe than the Indians; for the latter would return a falutation,[1] and did not fhow themfelves ftark naked in private houfes. This latter imputation caufed great irritation. Stubbs afferted that in nineteen years experience as a Quaker he had never feen a woman naked, and fome among the Quakers, who had been Williams' friends, were fo enraged that he deemed it expedient to drop the fubject. That Quakerifm would logically refult in arbitrary government Williams argued on the ground that thofe acting from the immediate in-

---

[1] Fox replies: "It is alfo falfe, that even the *Quakers* were againft *Taking by the Hand*, or true *Courtefy;* though to *Bow*, and *Uncover the Head* (whether *half* or *whole*) they are againft, and loft upon us in *Apoftacy*, if done by any of them."— *N. E. Fire-Brand Quenched*, i: 222.

fpiration of Grace would not need to be "cumbered with Lawes." An aged man, Thomas Arnold, "though much of late adhering to the *Quakers*," thought there was weight in this reafoning. With regard to the charge that the "Quaker Spirit tended to the fudden cutting off of People," Williams acknowledged that he had no facts to bring forward, and that he only charged them "with a tendency." Ravaillac, the affaffin of Henry IV, "that famous and wonderful man," had claimed to act as the inftrument of God, and a Quaker might do the fame. At this point Edmundfon retorted by accufing Williams of having approved the execution of Charles Firft. William Harris handed Edmundfon a book from which to fubftantiate this charge, but Captain Green, a Magiftrate, interfered, and the book was laid afide. The paffage, as Williams explains, expreffed fome approval of Parliament, but had no reference to the King's death, "which God knows I never approved to this day." Williams did not forget the part played by Harris in this epifode, and in the account of the difcuffion devotes to him a bitter paragraph.[1]

---

[1] p. 316, *infra*. William Harris was one of thofe who joined Williams at Seekonk. With John Throckmorton and others he is named in the "Initial deed" of the territory on which Providence was fettled. On the "Towne Street" his lot was next to Throckmorton's. When the town made its firft remove from pure democracy, in 1640, he was one of the four to whom the adminiftration of affairs was entrufted. In the winter of 1654–5 he feems to have been concerned, with Robert Williams and others, in fome difturbance. In confequence of this a paper was fent to the town afferting "that it was blood-guiltinefs and againft the rule of the gofpel, to execute judgment upon tranfgreffors againft the private or public weal." For afferting this doctrine Harris, two years later, was arrefted for high treafon on a warrant iffued by Williams in his capacity as Prefident of the Colony. The matter was referred to the Agent of the Colony, and feems to have been carried no further, but it was the beginning of a feud between Williams and Harris that only clofed with death. In 1660, Harris was one of the Commiffioners from Providence, and alfo in 1662 and 1663,

The laft point of the 14th Pofition, *that the Quaker Spirit tended* to *Perfecution,* Williams did not urge, as he had already touched upon it at Newport, and was wearied with the long debate. After he had withdrawn, Captain Green defired to return to the more ftrictly theological queftions, whether revelations were immediate, and whether the foul was a part of God, but the Quakers waved them as too abftrufe. Then Pardon Tillinghaft, "a leading man among the People called *Baptifts,*" raifed the queftion of Ordinances. After a brief difcuffion Edmundfon "fell to prayer," when Tillinghaft alfo withdrew, declaring "that he was free to difcourfe with them, but not to join with them in worfhip."[1] Thus ended the difcuffion at Providence, much in the fame way that the previous one in Newport had ended, each fide apparently well fatisfied with the refult. From Providence, Stubbs and Edmundfon went to Warwick, where the next day they had a meeting in which "the Lord's Power and Prefence were largely manifefted."[2]

facts which go to fhow that the charges of Williams was not endorfed by the majority of the community. In 1667, Harris brought a charge againft Arthur Fenner for riot, but Fenner was acquitted and Harris fined fifty pounds for caufing the Affembly to be called without caufe. Yet afterwards the General Affembly remitted the fine. A ftatement of the facts was drawn up by order of the town, and fent to other towns of the Colony in which Harris was defcribed as a " Firebrand." Notwithftanding this, Harris was reëlected Affiftant in May following, when the town addreffed to the Governor and Council a fecond remonftrance, in which Harris was feverely denounced. The circum-ftance that rendered Harris unpopular was his ufually acting as the attorney of Connecticut in the frequent difputes between that Colony and Rhode Ifland. He feems to have been the more fuccefsful before courts of law, while Williams had the greater influence with the community. Staples'*Annals,* pp. 20, 40, 143, 147. Arnold, *Hift. R. I.,* i: 254, 262.

[1] The Baptifts feem to have been very ftrict upon this point. As late as May 25, 1732, the Church in Providence agreed, "that if any brother or fifter fhall join in prayers without the bounds of the church, they are liable to be dealt with by the church for their offending their brethren."—Staples' *Annals,* 413.

[2] Edmundfon's *Journal* p. 75.

Thence Stubbs went to Narraganfett, while Edmundfon returned by boat to Newport.[1]

The following narrative of the difcuffion, though not publifhed by Williams until four years later, was drawn up, as appears from the title, foon after the debates took place. In preparing it he feems to have had no help beyond his memory; he endeavored to procure a fhort-hand writer, but could not.[2]   In this refpect his opponents were better provided, for when a difpute arofe, during the third

[1] Of the proceedings in Providence Edmundson gives the following account:

"When this Meeting (i. e. in Newport) was ended, which lafted three Days, *John Stubbs* and I went to *Providence*, accompanied with many Friends, to hear the other feven Propofitions, which lafted one Day, *John Burnyeat* and *John Cartwright* going another Way in Truth's Service. Now at *Providence* there was a very great Gathering of People, both *Prefbyterians, Baptifts* and *Ranters. Roger Williams* being there, I ftood up and told him in Public, We had fpent fo many Days at *Newport,* where he could make Nothing out agreeable to his *Challenge;* but on the contrary manifefted his Clamour, rash and falfe Accufations, which he could not prove againft us; that I was not willing to fpend much Time in hearing his Clamour and falfe Accufations, having other Service for the Lord, therefore would only fpend that Day.   So he went on, as he had done at *Newport* in *Rhode-Ifland.* We anfwered to all his Charges againft Friends, and difproved them."

"Now the old prejudiced Man was filenced; then the Profeffors defired to know our Belief, *What the Soul of Man was made of?*   I told them, I believed what the Scriptures faid, that when God made man, he breathed into man the breath of Life, and he became a living Soul; and that it was fufficient for me to know Chrift Jefus who redeemed my Soul.   But if any of them, that were great Profeffors and old Difputants, would undertake to fhow, what God made the Soul of man of, he might. Then one that was an ancient leading Man among them faid, *He would not meddle with it:* This ended the Difpute.   Then we had a feafonable Opportunity to open many Things to the People, appertaining to the Kingdom of God, and Way of Eternal Life and Salvation.   The Meeting concluded in Prayer to Almighty God, the People went away fatisfied and loving."—Edmundfon's *Journal,* p. 75.

Soon after this Edmundfon returned to England.   In 1676, directly after the excitement occafioned by King Philip's war, he again vifited Rhode Ifland.   He had "many bleffed and heavenly Meetings," but makes no further mention of Roger Williams. do. p. 93.

[2] See his Addrefs *To the People called* Quakers, *infra.* Short-hand was much ufed in the 17th century.

day's difcuffion at Newport, refpecting the precife words
ufed by Williams, Edmundfon infifted that thefe words
fhould be read by "one of theirs," who had taken them
down in fhort-hand.[1] But while Williams was thus compelled to rely upon his memory, Fox and Burnyeat, in
their Reply, although bitterly denouncing his ftatements,
do not queftion the general accuracy of his report.

Not only was the manufcript prepared, but the book
feems to have been actually in print before the fpring of
1673, fince in the addrefs *To the People called* Quakers,
the author refers to the pages as they now ftand. Why
the publication fhould have been fo long delayed does not
appear. Although Williams had affigned as a principal
motive in propofing the difcuffion the vindicating of Rhode
Ifland, much intereft feems to have been manifefted in
the work by prominent perfons in the neighboring colonies. Governor Leverett, of Maffachufetts, declared that
he would give twenty pounds rather than that the book
fhould not be printed, and to this the Governor of
Plymouth offered to add five pounds more.[2] Williams
himfelf attached fo much importance to the difcuffion,
that had he failed to fecure a publifher on this fide the
water, he had "great thoughts" of having his "large narrative of all thofe four days' agitation" printed in England.[3] He fpared no pains to fecure for his work the moft

---

[1] Burnyeat fays : "There is a Book in
Manufcript, of what was taken in *Short-
hand* of the Difcourfe at that prefent."
Truth Exalted, p. 54.

[2] Coddington's letter to Fox, in *New-
Eng. Fire-Brand Quenched*, Pt. ii : 246.

[3] See his letter to Samuel Hubbard, in
Backus, *Hiftory of the Baptifts* i : 511.

Williams feems to have had fome difficulty in getting his later works printed.
In a letter to Governor Bradftreet, in
May, 1662, referring to a propofed volume of his fermons preached to the Narraganfett Indians, he writes : "For printing, I am forced to write to my friends
at Maffachufetts, Connecticut, Plymouth,

favorable reception. It was prefaced with an "Epiftle
Dedicatory" to Charles the Second, a monarch whofe name
ftands in odd connection with fuch a controverfy, but whom
Williams thus addreffed becaufe His Majefty had been liberally provided with Quaker publications. Barclay's *Apolo-
gy*, which appeared in 1676, was alfo dedicated to the King
but in a ftrain of fober eloquence, for which we fhall
fearch in vain the pages of the following work. For
writing this Dedication, Fox charged Williams with
"manifefting a temporizing fpirit," and with now flattering
the King as he formerly had flattered the Parliament.[1]
But if Williams laid himfelf open to the charge of flatte-
ry in his Dedication to the King, he certainly guarded
againft any fuch accufation in the brief addrefs which follows, *To the People called* Quakers. He here accufers the
Quakers of denying the fundamental doctrine of Pro-
teftantifm; repeats in offenfive language his charge that
Fox purpofely avoided meeting him at Newport; and affirms that fpiritual pride was the "Root and Branch" of
the whole Quaker religion. His aim was "to give teftimony in his generation," with the expectation, as he con-
feffes, that few would be influenced by his arguments.
While, however, hoping little from the Quakers, Williams

and our own colony, that he that hath a
fhilling and a heart to countenance and
promote fuch a foul-work, may truft the
Paymafter (who is beforehand with us
already) for a hundreth for one in this
life."—Knowles' *Life*, p. 353.

[1] "And *R. W.* who hath now fo much
flattered the *King* in his Epiftle (in his
Book 1676) and would have us to be
punifhed; but let *R. W.* read his Book
called *The Bloody Tenant,* &c. (1652,)
and his Epiftle to the *High Court* of
Parliament, what he faith then of the
King. R. W.'s words are, as followeth:
The late King Charles *his* Confcience, to
opprefs the Confcience *of others, no fmall
Occafion of the Ruin of him and his.* So
Roger, read thy words in thy Book
(1652) and thofe in thy Epiftle to the
King now (in 1676) againft the Quakers."
N. E. *Fire-Brand Quenched,* Pt. ii: 241.

was anxious to conciliate the favorable judgment of another clafs.   Accordingly he added a third Epiftle, to the "*many* Learned and Pious Men" whom Fox had attacked, efpeci- ally Richard Baxter and John Owen.[1] Thefe Epiftles all bear the fame date, and were written after the body of the work had been put to prefs.   Appended to the account of the Difcuffion was a copious collection of Proofs of the Thirteenth Pofition, confifting of paffages from Fox's book.

The origin of the punning title of the book, Williams explains as follows : During. the firft day's difcuffion at Newport, Edmundfon reproved him for fpeaking of Fox and Burrowes "in fcorn and derifion," underftanding him to fay "Fox in his Burrowes."   Williams protefted at the time that he had ufed no fuch language, but afterwards, when he came to write his narrative, he wittily followed the hint of his antagonift, feeing in it "the finger of God directing and pointing him to fo proper and pertinent an ufe and application.[2]

However favorable in fome quarters may have been the impreffion made by the book, among the Quakers of Rhode Ifland it aroufed the moft bitter rage.   William Coddington, like Roger Williams long paft three fcore and ten, wrote to George Fox denouncing the author in unmeafured ftrains.   Richard Scot, a neighbor of Wil- liams for nearly forty years, wrote to the fame effect, and

---

[1] The impreffion made by the work upon the orthodox party may be inferred from the remark of Cotton Mather, in his account of Roger Williams: "And againft the Quakers he afterwards main- tained the main principles of the Pro- teftant religion with much vigour in fome difputations ; whereof he afterwards pub-

lifhed a large account, in a book againft George Fox and Edward Burrowes." *Magnalia*, ii : 499.

Mather, charitably remarks of Wil- liams "that many judicious perfons judged him to have had the 'root of' the matter' in him."

[2] p. 53 *infra.*

with equal acrimony.[1]   Fox feems already to have had his attention called to the work, which in its publifhed form was a ftill more direct attack upon himfelf than the difcuffion which it narrated.   The book was deemed worthy of an elaborate anfwer.   In June, of the following fummer, he attended the yearly meeting of the Quakers, held at London.   Immediately after, he went with William Penn to Worminghurft, in Suffex, a country place where Penn had eftablifhed his refidence not long before, and there, with the affiftance of John Bur-

---

[1] Thefe letters are interefting as illuftrations of contemporary opinion. Coddington under date of June 25, 1677, writes of Williams ; "He began with a *Thunder*, and had *Three Days* time to bewilder and befool himfelf, and fo ended in a great *E lips* of the *Sun* (which was taken notice of.) I have known him about 50 Years, a meer *Weather Cock*, Conftant only in Unconftancy ; Poor Man ! that doth not know, what fhould become of his *Soul, if this Night it fhould be taken from him.* He was for the *Priefts*, and took up their principles to fight againft the *Truth*, and to gratify them and bad *Magiftrates*, that licked up his *Vomit*, and wrote the faid *Scurrilous Book :* and fo hath tranfgreffed for a Piece of Bread."

" *Dear* G. F. I may yet more prove, what I have faid.   One while he is a *Separatift* at *New-Plymouth* in *New England*, Joining with them till they are weary of him (as from *Morton's Memorials* in Print deth appear :) Another time you may have him a *Teacher* or Member of the Church at *Salem* in *New England :* O ! Then a great deal of Devotion is placed in *Women wearing* of *Vails* in their Affembles, as if the Power of Godlinefs was in it ; and to have the *Crofs* out of the *Colors :* and then be againft the *King's Patent* and Authority ; and writeth a large Book in *Quarto* againft it.   And another time he is Hired for *Money*, and gets a *Patent* from the *Long Parliament ;* fo that it is not long, but he is *off* and *on* it again ;   One time for mens wearing *Caps* and not *Hats* for Covering their Faces ; and again *Hats* and no *Caps :* One time for *Water-Baptifm*, Men and Women muft be *plunged* into the *Water ;* and then throw it all down again.   So that Cotton (who in his day did know the Power of God to Salvation) faid of him, That he was a Haberdafher of fmall Queftions againft the Power." *N. E. Fire-Brand Quenched*, Pt. ii : 216.

Scot writes : "Concerning the Converfation and Carriage of this Man *Roger Williams*, I have been his neighbor thefe 38 years : I have only been Abfent in the time of the Wars with the *Indians*, till this prefent.   I walked with him in the *Baptifts* way about 3 or 4 Months, but in that fhort time of his Standing I difcerned, that he muft have the *Order-*

nyeat,[1] drew up the work which was publifhed in 1678, "*A New-England Fire-Brand Quenched,* Being Something in Anfwer unto a Lying, Slanderous Book, Entitled *George Fox Digged out of his Burrowes* &c. Printed at Bofton in the year 1676, of one *Roger Williams* of *Providence* in *New England.*"

The Reply of Fox was in two parts. The firft contained an examination, page by page, of the narrative which Williams had given of the difcuffions at Newport and Providence. The quotations that have already been made from this portion of the work, renders fuperfluous any further illuftration of its method and temper. The fecond part was an anfwer to the Appendix, with which Williams had reinforced his narrative. To the fecond part was added a " Catalogue of *R. W.'s* Envious, Malitious, Scornful *Railing Stuff,* falfe Accufations and *Blafphemies,* which he *foully* and Un-*Chriftian-like* hath Scattered and Difperfed throughout his Book, and calls it *Scripture-Language.*" The Letters of William Coddington and Richard Scot, to which reference has already been made, were alfo

---

ing of all their *Affairs,* or elfe there would be no Quiet Argument amongft them. In which time he brake off from his *Society,* and declared at large the Ground and *Reafons* of it: That their *Baptifm* could not be right, becaufe it was not *Adminiftered* by an Apoftle. After that he fet upon a Way of *Seeking* (with two or three of them, that had diffented with him) by way of *Preaching* and *Praying ;* and then he continued a Year or two, till *Two* of the *Three* left him."

" That which took moft with him, and was his Life, was, *To get honor amongft*

men, efpecially amongft the *Great Ones.*" *N.E. Fire-Brand Quenched,* Pt. ii : 247.

[1] "I ftaid at Worminghurft about three weeks, in which time John Burnyeat and I anfwered a very wicked and envious book, which Roger Williams, a prieft of New England (or fome Colony thereabouts) had written againft truth and friends."—Fox's *Journal,* p. 500.

From the circumftance that this reply was written at Penn's houfe, his biographer thinks it probable that Penn affifted in preparing it.—Clarkfon, *Life of Penn,* i : 177. But would not the fact have been ftated?

included in the volume. The example which Williams himfelf had fet of reforting to invective in place of argument, his Quaker opponents were not flack in following. Amply fupplied as his vocabulary was with the language of perfonal vituperation, it muft be confeffed that, on this occafion, he was fairly beaten with his chofen weapons.

It is well for the fame of Roger Williams that it does not reft upon his lateft work. Compared with his earlier productions it leaves the impreffion that what Cotton Mather terms "the long winter of his retirement" had as little promoted his fpiritual as his intellectual growth. Forty years inceffant contact with the petty animofities of a fettlement fingularly rich in difputes of every fort, ifolation from all external religious communion, bitter perfonal feuds with his neareft neighbors, had neither enlarged his underftanding nor fubdued his temper. The hot Welfh blood that courfed through his veins did not lofe any of its fire till his heart ceafed to beat. In his old age he is as quick to hurl denunciations againft thofe who differed with him as when forty years before he had queftioned the validity of the Maffachufetts charter. For one who had laid fo much ftrefs upon fpiritual liberty, he is fingularly harfh in his treatment of fuch as had exercifed that liberty in arriving at conclufions not coincident with his own. As an examination of the theological fyftem of the Quakers the prefent work is inconclufive and unfair. Not only does Williams fail wholly to detect, beneath wild eccentricities of fpeech and action, the "effence and marrow" of this great proteft againft the formal orthodoxy of the age, but in urging particular objections he continually forces the meaning of his opponents' language, and infifts upon drawing conclufions againft which they ftrenuoufly protefted. Much of the argumentation, if it may be fo called, is weak and quibbling. We fearch in vain for any fearching, difpaffionate difcuffion of the real principles of difference between the Quakers and their opponents. It may be urged, and with truth, that the firft generation of " old Foxian-Quakers" differed from the more moderate difciples of Penn and Barclay, yet furely his own experience fhould have taught Williams to treat with greater forbearance follies which, for the moft part, had been provoked by harfh perfecution. And when reproaching the Quakers for rudenefs of manners, he might have remembered his own former fcruples about taking off hats.[1]

But while the prefent work poffeffes no value whatever as a theological treatife, it is the moft interefting of all the author's writings for its local and perfonal coloring. There is no book that throws fo much light upon the heterogeneous fociety then ftruggling into being along the fhores of the Narraganfett. We find nowhere elfe the character and opinions of Williams himfelf fo clearly revealed. His love of difputation is illuftrated on every page. His vehement and inaccurate habit of fpeech is not lefs apparent. His tenacious recollection of real or imagined injuries is fhown in the evident fatisfaction with which he turns afide from George Fox to deal a blow at William Harris;[2] and his readinefs to jump at erroneous conclufions, in his repeated charge that Fox had " flily departed." Yet, at the fame

---

[1] "And he that could not put off his *Cap* at *Prayer* in his *Worfhip*, can now put it off to every Man or *Boy* that puls off his *Hat* to him." Letter of R. Scot, *N. E. Fire-Brand Quenched*, Pt. ii: 247.

[2] That Williams did not regret this part of his work is fhown in his letter to the Commiffioners dated Oct. 18, 1677: he fays of Harris; " I have prefented a character of him to his Majefty, (in defence of myfelf againft him) in my narrative againft George Fox, printed at Bofton."—Knowles, *Memoir of Roger Williams*, p. 498.

time, it fhould be remembered that the perfonal peculiari-
ties so confpicuoufly fhown in the prefent work do not reveal the whole man. Reading this alone we fhould be at
a lofs to underftand how he retained, till the day of his
death, the affection and efteem of the beft men in Connecticut and Maffachufetts.

Perhaps nothing is more ftriking in this volume than
the very flight difference which it reveals between the
views of Roger Williams and the prevailing Calvinifm of
his day.[1] We habitually think of him as " having a wind-
mill in his head," but he was a confervative in religious
opinion, and on nearly all fundamental points of belief
was fully in accord with the churches of New England.
Nothing can be more hearty than his commendations of
their doctrinal purity. On one point alone did he radi-
cally depart from them, in refufing to be connected with
any vifible body of believers. Still on this point he agreed
as little with the Quakers. They denied that there was
any Vifible Church, and held that external ordinances had
been forever done away ; Williams, on the other hand,
profeffed belief in a Vifible Church ; and rejected the miniftry and ordinances of his own day, fimply becaufe he
deemed them unauthorized.[2] For the earneftnefs, indeed,
with which he infifts upon a regular adminiftration of the
facraments, he almoft deferves to be reckoned a High
Churchman. He condemned as " unnatural " the preaching of women in public,[3] a practice which not only the
Quakers but the Baptifts encouraged. For a very brief

---

[1] " 'This is the main ground of my
controverfy with the proud Quakers,
they flie up in their Illuminations in
themfelves, and Condemnations againft
others, but they magnify (with the Papifts and *Arminians*) Curfed rotten Nature."—*infra*, p. 343.

[2] Compare *Hireling Miniftry*, p. 4, and
Winthrop's *Journal*, i : 307.

[3] *infra*, p. 134.

period, three or four months, Williams had "walked in
the Baptift way,"[1] but while in the prefent volume he
repeatedly refers to "the People called Baptifts," it is plain
that he did not regard himfelf as having the leaft connection
with them.   He denies that the doctrine of Baptifm is one
of the "great fundamentals" of the Chriftian Religion.[2]
It is no lefs plain, that as years had leffened the bitternefs
of his early fufferings, he had come to look with a far
more kindly feeling upon the Churches of the Bay.   He
commends the "heavenly Principles" of the "*Leaders* and
Corner Stones" of the New England Colonies; he confiders
that holding as they did to the neceffity of fome evidence
of an inward change, they "came nearer than others to
the *firft primitive Churches*, and the *Inftitutions* and *Appointments* of Chrift Jefus."[3]   It is alfo to be noted that neither
does Fox, nor the three Quakers who managed the difpute
at Newport, affociate Williams in any manner with
the Baptifts, on the contrary they repeatedly defcribe him
as a " New England Prieft."[4]

For thus bitterly denouncing the Quakers, Williams has
been charged with inconfiftency, but this is an entire mif-
apprehenfion of his pofition.   He fimply difcuffed their
doctrines; he did not feek to exclude them from the Colony, nor did he invoke againft them the interference of the
civil power.   It was becaufe of the full toleratiou extended to them that he deemed it neceffary to "vindicate the
Colony" from the reproach of being counted their abettors.   The only ground for the charge, which was firft
urged by Fox, was the declaration of Williams " that a due

---

[1] Letter of Richard Scot.
[2] *infra*, p. 177.
[3] Compare *infra*, pp. 103 and 343.

[4] Edmundfon's *Journal*, p. 74. *N. E.
Fire-Brand Quenched*, Pt. i: 36, Pt. ii:
177, &c.

and moderate reftraint and punifhing of incivilities" was not perfecution.[1] Williams has reference here fimply to breaches of ordinary decorum. The pofition he takes does not differ from that ftated with fo much clearnefs in his Letter to the Town of Providence.[2]

In point of ftyle the prefent volume is inferior to the author's earlier compofitions, a circumftance no doubt in part to be explained from the nature of the work. Yet it is throughout characteriftic of the writer. A feature which deferves attention is the marked preference, fhown in all his writings, for metaphors drawn from his experience of fea life. Thus in addreffing the King, he fpeaks of Charles V. as having his " Trick at Helm ;" he tells Baxter and Owen " that many able and honeft Sea-men differ in their Reckonings ;" he terms the declaration of the Quakers " an Englifh Flag in an Enemies Bottome ;" in his argument he was " glad to *hale* his *Tacks* and *Bolings* clofe home, and now and then *loof* up into the wind ;" of Edmundfon he fays, " upon a fudden, a violent, tumultuous, diforderly *Wind* filled all his fails ;" to one of Fox's anfwers he rejoins, " may not half an eye fee what a *fimple* Sophifter this is, to make fuch Yaws as not to come near the Ships Courfe and point in hand." Thefe inftances fhow how much force fhould be attached to the phrafe " fteered my courfe," in proof of the theory that Roger Williams came from Salem to Seekonk by water.[3]

In this reprint the NARRAGANSETT CLUB has made ufe of a copy of the original work, courteoufly placed at their difpofal by Charles Deane, Efq., of Cambridge. But

---

[1] *infra.* p. 307.
[2] Knowles' *Memoir*, p. 279.
[3] *Pub. Narr. Club*, vol. i. Biog. Introd. p. 33. Fox fays of Williams that he " went to the woods."—*N. E. Fire-Brand Quenched*, Pt. i : 172.

throughout, the volume has been carefully collated with a copy in the Library of Brown Univerſity, which contains marginal correčtions in the handwriting of the author. Unfortunately this volume is not perfečt, the firſt thirty-two pages, pages 97 to 104 incluſive, and the laſt ſeventeen pages, having been reprinted from the copy in the Library of Harvard College. In the Prince Collečtion there is a one in all reſpečts like that belonging to Harvard College, while the Boſton Athenæum has another in which the title reads G. Fox, and the Letter to Baxter and Owen precedes the Addreſs to the King. The latter change ſeems, however, to have been inadvertently made when the volume was rebound. As the paper and watermarks in all the copies are ſimilar, it is probable that the ſlight change on the title page was ſimply to improve the typographical appearance.

J. L. D.

Providence, October 15, 1872.

George Fox

Digg'd out of his

Burrovves,

Or an Offer of

DISPUTATION

On fourteen *Propofalls* made this laft Summer 1672 (fo call'd)
unto *G. Fox* then prefent on *Rode-Ifland*
in *New-England*, by *R. W.*

As alfo how (*G. Fox* flily departing) the Difputation went on
being managed three dayes at *Newport* on *Rode-Ifland*, and
one day at *Providence*, between *John Stubs, John Burnet*, and
William Edmondfon on the one part, and *R. W.* on the other.

In which many *Quotations* out of *G. Fox* & *Ed. Burrowes* Book
in *Folio* are alleadged.

WITH AN

APENDIX

Of fome fcores of *G. F.* his fimple lame Anfwers to his Oppofites in that Book, quoted and replyed to
By *R· W.* of *Providence* in N. E.

BOSTON
Printed by *John Fofter*, 1 6 7 6.

TO

The KINGS MAJESTY

Charles the IId: &c.

Whom the King of Heaven long and eternally Preserve.

Royal Sir.

THE Moſt High hath adorned you with an *High Birth,* with a *gallant Temper,* and Endowments of Nature, with *Princely Education,* and *rare Experiences &c.* The *Crown* of all, the *Sanctifier* of all muſt be *L'eſprit de Djeu,* or elſe all that is under the Sun *in fumum abeunt.*

Touching this moſt *holy Spirit,* and other heavenly Points in difference between the *Proteſtants* and the *Quakers,* I preſent your royal eye with a *Lantſkip* of a *Battle* fought this laſt Summer in your Majeſtyes *New-England,* between ſome of the eminenteſt of the *Quakers* and my ſelf, three dayes at *Newport* on *Rode-Iſland,* and one at *Providence* on the *Main* in the ſame *Colony.*

I am

I am humbly bold to preſent it to your *Royal Hand,*

1. That your own precious *Soul* (infinitely more precious then thouſands of *Brittains* or *Worlds* may ſee the *Grounds* and *Roots* of theſe *Proteſtant Diſquiſitions.*

2. That your *Majeſty* may ſee what your *New-Engliſh Subjects* are doing under the gracious *Wing* of your wonderfull *Favour* to us &c

3. Becauſe your Majeſtyes *Name* is often mentioned and concerned in theſe *Concertations.*

4. Becauſe it was affirmed by ſome of my Oppoſites in publick, that there were ſcarce any of their *Books* came forth, but the *King* had one: I thought it ſome obligation on me, to preſent the *Proteſtant Truth* (thus publickly and ſolemnly aſſerted) more juſtly then my *Popiſh* and *Arminian Oppoſites* to offend your Royal eyes with Smoak out of the *Deep Pit.*

Gracious Sir, I know your precious *Spirits* and *Minutes* are exhauſted in managing your *Warrs* abroad, and in preſerving your Dominions in *Peace* at home; I cannot therefore hope for one *glance* of your eye upon any more then this poor *Epiſtle.*

Charles the Great was one of the greateſt Princes of that name in the world. And *Charles* the fifth (both Emperours) had his wonderfull *Trick at Helm* alſo; but both (and all) turn into the *Cabbin* & *Pit* of *Rottenneſs. Charles* the 5*th.* in his 58*th.* year, *Charles* the *Great* in his 72*d.* year: But were every *drop* of water between your *Old-England* and *New,* a million of years, yet *Mors ultima linea,* and tis but *Momentum unde pendet Eternitas.*

By Gods moſt wiſe and righteous Permiſſion, the *Pope* and *Quakers* pretend their *Enthuſiaſmes* and *Infallibilityes*: I know and have detected much of both of their *Impoſtures,*

and

and I beſeech him who is the eternal *Pater Luminum,* to preſerve your *Royal Spirit* from both their *Cheatings,* that is from the *Oracles* of *Hell* in their mouths.

And I humbly importune your *Majeſtyes continued Grace* and *Patience* to this poor *New-England,* which (though a miſerable, cold, howling Wilderneſs, yet *L'eternel* hath made it his *Glory,* your Majeſtyes *Glory,* and a *Glory* to the *Engliſh* and *Proteſtant Name:* and if the moſt High pleaſe, *Old* and *New-England* may flouriſh when the *Pope* and *Mahomet, Rome* and *Conſtantinople* are in their Aſhes.

Providence in *N-England,*
March 10th. 167$\frac{2}{3}$.
(*ut Vulgò,*)

Your Majeſtyes moſt loyal and affectionate Orator at the Throne of Grace.

Roger Williams.

To the People called Quakers.

Friends & Country-men :

1. THe occasion of these *Discourses* you may see in the first Page: the 14 *Proposals* in the second Page, and the occasion of the Title in the 34.

2. The truth is (as *Edmund Burroughs*, and others of you say of your selves) from my Childhood (now above three-score years) the Father of *Lights* and *Mercies* toucht my Soul with a love to himself, to his only begotten, the true *Lord Jesus*, to his *Holy Scriptures*, &c. his infinite Wisdome hath given me to see the City, Court and Country, the Schools and Universities of my *Native Country*, to converse with some *Turks, Jews, Papists*, and all sorts of *Protestants*, and by Books to know the *Affairs* and *Religions* of all *Countries*, &c.

3. My Conclusion is, that *be of good chear thy sins are forgiven thee*, Mat. 9. is one of the joyfullest sounds that ever came to poor sinful Ears: how to obtain this sound from the mouth of that Mediatour that spoke it, is the great dispute beween the *Protestants* and the bloody *Whore of Rome*: this is also the great point between the true *Protestants* and your selves: as also (in order to this) about what man is (to the utmost) now by nature, what the true Lord Jesus Christ is, and all other controversies (discussed in this Book, not unworthy this your serious weighing (as *Mary* did) in the hearts and spirits, &c.

4. Bear with me while I say, that as the *Jesuites* pretend to deifie the *Pope*, but it is known, the end is to deifie themselves under the cloak of the *Popes* Name: so Satan

pretends

pretends to exalt and deifie you, under the name of *God*, and *Chrift*, and *Spirit*, &c. but his end is as *Peter* tells us, to exalt himfelf, and fill his hellifh Paunch with Souls.

5. I endeavoured, but could not procure a Short-hand writer, fo that I am forced to recollect Tranfactions from my Memory, and I believe (as in the holy prefence of God) that I have not failed to prefent the true fubftance of paffages without advantage to my felf, or difadvantage to my Oppofites.

6. I have ufed fome fharp Scripture Language, but not (as commonly you do) paffionately and unjuftly: I fometimes call you *Foxians*, (as *Nicolaitans* from *Nicholas*) becaufe *G.Fox* hath appeared the greateft Writer, and the greateft Preacher amongft you, and the moft deified that I can hear of, fure it is that here he fubtly run for it: he ordered that my Letters to our Deputy Governour Captain *Cranftone* (in which my Propofals to *G.F.* were, fhould not be delivered to the Deputy, until *G. F.* was fome hours under fayle, that he might fay he never faw my Paper, though it is as clear as noon-day that he knew all matters by Copies, Letters and Relations, perfectly many dayes before his departure.

7. My difadvantage (in our Contefts (efpecially at *Newport*) were great and many: for though *J. Stubs.* and *J. Burnet* were more civil and ingenious: yet *W. Edmondfon* was nothing but a bundle of Ignorance, and Boifteroufnefs, he would fpeak firft end all (though all three were conftantly on me at once) no man might fpeak at all in favour of my Pofitions: any might freely fpeak againft them: they fat in the midft of the Governour & Magiftrates (of their Opinion) and the whole Affembly (of their way) *W. Edmundfon* (though *J. Stubs* twice faid in publick, that I had not inter- interrupted them) yet *W. Edmundfon* would frequently and infolently interrupt me: fo that I was not only
forced

forced to bear patiently (through Gods only help) but to suppress my thoughts, which here I have added in some places. 8. I know that a great weight of your Opinions and Actings lye upon your believing your selves guided by the immediate Spirit of God: but I believe that I have proved that it is no more the holy Spirit of God, that speaks and acts in you, then it was the true *Samuel* that spake such heavenly words in the appearance of *Sam.* Mantle amongst a cloud of other witnesses you shall never perswade Souls (not bewitched) that the holy spirit of God would perswade your Women and Maidens to appear in publick (streets & assemblies) stark naked, &c. of which I have spoke more particularly in our disputations. 9. It is hard to perswade a Fox or a Wolf that he is so, &c. or that he doth Rob or Steal, or Murther; it is hard to per-swade a man while he dreams that he is in a Dream : yea though he be a filthy Dreamer as Gods Spirit speaks : In our Dreams we believe lyes and impossibilities to be true as that we are many thousand miles of, that we talk with dead men, &c. that we are at Marriages or Burials and are Kings and Queens. &c.

10. All that I can hope for (without Gods wonderfull mercy) is to give my Testimony in my generation: for (as *Solomon* speaks of the Whore) few or none of you return. Yet I know Gods foundation is sure he knows who are his amongst you as amongst other perswasions. I have proved, and will prove (if God please) that spiritual Pride, that is Pride about spiritual matters, is the Root and Branch of your whole Religion, and that the King Eternal, who did cast out proud Angels out of his Palace, will hardly open his Gates to proud and scornful Dust and Ashes :

Providence, March 10.   *I am one of your best Friends,*   *R.W.*
    1 6 7 $\frac{2}{3}$ (so called)

To thoſe many Learned and Pious Men, whom G. Fox *hath ſo ſillily and ſcornfully anſwered in his Book in* Folio

Eſpecially to those whoſe Names I have been bold to mention in the *Narrativt* and *Apendix,*

Mr Richard Baxter, *Mr* Iohn Owen &c.

Sirs,

THrough your ſides the Devil by the Clawes of this wily Fox, *hath tore at the heart of the* Son of God; *it is no wonder then if he tear at the* Heart *of his* Love-Letters, *and Inſtitutions, and the true Profeſſors of his name, who are innumerable in* Abrahams Boſome, *and the reſt travelling uprightly thither.*

For Brevity ſake I was forced to omit many excellent Paſſages, ſelected by Fox *out of your Writings & to ſelect ſhort Sentences of yours unto which he gives ſhort Anſwers. As to matters in* Difference *between yourſelves and me, I willingly omitted them, as knowing that many able and honeſt* Sea-men *in their Obſervations of this* Sun (*one picture of* Chriſt Jeſus) *differ ſometimes in their* Reckonings, *though uprightly aiming at, and bound for one* Port *and* Harbour.

Eternally praiſed be the Father of Lights, *and mercyes, that we are one in that moſt glorious ever fixed* Cynoſura (*about whom his true Prophets & Meſſengers ever have and doe and ſhall move: and he holdeth them in his right hand.*

I humbly beg of you. 1. *That you will more and more earneſtly, candidly and chriſtianly ſtudy the things that differ without reflecting upon Credit, Maintenance, Liberty and Life it ſelf, rembring who it was that ſaid it;* He that loves his life ſhall loſe it. 2. *More and more to ſtudy the Propheſies and the Signs of the Times, You know when it was that five Biſhops*

Bishops, twenty-two Ministers & almost three hundred other precious. Believers in the true Lord Jesus, were sacrificed in the Flames, for his ever blessed sake, against that monstrous Man of Sin and bloudy Whore of Rome. These Foxians fancy is but a feather to to those high Pico's and Tenariffs, the Pope and Mahomet whom some of you may live to see flung into the Lake that burns with Fire and Brimstone.

Were it not that the infinite Compassions of Heaven had made our gracious Sovereign the Breath of our Nostrills, the fiery Fornace had certainly burnt seven times hotter against Hananiah, Mishael and Azariah : Surely as for Conscience sake we ought to obey, so for Conscience sake we ought to be Instant and Constant at the throne of Grace for his Royal Preservation and Salvation.

Prov. March 10, 167$\frac{2}{3}$.   I am unworthy to be yours   R. W.

A Narration of
A CONFERENCE
OR
DISPUTE,

This laſt *Auguſt* 1672 (ſo called) in the
Colony of *Rode-Iland* and *Providence*, Plantations in
N.ENGLAND, between *Roger Williams* of *Provi-
dence* (who Challenged *Fox* by writing (which fol-
lowes) and all his Friends then met on *Rode-
Iland*, (and *G. Fox* withdrawing) *John
Stubs, John Burniat*, and *William
Edmundon* (three of their ableſt Apoſ-
tles) on the other, that is, (on the
pretended *Quakers*) Party.

Aving long heard of the great name of
G. Fox, (a man cried up by the Peo—
ple called *Quakers*) and having read The Occa-
his book in Folio (ſome years ſince) ſion of the
againſt, as I think above *ſix ſcore Books* and *Papers* *Diſputa-
tion.*
(written by pious and able pens againſt them) and
now this Summer hearing of his coming into theſe

Parts

Parts of *N England*, and the poor cheated Souls the *Quakers* with joy expecting his coming, as the coming of *an Angel of light* from Heaven: I read over his Book afresh (as in the holy presence and eye of God, (with a single Eye and Heart) and more clearly finding his *Answers* so weak and silly, so Anti-Christian and Blasphemous, and yet so Imperious and Scornfull, so Cursing and Censorious, [2] Damning and Reprobating all that bow not down to their new *Upstart Image*, my Spirit rose up within me, and I believe the holy *Spirit of God* (in answer to my poor Petitions and Meditations) resolved and quickened my Spirit to the present *Undertake* and Service. And therefore for his most holy Names sake, and the name of his most holy only begotten, the true *Lord Jesus* the *God-Man* and *Mediator* &c, And for the honour of the most holy *Spirit of God* (so horribly torn in pieces by this foul *Spirit of the Quakers*) For the vindicating of many of the precious Truths of the old *Christian purity*, and for the sake of so many precious Souls lying slain and bleeding before me, I made this Offer following to *G. Fox*, and any or all his Followers or Associates, then together at *New-port* on *Rode-Iland*. Tis true *G. Fox* was at *Providence* some few dayes before, and spake publickly; and it was free for me publickly to have heard him, and opposed him; But going the last year to one of their general Assemblyes at *New-Port*, and having begun to present to them some Considerations about the *True Christ* and the *false*, the *True spirit* and the *False* and being cut of in the midest, by sudden *Prayer* of one, and the

Singing

G Fox his Book in Folio weighed.

A Spirit of Confusion in the Quakers Meetings.

(3)

Singing of another, and then by the *Prayer* of
another and the fudden diffolving of the Affembly,
I refolved to try another way, and to offer a fair
and full *Difpute,* according to *Ed. Burrowes* (and
therein *G Foxes*) Offer in his large *Epiſtle* to *Foxes*
Book. To this Purpofe I drew up my thoughts
into fourteen *Propofitions* ; and knowing that *New-
Port* was the chief Town on *Rode—Iland* and *Providence* on the *Main,* and that G. *Fox* had fpake at
both places and *bewitched* many with his *Sorceries,* I
fent this Paper following to G. *Fox* at *Newport,* viz,

TO G. Fox *or any other of my Countrey—men*
at New-Port *who fay they are the Apoſtles
and Meffengers of* Chriſt Jefus, *In humble Confidence of the help of the* Moft High, *I offer to
maintain in Publick, againſt all* Comers, *thefe*
14 Propofitions *following, to wit, the firſt feven
at* New-Port, *and the other feven at* Providence:
For the time When, *I refer it to* G. Fox *and his
Friends at* New-port.

My Offer *of Difp.* on 14 *Propofi-tions.*

Only I defire

1 *To have three dayes Notice,before the day
you fix on.*

2 *That without* Interruption (*or many fpeaking at once*) *the Conference may continue from*
Nine *in the morning till* [3] *about* four *in the
afternoon.*   and

3 *That if either of the feven Propofitions be
not finiſhed in one day, the Conference may continue and goe on fome few hours the next day.*

4 *That either of us Difputing ſhall have free
uninterrupted*

uninterrupted liberty to speak (in Answers *and* Replyes*)as much and as long as wee please, and then give the* Opposite *the same* Liberty.

That the whole may be managed with that *Ingenuity* and *Humanity,* as such an *Exercise,* by such *Persons* in such *Conditions,* at such a *Time,* ought to be managed and performed, the *Propositions* are these that follow.

First *That the People called* Quakers *are not true Quakers according to the holy* Scriptures.

2 *That the* Christ *they profess is not the* True Lord Jesus Christ.

3 *That the* Spirit *by which they are acted is not the* Spirit of God.

4 *That they doe not own the holy* Scriptures.

5 *Their* Principles *and* Professions, *are full of* Contradictions *and* Hypocrisies.

6 *That their* Religion *is not only an* Heresy *in the matters of* Worship, *but also in the* Doctrines *of* Repentance Faith. *&c*

7 *Their* Religion *is but a confused mixture of* Popery, Armineanisme, Socineanisme, Judaisme *&c.*

8 *The People called* Quakers *(in effect) hold no* God, no Christ, no Spirit, no Angel, no Devil, no Resurrection, no Judgment, no Heaven, no Hell, *but what is in man.*

9 *All that their* Religion *requires (externall and internall) to make* Converts *and* Proselites, *amounts to no more than what a* Reprobate *may easily attain unto, and perform.*

10 *That the* Popes *of* Rome *doe not swell with, and*

exercise

exercise a greater Pride, *then the* Quakers *Spirit hath exprest, and doth aspire unto, although many truly humble Soules may be captivated amongst them, as may be in other* Religions.

11 *The Quakers* Religion *is more obstructive, and destructive to the* Conversion *and* Salvation *of the Souls of People, then most of the Religions this day extant in the world.*

12 *The* Sufferings *of the* Quakers *are no true evidence of the Truth of their* Religion.

13 *That their many* Books *and* writings *are extremely Poor, Lame, Naked, and sweld up only with high* Titles *and words of Boasting and* Vapour.

[4]   14. *That the Spirit of their* Religion *tends mainly,*

1 *To reduce Persons from* Civility *to* Barbarisme.

3 *To an* Arbetratry Goverment, *and the Dictates and Decrees of that* sudden Spirit *that acts them,*

3 *To a sudden cutting off of* People, *yea of* Kings *and* Princes *opposing them.*

4 *To as fiery* Persecutions *for matters of Religion and Conscience, as hath been or can be practised by any* Hunters *or* Persecutors *in the world.*

Under these forementioned Heads (*if the Spirit of the* Quakers *dare civilly to Argue*) *will be opened many of the* Popish, Protestant, Jewish *and* Quakers *Positions, which cannot here be mentioned, in the Dispute* (*if God please*) *they must be alleadged, and the* Examination *left to every persons* Conscience, *as they will answer to God,* (*at their own Perills*) *in the great day approaching.*

Roger Williams.
This

THis Paper above-said I sent inclosed in a Letter to my kind friend *Capt. Cranston* Deputy Governour of the *Colony,* that being such a publick person, he might timely be informed of such a publick Assembly, and as also might vouchsafe (as afterwards he carefully did) to afford his *Countenance and Assistance* to such *Peaceable* and *Pious Exercises.* But before the *Boat* went down with the Letter aforesaid from *Providence* to *Newport,*

The first usage to the *Author* & his *Proposals.*

I sent a Copy of my Positions to a Neighbour *J T.* whom I heard was inclining to them. He takes a Copy of them and reads them in their Meeting, before *John Crosman* Master of the Boat (one of them also) who presently the same hour, called me *Blind Sot* in the open *Street,* upbraiding me, how I durst send my 14 *Lyes* to such a man as *G. Fox* (one of them called him) *the eternall Son of God;* so that before my Letter went to *Newport* (which *Crosman* carried) by Letters, & *Crosman* his and

The deceit fulness of *Fox* & *Foxians.*

other Relations, all was known, even long before my Letters were opened, or delivered to the Deputy Governour: For in the *Junto* of the *Foxians* at *Newport* it was concluded for *Infallible Reasons,* that His *Holiness G. Fox* should withdraw, seeing there was such a Knot of the Apostles of Christ Jesus now at *Newport* together, (especially *John Stubs,* a man knowing the *Greek* and *Hebrew*) Therefore that it might appear that such a Nehemiah as he would not fly, it was [5] agreed that my Letters should not be delivered to the *Deputy Governour,* untill *G. Fox* was gone; so that it might be truly said, that he never saw the Paper which I sent unto him.   I had

had a touch of this *Leger de main* trick in our Dif- one of the subtil
pute at *Newport*, and the *Deputy Governour* did pub- *Tricks* of
lickly teftifie that my Letters to him were dated this subtil
the 13 of *July* (which he faid he wondered at) but *Fox* viz. to
were not brought to him untill the 26th of the faid ſteal hand-
ſomly from
Moneth, and untill G. *Fox* was ſome hours departed. the *Diſpute*
John Burniat profeſt that that he knew noth- & yet not
ing of the detaining of the Letters, only he knew all to run
that G. *Fox* never ſaw my Paper.   G. *F.* ſuppoſed for it.
I would be forced to be as plain in my *Proofs* as I
was in my *Poſitions*.   He knew that I was furniſhed
with *Artillery* out of his own *Writings*.   He ſaw
what *Conſequences* would roll down the mountaines
upon him from his proud and Inſolent, yet poor
and bald *Writings* ; and how far ſome of his preſent practices were fallen out with his *Writings*, and
therefore this old *Fox* thought it beſt to run for it,
and leave the work to his *Journey-men* and *Chap-*
lains to perform in his abſence for him.

Before I come to Tranſactions between thoſe
three left behind him [*John Stubs, John Burnet,*
William Edmundſon, and my ſelf] I think fit to tell A great
the Reader what a *preparatory Conflict* the moſt holy private
and only *Wiſe Lord*, was pleaſed to exerciſe me with, *Conflict*
before I came to the *Publick.* before my
publick.

My former antient Neighbour and friend *J. T.*
being bit by ſuch *infectious Teeth* himſelf, fell on
me, as a man would fall upon *a Toad* or *Serpent,* and
ſent me this following *Letter,* notwithſtanding he
was but newly bitten by them ; and for forty yeares
pretended no ſmall love and reſpect to God and
me.

He

He firſt *gave fire* upon me in this following *Letter.*

Providence. 18. 5. 72.

Roger Williams

J T. his Letter to me upon the ſight of my *Propoſitions* to *G. Fox.*

THy *Scurrilous* Paper *in thy* Propoſitions to G. Fox. *and others (who in ſcorn are called* Quakers) *I adviſe thee to refrain any further publiſhing thereof, and as it is written keep thee far from an evill matter, thy* paper *being full fraught with* impudent Lyes *and* Slanders, *with high flown airy imaginations, which if thou ſhouldſt live the dayes of* Methuſelah, *thou couldſt not perform. In Love to thy* Perſon *and* Name, [6] *which ought to be precious, I adviſe thee not upon a* ſudden motion (*as thou termeſt us to act by*) *but from the* ſpirit *of* Truth *and tender love unto thy ſoul, which* Spirit *by thy writing appears thou art a ſtranger to. Conſider thy latter end, leaſt with*

A Note of *Card Mazarin*

Cardinal Mazarin, *thou cry out in* a dying hour *Oh my poor* Soul, *what will become of thee? whither art thou a going? And ſaid if he ſhould longer have lived, he would leave the* Court, *and be a* Capuchin. Time *is precious,* Repent, Repent, *and mind the* manifeſtation *of the* Spirit, *which is given to every one to profit withall., and knocks at the door of thy* Heart, *for entrance, which being* rejected *will be thy* Condemation. *If thou rejecteſt this my faithfull witneſs for the* Lord, *I then ſay with* John *in the* Revelation, *let him that is filthy be be filthy ſtill, and ſo remaines*

thy friend and Neighbour *J. T.*

Having

Having read this Letter, and knowing this my Neighbour of late to have declined much from his former profession of *Godli,ness*, and many wayes by his *Loosness* had grieved my *Soul*, I wondered not much at his Lines, (though now much unexpected of him) as knowing the Quakers spirit, to be a ready Ditch or *Gulfe*, that readily sucks and draws into it Soules *afrighted* easily to skin over their Sores; Proud and Self-conceited ones, who gladly close with the *Spirit* of, and Children of *Pride*, and *Loose* fading *Professors*, of which sort the *Quakers* Meetings do much consist, as not being able to walk close *with God*, not daring to turn wholy *Profane*, or *Atheists*, and so daube up the breach with *untempered Morter* (the wild and foolish notions of the Devils *Whisperings*, under the cloak of the immediate *Inspirations* of Gods holy and heavenly *Spirit*) Many thoughts I had to pass by his Affronts, and *Insultations*: But considering that it was not my *Name* (not worth the while) but the most High, Eternall *Majesty*; and his most *holy Spirit* thus fouly pierced and debased, I return'd this *Answer* following.

Fuel for the Quakers Fire of Hell.

My ancient loving Friend,

 IF you pluck out the eyes of your Understanding, Profession, *and* Experience, *yet* (*through the mercy of the* Father of Lights *and Mercyes*) I *cannot do so with mine.* You tell me my Paper *to* G. Fox, *is* Scurrilous, &c. *full fraught with* [7] Impudent Lyes and Slanders, &c. *And you say you* write in Love, from the Spirit of Truth, *to* which

My Answer to the fore-going Letter from J.T.

which (*you say*) I am a ſtranger. *You mind mee of* Death *&c. and bid me* Repent, Repent, or elſe be filthy ſtill, and be damned.

To which I will not Anſwer as G. Fox *anſwered* H. Wrights *Paper with a ſcornfull and ſhamefull* Silence. *Thus I ſay in generall, you are my* Witneſs, *that I have long ſaid with* David *(and I humbly hope have made it good) I hate and abhor* Lying, *but thy Law do I love, for which I have loſt in my time ſomething, &c If I had not loved his* Law, *and abhorred Lyes, I had long ere this bowed down againſt my Conſcience, yea I had fired the Countrey about this barbarous Land (as ſome in this* Colony *have done) I had murthered the* Indians, *and* Engliſh *by the* Powder *and* Liquor *trade, to which you know I had Temptation, as much as your ſelf, or any others in* N. England, *but I loved the Name of God.*

For your ſelf, *if the God of heaven have terrified your Soul, (which I believe is the caſe of moſt* Quakers, *and of the* Devils *themſelves) and made it tremble at the* Wrath *to come, you muſt not think to run from his flaming* Eyes *and* Hand *(as* Adam) *amongſt the* Thickets; *you cannot talk of* Mercy *without a way of Satisfaction to an infinite* Juſtice. *(Who payes the* Old Score)? *It is impoſſible that all created Powers, in Heaven or Earth, can diſcharge for one ſinfull* Thought. *There muſt be an Equivalent diſcharge, not by* filthy Rags, *and menſtruous Clouts of our own* Holineſs; *which muſt be thought of before we can* ſay, We can ſin no more againſt God, than he

can

Crying ſins in N. England.

The infinite Juſtice of God muſt be ſatisfied.

can fin againſt us; *as you know who* Blaſphem-
ouſly *and* Horribly *maintain it.*

In your lines I pray you to Conſider,

Firſt. Your Irrationality, *for how can you
imagine that a ſerious Chriſtian, in humble Conſi-
dence of the of the mercifull Preſence, and gracious
Aſſiſtance of Gods* holy Spirit, *and of no little* Af- The
fliction *and Suffering, ſhould be ſo eaſily ſtird (as a* Bruitiſh
Rock *with a* Feather*) by your bare crying* Re- Simplicity
pent, Repent or be Damned, hearken to the of the
Light within thee? &c. Quakers
Spirit.

2. *Can* Reaſon *imagine, that after much* ſtrug-
ling *within my ſelf, and the* Birth *of my* Propoſitions *and* Reſolutions, *that I can ſo* ſuddenly
ſtrike Sail, *and bear up, and immediately* [8] Stifle,
and Smother, *and Burn my* Conceptions *and Reſolutions, as ſoon as I hear your ſimple and childiſh*
ſpirit *Countermand me?*

3. *Is it not unmanly* Childiſh *and effeminate,
to cry out* a Scurrilous paper, Lyes, Lyes, impudent Slanders &c. *and yet give me not one* Reaſon
or one Scripture *againſt any one of them? Is it
not too like the irrationall and brutiſh Anſwer of*
Humphrey Norton (*to a ſober and Sollid Paper of*
Thomas Olnys *ſen.*) *crying out,* Lyes, Lyes, 224
Lyes, *without any ſerious* Examination *of* Particulars?

2. *I charge your Lines with* Impiety, *where* The *Man-
you infer that the moſt holy* Spirit (*from that Scrip-* *ifeſtation
ture* [The manifeſtation of the Spirit &c.) *is* *of the
poured forth upon every Individuall perſon in the* Spirit. 1.
Cor. 12.
World.

World. Did the Oyl *moſt precious and holy, the holy* Ointments *and the* Blood *in the Law, reſpeſt the whole world, or the* Meſſiah *the* anointed *and his* Members (Chriſtians *or anointed alſo*)? *Was not* 1. Cor. 12. *written to the* Chriſtians, *or Saints gathered into the* Chriſtian *flock or Congregation at* Corinth, *unto whome the Father of* Spirits (*as in that place*) *vouchſafeth thoſe three heavenly Favours.*

1. Gifts *which he ſhews there to be different.* 2. Adminiſtrations, Miniſteryes *or Offices.* 3. Operations, *Works or Succeſſes, all wrought in the Saints by the holy* Spirit, *for the Glory of the ſame* Father, Lord, *and* Spirit, *the mutual comfort and edifiing of the* Saints, *yea and for the Convicting and drawing of other poor* Sinners, *out of the World to God.*

The Lord *mercifully awaken your Souls to the Love of God, and the Love of his holy Truth, for the not beleiving of which but the profane playing with it, the moſt high and righteous* Judge *of the whole world (in a way of Judicial Sentence) delivers up poor Souls to believe Lyes, and that ſo ſtrongly, as to give their bodyes to be burned for them.*

The Papiſts *catch hold upon a* Letter [This is my body] *You as ſimply as doe the* Generaliſts *catch hold upon the* Letter [All, every man that comes into the world &c.] *whereas the* Scope *and* Connection *in all writings, and in all matters in the world are rationally to be minded.* The Sence *and* Meaning *is in all* Speech *and* Writing, (*in*

Gods wonderful Juſtice.

The words *All* and *every one,* Conſidered.

(*in our own and other* Languages) *the very*
Speech *or* Writing *it ſelf. Theſe Words* [All
and every one] *in our own and other* Tongues,
[9] *are often uſed* figuratively: *it is ſo all the
Scripture over, and thrice in one verſe,* Colloſſ. 1.
28. *where Reaſon cannot imagine that* Paul *did*
literally *and individually admoniſh* every *man,*
teach *every* man, *and preſent* every *man that
comes into the world, perfect in* Chriſt Jeſus *which
could not, cannot poſſibly be true without another
Sence and* Expoſition, *then the words literally
hold out.*

4, *Again, you are dangerouſly bold to ſay that
you write from the* Spirit *of* Truth, *wherein you
Father theſe your childiſh* Irrationalityes, *your
profaning of the holy* Majeſty *of* God, *his holy*
Scriptures *and writings, and your raſh* Judging
and Examining *of others, upon the holy* Spirit *of*
God: *But I do humbly hope to evince, that the Spirit you boaſt of, is ſo far from the* Spirit *of* God,
*that it falls beneath the foot of a ſober and well
grounded* Humanity. *At preſent I only Inſtance
in that whoriſh and* monſtrous *act of your* Women *and* Maidens, *ſtripping themſelves* ſtark naked,
by your Spirit, *and with a face of* braſs *coming into*
the open ſtreets, *and publick* Congregations *of* Men
and Youths. *This* Spirit (*though defended by* G.
Fox *and others*) *is ſuch a piece of unnaturall and
bruitiſh* Impudence, *that I cannot hear of the like
amongſt* Jews *or* Gentiles, *yea not amongſt the moſt
Savage, Baſe and Barbarous of them all (all Circumſtances conſidered*).

The Im-
pudency
and Un-
cleaneſs of
the *Qua-
kers* Spirit.

5. In

5. *In the laſt place I obſerve your* Fickleneſs
*and Inconſtancy, what, and how often have I heard
you ſpeak of the* Chief *of the* Quakers *now at*
Newport? *How lately and how much have you
uttered of* John Croſman *his* Croſs *and froward
ſpirit (even ſince he pretended the* Spirit) *yea how*
inhumane *and* injurious *to your ſelf in the way
of his Calling? now all on a* ſudden (*for I heard
but little untill I ſaw your Lines) you are got up
into the lofty Chair of* Judging *and ready to ſay,*
God I thank thee I am not as this Publican, *I
beſeech the Lord to make you ſavingly to remember
that* Word [God reſiſteth *that is ſets himſelf in
Hoſtility againſt the* Proud, but he giveth Grace
unto the Lowly] *ſo prayes*

your old unworthy Friend *R.W.*

Providence 18th. 5th. 72.

I had hoped that I had Conjur'd down (at leaſt
for the preſent) that *Waſpiſh ſpirit,* but he flyes out
againſt me (within a few dayes) in this ſecond *Letter* following.

10]   Providence, 23. 5. 75.

J. T. his
ſecond
Letter to
me.

*A*Ncient *Friend and Acquaintance, I read thy Note
four dayes after the ſubſcribing it, that ſo thy
Councellors might throughly be informed of thy continued
Zeal in a dangerous Caſe. What I write to thee
in* Love *hath a contrary effect in thy* Spirit, *being ſo
prejudiced againſt us; according to the Proverb,* Nothing is well ſpoken, that is not well taken. *Upon
Diſcourſe*

Discourse thou didst say the Quakers could not be believed on their Words or Writings, having a secret Refervation within them, *which gives me to conclude, that wee are Judged before wee Speak.* For *my charging upon thee* Slanders and Lyes, *Examine but thy* Pofitions, *which will make manifest what I say.* As for the Terror *which thou fpeakeft of* &c. *I leave it to thee to confider what thou art about, leaft thou be called to Account for it before thou art ready.* As for charging me with Irrationality *for not alleadging Scripture for what I write, yet I alleadged three Scriptures, one of which thou wrefteft, adding what I wrote not, fo that if I had urged more, I fhould have had the like Catching :* But we both muft come to give an Account of what is done in the Body. *In this my Letter thou mayeft fee my witneffing againft moft of thy* Slanderous Propofitions. *Concerning the* Spirits manifeftations, 1 Cor. 12. 13. *I freely confent that they were the* Saints *by Calling, who are there Confidered.* As thou alleadgeft the Papifts *Catch at a word* [This is my body] *fo we catch at a word* [All] *and mifapply Scripture; fo that I perceive thou haft not a* Guide *to thy mind, but uttereft thine own Conceivings.* John. 3.16. *The Promife is to them that* Believe, *and not to* All.

Again, *Thou findeft fault with my rafh judging thee, and abufing Scripture: Take it to thy felf, for the word* Damning, *thou foifteft in thy felf, neither dare I pafs Sentence of* Damnation *upon any :* For Judgment *belongeth to the Lord, and we muft ftand or fall to our own Mafter.* As for my Ficklenefs *and Inconftancy, Lay thy hand upon thy mouth and Confider thy Windings*

ings and Turnings, in thy Judgment and Practice, how thankfull thou waſt to J. Burnet, whome thou highly commendeſt after thou cameſt home, and now reproacheſt the Truth, which then thou aſſenteſt to: and in thy 14 Poſitions, thou hinteſt (by thy wicked Surmiſes) what the ſudden ſpirit of the Quakers is, to take away the Lives of Kings, &.c. but I told thee in my firſt Letter, thou art a ſtranger to that holy Spirit we act by.

But further thy Malice appeareth in going to one thou ſaidſt, that [11] if the ſpirit of the Governour were to cut of his head, he muſt doe it. Call to mind what thou didſt to thy peaceable Neighbours ſeeking their Blood, crying out Treaſon, when the Court diſcerned thy Blood-thirſty ſpirit, which thy friends at Newport were aſhamed of, and thy Accuſations proved Invalid. How childiſh didſt thou act to ſwear againſt One, when another told thee of ſomewhat ſpoken to allay thy fury againſt William Harris? Call to mind thy Books written, and ſee thy Fickleneſs, wanting a Guid to thy mind, being for and againſt Perſecution. Thou chargeſt me to have gotten into the Chair of Judging: thy two Scripts I return upon thy ſelf, Phyſitian heal thy ſelf. The Wiſdom of man puffeth up; but the Wiſdom of God humbleth, that God may be all in all. I deſire thee to look back to thy Lines, and where thou mentioneſt the Satisfaction of infinite Juſtice: who payes the old ſcore? &.c. Alſo to conſider my Irrationality, that thy great Education, great Search &.c. as alſo thy great Travels and Struglings to bring forth thy Poſitions, all being in thine own will, and in the Apoſtacy wherin the great Whore hath made all Nations drunk with her Fornications, which the Lord

The high Opinion G Fox his Followers have of him yet he ſaild & run for it.

will

will in his Time, confume with the breath of his mouth.
I know thou haft undertaken a great Burthen *in Chal-*
lenging G. Fox *to anfwer thy* Pofitions; *I wifh thee*
to provide thy Armour of Proof, *as* Golias *that de-*
fied the Army of Ifrael. G.Fox *is furnifhed with that*
Armour *that thou haft no fkill to make ufe of; having*
alfo the Sword of the Spirit *to cut down all thy airy*
Imaginations: Therefore ceafe from further troubling
thee: a Word to the Wife is Sufficient, if thou haue a
heart to make ufe of it.

thy Friend and Neigbour, *J. T.*

To this Second Letter *I Replied* in this following

NEigbour, *in this your fecond Letter (mifdated*
as well as mine) you pafs by many Particulars
which I wrote concerning G. *Fox, Hump. Norton,*
your felf, and the ftripping your Women *Stark na-*
ked in publick, *&c.* you infift upon my Irrationall
dealing.

2. For your charging my *Pofitions* to be Lyes,
and Impudent *Slanders,* without giving me one
Scripture or *Reafon* to prove them fo; and here you Unreafon-
fay [*For my charging upon thee Lyes and Slanders,* able kind
examine but thy Pofitions, which will make manifeft of *Reafon-*
what I fay] But is this any more *Rationall* or Man- ing.
like? or is it not bruitifh to fay, you are a *Lyar* becaufe you are a *Lyar;* [12] Or you are a *Lyar*
becaufe you fay thefe *Pofitions* are true, and offer to
prove them. It is a *Man-like fpirit* to lead a *Beaft*
with an *Halter,* but a *Man* with *Reafon;* but to lead
or drive a Man with an *Halter* or Cudgel, and not
with

with a *Reason*, (in *Naturalls* and *Rationalls*, moſt of all in *Spirittalls*) is not the *Spirit* of *God* nor of *Humanity* : For what will my *Chargings*, and Cenſures and Clamors, and Curſings, and Damnings effect and beget upon a rationall Soul, without a proof of Reaſon, but an Opinion of my wicked falſe bruitiſh and irrationall *ſpirit* ?

3.   Tis true in your Exhortation to me, you bid me hearken to the *Manifeſtation of the Spirit* which is given to every man *&c.* This I acknowledg *Scripture.* You ſay I wreſted and added to an other Scripture, but you mention it not, ſo I am in the dark what you mean. And for this of the *Manifeſtation of the Spirit*, your ſelf now conſent to me, that it was ſpoken to the Saints or Chriſtians at *Corinth*, and therefore I ſpake true in ſaying, that as to my Poſitions (by you call'd *Impudent Lyes and Slanders*) you gave me not then, nor now any one *Scripture* or *Reaſon* to prove any one of my *Poſitions* to be ſo.

4.   As to *John Burnet*, I ſaid before him and afterwards, that he delivered many *Truths:* yet withall, I then at the ſame time (in their *Publick Aſſembly* at *Newport*) I told them, that it lay upon them to manifeſt to their own *Souls* and others, 1. That their *Chriſt* was *true* 2. That their *Spirit* was *Gods*, and the rather becauſe they were charged with denying the *Inſtitutions* of *Chriſt Jeſus*, and with the ſetting up of many *Will-worſhips*, as *Preaching of Women &c.* And I went on purpoſe to *Diſcourſe* of theſe matters (this being the time of their *Generall Aſſembly*, and a great *Concourſe*) I

I can give many Inſtances of their abuſing the Ordinance and Name of the Spirit of Prayer for a ſudden Silencing of their Oppoſites.

was

was ſtopt by the ſudden praying of the *Governour's Wife*, who alſo told me of her aſking her huſband at home (meaning *Chriſt* which I had toucht upon) I roſe up and ſaid, if a man had ſo alleadged, I would have anſwered him: But I would not Countenance ſo much the violation of *Gods Order* in making a Reply to a *Woman* in Publick: Hereupon *J. Nicols* ſtood up and ſaid [*In Chriſt Jeſus neither male or female &c.*] I was Replying to him and to *J. Burnets* Speech alſo concerning their *Spirit*, but I was ſtopt by *John Burnets* ſudden falling to Prayer, and diſmiſſing the *Aſſembly*. I reſolved (with Gods help) to be *Patient* and *Civill*, and ſo I ceaſed, not ſeing a willingneſs in them for me to proceed; which experience made me not to trouble [13] *G. Fox* and the *Aſſembly* at *Providence*, but rather to make a fair and Solemn offer of *Diſpute* about theſe matters: ſo that it is notoriouſly falſe, that I *Owned* or *Countenanced* any of their *Opinions*.

5 You tell me of my foiſting in that word *Damning*, and I tell you that thoſe words of *Condemnation* and *Damnation* are all one in your *Greek* and *Latine* and *Engliſh* and other Languages: So that in your telling me if I hearken not to you, it will be my *Condemnation*, you (all one) tell mee it will be my *Damnation*.

There are two *Damnations*, one which all Mankind is under, (*He that believeth not is condemned already*) the other, that finall Sentence [*Goe ye Curſed*] my *Charity* bids judge that you meant not the latter: But my *Knowledg* tells me amongſt

Jews

Jews and *Turks*, *Papiſts* and *Proteſtants* and *Pagans*
(with all of which I have converſed) I never met
with ſuch a Judging Cenſuring Reviling *ſpirit* as is
the *ſpirit* of the *Quakers*.

6.   As to my ſaying in my 14th Poſition, that
the ſpirit of the *Quakers* tends to a ſudden *Cutting
off* of people, yea *Kings* and *Princes:* It lyes upon
me to prove it, and you do only upbraid me with
it but offer no diſproof, nor can you or any other
evade it, when the *Roots* of *Affairs* and *Actions* are
dig'd up and examined.

7.   Next you cry out againſt my Blood-thirſty
ſpirit in *William Harris* his Caſe: and I anſwer
that it is not the ſign nor the part of Loyall and
gratefull ſubjects having received ſuch wonderfull
Favours and Priviledges from ſo mighty a *Monarch*, ſo to Slight and damn, to Null and make void
ſuch Royall *Grace* and Favour.   Is it not high and
monſtrous abominable *Preſumption* for any man to
quarrel with *Soveraign Majeſty* for granting Favour
and Mercy to the *Souls* and *Bodyes* of their *Subjects* (which he ought to doe, even in *Conſcience* to
God) and for diſpenſing with *Laws* made for *Super-
ſtitions* and *Oppreſſions*.   I think you have been an
Officer your ſelf in a *Corporation* in *England*: I
queſtion how you durſt then (or durſt now) omit
to take *Cognizance* of ſuch Actings, againſt your
Corporations ſafety, and the Honour and royall ſupream *Authority* of his *Majeſty*.

I was in place and ingaged more than others to
maintain the righteous ſplendor of the Kings *Crown*
and *Majeſty* and *Prerogative*, and the *Colonyes* ſafety
                                                     peace

*W.Harris
his late
Caſe of de-
nying that
the King
hath pow-
er to diſ-
pence with
his Sub-
jects in
Religious
matters.*

peace and Liberty, and yet I acted not without the Counfel and Concurrence of all the reft of the 14| *Magiftrates* who did no more but what belonged to our *Duty* and Alleagiance as faithfull *Officers* to his *Majefty* and this *Colony* under him: nor did we any more then *Neceffity* and common Prudence compeld us to, for who knoweth what *after Reckonings* may befall us? Did not *W. Harris* (when in place) more than juftifie us, by judging himfelf bound to hurry your felf, and about twenty more to *Newport*, to anfwer for Contempt of the Kings *Authority*, though but in an accidentall, peaceable, and (by his Covetous violence) occafioned Meeting. Was not *Mr Clark* (though favourable to *W. H.*) fo amazed at *W. Harris* his defperate *Prefumptions*, that he readily acted with us in *Examination* and *Commitment?* Yea did not *W. Harris* (upon the point) Confefs that we could not but Commit him, and therefore provided beforehand his Bedding, and other Conveniences for a *Prifon?*

8. It is not true that either in *Word* or *Writing* I cryed out *Treafon* againft him. But it is notorioufly known, that he and his *Complices* lay in Wait, and at Catch at every word as *Foxes* and *Lyons* for *Mr Greens* Blood and mine, as *Traitors* againft *King Charles* for our pleading the *Colonyes* proceeding againft *W Harris* in the time of the *Parliament,* and *Oliver Cromwell.*

Oh Friend, whither will thy poor Soul next be hurried? Is not the Gap and Gate now left open *His Majeftyes Declaration* for *W. Harris* or any man to Difpute openly againft the

the *Kings Prerogative*, and tell him that he knowes not, nor his *Councill* nor *Judges* the *Laws?* that he cannot diſpence with *penall Laws* on the *Conſciences* of his *Subjects, Papiſts* or *Proteſtants,* at *Home* or *Abroad?* But ſee the Finger of the moſt High! the *Kings Majeſty* (as if he knew all our proceedings againſt *W. Harris* his preſumptions, debaſing the *Kings Power* and *Prerogative*) in the preſent juncture of theſe Affairs, ſent forth his *Royall Declaration* to the World, aſſerting his *Supream Power* and *Authority* in ſuch matters, and by virtue of many Statutes and Acts of *Parliament.*

9. In the laſt place, that your ſelf and others may admire your *new ſpirit,* how much, and how often, and how long hath your own *Mouth* and *Hand* (and *Capt. Fenner* and diverſe with you) declared and remonſtranced to the *Generall Aſſembly* againſt *W. Harris* (which Aſſembly therefore fined him and outed him) as the reſtleſs *Fire-brand* of *Town* and *Colony* and who hath with all his power now kindled and blown this *Fire* between [15] *Conecticut Colony* and our ſelves. Yet now in your, and the Quakers boſom, muſt *W. Harris* be hug'd, as an innocent and peaceable Soul, and the *Kings* faithfull *Officers* reproached and threatned as Bloodthirſty and cruel *Oppreſſors.*

10. You bid me mind my Books, and my being for and againſt *Perſecution:* But through Gods mercy I can look at them with humble *Thankſgiving* and peace, without any recoiling thought to Perſecution (as you falſly intimate) from them.

11. As to *G. Fox* his *Armour, Sword, and Cuttings*

tings with which you threaten me; I defire to think as low of my felf, *&.c.* as you or *G. Fox* can think high of himfelf. It is infinite mercy that I live, and as a *Living Dog* may wait for *Crums* of mercy, clearly to *See*, dearly to *Love*, uprightly to *Follow*, and conftantly to *Maintain* the eternall *Crown* and *Glory* of the true *Lord Jefus Chrift*, and his moft holy *Spirit* and *Scriptures*, with whofe gracious *Affiftanee* I hope to prove that the *Quakers* fpirit, and *Chrift* have no *Communion*.

Roger Williams.

THe Ingenious and upright *Reader* might now well fuppofe that the Conteft were over: but it is not the *Light* of *Truth* or *Reafon* or *Scripture* or *Experience*, or the *Teftimony* of the *Prudent* or their own *Confciences* that will fatisfie this *white Devill* of this pretended *Light* and *Spirit* within them, and therefore muft I crave the Readers *Patience* while I produce I. T. his third and laftLetter to me and my Anfwer to it.

Neighbour,

COncerning the miftaking the Date of my Letter as J. T His
thou writeft, which could not be, feing I fent it third and
thee the fame day I writ it, but thine, I heard of it last Letter
to me.
fome dayes before I received it. As for my paffing over
many particulars (which did not concern the matter in
handling) I willingly omitted them, difcerning thy fub-
til fpirit, in no refpeEt anfwering by fcripture or reafon my loving Admonitions to thee: But in thine own
words, is it not bruitifh, irrationall, childifh to affirm

we

we are worſe then Barbarians, *which thy ſordid Po-*
ſitions *do hold forth?* How *childiſh, yea how fooliſh*
doſt thou ſhew thy ſelf in thy firſt Poſition, *for* G.Fox
to prove what he and all friends diſown, and in ſcorn
thou calleſt Quakers. *And in thy* 12th *Poſition doſt*
affirm, That our Sufferings are no Evidence of the
truth of our Religion, *Thou mighteſt have ſpar'd thy*

a *Whore* is *paines in bringing* [16] *forth this Brat, which is of*
as bold in *thine owne begetting:* But *we are ſure it is an* Evi-
her *whore-* dence *againſt thee, & all other of thy Spirit, which*
doms, as a *perſecute, that they have drunk deep of the Cup of*
Chaſt Wife *Fornication, upon whom the* Violls *of* Gods *wrath are*
in her Ino- *powred forth in* ſpirituall Fornications.
cency.

 How dareſt thou find fault with me in not alleadging
ſcripture, *nor* reaſon *in declaring againſt thy impious*
Charges mentioned in thy railing & impious poſitions?
Would'ſt thou have me to take the matter in hand
(which thou challengeſt G.Fox *to anſwer) to give like*
a fool ſcripture & reaſon for what thou aſſigneſt another
to doe? Oh *what Serpent-like ſpirit doſt thou act by,*
that doſt not own my plain dealing with thee in owning
the ſcripture & wreſteſt & foiſteſt in, as J *meant not,*
nor writ: Jf *thy ſpirit were reall (as before men thy*
words ſeem to import) thou wouldeſt not then ſhew a
ſmiling Countenance when War *is in thine heart, in*
witneſſing againſt thy Neighbours ſecretly, againſt that
Golden rule, Doe as thou would'ſt be done by.
Thou counteſt it open violence for a Woman *to ſpeak in*
the Church: *but if thou knewest what* Woman *that*
ſhould not ſpeake thou would'ſt have ſpared me theſe
lines writing, & have eaſed thy ſelfe of thy great
ſtruglings & ſtrivings within thee to bring forth on
            Abortive.

Abortive. *Thou chargeſt me in making a great Out-cry againſt thy Blood-thirſty ſpirit, concerning* W. Harris, *as though thou dideſt at no time cry out Treo-ſon Treaſon.* Anſw. *how doſt thou ſhift of as one that is guilty, and dare not mention the caſe I writ up-on, ſhufling it to be his laſt impriſonment, which I know not the ground of, but as I had it related by thee: But the Circumſtances conſidered, it cannot poſſibly be par-aleld (as my Letter declareth) with this laſt Caſe of* W. Harris. Firſt, *thy taking Oath againſt my wife upon an other mans word on purpoſe to allay thy furious ſpirit againſt* W. Harris, *he not thinking thou wouldeſt have proſecuted againſt her, as alſo againſt ſixteen of thy peaceable neighbours,* Can thou deny that at that Court *thou cryed not out* Treaſon Treaſon, *making all as guilty as* W. Harris? *Thou ſayeſt I bid thee mind thy Book written againſt Perſecution, and yet thy ſelf a* Perſecutor *of thy peaceable Neighbours even unto death.* Anſw. *How canſt thou in peace (through the God of peace, (as thou ſayeſt) look upon thy wicked Travels to murther the Innocent as thou dideſt at* Newport, *cry-ing out* Treaſon *being* Preſident.

Alſo what I have ſpoken againſt W. Harris *touch-ing his firing the* Town *and* Colony, *I thought ſo, and therefore contended againſt him, but I never ſought his life, note that* R. W. *Thou ſayſt* [17] *thou art not conſcious of any recoyling in thy* ſpirit, *ſo much as in a thought.* Here thou manifeſt's *an impious* ſpirit *that ſeekes to murther the* Innocent: *what* Fury *poſſeſſeth thee to talk of the* God *of peace & yet retaineſt a* murtherous mind, *not having repented of thy wick-edneſſe, how is thy heart hardned in ſeeking the lives of*

If there were any *Colour* for any of theſe hor-rible *Out-cryes,* I ſhould have heard of them

ſuch

from *W.*
Edmunſon
who rak'd
up all he
could
againſt me
both in the
Diſpute at
Newport
and *Provi-*
dence.

ſuch as thou thy ſelf haſt confeſt to be the Children of God? Oh murtherous man that hath not any Re-morſe for thy long-liv'd Wickedneſs, J am ſorry for thee, though thou ſlight all my writings & counſells, & take all in the worſt ſence; yet J beſeech thee to con-ſider thy latter end, & my deſire for thee is that the Lord would awaken thy Soul & give thee Repentance unto life.

In the laſt place thou writeſt how highly I eſteem of G. Fox. *and thou deſireſt to think as low of thy ſelf: How will this agree with thy boaſting of great* Education, *great* Experiences, *great ſtruglings and ſtriv-ings within to bring out thy* Poſitions *and* Concluſions, *which all my loving Teſtimonyes againſt (as iſſuing from a diabolicall ſpirit) did no more take place with, then a* Feather *againſt a* Rock. *Call to mind the preaching of* Jonas *to* Ninive, *yet forty dayes and Ninive ſhall be deſtroyed (a ſhort ſpeech) yet they repented and the Lord pardoned: And ſo I deſire thou mayeſt repent and find mercy with the God of mercy.*

Thy Neighbour *I. T.*

THus *Reader* it pleaſed the Infinite *Wiſdom* of the moſt holy and only Wiſe, to pierce through my heart with the thruſts and ſtabs of a of a foul-mouth'd *ſlanderous ſpirit,* by the hands of long pro-feſſed *friends* and lovers, yet pretending the name of God and of Scripture, as wel as my ſelf. How doth it behoove us then to make ſure that we can in truth ſay as *Jeremiah,* Lam. 3. *Thou art my por-tion ſaith my Soul O Lord*; Thou and none elſe, Thou alone without *Health,* **Strength,** *Beauty,* **Hon-**
our,

our, *Lands,* *Goods,* *Friends,* &.c. How fhould we
make fure that with *Thomas,* we may fay unto the
Lord Jefus, *my Lord and my God?* for whofe fake
we ought joyfully to bear what *falfe Chrifts, falfe
fpirits* and their Souldiers can dart from *Earth* or
Hell againft us.

<h4 align="center">*My Anfwer was as followeth.*</h4>

MY ancient Friend, it pleafeth the moft High
to give to all mankind (his *Children* alfo and
them efpecially) many *bitter Cups,* and that oftentimes by the hands of *dear friends* and [18] *dear
Relations,* that we might fall more in love with
himfelf then ever who isinfinitely more fweet, and
even Holinefs and Power and Wifdom and Love
it felf.

Your Lines(in this your third *Fury* againft me)
being full of *Bitternefs* in themfelves, are more bitter to my Spirit upon diverfe accounts. But the
moft High and *only Wife* will have it fo, and your
judgment and Confcience (and mine) will have it
fo, yet that will not acquit us, we both fay we muft
come to another *Barr,* and there ftand or fall eternally.

In this, *Firft.* You tell me you willingly omitted the Particulars I mentioned as not concerning
the matters in handling: I am not of your mind,
it is an *Eafie* yet a *fufpicious* way of anfwering, and
implyes not only unwillingnefs, but a *willing Ignorance* and *Guilt* alfo: For is it not concerning the
matter in hand (efpecially when fo perfonally provoked)

(margin:) My Anf-
wer to *J
T.* his 3d
Affault up-
on me.

(margin:) A deceit-
full way of
Anfw.

voked) to vindicate our selves and friends, our Teachers and *Apostles*, our *Spirits* and Religion also ?

2. Next you blame my subtle spirit, for not answering by Scripture or Reason your loving Admonitions : I gave you my Reason, shewing how simple it was for you to give fire upon me, and tell me my *Paper* was *Scurrilous, full fraught with impudent Lyes and Slanders*, and yet give me not one *Scripture* nor *Reason* to prove any of them to be so. 2. I shewed you how irrationall it was for you to think, that I should so suddenly renounce my understanding and *Conscience* and *Positions* upon the sudden sound of your Outcry *Repent, Repent.*

The horrid Nakedness of the Q Women shews the worse then barbarous nakedness of their Spirits.

3. You tell me it is childish, bruitish and irrationall, to say that you are worse then *Barbarians* : *Answ.* I said not so in generall, you and all the world ought to abhor the particular case, *viz.* the stripping *Naked* of your *Women* and Maidens ; a case worse then Savage and Barbarous, only practised by the *Bruites*, and sometimes by *Indians*, and *Whores* in their drink, when all *Modesty* and *Reason* is overwhelmed with more then common *Drunkenness.* Who can but abhor to think of such whorish and monstrous *Immodesty*, such an hellish *Incentive* to filthy Lusts, and that under the most holy name of the *Spirit of God.*

the name

Quakers.

4. *A*s to my first *Position*, you now tell me that it is childish and foolish for *G. Fox* to prove (I suppose you mean, for me to desire *G. Fox* to prove) what he and all friends disown, and thou in scorn callest Quakers : *Answ.* I know the Quakers
say

say [19] that name is given them in scorn, and
yet we also know it it hath its denomination from
those great bodily *Shakings* which have been believed to have come in mightily upon them by the
power of *Devillish spirits* (for many Reasons of
which afterward) However *G. Fox* in 370th. page
of his Book *in Folio* writes thus in the title of each
page [*The Quakers answer. The Quakers Answer*] I
know what may be said; and I know may be said
and justly to that excuse, and what shall be said in
the Dispute following.

5.   As to my 12th. *Position*, of Suffering of the
Quakers, and you say it is a *Brat* of mine own, and
that is an evidence against me, and all of my *Per-*
secuting Spirit. Answ. I shall (by Gods assistance
prove that you doe make it an *Evidence* of your
Religion, and then it must be your one *Brat* and
Bastard.

As to my persecuting spirit, the most High hath
been a holy witness to my Travelsand losses and haz-
ards and other sufferings, in my vindicatingand pro-
curing *Soul-liberty:* and I humbly hope in his mercy,
he will preserve me from being like many *Quakers*,
fouly fallen from their former *Christian Religion*

6.   You say, *How darest thou blame me for not*
giving Scripture or Reason against thy railing and
impious Positions, when thou challengest and assignest
another to doe it G.Fox, &.c.   *Answ.* I only blamed
J. T. for being so fierce and furious, so hot and
hasty in crying out *a scurrilous Paper fraught with*
lyes and impudent slanders, and yet gave me not one
Scripture or Reason against any one of them: common

*The Qua-
kers* Suffer-
ings.

mon *Modefty* and humane *Sobriety* would have
taught a little Patience, till *G. Fox* had anfwered,
or untill you had anfwered fomething of *Scripture*
or *Reafon* your felf.

7.   Nextly you tell me of my *Serpent-like spirit*
in witneffing againft my neighbour fecretly: To
which I lay before the moft High, I know not
what you intend 2. I know it not to be any
Crime (much lefs a serpent-like fpirit as your railing pen phrafes it) to give a true teftimony, and witnefs in private and publick, even againft the *higheft*
and deareft, in the matters of *God* and *Truth*,
which ought to be only *High* and only *Dear*
unto us.

Womens
Preaching.
8.   As to *Womens preaching* in the Church, you
tell me that I know not what that *Woman* is, *Anfw.*
I know the allegoricall Interpretations given of
both thofe Scriptures, to the *Corinths* and *Timothy*,
But where the holy *Scripture* is plain, and agrees
20] even with *Nature* it felf; where the holy *Spirit*
of *God* gives Reafons why Scripture fhould be fo
expounded (which is an extraordinary fignification
of Gods foveraign will and pleafure) where elfe one
part muft be *Literall* and an othei part *Allegoricall*,
(which is moft improper and not fuiting to the
Majefty and *Purity* of *Gods Spirit*) what can be
foberly in the fear of God and with any fober reafon collected, but that the moft High, the *God* of
Order (and all Order and Wifdom it felf) is pleafed
there to fet down the *Order* of his *Worfhip* in the
Chriftian *Congregations*.

9. Concerning *W Harris* you tell me I fhift
of

of the matter, for you meant not *W Harris* his laſt
Impriſonment: You prove it by my taking Oath
againſt your Wife upon an other mans word on
purpoſe to allay my furious ſpirit againſt *W Harris*. Theſe are your words, which may be taken
three wayes, but neither of them can I call to
mind: God knowes I truly deſire to See, Lament
and forſake every Idle word or thought, which my
ſoul may be ſatisfied is ſo: for I dare not goe beyond (as you proudly doe) that *Direction* of the
Lord Jeſus, dayly to cry [*Forgive us our Treſpaſſes*]
I dare moſt confidently deny that ſimple Charge,
viz. that I ſhould cry out *Treaſon* Treaſon, againſt
your Wife and others, labouring to bring them into the ſame guilt with *W. Harris.* whoſe facts and
courſes others (of no ſmall *Authority* and *Prudence*
amongſt us, with whome I adviſed) ſaw to be deſperate high *Treaſon* againſt the *Laws* of our
Mother England, and of this *Colony* alſo. When
W Harris, ſent his *writings* or *Books* to the *Main*
and to the *Iland,* againſt all *Earthly Powers, Parliaments, Laws, Charters, Magiſtrates, Priſons, Puniſhments, Rates,* yea and againſt all *Kings, and
Princes,* under that Notion that the People ſhould *W Harris
his former
practices
againſt all
Goverment
but that of
Saints as
the Qua-
kers now
ſpeak.*
ſhortly cry out, *no lords no maſters*; and had in open
Court proteſted, (before the whole *Colony* aſſembled) that he would maintain his Writings with
his *Blood.* Was it my Fury (as you call it) or was
it not *Honeſty* and *Duty* to *God* and the *Colony* and
the *higher Powers* then in *England* to act faithfully
and impartially in the place wherein I then ſtood
Centinell?

And

And it is not true that I fought his life as you upbraid me, much lefs theirs, who purpofely (as the moft high God is witnefs) were prefented, that fome prudent courfe might be taken by the Court for the preventing of their greater danger, and the *Colonyes* alfo. By your reafon the *Kings Majefly*, his *Judges* (yea all *Judges*) [21] yea the *King* him-felf, yea the *moft High*, and *King of Kings* fhall be condemned as *Blood-thirfty*, bloody feekers of the lives (though of high handed wilfull and dangerous *Tranfgreffors*) as though *Juftice* and *Mercy*, true *Pitty* and juft *Severity* might not harmonize, and make up the bleffed concord of Peace together.

10.   You mind me again of my Books againft Perfecution, and yet my felf a *Perfecutor* of my peacable Neighbours to the *Death*, murthering the innocent, yea that I ftill retain a *Murtherous* mind, and you cry out againft me, *Oh murtherous Man* &.c.   To which I fay, I am not better than *David*, nor (in this cafe) are you better than *Shimei*, who rak't up *Stones* and *Dirt*, and flung them with *Railings* at *David*, crying out *Come out thou bloody Man*, and this in the name of the holy *Spirit* alfo.

My Right-eoufnefs as to my deal-ing with *W. H.*

As to *W. H.* I never appeared In *Town* or *Colony* againft him for any private matter (although many wayes extraordinarily provoked and wronged by him) but alwayes in Witnefs (as I humbly appeal unto God) I fay in witnefling againft his *running down* and deftroying the *Publick*,(as at this day) for his Private *Covetous* and *Contentious* Ends.

The hor-rible Mur-thering of

And for your felf, who cry out fo much of *Blood* and Murther for my being impartiall to *God*, to the
King

King and the *Countrey*: I heartily wifh that your the *Indians* hands were wafhed from the bloody trade of by *Liquors* which the *Liquours* to the *Indians*, which even the *Quakers* Qu: have have practifed, telling the *Indians* that the *Quakers* notorious- only know God, and therefore would fell them tifed. *Powder* and *Liquors* cheaper, and they would not mix water with *Rhum* as others did: fo that by many fudden deaths, what by *Confumptions* and *Dropfies*, the *Barbarians* have been murthered, *hundreds*, if not *thoufands* in the whole Countrey, and more in this *Colony* than in any part of the *Countrey* befide that I have heard of, againft which I have witneffed from Court to Court in vain.

11 You afk me how I can think as *low* of my felf, as you *high* of *G. Fox*, when I boaft of *Education Experience &c.*

I anfwer, I boaft as *Paul* did, who confeft himfelf the leaft of all *Saints*, and the chiefe of *Sinners*; and yet reckons up the *Priviledges* end *Favours*, which God had vouchfafed to him, againft the foule Clamours of his malicious and envious Oppofites, the falfe *Apoftles*.

12. You conclude with advifing my *Repentance*, and you propofe to me the cafe of *Nineve*, telling me that forty dayes is a fhort *Speech*.

22] *Anfw.* I humbly befeech the *Lord* to help you and me, humbly and faithfully to examine our true laying of that *Foundation* of a true Repentance, which is a totall turning of our *Soul* or *Spirit* unto God; not out of *Fear* or felf ends, as *Diffemblers* do; but in *Mariage-love* with *God* that it might be faid unto us, *thy Maker is thy Husband.*

As

As to your fpecial Hint to me of forty dayes, I can fay it (through infinite mercy) that more than forty or fifty yeares, I have been acquainted with *Death*, and have (not feldom) familiarly difcourfed with the *Grave* and *Pit of Rottennefs* : I have defired to be ready at a *minutes warning*, waiting for a wind to tranfport me (as *Paul* fpeaks) unto *Chrift Jefus* in *Abrahams Bofome* which is beft of all. I pray you to know that I believe there is a *black Familiar* that haunts the *Quakers*, it may be he **They were the Dog-dayes when thefe hot and doged barkings were made at me.** *whifpers* to you that within forty dayes you fhall be ridd of me except I repent; he may fee into the crazy temper of my houfe of *Clay*. (Thefe *Dog-dayes* not to continue and abide a little of that time) Or God may fuffer him by fome immediate *Revelation* to employ fome malicious foul to *Murther* me, that this foul *Lyar* and *Murtherer* may extoll and predicate himfelf in print by your *Pens*, that he was a true *Prophet*, applauding and triumphing in the righteous Judgment of God againft a *Blafphemer* of your *gods* and *godeffes*. I believe that every *Hair of mine head*, and every *Minute* of my Life is in the mercifull hand of the *Father* of *Spirits*. I doe not fimply and blafphemoufly think **Death and the Refurrection.** as *G. F.* that my Soul is a piece or part of God; nor can I (as the unbelieving *Quakers*) flight the *Rifing* of my body; *Steven* fell afleep, and fo (among *Stones* or whatever his holy Wifdom pleafeth) I humbly hope fhall I, and rife again in the *Morning*.

R. W.

Prouidence, July 30. 1672. (fo called)

HItherto (gentle *Reader*) have been the *Skir-miſhings* of my *Forlorn-Hope*; I haſten now to the relation of the main *Battle*, for after this my third Letter and *Anſwer*, I heard no more of that *foul* and *ſlanderous ſpirit* : I ſhould rejoice to be inſtrumentall to his caſting out of my ancient friend *J T.* however he pluckt in his horns as *G Fox* himſelf did, and I have yet heard no further.

Within ſome few dayes after that our *Deputy Governour* had [23] delivered my Paper to them, the ſtrange *Quakers* (as was agreed with *G. Fox*) came to *Providence*. *John Stubs*, *John Burnet*, and others, and came to my houſe ſix or ſeven together : their *Salutations* were (like the meetings of their *dumb ſpirit*) in ſilence. I bid them welcome *&.c.* *John Stubs* began and ſaid, they had received a Paper from me, and they came to me to tell me, that they accepted my *Offer*, and that they had appointed (according to the liberty given them by my ſelf in my Paper) the 9th. of the preſent *Auguſt* to be the day at *Newport*. I told them they were welcome, and the more welcome becauſe they brought me tidings of their *Reſolution* : for I longed for *Opportunityes* of ſuch *Exerciſes*, to which I thought the moſt High invited us by our precious *Libertyes &.c.* I added that my Paper was in the firſt place directed to *G. Fox* : but they ſuddenly catcht at my word, and *John Burnet* told me that *G. Fox* was departed before my *Letters* were opened, and that *G.Fox* never ſaw my Paper (and probably as afterward in the diſpute he ſpake honeſtlie not knowing the Miſtery) *John Stubs* added that my

The firſt Interveni-ence at Provi-dence of the Qu. and my ſelf.

G Fox his cunning Departure

Paper

Paper gave liberty to *G. Fox* or his friends. I faid therefore I would not fail (if God pleafed) to meet them at the place, and by nine in the morning, on the day they had appointed.

They departed (after drink offered and accepted by fome) but the next morning being the firft of the Week I fent them word in writing, that diverfe of our Neighbours were grieved that the *Confer-ence* fhould be carried away from *Providence* to *Newport* wholly, (as fome of them had alfo fpoken) I told them that the accepting of my *Proffer* ne-ceffarily included the Conference about the latter feven at *Providence* : I told them their *Confciences* and *Credits* lay on it, and therefore defired them to fix on a day for the difpute of the latter feven at *Providence* before their departure hence. This Pa-per was delivered to one of their Company in the room where they were together, but whither on purpofe or (as tis poffible) by miftake, they fay the Paper was loft : fo receiving no Anfwer from them, I late in the evening fent them another writing, fignifiing, that I could not hold my felf ingaged to meet them at *Newport* about the firft feven, with-out their promife of difcuffing the latter feven at *Providence.* Then they wrote to me that I had feemed willing, and that they had given notice, and the Countrey would come in, therefore they challenged me to appear and prove my malici-ous [24] and bitter charges againft them, and with-all promifed that upon the finifhing of the firft feven at *Newport*, fome of them would give me a meeting a *Providence &.c.* Upon the receipt of this,

My care of ingaging hem to my whole Offer and of difcuf-fing the latter feven at Provi-dence.

this, I fent them a third writing fignifiing that I
refted in their Promife, and therefore (if God
pleafed) I would not fail to be with them at the time
and place appointed. And God gracioufly affifted
me in rowing all day with my old bones fo that I
got to *Newport* toward the *Midnight* before the
morning appointed.

Then I fent them a fourth Paper (with a Copie
of my firft that mifcaried as they faid) and fignified to them, that it would be convenient to agree
about fome *Order* of *Tranfition*, or paffing from one
pofition to another: as alfo fince they were *many*
and I but *One*, I prefumed their Reafon told them
that I expected but *One at once*, and that if
another defired to fpeak, the firft fhould hold his
peace; as alfo I fignified that fome were fcrupulous
of going into the *Quakers Meeting-houfe*, and ther- Scruples
fore I defired fome thoughts about it: they thought about
it convenient to fend *H. Bull* to requeft me to goe meeting in
to his houfe to them; I went; they urged the *Ca-* kers Meet-
pacioufnefs and *Conveniency* of their houfe, and I ing houfe
told fuch as fcrupled, that it was one thing to at Newport
goe into a *Jewifh Synagogue*, or a *Popifh Chappell* to
worfhip, or countenance their *Worfhips*: another
thing to *Profefs* and *Conteft* againft them, in which
refpect *Paul* difputed many dayes in the *Jewes
Synagogues* againft them, and I could freelie goe into the *Popes Chappel*, to difpute againft the *Pope*
and his *Worfhip*.

I knew our aged *Governour Mr. Nich. Eafton*
& other *Magiftrates* (of their judgment) would be *the way to*
there, & fo the *Civill Peace* maintained, & I had a *Conquer.*

ftrange

ftrange *affurance* given in to my *fpirit* from God in
anfwer to my poor requefts &*.c. viz,* that by *Mod-
eration* and *Patience* I fhould conquer their *Immod-
erations* and *impatiencies,* I therefore thought it in
vain to fpend time about a *Moderatour:* Tis true
they gave me no Anfwer either by Speech, or writing concerning their coming on me one at once,
but to their feeming great advantage they conftantly
fell on me *all at once,* and one of them *William Edmundfon* with grievous Language and infulting.

When I came into the place aforefaid I found
three able and noted preachers amongft them, *viz
John Stubs, John Burnet, William Edmunfon* fitting
together on an high Bench with fome of the
Magiftrates of their Judgment with them : I had
heard [25] that *John Stubs* was learned in the *Hebrew* and the *Greek* (and I found him fo) as for
John Burnet I found him to be of a moderate *Spirit,*
and a very able Speaker. The third *W. Edmundfon* was newly come (as was faid) from *Virginia,* and
he proved the *Chief Speaker,* a man not fo able nor
fo *moderate* as the other two: For the two firft
would fpeak *Argument,* and difcufs and produce
Scripture: but *William Edmundfon* was very ignorant in the *Scripture* or any other Learning: He
had been a fouldier in the late warres, a ftout portly man of a great voice, and fit to make a *Bragadocia* (as he did) and a conftant exercife meerly of
my Patience : he would often *Vapour* and preach
long, and when I had patiently waited till the *Guft*
was over, and began to fpeak, then would he ftop
my mouth with a very unhandfome Clout of a
grievous

The Per-
fons dif-
puting
with me.

*W Ed-
mundfon*
defcribed.

grievous *Interruption*: fo that fometimes I was forc't
to play the *Moderator*, and to proteft that fuch
practifes were againft the fober rules of *Civillity*
and *Humanity*. It pleafed *God* to help me with
fuch *Patience* to weather them, that *John Stubs* *J Stubs*
openly confeft twice, that though fome others had his Inge-
given them fome interruptions, yet that I had not nuity.
done it.

I took my Seat at the other end of the houfe The be-
oppofite to them, and began telling them that the ginning of
moft High was my witnefs, that not out of any pre- the *Difpute*
judice againft, or difrefpect to the perfons of the
Quakers (many of whome I knew and did love and
honour) nor any foolifh Paffion of pride or boldnefs (for I defired to be fenfible of my many de-
cayes of *my houfe of Clay*, and other wayes) nor any
earthly or *worldly ends* I had that occafioned this
trouble to my felf and them.

I was firft commanded this work from *Heaven*: The Occa-
Why fhould not this Argument be good for mee fion of it.
and for others as well as the *Quakers*? they fay their
commands are immediate (for *Interpretations* are
immediate) but I fay they herein fuffer *Satan* to
cheat them; for they fay they pray, they faft, they
wait, they liften, they judge of the motions that
arife within them, and fo have I done. The great
maker and fearcher of all hearts knowes, that none
but his holy *Majefty* was privy to the *Conception* of
this bufinefs.

1. My end was, the vindicating his *moft holy* My ends.
Name, which my Soul faw was trodden in the dirt
by *Sathan* clothed with *Samuels Mantle*, and the
bright

bright garment of an *Angel of Light,* which once he was, but pride deceived him.

26] 2. I had in mine eye the vindicating this *Colony* for receiving of fuch perfons whome others would not, we fuffer for their fakes, and are accounted their *Abettors* : that therefore together with the improvemeut of our *Libertyes* which the *God of Heaven,* and our *Kings Majefty* have gracioufly given us, I might give a publick teftimony against their *Opinions* in fuch a way and *Exercife,* I judged it incumbent upon my *Spirit* and *Confcience* to doe it (in fome regards) more than moft in the *Colony.* I may alfo truly fay that

Nicholas Davis drowned at Newport a little before the Difpute.

3. I had alfo in mine eye, that this exercife might occafion fome *Soul Confideration* in many. I told them that we had a dolefull *Alarum* and inftruction lately, we were taught what *Salvation* and *faving* was, in the late death and drowning of a perfon fo known to us (and all *N. England*) *Nicholas Davis.* I told them our cafe, and the cafe of all mankind is his (in Spirituall and *Soul matters*) *Oh a world for an Oar, a Rope, a Plank.* Only it muft be to all of us our work, to try whether our *Saviour* our *Salvation* be reall, and not failing in fo great a Straight.

Some of thefe bleffed ends it hath pleafed God to propagate by this occafion all this *Colony* over, and all of us round about have put forth our felves in *Difquifitions* and Searchings after the true grounds of the *Chriftian Religion* and *Worfhip.*

What Prayer was ufed.

I had many thoughts of beginning fuch an exercife with *Prayer* unto God for his Prefence : but I

knew

knew I could not joyn with them nor would they owne my *Prayers*: I had thoughts (as *Eliah* among the *Baalites*) to have prayed in the fingular number: But fome *Confiderations* made my fpirit content with this kind of Petition unto God: For not only in my *Clofet* and my heart, but publickly before them all I faid, *I doe humbly hope and beg of* God *the* Father *of Spirits fo to order and direct our Spirits in thefe our Agitations, that his holy name may receive glory, and the* Soules *of all of us fome* Soul-profit *and Advantage.*

I began with the firft Pofition, which I think *W. Edmunfon* alfo read out of the Paper. *viz.*

That the People called Quakers are not true Quakers according to the Scriptures. The firft *Pofition.*

1. I faid I knew they did not owne that name *Quakers*, as impofed on them by God, or taken up by themfelves, but given them in fcorn and derifion, as *G. Fox, Ed. Burrowes* (and I had heard *John Stubs* who joined with them) declared, and that 27] one *Gervace Bennet, a Juftice* in *Derby* firft fo called them in the year 1650 And yet I had caufe to judg that the name was given by *Juftice Bennet* and others to them from that ftrange and uncouth poffeffing of their bodyes. with quaking and *fhaking* of their *Bodyes* even in publick Affemblyes and Congregations, which extraordinary motions I judged to come upon them, not from the holy *Spirit* and Power of God, but from the fpirit and power of *Sathan* for diverfe *Reafons.* The name *Quakers.*

Firft. Although they pretend that *Mofes* and *David* and *Habbacouck* and *Daniel* were *Quakers*, yet

as

as to the Chriſtian Profeſſion, and the dayes ſince our gallant fore-Fathers in *Germany* (at *Spiers*) pro-teſted againſt the whore of *Rome*, and from that *Proſteſtation*, by the *Papiſts*, they were called in ſcorn and wrath the *Proteſters*, or Proteſtants (about 150 years ſince) unto this day. I ſay as to the Proteſtant Profeſſors and Confeſſors, the *Quakers* are but a new upſtart party or *Faction* riſen up little above 20 yeares ſince in the northern parts of *England, Lancaſhire &c.* Tis true, tis probable they are the Offſpring of the *Grindletonians* in the ſame *Lancaſhire* about two yeares before, who held thoſe two grand Points (though many wicked paths of *Doctrine* aud *Practice* were amongſt them) *viz.* 1 *That God doth all.* 2 *They could not ſin,* taking it according to the Letter. Theſe *Grindletonians* were the Offſpring of the late *Nicholaitans,* (as all of them are in truth juſtly ſo called) from *Henery Nichols* who put forth his Books of the ſame Poi-ſon in *K. James* his time, (which long ſince I read) and were confuted by many, and by Mr *Ainſworth* and Mr *Robinſon,* precious and powerfull *Witneſſes* of Chriſt Jeſus. *H. Nichols* aud his *Nicholaitans* were the Litter of thoſe *Spirittualls* and *Libertines* which ſpread in *Germany* and *France* in *Calvin*'s dayes; againſt whome that heavenly ſoul, gave his powerfull and heavenly witneſs in his Book againſt the *Libertines.* Theſe *Libertines* Satan raiſed up about the *Proteſtant Reformation* from the ruines and rubbiſh of the old *Manicheans* and *Gnoſticks,* and other blind Guides who ſwarmed in the firſt third and fourth Chriſtian *Centuryes,* until the *Pope* ſwallowed

The Riſe of the word Proteſtant. [marginal note]

The Grin-dletonians. [marginal note]

The Lib-ertines. [marginal note]

fwallowed up all the leffer *Serpents*, and fo became a *Dragon* with feven Heads and ten Horns, forcing all with fire and Fagot to deny *Chrift Jefus*, and to martch under Anti-Chrift (the *Anti-chrift* the man of fin) his Colours.

Some of these Particulars I could not then ex-prefs, but think ⌈28⌋ fit here to remember the for-mer dayes, for Information of fuch as doe defire it.

Thefe People came from *Lancafhire* and other northern parts to the Southward of *England* and to *London*. I fpake with fome of their Chief then in *London*, I knew it was the old proud *fpirit* which had appeared in fo many foul lyes in their former deceived and deceiving *Leaders*, and I was the more confirmed in my thoughts when I faw their foul *fpirit* fo tranfport them, not only in lying *Doctrines*, but lying *Quakings* and *Tremblings*, lying preaching through the Streets *Repent, Repent* : and lying and abominable *Nakednefs* of men and women, untill their ugly Child and Daughter *Rantifme* rofe from *The* Rant-their Bowels and practifed *Nakednefs* of men and ers *are but* women in the Streets and in their religious *Meet-* *the* Quak-ings, as *Adamites :* when it is notorioufly known ers *Daughter* they fell into many *uncleanneffes* and *Adulteryes*. To my face and to the world in print they maintaind, there were no fins in them : Saying *That the Saints could not fin, and God did all and was all,* and they were *as pure as Adam and God himfelf,* this is known by the Writings extant *&c.*

2. Again I faid unto my *Antagonifts* that the manner of thefe *quakings* and *fhakings* were not as of those *quakings* and tremblings of *David, Mofes,* and the

the *Corinths* receiving *Titus* with Trembling, or
the working out Salvation with *Fear* and *Trembling*:
for that may many wayes be proved to be the *Soul*
and *Spirit*, out of a holy Aw and *Dread* of the
Majesty of Heaven with whome we have to deal,
who only can pitty and help us in our deplorable
and forlorn conditions: Hee it is who worketh
the *Will* and the *Deed*, and therefore with deep
impreffions of *Aw* and *Dread* we ought to attend
upon all his holy meanes appointed, wherein (as of
old in the Tabernacle and Temple) he hath promifed to come to us. Befide, as it is naturall for the
Body to tremble when the mind doth, as we fee in
many Perfons in the beginning of a Battle, or going over a deep Water, or going to fuffer Death,
or looking over a high *Clift* into the fea &c. So
when the Bodies of thofe holy men, or any now
doe fo tremble *Experience* proves it that it is no
ordinary motion, but extraordinary, and upon
extraordinary occafions, and thofe holy and heavenly Occafions, as may be inftanced.

But the quaking and fhaking motions of the
Quakers (as I fhall prove) they proceeded not from
thofe holie Affections [29] proper to Gods Children, fo alfo they were horrid and monftrous cafting their bodies into horrid and monftrous motions
and Geftures which mine eyes have feen: Befides
the abundance of notorious Inftances, what ftrange
horrid motions are thofe which *Theora John* (as he
madly calls himfelf) and *John Toldervy* were toft
and tumbled up and down with? which cannot
be

True Qua-
king

The horrid
fhaking *of*
the Qua-
kers.

be imagined to proceed from the holy *Spirit of God*, but from Sathan to delude and cheat poor finners with.

To this purpofe I told them at the firft coming of this fpirit to *London* and *Weftminfter*, fome *Parliament men* told me that themfelves went to one of the *Quakers* Meetings about *Charing Crofs*, but were fo affrighted with the *fhaking* of their own bodies, and of their *Chairs* and Stooles under them, that they could never again be got into their *Affemblyes*.

I added, that fuch *Shakings, Motions, Extafies, &c.* were known to be the frequent workings of *Sathan* upon his Servants in all ages, Such were the furious motions of *Baals Preifts*, the motions of the *Poffeffed* mentioned in the *Gofpells*, and other *Hiftoryes*, and known to be amongft the *Barbarians*, our Neighbours about this time. *John Burnet* and *William Edmunfon* rofe up and faid that I had laid many deep and heavy *Charges* upon the people of the Lord, which I fhould never be able to prove: I had denied them to be *Chriftians*, and fo had wronged the good Spirit of God in them, and their Profeffion of worfhipping God in the Spirit: Yea I had taken away their being (as men) out of the World, as a dangerous People to *Nations* and *Kingdomes* & *Common-weales*, yea to *Kings* & *Princes*, and fo not fit to live amongft men in the World. Thefe Speeches were often uttered and enlarged by one or other of them, and that with Zeal (and Paffion in *W. Edmunfon*)

I waited patiently till thefe *Gufts* of their angry
Spirit

Satans Counterfeit motions.

The Quakers Anfwer.

Spirit was over, and then I told them I had not wronged them in a tittle : But by the help of the moft High I would make all good againft them, & toen leave it to every mans and womens Soul to judge at their own Perill.

About this time *John Stubs* alleadged that of *Paul*, Phil 2. *Work out falvatson with fear and Trembling.*

Quaking and Trembling I replyed I in no way oppofed the awfull and moft ferious impreffions of *Gods Majefty* in all his appearances & ordinances upon the Soules and Spirits, yea and *Bodyes* of Gods Children. [30] But I denied that thofe places to the *Corinthians* and *Philippians* concerned any fuch bodily fhakings and quakings as we now debated.

No Ordinance of God Befide I faid if *Quaking* and *Trembling* were a Command and an Ordinance, and inftitution of God to be practifed, then was it conftantly to be practifed (as the *Jewes* fay of *Cain* that the Mark which God fet upon him was a conftant *Trembling*) Or if not alwayes, yet alwayes in *Worfhip*, or if not alwayes in *Worfhip* yet at fome certain times. But

Counterfeit Quaking and Trembling the plain truth is, the *Devill* will be *Gods Ape* in moft things : He fubornes and fubftitutes a baftard *Quaking and Trembling* of the body in Imitation of *David, Mofes &c.* on purpofe to thruft out the true Fear and Trembling which ought to be conftantly in us, raifing up all our Affections and all within us to a due fence of the *Terror* of the Lord, the dreadfulnefs of our *Danger,* and the wonder of our *Deliverance* (which we can never make too fure) from fin and wrath to come to all eternity.

I

I alſo declared, that the *moſt High* and holy one, was free as he pleaſed to cauſe the trembling of the *Soules* of his People to over flow with influence upon their *Bodyes* alſo, asin *Moſes, David, Daniel, Habakkuk, Paul, &c.* this is like to be in ſome extraordinary caſes and *Converſions* or turnings to God, as *Paul's* was, and that eſpecially in bringing of *great Sinners* or *old Sinners* unto himſelf *&c.*

There were ſome few Speeches, ſome from the *Governour* and his Wife, and ſome few others that ſpake, ſome in favor of, and ſome againſt the *Quakers*, but neither did my Oppoſites nor I ſo far attend them as to engage with them, excepting ſome Turnes that were between *William Edmunſon,* and *William Hitchcock* (an Inhabitaut of *Newport*) who (as others did) witneſſed againſt their upbraiding me with my age (*Old man, Old man* &c.) as alſo for their *Interruptions*.

Mine own Brother Mr *Robert Williams,* School-Maſter in *Newport,* deſired to ſpeak : nor he nor others diſſenting from them could be permitted, except they would ſet their hands to my Paper. My Brother (unknown to me) put in a paper to them, which he took the liberty to read, deſiring that two things might be anſwered by the *Quakers.* 1. The matter of the true ſence of *Sin* as Sin. 2. Of the *Materiallity* of ſuch a Perſon as the *Lord Jeſus Chriſt,* and the materiallity of his [31] *Bloudſhedding.* This Paper they took but waved it. *W. Edmunſon* openly charged me with breach of Covenant, *viz.* That if any would ſpeak on my behalf, they ſhould ſet their hand to my *Propoſitions.* Tis true

A Paper put in of two great Conſiderations

true it was defired by one of them at my houfe at *Providence*, that if any joined with me, they fhould fubfcribe to my Paper. But I anfwered that I was *alone* in the Bufinefs, I had not confulted with any others but the God of heaven himfelf: fo that I denied vehemently that there was any fuch agree-ment, or any colour for it. Befides it was ridiculous to put either fuch a *Bar* and Limit upon any mans fpirit, and leaft of all upon Gods *Spirit, viz,* that no man fhould defire leave to object or querie *&c.* except firft he would fubfcribe my *Propofalls·* But I took the boldnefs juftly to charg them with palpable and grofs *Partiality* viz. that *W. Hitchcock* and others, (oppofing or diffenting) might not fpeak, but *W. Harris, W. Dyar* or any favouring of them might fpeak without exception, becaufe all that fpeak for their ptetended light, it muft be fuppofed that they fpeak from the Spirit of God himfelf: others out of *Ignorance, Malice and Envy*: this will appear more afterward.

However, there were thefe few debates about the liberty of fpeech in the Auditory and By-ftanders, and the *Quakers* deniall and enjoining of *Subfcription*: yet the moft High, *Father of Spirits* did fo compofe all fpirits, that it was wonderfull that fuch *Oppofites* fhould goe through fuch a work and Conflict all day untill night, without more *Interruptions* and *Difturbances*.

I was ready and waited to put forth my third Reafon to prove they were not true Chriftian Quakers, it was from Ifai. 66. *To this man will I look that is poor and contrite, and trembleth at my* Word. I
told

The unequall Termes of the Quakers enjoining Subfcription.

& their open Partiality·

told them that *G.Fox* in his Book all along was fo far from trembling at the *Word of God* in the holy Writings or *Scriptures*, that he could not endure they fhould have that name, or be once called the *Word of God*,   Tis true I know his pretence, that *Chrift Jefus* is called the *Word of God*, Rev. 19. But I know tis true alfo that he grants the Scriptures to be true, and infpired from the holy *Spirit of God*, and to be Gods words, though not his *Word*. Well, to pafs by the fimplicity of the *Diftinction*, and let us take what he grants, and is it not prodigious and monftrous Contempt that thefe holy Words, this holy Book and Writing of God fhould be fo undervalued and flighted, yea vilified [32] and nullified, if compar'd with their pretended *new found Light* within them, which was (fay they) before the *Scriptures*, and gave forth the *Scriptures*, and therefore was above the *Scriptures* and gave forth the *Scriptures*, and therefore was above the *Scriptures*, and therefore is not judged or tried by the *Scriptures*, but they by it.   Yea, and this light muft be in every one of mankind in the whole World: Hence it was that thefe holy Writings were fo difufed in their own private Readings, in their Publick Worfhip, and in their Families.

　　I told them God was little beholding to the *Pope* and the *Quakers* for their humble Reverence and great Affection to his holy *Letters, Declarations* and *Proclamations*.   The Pope had his *Infallibility* as well as they, his immediate *Infpirations* as well as they :   They both owned, and yet did not owne the *holy Scriptures*, the Pope and they only muft

　　　　　　　　　　　　　　　interpret

The Quakers evill fpirit toward the holy Scriptures.

The Light of each man in the World above the Scriptures.

The Pope and the Quakers great affection and ownnefs againft the holy Scriptures.

interpret *Scriptures*, they only give the *Sence*, they only judge all *Controverfies* : yea they difpence with the *Scriptures*, and if they were quite loft and burn'd and not a Copy of them left in the World, yet there were no lofs but a good Turn, a good Riddance, for then the *Pope* and the *Quakers Infallible fpirit* and its immediate *Infpirations*, would be more efteemed and fet by.

An Inftance of a long-haird profane *Qua.*flighting *Nature* and the *Scriptures.*

I produced an Inftance of one *Thurfton* an Apoftle of theirs who came to *Providence* with extraordinary long hair hanging over his fhoulders; It was fo long that an aged Soul (captivated for prefent amongft them) the wife of *C.S.* demanded of him why he ware it fo long fince Nature it felf did teach it to be a fhame for a man to wear *long Hair*, as the *holy Scripture* affirmed? He would not fay, He car'd not what *Nature* or the holy S*criptures* faid, but he faid as much in effeƈt (as fhe told me her felf, and may with true fear and trembling ftill think on it) *viz.* when that God that bid me wear it, bids me cut it off, then will I cut it off. As if he would fay, what tell you us of the teachings of *Nature* (as we fee in that monftrous cafe of their womens *Nakednefs*) or what tell you me of Scripture? I have a *Light* within me that made that *Light*, was before it, gave it forth, & is above it. This mans hair was fo offenfive and odious, that meeting of me, and faying, *Fear the Lord God*, I could not but anfwer him in thefe words, *viz. What God doft thou mean a Ruffians God?* alluding to that of *Paul* to *Titus*, *They profefs to know God, but in their Works they deny him.*

[33] I

33 | I told them the rage of the Devill in all Ages had been moſt fierce againſt theſe heavenly *Records,* in which the moſt gracious God and King, out of the infinite depths of his Wiſdome and Goodneſs, had provided for the Ages and Generations to come the glorious *Appearances* of the eternall *Inviſible King* in the former *Generations* of mankind from the Creation of the World, as alſo the *Wonders* yet to be finiſhed till time ſhould be no more, all which were in the holy *Scriptures.*

    I remembred them of a profane bloudy Wretch in *Ireland* who in the late horrid *Maſſacre,* hunting (among other bloudie Wolves) after the Goods and Lives of the *Proteſtants,* found a *Bible,* and with Indignation (the ſame which I believe is in moſt *Papiſts* and *Quakers*) he flung it into the *Kennell,* and *ſtampt* upon it with his feet ſaying, *A Plague of God take this Book, this hath cauſed all the Quarrels among us.* An hori-
ble In-
ſtance in
Ireland
againſt the
Holy Scrip-
tures.

    Whether I ſpake all theſe Particulars at one individuall time or Turn I cannot clearly remember, only I am certain thus I ſpake and more.

    My Oppoſites once and again had Turnes of Speech, but ſtill the only Sum of all was, that they owned the *Scripture,* but yet the *Spirit* that gave it forth was above it, withall they urged that I could not prove where in the Scripture, the *Scripture* was called *the Word of God.*

    I *Anſwered,* That many things were infallibly ſo, and true although not in ſo many Terms and Words mentioned : But yet there were abundance of *Scriptures* wherin the *Prophets* did expreſly ſay, The *Scrip-*
tures the
word of
God.

Thus

Thus saith the Lord, The Word of the Lord came unto me, and Hebr. 1. *The Lord spake diverse wayes, and at diverse times in the Prophets, but now he hath spoken by his Son.* Sure his Speech is his Word: Hence the *Word of God* is the Word preached, as *Paul*, 2 Theff. 1. *Not as the* word *of man, but as it is indeed the* Word *of God, Act.* 19 which preaching of the Word & growing of the word were not competent and proper expreffions to be affirmed of the perfon of the *Lord Jesus*; especially I told them I would use the words of the *Lord Jesus* when he fought with the *Devil* that famous *Combate, Math.* 4. No other Weapon did he use against him but γέγραπτοι *It is written*, and again, *It is written, It is written*, here *Chrift Jesus* quotes *Dut* 8. *Man shall not live by bread only, but by every word that proceedeth out of the mouth of God*: where *Moses* and *Chrift Jesus* affirm [34] that God hath many words, contrary to what some *Quakers* hath affirmed to me saying, *that God hath no more words but one*, and *Chrift Jesus* here affirmeth, That every appearance and providence of God, is a word proceeding out of the mouth of *God*, as well as this holy Scripture he alleadged. Though yet it is true, that *Chrift Jesus* is the *Word*, or declared Mind of *God*, incomparably above all his *spoken* or *written* or *providentiall* Words and Expreffions: He came out of the *Bosome* of the *Eternal Father*, and brought the brighteft Revelations of his eternal *God-head* & *Councels*, and therefore is moft juftly and eminently ftiled the *Word of God*.

I urged that the *Word* or *Words* of God were *Figurative* Speeches, for properly God had no *Mouth*,

nor

nor *Tongue*, nor *Lips*, nor *Heart* nor *Brains* &c. but
as our Kings Majefty his *Declaration* touching *Religion*, his royal *Charters*, his *Letters* from *Breda* are
often infifted on and urged by the *Quakers* as the
word of a King, though his writings contain many
hundred words; fo it is with the *King of Heaven* his
Scriptures and writings &c.

I had oft occafion to mention G. *Fox* and *Ed. Burrowes* their *Book* in Folio called *The great Myftery*
&c. upon which *W Edmundfon* reproved me for
fpeaking of G. *Fox* and *E. Burrowes* in fcorn and
derifion (fo his words were) I gueft he took me as
if I had fcornfully intended *G Fox* in his *Burrowes*, *The Occa-*
but I had openly purged my felf, protefting before *fion of the*
the Lord, that I had no fuch thought, yet this Paf- *Title of*
fage was the occafion of the *Title* of the *Book*: For *this Book.*
the finger of *Gods* moft wife and holy Providence
is often wonderfuliy feen in fmall, unexpected & in-
confiderable Turns and Occafions : In fuch poor
fhells oftimes may be found the *Kernels* of rich
and ufefull *Obfervations*. Sure (thought I) Gods
holy Finger is in it, that G. *Fox* and *Ed. Burrowes*
(Men fo qualified and named) fhould fo notorioufly confpire againft the true *Lord Jefus Chrift* in
their dark and fubtle hellifh Contrivings and *Imaginations*. It was alfo Gods overruling hand that
VV. Edmundfon fhould fo upbraid me, and firft put
the *Conceit* and thought of fuch a Confideration into me, which I apprehended as *Digitus Dei* the
finger of God directing and pointing me to fo proper and pertinent an ufe and Application.

Thus the only Wife and Righteous *King* catcheth
the

the craftieft *Foxes* in their own *Burrowes,* and turns their proud Surmifes & Cenfures upon their own *Pates.* This occafioneth me with Amaze-[35]ment and Aftonifhment to cry out *O God how deep are thy* Being, *thy* Attributes, *thy* Providences, *thy* Self *and all thy wayes beyond our thoughts and finding out* !

To proceed, I had obferved and prepared many *Quotations* out of *G. Fox* his Book, but they defired not to hear them read, as in the following dayes of *Conference* they were read by my continual importunate Urgings : I fay at firft I could not get oportunity to infift upon fome Particulars, a Taft whereof I think now fit to prefent the Reader with.

In *Page* 155. of *G. Foxes* aforefaid Book he brings in one *J Stallam* their Oppofite faying [*To fay the Light in every man gave forth* Scripture, *and will open* Scripture *to us, is palpable* Darknefs, *and contradicts the* Scripture] *G. Fox* anfwers, [*All be in utter* Darknefs *and know not the* Scripture, *untill they come to the* Light *that every man was in that gave forth* Scripture, *for the* Light *lets them fee to what it was fpoken, and* Chrift *the end of them.*

G Fox his prodigious Folly and Impiety. The englifh of that Anfwer is, That every man, that is all *Mankind* Men and Women if they will, can give forth *Scriptures,* or write holy *Scriptures* : I know they call this Light, *God,* and *Chrift,* and *Spirit,* the *Covenant* of *God,* the *Life, Truth* and *Grace* of *God.* I afked them in publick [Since this Light comes into this World in and with all Mankind, whether it comes into them at the *Conception,* or at the *Birth,* or when elfe ?

Pertinent Queryes and unanfwerable. Whether it was in all *Mankind* before the coming and

and death of *Chriſt Jeſus* or whether to thoſe that
are in the world ſince his coming, or both? Whether it be in the *Underſtanding, Will, Memory, Affections* in any of them ſeverally, or lodg'd in all of
them jointly? For it was a prodigious *Fable* to
imagine ſuch a *Sun* to ſhine in every Room of an
houſe, and yet none of the Inhabitants, nor any that
come into the house diſcern and ſee it: *Chriſt Jeſus* ſaith, *as the mouth is, the heart is, and before a
true turning unto God, we are in darkneſs,* we are
darkneſs, we hate the light of *God* and endure not
to ſee it, but wiſh there were no *God,* no *Father of
Lights* to diſcover and plague us for our dark
Courſes: yet our *Hearts* are ſo *cunning* and *cheating*
that they will tell us that we have *Light* and *Chriſt*
and *God* within us, and that we can ſpeak and write
holy Scripture, not remembring that (as *Chriſt Jeſus*
ſaid of the *Temple*) our hearts are *Dens* of Thieves
and (like painted *Tombs*) full of dead mens bones
and rottenneſs, [36] untill a ſecond *Birth* by the
VVord and *Spirit* of *Chriſt Jeſus.*

Again, in the ſame Page G. *Fox* brings his Oppoſite ſaying, [*And to ſay every mans* Light *is the true*
word of Prophecy *is* an old Fable, *no man ſhall be
able to ſpell out a ſyllable of the* Goſpel *by all that is
written in a mans* Heart.] This ſubtle Fox anſwers,
[*The Light that enlightens every man is* Chriſt, *and
the ſure* Word of Prophecy *to him he ſhall find it*]
In this Paſſage who can but ſee their *horrible* and
ſimple profaning and wreſting of plain *Scripture:*
Is it not clear as day to him that is not willingly
blind, that this *word of prophecy* in *Peter,* is the
Word

Word which the *Prophets* ſpake and writ of *Chriſt Jeſus*, unto whome the ſpirit of God in *Peter* ſends us, as being a more ſure and convincing *word* to us then that voice which *Peter* and *Iohn* affirmed that they heard from heaven in the Mount of *Tranſfiguration?* But thus *profanely* and *ſimply* do others of them affirm this *Light* to be that *Prophet* which *Moſes* wrote of, *Deut.* 18. whereas the *holy Spirit* in *Stephen Acts* 7. applyes expreſly that *Propheſie* to the perſon of the *Lord Ieſus*, that *God-man* in one perſon, whome *Moſes* and *Stephen* preached the great *Meſſiah*, or *Chriſt* the anointed *Prophet*, *Prieſt* and *King* unto all that receive or believe in him.

The tu-multuous ſpirit of the Quakers in Diſputing. Now diverſe obſerving and publickly expreſſing how unſuitable it was that three of the ableſt *Speakers* amongſt them ſhould *Conſult* openly and *whiſper* and utter themſelves one immediately after each other, and ſomtimes *all together* as one man againſt me : *W. Edmondſon* anſwered and excuſed it ſaying, that it was mine own *Paper* (which he often produced) which expreſt my Offer to make good my *Poſitions* againſt all *Comers*: But I replyed (once and again) That as God is a God of *Order*, and doth all things in *Number*, *Weight* and *Meaſure*, in moſt admirable *Order* and *Method*, ſo I had thought that (according as I writ and ſpake to them) they would have had ſo much *Ingenuity* to conceive, that nor I nor any man was ſo ſimple as to offer to Diſpute with, to oppoſe and to anſwer twenty or thirty or one hundred at once : But thus

Tis hard to hold the like ſubtle and impudent *Foxes* and *Ieſuites* they pleaded and practiſed from the beginning of the

Conference

Conference unto the end of the 4*th* day, refolving to make ufe of and (like dying men by drowning) to catch at any ridiculous *Advantage* though *unchrif-tian* and *uncivill.* Foxians *or any guil-ty difputant to a fair Difpute.*

But the truth is, this and many other *Difcourage-ments* and *Difadvantages* and *Difficultyes* the *Lord Iefus* gracioufly and faithfully [37] (For his name fake) enabled me to cut through, otherwife I faw the *Debate* would not have held on fo many *Hours* as it did *Dayes,* I knew they had as much mind to this work (no nor any guilty *Soul* in the world) as *Bears* to be tyed to a ftake to be baited; and I muft humbly declare and predicate it (to the praife of the *Father of mercyes,* and for the incouragement of others to be *Patient* for *Chrift Iefus* fake) that an hand from heaven caried me through to the end of each day, and to the end of the whole bufinefs.

Sometimes I offered to proceed to an other *Point,* but all this firft day was fpent upon the firft *Point* of *true* and *falfe Quakers:* For though many upon a fudden fpake as *Mr. Coddington Mr. Eafton* (then Governour, who fpake fharply) *VVilliam Dyer, VVilliam Harris* and others againft me, yet I minded clofely what my *Antagonifts* vented, who were placed on high in their *Defk* againft me : *Iohn Stubs* and *Iohn Burnet* were more fober and manly, but *VV. Edmundfon* (who was the junior of three) would fpeak all like *Solomons* foolifh woman, *loud* and *clamorous, fimple* and *knowing nothing,* being in truth nothing but a *flafh* of wit, a *Face of Brafs,* and a *Tongue* fet on *fire* from the *Hell of Lyes and Fury.*

One

One *Inftance* here fell out, for when I urged that
it was not what man had *within him* already, and
brought into the world with him, that made a true
Quaker, but the *Spirit of God* accompanying and
bleffing the *Reading* and *Hearing* of the *writings*
of *God preached* and *opened*: I faid the *Heart* of man
was fhut up lockt and barr'd up in *willing Ignorance*
and *darknefs* until the *finger of God* in the ufe of
thofe and other bleffed meanes, *pick* open in a more
gentle way, or *break* open by great afflictions and
and *terrours* the *Soul* and *Spirit* of man. I faid
that *Paul* preached the *word* by the River fide, but
the Lord opened the heart of *Lydia*: and while I
was faying that, *It was not Paul nor Pauls Preaching nor the word that he preached*----- at this word
VV. Edmondfon clamour'd out, *He fpeakes Blafphemy*: But it pleafed God to move the heart of our
Deputy-Governour Capt. *Cranfton* juftly and feafonably to witnefs againft this *Interruption* faying, *Let
him have liberty to make out his mind:* So I proceeded
and faid, it may be *VV. Edmnndfon* is offended as
thinking I fpoke againft the *word Chrift*; but *Chrift
Iefus* knowes that I had no fuch thought, but of the
words which *Paul* fpake. And I added that it was
not *Lydia* nor all her *Light* within her, nor *Paul*
nor [38] his *Preaching*, nor the *word* nor *words*
that he uttered, but the Finger of *Gods Spirit* (according to *Election*) that fet the *word* or *words* of
Paul home, opening her *heart*, and not every heart,
(fhewingwhat free grace is againft the *Popifh* and
Arminian and *Foxians* exalting of *Curfed Nature*)
and then it was that fhe being by the Lord turned,
fhe

*W. Ed-
mondfoo
juftly re-
proved by
the Depu-
ty Gover-
nor Capt.
Cranfton*

fhe turned to attend & apply to her foul the words which were fpoken by *Paul*, as a poor *Rams-horn* made ufe of in the hand of *God*.

Toward the end of the day *VV. Edmondfon* fell into a long *Invective*, how I had falfly flandered the *People of God*, not only in this place, but the whole Body of the People of the *Lord* called *Qua-kers* in all parts: For faid he we are a great people, many thoufands in *England*, many thoufands in *London*, befides in *Virginia* and *Barbadoes* and other places, and *N-England*. And he and they faid, haft thou any more to fay to make out thy *Lyes* againft them. *The Fo.:-ians boaft of their Number.*

I Anfwered (as at other times) that the *Papifts* the common *Proteftants*, the *Jews* and the *Mahumi-tans* and *Pagans*, *&c.* fited the world with their *Numbers*, and yet we jointly oppofed them in *Relig-ious matters* notwithftanding their *innumerable num-bers*: And as for more proof that they were not *True Quakers*, and fo truly *Feariug and Trembling* before *God*, I told them I would produce an Argument, that they were fo far from being *Chrift-ians*, that they were a to be *exploded* and *abhorred* of all *Mankind*, as being fallen beneath the common *temper* and *nature* of the *Humanity* of men and women, yea of the Savage and *Barbarous* in the world, *viz.* their ftripping *ftark naked* their *Men* and *Women* and *Maidens* and pafling along in publick places and *Streets* unto the *Affemblyes of Men* and *Youths* and fo were beheld and gazed upon by them! and this under a pretence of being ftirred up by God as a *Service* or *Worfhip* unto God,

God, as an act of *Christian Religion* proceeding from the immediate moving of the moſt holy *Spirit of God*, moſt glorious in purity, and purity and holineſs it ſelf.

Two of the Foxian women naked in New England. At firſt *W. Edmundſon* ſeemed to make ſtrange of the matter as if it could not be proved that any of their women ſhould ſo appear in the *Aſſemblyes* of People. I told them the matter of *fact* was ſo *notorious* that it would be loſs of time and *Impudence* to queſtion it, being ſo fouly and openly *practiſed* both in *Old* and *New England*.

39] Alſo I added further, that *G. Biſhop* of *Briſtow*, one of themſelves, in the ſecond part of the *Perſecutions of New-England*, relates in print the names of two women in *N-England* that did ſo practice: and he complains of *N-England Perſecution* becauſe thoſe women ſuffered *Whipping for* thoſe actions by the *Courts* and *Officers* of *N-England*.

John Burnet ſaid that the People called *Quakers*, were a People known to abhor all *Impurity* and Uncleanneſs and the *Appearance* of it, and if any of their women ſhould ſo practice, they ſhould condemn it in them, yet nevertheleſs if it ſhould pleaſe the *Lord God* to ſtir up any of his *Daughters* ſo to appear as a *Sign* and *Teſtimony* againſt the *Nakedneſs* of others, they durſt not condemn it.

John Stubs ſaid, that they did condemn all immodeſt *Appearances* in women, both in *Behaviour* and *Geſtures*. But if God ſtirred them up and commanded them to this ſervice to diſcover the *Nakedneſs* of others, they could not but acknowledge
Gods

Gods hand, and fubmit to it: And he further added, that it was a great *Crofs* to a fober womans fpirit fo to act, as well as an affliction and fuffering to her body.

John Stubs likewife alleadged the *Prophet Ifaiah*, (as alfo did *W.E.*) and the *Sign* of the Prophet *Eze-kiel*: and *John Stubs* read the 20*th* of *Ifa.* where *Ifaiah* was commanded to goe *naked* for a *Sign* to the *Egyptians* and *Ethyopians*, to prophefie and de-nounce that they alfo fhould go naked with their buttocks uncovered as the words are: and this is (faid they) a proof that the People of the Lord might be ftirred up by *God* to fuch actions for *Signs* unto others.

Ifai. 20 *dif-cuffed touching* Nakednefs

I Anfwered, that this was in the dayes of *Fig-ures* and *Signs*, Shadows and *Ceremonyes*: And though this was *G.Fox* his Anfwer(in his Book which I had there by me) yet *G.Fox* throughout all this his Book in *Folio*, turns of the Allegations and Arguments of many of his *Oppofites* with this Anfwer, *to wit*, *The* Subftance *is come, the* Body *is come*, Chrift *the* End *of the* Law, *the* End *of the* Command, *the* End *of the* Scriptures, *the* End *of the* Prophets, *and of all* Signs *and* Shadows *and* Figures.

2. Although it were fo threatned that the *Ethi-opians* and *Egyptians* fhould fo goe *totally* and *ftark Naked*, and that *Ifaiah* did fo, which is much quef-tioned: yet it is not to be queftioned but that the *Egyptians* and *Ethiopians* in their flight, would cover [40] their *Secret parts* with the firft cloaths or raggs they could get, as it is no queftion but the Prophet *Ifaiah* did.

3. The

3. The difference of *Nakednefs* of *Mankind* and *Womankind* is very great in all *Nations*. The *Sex* of *Women* is more fitted and framed by God for a *Covering*, for *Retirednefs* and keeping at home and for *Modefty* and *Bafhfulnefs*; nor do we ever read that ever God commanded fuch a thing to Women, or that ever it came into his heart, or that ever any *Godly Woman* did fo practice: there is no fhadow or colour of *Proof* from the holy *Scripture*, nor from any *Civill* and fober People, no nor from the naked *Barbarians* themselves, who though they fuffer their *Male Children* to go naked till about feven years old, yet cover they their *Females* from their birth : Tis true it is faid in *Brafil* and other bruitifh places fome *Savage bruits* go fo, but they are *Canibals, Men-eaters, &c*· and other B*arbarians* do not fo except in *Drunkennefs* and *Madnefs*.

They ftill anfwered, that they would not *Countenance* any fuch *Practice* but if the *Lord God* fo commanded his *Sons* and *Daughters* it muft be obeyed.

I demanded of them how it fhould be known that it was the voice and command of *God*, the *God* of *Holinefs*, and not the command of the unclean *fpirit*? for I told them that under that Cover that one of them might be fo commanded, and fent of God in fuch a pofture and behaviour amongft men, why might not ten or twenty, yea all the women in this prefent *Affembly* be fo ftirred up as it were by the *Spirit* of *God* to the horror and amazement of the whole *Countrey* yea of the whole *World?*

They feemed to me to be *Confounded* with this

The true voice of God, and many falfe and pretended.

Argumnet

Argumnet and weary to hear of it, and not willing to *Immeaiate*
speak to it : I therefore took occasion my self to say *Inspira-*
tions and
that it was true in former Dispensations. The Com- *Revela-*
mand of God came to *Abraham* to kill his own *tions.*
Child, his son *Isaac*, and this fact enjoined him did
seem as horrible *unnatural* and *cruel*, as this *Naked-*
uess of the Women unwomanly and *unnatural*. But,

1. It was in the day and dispensation of such
wonderfull *Signs* and figurative teachings unto men.

And 2. I said *God* did furnish them with a Spirit of discerning the *true* dream from the false, the
true voice from the false, the voice of *God* from the
voice of *Sathan* : But in our day wherein God had
altered his Dispensations and Revelations which
he [41] used to the *Fathers*, and had spoken to us
by his *Son*, and had left his mind both in the *old*
and *new Scriptures* or Writings : We have the example and President of the *Lord Jesus*, that is, to
attend to the holy *Scriptures* only, and to use the
weapon of | *It is written it is written*] against *Sa-*
thans immediate *Inspirations* and temptations.

Here *W. Edmondson* fel into a great heat against
me and said that I spoke *Blasphemy*, in saying that
Abraham and the *Saints* then had a way and Spirit
of discerning the Spirits which we had not, implying that Gods Spirit was not the same : He added,
that I had kept them long and had proved nothing,
and yet we had not done with the first *Position*. I
replyed, that I had produced such *Grounds* as should
never be shaken, and that I presumed did appear to
the *Consciences* of many, and I heartily desired might
also appear unto their Spirits, Soules, and *Consci-*
ences.

ences. Some of the Auditors fpake to this Purpofe, efpecially *W. Hitchcocks* who infifted upon the *Water Baptifme.*

And thus by Gods *Mercy* and Patience the Difcourfe of the firft day ended: which very day was *The Eclipfe of the Sun in the midft of the firft dayes Difputation.* notable and *fignificant* as to the created *Sun* in the Heavens, who in the midft of our Conteft was eclipfed, and hid his Face remarkably, and preached aloud to us, that although the true *Lord Jefus Chrift* the *Sun* of Righteoufnefs do fuffer (in his infinite wifdom and and Patience) falfe *Chrifts* and falfe *Prophets* and *Herod* and *Pontius Pilate,* and his enemies of all forts, *Jewes* and *Gentiles,* to cloud his *Face* and *Glory* a little from the World and his own People, yet he will break forth again in his eternal brightnefs, fplendor and glory.

When that heavenly young *Martyr* or Witnefs of *Jefus Chrift William Hunter* was burnt at *Burntwood* in *Effex* it was a clofe and gloomy day, but *A Note of W. Hunter burnt in* Effex *at* Burnt wood. this gallant young Champion of *Jefus Chrift* crying out aloud at the ftake, *Son of God look on me, Son of God fhine upon me!* immediately that moft wonderfull *Light & Fire* of Heaven the *Sun* tore the clouds and brake forth and fhined glorioufly aud remarkably upon the face of this bleffed *Witnefs* at the fuffering of the flames of fire, for *Jefus* his truth fake againft the *whorifh Principles* of both the *Papifts & Quakers:* and thus do the holy writings tel us, that this moft glorious light *the Sun of Righteoufnefs,* vifibly appeared in his glorious and glorified Form and Shape to the vifible eye of his fervant *Steven* while he patiently fuffered for the

true

true *Lord Jesus* sake the murthering Stones to lay him down to sleep.

42] **T**HE second day of our Spiritual *Contest & Battle* being come, (being the tenth of the sixth Moneth August (so called) I heartily wished that I might rather have kept my *Bed* then have gone forth to a whole dayes fresh *Dispute* with such (reputed) able and noted *Champions*. Not that the most high Lord *Jesus* whose cause and *Name* I was that day to manage, for the next point was about the true *Lord Jesus Christ*) not that I say he faild me in my *Resolution* to march on against *Men* and *Devils* for his Name sake; nor that he faild me in my cheerfull *Confidence* that he would carry me in the everlasting armes of his *Power* and *Goodness* through that dayes Conflict (as he had done the day before) but that he was pleased to try me with more than ordinary *Weakness* and mouldring of my *house of Clay*, that so my strength might be in a great respect immediately from Heaven, considering my great unfitnesf for this dayes Service : for thus it was, My continued *loud Speech* all the day before had left an impression of *Hoarsnesf* upon me, and much *rain* falling that afternoon (after the *Eclipse*) I took some wet in my feet that evening, so that my *Hoarsenesf* increased, and all that day my *Head* was afflicted with pain, and my voice with a painfull *Hoarsnefs*. I lookt up to heaven, and desired to wait as a *Begger* at the *Gate*, and as a *Dog* under the table of *Mercy*, and my Spirit was chearfully resolved not to give occasion of *Reproaching*

My great Indisposedness of body to the second dayes Contest.

Prayer and Patience.

the

the name of God to them who (I knew) waited and watched for it, nor any *Difappointment* to fuch as were refolved to attend the Meeting.

This day I chofe a middle Seat neerer to the Seat of my three *Antagonifts J. Stubs, J. Burnet. W. Edmondfon* that fo I might be heard the better with lefs *ftraining* of my *Voice* and *Breaft*.

I began and ftood up and faid, the holy Scriptures by the Prophet *Jeremiah* told us of certain *Bow-men*, fome that bent their *Tongues* as *Bowes* for *Lyes* and complain'd that none were *Valiant* for the *Truth* : I told my oppofites that they and I were met as *Bow men*, and I could heartily defire that all our *Arrowes* might fly one way, to wit in the defence of the true *Lord Jefus Chrift* againft the falfe : But fince I had charged them in my fecond *Pofition* to have fet up a *falfe Chrift* in ftead of the true *Lord Jefus* I fhould addrefs my felf to make probation of my fecond *Pofition*. Yet before I enter upon it, I pray the *Readers Patience* to be acquainted with fome *Particulars*.

Spiritual Bowmen & Gunners

43] *Firft*. Though my head was ill, and my *voice & fpeech* hoarfe and painfull, yet the Lord gracioufly carried me through the the whole day with little hindrance in my felf, and little difadvantage to the underftanding of the *Auditors*.

The fecond days Conteft.

Secondly. This dayes Difcourfe was but accidental and additional; for they and I defired to have finifhed the the whole firft feven *Pofitions* in one day at *Newport*, only in my paper I added, that if the whole feven were not finifhed in one day, the *Conference* might continue fome few hours the next

day

day following: on this second day therefore was a great Assembly, the *Governour, Magistrates, Inhabitants and strangers,* Men and Women, *&c.* And this dayes Contest also held unto the Evening.

Thirdly. As I had beg'd of God a Spirit of *Patience* to bear all their *Censures, Reproachings, Revilings, Vapourings and Insultings,* so it pleased God to exercise me with one notorious though private,[1] *That I was Drunk, and could not speak that day as I* had done the day before: But my Daughter *Hart,* at whose house I lodged, and *John Trip* sen. who lodged with me can testifie that I complained of *Illness,* and eat but a few spoonfulls of milk with Mr. *Trip* at Breakfast: and though my daughter kindly offered me a *Dram* for my *Illness,* but I refused it knowing it might curdle the milk I had taken, and so increase my cold and *Obstruction:* & this the most holy God knowes, and these Witnesses know was all I took that morning which might conduce to that foul *Slander ,* of being so *Drunk* that I could not speak plainly that day.

A black and sence- less Impu- tation.

Fourthly. This day also I encountred with that *Disadvantage* of all the three aforesaid *Disputants* at once with all their might fighting for their *Idolls* and *Images* against me: I spake of it, and so did others again and again; But *W. Edmundson* still bruit- ishly

The con- fused spirit of the Qua- kers.

In the copy of this book belonging to the Library of Brown University, are many manuscript erasures, corrections and annotations, in the well-known handwriting of Roger Williams. They were *possibly* made with the intention of correcting a second edition of the book, if such had proved desirable. These alterations will all be noted in this reprint and will be designated as Roger Williams' Manuscript Annotations.

[1] though private "Vizt." *R. W. Ms. Ann.*

iſhly pleaded that it was mine own *Offer* to undertake all *Comers*: I anſwered as before, that I took
them to be *rational Men*, and by all *Comers* not to underſtand *ten* or *twenty* or *an hundred* confuſedly at
once, but in a fair and equal way, one after an other:
it was grievous & often expreſt by ſome of the
Audience: But as before on the firſt day I reſolved
not to loſe time, or ſuffer a *Breach*: and the Lord
was pleaſed to make my *Yoke eaſie* and *Burthen light.*

The ſecond Poſition. Now to the proof of my ſecond *Poſition* which was,
That their Chriſt was not the true Lord Jeſus Chriſt.

44] Here I prayed their patience to ſuffer me to
Concerning true & falſe Chriſts tell them that they were not *Chriſtians*, nor Profeſſors of *Chriſtian Religion:* They might (with *Jewes
& Turks & Papiſts*) profeſs one God, yet *Chriſtians*
they could not be: but as the true Lord Jeſus told
us, many *falſe Chriſt* aud *falſe Prophets* ſhould come,
Traitors & Rebells againſt the King eter-nai & Murther-ers of him. who like *Mountebanks* inſtead of *true Phyſitians*, and
falſe and counterfeit *Money* inſtead of true, ſhould
with *Satans power* and *policy* paſs up and down and
deceive *Peoples* and *Nations*, ſo I muſt affirm and
declare that for their parts they had cut of the head
of the *Chriſtian Religion*, the true *Lord Jeſus
Chriſt*, and they had ſet up a falſe *Chriſt*, a falſe
King, an *Uſurper* in his ſtead, they had like *Michal*
put a wooden *Image* upon a pillow of goats hair in
Davids bed, but *David* himſelf was gone, the true
David, the true Lord Jeſus Chriſt was not to be
found amongſt them: this I ſpake expreſly and
they did hear me awhile.

My proof was, *Firſt*. Becauſe the *Deſcription* and
Character which the holy Scripture gives to the
true

true *Lord Jesus*, no way agrees with the *Image* which they have set up. I told them that it was known that the word *Christ* was a greek word sig- *The true* nifiing *anointed*, as the word *Messiah* in the Hebrew *Christ* *Lord Jesus* did. I said this true *Lord Jesus* was one Person made up of two *Natures*, *God* and *Man* united into one person, I said one Individual person, whatever *S Fisher* blasphemously utters against it. That as to his *humane Nature* or being *Man*, all the *Figures* and *Ceremonyes*, al the *Priests* and *Sacrifices* pointed to him as the great *Prophet*, the great anointed King and Governour &c. *His hu-*

2. As to his humane *Nature* and being a man *mane na-* and *One Man Moses* and the Prophets wrote of him : *ture woich* *G. Fox all* of his *Mother a Virgin*, of the place of his birth *night long* *Bethlehem*, of his bringing up at *Nazareth :* of his *so barks* *against.* Scourging and other sufferings, drinking *Vinegar* and *Gall*, the piercing of his hands and feet, the numb- ring of him with *Malefactors*, the parting of his *Garments* and casting *Lots*, his *burying, rising* and *Ascending* &c. and I said all those *Prophesies* and many more were exactly, literally, and punctually fulfilled in and upon that *Individual Person :* so that I affirm, there is such an exact *material and literal Harmony* between the *Prophesies* and the historical *Narration* of his *Birth, Life, Death, Resurrection,* &c. that he must needs be an Unbeliever, (*Jew* or *Gentile*) that doth not acknowledge the admirable Consent and Musick of [45] them in a *literal* and *historical Declaration*.

On the other hand I affimed their *Christ* was but *The Qua-* half a *Christ*, a *Light*, an *Image* or *Picture* or *Fancy* *kers Christ* of *allegorical and meerly Fancy, destroying the History.* of a *Chrift* made up of the *Godhead* and their *flefh*, I faid they had fet up a Chrift within them which was but an *Imagination*, an Image, a Chrift in the myftical *Notion:* but in reality *Nothing*: For as the *Papifts* make ufe of the name *Chrift*, and the *Pope* faith he is *Chrifts Vicar* and *Lieftenant*, and he doth all for *Chrift*, and the *Iefuites* (foaring above all *Chriftians*) pretend the name *Iefus*, and yet the *Proteftant Witneffes* have made it to appear that in many refpects the *Papifts* are infinitely againft both *Chrift* and *Iefus*, and fo are not *Chriftians* but *Antichriftians*: fo I told them did they, they blew a *Trumpet* for *Chrift Iefus*, God in Man, the everlafting Father, that we are *bone* of his bone and *flefh* of his flefh, that he was fo born at *Bethlehem* and dyed at *Ierufalem &c*, And yet all thefe fair *Flourifhes* and Colours are but as an *Englifh Flag* in a *Spanifh* or *Dutch* or any other Enemies Bottome: For do not all their Books declare that *Chrift is Spiritual*, that *Chrift, God and Man is within us, that his Birth, his Life, his Death, his Burial, his Refurrection, his Afcenfion are wrought within us,* fo that like the *Oracles* of *Apollo*, and the *Ecchoes* of the *Iefuites* the *Quakers* fay *Chrift was born at Bethlehem* and dyed at *Ierufalem*, but intend in truth and reallity no other *birth* nor *life* nor *death &c.* but what may be extant and wrought in the heart of man.

Humphrey Norton deales plainly againft the Perfon of Chrift To this purpofe I told them that *Humphrey Norton* (one that blew the *Trumpet* and beat up the *Drums* in the Name of *Chrift Iefus* as loud as any of them) exprefly writes openly in his Book printed at *London* after his return from hence, to wit, *Is not Chrift*

Chriſt God and is not God a Spirit ? you look for a Chriſt without you, from what coaſt or Countrey ſhall he come ? what Country-man is he ? You ſtand gazing up in the clouds after a man, but we ſtand by in white chiding of you. So that if you fix now really and truly upon a *Man* the *Manhood* and *Humanity* of Chriſt, and that he did confiſt and ſtill doth of body and ſoul (as we doe) then you are gone from, (and *Chriſtopher Houlder* in his late Anſwer to *Nathaniell Morton*) are gone from your former *Religion, Tenents* and *Principles,* or elſe you are miſerably bewilder'd in your Souls and Conſciences, and ſome of you moſt fearfully *equivocate,* and others muſt be fearfully up to the ears in *Boggs & Swamps* not knowing what to hold between this Chriſt without, and the [46] Chriſt within which you ſo much charge upon all except they be *Reprobates.*

The Equivoca-tion of the Foxians.

I told them I acknowledged *Chriſt* within as much as any of them, & infinitely more, for I did confeſs that every believing ſoul did bring home and apply the power and virtue of *Chriſts Birth,* and *Life* and *Death &c.* according to that clear Scripture *Eph.* 3. 10. *That Chriſt may dwell in your Hearts by Faith.* I ſaid there was a nearer union between Chriſt Jeſus and a Soul believing on him, then between a *Man* and his *Wife,* and between the *Soul* and the *Body.* That *Union* is *Earthly* and diſſolving : but that between *Chriſt Jeſus* and the *Believer,* it is *eternal* in Gods Decrees and Councells, it is temporary in *Gods* calling of his choſen out of the *World,* to *Repentance & belief* in the Mediator

Eph 3. 10. The true Union that is between Chriſt Jeſus & Believers.

Chriſt

Chrift Jefus, and it perpetuated and continues to *Eternity*.

I told them that (as the holy Scripture faith) they preached not *Chrift Jefus* but *Themfelves*, yea they preached the *Lord Jefus* to be *Themfelves*: that whatever were their Pretencfe (as the *Papifts*) of *God & Chrift & Holinefs & Mortification*, yet *The Qua-* they held not the *Head* (as the Scripture fpeaks) and *kers paint-* if their head be but a painted and an *Imaginary* *ed Chrift.* *Head*, they are but a painted and Imaginary *Body*. Their *Sun* of Righteoufnefs they talk of is but a *Sun* painted upon a *Sign* or *Wall* which is not the true Sun, but the picture of the *Sun* of Righteouf-nefs.

I told them they fet up this *Chrift* within, oppo-fite to *Chrift* without, as *Oppofites & Contraryes*, *Denying & Deftroying* one an other : for as it is with *Chrift* a *King* and his *Palace*, if his *perfon* be without, his *winhin and* *perfon* at that time is not within, though he be *Chrift* *without.* within by his *Right, Authority* and *Influence* : if his Perfon be within the Palace at that time it is not without. But the moft clear Truth is though thefe fubtle *Foxians* fometimes fpeak of a Chrift without that dyed at *Ierufalem* agreeing with the Chrift within, yet they prefently declare their mean-ing to be *Myftical* : For afk them but thefe two *Queftions*, and if they make any *Anfwer* you will fee *Two Quef-* the *Cheat*, the *Equivocotion* and the *Miftery of Ini-* *tions to* *quity* in it. *Quakers.* 1. Do they not hold the *Light* within every man to be *All*, to *doe All* and to *fuffer All* within which the Chrift without, *Is* or *Did* or *fuffered* without. 2. Afk

2. Ask them now what is become of this *Man*, this perſon that thus ſuffered at *Ieruſalem*, and they are forced to confeſs he ⌊47⌋ is within, and can give no other account of him, as they anſwered to me at *Newport* the laſt day of the Conference.

But to return, I told them what I ſaid I would prove out of their *Writings*, and eſpecially out of *G. Fox* atteſted by *Ed Burrowes* his large *Epiſtle*, and as it was thought by *John Stubs* preſent.

John Burnet declared not, (nor any of them) againſt what I ſpake: but ſaid (as ſaid the reſt) if *G. Fox* have ſpoken or written any thing that is not right and *truth*, we profeſs not to follow him : and they were willing I ſhould produce out of *G. Fox* his Book what I could that might make for my proof, *viz.* That they did not profeſs the *true Chriſt.*

I ſaid *G: Fox* had pickt out ſome particular Lines, Sayings & Sentences out of the Books and Writings of his *Oppoſites*, (it is not to be queſtioned but to his utmoſt *Advantage*, as knowing beſt how to *Anſwer* what he choſe and *cull'd* out) and ſince they were free and willing, I would produce ſome Inſtances: I took up the Book and read in the 3d. *page*, where he brings in his *Oppoſite Samuel Eaton* ſaying [The Sainſts have not Chriſt in the *Fleſh*] G. F. his Anſwer is [*Contrary to* Chriſt and the Apoſtles "*Doctrine, who ſaid they were of his* Fleſh, *and of his* "Bone, *and ſhould eat his* Fleſh, *and they that eat his* "Fleſh *have it in them.*] Whence I affirmed that Chriſt Jeſus had ſuch a Body as might be really and materially in the Saints, and ii was clear that they

G F x his Book in Folio produced. Page 3.

were

were one with the *Papifts* in their Sayings and *Doctrines* denying the Flefh, Body and Perfon of Chrift Jefus: For as the *Papifts* in ftead of a *Spiritual* feeding upon his *bloud* and Merits, they fubftitute and bring in a *Real*, *Material* and Carnal, in their horrible and fantaftical *Tranfubftantiation*; fo do the *Quakers* profeffing to eat Chrift *fpiritually*, wholy deftroy his *material* and flefhly being.

The Papifts & Quakers deftroy the Perfon of Chrift.

I proceeded faying, in the 4*th Page G. Fox* brings in the fame oppofite faying, *The Saints do not fee* Chrift, the Heavens contain him. And *G F.* Anfwers "*And the* Apoftle *faith they fate with* Chrift " *in* heavenly places: *fo he is contrary to the* Apoftle, " *and* Chrift *was in them and walked in them, and* God " *dwelt in them and* Chrift *in you except you be* Repro- " bates. I faid that as the *Papifts* were up *ridiculoufly & odioufly* with *Hoc eft Corpus meum, This is my Body* &c. fo they with *The Light within you, the Light that enlightens every man,* Chrift *within you except you be* Reprobates *&c.*

The being of Chrift in the Heavens

48] For if the Heavens do contain that Man Chrift Jefus bodily, (as they grant in word) faying They believed he *dyed, rofe,* and *afcended*: then in that fame fence and refpect the Saints cannot now fit bodily with Chrift in heavenly places, and therefore to alledge *Chrift* within, and their fitting with Chrift in heavenly places, was but irrational *Nonfence* and Jefuitical *Equivocation*:

The truth is they were gravel'd with thefe Confiderations, and they were willing that *G Fox* his book and his Anfwers fhould anfwer for them, and although the oppofitions of *G. Fox* his Oppofites were

The Quakers endure not trying

were mighty, and *G Foxes* were meer fimple *bark-* *but are willingly ignorant.* ings of dogs or foxes compar'd with the rational and prudential Anfwers of a man, yet when I be— gan to open and compare the *Affertions* of the Oppofite and *Fox* his anfwer, they would cry out (efpecially *W E.* like a *galled horfe* winching) *Why doft thou make thy* Obfervations *upon* G. Fox *his words ?* G.Fox *his words need not thy* Expofitions, *let* G. Fox *his words alone they are able to fpeak for them- felves.*

I told them it was a fencelefs bufinefs for me to alleadge, (and they to be willing I fhould) *G.Fox* his fayings and his *Anfwers,*and we fhould not de- bate and difcufs the *Sence,* and I make out my Proof out of *G. Fox* his words, and his *Adverfaryes* com- par'd together : when they had fpoken they knew their liberty to take of my *Anfwers* with their own, and leave what was fpoke to every ones Confcience in the fight of God.

They were *Obftinately* (that is in *Greek Hereti-* *Willing Ignorance.* cally*)* refolved to avoid this Courfe, therefore I was glad to *hale* my *Tacks* & *Bolings* clofe home, and make my beft of a *bare Wind* and now and then *loof* up into the wind, and get liberty to fay fome— thing and omit abundance of my Thoughts.

Once I was forced to fay to *W. Edmondfon* : Friend yefterday you quoted the 9 of *Nehem.* how it pleafed God to fend them his good *Spirit* to guide them : I pray remember now a word in the 8 of *Nehem.* *Nehem 8 they gave the Sence* They read and gave the *Sence* and caufed the People to underftand the *Reading.* Without this fearching for the *Sence* and meaning, the Pith and Marrow of

the

the holy *Scriptures*, or any other Scriptures or Writings we make use of, what are our Readings but the *Papifts Latine*, the *reading Minifters*, the pratling of *Children* and *Parrets*? yet notwithftanding all that I could fay and urge, it is known to all the *Audience* the Song was, *let G. Fox words alone to fpeak for themfelves, if thou haft any* [49] more to bring forth let us have them : fo that as before I was forced to wave my *Obfervations* and *Intentions*, and pafs on to new *Allegations* : Though now I fhall crave liberty to touch and point at (as with the finger) the *Oppofites Affertions* of *Truth* and *G. Fox* his unfavoury and rotten Anfwers

The Quakers non-fenfical Spirit.

In Page 8. He brings in *John Bunyan &c.* faying [*The Lord Jefus Chrift is afar in his bodily prefence*] and *G.Fox* anfwers, [*And yet he faith the Lord is at hand, and the Apoftle faid he was in them and Chrift faid he would dwell with them*] I here obferve and reply, the holy *Scripture* abundantly tells us of a twofold prefence of *Chrift*, 1. His bodily vifible *Prefence*, which *John Bunyan* fpeaks of and the *Quakers* in words grant. The 2. His *Spirituall*, invifible Prefence, of which many *Scriptures* fpeak and that moft clearly. *Eph.* 3. 10. *That Chrift may dwell in your hearts by believing &c.* Concerning this vifible bodily prefence, of which the Queftion is. *Firft.* *G.Fox* his impertinent and filly Anfwer is not to the *Point* no more then the *Eaft* and the *Weft* is to one point of the Compafs. 2. He fallacioufly, (moft *unchriftianly* and *impioufly*) denyes the body of *Chrift Jefus* to be any where, and as *Conjurers* do (*Hocas Pocas*) that which all now fee is

John Bunyan Chrifts twofold Prefence.

The Quakers Conjure with Chrifts Body.

is gone & vanifhed, fo that with the ancient enemies of *Chrifts Humane Nature,* the *Manicheans,* they *fay* and *unfay* and at laft affirm a *Chrift* only *God* and *Spirit* dwelling in them, and in all mankind alfo.

About this time thefe fubtle *Foxes* minded to fpin out Time, and wave the *clofe Fight* of examining Particulars concerning *Chrifts* humanity. G. *Fox* his Book was brought forth (the fame with mine (*John Burinat* took it and went along with me in the *Quotations,* I read and alwayes endeavoured to make my proof out of the *Allegation:* But *W*. *Edmundfon* kept ftrict watch and ftood Centinel, that no Obfervations of *Sences* or *Meanings* fhould pafs, refolving to keep out the Fire and Light of Chrift Jefus with *Stand,* or Ile let fly a *Fire* (from Hell) upon you. Well, I knew what froward Children and bruitifh Spirits I dealt with, & refolved to go *foftly* and to fpeak *foftly,* and as I could gain ground by *inches* (at leaft) for liberty to give my witnefs for the *Lord Jefus.* *The Qua-kers endure not Sences or Mean-ings juft as the Papifts and yet talk all of light*

In *Page* 9. He brings in *John Bunyan &c.* affirming that the Son of *Mary,* God-Man is abfent from his Church, G. *Fox* anfwers, but never touching Scripture about it. [*contrary to* [50] *Chrifts words, I in them and they in me: and I will be with you to the ends: and Chrift the Head of the Church. & where two or three are gathered &c. and the Saints are bone of his bone and* flefh *of his flefh. The old queftion of Chrifts Prefence.*

I Reply, here half an eye may fee as before, how he gives no other *Prefence* or *Abfence* of a Chrift but invifible and Spiritual, and fubtilly affirms that *Chrift Iefus* hath no bodily Prefence at all, in the

fence

fence which all Chriftians of what fort or Sect
foever (but thefe *Juglers* (and themfelves alfo in
word and horrible hypocrifie) do acknowledg and
profess,

*Fox &
Bonnet no
difference.*

In *Page* 10 He brings in the fame Author faying
[*Chrift. was not in his Difciples when he faid I am the
Light of the world*] G Fox anfwers. [*And fo cor-
rected by Chrift, I in you and you in me.*

Pag. 12. He brings in the fame Author, faying
[*The Body of Chrift is out of the fight of all his
Saints,*] G. *Fox* Anfwers, (they fat with Chrift in
Heavenly places, the Saints are *Flefh* of his *Flefh,*
and *Bone* of his *Bone,* were the Church which he
is head of his Body:) In which I Anfwer, and all

*The Qua-
kers pre-
tend to
owne
Chrifts
Bloud &
yet in truth
allow him
no Bloud
to fhed.*

his Book over (though he own a Chrift without,
and that died at *Jerufalem* in word yet he allows in
effect no other Body to *Chrift Jefus* but what is
Miftical and Spiritual: fo that with notorious *Jugling,* and *Jefuitical Impudence,* they would make
their fimple Followers believe that they own fuch
a *Chrift* as fhed his *Blood* at *Jerufalem,* and yet leave
him in his Body no more Blood to fhed then is in
a Spirit which hath no *Bones, Flefh* nor *Blood* to
fhed at all.

*Enoch
Howet.*

Pag. 17. He brings in *Enoch Howet* Affirming
[*That it is Blafphemy to fay that Chrift is in Man as
God Man,*] G. Fox Anfwers (ftill like the *Cuckow* in
one filly Note) How are they of his *Flefh* and of his
Bones: And doth not the Scripture fay, *Chrift* in
you, and God will dwell in you, and walk in you,
and are not his Saints of his *Flefh,* and of his *Bones,*
and there is one fentence added, are they not partakers of the *Divine Nature?*   I

I Reply, this *Participation* of the *Divine Nature* is (faith *Peter*) in the Saints by thofe precious Promifes, that is by receiving Chrift Jefus, by believing in him according to that *Ephef.* 3. 10. (That Chrift may dwell in your hearts by Believing) not that the Divine *Being* or *Effence* and *Nature* or *Godhead* is communicable to a finite Creature : from hence thefe proud *Simpletons* fancie (and fome have been fuch bold *Bayards* as to fay) they are Chrift and God, as much as he that died at *Jerufalem,* Chrifted with Chrift and Godded with God. *The divine and humane nature of the Lord Jefus.*

51 | It is remarkable that *Nicholas* the *Deacon* was the Father (as I believed)[1] of the old *Nicholaitans* and *Henery Nichols* in *King James* his time the Father of the new *Nicholaitans* in *London* and other places, crying up their perfection, their *Spirituality* and *Godhead,* all leading from the purity of *Gods Worfhip* and Authority of the *Holy Scripture,* and at laft to carnal *Filthinefs* as the Daughters of thefe the *Ranters* declare evidently. *Nicholas the Deacon and Nicholas Fathers of the old and new Nicholaitans.*

This Humane Nature, humane Soul and Body of Chrift Jefus is fo crofs, oppofite and contrary to their new whimfical Chrift Jefus (the Light within them) that *G. Fox* in all this Book cannot endure to hear of the word *Humane,* as being a new Name and never heard of in the *Scriptures.* *So Criftopher Houlder he boggles at the word Manhood.*

As to the word *Humane,* fuch an odious Word and *Bugbear* to *G. Fox* in all this Book : I faid in publick; many Words truely and properly *Englifh* were well and commendably ufed that were not in the *The word Humane confidered*

[1] "believe." *R. W. Ms. Ann.*

the Scripture in *Englifh* : it is true the word *Humane* comes from the word in *Latin Humanus*, fignifying partaining or belonging to Man : fo a *Humane Soul* or *Body* is no more but fuch a *Soul* or *Body* as all *Mankinde* have.   Hence I told them, that the word *Anthropinos peirafmos*, 1. *Cor.* 10. (I prefumed *John Stubs* knew) might have been turned *Humane*, but is truely turned no *Temptation* or *Trial* but fuch as is common to Men.   This *Fox* knows, that if Chrift Jefus be granted to have had fuch a Soul and Body as is *Humane or Common* to Men, down falls their *Dagon* before the *Cheft* or *Ark* of God, *viz.* their *Horrible, Monftrous Idol* of a Chrift called *Light within them.*

Ufed in the Scripture, 1 Cor 10.

We went on thus in alleadging Quotations, though not in a clofe Examination of them which they endured not, though ever and anon I made fome fallies out upon them and had fome *Skirmifhings*, and fometimes fharp *Difputes* before I would retreat from the *Quotation*.

In Pag. 282. He brings in *Daniel Gaudry* faying [*We fhall not fee Chrift as he is until he comes to Judgement, and then and not before we fhall fee him*] G. *Fox* Anfwers, (You where you are fee him not: nor know him as he is, we do believe you *:* but the *Saints* the *true Church* whom he is the Head of, in whom he is in the midft and in whom he is, &c.

Dan. Grudry Chrift not feen as he is until the day of Judgement

I was not defirous to trouble the *Audience* with more *Quotations*, but they ftill urged, hafte thou any more, haft thou any more, &c. upon their provocation I Quoted many more (to [52] make up an overwhelming Cloud of Witneffes againft

thefe

thefe *Proteftant Jefuites* and *Judafites*, Betrayers of the Son of God the true Lord Jefus Chrift.

In *Foxes* Anfwer to his Oppofite *Daniel Caudry* it is clear that he affirms the contrary to his Oppofite, *to wit*, that Chrift Jefus is as much now feen vifibly as ever he fhall be feen : in which I believe he fpeaks the heart of all the *Antichriftian Wolves and Foxes* who quake and tremble at the thought of Chrifts return again to judgment: and therefore thefe deluded and deluding Souls in their dark *Prifons* of willing *Blindnefs*, and the hellifh *Chaines* of the pride and hardnefs and fecurity of their hearts, they dream they fit in *Robes* of Glory themfelves & now keep open the high Court of eternal *Judgment* and pafs Sentence upon this Chrift without as a poor *Outfide Chrift* and all that worfhip him. *The perfonal coming of the Lord Jefus.*

2. I obferve in *Fox* his anfwer that he can not keep out of his *Burrow* of confounding a *vifible* eye and a *Spiritual*, a vifible and invifible feing : you fee him not faith he where you are, that is you that look upon fuch a real perfon indeed, fuch an one born living and dying as the Hiftory fets forth, you cannot fee him as he is, but we that look at *Chrift Jefus* and the hiftory of him as *Myftical, immediate, invifible*, though we ufe to pleafe you *children and fools* with the words of *Chrifts dying at Ierufalem* : we fee him he is in the mideft of us: and he is the invifible *Head* of the *Church* in God, while you talk of *Vifibles* and feing him as *Vifible &c*. *A vifible and invifible eye and object.*

In *Page* 276. he brings in *Richard Meyo* faying, that he did believe in a *Chrift* that dyed at *Ierufalem* : *Chrift ithin & Chrift without.*

lem : and that he doth not believe in a Chriſt *within*, and preach Chriſt within, is a Reprobate. *Colloſſ.* 2. 2. *Cor.* 13. And he is not in a true Belief of *Chriſt without*, that doth not believe in a *Chriſt within*, but is in the *Devils Belief*, and believes as the *Devils* do.

In this his anſwer an humble Soul may ſee how this ſubtle *Traytor* under the golden name of *Chriſt*, and Chriſt within in the heart, he ſtabs at the heart of the true *Lord Ieſus*, who ſuffered for poor Mankind in mans own nature at *Ieruſalem*.

2. I obſerve his virulent and venemous *Mind* and *Pen* ſtabbing damning and *reprobating* all that truly believe in the true *Lord Ieſus*, whome he confeſſeth to have been a real man dying at *Ieruſalem*, *&c.* except they can believe that he is now no where to be found but in every mans heart that cometh into the world, that is no where.

The Papiſts and Quakers Chriſt is no where

53] In *Page* 246. He brings in *Chriſtopher Wade* ſaying, [*It is whimſical to ſay Chriſt God and Man, Fleſh and Spirit is in them*] He anſwers, [*Contrary to the Apoſtles Doctrine who ſaid they were of his* fleſh *and of his* bone, *and Chriſt in you, and he would walk in them, and he that hath not the Spirit of Chriſt is none of his, and they are of his fleſh and of his bone, and Chriſt in you the hope of Glory*]

Chriſtoph Wade.

In the ſame Page he brings in the ſame Author ſaying |*Fleſh and bone cannot be a meaſure in one and a meaſure in an other*] He Anſwers [*wheras the Apoſtle ſaith, we are of his* Fleſh *and of his* Bone, *here thou art contrary to the Apoſtle, and that was more then one that had the* Fleſh *of* Chriſt, *and his* Bone *and his* Spirit.　　　　　　In

In *Page* 248. He brings in the same Author saying, [*It is a false thing to say Chrifts Perfon is in man*] He Anfwers, [*which is as much as to say, none are of his* Flefh *nor of his* Bone *nor eat nor had not his Subftance.*

And *Page* 249 *The Saints bodyes are not Chrifts body.* He Anfwers, *How are they Chrifts? How dwels he in them? and how are they of his* Flefh *and of his* Bone *then? and how bruitifh are you become in Knowledge? hath he not bought them with a price, and are they not his?*

And in the same *Page* he brings in the same Author saying, *that neither Gods Effence, nor Heaven, nor Chrifts Perfon was in* Peters *holy body.* He anfwers, *but the Apoftle said God will dwell with you and walk in you, and again, our converfation is in Heaven.*

And once more in the same page *There is not whole* Chrift God *and man in men.* Answ. *Then how muft men grow in the meafure of the fullnefs of the ftature of* Chrift: *and* Chrift *and* God *will dwel in man and walk in man,* God *that made all things, and* Chrift *by whome all things were made.*

I Reply, this Author *Chriftopher Wade* I know not many of his oppofites (living and dead, whome he here vapours to anfwer in his Book, I know were worthy of Chriftian efteem and honour for the grace and Knowledge of Chrift Jefus in them, and for other worthy refpects: and whither this Oppofite or any other whome he pretends to puffe at or Anfwer, have thought this audacious *Quackfalver* worthy of any Reply, I know not: For certainly (as he commonly concludes his Anfwer in

The Author whome G. Fox *oppofeth and in Pride and madnefs rageth againft.*

his

his Book(*Thy many notorious Lyes and Slanders and Blafphemyes are not worth the mentioning*: however for the proof of my *Pofition* I am occafioned [54] to follow this *Fox* into his holes and *Burrowes*, and to hale him out before God, Angls and Men as a moft greedy audacious *Fox* and *Wolfe*, not fparing the Son and Lamb of God, nor his precious Lambs and Sheep.

The Qua-kers Chrift but a whimfical Chrift

Now to all thefe laft *Quotations*, I fay (as the Oppofites to *Fox* faid) that this Notion of Chrift wit hin oppofite to Chrift without is a moft Frantick and Whimfical, Grofs and Blockifh Fancy: For though he grant Chrift Jefus to be a Man which *died at Jerufalem*, yet making him only Spiritual, and fuch a Chrift as is whole Chrift, God and Man in every man in the *World*, he makes Chrift Jefus to be but *Whimfical Chrift*, and that Man that died at *Jerufalem* but a *Babylonian* Fancy.

Hofanna to the Son of David

In Pag. 221. He brings in the Author to a Book called *Hofanna to the Son of David*, saying, [*Chrift is without the Sainfts in refpect of his Bodily prefence,*] He Anfwereth, (They are of his Flefh and of his Bone, and eat his Flefh and drink his Blood : and how have the Saints his Mind and Spirit, and he with them and they with him, and fit with him in Heavenly places, and he is the *Head* of the *Church*: how then is he abfent ? the[1] poor *Apoftates* from him who feel not Chrift with you, but he is with the Saints, and they feel him.)

I Reply, I obferve this *Viperous Tongue* faying to the unknown, heavenly *Author*, and *Fox* his other
Oppofitee

[1] "Ye" poor Apoftates. *R. W. Ms. Ann.*

Oppofitee [*Ye poor Apoſtates &c.*] what is it but a
heighth of Deviliſh Pride going before deſtruction
and condemnation? this proud ſwelling Bladder
puft up with a *Timpany* of *Wind* and *Vanity,* what a
huge ſwelling ſhew he makes? what a breadth of
confident boldneſs and bruitiſh impudencie he car-
ries before him? what a groſs, Frantick *Papiſt* is
he become, that cannot, will not diſtinguiſh between *Chriſts Spiritual preſence* and his bodily? that
cannot, will not conſider the difference between
Spirits and *Bodies,* a *Spirit* that hath no Fleſh nor
Bones, and a Body which hath both, as Chriſt his
Body had? that cannot, will not diſtinguiſh between
their ſinful *Fleſh* and *Bones,* and the ſinleſs *Fleſh* and
Bones of that Man Chriſt Jeſus? that cannot, will
not diſtinguiſh between God manifeſted in the *Fleſh*
and *Bones* of that Man Chriſt Jeſus, and manifeſted
in the *Fleſh* and *Bones* of *Believers* in him : O moſt
Holy and Righteous are thy Judgements, O thou
moſt High Judge of the World, who art a devouring fire and Juſtice it ſelf, who thus caſteſt down
the *Proud* and *Self-conceited* into the Dungeon of
ſuch *Black* and *Helliſh Ignorance!*

The Spirit of the Papiſts & the Quakers but one.

55] Pag. 217, Out of a Book mentioning the
Quakers Cauſe, ſaying, [*To ſay Chriſt within is never
to mention Chriſt without*] He Anſwers, There is
none knows Chriſt within, but he knows him without: the ſame yeſterday, and to day, and for ever :
And there is none knows him but they know him
within, revealed of the Father, which is beyond
Fleſh and Blood.

I Obſerve, This fooliſh *Fox* (for all his hiding
Craft)

The Quakers notoriously diffemble, for they do own and not own the Chrift that dyed at Ierufalem.

Craft) is here found out : He profeffeth (againft his Will and Heart) a Chrift that *died at Jerufalem*, and therefore is he forced to name a Chrift without : but when the *Hole and Burrough* is *Digged* the *Fox* is found : For Examine what is this *Chrift without ?* is he that litteral, real and material Perfon the Son of *Mary* (as all profeffing Chrifts Name generally agree ? Is this he whom the *Quakers* acknowledge to have *lived* and *died* at *Jerufalem ?* and do they intend a *Material Croffe*, a literal Death, a literal and real *Ierufalem?* fome of them will fay yes, but therein give the lye to others of themfelves, and alfo to the reft of their own ftory, in acknowledging no other Chrift but fuch as is in *every man*: fuch a Chrift as really and bodily *died at Ierufalem*, they fcorn and hate and fly from as the *Devils did*, crying out, *What have we to do with thee Jefus thou Son of the moft High God, art thou come to torment us before the time ?* Hence the former *Arch-deacon* or *Arch-bifhop* of thefe parts *Humphrey Norton* : he

Humph. Norton more plain in words then other Quakers.

mocks at an outward Chrift, he asks what Countryman he was and fhall be *:* He reproves the Fools that have their Eyes abroad, and gazing after a man into Heaven, he jeers at the Croffe, aud asks what manner of wood it was made of, feeing we muft take it up dayly *?* And *Fox* faith, this Jefus Chrift without and within, is Jefus Chrift yefterday, and to day, and the fame for ever : therefore

Chrift yefterday and to day.

in the *Logick* or *Reafon* of this *Bruite*, Chrift had no body that was born at *Bethlehem*, or died at *Ierufalem* : For he was born yefterday, and to day, and he is born forever : he dyed yefterday, and he dies

to

to day, and he dies forever, which is a moſt Heavenly Truth relating to Gods purpoſe, Chriſts Merit, and to Forefathers, our preſent times, and ſuch as yet muſt be born and follow after us.

But ſuch Myſtical and figurative Scriptures (which are in themſelves like *Sampſons Lion* and *Riddle*) through *Satans Policy*, and the proud ſimplicity of theſe ſimple *Foxes*, are made the common *Holes* and *Burroughs* where you may be ſure to find them : juſt like the *Jeſuites* (whoſe Coſens, if not Brethren of one belly of Hell [56] they are) who uſually confound clear Scriptures with Spiritual and Myſtical Illuſions, and fly from Diſtinctions and openings neceſſary in places more dark, figurative and allegorical.

In pag. 211. He brings in *John Burton* ſaying, *That the man that was crucified his body is now in the preſence of his Father, abſent from his People as touching his bodily preſence.* He Anſwers. *Doth not the Apoſtle ſay he is the Head of the Church? and doth not the Apoſtle ſay they are of his* Fleſh *and* Bone *and ſit it heavenly places, with* Chriſt, *and* Chriſt *ſaith, they muſt eat his fleſh, and he is in them.*

As I remember at the reading of this *Quotation*, I urged that herein *G. Fox* did plainly deny (as indeed in all the reſt I have quoted) Chriſt Jeſus to have had ſuch a body as could be born of a woman, wrapped in ſwadling Cloathes, &c. as could be *hungry, weary, ſleep, diſcourſe,* [1] *apprehended, buffeted, whipped, nail'd to the Gallowes, die, be buried, ariſe*

The Quakers endure not to be ſearched, temer of falſe and thieviſh ſpirits.

---

[1] Interline "be." *R. W. Ms. Ann.*

arife and afcend up vifibly into thefe vifible Heavens, now in the prefence of his Father, and abfent from his People on Earth, as touching his bodily prefence: But one of my *Oppofites*, (I think two of them) bid me not wronge G. *Fox* by my *Obfervation*, for his words were not fo. I Anfw. In *effect* and Subftance they were, for G. *Fox* here, (and in all his Anfwers) maintains the *Negative* to what his Oppofites *Affirm*. And 2. As to the grounds of his deniall it is clear that fometimes they are moft plain and clear, and fometimes moft fubtle, and commonly fuch as will bear a twofold Sence, on which they commonly ground fome *Jefuitical equivocation*.

The Quakers & Apolloes Oracles the fame.

In Pag. 210. He brings in *John Burton* faying, *Chrift went away into Heaven from his Difciples, and fo not within them.* He Anfwers, *Did not he fay that he would come again to them? Did he not fay he was in them, I in you? And did not the Apoftle fay Chrift was in them except they were* Reprobates? *the hope of Glory?* was he not revealed to the *Apoftle* and fo in him? and did not the *Apoftle* Preach Chrift within, and you preach Chrift without?

Iohn Burton.

Again in the fame Page [*Thofe Believers that are in the body at this day are abfent from the Lord*:] He Anfwers again, Doth not the Apofte fay Chrift is in them except they be Reprobates? and he is in them the Hope of Glory? and they have fellowfhip with God, and God will dwell in them, and walk in them, and he that believes believes in him, and Chrift and fo notabfent.

If ever there Equivocating Jefuites in the world the Quakers are.

Again in the fame Page, they fay [*He is abfent from them as touching his flefh*, He Anfwers, *Doth not the*

the Apostle say they [57] *are of his* Flesh *and of his* Bone? *and he that eates not his* Flesh, *hath no* life *in him, and they sit in* heavenly places *with him, and he that eates his* flesh *hath it in him.*

And again in the same Page they say [*There is not any* Heaven *within into which the Man* Christ *is ascended, or can any man contain a man four foot long?*] He Answers [*Christ is a Mystery, and is he not to be revealed within who is a Mystery?* He who did descend to be revealed and made manifest in his Saints in flesh and Spirit, that did descend, which is now manifested, that the World wonders at: that is ascended far above the Heavens, who is the Saints life living *Bread* and *Drink*: and where ever used the Ministers of Christ any such expression as thou doth, which shews that Christ to thee is a *Mystery?*

Reply, In all these four Passages *G. Fox* expresly denies that Christ is ascended into Heaven from his Disciples: That Believers now in the Body are absent from the Lord: that he is absent from Man as touching his Flesh: that there is a Heaven into which Christ is ascended: and that Chrifts Body is not containable in a place according to his stature and proportion. *The Qua-kers won-derful jug-ling about the true Christ*

2. In his Answers he notoriously jugles and equivocates as if he maintained *Christ in Truth,* he that lived and died at *Jerusalem,* and visibly ascended into Heaven though the whole scope and the plain open faced meaning of his words, with loud cries tend altogether to another business, *to wit*, to set up himself by setting up the Image and Picture, this *Imaginary Christ* which he calls the *Light within them.* The

The fame *Author* faith, *Pag.* 206. [*A falfe Chrift
hath a new falfe Faith to apprehend this Crucified
Chrift within,*] He Anfwers, [*Which is contrary to the
Faith of the Apoftles which Preached Chrift that's
Crucified within and not another*; *Him that was raifed
from the dead was rifen that* Lord Jefus Chrift
*within, the fame yefterday, to day, and for ever, by
whom the World was made glorified with the Father
before the World began: it was he that was manifeft in
the Saints, that was, and is not another, for the other
is Antichrift.*]

John
Burton:

Again in the fame Page, it is a *Sceipture* of the
Devils making to apprehend this Chrift within :
He Anfwers, Now I fay if there be any Chrift but
he that was crucified wit hin he is a falfe Chrift,
and the *Scripture* holds forth this, and the *Devil
never made it,* but he and his *Meffengers* are againft
it : And he that hath not this Chrift [58] that was
rifen and *Crucified* within is a *Reprobate* though
Devills and *Reprobates* may talk of him without.

This Quotation was read again in their own
Book by *John Burnet,* and they magnified the
Chrift within, but they would not fuffer me to
obferve the fence and argue from it, faying, G.
Foxes *Words were plain concerning the true Chrift*;
And fo indeed I fay they are to any penitent Soul
truly (like *Paul*) unbottom'd from weak and filthy
felf, and his own *Dunghil Righteoufnefs,* and burning with fincere *Affection* to the true Lord *Jefus* :
For thefe fubtle *Foxes,* and their Words difcover (as
the Sun at noon day) that as plainly as ever *Abfalom, Achitophel, Shimei, Sheba* rofe up in confpiracy
and

*The Qua-
kers Trai-
tors & Re-
bels againft
the true
Lord Jefus*

and Rebellion againſt *David*, &c. as plainly as ever *Judas* and *Peter* (for a time) and *Alexander* the *Copper-ſmith*, and *Hymeneus*, and *Julian* the *Apoſtate* denied *Davids Antitype* the true *Lord Jeſus*: ſo under the Cloak and Colour of *Chriſt Crucified* within, do their *Rebellious Traitors* bear Arms againſt the *Mediator* between God and Man, the Man Chriſt Jeſus: For although it be *Scripture Phraſe*, that we are *Crucified*, *Dead* and *Buried*, and *Riſen with Chriſt*: yet what a poor proof is this, that Chriſt was Born and *Crucified* &c. yeſterday, and to day within us, and there is no other *Birth* nor *Life*, nor *Death*, nor *Grave* but what is within us, and all are *Reprobates* and *Devils* that bow not down to this *painted devouring Monſter*.

Still my *Oppoſites* were catcht in their own *Craftineſs* they ſeemed well pleaſed that G. *Fox* ſhould be heard in his Anſwers to his *Adverſaries*, and I reſtrain'd and ſtopt from making out my Proofs from the *Senſe*, and *Scope* and *Meaning*: I was yet glad that ſo much was diſcovered, that I had (by *Catches*) liberty to give fire ſometimes, and intended to make uſe of this preſent Advantage (which I from the firſt intended, when I ſaw I ſhould be ſtopt, and they would not afford me the liberty I gave to them without the leaſt *Interruption*) as *John Stubs* confeſſed.

I have known the poor Lobſters catch the Foxes.

Page 135. He brings in *Thomas Moor* ſaying [*Chriſt is abſent from us while we are in this Mortal Body*] He Anſwers contrary to the *Apoſtle*, who ſaith, *the Life of Chriſt is manifeſted in their mortal Fleſh.*]

And

And Page 136. The fame Author faith [*Chriſt is diſtinct from every one of us, and without us in our particular perſons,*] He An- [59] ſwers, [*The Apoſtle ſaid Chriſt was in them except thed were Reprobates: and they were of his Fleſh and of his Bone, and they eat his Fleſh and drank his Blood, then it was in them, and he is diſtinct from none but Reprobates who hates the Light.*]

The wonderful blindneſs and hardneſs of my Antagoniſts Reply, I wondred not ſo much at this *Thunder,* and *Fire,* and *ſtinking Brimſtone* from this *Foxes* mouth, and that all are *Reprobates* with him that bow not down to his *Carved Image*: but I wondred at my Oppoſites, who declared (publickly as before) that they would not follow *G. Fox* but in the Truth, &c. and yet when I read all their [1] plain Evidences to them of *Foxes* denying the true *Lord Jeſus,* God andMan; and making only a *Spiritual Chriſt,* a *Myſtical Inviſible Jeſus, &c.* that yet they ſhould be ſo blinded and hardened, as to cover, excuſe and plead for *G. Fox* in all particulars, and ſtop me from drawing the *Curtain* and letting in the *Light* by Opening and Arguing from the Sence and Meaning.

I do not remember that any one of my three *Oppoſites* gave any poſitive anſwer to any of my Obſervations on *Foxes* Principles, Anſwers, and Evaſions: All their work was to keep themſelves within their Trenches or Burroughs, and to cry out [*Thou muſt keep to Foxes Words*] or, *Wilt thou go on to another?*

Frances Higginſon In Page 71. He brings in *Frances Higginſon* ſaying, [*Chriſts Humane Nature*] He Anſwers, [*Where doth*

[1] "the plain Evidences." *R. W. Ms. Ann.*

doth the Scripture speak of Humane, the Word Hu- The Qua-
mane *where is it written that we may search for it:* kers endure
Now we do not deny that Christ (according to the Flesh) word
was of Abraham, *but not the word* Humane: *And* Humane
Christs Nature is not Humane *which is Earthly, for
that is the first* Adam.]

Reply. This ignorant and simple Cavil (as I
have before proved it to be from 1 *Cor.* 10.) is
often brought by *G. Fox* in this Book, in an horrible equivocation to overthrow and destroy that
Humane Nature, that Flesh and Body of the Lord
Jesus, who yet had such a Body they say that died
at *Jerusalem* : These Traiterous Jesuits or *Judas-
ites* tell us *Humane* is of the Earth or Earthly, and
that is the *first Adam,* but Christ Jesus is of the
Seed of *Abraham* according to the flesh, that is, in
their mental Reservation, according to their flesh,
God in their flesh, Christ in their flesh suffering at
a *Mystical Jerusalem* within them: They are *Abrahams* Seed, *Isaaks* Seed in whom all Nations (by
this Christ the Light within them) must be blessed:
And all that are not this Seed, this Flesh, [60] this
Christ (which they are) are in the *Serpents Nature* Acts 13.
and *Reprobates.* But amongst all the most full and Opened of
heavenly *Scriptures* for the *Humane Nature* of the Humanity.
Lord Jesus : I shall touch but one at present, *Act.*
13. at *Antioch, Barnabas* and *Paul* in a *Synagogue* of
the *Jews* made the *Humane Nature of* the Lord
Jesus, (as also in other places) the great Subject of
their Discourse and Preaching : and concludes *ver.*
38. *Be it known unto you therefore Men & Brethren,
that through this Man is Preached unto you the For-*
                                                    givenes

givene∫s of ∫ins, and by Him all that Believe are Ju∫ti-fied from all things from which you could not be ju∫tified by the Law of Mo∫es. By the meritorious Suffer-ings, Death and Blood-∫hedding of this Je∫us (lit-erally in the *Hi∫tory* born at *Bethlehem* as the *Quakers* ∫ay, &c.) is only forgivene∫s of ∫in, and ju∫tification, &c. and not by a *Chimical* and *Diabolical* Chri∫t and Fancy within us, begot by the *Devil* on a proud and lazie Ignorance : Let therefore (as it follows) the Proud De∫pi∫ers wonder and peri∫h, believing not in him the true Light of the World, the true Brazen Serpent to all that look up unto him.

Tho. Col-lier

In Page 37. He brings in *Thomas Collier* ∫aying, [*If the very Chri∫t God Man be within tho∫e called Quakers he cannot come down from Heaven*] He An∫wers, ⌊Here he ∫tands again∫t the promi∫e of Chri∫t, that he ∫hall come and dwell in you, and walk in you *:* I will come again unto you. And he hath revealed his Son in me ∫aith the *Apo∫tle*, and know you not that Chri∫t is in you except you be *Reprobates* : and the Spirit of the *Father* ∫peaks in you, and ∫ee how contrary thou art to the *Prophets, Chri∫t* and the *Apo∫tles.*

The ∫econd coming of the Lord Je∫us

I urged that here *G. Fox* did plainly deny the expected per∫onal coming of the *Lord Je∫us* : but they charged me to give none of my *Sences* and *Meanings* to *G. Fox* his words : but now I have leave (by Gods merciful hand) here to ∫ay, that their *Hypocri∫ie* and *Deceit* (whereby they cheat them∫elves and others) is ∫o much the more gro∫s and abominable, becau∫e they pretend in words to own Chri∫t Je∫us *Humane de∫cending*, or *A∫cending*

as

as a Man into Heaven, and Chrifts there abiding until the time of the *Reftitution,* and Chrifts return the fecond time : They know alfo that all thofe *Scriptures* they produce (as *Chrift in you except ye be Reprobates, &c.*) concern an inward invifible and Spiritual prefence, and yet they bruitifhly cry out contrary to the *Prophets, Chrift, & the Apoftles.*

61] It comes to my mind that in reading & urging fome of thefe Paffages concerning thefe *Foxians* denying the *Humane Nature* and *Perfon* of the Lord *Jefus,* one of my Oppofites *John Stubs* infifted upon that 9. of *Ifaiah* where Chrift is called the *Ever-lafting Father* : and yet he faid, *He was the Son of Man born of a Woman, &c.* I Anfwered, the *Hebrew* word rendred by our *Tranflators,* the *Everlafting Father* is Tranflated by fome, the *Father of an age,* or *the Father of Ages,* alluding to the great increafe and fpreading of Chrifts Name, and the mighty increafe of his Spiritual Seed (as the Lord promifed to *Abraham* and *Ifaac*) as the Stars of Heaven. *John Stubs* faid the *Hebrew word* was [*Abi Haad,* &c.] and it was rendred *Pater Eternitatis* : I replied that it was rendred (and that more near the *He-brew*) *Pater feculi,* or *feculorum* : But I told him it was not a feafonable time and place for him and me to fpend much time about the Tranflation of the word : he faid he had brought the *Hebrew Bi-ble* with him, and it may be he underftood the *Hebrew* and the *Greek* and other Languages as well as my felf and better too : I was about to fay that they were wonderfully altered and changed from their former principles and practifes, for heretofore they have

The Ever-lafting Fath r Chrift Jfu. & how

The Qua-kers won-derfully changed & yet but in Diffimula-tion as to learning & the Scriptures

have profeffed to me that they had no need of
Books, no not of the Scripture it felf, for they had
the Teacher within them that gave forth Scripture,
&c. if now they were perfwaded to ftudy the Holy
Scripture and the Tranflation of it, and to examine
the Tranflations and the Copies of them, then they
did err and fin before, (which they fay the Saints cannot) in fo wonderfully neglecting and flighting
them as ufelefs and needlefs things.

Yea the truth is if their Light be fo Alfufficient
as they make it, to bring them to Heaven, to guide
them immediately and infallibly &c. what fimplicity is it in them to ftoop to *Pen and Ink*, and
mens fallible Tranflations, yea, many wayes charged
with many failings.

I know their Pretences of becoming *All to All*
to win the more, and of removing the offence and
ftumbling block, *viz.* as if they denied the Scriptures, but the truth is, they look at the *Holy Scriptures* ftill but as the *Ceremonies* which the *Apoftles*
difpenfed with for a feafon: they care no more for
the Scriptures then the *Papifts* do, they are forced
to make ufe of them for an end, but all their hope
is in their *Interpretations*, which both *Papifts and
Qua-* [62] *kers* bend their utmoft to fecure, *viz.* the
Priviledge of *Interpretation*, and chair of *Infallibility* to themfelves, or elfe down they tumble, for
moft fure it is the *Holy Scriptures*, and both *Papifts*
and *Quakers* are at irreconcilable difference, if the
one ftand the other muft fall for ever.

Although I defired to finifh all the firft feven
Pofitions that day, and offered once or twice to
proceed,

proceed, yet *W. Edmundson* (efpecially) upbraided W. Ed-mund. *leaves the Difpute & is hurried into Preaching*
me that I kept them long, and that I proved
nothing, and upon a fudden a violent, tumultuous
diforderly *Wind* or *Spirit* filled all his *Sails*, fo that
he rofe up and fell into a downright *Speech* or *Ser-*
mon to the *People* and *Auditory*: and firft he declared how notorioufly I had wronged them, in
laying and publifhing fo many falfe, and fome of
them dangerous *Charges* againft them. 2 And how
they had been fo long patient towards me and fuffer me to produce fo many *Allegations* out of *G.*
Fox his Book, and yet they fpeak nothing for me,
but *G. Fox* his words cleared him from all my unjuft challenges and charges. 3. He Appealed to
the People, how willing they had fhewed themfelves to own the Scriptures, and to have all their
Teaehings and Differences tried by the Scriptures.
4. He fell upon the two Hinges of all the Quakers common Difcourfes.

Firft, An Invective againft the *Priefts, Falfe*
Teacher, Falfe Apoftles, who had got on the *Sheeps*
cloathing, and fold the words of *Scripture* for their
Game and *Lucre* and he amplified this much how
all their care and ftudy was to get a good *Living*
or *Benifice* of 50. 6c 100. or 200 pounds a year
(more or lefs) and he that complained how I took
up time, now (tedioufly) made us all to hear a Story, which he faid he knew himfelf of one of the
Priefts that lived not many miles from the place W. Ed-mund. *his ftory concerning Benefices*
where *W. Edmund.* lived, who told with his own
Mouth unto *William Edmund.* viz. how that having
a good *Benefice*, another *Prieft* of his acquaintance

came

came to vifit him, whom he entertained kindly, and this his Gueft told him, that he was going to the *Bifhop* of *Dublin*, who was his Friend: and the *Prieft* the *Hoft* was afterward informed that this treacherous and ungrateful Gueft, did ufe all the art he could with the *Bifhop* of *Durham* (or *Dublin*) to get his Friends (that had entertained him) his Living from him.

2. The fecond part of his Sermon was (as ufually it is of all their Sermons) an extolling and magnifying of that Light which [63] he faid had appeared to him, which he advanced as the Principle and the Foundation, the Light, &c. he added how they had left all the Glory and Pleafures of the World for this Light: and how they had endured and fuffered much for Preaching this Light to ungodly and ungrateful men, who had ill requited them: for their Meffage and Work was only to bring good News unto them, to tell them that they fhould be free from fin and have Chrift Jefus live and dwell in them. I kept filence until this famous *Apoftle* and *Preacher* of *Chrift Jefus* had done this Speech or Sermon which he faid *he* was moved in his heart to make unto them & (as he often faid) to give an account of his Faith which he performed with very great zeal and fervency, both of mind and body.

And b vain extolling of their Idol Light

John Stubs his fermon I had thought then to have fpoke, but immediately *Jo. Stubs* ftood up being moved (as he faid) to Declare his mind and Thoughts unto the people alfo, and fo he began a large *Oration, Speech* or *Sermon* alfo (though not fo long as *William Edmundfons*)

mundſons) he declared how pleaſant a thing the
Light was, and how pleaſant a thing it was to behold it ? And he ſaid, *are you angry becauſe we bring
you the Tidings of the Light*? This was the principle,
this was the *Foundation* of all, the *Light, &c.* He
added (for *John Stubs* his was but *a* Repetition of
William Edmundſons his *Sermon*) that they had for-
ſaken all the Glory of Honours and Pleaſures of
this World for this *Light* : and they had left their
Wives and *Children,* and expoſed themſelves to hard
Travels and to many Hardſhips and Sufferings for
the *Light* ſake : I heard him alſo patiently and
gave him no *Interruption* (as he twice openly con-
feſt that I had not interrupted them : but when he
had finiſhed his *Sermon* and I had gained a little
calm and liberty of Speech, immediately before I
could finiſh one Sentence; that *Pragmatical and Inſulting Soul* W. *Edmundſon* ſtopt and Interrupted
me, ſo that I openly complained of incivility and
inhumanity : that hearing patiently their two Sermons, they were ſet down, and common Reaſon
ſaid that it was my turn to ſpeak, and every body
deſired what Anſwer I could frame to hear it, that
then I ſhould be *diſturbed* and *ſtopt* was no way be-
fitting the Societies of Civil and Morral men: I
then Anſwered, that thoſe very *Sermons* or *Orations*
which they had now made to the People were ſo
far beneath the merit of an Anſwer to them, that
they miniſtred and afforded to me a mighty and
invincible *Argument*, that the Spirit of God [64] was
not the *Author of them* : For we all knew that the
Spirit of God was moſt purely *Rational*, and a *Spirit*
of

The Quakers unruly and raſh interruptions

A ſhort Anſwer to 2 Sermons

of pure *Order*, and did not prompt or move men to break *Hedges* and leap over one *Ordinance* into another : We were engaged in a mutual *Conference* and *Disputation*, we were in the midst of it, how came we then to fall into *Popular Orations* and *Sermons*? is it comely when persons are *Disputing* to fall upon our knees and Answer a*n Argument* with a *Prayer* (as it is a frequent practice with the *Quakers*,) is it proper to break off *Prayer* and fall to disputing, or out of Disputation into *Preaching*?

The motions of Gods spirit not those of the Quakers

But I said my Opposites Spirit was far from the *Holy Spirit of God:* and his movings are far from the *Motions* with which my *Antagonists* were acted, for they had neither power to keep civil Order, nor to be patient, for not being able to answer nor bear my words *W. Edmundson* said expresly what should we sit here and suffer him to vent his *Blasphemies and Lies*? he hath kept us here two dayes, and have proved nothing, &c.

The Quakers not orderly nor patient

I took a little boldness and told them, that if *Paul* himself were present, or *Jesus Christ* himself in their bodily presence which they confessed he *died* in at *Jerusalem*, yet they would say unto them, even unto Christ himself, thou hast falsely *charged* but thou hast proved nothing : *Paul* himself should be an Enemy, and Jesus Christ should be a *Blasphemer* and a *Beelzebub* because he brought glad news of the Truth from Heaven to them.

I further said, that I had more to offer in the name and in the cause of the true Lord Jesus Christ, and after I had got liberty of speech, I said that as they which *denied* the person of the true

Lord

Lord Jesus denied the true *Lord Jesus* himself, so they which denied the Offices which God the Father had invested him with and *designed him* to fulfil, the *denied* the true *Lord Jesus Christ*.

They *demanded* of me wherein *they denied the offices of Christ Jesus*: I Answered, *I had many things to declare in which they denied the* Offices *of Christ Jesus* (as well as the *Papists* for which we seperated from them as *Antichristans*, not holding the Head the true Lord Jesus the *Sacrifice and Sacrificer*, the only *Prophet*, *Apostle* and *Messenger*, bringing in *the last times, the last Dispensation and Will of his Father*: contrary to the *Papists* who set up (some of them) *the Pope* and (some of them) *the general counsel above the* Lord Jesus declaring his mind in the *Holy Scriptures*: and con- [65] trary to the *Quakers* who set up a voice or motion within them overtopping and over pouring the voice of Christ Jesus in the Scriptures, some of them maintaining that this *Light* within them is that *great Prophet* that was to come which *Moses* Prophesied of, *Deut.* 18.

I said I would contract my thoughts, and speak at present only a little of his *Kingly power and Office*, and I plainly denounced that they were all notoriously guilty of *High Treason* against the King of Kings, the Lord Jesus, yea as far as in them lay, they robd him of his Crown, and Life and All.

In particular I told them I had abundant proof there ready to bring forth from G. *Foxes* Book, that he and his Associates denied (yea all of them) that visible Kingdome and *Church* and *Institutions* which

he

he as *King* over all his *Subjects* hath *Sovereign Right* unto, and moſt faithfully and wiſely ordained to continue until his coming again.

*The viſi-
ble Chriſ-
tian
Church
& Ordi-
nances.* I told them that *G. Fox* his Book and all their Books and Profeſſions denied any viſible Church of Chriſt at all : and though they maintained and kept up *Congregations* (of pretended Chriſtan) *Wor-
ſhips* and *Worſhippers* (in a direct contradiction unto their own Tenents, yet) they maintained the Church was in God and ſo not viſible : the Officers of the Church were inviſible and immediately made by the immediate and inviſible Spirit. The *Baptiſme* was within, and only the *Baptiſme* of the *Spirit* and of *Fire* : The *Lords Supper* appointed by the Lord Jeſus to be a Spiritual Feaſt remembring him until his coming was with them nothing elſe but Spiritual joy, which they have one in and with another, which they have by the ſecond com-
ing of the Lord Jeſus to them, who they ſaid was come again to the Apoſtles the ſecond time, and unto themſelves alſo.

Upon this (as I remember) there fell out ſome words between my Oppoſites, and ſome of the people called *Baptiſts* : But ſome of them (eſpecially *John Stubs*) demanded of me, why I thus charged them and was my ſelf ſo guilty, not liv-
ing in *Church Ordinances* my ſelf.

*Touching
the ſeveral
Churches
extant.* I Anſwered, that it was one thing to be in Arms againſt the *King of Kings* and his *viſible Kingdome* and *Adminiſtration of it*, & to turn off all to *Notions* and *Fancies* of an inviſible Kingdome, and inviſible Officers and Worſhips as the *Quakers* did : Another thing

66] thing among fo many pretenders to be the true *Chriftian Army* and *Officers* of Chrift Jefus) to be in doubt unto which to affociate and to lift our felves.

After all my fearch and examinations and confiderations I faid, I do profefs to believe, that fome come nearer to the *firft primitive Churches*, and the *Inftitutions* and *Appointments* of Chrift Jefus then others, as in many refpects fo in that gallant and heavenly and fundamental Principle of the true matter of a Chriftian Congregation, Flock or Society, *viz. Actual Believers, true Difciples & Converts Living Stones,* fuch as can give fome account how the *Grace of God* hath appeared unto them, and wrought that *Heavenly Change* in them; I profeffed that if my Soul could finde reft in joyning unto any of the *Churches* profeffing Chrift Jefus now extant, I would readily and gladly do it, yea unto themfelves whom I now oppofed.

Churches nearest to Christ Jesus

This was and I hope is the principle of the N English Church.

But *Thirdly.* Not finding reft, they themfelves knew, there is a *Time* of purity and *Primitive Sincerity*: there is a time of *Tranfgreffion & Apoftacy,* there is a time of the coming out of the *Babilonian Apoftacy & Wildernefs*: there is a time of many *Flocks* pretending to be Chrifts and faying. *Loe here he is, &c.* and a Command of Chrift Jefus, goe not into the *Wildernefs,* goe not into the private *Chambers:* There is a time when *Chrift Jefus* his Doves and Loves cry out to him, *O thou whome my Soul loveth, tell me where thou feedeft, where thou makeft thy Flock to reft at noon; for why fhould I be as one that turns afide to the Flocks of my Companions?*

The various appearances of Christ Jesus

ions? I doe not remember that any *Reply* was made to this by any of my *Oppofites,* nor heard I any more of this *Objection.*

I now praied there[1] patience to hear me a few words : I faid we had fpent two whole dayes from *My offer in the end of the fecond dayes con- ference* morning to night and had proceeded no further then the Debates of the two firft *Pofitions,* I told them if they were free I would attend them again in the Morning (being the firft of the week) to fall upon the proof of my other five pofitions remaining for *Newport* : or if they were not willing to that, I would (if God permitted) attend them there on the fecond day called *Munday,* in the Morning to proceed upon the reft.

Lying pre- tenders to Gods fervice *W. Edmundfon* faid, they had fpent fo much time already upon but two of them : and both he and *John Stubs* faid they had other bufinefs in hand then to attend unto my *falfe Charges* which in all 67] this time I could not make out : they faid they muft go about the work of the Lord to which he had called them.

The Authors juft Apolo- gie agaiſt I told them I had ufed all diligence, I failed not to meet them about the exact hour appointed, and always before the audience was come. I never withdrew nor abfented a *Minute,* but put my old *Carcafe* to conftant purfuit of my promife which lay on me to fulfil, and to make out my proofs, although they had fpoke never a word until I had finifhed : I ufed all poffible brevetie, and oft times fuppreffed my thoughts preffing in upon me for

Utterance

[1] " their." *R. W. Ms. Ann.*

Utterance and Audience; I rather chofe thus to *the unjuft*
Apologize for my felf, then down right to blame *clamors of*
them, on whom (they faw well enough) I laid the *the Qua-*
blame of our long proceeding. I told them I had *kers*
fpoken nothing to them but the *Eternal truth* of
God, which fooner or later would arreft them,
and ufing aloud the words of the Lord Jefus [*viz.*
The words that I have fpoken fhall judge you at the laft
day.] I withdrew.

Within a quarter of an hour they fent one to
me to defire my coming in again to them, and
William Edmondfon (commonly their proud mouth)
told me that I had deeply charged them and laid
many *falfe Accufations* upon them, and fome of
them dangerous, both as they were *Chriftians*, and
as they were men: they had ufed long patience in
hearing of me, and yet becaufe it fhould be feen
that they were willing to hear the utmoft that I
had to fay they would meet and fpend a few hours
with me on the fecond Day following at *nine in the*
Morning, only they would not endure any long and
tedious Difcourfes.

I anfwered that their own fouls knew, and the *A mutual*
Auditors knew I ufed to be brief: and if they had *agreement*
for a third
pleafed to have given me leave, I would have fin- *dayes con-*
ifhed the whole feven by noon the firft day: and I *ference.*
would now promife them (by Gods help) to finifh
what I had to fay to the other five remaining in a
quarter of an hour, fo that in five quarters of an
hour I would prefent them with what I had to fay:
W. Edmundfon faid they would expect I fhould fo do,
and all of them feemed well pleafed that I offered

to

to difpatch each Pofition in a quarter of an hour ; I faid they muft not count me falfe& a *Promife-breaker* if I was not exact to a quarter of an hour poffible I might be within a quarter, poffible I might fomething exceed it, but I hoped not to exceed above a quarter.

W. Edmundfon replied, Nay *Roger* thou muft be punctual if [68] thou wilt be a Chriftian : and indeed afterward at *Providence* he unjuftly more then once upbraided me faying, *Is this your quarter of an hour?* I anfwered that Chriftians nor any prudent man would be fo curious and critical as to raife Cenfures and Accufations upon the nicityes and uncertaintyes of a few *Minutes*, for unless we had Clocks and Watches and quarter-Glaffes (as in fome Ships) it was impoffible to be exactly punctual : however by Gods help I faid I would ftudy fuch *Exactnefs*, that I would rather omit much I had to fay then fail in my promife to them.

After this (as I heard) *W Hitchcock* of *Newport* held difpute with them about Water-Baptifme, I was withdrawn being evening and weary.

I was told by many of *Providence*, that I knew them they would not ftand a *Difputation* : or if they did they would not continue without great *Advantages* and be as flippery as *Eeles*, and break off abruptly, as their fpirit hurried them, I therefore ftudioufly endeavoured to tole and drive them to the finifhing of my remaining five at *Newport*, and the other feven at *Providence*. And thus by the moft wife and gracious hand of God we came to the end of the fecond dayes work, and the fecond Pofition and the end of the Week. It

A quarter of an hour much canvafed.

The Quakers fpirit & policy

It was queried by fome why (at *Newport* and *Providence* afterward) they appointed the end of the weeks for the *Difputation?* and why fince it was not finifhed they would not proceed on the firft day? It is not immaginable that they cordially owne that day, (for the *Quakers* work upon it) but they wifely refolved to have the whole firft day with the People to make up their *Breaches*, ftop *Leakes* drefs wounds that might be in the foregoing *Agitations* againft their *Confciences & Credits.* It is dolefull that men of excellent parts, and of great knowledge in the *Scripture,* fhould yet fo ly under a Sentence of *Gofpel juftice,* that they cannot but *deceive* as they are *deceived,* that they cannot but *believe Lyes* and *tell Lyes,* horrible and blafphemous Lyes, as confidently as the *Pureft Truths,* and fuck in and, powre out the poyson of Dragons, the great *red Dragon,* the *Father of Lyes,* inftead of the fweet *Milk* and *Wine* from the *Breafts* of the *Way, the Truth, and the Life,* the fon of *God Chrift Jefus.*

The Quakers would not difpute on the firft day and why.

69] THe third day of our *Conference* being come, being the fecond of the Week as was appointed, *W. Edmundfon* began and faid to this effect, *Roger,* we have waited upon thee two dayes already to hear what thou hadft to fay to prove thy falfe *Charges* againft us: we are here according to promife to fpend fome hours about the reft of the feven which yet remain: we muft tel thee that we will not give thee leave to make a long work of it: if according to thy promife thou wilt difpatch each

The third dayes conference at New-port

af

af the other five in a quarter of an hour, we will
keep our promife and hear thee.

I knew it was in vain, (as in the other two dayes
paft I found it) to infift upon their obftinately continued *Advantage* of three conftantly engaged againft
me (befide their accidental fpeakers who had liberty when others were forbidden) I fay notable and
Chief men in their way and *Sect*: and having juft
then read a Letter as I fate there directed to my
felf and all of us to be read in the *Affembly*, I begun with prefenting the Letter to them, and told
them that juft now it was delivered to me &c. I
knew not certainly from whome it came, nor of
one Tittle of the Contents of it: only I judged it
to be my Brother *Robert Williams* (*School-Mafter*
of *Newport*) his hand: I read the *Superfcription*
and offered if they pleafed to unfeal and read it,
or I would deliver it into their hand fo to doe.

W. Edmundfon anfwered that they came not
thither to hear *Papers*, but to hear how I would
make out my falfe *Charges* againft them and this
he fpeaking none would whift againft it, and this
he did fpeak becaufe my Brother beyond my expectation and thoughts fpake fome words the firft
morning againft their *Infulting* and *domineering*
over me, as alfo delivered a paper to them which
was with much adoe handed and delivered to them
but never read, containing thefe two great *Points*
in every true penitent Converts eye, *viz.* the fight
of *Sin as Sin.* And 2. The fight of the material
Lord Jefus as the true *Meffiah* or anointed, thefe

were

A Letter
fent in to
all of us.

were the two *Daggers* which they knew ſtab'd at the heart of their feigned *Chriſt* and *Light* within them.

I knew my Brother patiently waited there the two firſt dayes, and was (with others) ſilenced : and now I gueſſed he had ſent them his mind and would trouble them no more. I told them [70] the whole *Aſſembly* had Intereſt in the Letter, as directed to us to read to the reſt. *The Letter refuſed to be opened by the Quakers*

W. *Edmundſon* and the reſt deſired the *Auditors* to ſpeak if they deſired to have it read : ſome of the *Quakers* ſaid it might be read when the buſineſs was over : ſo I to make no breach put it up, and in the end of the day offered it again, claiming their *Promiſe*, but they regarded it not, ſo that after the *Conference* ended (we of *Providence* being called away by a Boat preparing to depart) I ſtept to my Brothers houſe and acquainted him with Paſſages, who ſaid that not only the *Superſcription* was his hand but the Letter alſo, and I might open and read it, and (if it might be) preſent it to the intended *Aſſembly* at *Providence:* of which we ſhall hear when it pleaſeth the mercifull hand of the Lord to bring us to thoſe Tranſactions. In ſhort, it was refuſed there alſo, & therefore I have judged it fit, ſince it was ſo ſolemnly flung out both at *Providence* and *Newport* that it ſhould have as ſolemn a *Publication* to the whole world, and the rather becauſe it is a *witneſs* of Truth as to the two firſt dayes tranſactions, impartially reproving my *Oppoſites* and me alſo where he conceived we were failing : It is true I am not of my Brothers *The Sum of the Letter*

My ſelf reproved in the Letter in 3 particulars

Conſcience

*that under hand writing.   And herein (loving friends)
you have infringed upon those great Liberties and Mercies which God hath bestowed upon these parts, and
which you do enjoy, and cannot enjoy else where: And
will you now shut up your common Wine-presses that we
can have no fruit nor refreshing but what comes from
your private Presses?   Know (Loving Friends) this
is a sad grievance that lies upon us.   Yea, you do in-
fringe not only upon our Souls but upon our* Temporal
Liberties.

*For in our Courts of Judicature there is a funda-
mental liberty stated for any to speak freely for Conscience sake in any Cause in the Bounds of Sobriety
and Modesty.   But this appears against the Rules and
Practises of all* Christianity, *not practised by the*
Judicial Convocation, *nor by the high* Commission
Court *in our Native Couutry, where often I have been,
and the* Metropolitan *with the rest of the* Bishops *in
Gravity and Christianity (though their pleadings were
by Proctors, yet) gave liberty especially for Relations
to speak: As in one Instance of a person whom you
all have heard of, when he was to come upon Examination, his wife being big with Childe came with him,
the* Arch-Bishop *(though otherwise he might be improper, yet herein shewd great civility by considering
the Womans condition, and gave liberty for speaking to
the full, with replying no discomfortable Words, yea in
Christianity delayed further prosecution until she was
delivered, though afterwards they acted their improper
persecution.*

*But into what a condition shall we be brought (I
hope not into an high* Commission *nor* Inquisition
Court)*

Court) *if this* Imprimator *goes on, that none fhall fpeak, no not fo much as fuffered to defire to fpeak, though they are great with Childe with the Man Chrift Jefus:* But I hope the People will fee their Liberties, and your felves know this was not the true Apoftles practifes.

2. Your fad quenching of the Spirit when the motion of it arofe in any for Soul-fatisfaction in any to fpeak, you would not fuffer them to be expreffed but ftifle them in their coming forth : O dear Friends confider, you would not be fo dealt with : For what did you know but [74] the Lord might bring forth from any of the Auditors for witneffing his Eternal Truth and Glory? therefore as your Heavenly Mafter is bountifully free, be not you Niggards in fhutting up his Bounties and fuffring none to pafs but through your own Purfes : I fpeak as the Apoftle did after the manner of men.

Quenching of the Spirit

3. Your Indecorum Behaviours both in words and geftures unto your elder Fellow-Servants & aged Father complaining as not performing your duty as young men according unto Rule of honouring gray hairs

The infulting Spirit of the Quakers

1. But by unfeemly fmiles of Derifion, faying often (for a time) *Thou old Man, thou old Man,* thereby appearing to provoke to paffion :

2. When that would not move his exceeding great patience, then charging of him with Blafphemy, and to prove his Blafphemy :

3. Again (*not* Apoftle *or* Gofpel *like*) feeking and taking advantages againft the Aged, and contrary to Covenant by three or four baiting him at once, unto the confounding of his memory, or ftopping of his utterance,

                                                            under

under the pretence of challenging all comers (when reasons considers of coming in Order) But your defence was that you were but one Man, then you should have been but one Mouth.

Again your improper charging of the complainant with mispending of time, when in Truth it was your selves (in not suffering of him orderly to proceed) But by your often Iterations, Tautologies, Indecorum Behaviours and Expressions, with improper Preachments at that time, and yet lay the defect upon the aged, and would not be satisfied with his substantial Proofs, divine Reasons and Argumental Demonstrations. And herein your Conscience (if unsatisfied) had liberty in timely Order, to have made your substantial Defence, if patience had been suffered to have had her perfect work. It is acknowledged by Auditors, that as the Complainant brought substantial proof (for so far as he proceeded) so you the Defendants also brought substantial defence (in what was substantial) but now who shall judge? ye will not suffer the Gospel rule, that the standers by, the Spirits of the Prophets shall judge. Then both of your own private Interpretations doth aim to be judges, and so will be endless and true judgeless: And by proceedings, the cause of Christ Jesus (being now at stake) much dishonoured unto the sadness of my Soul and unsatisfied Conscience, and also the expectation of the Auditors which was for Soul-edification frustrated, and unto publick shame (as yet) only self contendings hath the supream Appearance. Therefore (Loving Friends) [75] pleading and defending for your Lord and Masters sake, shew your selves faithful Servants of Christ Jesus in all Humility, self-denial,

The true cause of our long discourse at Newport

self-denial, Love, Charity, Tenderness, in bowels of
compaffion, in Gofpel Peace and Unity : only unto
your Mafters praife and Glory : that the Auditors
may receive the plain naked Truth of the Lord Je-
fus unto their Souls Edification, even the real Truth
as it in Jefus, and not as words of man which is only
Vanity and vexation of Spirit under the Sun *of*
eternal and univerfal Righteoufnefs, *whofe infinite*
glory is witneffed by

Robert Willams.

Newport Auguft. 6.
  1 6 7 2.

THis was that poor Letter (condemned unheard
by thefe high Saints who now keep Judgement day) to the fire and everlafting filence : this
was the two edged Sword which fmote in the hon- *The*
eft upright intentions of the Author every way *modefty of*
reproving me, reproving them, and yet having fo *this letter*
much Sugar with his Vinegar and Honey with his
bitter Powder, that had it been unfeal'd and read
at *Newport*, or read at *Providence*, whofe tafte could
it have offended, but theirs only who like the men
of *China*, judge all the World to have no eyes but
themfelves excepting the Men of *Europe* to whom
they will grant one eye, and that is more then our
proud *Pharifees* will do to any that bow not down
to their moft groffe *Phylacteries*.

  But from this finger of God this providential
Letter appearing upon the Wall before us : I return
to the work of the day, which was the Difcuffion

and

and Probation (on my part) of the other five Proposals remaining.

I therefore (after the Letter was put up unread into my pocket) requested their Patience, while I produced my Proof of the third Position, which was, *viz.* [*That the Spirit by which they were acted was not the true Spirit of God:*] Tis true I had many things in my mind and memory) some of them I here express) but I was forced to pick and chuse and lay by : for I told them that according to my promise, and their expectation I would present them with the Substance of my proof of this Position in the compass of about a quarter of an hour.

The third Position against the Quakers spirit Discussed

76] I reminded them first of the nature of the Word Spirit in Latine *Spiritus,* in Greek *Pneuma,* in the Hebrew *Ruch* and *Ruach,* signifying sometimes *Breath,* sometimes *Wind,* and from thence applied unto God himself, unto Angels, unto Men, as denoting a spiritual, powerful, invisible fine Substance distinct from flesh and earthly Bodies: Hence God was said to be a Spirit, not properly but that his Being was pure, powerful, invisible, &c.

The word spirit

1, Whether God was properly a Spirit (as the Quaker affirmed) we had some controversie at *Providence* of which hereafter.)

2. Concerning Spirits, I observed two great Sects : 1 Those of the *Pharisees* (who were accounted the most Orthodox, Sound and right, holding such a Spiritual Substance in Angels and Spirits and a Resurrection. 2. The Sadduces which held neither Angel, nor Spirit, nor Resurrection, as at this day, &c. 3. It

3. It is clear there is a two-fold Spirit: 1. Holy and pure: such a Spirit is God himself, and the *The quality of Spirits* Holy Spirit proceeding from the Father by the Son, such are the Spirits of the Angels, the Spirits of Gods Children in part, and the Spirits of juft men made perfect (the *Quakers* fay here, we fay in the life coming.)

The other Spirit is a wicked Spirit, a lying and a murtherous Spirit in Sathan and his Children, yet often counterfeiting the Holy and pure Spirit, like the Oile and Ointment which God prefcribed and forbad the like of it to be made on pain of death. Therefore we are commanded not to believe every Spirit, but to try even the very Spirits, not only of men but of *Doctrines, Churches, Religions,* pretend- *All fpirits muft be tried* ing the Name of God, (as do the *Turks, Jews* and *Chriftians*) and of the Son of God, as do all the Antichrifts and Antichriftians extant.

4. The Holy Spirit of God (being the *feven Lambs of Fire, the feven Eyes, and feven Horns,* Rev. 5.) he is pleafed to work varioufly.

Firft in an ordinary way of Regeneration and Sanctification, &c. common to all the loweft and youngeft of Gods Children, (*John* 3. *that which is born of the Spirit is Spirit*) Hence we read of the Spirit of Prayer, and of Holinefs wrought in the Soul by the finger or power of God: fo that the knowledge of God, the fear, the love, the trufting to and in God, the calling upon God is natural to all Gods Children, *Gal.* 5. *Abba Father,* &c.

77] The fecond is extraordinary and 'immediate, fuch as was pour'd upon the Lord Jefus, *Ifai.* 11.

fuch

such as Chriſt breathed upon the *Apoſtles*, and by the *Apoſtles* hands upon others when they ſpake with *Tongues*, fortelling things to come, and penning the Holy Scriptures or Records, as did the Prophets of old, and the firſt Meſſengers the Apoſtles of Chriſt Jeſus.

I told them I had many things to ſay as to the falſe Spirits of the falſe Chriſts, and falſe Prophets, the Spirits of Devils as well as the Spirits of God (in the *Revelation*) and the three wayes of deceit mentioned, 1 *Theſſ.* 2. by Spirit, by Word, or by Letter: but I would contract my ſelf, I ſay that their Spirit by which they were acted was not Gods Spirit.

1. Becauſe the Holy Spirit of God was given *Gods Spirit* by means, but the *Quakers* pretended all along in *given by* G. *Fox* and other Books, that their Spirit was im- *Gods* mediate or without means: I ſaid in the 8*th* of the *means* *Romans* was a *Golden Chain* of *Gods Order* or *Method* of *Working* from *Predeſtination* to *Glorification* : In the 10*th.* to the *Romans* was a *Golden Chain* of the *Means appointed*, &c. How ſhall a Man be ſaved? *The Spirit* by calling upon God? How ſhall he call on him *of God* except he believe in him? how ſhall a Man be- *working by* lieve in him except he hear of him? how ſhall a *means* Man hear of him except ſome Preach? how ſhall a Man Preach except he be ſent, &c. Hence *Peter* Preaching Chriſt Jeſus to the firſt Converts, they were ſome thouſands brought to Chriſt, when they were pierced to the heart, and cried out *what ſhall we do? Peter* ſends them nor to a light within them, but bids them *Repent and be Baptized*, Act. 14.

14. *Paul* fo fpake that many believed, *Act*. 16. *The Qua-*
while *Paul* fpake the Lord opened *Lydias* heart : *kers at*
and I appealed to the Confciences of thofe called *appealed*
Quakers at *Newport* there prefent, whether in a *too pub-*
contradiction this Spirit they now profeffed, de- *lickly*
fcended immediately upon them from God (as they
fpake) or was not conveyed unto them by the Miniftry of the former Preaching *Quakers* that came
unto them : fo that thefe now are but the waterers
and confirmers of this Doctrine of the Spirit in
them.

2. As Believing and Converfion comes by hearing, &c. fo thefe extraordinary gifts and powrings
forth of Gods Spirits was generally by means alfo :
Chrift ufed Breathing upon the *Apoftles :* the Spirit
of God defcended, *Act*. 8. 19. in the laying on of
hands : in *Peters* Preaching, *Acts*. 10. the miraculous Spirit of [78] *Tongues* and *Prophecy* defcended
upon *Cornelius* and his company, and not before,
yea, and what is that waiting in filence ufed in private, and in the publick Affemblies of the *Quakers*,
but a confeffed means in which they wait for the
Spirit of God (as poor Souls they think) defcending
on them.

I was then forced to omit the *Allegations* out of
G. *Fox* his book then by me and ready, but I will
now recite a few of them.

In page 6. of this Book in Folio, G. *Fox* brings *Samuel*
in *Samuel Eaton* faying [*The Prophets and Apoftles* *Eaton*
drew people to an outward Word] He Anfwers, Now
is that which lives and endures forever, outward ?

and

and did not they bring them to Chriſt the power of God, which is the end of words which is immediate.

Again in the ſame Page *Samuel Eaton* [*Is not the Goſpel an External way*] He Anſwers *No*, the Goſpel is a Living way which is revealed within, and is the power of God to Salvation.

In the ſame Page *Samuel Eaton* [*Are not they ſeduced who are drawn off from the External means by which the Spirit is given and Faith wrought, to wait for the receiving of the Spirit without any Word to convey it to them, which Spirit when they have it is not the Spirit of Truth but of deluſion*] For Anſwer, [The Spirit and Faith is not conveyed to any Man without the Word, and they are ſeduced which reſts in the *External* from the Eternal, and the Spirit is not given by Eternal means, neither is Faith wrought.]

I Reply, and obſerve how the wiſdome of Men is enmity againſt God, and how witty this *Fox* is to catch himſelf and others in the Traps of eternal Howling? how doth he here confound the audible words or preachings of Gods mercy in Chriſt Jeſus, with the inaudible, inviſible, myſtical and metaphorical word, Chriſt Jeſus himſelf.

2. Who ſees not his groſs and impudent denying of the *Spirit* and *Faith* to be conveyed by means from God unto us.

In Page 15. *G. F.* brings in *Henoch Howet* ſaying [*There is nothing in Man to be miniſtred to but man*] He Anſwers, How then miniſtred the Apoſtle to the Spirit? and Chriſt ſpake to the Spirits in Priſon : and

Henoch
Ho vet

and *Tim.* was to ftir up the Gift that was in him and the Spirit of the Father fpeaks within them : and the Light fhines in the Heart : and the Son of God is revealed in me faith the *Apoftle* : that which may be known of God is manifeft in man, for God hath fhewed it unto them, *Rom.* 1. and the *Apoftle* was [79] manifeft to every ones Confcience in the fight of God, and that was of God which the Children difobeyed.

I Reply, 1. (As in his late Book exalting his *Heathen Light* above the *Holy Scriptures*) he fimply and prophanely joyns the *Philiftian Priefts,* and *Egyptian Conjurers* with *Holy Job* and his Friends, &c. fo here he confounds and jumbles together the natural powers and faculties and *Humane Light* in all Mankinde with the Grace and Spirit of God both ordinary and extraordinary as may be feen at the firft view.

2. His Scope is (abominably and horribly,) to make the holy Spirit of God capable of being preached unto, to be converted and turned unto God, yea to refufe and be damned, for it is not *Man* he faith that is preached unto.

3. How *Sottifh* and *Blind* doth this *Deceiver* proclaim himfelf in the *Chriftian Doctrines* of Preaching, *Converfion, Faith* and the *Grace* and *Spirit of* God confounding *Gold* and *Droffe, Pearls* and *Pebbles, Harps* and *Harrows* (as all one) altogether. *G. Fox ignorant of the true fpirit of God*

In Page 136, 137. He brings in *Thomas Moor,* faying [*Nor are we to wait for a further Revelation to be given forth then the Scripture for the Word of God came not firft immediately to the Gentiles but to* *Tho. Moor.*

the

the Apoſtles:] He Anſwers, The Apoſtles that Preached the Word of God, it was immediate to whomſoever they preached it, for they had read it immediately, for the Word it ſelf is immediate with more that follows to the ſame ſenceleſs and abſurd purpoſe.

Reply, As if all that receive *G. Fox* his Book ſimply pretended to be from the Spirit of God re-
The uſe of ceive it without *G. Fox* his *Brain* and *Hand,* and
means Pen or *Paper, Printing* and *Letters* : or becauſe a King delivers his minde to his Secretary, and commands him to *Pen it* in a *Proclamation, Declaration,* &c. therefore the Kings Word or Will comes to every man immediately without any ſuch means, as the Secretaries compoſing his *Clarks* Tranſcribing, the uſe of *Printing, Letters, Paper, &c.* to talke after this ſort, what is it but to talk Frantick and Bedlam, and without the guidance of a common rational Spirit.

In Page 5. he brings in *Samuel Eaton,* ſaying [*Though all the Saints have the Spirit of Chriſt dwelling in them, which is Eternal and Infallible, yet that this Spirit ſhould do all which Saints do, and ſhould ſay all that Saints ſay, and ſhould judge for them, both perſons* [80] *and things after an infallible manner, and*
Fox and *that they ſhould neither ſay nor do any thing by any*
the Qua- *underſtanding of their own but the Spirit*: *all this we*
kers above *deny*] He Anſwers, [Which is contrary to the Apoſ-
all Kings tle, who ſaith, as many as are the Sons of God are
and led by the Spirit of God : and Chriſt acts all in
Princes, them and for them : and the fruits of the Spirit,
Popes & &c. and the Spiritual man judgeth all things : And
Emperors
Saints and
Angels that

that is it which leads the Saints to divide and dis-
cerne all things both temporal and spiritual; the
spiritual Wisdome of God which gives them a
spiritual understanding, which men must rule
withal, but not with their own which comes to
nought : and you that have not that which is infallible to judge in you, know not the Spirit of
Christ, neither can you judge of persons or things
that have not the infallible judgement, nor have
the Spiritual man : neither have you the Word of
God in your hearts, nor Christ which is eternal
and infallible all which the *Quakers* have to judge
persons and things.]

I Reply, *Mahomet* the *Grand Segnior*, or *Elder*,
and *Prophet* transcending *Moses* and *Christ* (as he
and his followers *Mahumetans* say) he pretended *The Ma-*
that he had the mind of God by immediate Reve- *humetans*
lation, and that by Revelation of the *Holy Spirit* *& Qua-*
kers con-
in the shape of a *Dove*, he wrote the Minde, the *sidered and*
Word or Scriptures of God the *Alcoran* : But poor *found one*
silly Souls were *Mahomet* and all his Disciples compared with the *Seraphical Doctors*, the *Foxians*, who
neither say nor do any thing with any understanding of their own, but the immediate and infallible
Spirit of God says and does all in them : who are
fit to be Kings and Princes, Governours and Judges,
Masters of Ships and Families, &c. indeed of any
place of power or trust, but these walking *Gods*,
and *Christs*, and *Spirits*, even the meanest of the
Quakers ? May not the meanest Youth or Wench, *The Qua-*
if but a pretended *Quaker* (according to this rule or *kers Gods*
rate of being immediately inspired in all they do *upon Earth*
or

or say) transcend all other *Teachers, Translators, Interpreters, Kings* and *Counsellors, Navigators, Histori-
ans, Geographers, Rulers* and *Judges,* &c.   It is true
that *Thomas Munster* and *Becold,* and *Knipperdoling,*
and *Fifer* pretending immediate *Revelations,* and so
have other Leaders of these *Nicolaitans* in *France*
and *England,* &c. but none were so large and open
hearted as to communicate so freely and bountifully to all their followers, the immediate Inspirations of their pretended holy spirit, as these [81]
foolish and filthy Dreamers do: for so saith *Fox*
[*All the Quakers say or do is by the infallible and
eternal Spirit*] but how horribly their Spirits, Principles, Divisions, Miscarriages (in many sinful practises) and Apostacies amongst themselves give the lye
and contradict this their infallibility is notoriously
proclaimed on the house top: and I may say something more to this Head afterward.

   At present I return to my *Antagonists,* who (while
I was Arguing against their immediate Spirit) could
not hold until my quarter of an hour, and this Head
The lead-
ing of the
Spirits
debated. (about their Spirit) was finished but brake silence,
and they said (*especially John Stubs*) doth not the
Scripture say, if any man have not the Spirit of
Christ he is none of his: And as many as are led
by the Spirit of God they are the Sons of God, and
ye have an unction, and need not that any man teach
you, and you know all things?

   I then answered that there was a leading of a
Beast by an *Halter* or *Bridle,* and there was a leading of a Man with a *Reason* when his understanding and judgement is satisfied, and if so, I presumed
                                                    they

they intended, that the leading of the Spirit did
not lead them as *Beafts*, but as Rational, fatisfying
their Reafons and Judgements : and if fo Reafon
grants that there are falfe Spirits, lying Prophets,
Seducers and Deceivers, &c. *Reafon* therefore further faith, that every Soul muft be fatisfied, whether this *Leading*, or *Anointing*, or *Teaching of the
Spirit* be by means of *Praying, Preaching, Reading,*
Meditating, Conferring, &c. or immediate without
the ufe of thefe : if motions without the ufe of
thefe be pretended *Reafons* tells us that a *Rational
Soul* muft be able to try whether the Spirit pretending to be a true or lying Spirit, and that it
muft have fome *Rule* or *Touch-ftone* to make their
Tryal by, that the Rule muft be my own Reafon,
or fome Teftimony of unqueftionable Witneffes
fatisfying my Reafon, or fome heavenly infpired
Scripture or Writing which my Reafon tells me
came from God : *Reafon* alfo tells each rational
creature, that it is very fufpicious to be a falfe, lying
and develifh motion, which flights the *Holy Scripture* and other holy means wherein the *Holy Spirit,
Prefence* and *Power of God* hath appeared to Gods
People formerly Reafon tells me, that if I finde
my felf weak (as who doth not) to fight againft the
Devil (the roaring Lion and old Serpent) and I am
bound to feek out for help, and what help more
powerful [82] and proper then that of the eternal
and all powerful Father of Spirits : and that it is
beft to take *James* his *Counfel*, if any Man wants
wifdome let him ask of God who gives to all Men
liberally and upbraideth not : if fo, then *Reafon*
tells

*The tryal
of Revela-
tions*

*Reafon
fanctified
and rightly
improved*

tells us, that except we fuffer our felves to be led as *Beafts* by *Sathan* (as the poor *Quakers* are) we muft come to the ufe of Means, or a mediate leading and teaching, and then what is become of thefe hellifh fancies of only immediate *Teachings* and *Infpirations?*

I told them that befide this *Counfel* and *Command* of God in *James,* the Lord Jefus tells us by an admirable fimilie, *that the holy Spirit of God is given in the ufe of means,* Luk. 11. *If you who are evil give good gifts unto your Children, how much more fhall your heavenly Father give the holy Spirit to them that ask him?* and that is *Ifa.* 11. the Spirit of Wifdome, the Spirit of Knowledge, the fear of the Lord and all the Graces of the holy Spirit. It is clear that the Pen-men and holy Scribes of Gods will unto us (in whom God did fpeak, and by whom he wrote immediately and infallibly thofe blefled chofen pens of his were not infallibly guided by an immediate Spirit in all that they faid and did about this Scripture, as thefe poor *Dreamers* fay of themfelves, and therefore muft necefiarily dafh againft the *Holy Scriptures,* and all holy means formerly ufed by the firft Chriftians, yea and all rational means to pieces; for all that they fay or do is the immediate Spirit, and Chrift and God himfelf as *Fox* here affirmeth.

I anfwered further, that if that *Scripture* alleadged by *John Stubs* [*To know all things*] be to be expounded litterally, and (as *G. Fox* in this Book) *viz.* that the Saints know all things as God, then why are not the *Quakers Omnipotent* and *Almighty*

The Spirit gotten of prayer

The Quakers Spirit

The omnifciency of the Quakers

Almighty as well as *Omniscient* : yea as it is said of the
Pope, if he can deliver all Souls out of *Purgatory*
(if he please) without *Money*, surely he is very inhumane, impious and cruel that he doth not : so I
said what impiety is it, what cruelty and inhumanity is it in the *Quakers* said I, so infallibly knowing
all things as God, not to reveal unto Men, and
especially in their publick Assemblies so many
deep points of the Godhead, of Creation of the
Holy Three in Heaven and Earth, (which they con-
fess) and all the deep Mysteries and Prophecies in
the *Holy Scripture* especially in *John* and *Daniel*
their *Revelations*, &c. the *Most Holy*, *Omniscient*,
and *Eternal Jehovah* knows that the *Pope* and his
Purgatory, the *Quakers* and [83] their *Omnisciency*
are but *Childrens* and *Frantick Persons Dreams* and
Phantasies, and that the Saints knowing all things
is the same with their doing all things through
Chrift which strengtheneth them that is not all
things litterally, (for that were ridiculous and blafphemous to affirm it) but all things *figuratively* and
Comparatively, which his holy Wisdome thinks fit
to require them to know and do in order to his
Glory and their *Salvation*.

But *John Stubs* insisted how they knew the *Mystical number* of 1260 dayes, the 42 Months, the *Time
and Times* and *half a Time*, and that the *Woman* was
come and coming out of the *Wilderness* in them,
and that now they were *Preaching* the *Everlasting
Gospel* to them that dwell upon the Earth.

I Replied, it is notorious how many excellent
men have been bewildred, and missed in the opening

ing of thefe *Myfteries*. I faid that if their infallible and their all-knowing *Light* could open all
things and was now the *Everlafting Gofpel* or *Glad
News*, the Word *Eternal, &c.* and that it was not
only in the *Quakers* and their *Saints*, but in all
Mankind, I defired to know what they meant by
this Word within, whether they meant in the underftanding (the eye of the Soul) or in the Will, or
in the Memory, or in the Affections, or in all of
thefe joyntly : for Light is only feen with the Eye,
not with the Tongue, nor Ear, nor Hand : it is
true in the 2 *Cor.* 4. it is faid; *that God hath fhined in
our Hearts*, but there the heart muft be underftood
the Underftanding the Minde which is properly
and nextly the feat of the Light and Knowledge
of God, and this fhining (though *Fox* make it to
be natural or born with every Man) is faid to be by
Pauls Preaching as is there abundantly proved
where it is as clear as the Noon day fhining, that
God fhined, Chrift fhined, and *Paul fhined* before the
Light or *Notice* of the glad news of a Saviour come
to the heart or ears of poor Sinners, and fo thereby
are turned from their natural hellifh *Darknefs* to a
Supernatural Heavenly Light.

Who knows not (with *Jeremiah*) the heart of
Man to be naturally dark, deceitful, defperately
evil and wicked, & *Gen.* 6. the imaginations of the
heart of all men to be *only Evil* and that *continually,*
and that it may be faid of all men (as it is faid of
the holy God, in him is Light and no Darknefs fo)
in them is *Darknefs* and no *Light,* fo that to
hearken to, to turn to, to liften to any voice or
motion

The Light within.

*2 Cor. 4
God hath
fhined in
our hearts*

*The dark-
nefs
within*

motion within in heavenly things, in matters of
fupor- [84] natural light, is as proper as in matters
of law to go for Counfel to a cheating thief or
rogue, in matters of health, to a known cheating
Mountebank, as to turn within to a mans heart
which was the arranteft *Jugler* and *Cheater* in the
world.

At this word *W. Edmundfon* cryed out, *Blafphemy, He fpeaks Blafphemy.* I conceived he meant I
called their *immediate holy fpirit* which they pretend
to, the arranteft *Jugler & Cheater* in the world: *An Evidence that*
My heart was warm, and my tongue breaking *the Qua-*
filence, and longing to fhew him his willing mif- *kers fpirit*
take, and that I mentioned not nor thought of the *and a deceitful*
Holy Spirit, but every mans own deceitful heart *Heart are*
(though clearly I have thought and proved their *one*
holy Spirit is no other but Sathan himfelf and every
Mans own deceitful Heart: but I was prevented,
for fome of the Auditory fpake aloud that he miftook me, and amongft others our *Deputy Governour* *The teftimony of*
Capt. *Cranfton* openly faid that *W. Edmundfon* mif- *the Deputy*
took me, for I exprefly faid that the *Heart* of man *Governour*
was the arranteft *Jugler & Cheater* in the world. *Cvpt.
Cranfton*

This did not fatisfie *W. Edmundfon,* but he re- *and others*
plied, let the words be read then by him that took *againft W.*
them in fhort-hand: fo they cal'd upon one of *E. flander-
ous rafh-*
theirs to read what he wrote: now I knowing *nefs,*
what fhort-hand could doe as well as moft in *England* from my *Childhood,* and that it is impoffible for
any to write *Verbatim* fo faft as I then fpake with
vehemency, I concluded he had not exactly my
words: yet I am confident in a faction and partiality
he

he feemed to read fome words favouring my calling their *fpirit* the arranteft *Jugler and Cheater* in
the word, extreamly contary to my certain knowledg of my intentions, and of what I uttered, befide
the fndden and quick exception of our Deputy
Governour and others: but alas this was a fmall
bufinefs: but I was about to fay (as before I did fay)
from the holy Scripture *Pro.* 28.   *He that trufteth*
to his own heart is a fool, and till a fpirit of Regeneration and Converfion change the heart of man,
there is no other *Chrift* nor *Spirit* within, but the
fpirit of Sathan, which is the fpirit by which the
Quakers are acted, and is the arranteft *Jugler* &

The great *Cheater* in the world: This *Jugler* is fo cunning
Cheater that he out-jugles the *Juglers,* he catcheth the
who cheats craftieft foxes that catch fo many others, he takes
all Cheat- Captive and leads away in chains the *Wife* and
ers. *Prudent,* the High and Mighty, til the holy *Spirit*
of Chrift Jefus difcover and break his fnares and
lead him Captive alfo.

The great 85] 2.   I was adding another Argument from *Ifai.*
Magna 59. and I did mention the place where the great pro-
Charta xi mife, *Grant* or *Charter* is given by God the Father
Ifa. 59. to *Chrift Jefus* and his Pofterity, *viz.* that his word
and his Spirit fhould be in Chrifts mouth, and in
the mouth of his *Seed,* and in the mouth of his
Seeds Seed from thenceforth and for ever.

I faid that that bleffed *Son of God* and *Son of*
Man the man Chrift Jefus, lived and dyed a *Batche-*
lour, he never had any natural *Seed* or *Iffue*: Be-
lievers are his *Offpring, his Seed,* his *Children* and
Grand-Children and fo downward to as many as the
Lord

Lord fhall call. And that *Fox* fhould not fay the *The true Seed.*
Word and the Spirit are all one (as commonly G.
Fox doth) and that the Father and the Son are one
without Diftinction (as boldly and Babilonically he
doth) Here is (moft diftinctly and exactly diftinguifhing) 1 The *Father promifing.* 2. The Son
the *Mediator* receiving this Promife. 3. The
Promife it felf, which is of a *Word* to the Son
(though that bleffed Son is alfo called the Word)
viz. of the revealed Doctrine, Will and Mind of
God recorded from and by the holy Scriptures, *viz.*
that this Word fhould be in his mouth and in the
mouth of all his *Seed,* or *Chriftian Children* after
him, efpecially his *Meffengers* and *Preachers* to the
end and Confummation of all things.

I told them it was notorioufly known how they
flighted this holy *Charter,* how they joyned not
the holy *Word* and *Spirit* together but trod upon
the *Word of God* under a cloak of advancing the
Spirit, *&c.* But of this I fhall fpeak in the next
Pofition following.

I was alfo mentioning a *third Argument* againft
their fpirit from the *Irrationallity* and Unrulinefs of
it, contrary to the *Wifdome* and *Rationallity* and
Order and *Holinefs* of the holy *Spirit of God*: this
is apparent from their bitter *Reviling,* and often
fencelefs and frantick *Reviling* in fome of them,
Devil, Devil, Devil The devillifh *Inquifitors, Monks* *The rail-ng fpirit of the Quakers.*
and *Fryers, &c.* exceed them not in fpattering
out *Diablo, Diablo* againft fuch as dare to oppofe them: indeed they are both *Poffeffed* by one
fpirit of blafphemous *Railing* and *Reviling* againft
the

that Writings of the *Old Teſtament* and the *Papiſts* owned both old and new but it is known that in many particulars they do in effect deny and damn them. 1. They both ſet up their rotten *Traditions*, their unwritten *Verityes* (as they ſpeak) of equal authority with, if not (in caſes) above the *holy Scripture.*

The Jews and Papiſts and Qua-kers all of them in effect deny the holy Scriptures.

2. They ſet up the Papiſts by the authority of the Council of *Trent,* a moſt defective *Tranſlation,* notoriouſly falſe in many places all over above the firſt Copyes of the *Hebrew* and *Greek* whence all *Tranſlations* as *Counterpanes* and ſecondary Copyes or *Duplicates* ought to flow.

3. The Papiſts ſet up the *Pope* as the only in-fallible Judg & Interpreter in all *Queſtions* about the *Scriptures* and the Jews make their *Rabbies* as ſo many *Popes* alſo.

4. Their *Interpretations* are ſo forraign and ſtrange and many of them ſo abſurd & mon-ſtrous from the genuine & proper Sence of the Scriptures, and adulterated with *Wreſting and alle-gorizings &c.* that is truly ſaid of them that they bring not their *Doctrines, Diſciplines* and *Converſa-tions* to the *Scriptures* but force the [89] holy *Scrip-tures* of God to attend and wait upon their Abomi-nation as a Negro Slave and Lacquey.

I ſaid the Jews and Papiſts did not more diſowne the holy *Scriptures* upon the account of their *Popes and Traditions* and Interpretations than the Quakers did upon the account of their *Light* and *Spirit* and *Interpretations* alſo. Who knows not that in the beginning of their Profeſſion, they generally fell from

The Qua-kers ſlight-ing the holy Scriptures

from the reading of them by themselves or in their *in many horrible* Families, or in their *Publick Assemblyes*, only crying *Particulars.* up the *Light within, the Spirit within, the Scriptures within, their Teacher within.* They ftil say *The Scripture was not the Word of God, the Scripture is but a dead Letter,* they have no need of *Paper-Teachers* having the spirit that gave it forth? Yea as the Papifts say, if the Scriptures were loft and burnt out of the world, the *spirit* within them could give new *Scriptures.*

Tis true the *Quakers* in this Difpute profeffed to *A diffembling Show of Quakers refpecting the Scriptures.* be tryed by the *Scriptures,* which the firft *Quakers* among us wholly denied, but only by the *Spirit* within them: But what avails this *Confeffion*? Is it not but a fubtle trick of *Equivocation,* when ftil they profefs to owne *G. Fox* all along, and he profeffeth the Soules of all men to be a part of God and the divine Effence, and that their is no diftinction between *God, Chrift, and Spirit* and *themfelves*; what fhould hinder but that the Scripture is but a *dead Letter,* and (compared with their fpirit) a weak and needlefs *Paper* unto them that hath fuch a *light* and *Spirit* within to guide them?

I told them before and now that there was an *Irifh Papift* in the late warrs that fpoke the very *An Irifh Papift confeffing the Truth.* heart and foul of *Jews, Papifts* and *Common Proteftants,* and the *Quakers* themfelves, as to the holy Scriptures. In plundering and rifling a *Proteftants* houfe he found a Bible and flung it in the Kennel, and kickt and trod upon it faying, *The plague of God take this Book, it is the caufe of all thefe Quarrels.*

My Oppofite faid they owned the *Scriptures* in
their

their place as a *Declaration* of the Saints Conditions, & *John Burnet* took a *Bible* and read publickly that Paſſage in *Luke* 1. where *Luke* calls his Writing a *Declaration*. I urged that this will of God. (for this *Declaration* of what Chriſt ſaid and did, and of all the reſt of the Scripture, was a *Declaration and Revelation* of *Gods* Will to his People and to the whole World) this written and revealed [90] will of God I ſaid was the Judge and Decider of all Queſtions, the tryer of all *Spirits*, all *Religions*, all *Churches*, all *Doctrines*, all *Opinions*, all *Actions*. They anſwered they did owne the *Scriptures*, and would be tryed by the *Scriptures* (which is a new trick, meaning according to their own not to be queſtioned *Interpretations*) I urged that they ſet up their Spirit above the Scriptures, (fathering all their Revilings Curſings and Abominations upon the holy Spirit) I asked whether they owned the Scripture as the ſquare Rule or Guide according to whoſe ſentence all the Knowledge of God and of our ſelves, the Knowledge of Gods Worſhip and Service and our own Bleſſedneſs and Salvation was to be determined, yea and the Spirit within them to be tryed, determined, approved and condemned alſo.

The Scriptures miraculouſly preſervd to be Gods ſtanding outward Record & witneſs.

They ſtill fled to this *Burrough*, the Spirit that gave forth *Scripture* is greater then the *Scripture :* the ſpirit is in us, that Spirit only opens the Scripture *:* the Spirit is immediate and infallible and they only who have this Spirit know the Scriptures. I anſwered that I maintained the inward breathing of the holy *Spirit* more than themſelves, for

for I quoted before *Luke* 11. *viz.* that we ought in all our *Preachings, Hearings, Readings, Prayings, &c.* to beg the help of the *Spirit* called the Finger and Power of God: and yet I also maintained that this Record, this Word Will or Mind of God written and pen'd by chosen Pen-men as Pens in the hand of his holy Spirit, and so miraculously preserved from the Rage of the Devils fiery Instruments, *Babilonian, Assyrian, Romane* and *Popish Tyrants* and that much among the Jewes and Papists (and much by their meanes also though they hate it) I say this Record is the outward and external *Light, Lanthorn, Judge, Guide, Rule* by which God witnesseth himself and his Truth in the World, comforteth and feedeth his saints in their Dispersions, discovers and reforms the defects and wanderings of his People (as in *Josiah* his finding this Record, and *Ezekiel & John* eating the Book, out of which the holy Spirit inspired them to prophesie to Kings and Peoples *&c.*

Tis true who doubts it but that God and the Spirit were before the Scriptures, and so he was before the Creation, before Christ Jesus was born, and his Redemption actually accomplished: are the works of God therefore, and the several Dispensations and Institutions and Instruments of God in their several times and [91] places of any whit less power or esteem because the most holy *God* and his most holy Spirit were before them? *John the Baptist* saith that Christ Jesus was preferred before him, for he was before him and he was not worthy to unloose the Shoe-latchet of Jesus the *Lamb* of God;

God; and yet for the fulfilling of all Righteousness the *Lord Jesus* must come to *John* to be baptized of him, and the holy *Spirit* of *Light* will declare himself to be true by the holy *Scriptures*, and discover all other Spirits to be spurious false and Bastards and notwithstanding their cracking and prating of Light if they slight this outward standing *Record* and Witness of God in the World it is because there is no light in them,

One of these two must be done either we must subscribe to the *Papists* and by their pretended *The holy* Spirit and Church find out and authorize the Scrip-*Scripture* tures, just as the *Foxians* say, or else we must with *the only* *Luther* and his Associates, *Calvin* and his followers *outward* maintain Learning study the Scriptures, search the *standing* Originals, Copyes and Translations, and vindicate *Rule &* their Purity and *Perfection*, their Authority and *Record* *like the* sole external Direction how to judge of all pre-*Records in* tending *Christs and Prophets* and *Doctrines & Churches* *the Tower* and Spirits.

The Holy While we were thus discoursing *W. Edmundson* *Scriptures* propounded this Similitude, if I should write a letter *are Gods* to a friend and subscribe my name *W. Edmundson*, *Love-let-* doth it follow therefore that the Letter is *W. Ed-* *ters* *mundsons?* I answer that the Quakers do affirm that the Scripture is within them, what is the english of that? but that the Light which they and every man in the World hath within them (the Christ the Spirit which every one hath) is Scripture, and in a sence I said it was a Truth that *W. E.* his letter to his friend was *W. Edm.* not only a *Declaration* of his word, mind or will to his Friend, but

but in a refpect his mind and will it felf that he
fent in Writing to his Friend, and fo the Scripture
in a Sence is Gods mind and Will to us.

Upon this occafion I told them that the Scriptures were the *Love Letters of Chrift Jefus* to his
Church, as the *Love-Letters* of fome mighty *Monarch* to his Betrothed Queen or Empress, they are
dear, not as common *Paper* and *Ink*, but as the
Good-Will, the deareft Love and heart of the King
and Emperour himfelf: and thus are holy *Scriptures* highly prized and embraced, and laid up in
the heart and bofome of the true *Children of God*,
92 | believed liftned to, and followed as the voice of
Chrift Jefus to his true fheep and Spoufe: the
Baftard Children and the *Wolves* covered only with
the *fheepskins*: they have other *Words, Letters* &
Spirits, 2 *Thef.* 2. whatever they prate of Scripture,
and fpeak brave fwelling empty words as *Jude*
fpeaketh.

Tis true as *G. Fox* all along in his Book vapours
that the Spirit was before Scripture, and gave forth
Scripture: but I proved before, that their Spirit,
their Light, their Chrift, were but hellifh *Darknefs*, the fpirit of Sathan, and a falfe lying Chrift,
&c. 2. The Difpenfations of God were many and
divers (as before the Law and after (but in this laft
and third difpenfation, he hath fpoken (that is his
word, mind and will whatever) the *Quakers* as well
childifhly as Blafphemoufly prate to the contrary *The admirable ex-*
by his Son: And as the Son himfelf the Lord Je- *cellency of*
fus in his own perfon, when he perfonally main- *the Scrip-*
tained that famous combat with the Devil ufed no *ture*

other

other weapon but Prayer and Fasting and the Holy
Scripture, so he left written this holy patern and
example, that we through Patience and Comfort
of the Scriptures might have hope, *Rom.* 14. *Lu-*

ther being demanded how he gain'd such knowledge and abilities in such blind *Popish darkness*, he
freely confessed that the holy Scripture was his
first help, the second Meditation, the third earnest
Prayer to God to vouchsafe his Spirit to bless the
two former unto him. The Lord Jesus therefore
not only ordained his Messenger or Preachers of

his glad Tydings to *Jews* and *Gentiles,* but his Pen-
men also, *Joh.* 20. for those two great ends (as to
us) to wit,

1. These things are written that you may believe
that Jesus is the Christ (to wit, that that individual
person and man called Jesus was the *Christ*, the
Messiah so long promised and expected (contrary to
the Blasphemous Fancies of the *Quakers.*)

And 2. That Believing in him (that individual
person called Jesus, and not in a Fancy within) we
might have Life and Blessedness.

It is no wonder therefore, that the *Devil* (the
great *Thief*) as he compasseth Sea and Land with
the *Pharisees, Jesuites* and *Quakers* to make *Prose-
lytes,* so wherever he comes he labours to blow out
the *Candle of the Holy Scripture.*

It is the Spirit Breath or wind of the *Devil* in
the lips of *Atheists, Jews, Papists, Quakers, Ranters,*
&c. that puffs and blows |93] against this Holy
Light (more precious infinitely then the Sun in the
Heaven :) it hath been most wonderfully to amazement,

ment preserved like the Sun in the Firmanent, and shines most gloriously again and again, after the blackest and longest storm and night of *Apostacies* and *Persecution*.

The *Turkish History* tells us of a Woman appearing in the Heavens with a Book open in her hand, some of their *Mahumetan Priests* dared to say (for which one greatly suffered) that the Woman was the Christian Church, and the *Book* was their *Bible* or *Scriptures* which threatned ruine to their *Mahomet* and *Alcoran*: *John* was not commanded (and in him the *Protestant Witnesses*) to stand still and listen to a Light, to a motion or voice within, but to eat up the little Book open (once again) in the hands of Christ Jesus, *Rev.* 10. and after this eaten up to prophesie to *Peoples* and *Nations*, to *Tongues* and *Kings*. *A famous vision in Turkey*

Whether this Book be the Book of the *Revelation* or the Book of the whole Bible or Scripture, it is apparent that during the 42 Months of the *Papal Reign* and *Darkness*, *Christ Jesus* hath given Authority and power to his Witnesses to search after the Holy Records in the *Original, Hebrew and Greek* Copies, and to bring them forth by Translating and Preaching the Doctrine of them, &c. for which they have suffered Death and Burning, as *Tindal* and many other excellent men of God. The Walls of *Rome*, yea the Gates of *Hell* have shaken and felt the might of this *Heavenly Artillery*: It lies therefore the Devil and all his *The two Witnesses eat up the book of Script.* *Tindal the first heavenly Translator burned*

Messengers

Meſſengers in hand to break to pieces, or to nail up their[1] heavenly Ordinance.

The Jews
outward
reverence
to the
Script.

It hath been obſerved that there never were any (more than others) famous for Chriſtanity, but they firſt were famous for an admirable Love kindled by God in their Hearts to the *Holy Scriptures* : It is true the *Jews* (to whom the Oracles of God were committed, *to wit* in the *Old Teſtament* : how ſtudious have they been in it, even to every Word, and Letter? they accounted it a crime for any Book to ly upon it, but this alwayes to lye uppermoſt. My ſelf have ſeen the *Old Teſtament* of the *Jews* moſt curious writing whoſe price (in way of trade) was threeſcore pound, which my Brother a *Turkey-Merchant* had and ſhewed me : But I ſpeak of an inward love, a *Soul-love*, &c. It is wonderful what

The firſt
Proteſtants
aſſ ction
to the
Scripture

Luther relates of that bleſſed *Duke of Saxony*, whom [94] God ſtir'd up to favour and cheriſh *Luther*, &c *viz.* that he cauſed his ſix Pages each of them to read to him daily everyone his hour in the Holy Scripture. This was the affection in all the firſt Witneſſes the *Waldenſians, the Bohemians, the Engliſh, French, Dutch, Scotch*, &c. who together with the Scriptures had mighty Affection to the ſtudy of the *Hebrew* and *Greek* in which golden *Cups* and *Bowles* the *King of Kings* was pleaſed to convey the Wine (like *Ahaſhueroſh*) of his Eternal Majeſty and Goodneſs to us.

It is wonderful to conſider how much the ſtudy of the *Scriptures* and of the *Hebrew and Greek Tongues*

[1] "nail up this." *R. W. Ms. Ann.*

Tongues confounded and put to flight the *Papists*, and forced them to study the *Scriptures* and the *Tongues* also, both which the barbarous dark Spirit of the *Quakers* hate, as darkness hates the Light.

The Scriptures put both Papists & Quakers to flight

It is no wonder this Spirit of Lying cries out so fiercely against the Schools of Learning in *Old and New England*, it knows that the right and regular propagation of natural, of civil, and especially of *Divine Knowledge* scatters the thick Fogs of the *Quakers* affected hellish ignorance.

The blessed *Martyrs* and *Witnesses* of Jesus in all ages have been ravished with holy delights like *David* in the holy Scripture, in *Q. Maries* dayes, that famous *Ridley* (called *Bishop of London*) he had got most of the holy Epistles in *Greek* by heart, even before he left *Pembrook Hall in Cambridge*: and as the fire of persecution grew hotter, so did those blessed Witnesses (like Jesus with *Moses* and *Elias*, and *Paul at Troas*) spend hours and nights in Prayer and holy Conference upon the Scriptures, and those things which the Lord Jesus should and hath now accomplished according to the Scriptures.

Christs Martyrs or Witnesses love to Scriptures

It is true (in print) *James Parnel* spake like a *Papist* an *Atheist*, and a *Quaker* of the holy Martyrs or Witnesses of Jesus Christ, and of the book of Martyrs it self. It is no wonder that the most Righteous and jealous Lord left him not to dye the common death of all Mankinde, but to Murther himself by a proud presumptuous attempt of declaring himself to be Christ by fasting 40 dayes and 40 nights, I believe this to be a Truth from the Testimonies I have seen of *Parnels* case (being my

James Parnel his horrible sin & Judgment

self

felf then in *London*) whatever, *Fox* & the *Quakers* impudently affirm to the contrary.

95] It is true that *James Parnel*, and *Fox*, and all of them fometimes miferably (and after the Devils Method) make ufe of *Scripture* as a Shield or Buckler to fence themfelves againft the Scripture, and as a Sword to run through the Heart and Bowels of the Scripture, the Saints, and Chrift, and God himfelf: they make ufe of it as *Stirrops, and Ladders,* and *Scaffolds* for their counterfeit Chrift (in pretence but in reallity themfelves) to mount up into their *Saddles* and *Thrones of the Eternal power and Godhead* that fo the Earth may be theirs by Authority: So that as the Lord fpeaks of the *Jews Sacrifices* that they were not his: and of *Jehoiakim that he did not know the Lord,* Jer. 22. and of the *Corinthians,* 1 Cor. 11. *that they did not eat the Lords Supper* though *they did eat it*: fo I affirm (from all the premifes alleadged) the *Quakers* do not own, that is truely and Chriftianly (as they fay *Bonâ fide* and *in reality*) but flight, and villifie, and abominate, and nullifie the holy Scripture, that their unwritten Lies and lying Spirits may be exalted.

How the Quakers own Scripture

2. King. 17. the Samaritans feared the Lord and yet feared him not.

We have a great word in ufe amongft *Merchants* and others, to wit the word [*Effects*] they defire to fee *effects* of money or Goods, for want of a real and effectual prizing and loving & obeying and magnifying the *holy Scriptures.* The *Jewes* & *Pharifes,* the *Papifts and Quakers* do not owne the *perfection* & *Authority* of the holy Scriptures, but fet up their *Traditions and Popes Councils* &
Spirits

The word Effects

Spirits above them, and therefore the *Jewes & Pa-pisfts* and *Quakers* do not owne the holy *Scriptures.*

I freely acknowledge that many of thefe Particulars I could not then exprefs becaufe of my Confinement to a quarter of an hour, and fometimes the *Interpofure* of my *Oppofites.*

I remember I urged that dead and rotten efteem that both *Papifts* and *Quakers* fling as dirt in the face of the holy *Scriptures,* calling it *a dead Letter,* *a Nofe of wax, a leaden Rule* which may be pincht and bow'd to every mans Opinion : But *Firft,* They horribly bow and pinch that *holy Scripture,* 2. *Cor.* 3. which meddles not with all the *Scripture* but with the *Covenant* of the *Law* and *Juftice,* oppofite to the *Covenant* of *Grace & Mercy,* & calls the *Law a killing Letter* compar'd with the Grace & Mercy of an offended God now reconciled by *Chrift Jefus.*

The Papifts and Quakers call the holy Script. a dead Letter.

But *Secondly,* Thefe poor *Foxes* fly to their *Burroughs* and confound the matter of the *Scripture* or *Writing*; being Paper [96] and ink, &c. with the contents the purport, and (as I may fay) the matter contained in the matter : we ufe to fay what have you to fhew for it ? what evidences have you ? what Records, and fometimes when no Witneffes are living or can be had, an old poor Record is produced which proves the life and fpirit of the bufinefs : what *Simpletons* do thefe (only) wife ones fhew themfelves in affairs of men that know not, that (as *Solomon* fayes of the *Tongue, Life* and *Death* is in the power of the *Tongue* fo) *Life* and *Death* is in the power of a piece of Paper : what hath an *Executor* (yea many thoufand Executors to fhew for

The power of Writing in all Affairs.

their

their Eftates fometimes of hundreds, yea thoufands years but a little paper, and ink, and wax from the Teftators? what gives life to a condemned foul but a *Pardon* or *Reprieve* in a piece of *Paper?* who knowes not that a Writ or Paper figned by his *Majefty, the Lord Chancellour, the Lord ceief Juftice* hath Death in it, and fetcheth off the heads of many, yea the *higheft Offenders?*

The *Quotations* out of *G. Fox* which then I could not infift on, I fhall prefent a few and then pafs on to the *fifth Pofition.*

Jofh.
Miller.

In the 47*th.* Pag. *G. Fox* brings in *Jof. Miller* faying, *It is an Errour (if not damnable) to fay Chrift is the meanes, and that there is no other meanes of Salvation.*

He Anfwers, *And Chrift faith no man comes unto the Father but by me: and he is able to the uttermoft to fave? and he fhall be my Salvation to the end of the Earth faith the Lord: and faith the Apoftle, God is in Chrift reconciling the World to himfelf, and he that hath the Son hath Life, and the Father and the Son are one, and there is no falvation in any other.*

I reply: I fhall now freely declare to the Sence cf this *Allegation,* though in the Difpute my *Adverfaryes* would not fuffer me to meddle with the Sence of *G. Fox* his words, contrary to our Coven-
The Quakers notorious Covenant-Breakers. ant in my Writing, *viz.* that each Party fhould fpeak as long as they pleafed, which Liberty they enjoyed without my *Interruption:* and firft I doe not think that *Jof. Millers* words run fo loofely in his own Book: I do not think that a man of Wifdom would call it an error to fay that *Chrift is the*

meanes

meanes of Salvation: But to the second part, to which *G. Fox* opposeth, I believe it is an *Error*, and a damnable *Error*, and a Doctrine of *Devils*, to say there is no other meanes of Salvation: for this wretched *Jugler* subtilly confounds the *Instrumental Causes* of *Salvation* with [97] the *Efficient* in God the Father, and *Meritorious* in God the Son, Christ Jesus. 'Tis true, there is no *Redemption* and Forgiveness of sin, but in his Blood, *Ephes.* 1. though I know this *Jugler* (as before) means not a Christ, nor his Blood, nor Death as we do mean, but *Imaginary within*, &c. And yet as *Means* and *Instruments*: Christs Messengers are said to save themselves and others: The holy Scriptures are said to *make wise to Salvation*: A man may be *Gods means* or *Hand* to save his *Wife* and the *Wife* her *Husband*: *We are saved by hope* saith *Paul*, and saved by *Baptisme* saith *Peter*, yea, Women are saved by Child-bearing, as God blesseth those *painful Curses* to be blessed means of bringing to, or growing up in Christ the Saviour. All these subtly and wickedly *G. Fox* sets at variance with the *Meritorious Salvation* by Christ Jesus, between which there is an *Heavenly Union* and *Concord*, as between a man saving his Brother by throwing a *Rope*, or *Oar*, or *Board* unto him, &c. or a *Midwife* saving both Woman and her Birth in *Child-bearing* by the Means of Women, and Helps which her Skil and Labour administreth to her. To talk of this *Immediate Christ* and *Spirit* without Scriptures, without Preaching, and oth . holy means, is as silly, as Impious,

as

Means of Salvation.

A Union between the Meritorious Cause and means, and the Instrumental and Efficient or worker.

as Blockiſh, as Blaſphemous, and as Bedlam, and
Frantick, as wicked and *Anti-Chriſtian*.

Would not every body laugh at *G. Fox*, if he
ſhould ſay, that becauſe the *Kings Majeſty* gracciouſly
pardons *Condemned Rebels* at the *Mediation* of the
Prince his Son, therefore the Compoſing the writing,
the proclaiming of the pardon, the bring- of it to
the *Rebels hands* written and ſealed with the *Kings
broad Seal*, are no means of their Salvation and
Deliverance?

Hoſanna
to the Son
of David.

In *Pap.* 221. he brings in the Author of *Ho-
ſannah to the Son of* David, ſaying, [*The ſure Word
of Propheſie the Apoſtle ſpeaks of, is the Propheſie of
Scriptures.*]

He Anſwers, Doth the Scripture ſhine in a dark
place until the Day dawne? Are they them them
that muſt be taken heed unto as to a Light? Can
any ſee the Scripture, and know the Scripture, but
with the *Light within*? Can not a *Cain*, a *Baalam*,
a *Core* bring Scripture that is gone from the Spirit
of Propheſie within, and then put the Letter for it?

The more
ſure Word
of Pro-
pheſie.

98] I Reply 1. I know that *Fox* makes their *Idol
within* called *Light*, to be the more ſure word of
Propheſie, and his uſual proof is, [*The Teſtimony of
Jeſus is the Spirit of Propheſie,*] But firſt, why muſt
all the Prophets or Meſſengers of God, who from
the beginning of the world were Gods mouth and
Pens, Concerning the *Birth, Life, Death, Burial,
Reſurrection, Aſcention* and coming to Judgement
of the Lord Jeſus be here caſt out from the Word
of Propheſie? Is it nothing, *Luk.* 1, that God
ſpake (ſurely Gods ſpeaking is his word) *God ſpake*
by

by *the mouth of his holy Prophets, which have been* Gods
since the World began. And *Heb.* 1. *God ſpake ſun-* ſpeaking
dry times and in divers manners in Time paſt unto the Prophets
Fathers, but how did God thus ſpeake or utter his is his
word, but by the Prophets: And *Rom.* 16. But Word.
now is made manifeſt, and by the Scriptures of the
Prophets, according to the Commandment, *&c.*
Therefore how oft is it written concerning the
Lord Jeſus. *Theſe things were done that the Scriptures
might be Fulfilled,*] in which regard, (as to our ſatisfaction and belief) the written word of Propheſie
of the Prophets are a more ſure Word and Evidence to us concerning the Lord Jeſus then the
Miraculous Appearance from Heaven of *Moſes* and
Elias, and the voice from Heaven of which *Peter*
here ſpeaketh; though in it ſelf a true Teſtimony,
yet not ſo ſure, ſo firm and pregnant as the Word
that God ſpake by the mouth of his holy Prophets
from the beginning of the World, *&c.* Hence the
Anſwer of *Abraham,* and indeed of Chriſt Jeſus:
If they, hear not *Moſes* and the *Prophets, neither
will they believe though one ſhould riſe from the Dead.*

2. How ſure is the *Quakers Light,* their Word of The mad-
Propheſie? A ſober mind can not but admire that leaving
Face and Forehead of Braſs and Adamant with the Scrip-
which God the Righteous Judge of the whole tures and
hath plauged Satan and his Followers, ſo that they a Spirit
bluſh not to prefer ſuch a ſimple Image, a *meer Ba-* within.
bie and *Childs Puppet* of their *Immediate Word* of
Propheſie before the Word, the mind and will of
God by the mouth of all the Prophets?

For is it not known in the holy Scripture, in all
Hiſtories,

Hiftories, in all Ages, in all Nations, what Curfed Opinions, horrible Uncleanneffes, Bloody Murthers and Slaughters have been Conceived and brought forth from the Spirit within, and Revelati- [99] ons from *Divilifh Lights* and *Spirits*, and the horrible End that generally the Authors and Promoters of fuch Spirits and Infpirations have come to?

The workings of Satan by Spirits and Infpirations in all Ages.

3. This Scripture, *Revel.* 19. *The Teftimony of Jefus is the Spirit of Prophefie,* what is it but *Goliahs Sword* to fetch off the head of this proud Philiftin, for, doth not the *Angels* forbid *John* worfhipping of him upon this ground, *viz.* that the *Angel* was his *Fellow Broker, Fellow Servant, Fellow Worfhipper, Fellow Witnefs?* Is not this the Argument whereby he prohibits him, *viz.* that one Teftimony of Jefus was the work of Gods Spirit in the *Angels,* in their way, as well as in *Iohns* and *Peters* in theirs, *&c.* and fhall we fay that the Angels too are *Quakers,* and Chrift hath enlightened them alfo, as well as every man that comes, *&c* And *Revel.* 22. Doth not Chrift threaten the *Adders* to, and *Diminifhers* from the word of this Book of this Prophefie: what *Affinity* hath a written Book a written Prophefie with *Immediate whifperings* and *Infpirations?*

The Devil and the Quakers alleadging Scriptures

2. Why fhould G. *Fox* here mention *Cain, Balaam, Core?* what Scriptures could they bring? what Scriptures were written in their times? I think it no breach of Charity to guefs that the *Quakers* and G. *Fox* are fo ufed to Curfing and Cenfuring their *Oppofites* (at the firft dafh) for *Cains, Baalams, Cores,* that they could not well tell how to mifs them:

Such

Such perfons no queftion, and the *Foxians,* and the *lying Spirit,* the *Old Fox* and *Serpent,* bring Scripture : But doth the Divel cordially prize and love the word of *Prophefie,* the *Teftimony* and *Witneffes* of Jefus? However he plainly here Confeffeth that the holy Scripture is fo powerful that the very Counterfeit, the picture and Name of it will do him good Service, with fuch whom he defires to cheat and Ruine. And yet *fecondly* this fhews the *Quakers horrible wickednefs,* that although they love the holy Scripture (for the general of them) as well as doth their *lying Father,* yet turn they the Truth of God into a lye, and with the ugly Spider fucks that which he turns into poyfon, even from the fame Flowers of Paradice, the holy Scriptures, from whence the *hony Bees,* the true Believers, fuck the pure hony of Eternal Truth and Comfort.

3. Again, what madnefs is it for this *blind Dreamer* to ask his Oppofite, whether the Scripture fhines in a dark place until the [100] dawne? & whether they muft be taken heed unto as to a Light? For, how often is the holy Scripture even the very Law before the Gofpel, or glad News was preached, adorn'd and beautified with the *Illuftrious Title* of Light? and all the *fubtle Foxes* in the world muft know that if they attend unto whifperings and peepings, *Ifai.* 8. and leave the written Law, the Word, and other Prophefies of *Scripture,* or written Prophefies, Words and Oracles of God! For all their Childifh Vapourings and pratings of their Light, the *Eternal Father of Lights* proclaims them to be Children of *howling darknefs* and that

No Light in the bold pretenders (to fo much) the Quakers.

there

there is no Light within them : I ſpeak it with horrour and Amazement, and alſo with ſorrowful Confidence that he that ſhall find a ſpark of true Light either of the knowledge or grace of the true Lord Jeſus in this their *Fantaſtick Light*, he ſhall find the Living among the Dead, he ſhall prove the Prophets that ſpake, and the Lord God of the Prophets whoſe word was ſpoke, to be Lyars, for ſaying there is no Light within them.

But *Fox* again demands, (*Can any know the Scripture but with the Light within?*] And I ask him what Light have the *Papiſts* and *Iews*, and the *Divel* himſelf, when they and he bring Scripture to Chriſt himſelf? I know very well what he means in his *Ieſuitical, Diabolical Reſervations*, by the *Light within* and by knowing the Scripture, his meaning is known and Common, *viz.* except he be one of thoſe dark Souls called *Quakers*: But did not the Devil bring a pertinent Scripture and promiſe to Chriſt Jeſus as ever *Papiſt* or *Quaker* could have alleadged, though pointed and directed as are the *Papiſts, Iews* and *Quakers Allegations* to a *Venemous* and *poyſonous End.*

The pure Scripture filthily abuſed.

He brings in *Henoch Howet* ſaying, [*The Scripture to be the only Weapon whereby Chriſt overthrew the Devil.*]

Pag 14: Henoch Howet. By the Weapon of the Scripture only Chriſt Conquered the Devil-

He Anſwers, who bruiſeth his Head, and was before Scripture was, yet the Scripture is for Correction and Doctrine, furniſhing the man of God in his place, and Chriſt the Seed was before the Scripture was: And all them that hath Scripture and not Chriſt cannot overcome the Devil, you and the

the *Papiſts* doing his work : for they that overcome him that is with the Power, and thoſe have
the Scriptures of Truth, which the Devil is out of.
101] I Reply, How doth Chriſts bruiſing of Satans Head, and being before Scripture was, diſprove
Fox his Oppoſites ſaying, *viz.* the only weapon
whereby Chriſt Jeſus overcome the Devil was the
Scripture ? what is this to the point of the Com-
paſs ? may not half an Eye ſee what a *ſimple
Sophiſter* this is, to make ſuch Yawes as not to come
near the Ships Courſe and point in hand.

2. Who ſees not *Fox* in his *Burrough* of the divers Acceptation of the Word Chriſt ? For in the
Senſe of his Oppoſite that man Chriſt Jeſus who
fought the Devil, and *Fox* Confeſſeth died at *Ieruſalem* : was not before the Scriptures, But his Birth,
and Life, and Death, *&*.. were Proppeſied and declared by the Scripture long before he was born.

3. As for this ſaying, [*They that have the Scripture
and not Chriſt can not overcome the Devil*] What
News doth *Fox* tell the World, which no Body
denies ? and how doth this deny that Chriſt Jeſus
overcome the Devil by the Scripture ?

4. Is all Scripture or writing given by Inſpira- The
tion of God, *and is profitable* (though *Fox* alleadg- Scripture
eth this Scripture by halves) *for Correction and Doc-* moſh fit
trine, &c. then it clearly follows, that as Chriſt and pro-
Jeſus overcome the Devil by the Scripture, ſo by per Wea-
the ſame Weapon this *ſubtle Fox,* and all other of pon
Satans Foxes muſt be Corrected, Confuted Catcht againſt the
and deſtroyed, (except they repent) for ever : But De.
what is this Confeſſion that the *Scripture is profitable*
for

for Correction, &c. but a kind of grant to his Opposite that Chrift did overcome the Devil by this
Weapon, for he Confeffeth it profitable for Correction, *&c.* though yet all this running about in
and out into his holes in this Anfwer is a whifpering, and yet loud enough to be heard, *viz.* that
Chrift did not overcome the Devil by the Scripture,

5. As for the *Quakers Power* here pretended in
Oppofition to the Scripture, as being thofe that
have Scripture within them, and fo overcome the
Devil? How doth the Devil deal as one that pretends to Fight, with Children who lies down and
Cries as if thofe poor Childifh Souls had Overcome
him? Thus fometimes a Devil of Drunkennefs,
of Swearing, of Stealing runs away from the Sermons of the *Quakers*, as a *naughty Devil*, fometimes
at the Chiding and Conjuring of a *good Witch*!
That he may get the fafter hold by fpiritual pride,
hypocrifie, [102] felf Conceit, and Contradiction
to the Scripture, by will worfhip and Superftitious
Inventions againft the holy Inftitutions and Commands of the true Lord Jefus Chrift.

Pag. 289. He brings in *Francis Duke*, faying,
[*When Chrift told the Devil that man fhould not live
by Bread alone, but by every Word that proceedeth out
of the mouth of God, that was believing the Scripture :
And this Word of God in the Scripture was the Ground
of Chrifts Faith, and fo to all that are his*

He Anfwers, Many may have the Scripture and
never hear the voice of God, as the Jews in the
fifth of *John*, and they faid they believed the Scriptures though they were out of the true belief:
But

But receiving the Word from God, is, as they that gave forth the Scriptures : which man lives by and not by bread alone, and so knows him who was before Scripture was given forth : And for saying that the Scripture was the Ground of Chrifts Faith, he was afore the Scripture was writ, and fo fulfils their Words, and is the Author and the Finisher of the Saints Faith, which was before the Scripture was given forth, him by whom the World was made, and is the Author of the Saints Faith, that bruifed the Serpent under his feet, which was before the Scripture was.

1. I Reply, How Notorious for *Tautologies* are thefe *brutifh Clamours*? Thrice in this fmall Anfwer have we of Chrift, which was before Scripture was, who was before Scripture was, &c. fhall we believe their Notorious Lyes, *viz.* that the Light within them gave forth *S*cripture, and that they fpeak and write as they are moved by the moft holy and Infallible *S*pirit, when their writings are fo weak, lame and Childifh, juft like the talk of Aged doting Women, and fo full of Idle Repetitions? ^{The Quakers Riei-culous for and in their *Tau*tologies.}

2. What Anfwer is this, how brutifh and Impious, *viz.* that a man may have the *S*cripture and yet not be in the belief, therefore the Word of God was not the Ground of Chrifts belief, fo again, the Devil and wicked men may have the *S*cripture, and yet believe not in them, therefore Chrift Jefus and his faints believe them not neither : this Inference is clear, you fay Chrift was before *S*cripture was, &c.

I Reply,

I Reply, He was, and he was not,: But let Heaven and Earth Hear and abhor the *Sophiſtry* of theſe *Deceivers*, they would fain [103] have no ſuch Chriſt as man, a Chriſt without, an *out-ſide Chriſt*, but a *Spirit* and God only, and that in their Fleſh: yet again, (for ſhame of the world) they are forct to Confeſs that there was ſuch a man or perſon, *&c.* and yet to Cloak and Cover that Confeſſion from Croſſing their Principle, they ſay ; that before Scripture was Chriſt bruiſed the Serpents Head, that is Chriſt that made the World, Chriſt the Light, the Word, : But this again., we ſay is falſe alſo, for the Promiſe is, *Gen.* 3. that the *Seed of a Womau* which was Chriſt in his Manhood, born in the Fulneſs of Time, *Gal.* 4.

The Quakers mad Fancies as to Chriſt and the Scripture.

And let G. *Fox* or any of their *Juglers* Anſwer: If they ſpeak honeſtly, and (*bona fide*) if there was really ſuch a man called Jeſus at *Jeruſalem*, &c. as there was ſuch a man called G. *Fox* lately in *New-England*, was there not ſuch a man called Jeſus, after the Scripture was written or penn'd ? was dot this ma*n forty dayes tempted of the Devil*, and did not this man called Jeſus Chriſt Overcome the Devil by the Weapon of the writing or Scripture : and was not the holy Scripture the Ground of his Faith, as he makes the Will or Word of God declared in this holy Writing or Record the Ground of his ſaints Faith alſo ?

The Humanity of Chriſt.

He brings in *Iohn Timſon* ſaying, [*The Scripture is the Rule of Life.*]

Pag 16 John Timſon

He Anſwers, Contrary to Chriſt, who ſaid, *the Spirit ſhould lead them into all Truth*: *And they that are the*

Sons

Sons of God are led by the Spirit of God : and the Churches was to hear what the fpirit faid, for the fpirit lead them to fpeak forth *Scripture.*

I Reply, If among the feven things that God hates, he is an Abomination that foweth Difcord, what is he that would Oppofe and fet at Odds the moft holy fpirit, againft the holy fcriptures Infpired by him? and in Effect declares that Gods Children are not to attend to the voice of God in thefe his holy Infpired writings, but to a fecret Voice or whifpering within them : Contrary to the fcriptures Voice both before and fince Chrifts coming, as I have and fhall further manifeft.

2. As to the fpirits leading into all Truth, and the fons of God are led by the fpirit of God : Is not *Fox* here in his *Burrough,* not diftinguifhing between the Extraordinary leading of the holy Apoftles Appointed to be the Eye Witnyffes of Chrifts Death [104] and *Refurrection,* &c. and the firft Meffengers or Apoftles to the Nations, in which Refpect, the one Author of thofe three Gifts, Adminiftrations, Operations, 1 *Cor.* 12. peremptorily asks the Queftion, *Are all Apoftles, are all Prophets, have all the Gifts of Miracles?* and yet all Gods Children are Regenerated, are fanctificd, are guided and built up an habitation of God through the Spirit : and yet alfo the gracious prefence and working of the holy Spirit, may be hindred and quenched, by neglecting of the holy Fuel of the holy Scriptures and other holy means appointed. And therefore the Lord Jefus Commands us to pray for the Spirit : and *Daved* cries out, *Thy Spirit is good*

lead

The holy Scriptures the Rule

--- leading of the Spirit.

Gods Spirit given by means.

lead me, &c. *and take not thy holy Spirit from me.*
And this is the Devils (the *Old Fox*) his *Devilish
Subtlety* to make the Cloak of the Spirit Extraordinary Affiftance, and the Angels Extraordinary
protection, a ground of Chrift Jefus, and his Servants
flinging themfelves down from the *Pinacle* of the
Temple, and this I fay from the God of Truth will
be the *Breack neck* of the People called *Quakers*,
(without Repentance) every Soul of them.

The fifth Position

We now defcend to the proof of the fifth Pofition with their Confent, which was, their *Principles and Profeffions are full of Contradiction and Hypocrifies.*

The danger of being deceived

Depths of Hipocrify

I told them, that they knew well, that the Spirit
of God had given us abundant Warning againft
*falfe Gods, falfe Worfhips, falfe Chrifts, falfe Spirits,
falfe Prophets* : He Commands us in Scripture not
to believe them, &c. but to try them, to try all
things, as we do with *Touchftones*, and with *Bal-
lances*, yea, with Fire it felf. For, fome *Counter-
fiet Coyne* hath been fo like pure gold, fo double
guilt in the middle, and the Ring round about pure
gold, that it hath deceived the *Touchftone*. The
Devil himfelf as black a *Fiend* as he is, the Spirit of
Darknefs, yet he knows how to wear *Samuels Mantle*, and the *white Robe* of an *Angel of Light*, &c. I
told them it was Common for *Spanifh*, *Turkifh*, or
any other Enemy in Time of Warr to hang out
Englifh Colours, the more easily to deceive & Catch
the poor Merchant man, and *Judas* the Traitour
gave no other figne to the *Jews* in his betraying of
his *Lord* and *Mafter*, the Lord Jefus, *but God fave my
Mafter* and a Kifs.   Moft

105 [1]] Moſt of this I Remember I ſpake, and then ⸾Lies in Hipocriſie.⸿ I told them that *Paul* tels *Timothy* of ſome that ſhould ſpeake Lyes in Hipocriſie : I told them of theſe, there were two ſorts.

1 Such as knowingly (for wicked andDeviliſh Ends of Profit or Preferment) take the *Leading Staff* in hand,as 'tis more then probable, that the *Miſleader* of ſo many Millions of *Mahumetans* did : and as one of the *Popes* in Merriment to his *Cardinals* Con-feſt it, ſaying, *Quantum Lucri fecimus ex hac Fabula Chriſti*? What gain have we made of this Fable of Chriſt? Thus *Judas* knowingly, for his Gain ſought Opportunities to betray Chriſt Jeſus.   Thus ⸾Two ſorts of Soul Deceivers⸿ the *Schechemites* (and Millions are their *Succeſſors* as they are to *Nebuchadnezzars Idolaters*) underwent that painful and ſhameful Ordinance of *Circumciſion*, partly to pleaſe their Princes, and partly for that hope as (*Schechem* told them) that all that *Iſrael* had ſhould be theirs.

A *ſecond Sort* of *Soul Deceivers* that are, and yet know not in their Conſciences that they are *blind Guides* or *blind Followers*, but for not loving Truth God hath given them up to believe Lyes, for Truths: falſe Chriſts and Spirits, for true Chriſts and Spirits; yea, and with *Paul* to think that they verily ought to do many things againſt *Jeſus of Nazareth*, yea, and as the Lord Jeſus *Poſitively Foretold* they ſhall think to do God Service to kill himſelf, in killing his Servants.

I told

---

[1] In the copy in poſſeſſion of Brown Univerſity, Roger Williams has placed his autograph acroſs the outſide edge of this page.

I told them my Charity, bid me hope that the *Quakers* and themfelves prefent were not of the *firft*, but of the fecond fort, and I prayed them to be as patient as they could while I muft prove that their Principles and Profeffions were full of Lyes and Contradictions, and of Hipocrifies, and Diffimulations. I wondred that my *Oppofites* and *Auditors* bare all this Load fo filently? But at this word *W. Edmundfon* and the reft brake out faying, We regard not what thou thinkeft and fayeft of us, nor do we need thy Charity, but go on to thy proofs, *&c.*

The Quakers of late have Changed much of their Spirit, or elfe more notorioufly Equivocators.

I then faid, that their many Books, and G. *Foxes* (that thereby me) and their Profeffions, did fo exceedingly Clash one with another : and fome of their latter Books (as *Chriftopher Houldsworths*) and fome of theis latter Profeffions and Practices were fuch that many of their Obfervers Conclude, that either they had altered their Religion in many of their Principles [106] and Practices, and were turned from what they formerly held, and were amongft us : Or elfe their Hipocrifies and Diffimulations were more and more prodigioufly Abomina-

The Juggling of the Quakers about Chrift.

ble. I came to Inftances, and told them that when they were Charged to deny that man Chrift Jefus, they profefs and preach they are wronged, for they believe in that Chrift which was born of a *Virgin,* and died at *Jerufalem,* and yet for all this, it is but in Truth a *Spiritual,* and *Miftical,* and *Allegorical Chrift,* which under boord andin the bottom) which they hold. For, in *New-England* (before G. *Fox* came) H. *Norton* and others fay, is not Chrift God, and is not God a Spirit, and is there not a *Spiritual Virgin,*
a *Miftical*

a *Miſtical Bethlehem*, an *Heavenly Ieruſalem*? And do not G. *Fox* and *Ed. Burroughs* all along hold out ſuch a Chriſt, whoſe Body is not now to be found? and ſuch a man as is in every *Saint*, or *Quaker*? and in every perſon in the world except he be a Reprobate?

Again, 2. They ſay, they hold the Chriſtian Church, the *Chriſtian Ordinances*, the *Chriſtian Miniſtry*, the *Chriſtian Baptiſme*, & *Supper* the *Reſurrection*, the *Iudgement*, the *Life Everlaſting*, but ſearch their Books, Examine their preachings and profeſſings, and you ſhall ſee, and may admire their Juglings and Diſſimulations: Do not *Fox* and *Burroughs* all along diſclaim any *Church Miniſters*, *Baptiſme*, &c. but what is *Immediate* and *Inviſible*? Do they really own any Supper but Chriſts inward Supping with them, and they with him? Or any *Reſurrection* but the tiſing of their *Bodies* to *perfect Holineſs*? or any *Iudgement* and *Eternal Life*, but what they have now attained, and are now paſſing Judgement upon the world? *About the Church and Ordinances.*

3. Again, though they do deny any Church but *Inviſible*, yet their Churches and Congregations are known and *Viſible* and ſtated (not attending *Inviſible Motions*) both firſt day and other dayes with prayers and Preachings, and ſingings, and real joynings or Addings to them & Caſtings out: Theſe things neceſſitty forceth them to practice, or elſe they cannot poſſibly keep together, although in *Monſtrous Diſſimulation* they diſclaim it.

4. They profeſs that their Saints have an *Unction*, yea, that every perſon in the world is ſo enlightned *Inward and outward Preachers.*

by

by Chrift Jefus, that he hath Chrift and Spirit, and the Kingdom of God in them, [107] (as the *Phari-fees* had, and the very fame the Saints have) and if they will, they have Teaching enough to Juftifie, Sanctifie and fave them : and yet again what a noife is there in the World about the *Quakers, Teachers, He Apoftles,* and *fhe Apoftles,* fnch as the Lord Jefus never fent either the *Twelth* or the *Seventh,* or their Succeffors. How do they boaft to be the only Min-ifters of Chrift Jefus fent into *Old England* and *New-England,* into *Scotland* and *Ireland,* yea, into I*taly* and *Turky,* and other Nations as diligent and zealous as the *Pharifees* to pervert and poyfon Souls with a falfe Converfion and Salvation.

5. You profefs the Scriptures to be the words of God, but not the Word of God, and yet now you profefs to be tryed by them : Anon again, you need not the Scriptures, you have that Light and Spirit within you that gave out the Scriptures, and if all the Copies in the World were burnt yet you have the Scriptures within you, therefore you not only (as the Spirt of God faith) deceitfully handle the Scriptures by deceitful Interpretations, but by de-ceitful owning, and not owning, and as G. *Fox* in his late Book in Exalting *Heathens* above *Chriftians* owning them, and yet Exalting the Spirit in the *Philiftian* and *Egiptian*Sorcerers above them.

6. As to *Magiftrates,* how full are their Books and Sermons againft Perfecution and Perfecutors, and yet how plainly do their Principles perfecute all others that fubject not to their Light, when they have attained fuch *godly Magiftrates* as they arc (as they

As to the Scriptures

G Fox his laft Book Exalting the Hea-then

As to Mag-iftrates

they ſpeak) in the Light. I told them I was Concerned to make this out more fully in the proof of
my *Fourteenth Poſition*, and therefore at preſent I
would trouble them but with one *Quotation* out of
G. *Fox, Pag.* 170. where I Read, and *Iohn Burnet* ^{Pag 170}
Read alſo, how G. *Fox* brings in *Iohn Stallam* ſay- John
ing, [*And the Magiſtrate is not to Level the Law with* ^{Stallam}
the Light in every mans Conſcibnce, Again, if the
Magiſtrate be in the Light and diſcern the mind of The Qua-
Chriſt, and diſcern his Law, is he to Compel all the Na- kers Prin-
tion and Common-wealth to come to the practice of his ciples are
Light?] for Perſe-
cution

G. *Fox* Anſwers, the Magiſtrate of Chriſt, the
help, Government for him, he is in the Light and
power of Chriſt: and he is to ſubject all under the
power of Chriſt, into his Light, elſe he [108] is not
a faithful Magiſtrate: and his Laws are agreeable
and Anſwer according to that of God in every
man: when men act contrary to it they do evil, ſo
he is a Terrour to the Evil doers, diſcern the precious and the juſt from the vile, and this is a praiſe
to them rhat do well.

I urged from hence, that the *Quakers* (and G, *Fox*
in his Book in many places) owne no Magiſtrates The Qua-
but ſuch as are godly that is in their dark Sence, kers Zeal-
that be Magiſtrates for their Chriſt, be in the Light ous Perſe-
and Power of Chriſt, for then ſay they, their Laws cutors.
are agreeable to that of God in every man.

2. Theſe their Magiſtrates (in the Light) ought
to ſubject even the Conſciences and Souls of
all that be under them, by *Corporal puniſhments* to
come under the Power of Chriſt into the Light.

3. This

3. This is Confirmed and fealed with a *peremptory Doom* upon the neglecter and failer, *viz.* [*Elfe he is not a Faithful Magiftrate.*]

4. I obferve the Reafon and Equity which they alleadge of this fubjecting all Subjects to the Light of Chrift, becaufe fuch *Magiftrates*, *Laws* and *Edicts* are witneffed by God in every man, and therefore he fins againft God himfelf who breaks fuch a *Magiftrates Command*, and therefore is juftly punifhed, *&c.*

Upon my urging of fome of thefe particulars fome of them defired to hear the *Quotation* read again: fo *Iohn Burnet* read the whole paffage again, and faid, that G. *Fox* fpake not there of matters of Religion and Confcience, nor of the Magiftrates compelling men to be of his Religion and Confcience, but of punifhing them for matters of wrong between man and man, which are againft the Light in every mans Confcience, as *Drunkennefs*, *Whoredome*, *Murther*, *Stealing*, and the like.

I Replyed, the Terms were fuch both of the Queftion by the *Oppofite*, and the Anfwer by G. *Fox* which argue and Comprehend the matters of Religion and Confcience, *viz.* If the Magiftrate be in the Light, and difcern the mind of Chrift, *&c.* and G. *Fox* his Terms are the fame about Chrift and the Light and bringing them fubject to Chrift.

2. It is not Imaginable, that the Oppofer would queftion whether the *Civil Officer* ought not to punifh fuch incivilities and [109] Incivilities and Inhumanities as *Drunkennefs*, *Whoredome*, *Stealing*, *Murther*, &c. Therefore G. *Fox* muft intend that their Magiftrates for Chrift muft Fight for their

Chrift

Chrift againft all their *Oppofites*, though they cry *Perfecutors, Perfecutors*, &c.

In *Pag.* 221. G. *Fox* brings in the Author of the Book called *Hofanna to the Son of* David, faying, [*They know not abfofolute Perfection that are admitting of Meafures and Degrees, nor come to the Day and the bright Morning Star, is not Rifen.*] The Qua-kers Per-fection, and yet in Meafure Pag. 221. Hofanna to the Son nf David.

He Anfwers, did not the Apoftle fpeak that they were Children of the Day, and the night was over, and knew the whole Body, and yet faid, he would not go beyond his Meafure? And doth he not fpeak of the *Stature and Meafure and Fulnefs* of *Chrift*? and were they not come to Perfection, and fpoke wifdome among them that were perfect?

I Reply: As to their *Monftrous pride* I fhall fpeak, when I come to Compare the *Pope* and them in the *Tenth Pofition*: At prefent I Ask them, whether *Paul* fpeak of his Meafure in Holinefs and Grace, or no? Some of them fay that they are not only perfect as God in Holinefs, but alfo in Power *Omnipotent, Omniprefent, Omnifcient*, &c. But if *Paul* be not brought in to fpeak of fuch a Perfection in Holinefs as is in God, G. *Fox beats the Air*, & comes not near the Queftion: to fave their Doctrine of Perfection from being a perfect Contradiction & Lie, and they would fain make themfelves & others believe that they are as truly perfect in their Holinefs as God is, though their Holinefs be not fo much: As if they were perfectly Gods, (though but little Gods) as God himfelf being a great God, and fo are forct to fhow their Contradictions, and wheel about to Perfection of parts as a Child is mankind though The Old Romans with their Dii Min-ores or lef-fer Gods and the Papifts and Qua-kers all one.

The Per-fection of the God-head

not

not a perfect man, and a drop of water is true water, and may be as Salt as any drop in the *Ocean*:
having theQuality of, but not the Equality with the
Ocean As otherwise G *Fox* foolishly & blasphemously speaks of God in this Book, Moreover, since
these high minded Souls dare to say that they are
as pure as God, and (some say what they think)
that they can no more sin against God, then God
can sin against them, *&c.* I Ask them whether
there be any Measures and Degrees in God? whether
his Perfection in Holiness be notHoliness it self?
Wisdom it self, goodness it self, unto which there
there can be no Addition or [110] growth as we
are Commanded *to grow in the grace and knowledg
of Christ Jesus.* To talk therefore of *Measures* &
*Perfections,*is as silly as forG.*Fox*when he hath begun
to sow a Shoo,and hath as yet taken but a few stitches,
yet to boast Confidently that the Shoe is perfect.

**The Qua-
kers Falla-
cious Per-
fection.** We deny not, but a Dram Cup may be as perfectly full of wine as a Pipe or Butt, and so *Johns
little Children* as perfectly, that is, as truly Gods
Children, as his strong men or Old men : But to
say this Cup or Spoon is equal in quantity to a Pipe
or Tun, a Child is equal to a strong man, much
more for a *poor Potsheard* to say he is equal with his
*Porter,*and a *Worm* of the *Earth* equal to his *Maker,* what is it but a *bloccish* and *blasphemous Fallacy*
and *Contradiction*? and a wheeling about to a Per-
**Hosanna
to the Son
of David.** fection of parts which none deny.

In 222. He brings in the same Author saying,[*Christ
is without his Saints in respect of his bodily presence.*]
He Answers, How are they of his Flesh, and of
his

his Bone, and how do they eat his flesh, and drink his Blood? And how have they his mind and Spirit? And he with them, and they with him? and sit in *Heavenly Places* : And he is the Head of his Church, and how then is he absent? yea, *poor Apostates* from him feels not Christ, but he is with the Saints, and they feel him.

I Reply, and Ask, is this Eating of his Flesh, and drinking of his Blood after a *Corporal, Bodily manner*, visible and real as to other Senses Or is it Miraculous and Spiritual? Or is it *Spiritual & Misti-cal* by Faith, and by believing as the *Protestants* say? After the first *Corporal way* the very *Papists* affirm not: After the *second way* you will not say it is: Nor would you be thought to be so *gross Papists* as to hold *Transubstantiation* ? and therefore must it be the *third way* whichis by believing : and then you *poor Jugling Souls*, what is it to a *Bodily pres-ence*, that you Eat him by believing? G Fox his Falla-Presence of Christ Visible and Natu-ral or Mi-raculous and Super-natural Eating of Christ.

2. Whereas you say, you *sit with him in Heavenly Places*, you are one wiih him, &c. he is Head of the Church, &c. Here I must Ask you you hold him to be such a *Visible Head* of the Church, as the *Pope* saith He is, and if you say yea, I then Ask you where will you direct us to such an *Individual Man*, or person as the *Pope* is, and may be directed to, as we know from so great Art all the World over, If you say No, what is this then to talk of a *bodily* |111 *presence* of Christ (which is the point) and then Flap me in the mouth with a *Fox Tail*, and tell me (in a *Childish* and *Equivocating Contradiction*) that you mean not a *Bodijy presence* but a *Spiritual*. Christ Head of the Church

3. As

3. As for the *poor Apoſtates*, and your feeling of Chriſt, which the *poor Apoſtates* do not.

I Reply, An *Adulterous Wretch, Accuſed* Ioſeph of *Whoredome*, who was a pattern of *pure* and *holy Chaſtity* : For, whom do this *Whoriſh Brood* of *Foxians* thus brand for *Apoſtates*, and ſling among them *Firebrands, Arrows* and *Death ?* Are they not all the Children of God that are, or ever were, or ſhall be called ? Are they not the Souls under the *Altar* who have been ſlain *Thouſands* and *Ten Thouſands for the Teſtimony of Ieſus* againſt theſe *horrid Deluſions*?

His Bodily preſence.

Are they not the very *firſt Churches*, and the *Apoſtles* of Chriſt Jeſus, from whom Chriſt in his *Bodily preſence* was departed, as he often Forewarned

The Quakers Count all Gods Children Apoſtates.

them, and (as the holy Scriptures abundantly Recordeth) is Fulfilled ? For, ſee the Jugling of theſe Deceivers, when this *Bodily preſence* is Examined, they mean no ſuch *Individual Man* and perſon, but a mind and Spirit, and ſuch a Chriſt as hath no *Individual Bodily Preſence*, as we and all men have.

G Fox his Juglings and dreams about the perſon of Chriſt

If G. *Fox* when he is in *New-England* ſhould ſay he is in *London* in his *Bodily Preſence*, and that his Friends feel (as he ſpeak) his *Bodily Preſence* there, becauſe they feel his Love and his Affections in their minds and Spirits : What *Hocas Pocas* and *Iugling Chriſtianity* is this ? All the Saints and Children of God muſt all be *Apoſtates*, fallen from God and Chriſt, and Grace, that cannot Skill and Feel this *Horrible Egiptian Canting Language*.

I will turn my Thoughts higher. O thou moſt *glorious Sun* of *Righteouſneſs, Truth* and *Holineſs* ſhine

ſhine forth, and let it be ſeen, how the Devil called
the Lord Jeſus *Beelzebub* : The *Treacherous Revolt-*
ers and *Apoſtates* from thee, they call thy ſelf, and
thy Saints *Revolters* and *Apoſtates*. They boaſt
with the *bloody Papiſts* and other *Traitorous Rebels*
againſt thee, of their Right and Intereſt in thee, of
their poſſeſſing and feeling of thee, feeling thy
Scriptures and thy *Bodily preſence* within them : Oh
let thy *glorious Light* declare, who theſe *poor Apoſ-*
tates and *Revol-* [112] *ters* are, *who break down thine*
Altars, burn thy Temples, ſcoff at thine Inſtitutions,
Cry up a falſe and *Helliſh Chriſt* within them,
Chriſten him with the Name of *Light*, though he be
thy *Conquered Slave* the *Devil,*telling us he is thine
Angel of Light, who with his *Counterſiet Souldiers* of
Light, Crucifie thee and pierce thee, and mock and
Curſe thee, (the only true Son of God and Son of
man) as ever *Herod* and *Pilate,* the *Preiſts* and *Iudas,*
the People and Souldiers did.

An Apoſ-
trophe or
Pe tion to
the Lord
Jeſus

In *Page* 259, he brings in *James Browne* ſaying,
[*the Kingdome that is in the Saints, is not in the*
Phariſees.]

259 James
Brown

He Anſwers, [That is, in the *Saints,* is in the
Phariſees in a *Meaſure,* though it be but as *a Grain*
of Muſtard Seed, which is like to *Leaven little.*]

I Reply, 1. What If I ſhould ſend you to ſome of
your *Margents,* where the Greek word [*Entos*] is
rendred amongſt you : that is, unto you, upon you,
as *Luke* 11. *If I by the Finger of God caſt out Dev-*
ils,ſurely the Kingdome of God is Come upon you?
The Phariſees expected (and ſo did all the *Iews,*
and *Chriſt Diſciples* were not free) I ſay look for a

Chriſts
Kingdom
in,or
among the
Phariſees

glorious

glorious Temporal King that fhould make his *Ingrefs* with Pomp, and [*Meta pur oterefio*] as the Scripture fpeaks with Obfervation, but he came in as fome Kings in difguize, and (as they fpeak) *Incognito*, and yet his Kingdome was among them, in the midft of them, by his *per onal prefence*, his *powerfulp eaching*, and his *glorious Miracles.*

2   Since (in Oppofition to *Chrifts Vifible Kingdome* his Church) you predicate a *Kingdome within, Confifting of Righteoufnefs, peace, and joy in the holy Spirit* : do you think indeed that the Hipocritical Curfed Pharifees were fnch Righteous, peaceable and joyful Souls as your felves: As fure as God is Light: They and their Succeffors your felves, will find your felves when you wake, in *horrid Quaking*, and except you repent HellFlames about your Ears, as the Lord Jefus told thofe *whited Walls* and *painted Sepulchres.*

Horrible and hipocritical Chiftianity

3. Muft you take Meafure of the Pharifees, and tell us that the Pharifees in a Meafure as a grain of Muftard Seed and Leaven are the fame with your felves ? Do not you Cry out that you are perfect, not in Meafures and Degrees, but that you are all one in *Quality* and *Equality* of Power and Glory with God ? and muft [113] this muft be the fame with Chrift Jefus and his Saints, and you and the *Pharifees* all together ? *Can two walk together,* live and love together, board and bofome together *and not be agreed* together, no other wayes then *Light* and *Darknefs, Chrift* and *Belial, Righteoufnefs* and *unrighteoufnefs* ? What ftinking work do thefe *provd Pharifees* make of *Chriftianity* ? How juftly doth the Son of God give them their proper Titles, *Ye Fools and Blind?*

4. If

4. If it be the same Kingdome in Christ Jesus and in Saints, and in the *Pharisees*, and every wicked man in the world, though but *as a grain of Mustard Seed*, and *Leaven*, what is the Reason this *Mustard Seed* grows not up, this *Leaven* spread not in them? Can a Nation be subject to the King of *England*, of *Spain*, or any osher Ptince or *Monarch*, and yet not know how, nor have no knowledge nor feeling of it at all? Can there be such a God, such a Spirit, such a Fire? yea, but such a *Mustard Seed*, or *Levven*, such a T*eacher*, and yet not grow, not prevail, not prosper, nor be perceived? ye *Fools* and *Blind* are all your *Mustard Tree*s stunted all the world over, no Shelter for the *Heavenly Birds*, your pure flowre of Holiness and sincerity, mixt and-blended with the *black Weeds, Cockle* and *darnel* of *open Idolatries* and *prophaneness*, and *Pharisaisme*, and *Hipocrisie*: What abominable Contradictions and Lyes in *Hipocrisie* are here? The *Pharisees* have Christ and his Kingdome of *Righteousness, peace* and *joy* in the *Holy Spirit* within them, and yet live in pride and Covetousness, and Extortion, and Excess, and Cruelty, and Hipocrisie, and Blasphemy, and all this *Rottenness* and *Dead mens bones* stinking and ruling all within, notwithstanding all the *white* and *paint*, and *garnishing without* your selves, (their *Hipocritical Off spring*) have, and live in, you say, this Kingdome of Christ Jesus, this *Kingdome of Righteousness and Joy in the holy Spirit*, as perfect and pure as God himself: all one with us, Infinite in *Majesty, Holiness, Power* and *Glory*, not only in *Quality*, but *Equality*, &c. (as this wretched G. *Fox* affirmeth) And yet within and withont

A Monstrous King and Kingdome of the Quakers.

Abominable lyes in hipocrisie.

The Pharisees and Quakers hipocrisie wonderful

withont *Idolatrous* and *Superftitious, Inhumane* and *uncivil, paffionate* and *fierce, Cenforious* and *Curfing*, and moft *Impudent* and worfe then *Barbarous*, in fome *of your Impudently, monftrous and avowed practices*

Having difpatched our Agitations about the *fifth Affertion,* [114] and the *Quotations* out of G. *Fox* which I could not then Infift on in publick, I defcended to the *fixth Pofition* which was, *viz.* [*The Religion of the Quakers is not only an Herefie in the matters of Gods holy worfhip, but alfo in the Doctrines of Repentance, Faith,&c.*

This *Affertion* hath two main Branches : *Firft,* that the Quakers Religion is an *Herefie,* and themfelves *Hereticks* in the matters of Gods worfhip.

2. Not only fo, (about the Circumftances of which Gods own dear Servants themfelves greatly differ) but alfo (which is more Lamentable and dangerous) in the Doctrines of Repentance and Faith, and the reft of the graces of Chrift Jefus.

I told them *firft,* that the word *Hairefis* Herefie, in *Greek,* (from whence the word *Hairetikos* an Heretick) fignified an *Opinion* or *Opinions,* chofen and ftood in by one or more againft the *Chriftian Religion.* I faid the matter mighr be aggravated, and a ugmented from the Greatnefs and *Vitallity* of the matter of the Opinions, but the *Formality* and *Nature* of it lay in the will and obftinacy thereof.

John Stubs ftood up and faid, that *Herefie* was defined by fome to be an Opinion obftinately ftood in againft the *firft Chriftian Purity* : I Anfwered, yea, and the Opinion of fome was, that *Herefie* was an
Error

Error in the *Foundation* obſtinately ſtood in : But
I ſaid we had not time to enter upon a Diſpute
about the word or thing at this time, the Subſtance
of my *Affirmation* was, that their Religion, Sect or
way was falſe, and gone from the *Inſtitution* and
way of the Lord Jeſus delivered by himſelf and his
Apoſtles, or *Meſſengers* :

1. As to worſhip, they denyed the Converting
and gathering of the Saints into *viſible Aſſemblies*,
or *Congregations* : affirming the Chnrch to be *Inviſible*, the *Miniſters Inviſible*, the *Baptiſme* and *Supper Inviſible*, &c.

The ſecond (which was aur *Poſition*) was in thoſe
two great Fundamentals, the *Beginning*, or *A. B. C.*
of the *Chriſtian Religion*, viz Repentance from dead
works and Faith towards God:As for thoſe two
Doctrines of laying on of hands, and of *Baptiſmes*
they concerned the Church, and worſhip, (concerning the Circumſtances of which God is pleaſed to
permit his ⌈115⌉ Children to be lovingly differing
and diſcuſſing; the other four *Repentance*, *Faith*,
Reſurrection and *Judgement* (in which generally
Gods Children agree) in theſe alſo as well as in the
matter of worſhip, theſe wandring Souls are *Hereticks*, that is, obſtinately maintaining *Notoriouſly*
falſe and *Anti-Chriſtian Abominations*, In ſo much
that the many Sects amongſt the *Proteſtants*, yea,
and the *Papiſts* themſelves do not ſo differ from *a
true Proteſtant* and *true Chriſtian* as do theſe *wilful,
ignorant*, and *wandring Souls*.

1. Then as to Repentance, I ſaid it was the firſt
heavenly and ſaving work of God upon the Soul,

The Quakers Hereticks againſt all the Chriſtian Principles, and more Heretical againſt the firſt Chriſtian Religion then any Proteſtauts or Papiſts.

The Quakers Here-

wherein

wherein he turned back home again the whole Soul unto himſelf, being revolted and run from him into the Arms of Rebellion in the Fall of our *firſt Parents.*

This was the great point preached by *Moſes* and the *Prophets*, and more expreſsly by *John the Baptiſt*, and by the Lord Jeſus himſelf: and when he ſent abroad his Apoſtles or Meſſengers into all Nations, they were to preach the Goſpel or glad News of the Forgiveneſs of ſins according to *Luke* 24. viz. that Repentance and Remiſſion of ſins ſhould be preached in his Name unto all Nations, beginning at *Jeruſalem.*

Here about I remember they told me that it was known that they preached the Doctrine of Repentance and of turning from all ſin unto God, &c.

I Anſwered, that the *Papiſts* and they made a ſhew and Colour of Repentance, but it had not the Life and Subſtance of Repentance in it: It was no more but an *empty Title* and *ſhadow* of Repentance: we know the *Papiſts* define their Repentance by theſe three. *Firſt*, Contrition, *Secondly*, Confeſſion, and *Thirdly*, Satisfaction or Reſtitution.

But I ſaid the *Proteſtants* proteſted againſt this Repentance of the *Papiſts*, and ſo againſt the *Quakers*, for, who knew not the ſorrow and Confeſſions of *Saul*, and *Ahab*, and *Pharaoh*; and the *Philiſtins*, and *Judas*, yea, and alſo the Reſtitutionwhich *Judas* made, (not daring to keep in his hands that which he had unjuſtly and wickedly gotten) and yet who can truly aſcribe unto theſe mens Repentance, the Character and bleſſedneſs of a true Chriſtian returning and coming home to God.   2.   I

2. I said it is known in daily practice, that when some times [116] *Notorious* and *openly Flagitious Perfons* profefs to be *Quakers,* (for all their craking of fear and trembling and Quaking) there hath appeared no Senfe of godly forrow, of godly Contrition and brokennefs of heart in them, for their finful Nature and Life againft fo *Infinitely pure* an *Holinefs* and *Majefty*? but immediately (upon their bowing down to Satan, and owning him as a *Light,* and *Chrift,* and *Spirit* within them) they are, having lefs Prophanenefs now pure and holy as God is, they can no more fin then Chrift can! *the Miftery of godlinefs is God manifefted in their Flefh,* I know fome of them fay they come to perfection by degrees, yet they fay the leaft of their *new-born Quakers* can not fin, and what is that but Perfection? yea, they are Chrift and God: and therefore why fhould they give refpect to any *King,* or *Kings,* &c. why fhould they not *Thee* and *Thou* the *Aged, Learned, holy, and High,* why fhould they not fit filent even fcores and hundreths of them (poffeffed with a dumb Spirit) as in a Form and Order of Chriftian worfhip waiting for this Spirit, and then be perfect Chriftians?

The Quakers Converts.

3. The *Proteftants* both *Englifh, French* and *Dutch,* &c. have manifefted againft the *Papifts,* and therein againft the *Quakers,* that Repentance is a turning of whole Soul from all fin as fin to all of God as God: from the fin of Nature, and that *Heart filthinefs* which we bring into the world with us, and from whence, even from within, as Chrift Jefus tells us? what ever Satan and the poor Quakers

The Proteftants true Repentance.

kers

kers prate *proceed our evil thoughts, Adulteries, Forni-cations, Murthers, Thefts, Covetoufnefs, Wickednefs, Deceit, Lafcivioufnefs, an Evil Eye, Blafphemy, pride, Foolifhnefs*, Mark 7, *&c.*

4. I urged that their *Profelites* and *Converts* are but like the *Pharifees* of old, though oftentimes dearly bought by Sea and Land, I fay, but tnrned from one fin to another, from one Image to another, from one Devil of Drunkennefs or Swearng; *&c.* to a Devil of *Pride, horrible pride,* the worft of all prides in Earth or Hell, to wit, a *Spiritual Pride* fwelling with the *Dropfies* and *Tympanies* of their *Conceited knowledge, Conceited Repentance, Conceited Faith, Love, patience, joy, holinefs, Juftification, Sanctification, Mor-tification* and *Salvation.*

2. How horribly do they defpife the *true broken hearted Pub-* [117] *licans,* who can fee nothing but

The Qua-kets defpi-ling sin and Damnation in themfelves, and cry out for mercy and Forgivenefs? How do they *Supercilioufly* and *Pape-like* belch out as from Hell, *God I thank thee that* I *am not like thefe Publicans?*

AndRevili others. 3. How bitterly do they Inftantly raile and re-vile, Condemn and Curfe, breathing out Fire of Damnation as Fire and Brimftone from the Moun-tains in *Sicily,* or elfe Hell it felf againft all that op-pofe them? as far from the Teaching of Chrift and his *firft Meflngers* as *Lambs* and *Doves,* are from the *Ravenous, popifh* and *Devilifh Lyons* and *Eagles.*

4. To name no more at prefent, How doth the Devil of worldlinefs and Covetoufnefs domineer

Their Covetouf-nefs. over many of them? By a ftrict Profeffion all per-fons are taken off from Drunkennefs, Whoredome, Swearing,

Swearing, &c. und put on *Theiftinefs* and *Induftry*,
and if their hearts Centre and fix not on Chrift Jefus, and the *Heavenly Records* of Chrift, the Scriptures: and on the Life to come, but upon *Self, Exalting felf, a felf Chrift*, and *Spirit*, and *Heaven*, and
Refurrection, &c. which is the Truth and bottom
of the Quakers Religion, what can the moft of
them run in but a Courfe of *greedy gaping* after,
and getting, and raking, and gathering the *muck*
and *dung* of this *prefent Life*?

It is true, that many that hold the fame *Fanciful
Notions* with the *Quakers*, yet are of *Ranting, jovial,
fpending Spirits,* but the Spirit that haunts the *Quakers* moft is a *foure, proud,* and *Melancholy Devils,* A fowre
and his Commiffion is to turn fuch perfons into the Spirit is
Gadarens Swine rooting up all that ever they come the Com-
at for their own Ends and Belly: How many are mon Spirit
the Inftances even in this *Colony* in fome efpecially, of the
as able and as active Souls as any in this *Colony* or Quakers.
Country, and as guilty of murthering the *Natives*
by the *Liqour Trade* as any: and as fuddenly and
ftrangely fnatcht away by the hand of *Gods Power*
and *Iuftice*, as any ufually can be, but being departed
I will touch no more upon this ftring.

From their Doctrine of, and their Herefie or Obftinacy in a *falfe Repentance,* I touch next npon
their *falfe Faith*: I faid it was true they fpoke much The Qua-
of Faith and Juftification, &c. as the *Papifts* did, kers Falfe
and as G· *Fox* in his Book (by me) did: yet if they Faith.
pleafed, I would demonftrate by Inftances out of
his Book all along that he Confounded and made
all one, both Faith and Ju- [118] ftification, yea,
and

and Sanctification, and made believing in Christ Jesus but a *meer Babel* and *Chaos* of *Nonsence* and *Cnnfusion*. For although (which is *Foxes Common Burrough*) he that Faith hath Repentance, hath Justification, Sanctification, and all *Christian graces*, yet to Confound and make them all one, is as to go into a *fair Garden*, and say a Rose is every Flower in the Garden : or to say, that the Letter *A*, or *O* is every Letter in a *Printers Box*, or Book : Or to say, that a *Rebels* receiving the *Kings pardon*, that is the *King himself* : his receiving it is the pardon it it self, that is the *Rebels Conviction, Converfion, Condemnation, Execution, Resurrection, Acceptation, Exaltation*, and *Adoption* into the *Favour* and *Communion* with the *King* for the Future. All this *Monstrons* and *Nonfensical Language* is the Tongue or Speech of the *Quakers*, and G. *Fox* especially.

G Fox his horrible Confounding of Faith and all other Chistian Virtues and Graces together.

2. I told them that although (with the *Quakers* and *Papists*) G. *Fox* talkt much of Faith in Christ : yet I had proved and further should, that the *Quakers* put out and obliterate the true Christ or Object to be received and believed on, as before in the matter of Faith, they put out the true living Eye of Faith, and put in a painted, or *Glass Eye* in the Room of it.

True Faiah what it is

True Faith is a Receiving of Christ Jesus as my only King, Priest and Prophet : It is a believing on, or receiving of Christ distinct from God, *Iohn* 14. You believe in God, This true Lord Jesus Christ the *Quakers* turn into a *meer Fiction, Dream*, or *Imaginary Chrift* in the mind of a man, or Woman : a *Popish Transubstantiated Chrift*, all Spirit and

The Quakers Tranfubstatiarion worfe then the Fantastick

and no Body, and fo not confifting of Flesh and
Spirit : He hath no Flefh of his own, as you make
him : and yet Flefh of his own, becaufe your Flefh
is his Flefh, and yet your Flefh you fay alfo muft dye
and rot, and never rife again, and fo you have blown
up and Jugled away the Flefh of Chrift Jefus, both
his and your own alfo altogether.

This is a Trick of *the Father of Lyes*, and *Iuglings*
beyond that *Monftrous* *Fancy* of the *Papifsfts Tran-fubftantiation*, for although they turn the Bread into
the Flefh of Chrift, yet they turn not the Bread of
Chrift, nor the Flefh of Chrift into their own
Flefh : The *Quakers* can give no Account what is
become of the Flefh or Body of that man Chrift
Jefus, thefe *Foxes* have devoured the Lambs of God.
Miraculous and Monftrous is [119] the Papifts *blaf-phemous* and *Bloody Fancy* of *Tranfubftantiation*, but
not more miraculous and monftrous, *&c.* then that
of the *Quakers*, which granteth Chrift Jefus to have
been born, lived and dyed as We,&c and yet now
Tranfubftantiated into a Spirit, and the *Quakers*
Flefh. So that in the Upfhot, the Chrift in whom
they believe is vanifhed (by an *Hellifh Chimiftry*)
into themfelves, and it is moft certain, (the Lord
open in great mercy fome of their Eyes to fee it)
they do believe on themfelves, and that lying Spirit
within them.

I remember, that hereabouts *Iohn Burnet* faid, that
it was not true that they preached not true Repent-ance, and herein he fell into a Speech or Sermon to
the People, profeffing that the *Quakers* maintained
Repentance toward God and Faith in Chrift and
Godlinefs,

Godlinefs, and Righteoufnefs, &c. and he continued
I Judge above half an hour, (though not fo long
nor fo furious as *William Edmundfon* the day before.

I liftned carefully and watcht his Ending (being

And my
Anfwer
defirous to fay fomething leaft another of them
fhould fall into a Sermon alfo and put me by) and
I fpeedily faid (to this Effect) Friend you have here
delivered many holy Truths of God (at this there
was deep filence, as if I had turn'd a Profelite, at
leaft it pleafed them to be applauded, I went on and
faid concerning Repentance and turning from all
fin, of the Blood of Chrift, and of being faved by
his Blood, *of living foberly, Righteoufly, and godly in
this prefent World*, &c. but withal I faid, they did
not reach me nor any thing that I had fpoken as
proof againft them, for I and all their Adverfaries
the Proteftants preached Repentance and Faith,
&c. but theirs was an *Anti-Chriftian Repentance*,

The Qua-
kers and
the Papifts
general
Faith and
Repent-
ance
and Faith, &c. becaufe either not true Repentance
and Faith as Proteftants argue againft the Papifts
and Quakers, or elfe in general Terms not diftinguifhing between true Repentance and falfe, and
fhewing the difference between the true Faith and
the falfe : So that I faid you might have preacht
this Sermon even in *Rome* before the Popes face in
his own Chappel, yea, the Pope and the *Cardinals*

The Jug-
lings of
the Papifts
and Qua-
kers
and *Friars*, and *Iefuits* deliver the fame Doctrines
(in general Terms) daily : But as *Thieves Iuglers*,
and *Counterfiets* when they come to Examination,
their Impudent fayings and Swearings prove but
the paints of *Whores* and *Har-* [120] *lots*? So do
the Devilifh Doctrines and Devilifh Conceit and
Fancies

Fancies of *Papiſts*, *Quakers*, and all Fantaſtick, Formal, Carnal Proteſtants, who Cry *Lord, Lord*, &c. but are Anſwered by Chriſt Jeſus with I *know ye not, Depart from me ye that work* Iniquity.

I cannot Affirm that I ſpake all theſe Individual words, nor have omitted ought that I or they ſpake: yet I remember no more, though being Confined (by their great deſire and my ſelf) to a puarter of an hour, for each point I was forced as all may judge to omit many Amplifications and Illuſtrations which now I crave the Readers patience, while I preſent him with ſome of them.

I intended to have Charged them with the falſe- neſs of their Hope, and Love, and Peace, and Joy which they often Crake, (though they pretend quak- ing and Trembling) their Heaven confiſteth, and all the Eternal Life to come, they look for, they are now in preſent, full Poſſeſſion of. _{The Hope peace and Joy of the Quakers}

What Scripture is more common in the mouths and pens of the *Quakers*, then that of *Paul* to the *Coloſſians, Chap.* 1. which is, *Chriſt in you the Hope of Glory*: whereby they Infinuate two of their grand Deceits and Lyes, *Firſt*, that their is no other Chriſt but what is in every man in the World. *Secondly*, That there is no other Glory to be hoped for in, or by, or with the Lord Jeſus, but what the Saints, that is the *Quakers* enjoy, and are already poſſeſſed of within them in this Life. _{Chriſt the Hope of Glory}

To which I ſay, how many painted Anchors and painted Hopes are there? How many Hopes as in *Iob* like the Spiders web ſwept away to Eternity?

If

If there be e're a painted Anchor or e're a Spiders web in the world[1] this of the *Quakers*.

Hope is one, as in time I may furthet demonstrate.

For, do they not overthrow the very Nature of Hope which they prate of, and give rhe Spirit of God *Rom*. 9. the Lye, which tells us that Hope is not of things in poſſeſſion, or which we ſee? doth not *Paul* there tell us almoſt in plain Terms, that it is ſimplicity and Non-Senſe to talk concerning Hope after ſuch a Rate? Doth not 1 *Pet*. 1. tell us of a *Living Hope* (oppoſite to painted and dead Hopes) and this *Living Hope* called in other places *the Hope of Righteouſneſs, the Hope of the Redemption of our Bodies* ? the Hope as of Heirs for an Inheritance? of the Glory that [121] ſhall be revealed in us, which is a ſtate of the manifeſtation of the Sons of God, though ſaith *John, We are now the Sons of God*, 1 John 3. we know not what that is, all that is now enjoyed is but as the *firſt Fruits* to the *Harveſt*, as the Spirit ſpeaks.

The Simplicity as well as Impiety of the Quakers Hope

2. Again, what Ignorance and ſimplicity is it to call Chriſt or God, the Glory or the goodneſs, or good things which we hope for, Literally and properly upon the Promiſe, and the Power, and goodneſs of God, no Chriſt Jeſus? Can the *Eternal God* in any *Literal Senſe* be called the Hope of *Iſrael*, Jer. 14. but in the ſame *Figurative Senſe* whereby *Moſes* cals him *Our Life and the Length of our Dayes* ? and we in *Common Speech* call ſuch a man, or his

Promiſe,

---

[1] Interline "it is" after world. *R. W. Ms. Ann.*

Promife, or any Creatures dear to us, *Our Hope, our Love, our Joy,*&c. that is theGround or theObject of ourHope&c

Their *great Blunderer Humphry Norton* he deals as plainly and roundly as G. *Fox* (his *æmulous Corrival*) falfly and fraudulently, when that holy Scripture [*If in this Life only we have Hope,* &c.] was here objected to *Humphry Norton,* he clapt his hand on his Breaft faying. He had it there already, that is oppofing it to (and denying the Hope in) the Life to come, efpecially, as to their Bodies which are not raifed up (they fay) *Spiritual Bodies,* being (though of late) more fubtly and hipocritically all one with thofe deceived Souls that faid the Refurrection was paft already. It is true, they will pretend to owne the Scriptures, Chrifts humane Nature, the Refurrection, and Judgement, and Faith, and Hope, ahd Repentance, &c. as true and found as any Proteftant : but ftill it is no otherwife, but as G. *Fox* and *Ed. Burroughs* fay in this Book, that is, (as I have and fhall open) in a moft *Jugling* and *deceitful Senfe* and meaning.

It is reported that fome of them at their Death have ufed thofe words [*Lord Jefus receive my Spirit,*] fome have Charitably thought that they intend thereby their going prefently into the prefence of Chrift Jefus, but as the Truth and bottom, however they blind the world, and the weakeft of their Followers, (until they be fit to wean and fall to ftrong meat) others of them Covertly fay & write, and others of them more plainly fay, *viz.* That they believe no more Rifing of their Bodies then the

rifing

[marginal notes:] Humpry Norton his Hope

The Quakers Hope of life to come

rifing of a Dog: and as to their *Spirits* they believe
Souls are [122] patts of God, and go unto God and
into God: and therefore their faying, *Lord Jefus
receive my Spirit*, is no more then Lord Jefus receive thy felf, according to fome of their plain Expreffions: To whom fhould I pray? my felf? to
whom fhould I give Thanks? my felf? wherein
their *woful, black,* and *filthy Spirit* Contradicteth
it felf amongft themfelves, though they agree in
the *Devils Bait,* (which Catcht himfelf, and with
which he Catcht our *firft Patents* and all his *Pofterity) viz. Ye fhall be as Gods,* live as God, know as
God, be Gods and Chrifts for Evermore.

I fhall now crave the Readers patience to hear
fome fewQuotations out of G. *Fox,* which my quarter of an hour would not then permit) declaring
thcir *Apoftacie* and *Herefie* in the matters of *Repentance, Faith,* &c.

In *Pag.* 127. he brings in *John Bunyan* faying,
[*It is a Counterfietlng of the New Birth for men to
follow the Light wherewith men coming into the World
are enlightned.*]

G. *Fox* Anfwereth, [*which none comes to the New
Birth,but who comes to the Light, wherewith every man,
&c. which believing in is a Child of the Light: believing and receiving comes to receive power to be the Sons
of God.*]

I Reply, none are truly Converted, born again,
&c. but in a true Senfe they come to Chrift Jefus:
For the Scripture faith, *he gives Repentance to Ifrael,
He is the Author and Finifher of our Faith*: But that
Jefus Chrift as God, (fo the *Quakers* owne him) and
as

Marginal notes:

The Qua-
kers bait
by which
Satan takes
them

John
Bunyan

The new
Birth of
thc Qua-
kers

as man (for fo they alfo owne him) fhould be in
every man, and Woman, and Child in the World,
I have proved and fhall prove it to be a *blockifh* and
Devilifh Fancy.

2.   If this Light, this Chrift the Mediator between God and man be only a Spirit and not man,
why do the Scriptnre, why do the *Quakere* madly
fay there was fuch a man, though they cannot tell
now what is become of him except he be (as they
fay) within, *&c.*

3.   If this Light, this Chrift, this Mediator be
in every man, what fhould be the Reafon that fo
many *Thoufands* and *Ten Thoufand* of *Millions* fee
him not? Only a few perfons Curfing and Reviling
all the reft, and that fay all but the *Quakers* are deceived? Can the Sun be in a Chamber and perfons
not blind, but [123] feeing and awake, and ufing his
Light and yet not fee it. Certainly it is but a *painted
Sun* that doth not fhine equally on all, it is but a
painted Fire that doth not burn, and the *Quakers* are
but *Pictures* of *Chriftians,* and pictures of men to
argue aftet fuch a Rate, that Chrift not only as
God, and Creatour fhould be in every man, but alfo
as the Mediator, as the Spirit, and yet not operate
according to the Nature of the Sun and Fire: It is
true, the Lord Jefus came into the dark world, and
their darkness comprehended him not to be He
that was to come, the *true Meffiah*: but when Chrift
Jefus as Mediator, the true or only Light fhall
dwell in the Undeftanding and Will, and Memory,
and Affections of a man or Woman, and thofe perfons be favingly inlightened by him as you write,
                                                        and

and yet not Converted and faved by him, it can be
the Language of none but thofe that peep and mut-
ter *Ifai.* 8. but have no true Light, but a falfe and
painted Light within them.

The true
and falfe
new Birth.

Laftly, faith *Fox* this turning to the Light within
is the New Birth: But the *Holy Record* faith, that
till the preaching of the Word, or Gofpel, or glad
News come to the mind of a man, (ordinarily by
the Ear, and hearing, and preaching, *Rom.* 10.)
there is no *Faith,* nor *Covenant,* nor *Chrift,* nor God
in the Soul, *Ephef.*2. and we are not only in darknefs, but darknefs it felf, *Ephef.* 5. and only by the
holy Word and Spirit preached[1] the bleffing, *Ifai.*
59., God fhineth in our hearts, and not by any fuch
Immediate Fantaftick Faith or Spirit, as the *Anti
Chriftian Quakers* dream of, yea, againft the Light
of a twofold Experience in their own Souls.

The Qua-
kers put
out the
Eyes of
their own
Experi-
ence.

1. That many of them being enlightened and
formerly Convicted by the reading or preaching of
the Doctrine, Word or Will of God revealed in
the holy Scripture.

2. That of their new Light (as they falfly and
foolifhly prate) pretended to be brought unto their
Ears and knowledge by the means of thefe *new
Apoftles, Preachers,* and *Minifters,* fo pretended of
Chrift Jefus.

When God hides (that is by *Spiritual Judgements*)
the Light of Scripture, of the Spirit of Reafon,
and of Experience, *&c.* who can find it out? No
man, no nor Devil can fubfift one minute without the power of *Chrifts Eternal Power and Godhead:*

[1] Interline "is" after preached.   *R. W. Ms. Ann.*

head: [124] but when Chriſt Jeſus comes into the
Soul as *Mediator* of the *new Covenant,*and be thus
idle and not operative in all mankinde in the
World, and not to Convert,and work belief in them,
which muſt be either becauſe he cannot, or becauſe
he will not, as the *Leaper* ſaid, is as black and blaſphemous a Fancy as any *Atheiſtical* or *AntiChriſtian
Soul* can harbour.

He brings in *George Willington* ſaying, [*He is Iuſ-* ^{Pag 44.}
tified by Faith alone without good works]He Anſwers; ^{George Willing-}
[*What without Faith that works by Love.*] ^{tou}

I Reply: In this paſſage, and in many others, this
ſubtle man clearly diſcovers what he makes true
Juſtifying Faith to be, *viz.* not one hair breadth
more then the Faith that may be to God in the
firſt Covenant, the Covenant of works, and a looking
to be Juſtified and ſaved be God for a mans own
Abilities, performances and Righteouſneſs, far from
the Faith of the Goſpel, which though good works
in Love follow it, yet not one good work in the
world goes before it: Nor one good work in the
world goes with it in the point of Juſtification, or ^{The Qua-}
pardon of our Tranſgreſſions: and therefore G. <sup>kers meer
Jewiſh and</sup>
Fox hath not only *George Willington* his Oppoſite, ^{Popiſh}
but the expreſs word and Declaration of the Spirit
of God ſaying, [*Rom. 3. Therefore we Conclude that
a man is Iuſtified by Faith and not by the works of the
Law.*]

^{The dole-}
Alas *porr Bankrupts* who owe more Infinitely to ^{ful ſtate of}
God then we are worth: who are over head and ^{all men}
Ears in Debt to God, to our own Souls,to Men and <sup>till mercy
not juſtice</sup>
Angels,and the whole Creation, having ſinned againſt ^{pitty them}
Heaven,

Heaven, &c. that have not one farthing toward the
difcharge of fo many *Infinite Millions* of *Talents*:
God of his rich Infinite mercy convinceth fome of
the proud Sons and Daughters of men of their *deplorable Condition*, makes them cry for mercy, and
for Chrift Jefus fake and Mediation, he freely Iufti-
fies and forgives them. Thus faith the Scripture
all along, and that our Faith, our believing or receiving of this grace though it be followed with
Mary Magdalens Love, contributes not one farthing
toward the payment *of our Infinite Millions*, no not
fo much as one good Thought.

He brings in *Iofeph Miller* faying, [*It is an Errour to fay, we are Iuftified by that which Chrift doth
in us.* He Anfwers, Contrary to the Apoftle, who
faith, We are Iuftified by Faith in his Blood: [125
And the Faith is in the Heart, and the Blood is in
the Heart that purifies it, and held in a *pure Confcience*: And the Word of Faith is within, *Rom.* 10.
And Faith gives Victory over the World, and that
which gives Victory Juftifies, And Chrift is within you who is *Juftification, Sanctificotion* and *Redemption*: either of them is found within, and thou
art in the Errour, and not fit to talk of thefe things
thou underftandeft not.

I Reply: Grant that in a true Refpect and Senfe,
Faith is within, and the Blood within, and the
Word of Faith within, and Chrift within, and *Juftification* and *Sanctification* within, will it therefore
follow I fay, will it therefore follow with any Colour
of Common Reafon, that therefore in one and the
fame Senfe they are all within, and they are all
one,

Pag 47
Jofeph
Miller

The Qua-
kers Jufti-
ficatson
within us.

Fox his
Babilonifh
tumbling

one, and they were not without before they were _{of all in a}
within ? I know this *fubtle Fox* and he that helps _{Croud and Heap to-}
his deluded pate to bind up fuch a *Bundle* of *wrefted* _{gether.}
Scriptures, would have it fo, that he may *jumble* and
blend all together in a *Babilonifh Myftery*, and fubtly
deny the Truth of the holy Scriptures Hiftory.

It is true, *Cheift dwels in our Hearts by believing*,
Ephef. 3. and Confequently his Crofs, yea, his *Manger*, yea, his *Blood*, yea, his *Grave* are within, *&c.*
But that Chrift Literally fhed his Blood within
us, as a *Ranfome* to his Eather for the fins of the
whole world, is as *Fine* and *bruitifh a Fancy*, as that
the *Crofs*, the *Spear*, the *Soulders*, the *High Priefts*,
Scribes and *Pharifees* and *People*, *Pilate*, the *Romans*,
Ierufalem, Iude, & the whole world (as fome of them
have idly & ofteuprated) are Literally within us.

It is true in a Senfe, the King and his pardon,
and Counfellours and Scribes, and writings, and Seals,
&c. are all in a *Rebels heart*, as he believes and ap- _{Juftifica-}
plies all thefe within him, and his belief works by _{tion opened.}
love : But if they be within otherwife then we Af-
firm, *&c.* and as G. *Fox* would have it, then they
are not withont alfo, (which is the mark all thefe
Arrows from *Hell* fly at,) and Confequently Chrift
Jefus and his Blood fhedding, and a *Literal Ierufalem*, and a *true* and *real man* Chrift Jefus, and the
holy, real Literal Scriptures are blown up and vanifhed altogether.

Pag. 10. He brings in *Iohn Bunyar* faying, [It *is
not Faith and works that juftifies a man before God,
but it is Faith and good works which juftifie in the
fight of men only, and fuch works will not* [126] *juftifie in
the*

*the fight of God: and he faith, that works is only to
juftifie their Faith to be true before men.*]

G. *Fox* Anfwers, *Abraham* was not Juftified only
to men by his Obedience, but to God: And where
there is *Faith* there is *Iuftification* which works by
Love: And the *Saints Faith* and *works* were not
only to Juftifie them in the fight of men. For the
work of God is to do what he faith,& the will
which who doth not is not Juftified by fo doing,
but to be beaten with ftripes: who feek to be Juftified by their Faith and works in the fight of men
are dead, Faith and works both.

I Reply, He that reads this paffage may without
doubting Conclude that G. *Fox* and his *Foxians* are
as *perfect Pharifees* (*Iewifh* and *Popifh*) as ever bur-
roughed in *Rome* or *Ierufalem*, maintaining a Covenant of works, Juftification by works, and renounc-
ing Chrift Jefus his Blood and merits: For if *Abraham* was Juftified and received his pardon by his
Obedience to God what need was there for him
and us,to look out for a *Surety*,a *Redeemer*, a *Mediator* to pay his Blood for our Ranfome, and to fetch
us out of the *miferable ftate of Sin*; *Death*, and
Hell,&c.

2. Whereas G. *Fox* asketh what is the work of
God, but to do what he faith.

I Reply, 1. The work of God (according to
Chrifts Doctrine) is to believe on him whom God
fent. It is true, it is the Command of God to
keep his Commands,but fince the deadly Fall of
man,none,not one being able, *Rom.* 3.(though *Fox*
deny it,) it is the work,the *great work* of God to fly
to

to that *bleffed Propitiation* for poor finners,(throughout the world :) But G. *Fox* cannot diftinguifh between the *Covenant of works,* of *Iuftice,* and of *Debt,*
and that of *mercy,* and of receiving all as a *Beggar,*
and Condemned Rebels, *poor proud Souls* they know
not any difference between the Blood of Chrift
Iefus and their own Blood, as we fhall fee afterward.

3. Whereas he faith, that they do not Gods will
are not juftified in fo doing :

I Anfwer, therefore it follows ronndly as his Conclufion, that they that do Gods will are juftified in
fo doing : that is their fins are pardoned as *David*
and *Paul* by pardon of Sin defcribe juftification,
127] Who fees not the fubtlety of this *Fox* cheating himfelf and others with the divers fignification
of this *Latin word Iuftification*? It is true, a man
can not be juftified or defended for *Thieving, Whor-*
ing, Murthering, &c. Doth it follow therefore, that
they that do not *Steal, whore, murther,* &c. by this
abftaining from Sin, and by this their work they
obtein the pardon, and ftand by this their work,
legally right and juftified in the *Court of Heaven*!

Fox his playing with the word Juftification

I Conclude, that by thefe hints a broken hearted
finner, who hath feen Sin as Sin, the fin of his Nature, his chief fin, *&c.* will fee how far from the
Doctrine of true Repentance, true Faith, &c thefe
mens Teachings be, and (for all their boafting) what
need they have to Examine themfelves whether
they be in the Faith, and whether there be any other
Chrift Iefus within them then a *Counterfiet* and *paint-*
ed Meffiah, and whether their *Counterfiet* and *painted*
Faith, Repentance and *Hope* will yield them another
Fruit then a *dolefully Counterfieted and perifhing Sal-*
vation. At

At laſt by Gods merciful held I come now (with their glad Conſent) to the ſeventh and laſt Poſition propounded to be diſcuſt at *Newport*, viz. that their Religion was nothing elſe but a mixture of *Popery*, *Arminianiſme, Socinianiſme, Iudaiſme*, &c.

The laſt of the ſeven Poſitions at New-port

Herein I knew I was not to exceed my quarter glass, and there.fore I take liberty now a little to inlarge, to remember the Reader of the old Pro-verb, *that where God hath his Church, the Devil will have his Chappel*. And that where Chriſt Ieſus hath his Field of *good Seed*, while the Servants ſleep, the Enemy will ſow the *Tares*, of *rotten Doctrines*, and *rotten Profeſſors*, who like *Windefals*, and *Revolting Rebels* fall from the *holy Truths* they have profeſſed, being looſe aud weak believers or only *affrighted* and *Terrified Hipocrites*, by Gods righteous Iudge-ment delivered over to liſten too, and believe Lyes as the only *heavenly Truths* of Ieſus.

The Qua-ker Religion pieced up o many old Here-ſies

I had purpoſed to have ſhewed how in matters concerning God, the Son of God, the Spirit of God, &c. the *Quakers* have followed, the *Cerdonians*, the *Priſcillians*, the *Valentinians*, the *old Gnoſticks*, and *Manicheans* : but I Confined my ſelf to the Terms of the *Poſition*, and declared that the *Quakers* were *downright Papiſts* in many points, ſome I then In-ſiſted on, and the reſt [128] intended, I ſhall now mention. *Firſt*, In magnifying the *rotten ſtrength* and *Arm* of *dead* and *rotten Nature*: when it is Ob-jected to G. *Fox* in his book, that *by Nature we are all dead in ſins and Treſpaſſes*:

G. *Fox* Anſwers, by d,viding all men into three ſorts: Some are born holy from the wombe, as *Ier.* Some

Some the Saints that is, only their Children born
holy without any finful corruption. *Thirdly,* the
wicked who will not turn to the Light within them,
and they are only the *Unbelievers dead in fin.* But
the *Proteftants, David* and his *Followers* Confefs
their *Natures, Births,* and *Conceptions* to be all defiled with fin, and with a *finful pronenefs* to all Iniquity, though *miraculoufly* fome are Sanctified, or fet
apart to God from the wombe as *Ieremiah, Iohn the
Baptift,* &c. Some after a more peculiar and miraculous manner, as the Lord Iefus : Some by *New
Birth,* and the *wonderfal Supernatural Power* of the
holy Spirie *Changing, Regenerating,* and as it were
New Creating the *Soul* and *Spirit,* in *Everlafting,
Unchangeable Holinefs* and *Righteousnefs* after the
Image of his first and fecond Creatour.

It is true, that the *Papifts* come nearer the Truth
as to *Birth, Corruption* and *Defilement* then the *Qua-*
kers, acknowledging all *,o be Conceived and born in*
Sin, not that the Devil or the *Papifts* care to acknowledge this Truth, but that they may ufe it as a
Cridge over which they may pafs to the Neceffity of
Baptifme on pain of *Damnation* : on which they
may alfo build many other *Superftitious Fanciee* as
to the holy Ordinances.

But the *Quakers,* although they hold only their
own Children to beConceived and born holy &with-
out Sin, yet they jump into one ftep with the *Pa-*
pifts, as to the Power of Nature in Spirituals, ane
that every man and woman in the world hath a
fufficient Light within him to fee God and Chrift,
&c. and to turn themfelves unto them to *Eternal
Life.*

Life. Contrary to the *Proteſtants,* who from the holy Scriptures maintain mans Natural Blindneſs and Darkneſs, *Epheſ.* 5. Mans Natural Deadneſs, *Epheſ.* 2. and that our wiſdome can not diſcern any Spiritual thing, that is, Spiritually, 1. *Cor* 2. That our *Quinteſſence* of *Nature,* our very *wiſdome is Enmity to God:* He hates us as we hate him, and are at *deadly fewd* and *mortal Hatred* like two men of War [129] giving Fire one upon another, we *re-*

The way of Converſion both of the Papiſts and the Quakers *ſolving* to ſink by *Ejods ſide,* rather then to yield to God: but God in *Infinite pitty,* ſeeing our weakneſs and madneſs, and certain Deſtruction hangs out a *white Flag* and offers a *Parly,* on purpoſe to ſave us from our deſperate minde & Ruine, which by many heavenly means of *Free mercy* he Effecteth ? The *Papiſts* ſpeak more like Men, and at laſt yield that men and Women have left them (ſince *Adams Fall*) power to liſten too, and obey *Moral Perſwaſions,* and offers which God makes : The *Quakers* talk only (like *Bruits*) of no means, no means but *Immediate Revelation* of the Spirit : and yet in Contradiction to themſelves they make theSpirit an inward means, and their *Apoſtles* or *Meſſengers* an outward means, or elſe they make themſelves *idle Embaſſodors,* in vain and to no purpoſe. The *Pro-*

The way of the trne Proteſtants *teſtants* affirm from 2. *Cor·* 3. that we have not one good Thought but from God, that it is God, not we, that turns the will, *Phil.* 2. that when the Word of Faith is preached, *Rom.* 10. and Faith or Belief is wrought by hearing, : yet is it *Gods free Grace* that makes the difference, 1 *Cor.*4. when ſeveral Hearers are Aſſembled, and God opens *Lidiahs heart* and

not

not others, *Acts* 16. the *learned Academians* mock, and only *Dionisius* and *Damaris*, and a few believe, becaufe *God sheweth mercy on whom he will, and whom he will, he hardneth.* Acts 17. Rom. 9. 2.

The *Papifts* and *Quakers* both maintain that *dole-fully, uncomfortable*, and *defperate Doctrine* of falling away from *true* and *faving grace*: The Truth is, neither of them feem to know *Experimentally* what *true* and *faving grace is*: It is true, they differ, the *Papifts* make *Saving Grace* the Property only of the *Regenerate*: The *Quakers* fay it is in every man and Woman in the world, they have it, though they know it not, and will not turn to it, and believe in it: yet both agree that they loofe it, whereas the *true Proteftants* though they grant great Failings and Falls, and Defertions of Gods Children, yet they hold the *Seed of God*, the *holy Spirit* and Word of God, *Ifai.*59. and 1 *Cor.*3. that *Incorruptible, Eternal Seed*, of which they are begotten, never *Final-* [130] *ly?* nor *Totally* to be Ecclipfed, and they juftly account that Doctrine of *Interceffion*, viz. when *Son-ship* or *Childship* is cut off by Sin, and Renewed by Repentance, to be a *fimple Fantaftical Notion*, as if *David* were a Child of God to day, a Child of the Devil to morrow, a Child of God this hour, and a Child of the Devil the next, &c. only they fix this impiously upon mortal and great fins only, as if *Adam* Eating of an *Apple* were not fufficient to his and our Deftruction, as well as *Davids* finning with *Bathsheba* and *Uriah*, &c

Falling from Grace

The true Proteftants Doctrine as to Falling away.

3. I muft be briefer, though not fo brief as I was

forced

The Papifts and Quakers agree againft the holy Scripture

forced to be in our publick probations : I told them that the *Papifts* and the *Quakers* were *great Confederates* in their Endeavours to raze the *Records of Heaven,* and to rob the Saints and the world of this *Ineftimable Jewel* and *Treafure* of the holy Scriptures.

1 The Papifts own it not to be all the word or will of God revealed, but that there be unwritten Verities,that is, Gods mind revealed from Father to Son, by Tradition.

The Quakers will not vouchfafe it the Name of the word of God, out of a fimple pretence, becaufe Chrift is the word of God, that is, he isindeed the chief manifeftation of all the Appearances of God.

2 The *Papifts* horribly abufe it,calling it a Nofe of wax,a *Leaden Rule,*a *dead Letter, &c.* and fo do the Quakers triumphing over it with base Infultations, as over a *dead Letter,* a *Carkafs.* &c.

3. The whole world of *Papifts* affembled in *eighteen Years Labours,* (& *Chymical Laboratories*at *Trent*)at laft thundred out their *Anathamaes* and

The Papifts and Quakers Enmity againft the Hebrew aud Greek

Curfes againft all that fhould not prefer the *Vulgar Latin Copies* before the *Hebrew Copies* and the *Greek* (in which it pleafed the holy Spirit of God firft to write his mind and will or word unto us:) And do not the *Quakers* as *fimply* and *bruitifhly* bind themfelves to the bare Letter of the *Common Englifh* ? Though they know the *Hebrew* and *Greek Copies* are the *Foundation* and *Touchftone* of all other (though millions of) Tranflations : Though they know there be more *Englifh Tranflations* then one ; Though the Englifh Tranflations *wonderfully* [135 *differ*

differ; Though *Ravius*(that *Famous Oriental Hebrician*, &c.) proclaims above a *Thoufand Faults*, and fome grofs in our laft Tranflation : though fome of them (as *John Stubs*) boaft of their humane Learning produced his *Hebrew Bible* in our Conference : yet will thefe Ephefians cry out (like *Frantick mad*) great is our *Latin Tranflation*, great is our *Englifh Tranflation* : Yea, one of them boafted to my felf, that the Spirit of God would teach them Scripture without the *Hebrew* and the *Greek*, or the *Englifh* either.

4. The *Papifts* fet up a Judge in Controverfies above the holy Scriptures, who can difpenfe with Scriptures and do all that God can do. And fay not the Quakers the fame of their Spirit which is above the Scriptures, for it gave forth the Scriptures, and is in every man

The Papifts and Quakers Judge of Scripture

5. The *Papifts* though they will not deny to make the Scriptures the Rule, and profefs to be tried by it, yet their Church, and the head of it the *Pope muft Interpret* : And do not the *Quakers* herein the fame concerning themfelves, though fome think more bruitifhly, for they will allow no Interpretations, nor meaning at all, but you muft take the words as the *Tranflators* have given them us (right or wrong) and you must not enquire either into the meaning of words, or the meaning of mind of God in the place. Oh what a *black, deaf* and *dumb, Lazie Spirit* hath poffeffed the Souls of thefe great pretenders too and *Monopolizers* of the holy Spirit of God, both *Papifts* and *Quakers* ?

Interpretation of Scripture

6 The *Papifts* generally ufe not, nor have the
holy

holy Scripture, (no not in their Devotions) in their own Tongue, but in the *Latine*, (the *Whores Tongue of Italy :*) therefore no wonder they prize it not: but even the *Lights* or *Luminaries* fo pretending, amongft them difufe it, Care not for it, read it not, *&c.* many have it not : So that *Luther* tels us that in *Thirteen years* or more he faw not a Bible in his College at *Erford*, until by Gods merciful providence he came to fee one, to his own & the Comfott of *Thoufands*, & *Luther* tels us that at one great Affembly of the *Emperour* and *Princes*, the *Proteftants* of *Germany* had Conveyed a Bible on the Table : The *Cardinal* being firft come he opened the Book, and read here and there in it, (it is like he had not feen [132] it before in his Life,) In comes one of the *Popifh Princes*, and askt the *Cardinals Eminency* what Book he had there?

The Papifts and Quakers flighting holy Scripture

He Anfwerred, I know not : but I am fure it is agaiuft us, and it is laid here for that purpose. Oh the *I*nfinite mercies of God to us in our times, and our Infinite Debt to his Infinite goodnefs, and our Infinite guilt in neglect of it:

The Papifts and Quakers would be rid of the Scripture

The *Quakers* at firft took off themfelves, *Families* and *Affemblies* from any use of it : Their Spirit they Crake that made theScriptures fupplies all, *&c.* The *Papifts* and *Quakers* both have faid and printed, that if the Scripture were confumed & quite taken out of the world, there would be no Lofs, fo long as they have theSpirit. The Truth isIcould byArguments many make it appear that the *Papifts* and *Quakers* love the holy Scriptures no better than *Goliah* loved
                                                                  Davids

Davids ftone and fling? nor no better then the Devil loved *Chrifts* Gegraptai, *It is written* : *It is written* : for the *Papifts* and the *Quakers,* and the Devil knows that if the holy Scriptures be Exalted, as the revealed will or word, or Declaration of the mind of God, down-falls their pretences of *Traditions* and *Revelations,* whereby the *Devil deceivs* themfelves and *himfelf alfo.*

4. The *Papifts* and *Quakers* fhake hands in the moft *hellifh Doctrine* of Juftification by what is within us, by what Chrift works within us, in fhort, by what is called Sanctification put for Juftification, and the forgiveness of fin, in and for the merits of the Lord Jefus freely imputed and given to us : The *Papifts* ufe the word *Inherent Righteousnefs,* but the *Quakers* bogle at the word not finding it in the *Englifh Bible,* yet they agree that by the works of Obedience, yea, and alfo by the Acts of their own *Inventions* and *Superftitions,* they can make a pardon under a hedge to themfelves, and Crake that they have received a pardon and Juftification fealed under the *Broad Seal of Heaven* to them, but it is againft the glory of *the King of Heaven,* and againft the glory of *the Son of God,* and his *glorious Sufferings,* and their own *Salvation.*

The Papifts and Quakers unite againft the Blood of the Lord Jefus

5 The *Quakers* are P*apifts* in that Spirit of *Infallibility* which they arrogate to themfelves, pretending that the holy, Spirit *fhall lead them into all Truth,* fpeak *Immediately* in [133] them, *&c.* though herein they differ, the Pope infallibly expounds Scripture, but the *Quakers* fpeaks Scripture, and his word is Gofpel, *&c.* yea, all men have this Spirit, and

The Infallibility of Papifts and Quakers

and need no *Teacher*, and yet what an *horrible Contradictious noise* is there of the *Quakers, Apostles, Messengers, Ministers, Preachers* He and she sent into *Old-England*, and *New-England, Scotland, Ireland, Turky, Italy*, to bid people hearken to the *Immediate Spirit* within ?

The Quakers Popish Perfection. 6. The *Quakers* are *Papists* in that high lofty Conceit of their Perfection, when *Calvins time* this Spirit came from Hell under the name of *Spirituals*, and when of latter years in *Lancashire* under the Name of *Grindletonians*, all their Religion turned chiefly upon these two Hinges.

1. They could not sin, were perfect, *&c.*

The Popish Revelations of the Quakers 2. They did nothing, said nothing, but God and the Spirit did all.

7. The *Papists* and *Quakers* are great Friends in their Notions & practice of *Revelations, Visions, Dreams, Impulsions* and *Inspirations* : He that hath known so much as I have known of both their Spirits this way, and hath read their *Legends* as I have done, and can Instance in particulars as I can, will say, it is a *foul, Popish, Devilish Spirit* that haunts them (both under this fine pretence)to turn *both off*

Pbpists and Quakers one in Ceremonies and Inventions *from the words of Jesus*, Luke 10. How readest thou ?

8. What *Cart Loads* of *Traditions* and *Ceremonies* have the Papists, and I believe if the *Quakers* have opportunities and means (as the Papists have had) they will not be behind them : what a noise is made about uncovering or bowing the Head, Knee, for

Courses

Courfes of wearing of Lace, (yea, *Bands* and *Hat-bands* by fome of them :] Of faying you or *Thou*, of ufing *Mufick, Carving, painting,* of *fitting filent,* (fome hundreths together) of *fighing* and *fhaking* of the Body ? all which, as relating to *Religion* and *Chriftians*: &c they are but *fimple, Infignificant,* and *Idle, popifh Trafh* and *Trumpery.*

9. The Papifts and Quakers are Biethren in Iniquity in their Affirmations that the Pope is not *Anti-Chrift,* and that [135] the Church of *Rome* is not the *great Whore*: The Papifts Affirme that *Anti-Chrift* is not yet come, and that he fhall come juft in the end of the world, and fhall finifh all thofe wonders in the *Revelations* in three years and a half: The Quakers though they hold Papifts and Proteft-ants (all except the Quakers (to be *Anti-Chriftians*; (& as *Fox* doth) caft back all the Prophefies of falfe Chrifts, falfe Prophets, and *Anti-Chrift* to the time of the Apoftles themfelves : yet the *great Whore* and the Devil, and fin, (upon the point) they fimply Confound and make all one ; as may be feen in *Fox* his Title to this great Book, and other of his and their writings.

The Quakers and Papifts agree that that hge Pope is not Anti-Chrift

10. It may be wondred why the Popes when made or created by an hnmane & Devilifh *Fiat,* they change their Name, and why the Quakers guided by the fame *Hellifh Spirit* and *Fancy,* are fo dainty and tender about owning their Old names : The Hiftories fay, the *Original* with the Popes was with hiin who was *Os porce,* or Swines fnout, by Name, and was not thought fit being raifed fo high to bear

The Quakers not owning freely their Names.

fo

1. In that great point of *Righteoufnefs, Reconcili-ation* with God, and *pardon* of Sin: They were *Zealous* (as the *Quakers* are) in the works of *Right-eoufnefs,* thinking thereby to pleafe and pacifie God, and to fatisfie his Juftice, putting their own *dirt* and *dung, Swines Blood* and *Dogs necks* upon *Gods Altar,* inftead of that *One fpotlefs Lamb of God,* that Man Chrift Jefus who alone *Expiateth,* and *taketh away the fins of the World.*

2. The *Jews* were *Zealou*s for their *Additions,* Traditions and *Superftitious Inventions,* which (as the Lord Jefus fpeaks) they pteferred before rhe Com-mands of God: as the wafhing of their hands, and of their Bodies, and of Pots and Cups, and Beds, and Platters, and other things upon a *Confcientious* and *Religious Account.*

The Qua-kers Ju-daifme.

The *Quakers* (if they had their Scope) fcorn to come behind the *Jews,* or *Papifts* for *Ceremonies* and *Traditions,* which it was neceffary for them both to add (as *Apples* and *Nuts,* &c. to ftill poor Children from Crying after Gods Worfhip.

1. I named fome of the *Quakers Traditions* and I*nventions* in our *publickConference,* (unto which I fhall now name [138] fome more) I told them, and now do, of the *Un-Chriftian* and *unnatural Inven-tion* of *Women Minifters, Women Apoftles, Women Embaffadors* to all *Nations*: a bufinefs that all the *Apoftolical firft Chriftian practice,* and all *fober* and *modeft Humanity* abhor to think of.

The Qua-kers Tra-ditious and Ceremo-nies

2. Their *dumb* and *filent meetings* (their *dumb* and *deaf* Spirit) without Colour of *Common Humanity* or *precept* or *practice,* or *promife* of Chrift to fuch a worfhip.   3. Their

Dumb Worfhip

3. Their *bruitiſh* *Salutations* of ſtrangers, yea, and of acquaintance, Foes or Friends : It is true that ſome of them will admit of thoſe two words, How do you, and Farewel, as if there were ſome holineſs in theſe two, and in none other, and they might practice this holineſs toward the world, &c.

Either none or Immodeſt Salutations

4. Their *New Way* of *feeling* and *grabling* the *hand* in an *uncouth*, *ſtrange* and *Immodeſt way*, and this inſtead of kiſſing, called the *holy Kiſs* amongſt Chriſtians, and a token of Love and Reverence to men alſo in ſober and Civilizd Nations.

5. Their *bruitiſh* *Irreverence* to all their Superiours either in Age, or in any other way of *Prehemi-nence*, a moſt *proud* and *monſtrous Beſtiality* againſt ſo many Commands and Examples of holy Scripture, and againſt the very Light of *Barbarous Nature* it ſelf, for the *Indians* uſe both Reverent words and Geſtures towards their *Sachims*, *Wiyouhs* and *Rulers*. Contrary to which, ſome of us have heard the Children of the *Quakers* brought up and taught to ſay to their Fathers *George* thou lyeſt : *Mary* thou lyeſt to their Parents, a Language which deſerved little leſs then Death by the Law, which God delivered to the *Jewiſh Nation*, and ſurely deſerveth ſevere Puniſhment at this day.

The Quakers diſreſpect to all Superiours.

6. Their Crying down of *Muſicians* ond muſick, (ſo Excellent a gift of God) as a *fooliſh* and *Deviliſh practice*, though confirmed by ſo many Reaſons from, and before Chriſts time in Scripture, and in all ſober Nature and Civility, though it is abuſed, as all the gifts of God are.

The Quakers againſt Muſick.

7. Their

Fantaſtical
finging

7. Their own *un-Chriſtian, Fantaſtical, abſurd,* and *unprofitable way* of *Toning* and *finging.*

Carving,
painting

139]   8. Their Condemning of the Commendable and Ingenious Arts of *Carving, Embroydering,* and *Painting,* ſo approved of,andCommended by God himſelf in Scripture, *&c.*

Orna-
ments

9. Their Crying out againſt Ornaments of Garments, and otherwiſe, againſt that Order God hath ſet in his works, and that Variety of his gifts for neceſſity, for Conveniency, for delight, even to *Aſtoniſhment* and *Admiration* in all his glorious works.

All theſe particulars (and more) I had not time, nor have I now to reckon up and amplifie, I remember no *Material Exception,* or Objections I had from my *Antagoniſts.*   Only *Iohn Burnet* ſpake againſt my great charging of them,and *William Edmundſon* he thundred out continually how deep my Charges were, and how weak my proofs, and that I had proved nothing.

The Con-
cluſion of
the Con-
ference at
Newport

I told them that if *Paul* or Chriſt Jeſus himſelf were there in preſence, they propably would be Anſwered as I was,*viz.* that they made many deep and falſeCharges againſt the people called *Quakers,* but they could prove nothing: but I ſaid,I ſubmitted the *Examinatoon* and *Conſideration* of all paſſages unto every mans Conſcience, and the praiſe and Iſſue only unto God.

The
quickeſt
and laſt
turn about
where
Chriſt is

After ſome turns of this ſort, *&c.* I praid their patience to Anſwer me one queſtion, *viz.* where is now that Man Chriſt Jeſus which they had Confeſſed to me was born at *Bethlehem,* and died at *Ieruſalem,*

Ierufalem,&c. At this they were all a while filent, and then *Iohn Burnet* Anfwered faying, he is where the Scriptures fay he is.

I Replied, where do the Scriptures fay he is, *Iohn Burnet* Replied, the Scripture fay he is *within*: I rejoyned to this purpofe: Then muft his Body be *Ubiquitary*, (as the *Tranfubftantiators* and *Confubftantiators* are forced to hold:) Then muft he have Infinite multitudes of Bodies, then muft his *Monftrous Body* or Bodies come from within his Saints, yea from within all mankind to Judgement, &c.

Juft here it pleafed God fo to Order it, that from the *Boat* (ready to fet Saile for *Providence*) I and others were [140] called upon to depart: So I was ftepping down, the Lord opened the mouth of *Elizabeth Williams* my *Brothers wife*, one of the Society of the *Baptifts* in *Newport*, who hearing their Clamours, their only Refuge, he hath proved nothing and faid aloud: The man hath difcharged his Confcience: He hath fully proved what he undertook to prove againft you, and the words that he hath fpoken fhall Judge you at the laft day. And thus the *Father of Lights, the firft and laft, the Alpha and Omega* gracioufly carried me through all alone thefe three dayes Contefts, as in a fhadow of Death with thefe *Deceived,* and *Deceiving Souls*: through my Labours of making out my proofs, the burthen whereof lay wholly upon me though they had been filent, (through their

Cenfures

An Unexpeƈted yet Seafonable and true Teftimony from Elizabeth Williams

Cenſures Reproaches, Falling on me ſo many at once, their *Interruptions,* and other *Diſadvantages* and *Provocations,* his *holy Name* be ever *praiſed* and *magnified.*

Our

141] *Our Conferences and Disputes at*
P R O V I D E N C E upon the seven other
Positions mentioned in my Paper sent to G.
Fox and his Associates.

Fter we were thus(as above said)parted:
They Remembered their Promise to
me of discussing the other seven at
Providence, and accordingly *Iohn Stubs*
and *William Edmundson* sent me a Note

The Con- of their willingness to come to *Providence* the last
ference at
Provi- day of the next week being the 17th. day of the
dence· *sixth Moneth* called *August*.

I Returned them from the *Shoar side* another
Note signifying, that (if God permitted) I would
then and there be ready to Receive them.

That day it pleased the goodness and patience of
God to bring us to, and being met thus at *Provi-*
dence, I first presented them with the Letter which
was sent to them and me (God knows) without
my thought or knowledg, at *Newport*, in publick
Assembled. But there they thrice refused it, and
here at *Providence William Edmundson* Answers, that
they

they came not to *Pro-* [142] *vidence* to hear *Papers*, but to hear me make out my Charges againſt them: One of my Neighbours *Thomas Olny Senior* an able and *Leading man* amongſt the People called *Baptiſts* at *Providence*, moved alſo for the Reading of the Letter, *William Edmundſon* ſaid to him who art thou? Art not thou a *Baptiſt*? haſt not thou ſeen it already? and further ſaid to him, Thou art an *Envious* and *filthy man*, upon no other *Provocation* but his *Rational deſire* the Letter might be Read. *William Edmondſon* thongh he had on either ſide of him an *able Iohn*, viz. *Iohn Stubs* and *Iohn Cartwright* ſpake all, and at laſt was forced to ſay that if the Letter Contained matter tending to prove my *Poſitions* it ſhould be read. But in the End I put up my Letter again, at the motion of *Captain Holden* of *Warwick*, as I did at *Newport*, in the morning of our *third dayes Conference*, for I obſerved that for all their *bruitiſh Clamour* of *Diana*, their *Light* or *dark Lanthorn*, rhey could not endure to be *Informed*, *Admoniſhed*, *Counſelled*, leaſt of all Reproved by any: and I alſo reſolved to wait upon Gods mercy for a Seaſon of publiſhing it on the *Houſe Top*, and therefore the Reader hath it *Faithfully preſented* in the *Eighty ſeventh Page* in the beginning of the *third dayes Conference* at *Newport*, this time ſtood up *Captain Iohn Green* of *Warwick* one of our *Magiſtrates*, who obſerving the *Inſulting Carriage* eſpecially of *William Edmundſon*, he deſired leave to propoſe one Query, which being granted he ſaid, he ſpake not as a *Magiſtrate* with *Authority*, but as an *Auditor* and ſitter by, and he ſaid, I deſire ro know whether

Mr.

Paſſages about Reading the former Recited Letter. Thomas Olny

About a ſtrange Query put to my Antagoniſt by Captain Green.

Mr. *Williams* be here as a *Delinquent* Charged to Anſwer at the Barr, or as a *Diſputant* upon equal Terms.

This *Query* they waved as well as they could, and I waved it alſo, and bore what ſeemed *Intollerable* to ſome that we might not be discouraged to go on in our buſineſs, about this time Mr. *Caverly* of *Warwick* deſiring leave to ſpeak, motioned for the Choice of a *Moderator* between us, *William Edmund-ſon* Anſwered that *Roger Williams* had himſelf pro-143] vided a *Moderator*, and he produced and Read my *Paper* of *Poſition*,, wherein I deſired that all matters might be left to every *man*s *Conſcience* and *Iudgement. &c.*

I knew with whom I had to deal, and therefore purpoſely waved, what ever I thought they would bogle at,& purpoſely gave them all *poſſible Advantages*, &c. and I humbly waited on God for patience for his ſake to bear with all Inconveniences, Inſultings, Interruptions, *&c.* and then, *I knew there would be no great need of a Moderator.*

Having thus cleard the way, I told them, I would briefly fall on my proof of the *firſt*, of the *ſeventh Poſitions* to be debated at *Providence*, *William Edmundſon* took forth his *Paper* and Read it, *viz.* [*The People called Quakers in Effect hold no God, no Chriſt, no Spirit, no Angel, no Devil, no Reſurrection, no Iudgement, no Heaven, no Hell, but what is in man.*

I told them that it was true, that in words and Terms they profeſſed and maintained all theſe, as other *Proteſtants* did, but if their writings were Examined, and eſpecially this of G. *Fox* which I had there

A Moderator motioned.

The firſt of the Poſitions debated at Providence

there by me it fhould appear that what they pro-
fefſed in one place they overthrew in another: I
told them that they had there *George Fox* his Book
as well as I, and if *Iohn Stubs* would turn to them I
would name the *Quoted Pages*, and read them and
he might read them alfo.

I named *Pag.* 273. where *George Fox* brings in _{Alexander}
Alexander Rofs faying, ⌊*It is horrible Blafphemy to* _{Rofs}
*fay the Scripture is not the Word of God, and to fay
the Soul is a part of God.*⌋

He Anfwers, ⌈The Scriptures are the words of
God, *Exodus* 20. and the *four Books* of the *Revelations*, but Chrift is the word in whom they End.
And it is not *Horrible Blafphemy* to fay that the Soul
is a part of God, for it comes out of him, and that
which comes out of him is of him, and Rejoyceth _{G Fox}
in him, I faid here what *George Fox* meant by the _{his Non-}
four Books of the *Revelations*, I knew not, and if _{Senfe}
they did they fhould do well to declare.

145] But they paft it by and fo did I and I infifted
on the matter which was that *G. Fox* imagined fuch
a *God* and *Godhead* as is partible and divifible, which _{*Quakers*}
might be divided into parts and pieces, and by this _{*ous opinion*}
_{*blafphem-*}
ftrange communication of his Effence, made him _{*about Goa*}
diffolvable, and fo corruptible, *&c.* againft the *Puri-* _{*and the*}
_{*Sovl*}
ty & Majefty & Eternity of *God*: For this renders
the *Effence* or Being of God capable of falling
from his purity as man hath done and doth, and
capable of punifhment and condemnation in *Hel-
Fire* as the Soul of man is; all which and more
neceffary Confequences of of that opinion are horrible and blafphemous to imagine, much more to
be

be uttered of the eternal invifible and infinitely and only *Wife God*.

About Gods Breath. *John Stubs* here read the words of *G. Fox* and faid, the reafon was to be weighed which *G. Fox* ufed which was; For it came out of him, and that which came out out of him is of him, and rejoyceth in him. To this end he defired the word in *Gen.* 2. might be viewed, which he turned to and read, viz. *God breathed into him the breath of life and man became a living Soul.*

About this time *Sam. Gorton* fen. defired to fpeak, and faid, If it be affirmed that God can be divided, & that man was a *Part of God,* the *God-head* was deftroyed and the *Soul of man,* and upon this *Bafis* all the reft would follow which was afferted in this *Pofition.* And whereas *John Stubs* read it as it is in our *Tranflation,* viz. *God breathed into him the breath of life, Mr. Gorton* faid it was *Lives* in the Margin, the breath of *Lives,* which *John Stubs* acknowledged.

It is frequent in their Books, (when they will fpeak plainly) for them to confefs that God breathed forth himfelf into *Adam,* and that ther fore mans *The Quakers Grofs conceit of soul & body* Soul or *Spirit* is a part of the *Divine Effence,* that the Soul is an increated fubftance: that as for the *Body,* it comes from the *Earth,* and returns to the *Earth,* and duft and rottennefs, and however they fometimes preach and print hat the *Body* fhall rife again, yet others again of them fpeak plainly, that as the body of a dog or beaft fo it vanifheth: But as for the *Spirit,* they fay that returns to God, that is into God. And although they talk to blind our eyes of a *Refurrection and Judgment,* and of *Souls being*

being punifhed with the Devil and his Angels, yet
others of them affirm that all Souls return into God,
and that the foul of *Judas* is now as happy in God
as the Soul of *Peter,* yea others of [146] them fpeak
plainly that they are *Chrift & God :* therefore one
of them being defired to give thanks at dinner,
asked roundly, *to whome fhould I give thanks ? to my
felf ?* and *Calvin* relates how (long ago) one *Quiniti-*
nus in his time a Leader this way, being demanded *Their high*
how he did? refolutely anfwered, *How can Chrift blafphe-*
doe but well ? and yet at that time he was very fick.*myes.*

About this time *W. E.* faid, what doft thou tel
us of ftoryes what this man faid and that man faid
we will not believe thee! But juft here rofe up a
neighbour *Jofeph Jinks,* who faid he had no preju-
dice againft the Quakers, yet he could witnefs to
the truth of thefe fpeeches of the Quakers, for one
of them had fpoke as much to his face lately at
Newport on *Rhode-Ifland :* but I ftill laboured to
keep down heat and therefore I told them I would
not trouble them with *Proofs* from elfewhere, but
from their own *writings,* and from that of G. *Fox*
there prefent, and therfore I prayed them to turn
to *Pag.39.* where G. *Fox* brings in *Magnus Bine* *Pag. 89.*
faying, *The Saints are neither in the fulnefs of the* *Magnus*
God-head nor part, away with this Blafphemy which *Bine.*
faith this is, &c. *Fox* anfwereth, The work of the
Miniftry was to bring People to the Knowledg of
the *Son of God,* to a *perfect man,* to the unity of the
Faith, to the meafure of the ftature of the fullnefs
of *Chrift :* and *Chrift* will dwell in the *Saints,* and
God will dwell in them : and thou fayeft they have

no

no part of the *Fulness* of the *Godhead*, and *John* faith, *of his fulness have we all received, in whome dwels the Godhead bodily*, and ye be all in the *Blasphemy*, that be out of this part of the *Fulness*.

I faid, that *G.Fox* rofe up contrary to what *Magnus Bine* affirmed, to wit, *That the Saints are not in the* fulnefs *of the* Godhead. But *W.E.* bid me let *G.F.* his words alone, his meaning alone, and keep to the words. I told them the fubftance of my proof lay there in the fubftance of *G.Fox* his anfwer to his Adverfaryes : I took *Fox* his own word for the *Quotation* out of his Adverfary, which may be thought to be taken with as much Favor and advantage to himfelf as may be : and therefore if they ftopt me from opening and comparing the words in a rational and juft way, they ftopt me in the bringing forth of my *Proofs and Arguments*.

About the fulnefs of the God head.

Unreafonable Reafoning.

I think here it was that *W.E.* faid further, If thou goeft on to make out *G.Fox* his Sence and meaning, we tell thee that we will ftop thee, *&c.*
147] But fince our bufinefs is with *G. Fox*, as well if not more than with *W. E.* efpecially becaufe of his *Book*, we fhall now more freely inlarge upon the words *&c.* and Sence and *Meaning* alfo.

For the *Fulnefs of the Godhead* is one thing, and another thing our (and all his works and Creatures) partaking of that *Fulnefs*, in fome mercifull likenefs and coformity, as *Mofes* and we behold his *Back* or dark *Refemblance*, and by Reflection, (as we behold the Sun) take in fome weak low thoughts and conceits of the Eternal and Invifible incomprehenfible and inconceivable *Power* and *Godhead*.

Thus

Thus to partake of fome drops of the Ocean of *The great* his *Wifdom, Power, Goodnefs, Holinefs, &c.* is not to *temptation of knowing* become an *Ocean* of *Power, Wifdom, Goodnefs, Holi-* *and holy* nefs, yea *Wifdom it felf, Power it felf, Goodnefs it* *People.* felf, Holinefs it felf* as God is. This devilifh *Pride* was the Sin of the *Devils,* or *wicked fpirits,* this was the Sin of our firft *Parents* unto which the Devil beguiled them; and this is *Sathans* bait ftill to catch all *Wife & Rich & High,* and efpecially *Holy People* with, *viz.* to be as God, to be in the fulnefs of the *Godhead,* to be *God himfelf.*

2. However this *Jugler* fpeaks here of the *Ful-* *The Qua-* nefs* of the *Godhead bodily* in *Chrift,* yet if he be ex- *kers make* amined and fearched it is clear that by *Chrift he* *themfelvs* *God and* meanes the *Body,* the *Quakers* and every one of *Chrift.* their *Bodyes* is *Chrift* in whome the *Godhead* dwels bodily : and the great Myftery of which the *Holy Scripture* fpeaketh, 1 *Tim.* 3. Is God manifeft in their flefh, and therefore *Sam. Fifher* ufeth in his Writing, *Chrift Jefus)* as *Peter* did in his denying of him faying [that Perfon whome you call *God-Man*] is as high Treafon againft the *King of kings,* and *King of Saints,* as hath ordinarily been acted fince God moft wonderfully gave life to a lump of Clay, which now perks up to the eternal *Power* and *Godhead.*

Pag. 90. G. *Fox* brings in the fame Author fay- *Magnus* ing, *There is a kind of Infinitenefs in the Soul, and it* *Bine.* *cannot be Infinitenefs it felf,* He anfwers, *Is not the Soul without beginning, comeing from God and returning into God again which hath it in his hand? which hand goes againft him that doth evill, which throws*
down

down that which warrs againſt it, and Chriſt the Power of God, the Biſhop of the Soul which brings it up into God, which comes out from God, hath this a beginning and ending, and is not this infinite in it ſelf, and more than all the World?

The Soul
of man
infinite

148] I Reply, in theſe few lines, let him that hath his ſences make common ſence and Engliſh of ſome of them.

However this is expreſs that the Soul is without beginning or ending, coming out of God, and returning into God : ⌊*Hath this* (ſaith *Fox* (*a beginning or ending, and is not this infinite in it ſelf and more than all the World*⌋

I know I have had better Opinions and better Reaſons from theſe poor Natives of *America* then this poor ſelf conceited God and Chriſt. G. *Fox* expreſſeth concerning the Soul and Spirit of Man : what is here but a bruitiſh notion of the Spirit of man, and a bruitiſh notion of the Eternal Power and Godhead?

Among the ſix or ſeven Opinions of the Soul of man, this is one (and one of the groſſeſt) *viz*. that Mans Soul is an efflux, efflation, that is a flowing or breathing out of the Eſſence of eternal and infinite Godhead. This worſt and moſt Blaſphemous Opinion of the reſt, the old Serpent hath taught theſe *Foxians*, in ſo much that theſe bewitched

The Qua
kers are the
old Mani
cheans

Souls ſay and print, that this World is God, and the Godhead, manifeſt no[1] variety of appearances, and returning all again into the center of the Godhead :

in

---

[1] Change " no " to " in," *R. W. Ms. Ann.*

in which they fhew horrible ignorance and Block-
ifhnefs in heavenly or earthly matters : for reafon
tells us that Finites be innumberable and yet nu-
merable in time, but Infinite is but one. The *Quakers* and *Manicheans* are but one in many particulars *Manicheus* held two infinite powers or princes :
One infinitely good, the other infinitely as bad,
which they fay is the reafon (in fome Difputes I
have had with them) why God nor the Devil, good
nor evil gets the final victory one over another in
this World.   But this notion of two infinite or
boundlefs Beings, is foon found fimple and bruitifh
for an infinite or boundlefs Being, cannot poffibly receive a Neighbour a Competitour, or fecond infinite
or boundlefs, for then the fecond would terminate and
bound the firft and it felf alfo and fo not one infinite
at all be granted. Beware of *Dogs* faith *Paul* & the
Holy Spirit faith (*Cant.* 2. *beware of Foxes* [*take us the
foxes*] fure it is : we are to fly from bruitifh fellowfhip, with them in thefe bruitifh Fancyes, fo alfo to
fly from thefe their brutifh Barkings and Blafphe-
mings againft the infinitely Glorious and inconceivable Excellencies of God, and among the reft
his incomprehenfible patience, which could not bear
fuch horrible provocations were not his patience
himfelf, infinite and incomprehen- [149] fible :
Alas poor lump of clay and duft and afhes : poor
finite vapours we are, that are fo far from being infinite that (in a fence) we are infinitely Blocks and
Beafts, and not able to give a guefs at what Infinity,
and an infinite Majefty and Godhead is.

I quoted *Pag.* 67. where againft *Fr. Higinfon* he
faith

*Municheus
his 2
Principles*

*The infin-
ite patience
of God*

*The Qua-
kers obfti-
nate in hor-*

immortal and only wife God, which no truly humble Soul can but tremble to hear and think of.

*The Qua-
kess make
themfelves
Fa her,
Son &
Holy Spirit*
It is clear in thefe Paffages,   1. That the *Qua-
kers* make themfelves *Father, Son* and *Holy Spirit.*

2. They make no other work of *Redemption* on
Juftification, &c. but what is wrought in their *fpirits, minds* and *fancyes*, called *within them.*

3. They make no other ftate of *Heaven, Ref-
urreƈtion, Judgment or Life to come*, then is in them
and their Bodyes at prefent.

Now concerning their bold and blafphemous af-
cending into the Throne of God we fhall hear a
little more in *G. Fox* making no Diftinƈtion between the *Father* and the *Son*, with that known
Heretick *Sabellius.* and 2. In his making no diftinƈtion between Chrift Jefus himfelf, and his Saints
or Believers in him.

In *Pag.* 246. He brings in *Chriftopher Wade* faying, *God the Father never took upon him humane Na-*
*Chrift.
Wade* *ture. G F.* anfwers, *God was in Chrift reconciling the
world unto himfelf And art ignorant of the great
myftery, God manifeft in the flefh; and his name is called
the everlafting Father.* As for the word *Humane*,
which is *from the ground*, it comes from thy own
Knowledge which is *Earthly, And Chrift took upon
him the feed of* Abraham *and* David *according to the
flefh*, and this is *Scripture-Language.*

*H. Nortou
more plain
then G F.* 151] I reply, in the former part of this *Narrative* I have fhewn how fimple & irrational *G.F.* his
clamour is againft that word *Humane*, and that the
bottome is their impious, unchriftian and hypocritical denying of Chrift Jefus to be a man, one
individual

individual perſon as every man is : therefore *Humph.
Norton* (*G. Fox* his Corrival) is more plain and down
right,ſaying,is not Chriſt God, and is not God a
Spirit, and chiding us for gazing after a man, &c.

I ad to the former page 293. where *G. Fox*
brings in one *Fergiſon,* ſaying, *that Chriſt and the
Father and the Spirit are not one, but are diſtinČt,* &c. *Fergiſon.*

G. Fox anſwers, this is a denying of Chriſts Doctrine, who ſaith, *I and my Father are one* : and the
Holy Ghoſt proceeds from the Father and the Son :
and he was conceived by the Holy Ghoſt, and they
are all one and not diſtinČt, but one in unity : that
which comes out from him leads the Saints into
all Truth that ever was given them from the Spirit
of truth, and ſo up unto God the Father of truth,
and ſo goes back again from whence it came. *G F
againſt the
myſtery of
Father
Son and
Spirit*

Again the ſame *Author* ſaith, *it is Blaſphemy to
ſay the Son is not diſtinČt from the Father,* &c.

G. Fox Anſwers, the Father and the Son are one,
the Father in the Son, and the Son in the Father :
ſo that which is in him is not diſtinČt from him,
and they Blaſpheme which ſay, the Son is not in
the Father, and deny Chriſts DoČtrine.

I reply, *G.Fox* all along his Book calls that blaſphemy which the moſt holy and eternal *Lord* calls
heavenly *Truth.* He hath like ſome *Witches* and
other notorious wretches ſo inur'd himſelf to poyſon,
that it is all one to him to ſwallow down the moſt
ſenſual and ſenſleſs *Dreames,* even concerning the
fearfull myſteryes of the *Father, Son,* and *Holy Spirit,* when the *holy Scripture* tels us concerning theſe
Myſteryes, that in this life we know but in part, as
through a glaſs darkly *&c.* *The Quak
blaſphe-
myes as to
the moſt
holy Spirit*   2.   For

2. For his Proof, it is *the Childs song in the streets*, they are one and therfore not distinct: I fear he knows, but will not know the nature of several respects and accounts, *viz.* that in one respect *Christ Jesus* saith, I and my Father are one, and in another respect my Father is greater then I; thus in one sence *a Father* is one with his Children, an *Husband* with his *Wife*, a *Captain* with his *Souldiers*, a *Skipper* with his *Sea-men*, a *King* with his *Subjects*. And yet in another respect, the Son is not the Father, the Wife is [152] not the Husband, the Master is not his Servants, the Captain is not his Souldiers, the Master is not his Sea-men, and the King is not his subjects.

And thus though *GF.* and *MF.* be one in mariage, and one in a *spirit* of notorious railing, yet she her self will not say but she is the *Woman* and he is the *Man*, she the wife and he the husband, and this Distinction God in Nature the Law of our Countrey and all Nations will force them (will they, nill they) to acknowledge: otherwise (like the man possessed in the Gospel) I fear no Chains of Humility nor Modesty would hold them from throwing off all Chains of Conscience, and from flinging all upon heaps of confusion without all due respective respects and distinctions.

Tee Quakers Chaos & babel.

There are four great points of the *Christian Belief*:

The Quak. dig up the root of al Christianity in the 4 great Doctrines thereof.

1. The Doctrine of the Father, Son and Spirit, and these they will not distinguish but make all one, and all to be in man.

2. The

2. The Doctrine of the Fall, Redemption, Justification, Sanctification, &c. and these are all in man
by their Tenents.

3. The Doctrine of the Church, the Officers,
Baptisme, the Lords Supper, and these (say they)
are all invisible, and within man.

4. The Resurrect on, eternal Judgement, Eternal Life. Heaven and Hell, Angels, Devils, & these
their Professions and Printings proclaim to be in
Man also : yea, so within him that they are only
within him, and that without [1] there is no God, no
Chrift, no Heaven nor hell, &c.

In Page 38. *G. Fox* brings in *Tho. Collier,* saying *Tho Col-*
[*The Kingdome is not come, nor the refreshing from the* *lier*
Spirit of the Lord.

G. F. Answers, *which shews they are unconverted,*
gadding here and there, : And Chrift tells them *the*
Kingdome was in them. And they that are not turned to
the Light which comes from Chrift the Refresher where-
by refreshing might come, and so are not come to Re-
pentance yet.

Reply, Who sees not that G. F. speaks not here
of the Kingdome of Chrift (so often promised in
the future and to come, and the time of refreshing,
Act. 3.) but that he cuts off all future hopes and
expectations to come, and appropriates aud con-
fines and fixeth, and stakes down all to the present
moment of this vanishing life, and to what is (in
this moment) in the minds of Men and Women ?
153] The Holy Scripture tells us, and Experience
tells

[1] Interline " man." *R. W. Ms. Ann.*

The Quak. hold no Heaven nor Hell to come tells us that *Hypocrites* have no solid peace and joy here, nor solid hope of joy or glory to come : and yet (to still the deen and clamour of Conscience) abhorring the thought of a judgement and reckoning to come, they foolishly and atheistically please themselves with a childish *Dream* of no Heaven nor refreshing, no Hell nor torment but what is now within us.

Pag. 101 he brings in *John Clapham*, saying [*To witness Heaven, and Hell, and Resurrection within is the Mystery of iniquity.*] G. *Fox* Answers, [*which shews thou never knew Heaven in thy self nor hell there, nor Christ the Resurrection and the Life, which they are blessed that are made partakers of the first Resurrection, on them the second Death shall have no power, and the Scriptures do witness Heaven within, and if Christ that was offered up, the Resurrection and the life be not within thee thou art a Reprobate*]

John Clapham

I Reply, If G. *Fox* would speak of Heaven, and Angels, and Hell, and Devils, and of the Resurrection and Life to come, by way of allusion and similitude, or by way of first Fruits or Taft of them, he might profitably do it, but to speak of them in opposition to a rising again, an Heaven, an Hell, &c. to come, what is it ?

I say, what is it but to proclaim their Revolt from, and their Rebellion against all the Christian Faith and Religion, and their wonderful hardening against whatever is yet to come, either here or in the eternal State approaching ?

Pag. 214. He brings in some (namelefs, saying, [*To say Heaven and Glory is in man, which was before*

fore man was, they are fottifh and blinde.] He Anf-
wers, |*There's none have a Glory and a Heaven but
within them, which was before man had a Being.*]

Unto this I adde, *Thomas Pollard* faying, for a *Tho Pol-lard*
perfection of Glory to be attained to on this fide
the Grave, I utterly deny.]

G. Fox Anfwereth [*Where Glory is (in the leaft de- The epi-curian Phi-lofophers &
gree) it is in perfection, and who have not Glory, and the Qua-kers one Sect.
doth uot attain to Glory on this fide the Grave they are
in a fad condition : for the Saints rejoyce with joy un-
fpeakable and full of Glory, &c.*]

I Reply, as the Swinifh Epicures and *Dives's* of
this World, what ever they formally and loofely
profefs) have no solid hope of peace and joy to
come after this life, and therefore (like Biuit
Beafts) practically confefs it faying, (in their hearts
and Life) [154] let us eat and drink for to morrow we fhall dye: fo do this cynical and doggid
kind of Philofophers (the Quakers) profefs plainly
(though fome would cover it) no hopes of a rifing of
the Body but what they have here, no hopes of a
Heaven but what they have here, no hell but what
they (in their minds) have paft through : no Judgement but what (as Saints) they are now executing.

I know that fome of the *Quakers* will not believe that *G. Fox* and others of them deny the
Refurrection, &c. but (if they will not willingly
fifh[1]) let them read and confider thefe my *Quotations* from *G. Fox, Ed. Burrowes* and *John Stubs*
their Book in Folio, and let them alfo know that
whatever they profefs againft this that I have faid,
that

[1] Change to "err." *R. W. Ms. Ann.*

that is but horrible Hypocrifie and Deceit, for they would not in all our Difputations depart one hair from thofe horrible and monftrous *Blafphemies, and bruitifh Reafonings in G. Fox and Edward Burrowes.*

The 9th Pofition proved

We came to the ninth Propofal, the fecond in order to be debated at *Providence,* viz [*all that the Quakers Religion requires externally and internally to make Converts or Profelytes, amounts to no more then what a Reprobate may eafily attain to and perform.*]

I did not (the Father of Spirits is my holy witnefs) fling this in as a Firebrand of *Reprobation* againft either Teachers or Followers called *Quakers* : it is true they do fo againft all that ever were not or are not or fhall not be in their Opinion, but my hope is, that many amongft thefe mifled and wandring Souls may come to *Abrahams Bofome,* &c. yet this I affert, that thoufands and ten thoufands may be of their Religion, and may have gotten all that their Religion requires or performs, yea, all that their Principles call for outwardly or inwardly, and yet not be accepted but rejeĉted from the holy and gracious prefence of God.

I told them that I had this notion from a man famous in his day (Mr. *W. Perkins*) who having been a deboift young man in *Cambridge* after the call of God to him he proved famous in Preaching and Writing, and (with a lame Club hand) he wrote admirably againft the Papifts, and maintained that all Popery preacht to the making of Converts or Profelytes amounted to no more then what *Reprobates* may eafily attain unto.

Mc. Perkins faying of the Papifts and mine of the Quakers.

I fay the fame of common Proteftants, and of the
Quakers,

Quakers, they may have a great meaſure of ſorrow for ſin: great reſolu- [155] tions, great Reformations, great Rejoycings, great and wonderful performances endure great perſecutions, endure burning of the Body in the Flames, and yet be far from the true Proteſtant Religion either in the true Doctrine and Principles, or in the true life and practice of it.

For the Foundation both of the *Papiſts* and *Quakers Faith* is laid upon the Sand of *Rotten Nature* which they (both) only adorn and trim as the dead *Carcaſſes* and *Coffins* with Roſes and Lillies and other *Flowers and Garlands*, their own penances ſatisfactions, Alms, Prayers, Faſtings, Suffrings, which are but Womens filthy Clouts, and Dung of Men and Beaſts put into the ballance of Gods infinite Juſtice, inſtead of the infinite Righteouſneſs and Satisfaction of the Son of God : poor Souls, they know not that the whole Creation (viſible and inviſible, ſeen and unſeen, known and unknown, cannot reach Gods moſt holy and inconceivable juſtice, for the leaſt evil word or thought. Neither of theſe (nor millions of *Proteſtants*, much leſs millions of millions in one evil word or thought, then in all the ſorrows and calamities felt in this life, or juſtly feared in the life a coming.

Neither Papiſts nor Quak ſkil bow to pay Gods juſtice

With the *Quakers* 'tis known, that if a notorious Drunkard,&c be convinced, and come to hearken to a Spirit within him, to ſay, *Thou and Thee*, and think himſelf equal and above all his former Superiours, &c. he is Juſtified, he is Sanctified, and ſo

The Character of a Quaker

Holy

Holy that he cannot fin in Thoughts,[1] Words, and
from this high Mount looks down on all others
(efpecially if oppofite) as *Pharifees, Publicans,
Cains,* &c. Thus they pretend *Repentance, Faith,*
and a change of heart becaufe they have changed
their talk, their Garments, &c. But,

1. I told them that true Repentance lay in a
difcovery of fin as fin, as greater than the greateft
filthinefs in the world: no poverty, no fhame, no
lofs like unto it, &c.

What true
turning to   2, In an utter inability to contribute one mite,
God is. either from felf, , or from the whole Creation toward fatisfaction to infinite Majefty and Juftice for
the leaft evil thought or imagination.

3. That as bleffed *John Bradford* faid to God :
Lord thou art Heaven, I am Hell, viz. that in the beft
natural Soul in the World, there is nothing but a
Kennil, an *Hogftie,* a *den of Atheifme, Murther, Theft,*
Fornication, Adultery, and all kinde of Wickednefs.

156]   4. That I have not fo much in me as to defire *Deliverance,* nor to be fenfible of any need of it.

5. That it is only mercy and rich free Grace
Jacobs
Ladder of that worketh in me or any Soul a Sence of my
true Chrif- Condition a Sence of Juftice a Sence of Mercy.
tianity.
6. That it is Mercy only worketh a willingnefs,
a new defire, new Affections towards my Maker,
towards my Ranfomer, who paid his *Bloud,* his
Heart-Bloud, the *Bloud of God* to ranfome and re-
deem me.

7. That in this work, Mercy not only worketh

a

---

[1] Interline "or."   *R. W. Ms. Ann.*

a Sence, a thirſt after Pardon and Peace with my
Maker, but alſo after a *Conformity* and *Likeneſs* unto
God.

8. Becauſe I cannot reach this, the Mercy and
Pitty of God worketh in my Soul a longing after
God, and after the turning of the whole Soul unto
God, and after thoſe ſeven Evidences of true Re-
pentance, 2.*Cor*.7.

9. This is in true Chriſtian *Repentance* and turning of the whole Soul unto God, *viz.* to receive
every *thought*, every *motion*, every *deſire* upon the
account of Mercy and Pitty, as ever poor Dog received *Crum* or *Bone* under the Table.

Much of this I ſpake publickly, as alſo that no
Papiſt nor *Quaker* by their grounds could get up
this *Jacobs Ladder*, much leſs upon thoſe higher
grounds and ſteps of caſting off *Self*, of doing all
purely for God, and in Gods eye : of meekneſs and
Mercy to other poor drowning Soules, of pure Love
to God for *Himſelf* for his *Holineſs*, *Mercy*, *Goodneſs*, *The Qua-*
yea for his *Juſtice* : of quiet and patient and thank- *kers ond*
full reſting in his holy Pleaſure, whatever he take *moſt mens Shipwrack*
from us or bring upon us.

I ſaid and ſay, that neither the teachings of the
Papiſts or *Quakers* will help them to get up one
Step of this heavenly *Ladder* ; for by the utmoſt
ſtrength and activity of *Nature* no man can advance and climbe higher then to love *God* and *Chriſt*
and *Heaven* for it *Self*, and *Self-ends*, which is no
more but *Flattering* of God, baſe and dog-like
Fawning and *Hypocriſie*.

I cannot call to mind ought that was oppoſed by
my

The Qua-
kers Min-
isters and
their Plea. my *Antagonists* against thefe Confiderations : but
John Stubs faid, Doft thou count our *Religion* an
eafie *Religion*, for my part faid he, we have not
found it fo eafie to forfake all the glory and pleafure of this world, to forfake wife and children *&c.*
to goe about the work of the Lord in ftrange
Countreys, *&c.*

157] And *W. E.* faid thou fayeft our Religion is
an eafie Religion : For my part faid he I have not
found it fo, I have not found it fo eafie to forfake
all the glory and honour and pleafures of this
World, and to expofe our felves to hardfhips, to
forfake our Wives and Children, Friends and Relations,and to goe about in ftrange Countreys *&c.*
And *W. E.* further faid in that thou faift our Religion is an eafie Religion, it is a plain evidence
that thou that talkeft fo much of Religion, and of
the Religion of the *Quakers* thou yet never knew-
eft what Religion is, with more to this effect : and
they (according to their wild fpirit) infifted vehemently on the wronge which I did them, and the
People called *Quakers* : and that as for themfelves
they were but a few, but the people called *Quakers*
were a great *Body* : they were many thoufands all
over *England*, they were many thoufands in *London*, as alfo in *Barbadoes*, and *New-England* and
Virginia, and other places.

I replyed, that my time would not give me leave
as they knew, to fay much to their greatnefs and
number, yet I faid their Religion like the *Papifts*,
was easie and agreeable with *Nature*, they had the
wind and tyde of *natural corruption* to joyn with their
fpirit, which knew this well enough.   I. It

*A clofe
fight as to
Religion*

*The eafi-
nefs of the
Quakers
Religion*

1. It was easie to perswade the *Quakers* to change one fowle *Spirit* and *Devil* for an other, a Devil more grofs and ugly, for a Devil more refined painted and guilded: their pride in *Cloathes* and fantaftical *Fsbions*, to pride in *felf conceit* and *fantaftical Opinions*, their Drunkennefs and Gluttony, with Wine and Flefh to Intoxications, with high and proud Vapours: How many millions travel on the broad way to Deftruction, and yet prate of a ftrict and narrow *Path*? What wonderfull hardfhips doe both *Turks* and *Papifts* endure in their religious *Pennances*? How doe they *macerate* and *whip* themfelves, even till the bloud of their tender *Women* hath ftreamed down upon the ground from them? Yea how zealoufly (in the caufe of their Religion) have the very *Jewes* themfelves caft away their Lives, as *Spain* and *Portugal* can witnefs.

One Devil changed for another.

yea fometimes one for feven

Befides, I told them it was a poor lame thing to talk of *numbers* when the Council of the only *Wife* was fo clearly revealed concerning his *Little Flock*, oppofed to the vaft and monftrous *Herds* both of civiliz'd and wild *Nations*.

158] I put them in mind of the innumerable multitudes that followed after that ftupendous *Cheater Mahomet*, even *thirteen* parts of the world, divided into *thirty*, as very knowing *Cofmographers* or *Defcribers* of the World have computed. And if fo be that the *Pope*, and Church of *Rome* be the eight *Head*, the great *Whore* that fits upon many *Waters*, *Kingdomes* and *Nations*, what a poor Slut is the *Quakers Fancy* compar'd with the *Baals Priefts*,

The Quakers fimple boaft of numbers

the

the *Romish Proselites*; the Beaft whome the whole world wonders after?

3. Again it is to me and may be to all men, wonderfull that fince the *Religion* of the *Quakers* is fo eafie &c. that ten thoufands more of people in old and new *England, Scotland, Ireland* and other parts, have not lifted themfelves under this new *Mahomet*, pretending fo much from the *Dove* from Heaven as *Mahomet* did.

The carnal weapons Tis true *G. Fox* and *Foxians*, pretend the two horns of the *Lamb*, and that their weapons are not *Jehues* nor *Baals Priefts*, but that they have forfaken all *Carnal Weapons*: but this I fhall fhew to be an horrible Lye when I come to the laft *Pofition*.

The *Devil* and the *Papifts* and the *Quakers* know that the *Quakers* only want a *Sword* to fubdue as many *Profelites* as either *Mahomet* or the *Pope* hath done. The *Quakers* fome prate fubtilly, others childifhly againft *Carnal Weapons, Carnal Weapons* &c. but I fhall fhew (if God pleafe) in my 14*th*. and laft Pofition, what a *Devil* of *Pretence* this is.

At prefent the *Devil* knowes they want but a *Sword* (not *Hearts* nor *Hands* nor *Principles*) whereby to fubdue as mauy *Profelytes* as the *Pope* or *Mahomet* hath, and literally and materially *thrafh* the *Mountains* with *Flails* of iron, and make the *Nations* turn (in an eafie *Hypocrifie* and *Diffimulation*) *Diffembling Quakers*. I wonder and adore the *Councels* of the *Eternal*, that any of thefe three fhould be *Cheated* by this *fpirit*.

Firft, Any of thofe truely fearing *God*; for their *Principles fpirit and practices* being fo notorioufly oppofite

oppofite to the meek and patient *Spirit* of true *The Qua-kers Spirit far from purity and Holinefs.* *Purity* and *Holinefs,* and evidencing them to be lead by a dumb and dogged *Spirit.* 1. Their high and fhamelefs *Pride* and *Vapouring* is notorioufly known, of which in the next Pofition. 2. Their mouth full of *Curfing* and *Railing* above any or all that profefs to march under the *Chriftian Name* and 159| *Colours.* 3. They fpit not out their *Venome* fo fiercely againft any as againft the moft confcientious *Preachers* and *Profeffor* of the *Proteftant Faith,* as appears all along in this railing of *Fox* in Folio againft them.

4. They eafily fall in with openly profane and ungodly *perfons,* and with carnal and luke-warm *Laodiceans,* who can fwim with the tyde, fail with every wind. If they can but fay *Thee* and *Thou &c.* *The Spight-og the Quakers Spirit*
5. It is wonderfull how their fpirit (profeffing to be *Proteftants*) can fo wickedly ftrike in with the bloudy fpirit of the *Papifts,* againft the Witneffes and Martyrs of Jefus, compiled by that heavenly *J. Fox.* in the Book of *Martyrs* which this bloudy fpirit (in *James Purnels* Watcher) upbraidingly calls [*Your Record*] as if it were none of theirs, nor the bloudy Papifts, againft whofe bloudy practifes under their *Popes,* and the old proud *Romans,* the *Romane Gods* and *Emperours,* that heavenly Book fhews how thofe heavenly *Martyrs* or *Witneffes* over came by the *Bloud of the Lamb,* the word of their *Teftimony,* and not loving of their *Lives* unto the *Death.*

6. That moft Savage and worfe then *Indian Spirit* of their ftripping their women ftark naked,

and

and fo to enter into the *ftreets* and *Affemblyes* of men and youths, which Piety *Chriftianity* and common *Womanhood* and *Modefty* abhor to think of.

Secondly. As I wonder how any *godly Soul*, fo how any *Learned Soul*, who hath ftudied the primitive Copyes of the *Hebrew* and *Greek Scriptures*, can yoke with fuch rude *Bablings* and Repetitions of fimple ignorant *Praters*. Tis true the Lord Jefus and his Embaffadors were not all traind up as *Paul* was at the feet of *Gamaleel*, yet had they before the whole World the miraculous effufions of *Fiery Tongues*, and heavenly Oyl upon them, which thefe poor *Simpletons* ridiculoufly like Puppets in a Shew pretend too. Befide, the *Commons* among the firft Chriftians were as learned if not more then our primeft *Academians*, the *Hebrew* being their Mother Tongue, and the *Greek* and *Latine* familiar, by the *Greek* and *Romane Conquefts* over them, all which Helps the moft of the Leaders of the *Quakers* want, only pretending to underftand fupernatural and miraculoufly (in a trice and immediately) what is to be gotten by honeft and faithful Labour and induftry, the holy will and mind of God from the true Original Copies.

160] *Thirdly,* I do admire that any fober, modeft *Woman* (made fo by nature, and much more by Grace (fhould ever dare to come into their Affemblies: it is certain that the *Ranters* is a Sifter or Daughter of them: though they quarrel, and fight, and fcratch one the other: The *Ranters* more plainly (according to their Principles make the *Nakednefs* of Men and Women, a part of *worfhip* unto God,

God, unto which they fay they are reftored by *Chriſt Jeſus* the ſecond *Adam.* This *Adamites Fowle ſpirit* is no *New-come ſpirit*, I have know nit almoſt ſixty year, and what a motion was made and urged by ſome (whome I can name) for Plantations in warmer *Countreyes*, where they might practice that *Ordinance of God* viz, *Of Nakedneſs of men and women in Gods worſhip.*

Theſe our *Adamites* are led by a more Savage and Barbarous, and Monſtrous Spirit, the which under the vizird and mantle of Religion deceives them, and of being a ſign to others : And this very bruitiſh practiſe have kept ſome Women (too much inclin'd to them) from falling into their filthy puddle, and of returning ſome which were left by Gods Juſtice to go too far amongſt them ſure we are the holy ſpirit of God (all along) abhors the appearance of uncleanneſs, and commands the vailings of Women (eſpecially in Chriſtian Meetings) *Quakers driven on by the old Spirit of the Adamites*

I have been too long upon the eaſineſs of their Religion, and of the agreement of it with corrupt and rotten Nature which ſlides into it as eaſily as Brooks and Rivers ſlide and run down into the Ocean.

There be two other cauſes of falling into falſe Religions or ways of worſhipping God.

1. Hope of Gain, which was the *Sechemites* Bait : (the ſweet Muſick propounded by *Nebuchadnezzar.*) &c.

2. The fiery Furnace, &c.

Theſe moderate times have not driven the *Quakers* to bow down to their Spirit for fear of perſe-ſecution,

The rising of the Quakers cution, and the fiery Furnace but Sathan knew well enough that the Corruption of Nature, and the hope of Gain and Glory would cheat to purpose (as all may see it hath done:) Sathan knows that some have a moving and travelling Spirit, and cannot rest in a sedentary or quiet life:) Some are of a rising, aspiring Spirit (though neither from Birth nor Breeding, nor abilities) and therefore cry down all Honour or respect to be given to any (but themselves) some are false and [161] rotten in their *Profession,* and ready to fall and tumble when any *strange wind* of Temptation blowes upon them.

7. Some may be *Sincere* and upright to God in the *Root,* but *Weak,* and not so rooted in the *Holy Scriptures,* as the Disciples themselves, who wondered for a time what the *Rising* from the dead *Diverse Sorts suffered by God to fall into the Quak Ditch.* should mean, and had need of their *Lord* and *Masters Take heed and beware* of the *Leaven* of the *Scribes,* and *Pharisees,* and *Sadduces,* &c. Some truly fear God, but have neglected the purity and chastity of *Gods holy Worship,* and have reserved in a weak Conscience a liberty of playing the *Whore* against a jealous *God* and *Husband.*

But generally they that are taken by the *Quakers Bait* are such as never loved *Christ Jesus* in Sincerity as the Scripture speaketh, neither within nor without, and therefore suckt in *Nicolds* and *Nailors,* *But especially for Male and Female Protestants.* and *Foxes* dreames of a *Christ,* within them opposite to *Christ* without : of a *Christ* a *Light* a *Spirit* within, which had no *Humane Body,* or if he were humane, or a man they know not now what is become of him.

The

The *Lord Jesus* tels us that some will plead with him at the last day, that they have heard him *Preach*, that they have been at his *Table*, that they have prophesied themselves, *cast out Devils* in his Name, and in his Name done many *Wonderfull things:* should not this make every Soul that calls it self *Christian*, startle and look about them, especially when they hear Christ Jesus say, *depart from me I know you not ye workers of Iniquity.*

I told the Quakers that their *Theora John* pretended to write after the *Spirits* Dictate, a volume in *Hebrew, Greek, Latine, Arminiack,* &c. which he confessed he understood not: what if it should please Gods infinite Wisdom, to suffer the Quakers or others to speak and understand all *Languages*, to work great *Miracles*, yet if they come under the Note Christ gives them, of *Workers of Iniquity*, they fulfill the termes of my *Position*, and prove but *False* and *Reprobate.*

    This is the true and infallible distinguishing *Character* between the true *Legitimate* and the *Bastard* and false *Christian*: The soul of the *True* is broken for Sin, as Sin, as opposite to God, as filthy in his eye: The soul of the *False* is broken for Sin as bringing temporal Loss or shame, or pain, and beside temporal, Eternal. The soul of the true, is broke off from Sin, from the least Sin, [16z from the appearances of sin from the occasions of Sin, from the thought of Sin as worse then all the Afflictions of this life, or the Torments of Hell to come. The soul of the False, hath secret Friendship and Correspondence with Iniquity (as *Church-Papists*

The great distinguishing Character of true and false Pretenders

Papiſts with Popery &c) in the ſecret chambers and *C*loſets of the heart, at which they willingly wink, and to find it (when they are put to it, yea and ſeem to doe it) they are willingly remiſs and negligent.

Hence it was a famous Principle of the firſt *New-Engliſh Reformers*, viz. to be *C*hriſtianly carefull that their Members gave *Chriſtian Evidence*, (ſo far as godly eyes of Charity could reach) of the truth of their Converſion and turning unto God, which for ought I know is not changed by their Succeſſors.

It is dolefully true that many ſeemingly *Elect*, prove *Reprobate*, and many truly *Elect* fall into many great *Sins* and *Sorrows*. How black and dolefull then is their Condition (ſuch as the *Papiſts* the *Quakers* and others) whoſe *Religion Principles* and *Practices*, ariſe no higher then what a *Reprobate* may attain unto.

The 3d Poſition debated at Providence. We came to the tenth *Poſition*, (the third in order to be diſcuſſed at *Providence*) which they read out of their paper, viz. *That the Popes of* Rome *do not ſwel with; and exerciſe a greater* pride *then the* Quakers *have expreſt, and would aſpire unto, although many truly humble Souls may be captivated amongſt them.*

Two great Competitors the Popes and Foxians. I have here two mighty *Fields* to expatiate and walk in, viz. The pride of *Chriſt Jeſus* his pretended *triple-crowned Vicar*, and the pride of the new *Papiſts* pretending to be *Chriſt himſelf*: of which the holy *Spirit* ſpeaketh, *There is a Generation, oh how lofty are their eyes and their eye lids are lifted up?* In publick Diſcourſe I knew I was but to take

take a fhort turn of a quarter of an hour, I am
now at more liberty of inferting what I intended,
but was forced to abbridge wlth all poffible brevity
at that time.

I told them there was a *pride* in *outward* and ex-
ternal things, in *Parentage*, in *Perfon*, in *Beauty*,
Strength, *Wit*, *Aparrel*, *Houfes*, *Money*, *Shipping*,
Land, *Cattle*, *Offices*, *Relations*, &c. this I now paft
by : All thefe (like *Diogenes* on *Platoes* carpets) the
Quakers fay they tread on &c.

There was 2. the devils *pride*, and the devils *Con-* *Spiritual*
demnation, a pride in Spiritual *Knowledg*, fpiritual *pride the*
devils
Gifts, fpiritual *Priviledges* and *Excellencies* : This *pride*
was the Devils *Break-neck*, and will be [163] of the
Popes and *Quakers*, and of all tha*t* afpire to the
Eternal power and *Godhead*; for God or they muft
fall to all eternity.

I named then diverfe Parallels betwecn the *Popes*
and *Quakers*, I will now name all I can remember
I named, and will name fome more at this prefent,

Firft, The *Popes* have exalted themfelves above *The Popes*
all that is called *God*, above all *Civill powers*, *Kings* *& Qua-*
and *Princes*, riding upon their backs, difpofing of *kers pride*
their Crowns, making them lead their horfes, hold *compared*
their ftirrups, kifs their toes, yea lye down under
their feet bodyes and fouls, and fubmit their neck
to this abominable foot of pride, as the *Scripture*
calls it.

As to the *Quakers* they know it is not yet time
to put on the *Lions* and the *Eagles*, but the *Sheeps*
and the *Foxes* Skin : but no man need queftion that
if God fhould pleafe to let loofe the *Quakers fpirit*
to

to the full length of its tedder, as he hath done
that of the Popes, the ſpirit of the *Quakers* would
ſcorn to come behind the *pope*: For who ſees not
how at the firſt, *fledging* and creeping out of the
Shell how they boaſt and vapour of their numbers?
We (ſaid W. E. to me in publick at *Newport*) are a
great People, many thouſands in *England*, many
thouſands in *London*, beſides *Virginia*, *Barbados*,
N-England and other places: what would they ſay
and doe if they had the *popes Univerſality*, and
could boaſt of the many *Waters*, *Peoples*, *Nations*,
Tongues and *Multitudes* upon which the *Whore*
ſitteth?

Beſide, W. E. (a man fit to make a *Bonefacius* or
a *Hildebrand*) *John Stubs* alſo though of a more
prudent and moderate ſpirit) was up with the ſame
boaſting of their *Numbers*, and all of them are
ready to cry up their *Diana* whome all *Aſia* and
the *world worſhippeth*. But,

2. In their firſt creeping (like Hercules out of
the Cradle, how doth this Spirit dare the Spirits of
Kings, and Keyſars, and Popes themſelves (under
the pretence of Tranſlations and acceptations of
words) to *Thou* and *Thee* to the faces of mighty
Monarchs? with what *Braſen Faces* have they addreſt the *Royal preſence* of our *Gracious Dread Soveraign*, without either bowing the knee, or baring
the Head (ſigns of Engliſh reverence and civility)
and this out of an horrible and lying pretence, that
Chriſts amity (even in Civil things) reſpecteth no
mans perſon, that they may trample as Gods on all
man-kinde, &c.

3. I

164] 3. I can fay what mine eyes and ears have *Pope Ed-mond com-manding & filenc-ing the Governour* feen and heard, *viz.* our Honoured and Aged Mr. *Nicholas Eaſton, Governour* of this Colony under his *Majeſty*, offering to ſpeak once and twice in our late Conteſts at *Newport* (and no queſtion would have ſpoke for the *Quakers* againſt me, yet) *Pope Ed-mundſon* put forth his hand imperiouſly toward the Governour, ſaying, *Whiſt, Whiſt*, which whiſting and ſilencing Language if they uſe to their Friends in Authority, what will they ſay or Thunder to their Enemies if ever they get up into the *Papal Chair* ?

2. The *Pope* ſits in the *Temple of God*, as over *A ſecond Paralel be-tween the Pope & Quakers* the Churches and Conſciences of the Chriſtian Name and Worſhip, giving *Canons* and *Decretals* to be obſerved by all Chriſtian People on peril of loſs of *Earth and Heaven*, &c.

And do not their[1] new *Popes* (not regarding as the *Apoſtles* and *Bereans* the Holy Scripture) lay on the common *Quakers* Conſciences and Congrega-tions their *Decrees*? tis true *G. Fox* in his Book in Folio gives the immediate Spirit of Infallibility to all his Saints : yet muſt they (in a ridiculous con-tradiction) ſit ſtill poſſeſt with a *Dumb Devil*, ex-cept ſome He or She *Apoſtle* come amongſt them, who ſend word of their coming to call the Coun-try in many dayes before, and ſeem to have a Com-mand of their *Diabolical Spirit* more then other *Quakers* have, though they (as I ſaid before) in a ridiculous Contradiction) aſcribe it unto all their *Saints* and *Quakers*.

Thus

" thefe" *R. W. Ms. Ann.*

Thus did *Humphrey Norton* (a Pope) in his day in

The Pope and Qua-kers usurp over the Souls of all men

these parts) overtopping and rating *W. Brand* at *Newport*, he confirmed the *Decree* for the *weekly Meetings* not only on the first dayes, but on the week dayes at *Newport* and *Providence :* he ordered their fitting and departing Dumb, unless a He or She Apostle came amongst them, he left in writing (which I can produce) an overthrow of all civil Order and Government except in the hands of his Saints, entituling his Paper thus, the Saints Law and the Sinners Law as *G. Fox.* his decree under the title of the Law.

Hump h Norton & G Fox compared.

G. Fox succeeds (as Pope) *Humph. Norton* in these parts, and being angry with his Predecessour (as some Popes have been) he lets loose the *Dumb Devil* and gives Liberty to all to speak as the Spirit gives them utterance : this shews what a lying Spirit of Unity they boast of (such an one as was in *Nailors* business) though they most proudly deny Unity to all but to themselves, as [165] the *Papists* do : *G. Fox.* also gave forth his Decree of loosing them from that bruitish and doggid Behaviour which *W. Brand* and *Humphrey Norton* left them in, and by *Word* and *Example* commanded them to be more sociable and manlike, so that many of

G F. a subtler Fox then. Hum. Norton.

them will speak in Salutations, and shew some reverence by bowing the Heads, or uncovering it, as *Fox* himself did after his Sermon at *Providence*, uncovering his Head and bowing to the People, and passing through the midst of them (his Hat in his hand) with much respect and civility. And he blames those (as I hear) which violently and madly

have

have flung themfelves upon unneceffary temptations
and dangers: whence follows (in the eyes of the
whole World) that either the latter or the former
Spirit was not Gods, and perfect, and the Spirit of
Unity of which they childifhly fo crake and vapour, as the chiefeft Flower in their Crown of
Pride.

3. The *Pope* lifts up himfelf as God over the *A third*
Holy Scriptures: He is the fole Judge and Inter- *parallel*
preter of them, and the fole decider of all contro- *the Pope*
verfies in Religion about the expounding of them: *& Quak.*
yea, he hath power to difpence with *Peter* and *Paul*,
&c. yea, what Chrift and God can do that gave
forth Scripture, that can the *Pope* their *Lieutenant*
do: hence all this *Difpenfations* of Oaths, of Marriages, &c.

Do not the *Quakers alfo tread* this Holy Scripture,
this ineftimable Jewel of Gods Writing and Book
under their proud feet, as formerly I noted upon *Both Pa-*
the fourth Pofition of their not owning the Holy *pifts &*
Scripture? Do they not (upon the point) fay that *their Pride*
they made, they wrote and gave out the Holy *above the*
Scripture? and though in our late Conference they *Scriptures*
faid they would be tryed by the Scriptures, yet (as
the *Papifts*) they admit no Interpreter but themfelves, for the Spirit within them they fay gave forth
the Scripture, and is above the Scripture, and both
they and the *Papifts* have faid that there would be
no loffe if they were gone out of the World, for
the *Papifts* fay their Traditions, and their infallible
Spirit would fupply the lofs: and the *Quakers* fay
the Scriptures is within them (in effect) they fay

that

that all that they do and fay is Scripture : fo far
are both *Papifts & Quakers* from a Chriftian and
Candid Profeffion of being tried by the Holy Scripture : that they moft Horribly and moft Hypocritically trample it under their proud feet.

166] 4. Thefe *Romanifts* or *Proud ones* (as the *Hebrew* fignifies) both *Papifts* & *Quakers* moft infultingly lift up themfelves againft the Servants and
Children of God all the world over that bow not

*The Pope
aad Qua-
kers borri-
ble revilers
Slander-
ours &
curfers of
the Righte-
ous*

down to their Images : be a Soul never fo humble
and penitent, never fo holy and mortified, believe
the Scriptures, &c. and give his life for the truth of
of them, yet he is damned if he believes not the
Pope to be the head of the Church : and fay not
the *Quakers* the fame of all that believe not in their
pretended Lights : your Repentance is nothing,
your Holinefs nothing, your Zeal, Praying, Preaching, Fafting, Suffrings nothing : and they think
they have reafon to fay fo, becaufe you believe not in
the true Chrift, and therefore you are in *Cains* Nature, in the *Satanical Delufion*, Reprobates, &c. fo
that all the bleffed Souls under the Alter calling
for vengeance againft the fhedders of their blood
the *Roman Emperour*, or fince the *Roman Popes*, they
are all branded with a black cole of damned Souls
and Reprobates by *G. Fox*, becaufe they profeffed,
preacht and died for a Chrift without them though
that Chrift without them dwelt in their hearts
(*Ephef.* 3.) by believing *and for his fake they loved
not their lives to the Death.*

*The 5.
parallel*

I told them that the *Pope* and they were one in
the great point of the Infallibility : they both pretended

tended the Spirit of God as did the *Apoſtles*, &c.
but I have proved their pretence is as true as that
of *Apollo's Worſhippers*, by whoſe *Prieſts* the Devil
gave *Oracles* (*Extripode*) from their threefold ſtool, *The infal-*
and that ſo ſubtilly and cunningly that whatever *libility of*
Oracle or *Voice* it was, and whatever the event were *the Popes*
yet the Devil would ſave his own: *Apollo* ſhould *and Qua-*
kers
be the true God of Wiſdome, and *Apollo's Prieſts* *Oracles*
true *Prophets*.

At laſt when Chriſt came *Apollo* being conſulted
and failing to give anſwer, the Devil was forced to
anſwer that there was an *Hebrew Childe* borne that
ſtopt his mouth: I am ſure this *Hebrew Childe* (the
true Lord Jeſus Chriſt) hath often alſo ſtopt the
mouthes (in one ſenſe) of *Pope & Quakers*, for their
Predictions have not come to paſs, (though ſome
which the Devil could gueſs at) have: and he will
ſhortly ſtop their mouthes forever.

It was truely ſaid of (that long eighteen years *The Holy*
hatching) Deviliſh Junto of *Trent*, that the Holy *Spirit in a*
Cloakbag
Ghoſt, (that is the *Popes* Holy Ghoſt) came every *at the*
week from the *Pope* at *Rome*, &c. to his *Legates* at *Councel*
at Trent
Trent, in a Cloak-bag: and do not *G. Fox* his
Books [167] and all their writings declare for their
corrivality and competition with the *Pope* for this *The Pope*
their pretended Holy Ghoſt: do they not upbraid *and Quak*
the two
all other Miniſters and People for being out of the *great pre-*
infallible Spirit: Do they not ſay their Miniſters *tenders and*
and their Commiſſions are inviſible becauſe imme- *corrivals*
for the pre-
diate and infallible? do they not aſſigne this to be *tended*
the cauſe of all the Sects and Diviſions among the *Holy*
Ghoſt
Proteſtants, becauſe they have not the infallible Spirit as the *Quakers* have?   Here

Here (as I remember) *John Stubs* ſtood up and alleadged that place in 1 *John* 4. Hereby we know that we dwell in him, becauſe he hath given us of his Spirit.

And again, you have the unction and know all things. And *W. Edmondſon* boaſtingly, and proudly ſaid, that they had the ſame immediate and infallible Spirit which the Apoſtles had, and that *John & Peter* were but their elder Brethren.

The Quak pretending to be Apoſtles

Unto which I anſwer, *Peter* I know, and *John* I know, but who are you? For 1. They were *Eye-Witneſſes* of the Lord Jeſus his *Life* and *Death* and *Reſurrection*. 2. They were immediately endowed with *fiery Tongues*, and *fiery hands* to preach in all *Languages*, and to pen from Gods mouth his holy word and Pleaſure and to work real Miracles, not metaphorical ones only (as *G. Fox* ſaid at *Providence* the *Quakers* did, that is open the eyes of the *Blind* by *Converſion* &c.) I added that it might pleaſe the infinite Wiſdom of God to ſend higher Pretenders to *Apoſtleſhip* then the *Quakers*, who ſhould ſpeak all *Tongues* 1 doe *Miracles*: But as Gods Servants had a *Rule Iſa.* 8. the written Law and Teſtimony, and were not to believe their *Dreames* though they came to paſs, *Deut.* 13. So have Gods Servants now, *viz.* The *Doctrine of Chriſt Jeſus* both concerning *Faith* and *Order*, and to ſtrive earneſtly for the Faith once delivered.

F F his Counterfeit mirrcles

A 6 Parallel between the Pope & the Quak.

The Pope like *Baalam* ſayes, he is the *Mouth* of God: whome he bleſſeth, they are bleſſed, and whom he curſeth &c. therefore ſendeth he his

Curſes

1 Interline "and." *R. W. Ms. Ann.*

Curſes like *Thunderbolts,* yea among *Kings & King-domes* in other Nations, and our own as *K. Henery 8th. K. Edward. 6th. Queen Elizabeth* experimented *&c.* and is there any People bearing the name *Chriſtian,* ſo like the pope their Father as theſe, whoſe *Mouth* (faith *David*) is full of *Curſing* and *Bitterneſs,* like Floods out of the *Dragons Mouth,* and *fire-brands arrowes* and *Death* crying out againſt the moſt *Humble* and *Con-* [168] *ſcientious Cain, Saul, Judas, Viper, Serpent, Reprobate Dragon, Devil* (yea one of their *Shee-Apoſtles, Devil, Devil, Devil,* all at once to one that oppoſed her amongſt us) and ſuch foul ſtinking expreſſions (like the *Quakers* in *London*) about the Dung of Mankinde, that modeſty eſpecially the baſhfulneſs and modeſty of Women would have been far from.

A ſeventh is that great point of horrible Pride in both *Pope & Quakers,* exalting the Dung and Dirt of their own Qualifications, Excellencies, Graces, Labours, Faſtings, Satisfactions, Believings, Sufferings as a price and ſatisfaction to Gods Juſtice, as a *Merit* or *Deſert* for the pardon of their ſin, for though they both Sophiſtically and Hypocritically mention the *Blood of Chriſt* ; yet they count the buſineſs of this *Chriſt* (as the Pope faid) but a *Fable,* and indeed and truth through the Pride of their high ſpirits they think God is beholding to them : I have ſpoken to this already, and of that deviliſh Pride of their being without ſin : yet in this Doctrine of *perfection* the Quakers exceed the Doctrine of the Papiſts: for generally the *popes* attribute this purity but to ſome of their rare Saints. And 2. Generally the Popes themſelves confeſs themſelves *A 7 parallel between the Pope and Quakers*

8 Parallel as to the ſinleſs condition of the Quakers

to

to be finners. 3. They give refpect and civill honour to all eftates, although in *Spirituals* and *Civills*
too they overtop them : But the high and lofty
Devill of the *Quakers pride* tranfcends all this : G.
Fox makes all his *Saints born of God*, that (literally
expounded) they cannot commit fin ; yea, G. *Fox*
tells us that the Saints (that is his *Foxians*) are as
holy and perfect as God, not only like to God in
quality, but in equality alfo. They have the fulnefs of the Godhead in them bodily. That the
myftery of godlinefs is God manifeft in their flefh!
Hence he faith there is no diftinction between God
and Chrift, and the Spirit and themfelves. Hence
it follows, that they are the Father, Son and Holy
Spirit (which by Devilifh Chymiftry) they can
prove *:* and that they are the *Three that bare Record in Heaven,* and the *Three that bare Record in
Earth* : The Scripture is within them : They made
it, and all that they fay and do is Scripture, what
they fay God faith, what they advife God advifeth,
what they do God doth, &c.

It is true, this is not believed (no not by fome
Novices among them but this and more, many of
their lying *Foul mouths & Books* exprefs, which may
make a Soul that is truly humble to quake and [169
rend his heart at fuch *Blafphemy*, the firft Perfectift
in thefe parts was one *H. B.* who came from *Bofton* to *Providence*, who affirmed that what he fpake
God fpake, what counfel he gave God gave, &c. It
pleafed God to leave him (though a fubtle man) to
ridiculous Folly amognft us, and at *Barbadoes* and
London fince, to worfe practices : as commonly God
punifheth

G F his proud Blaf-phemy as to God himfelf

H B the firft Per-fctift in thefe parts, and moft notorious for Imper-fections.

punisheth such height of *Pride* even in this present life before Death seize upon them.

I remember while we were declaring their proud *Disrespect* to all men, *John Stubs* said, That it was their practice to pay tribute to *Cæsar*, and to give Honour to whome Honour belonged. And I answered to this effect, that it was against their Principles and practices to shew respect to any mans Person in the World. As for tribute they paid none but what necessity and policy forced them to, and notoriously backward here: But they knew that I and *G. Fox* knew, and all the world might know out of *Fox* his *Writings*, that the *Quakers* are the *Higher powers*, the *Dignityes*, the *Most High God*, and ought to have all Honour and Tribute paid to them by all the whole Creation. Tis true there seems to be a Change and some relenting and *Giving* of the *Weather* in *G. Fox* his own practice of Courtesie, and others from him: but while they own what *G. Fox* hath written, and that he writ it with a perfect spirit: I say untill they do make some *Recantation* or *Retractation*: or shew the Reasons why they doe not, *H. Norton* who keeps more plainly to his *Principles* is to windward of them, and the *Foxians* do but strip themselves naked to be more derided and scorned as the more notorious *Juglers* and *Dissemblers*. *The difference amongst the Quakers as to these things.*

We came easily (with their Good-will) to the 4th. *Position* of the latter seven, which they read out of the Paper (as willing to be out of ther pain) viz, *The Religion of the Quakers is more obstructive and Destructive to the Conversion and Salvation of Soules* *The 4th of the seven last Positions.*

of

*of People than moſt of Religions that are at this day
extant in the World.*

I ſaid for the proof of this it was requiſite to take
a ſhort view of *Religions* and *Worſhips* in the world.
We knew that the Sons of Men were juſtly divided
all the world over into two Sorts,

Firſt, The wild and Pagan, whome God hath
permitted to run about the world as wild Beaſts all
this great fourth Part of the World, and in ſome
of the other three.

170] They acknowledge a great ſupream God
and Deity, Maker of all things, yet they acknowledge (as other famous *Civilized Nations* formerly
have done) that there be many other Petty-Gods
and Deityes in Heaven and Earth, yea within their
own Bodies, yea whatever is extraordinary, excellent or ſtrange to them, they are preſently apt to
aſcribe a Deity unto it, though it be but *Beaſt, Fowle*
&c. and ſay it is a *God.* It is commonly known
that as their garments hang looſe about their
Bodyes, ſo hangs their *Religion* about their Souls :
So that (to my knowledge)they are ſo far from
hindring any to come to God, that when they have
ſeen the grave and ſolemn *Worſhip* of the *Engliſh,*
they have often ſaid of themſelves and their own,
that they are all one *Dogs* in compariſon of the
Engliſh.

The ſecond ſort of men are the *Civill* brought to
Cloaths, to *Lawes &c.* from *Barbariſme* : theſe alſo
the infinite Wiſdome of God have pleaſed to leave
to variety of wayes of *Worſhipping* the *Heavenly
Majeſty,*

Amongſt

Amongft others we find four moft known and eminent,

Firft, The *Jewiſh Worſhip* famous from Gods own appointment by *Moſes &c.* 2. The *Turkiſh,* famous for ſpreading from *Mahomet* to moſt of thirteen parts of thirty in the World.

The four chief Re-ligions of the World.

3. The *Popiſh,* famous for ſpreading over *Europe* and other weſtern parts of the world. 4. The *Proteſtant* famous for ſo wonderfull a *Revolt* and Seperation from the Popiſh. All theſe four profeſs one God and ſupream *Deity* : but they differ in two things, 1. In the *Prophet* or Meanes by whome God ſpeaks to man; the *Iews* cry up *Moſes,* the *Turks Mahomet,* the *Papiſts* the *Pope,* the *Proteſt-ants Chriſt Jeſus* in the Scriptures,

The ſecond great difference is in the *Form* of Worſhip, which every one of theſe four great Partyes practice in various and different wayes as they are perſwaded.

Our ſelves the *Proteſtants* are divided into two Partyes,

The firſt is entituled *Epiſcopal* and *Preſbyterian* in Parochyal or Pariſhional Aſſemblyes.

The ſecond is *Seperate* from thoſe National and Parochyal Aſſemblyes, ſome more ſome leſs, and thoſe are now known to be Firſt, the People called *Independants.* 2. The people called *Baptiſts.*

We that pretend the Chriſtian Name againſt the *Jewes* and the [171] *Mahumetans,* we mainly differ, 1. In matter of *Doctrine,* as *Repentance, Faith,* &c. 2. Of *Worſhip, Diſcipline* &c. And we generally agree, that as the *Mahumetan* and *Jewiſh* Worſhip

The religi-ous Differ-ences among the Proteſtants

Worſhip have little in them to tempt a Soul to turn into them compar'd with the *Chriſtian*, ſo thoſe Chriſtians that differ each from other in point of Doctrine and Worſhip both, as the *Papiſts* and the *Quakers* doe to be farther from the truth of the Profeſſion of *Chriſt Jeſus*, and more obſtructive and deſtructive to the Souls of men then the other partyes; yea and the *Papiſts* not ſo much as the *Quakers*, who wildly profeſs all *Ordinances* and *Miniſters* to be inviſible, and yet are hypocritically and ridiculouſly found to be as viſible and open as any.

If the true *Foundations* of *Repentance* and *Faith* be caſt down it is in vain to talk of ſaving of *Soules*, it is in vain to talk of Worſhipping of God. The *Quakers* (for all their craking of *Quaking* and *Tremhling*) their way is more eaſie of *Worſhipping God*, and of bringing perſons to their *worſhip of God*, then the way of *Jewes* or *Turks* or *Papiſts*, who to my knowledge take more paines in *Religion* then do the common Proteſtants: I confeſs they all do but paint and guild over natures old and rotten Poſts, only the real Proteſtants have and profeſs the greateſt care of any in the world for true *Faith* and *Repentance*.

The *Quakers* came not neer that care of *N-England* (I am ſure at firſt) for the perſonal true *Repentance* and *Holineſs* of their *Church* s and *Congregations*: For it is notoriouſly known, that if perſons notoriouſly *Deboiſt*, come but to acknowledge a *God and Chriſt within them*, that is in *Engliſh*, that themſelves are *God* and *Chriſt*, and can practice *Thou* and

Fundamental Differences.

The Quakers eaſie

and *Thee*, and *Cheek by Joll* with all their Betters, *Converfion and Churches, not compa- rable to the way of N-Eng- land.* and can rail at and curfe all that oppofe them, and can come and bow down to a dumb Image and *Worfhip* without any great bufinefs of *Contrition* and *Brokennefs* and *Godly Sorrow*, they are enrold and canonized for *Saints* and *Gods &c.* they are free from Sin, born of God and cannot fin, they now fit upon the twelve thrones and judge the unbeliev- ing *Jews* and *Gentiles* in their *heavenly places*.

The wound lyes here (as it is with *Papifts*, *Ar- minians*, and indeed with all mankind) in the footh- ing up and flattering of *rotten Nature*, from whence (from within the *Lord Jefus* tells us) proceed all the rotten and hellifh *Speeches* and *Actions*.

172] I told them it was in this cafe as it was with *Kings* and *Princes*, there were two great Enemyes that haunted the Pallaces of Kings and Princes. 1. *Traiterous Spyes &c.* 2. *Traiterous Flatterers*.

Juft here it was (as I remember) that *W. Ed- mundfon* ftopt me faying, thou haft here been tell- ing us Storyes of *Turks* and *Jewes*, but what is that to thy Charge againft us? we are none of thofe that flatter *Kings* and *Princes*, we deal plainly with all men. *Flatterers of Kings*

I faid they miftook me: for I did not fay they flattered Kings, I ufed a fimilitude only, viz. that as *Flatterers*, &c. of Kings and great men, were their deadlieft Foes, fo fuch Religions and Doctrines as moft flatter and footh up our rotten hearts and na- tures they are moft dangerous and deftructive to us: I intended to add that the *Quakers* pretended to be as fine Flower fifted out from the *common Proteft-*
ants,

The whor-
ifh Quak-
ers, and
whore of
Rome.
ants, yea, from the *Independants & Baptifts*, that
Sathan was too fubtle for the fubtleft *Foxes* of them
all, for he knowes that by pretence he more eafily
& dangeroufly conveys the Poyfon of exalting corrupt and curfed nature in the room of true Soul-faving Humiliation.

I did fay as the *Whore* of *Rome* deceived whole
Towns, Cities, Nations and Kingdomes with her
glorious Trimmings, and her Golden Cup : fo that
the *Painted Quaker* (as a Drunken Whore) fhould
follow the *Drunken Whore of Rome*) drunk with the
blood of Jefus, &c.) for the obtaining of (the fmoak
of a *Tobacco-pipe*) the Riches and Honour of this
World.

There are two forts of godly Soules catcht up a
while by the Devils Craftinefs.

1. Weak and unftable (for there are Children,
ftrong Men, & old Men in Chriftianity.)

The Devil
a roaring
Lion
2 The unwatchful and fecure. The holy wifdome of God difcovers in Holy Scripture, what the
Devil, that Sathan an old Serpent is, *viz.* not only a
Roaring, but a *vigilant Lyon*. *David* (Gods beloved
as his Name is) he fails in his managing of Government, therefore the Devil ftirs up *Joab and Achitophel* to help (the grand Rebel) his Son *Abfolom* : and
afterwards *Sheba*, and all in wonderful Figures, in
all Ages, and in this our age and day.

A famous *Jefuit* prints it, that all the Religion
in the World lies in competition between the *Jefuits* and *Puritants*, &c. About [173] this time *John
Stubs* told me that they (and I fay fo do the
Jefuites pretend to do) had left the Glory and Pleafure

sure of this world their Wives and Children, Friends
and Relations, to Preach the Everlasting Gospel;
For the Woman had been 1260 years 42 months in
the wilderness, and she was now come and coming
forth, and they were now preaching the everlasting
Gospel, and therefore they advised me to make
haste and dispatch and not to hinder the Lords
work.

I spake what then I thought fit, and now adde *The Quak*
that the *Pharisees*, the *Apostles*, the *Quakers* and *pretences*
Jesuites do compass Sea and Land: but the *Phari-* *all pre-*
sees, Jesuites and Quakers will be found at last to be *tending*
the *Apostles* Messengers, Heralds, Envoys, Embassa- *Preachers*
dors, and *Emissaries* of Sathan sent out from Hell
to predicate the goodness of rotten nature, hell and
damnation, and that false and hellish Gospel (or
good news) of poor rotten Natures *Righteousness,*
Satisfaction, Penances, and to the damning of
Souls, &c.

The Devil knows that after the witnesses have *True*
done their work against Antichrist, and after their *Preachers*
slaughters! the Lord Jesus will send abroad his *gers*
Messengers to other Nations (*Jews & Gentiles*) and
New Jerusalem, or a new vision of peace shall then
come down from Heaven among the Sons of men:
but for the present he stirs up these Jesuites and
Quakers (with brave titles and pretences) like so
many *Mahomets* (under pretence of *Diogenes* tread-
ing on *Platoes Carpets*) to fish for the smoak of this
Worlds *Sodome,* and no doubt but the *Quakers* will
use the Sword as much as *Mahomet* or the *Jesuites,*
under

under the cloak and colours of love to Jefus and faving of Souls.

I confefs that Charity hopes and believes all things, and yet I fay, curfed is that charity that puts out the eye of Reafon, the eye of Experience, the eye of true affection to Chrift Jefus, his Father and his Wife to the Souls of his followers, and the Souls of poor finners *Jews & Gentiles*.

The Earthly & Heavenly Sword

As to the faving of Souls, it was a Thunder from the heavenly mouth of Chrift Jefus. They that take the Sword fhall perifh by the Sword : as if he fhould fay, *the Sword is not a faving but a deftroying Tool*, in Soul-humbling, and Soul-faving : making worlds of *Hypocrites*, but not true *Proteftants*, true *Chriftians & Followers* of the true Lord Jefus, and of his Father, and of his Holy Spirit.

174] The *Spirit* fay the *Quakers*, why thats our *Weapon* ! the *Sword of the Spirit* the *Word of God*, why thats the word of God Chrift Jefus our Weapon : So faith *G. Fox* and all our *Fantafticks* out of weaknefs and madnefs, not weighing what a perfon

A great myftery amongft Papifts and Proteftants

the holy Records defcribe Chrift Jefus to be, but as foolifh Children and Anticks in the Lord Mayors fhews, they cry out *Chrift* and the *Spirit* only for a fhew and colour, I know it that the true Lord Jefus his holy Father, and Holy Spirit is as odious both to *Jefuits*, and moft *Papifts & Quakers* as the Devil, yea infinitely more then the Devil himfelf, as with Gods help I have and fhall make it as clear as the Noon dayes Sun.

O you confidering *Proteftants*, fee you not how the Devil would rob you of that Sword with which Chrift

Chrift Jefus overcame him [*The Holy Scripture*] un-*A word to the Pro-teſtants* der the colour and cloak of the Spirit in the mouths of the *Quakers?* how, if the Holy writings muſt yet live, why he hath *Fiſher*, and *Stubs*, and *Pennington*, and *Biſhop*, and others that skill Tongues, and yet own the *blockiſh Spirit* of the *Quakers*: how if you blame the *Popiſh Devil* for a Blockhead, he can puff up his Bladders the *Jeſuites*, to a late won-derful ſwelling of Tongues and Hiſtories, and all kinds of Knowledge, as in *Bellarmine* and his Aſſo-ciate and Followers and of late in thoſe great Wri-ters *Petavius* and *Morinus*.

The eternal Word, and Son, and Sun of God the *The myſti-cal Farmers* true Lord Jeſus will more and more diſcover who are his true friends, his true Loves (that love *Alex-ander* more than the *King*) that are true Chriſtians, true *Jeſuites*, and that truly love and pity poor Souls: he will diſcover who are the great *Farmers*, who having a minde to the *Farm* themſelves con-ſult and ſay, *come, this is the Heir* (that is Chriſt Je-ſus in his true Meſſengers) *let us kill him*: kill him with Tongue, and Pen, and Sword, &c. the *Inheri-tance* of Heavenly and Earthly Glory ſhall then be ours, &c. and to this end only they talk of Souls, &c.

We now deſcended to the fifth and ſorrowful *The 5th. of the laſt 7 poſitions* point of ſuffering which they read, *viz.* [*That the ſufferings of the Quakers are no true evidence of the Truth of their Religion.*]

At the reading of this they told me, that although their *Sufferings* were great in all places whither the Lord had ſent them, yet they made not their *Suf-fering* an Evidence of the truth of their *Religion*, & therefore

*The suf-
frings of
the Qua-
kers*
therefore I might have been better advifed then to
175| put this in among the reft of my *Lyes* and
Slanders as not confiderable, and now not worth the
mentioning, &c.

I Anfwered, that I underftood what they faid, and
I undeftood mine own affirmation alfo; and defired their patience alfo while I offered my Proofs
to two Particulars,

1. That in their *Books* and *Writings* &c. they do
make their *Sufferings* a great Evidence to themfelves and others of the truth of their *Way* and
Spirit.

2. This their *Suffering* is not valid as to the
proof of their *Religion*, *Way* and *Spirit* to be of
God. So then they bid me prove it if I could.

*Pauls and
the Quak
fuffrings*
I told them that I could find no *Jewes*, no *Papiſts* no *Proteſtants*, that did fo magnifie and fo exactly infift upon their *Sufferings* as the *Quakers* did.
Tis true that *Paul* did more particularize his Sufferings then other Saints in Scripture; but it was
alfo true that they were fo exceeding great that
Paul feemed a *None-Such*; but befide that it was
upon fome great *Infultings* of the *Falfe Apoftles*
againft not only himfelf, but againft the Truth of
Chrift Jefus: neither of which is the *Quakers* cafe.
Befide, the *Quakers Sufferings* generally were not to
be compar'd with *Pauls*, and yet they fet down fuch
exact accounts of every *hour* in prifon every *Stripe*
*The Quak.
fufferings
in Hyſtory
of G. Biſ-
bop re-
corded.*
in *Whipping*, every pound loft: and this publifhed
to the world in print, as if it were a Sign hung out
with this Infcription, *Loe people thefe are the* Evidences *of Gods holy* Truths, *and Gods holy* Spirit, *of*

our

our Perfecutors wickednefs, *and our* Chriftian Faith
and Patience, *who for his Truths fake can endure all
this.* I faid it was not rational to think, that men
profeffing fuch high *Wifdome* and *Confcience,* fhould
declare fuch *Lyfts* and *Catalogues* of *Sufferings* (as
G. *Bifhop* doth to the world, of the *Quakers Sufferings in N. England,* in his firft and fecond *Hiftory*)
only in a childifh Vapour, Oftentation and Vain-
Glory, much lefs in hopes of *Reparation* or .any
worldly advantage, either in *England* old or new,
Scotland or *Virginia,* &c. and therfore Reafon per-
fwades that thefe Sufferings are held forth (as the
holy Spirit fpeaks of the Sufferings of the *Theffa-
lonians,* 2. Theff. 2.) as a manifeft Token of the
righteous judgment of God rendering *Tribulation* to
their Perfecutors, and *Reft* to themfelves fuffering
for the *Kingdome* of *God.*

As I remember, *John Stubs* faid, they did not
boaft of their [176] Sufferings, but bare them patiently for the Truths fake which they preached
and profeffed.

I faid I did not charge them to fay in exprefs
terms, We have loft fo much outward *Gain, Favour,
Friendfhip, Worldly Advantage* for the Name of
Chrift within us, can you fay the like for the Chrift
without you? We have endured *Imprifonments,
Whippings, &c.* have you done the like? only this
I fay, that as all *Religious Jewes, Papifts, Proteftants
&c.* are confirmed in their Perfwations by their
Sufferings, and do predicate them to others as *Arguments* and *Signs* of the truth of their *Doctrines,*
and of Gods prefence and Affiftance with them : fo
do

do the *Quakers* and that with more Particular and exact *Accounts* then moſt of all the reſt have done.

I told them, I had obſerved much to this purpoſe in *G. Fox* & *E. Burrowes* in the Book by me.

E. Burrowes *his* Epiſtle *quoted.*

They bid me alleadge what I could out of them : I took up the Book, and they theirs, I directed them to the 12*th.* Page of *Ed. Burrowes* his large *Epiſtle* to *G. Fox* his Book in Folio where I read this paſſage viz. *And this we did with no ſmall oppoſition and Danger : yea oftentimes we were in danger of our Lives, through beating, abuſing, puniſhing, haling, caſting over walls, ſtriking with ſtaves & Cudgels, and knocking down to the ground :* Beſide, Reproaching, Scorning, Revilings, Hooting at, *Scornings and Slanderings, and all abuſe that could be thought or acted by evil hands and tongues, and oft carried before* Magiſtrates *with grievous Threats, and ſometimes put in the Stocks, and whipped, and often impriſoned, and many hard dealings againſt us , the worſt that tongues or hands could execute, ſparing life.* Of this all the North Countreys *can witneſs. And all theſe things are ſuſtained and ſuffered from People and Rulers becauſe of our* Faithfulneſs *to the Lord, and for declaring againſt the falſe Deceivers. For nothing ſave only the hand of the Lord and his power, could have preſerved us and carried us through all this : neither for any* Reward *outward whatſoever, or advantage to our ſelves would we have expoſed our ſelves to ſuffrings, violence and dangers which befel us daily. But the Lord was our exceeding great reward through all theſe things, and kept us in the hollow of his hand, and under the ſhadow of his wings, and gave us dominion in*
                                                    Spirit

*Spirit over all our enemies, and subdued them before us :
and though Rulers and People were combined against us,
and executed their violence and in-* [177] *justice against
us, yet the Lord made us to prosper and grow exceedingly
in Strength, Wisdome and Number, and the hearts of
the people inclined to us, and the Witness of God in
many stirred for us : for to that in all Consciences,
Words and wayes we did commend our selves to be known
and approved.*

Hereto they suddenly said, What canst thou
make of this, but that *Edward Burrowes* said the
truth, that the Sufferings of the people called *Quakers* were very great, & that he acknowledged the
powerfull hand of the Lord toward them in sup-
porting and delivering them : But this was far
from boasting or making it any *Evidence* of the
truth of their *Religion* and *Principles.*

I replyed, I prayed them to consider why pious
and conscientious Souls (as they would be reputed)
should give so large a *Catalogue* of their *Sufferings.* *The Quo-*
2. Profess it was only for their *Faithfulness* to the *tation*
Lord.   3. Declare that it was the hand of the Lord *weighed.*
that kept them,   4, That he only could do it : I
sayd the *Weaving* and *inter-weaving* of these Particulars, speak plainly that for their *Faithfullness* to
the Lord and his Truth in declaring and suffering
for it, the Lord had been faithfull to them in sup-
porting them and comforting them in all these Suf-
ferrings for his Name sake. Why should wise men
use all these words but to this end, of *Evidencing*
their *Faithfulness* to God, and Gods *Faithfulness* to
them.

After

After some words had about these kind of passages in *Ed. Burrowes* and other of their Writings, I told them that we must come to that ancient and true Maxime, *Causa facit Martyrem*, not the Suffering of *Burning* it self that is the evidence of a true matter. I therefore told them that as it was in the case of Signs[1] Wonders *Deut.* 13. though they be Signs which false *Prophets* give, which come to pass, yet God commands his Children not to be moved from his written word, and his holy revealed and recorded *Ordinances* and *Institutions*.

What true Suffering is.

I told them that I had other places which I had turned down in *Edward Burrowes* to produce; but these I had suppressed in my thoughts for expedition sake, and would if they pleased pass on to my proof of my next *Position*, to this they readily assented : but being now out of my Shackles of a quarter of an hour (to which I wink'd to draw them on) I crave the Readers Patience and leave to hear me say something now which then I could not say.

True Scripture Language.

178] First. To what I have said before of *E. Burrowes* insisting so largly on the *Sufferings* of the *Quakers*, and yet my *Antagonists* denying them to make their Sufferings an *Evidence* of their *Truth*, I present the Reader with a witness of *G.Fox* his words in his *Pag* 64, [*And there is a Proof to thee that the* Quakers *are sent of God who speak to thee of the Scripture right as they are*] He that reads the place shall see that *G.Fox* useth these words against his Opposite *Jeremiah Jewes*, because that his Opposite

[1] Interline "and"   *R. W. Ms. Ann.*

polite had faid, viz. That the *Word of God* was contained in the *Scripture* : and *G. Fox* checks him for it and faith if he had faid [the word which it fpeaks of] he had fpoken right &c. And this *G. Fox* makes an *Evidence* of the *Quakers* being fent of God, that they only can fpeak *properly*. How much more is what I have produced (and have much more to produce) a *Proof* that they do roll their Souls upon their *Sufferings* as an *Evidence* and Confirmation that they are fent of God?

2. It is wonderfull what the *Jewes* and *Papifts* have fuffered for their *Lyes* and *Blafphemyes* : What *The won-* a wonderfull Story doth *Manaffeh Ben-Ifrel* relate *derfull* of a Noble man, a *Portugal*, turned *Jew*, burn'd *of Here-* in *Portugal* for the *Jewifh Faith*? What *Devotion* *ticks* and *Zeal* have many of the *Popifh* Party fhewn at *Tiburn*? Sure it is that a natural *Valour* and *Magnanimity*, a natural *Melancholy* and *Stoutnefs*, a natural *Pride* and *Vain-Glory* will give wings which fire and Burning cannot fcorch and conquer.

3. I doubt not but that tis poffible for not only *Chriftians*, but alfo *Jewes* and *Papifts* &c. like *Paul* in his mad *Confcience*, to be zealous for his *Confcience*, and to put others to death for their *Confciences*, and yet neither of them to fin againft their *Confciences*, but ignorantly as *Paul* did.

4. I believe that not only *Paul*, and fuch as he, *Great fail-* in Unbelief may fo practice, but even the true *ings of* Saints and Children of God. He that fhall ponder *dren in* the Fathers *Poligamy*, the beft Kings of *Judah* fuf- *this life.* fering the *High places,Davids* flaying *Uriah,Afahs* imprifoning the *Prophet, Peters* rafh ufing the Sword,

Davids

Davids and *Nathans* unadvifed *Advife* to build God
a Temple, the *Difciples* calling for Fire from Heaven, and fhall fee caufe to reprove the *Quakers* for
their rafh damning of others from whome they
have fuffered. For,

5. As tis poffible for Gods own Children to hold,
and that [179] obftinately, falfe *Principles*, fo it is
poffible for other of Gods Children as obftinately
to afflict and punifh thofe others to *Death*, and fo
bring *Affliction* and *Deftruction* one upon an other
which is that the Devil aimes at.

6. Becaufe the *Quakers* do fo abundantly glory
in their *Sufferers,* and (in comparifon of them)
flight the *Saints* under the *Altar* (in our *Book of
Martyrs,* as *James Parnel* impioufly calls it) cafting
all that differ from them into the *Satanical Delufion,* and *Serpentine nature,* as *Fox* doth, *Pag.* 5. *and*
253. and 99. Who forbids to receive into their
Houfes, no not Kings and Princes, nor to bid them
True and God *fpeed* that are not in their Light. I think it
Falfe Suf- fit to obferve at this Turn fome Differences between
ferers for
the Name true *Sufferers* and falfe, both pretending the Name
of Chrift. of *Chrift Jefus.*

First, The Perfons whome the heavenly man
John Fox defcribes, they were men and women
known to be of holy and heavenly Spirits towards
God, and of low and meek Spirits towards all, yea
their very enemyes. I would I could fay fo of the
Quakers (though no queftion but a *a gold Ring* may
The Qua- fall into the *Channel,* and[1] *Jewel* into the *Dirt* of
kers de-
fcribed. worldly and *Antichriftian errors*) But for the *Qua-*
kers

---

[1] Interline "a." *R. W. Ms. Ann.*

kers I have caufe to fear that generally they are *Proud, ambitious,* and *Worldly-minded* Wretches. Some of them have literal *Knowledge* of the *Scripture,* and fome ftirring *Affections* with the ftony Ground, others with the thorny Ground have fuffered formerly, but the Cares and lufts of this world have drild them into this way of Antichriftian Worfhip. others are *Fierce, Pragmatical. Difcontented &c.* and they muft travel and be *Apoftles* to preach and bring in Profelites.

The Caufe of *John Foxes* and *G. Foxes* Martyrs differ as much as Day from Night, and Light from Darknefs: For it is known that *J. Fox* his *Martyrs* or *Witneffes* (thofe bleffed Souls under the Altar) were flain for maintaining the Authority and Purity of the *Holy Scriptures* as the revealed word or will of the *Eternal God* againft the *Traditions* and *Inventions* of men.

J Fox & G Fox their Martyrs the contrary caufes of their Sufferings.

But *G. Foxes Sufferers* have generally fuffered for their *Childrens Baubles,* fantaftical *Traditions* and *Inventions,* for fetting up a *Dream* of a *Light* and *Chrift* within all Man kind, above the *holy Scriptures,* above the *Son of God,* above all *Earthly Dignityes,* and all their *Betters* : endeavouring (with the Pope) to trample all *fouls* and *Bodyes* under their proud feet.

180]   3. The carriage of thefe two Sorts of Sufferers differ as much as *Eaft* from *Weft,* and *Heaven* from *Hell.*

1. The ground of *Johns* Sufferers was that which *John* fo much writes of, *viz.* love to the Heavenly Bridegroom, without which *Paul* flights burning
ing

Heavenly love carried on. G Foxes even felf, God and Chrift & Spirit.

ing it felf: this appears in their wonderfull Love to the holy Scriptures, (the Love-Letters of *Chrift Jefus*) and unto all that loved *Chrift Jefus* alfo. The Quakers are known to be Fierce, Heady, Proud, Self-conceited, Stout, Bold, and driven on by an Audacious and Defperate *Spirit* (which *G.Fox* and fome fubtle *Foxes* with him have of late blarred in *H.Norton &c.*) No queftion but fome of them have a notion of *Wrath* yet to come, and therefore rather then to endure *Hell Fire* they will give up their lives to the Flames, others of them faft 40

Virgin love to God, &c.

dayes, and yet be far from true *Virgin Love* to the *Son of God*. *A Virgin* that loves a man for *Himfelf*, will not flight his *Love-letters*, nor his *Near Relations* (leaft of all abhor them, and fink and burn them as thefe *Foxians* doe.

2. The carriage of *J. Foxes Witneffes*, though (in refpect of Gods holy Truth) it was couragious and gallant, yet their lowlinefs and humility did fhine forth glorioufly alfo.

1. As to God, being more fenfible of their fins then of their fufferings: confeffing with many tears that although God did turn their fufferings

The humility of Chrifts fufferers

unto his Glory, and although ungodly men (like Foxes and Wolves) hunted them like innocent *Lambs* and *Chickins*) yet they had deferved and calld for this Storm by their unthankfulnefs for their former peace and liberties, by their drowfinefs and fleeping upon the Earthen bed of worldly Profits and Pleafures.

Contrarily it is known to all, that although fometimes the *Quakers* will fay we come in love to your
Souls

Souls yet (the *Quakers* are far from confessing their *Devilish pride*
sins, as having no more sin then God hath, and
(according to their Principles and some of them
say it) they can no more sin against God then God
can sin against them.

As to Men Chrifts sufferers were meek, patient;
refpective, contented, thankful.

But as the *Quakers* hearts have an infensible
brawninefs and hardnefs (like frozen Rivers come
over their hearts) in matters of God fo as to men.
181] 1. Was there ever a People (Men and Women profeffing fuch an height of Chriftianity) fo
fierce fo heady, fo high-minded and though generally not hardned) fo cenfuring, reviling, curfing and
damning: and fo favage and barbarous as in the
ftark nakednefs of men and women, &c.

2. As to Revenge, how patient, and pitiful, and
praying for their Enemies were *J. Foxes Martyrs*
or *Witneffes*, and *G. Foxes*, how fpitting *Fire &* *The pre-dictions of the Qua-kers*
Brimftone? (witnefs the fecond part of *N. England*
judged by *G. Bifhop*) becaufe Chrift in them is
come to judgement) wherein he pronounceth *De-ftruction* to Bodies and Souls of *N.England men*, faying in his Epiftle, *that their judgement lingreth not,*
nor doth their damnation flumber.

Tis true fome of their Predictions have and may
come to pafs as do many alfo of *Conjurers & Witch-es*, for the Devil knows the Complexion of perfons
and things, and what is like to come to pafs (as in
Sauls cafe and in other events) and ftill the poor
Quakers (and other his *C*aptive Slaves) with fuch
Bables as thefe. I told you what weather it would
be,

A bleſſed
ſaying of
bleſſed Mr.
Dod. be, I told you where the Wind would blow : I told
you what would come to paſs,] and yet as bleſſed
Mr. *J. Dod* uſed to ſay, *though the Devil was up
early, God was ſtill up before him* : for the Proverb is
here true, *God hath ſent curſt Cows ſhort Horns* : his
infinite Wiſdome, Power and Goodneſs is pleaſed
to put an Hook into the Jaws of Sathan : he ſhews
himſelf the pitiſui ſparer and preſerver of men :
When the Devil is a *Fiſher* longing for troubled and
bloody waters, yet God hath graciouſly proved
many of the bloody propheſies of his waſpiſh Prophets and Propheteſſes, (as I can prove) to be lying
and falſe already.

The 13 po-
ſition
diſcuſd. We now deſcended to the thirteenth Propoſal
(the ſixth to be diſcus'd at *Providence*) which was
read by them, and is this, *viz.* [*Theſe many Books
and Writings are extreamly Poor, Lame, and Naked,
ſwelld up only with High Titles and Words of Boaſting and Vapour.*]

I told them that I had not ſhun'd (as in the
preſence of the moſt High) to read any of their
Books or Letters I could come at : but the truth is,
I could never pick out any Wheat (of ſolid, rational
and heavenly Truth) out of their heaps of Chaffe,
and Dreams, and Fancies of new Chriſts, new
Spirits, &c.

It is true that *W. Edmund.* ſaid, that the Word
of the Lord [182] was a Fire, and a Hammer, &c.
But I ſaid the word they meant was but a painted
Fire, and a painted Hammer, and that never broke
nor burned up ſin as ſin.

Let a man read the Works of the *Papiſts, Lu-
therans,*

therans, *Arminians*, and amongſt our ſelves, the *Epiſ-*
copal and *Preſbyterian* Writings: a man ſhall have
wherein to exerciſe his Judgement, Memory, &c.
he ſhall have Scripture propoſed, Arguments al- *compared*
leadged, yea he ſhall read Anſwers and Replies,
whereby to ſatisfie a rational Soul and Underſtanding.

But in the *Quakers Books & Writings*, Peter &
Jude tells us (what I have found) clouds high of an
imaginary Chriſt and Spirit: high ſwelling words,
ſtrange from the Holy Scripture Language, and all
ſober and Chriſtian Writers and Speakers.

Let *Jo. Chandlers* Writings, and the Writings of
Theora John (that Monſter of Deluſion) be viewed,
whoſe bodily Raptures, and frantick Writings of
the *Quakers* Principles, and of the *Jews* (in *Hebrew*,
Greek, Latin & Arminiack Writings (which he con-
feſt he underſtood not) and let the reſt of their
Writings be brought to the *Touch-ſtone*, and ſee if
an honeſt *Goldſmith* can find ought elſe but the
Droſs, Dreams and Fancies, in ſtead of the ſolid
Gold of Heavenly Scripture.

I have read *Nichols*, and *Nailor*, and *Howgel* and
Burrows, and *Parnel*, and *Farnworth*, and *Fox*, and
Dewsbury and *Pennington*, and *Whitehead*, and *Biſhop*, *G F. his*
&c. And I could readily and abundantly prove my *Writings*
poſition out of all of them, but my deſire and inten-*poor and lame*
tion was (as by my Paper to *G. Fox* appears) to
have made it good to *G. Fox* himſelf, and to all
Chriſtians, how poor and lame, and naked *G. Fox*
his writings are, who ſeems to be as *Pighius* and
Echius amongſt the *Papiſts*, and as *Bellarmine* the
greateſt Writer amongſt them.

I told

G F his
book in fo-
lio confide-
red

I told my *Oppofites* I would therefore Anfwer this *Bellarmine*, and I would not fay *Bellarmine* thou lieft: but I would by Holy Scripture fhew *G.Fox* and his deluding *Foxians*, how the old *Fox* the old *Serpent* was too crafty for them all, and had brought them and their Followers to the brim of the Lake that burns with fire and brimftone.

Firft. then I faid, let who will that underftands true Englifh, and are able to read and write true Englifh, (though he know no more) take *G. Fox* his Folio Book in hand, and tell me whether ⌊183 (through his whole Book) he writes like an *Eng-lifh-man*: And though he upbraids all his Op-pofites fcornfully and ridiculoufly (as poor Children that know not the Bible nor their Accidence in faying *you* to a fingular, &c.) whether in many fcores of places in his Book he confounds not the fingular and the Plural : I confefs when I urged this in pub-lick, my Oppofites defired of me no proof of this out of *Foxes Book* and therefore (remembering my quarter hour Glaffe) I fpared Quotations, but now (through Gods patience and my Readers) my Ted-der being longer, I fhall give one or two brief Proofs and Inftances.

In page 282. in *G. Fox* his fecond Anfwer he faith, [*You where you are fees him nor*] where it fhould be the Plural fee him not, if this *Proud Bruit* had known either his Accidence or the Bible.

In Page 300. he faith [*The Scriptures is able to make wife unto Salvation*] which fhould be are able, &c.

In Page 16. [*The Churches was to hear*] for, were to hear.   In

In Page 110. [*As thou doth*] which fhould be, as G F his ig-norance of common Englifh
thou doft: And abundance more of this Boyes
Englifh all his Book over, which I cannot impute to his *Northern Dialect* (having been fo long in
the South, and London, and read and anfwered (as
he dreams) fo many Englifh Books: nor to the
Printer (the faults of that kinde being fo numerous) but to the finger of the moft High, and moft
Holy, whofe property it is, and therefore delights to
run thwart and croff the fhins of proud and infulting Souls and Spirits.

2. I obferve throughout his Book a Devillifh
Black Line of defpifing thofe that are Good (as the
Scripture fpeaketh) He counts none Godly but himfelf and his *Foxians:* yea there is no *God,* no *Chrift,*
no *Spirit,* but what is in him and them feelingly,
though they fay he is in every man and woman in
the world, and *Chrift Jefus the Sun of Righteoufnefs,* Horrible contradic-tion
and the *Holy Spirit,* and the Kingdome of God,
which they confefs confifts in Righteoufnefs and
peace and joy in the Holy Spirits,[1] and yet (as they
impioufly and fimply fpeaks) thefe Inhabitants and
Hofts to all thefe Guefts know nothing of their
lodging and dwelling within them.

G. *Fox* gives a fhrewd fufpition that he never knew
what the true fear, and love, and peace, and joy of The ex-cellent men.
God mean; if he did, is it poffible that he could
puff at fo many Writers (excellent for great Knowledge and godlinefs, denying any thing of God or Whom G F in his
184] Chrift, or Spirit, or Grace to be in them:
fome

[1] "Holy Spirit." *R. W. Ms. Ann.*

book in folio trampleth on as Diſhclouts Dogs & Devils ſome of them (eminent ſervants of God) I have known : of others of them I have ſmelt the *ſweet Odour* of an Heavenly report from the mouthes of others and in their Writings.

But as *G.Fox* will be found to adore an *Image & Crucifix* for the true Lord Jeſus, ſo whatever he ſay of others will his Faith, his Love, his Spirit of Diſcerning, and *Hope of Glory* and *Salvation* prove (without Repentance) dolefully falſe in the latter end.

For, doth not this *Proud Cenſor* know that men may be true Saints in their perſons, and yet be ſubject to ſudden *Epileptical & Falling Fits?* may not *David* walk with God with a perfect heart, and yet in the matters of *Bathſheba* and *Uriah* (and many other particulars) fall down like a Jewel into the Dirt? that Chriſt Jeſus owns *Peter* and his *Confeſſion,* &c. and yet in another caſe, *get thee behind me Sathan?* That *Peter* reſolves to dye for Jeſus, and yet denies with Curſing and Swearing, that he never knew him, and after *Chriſts Reſurrection* and *Aſcention,* even *Peter* plays the *Hypocrite & Diſſembler.*

Yea did not the high Fathers in Godlineſs, famous Kings in Gods Church live long in the incivility of many Wives, and the impiety of Wor- *A difference of Sinners* ſhipping in the High places, &c. to what purpoſe doth the Lord inſpire his holy Pen-men to write theſe holy Hiſtories : was it to ſhame his Saints departed, or to ſhame his own Holineſs, and to caſt a ſtumbling block, and a protection for after ſinners and tranſgreſſors? or amongſt other holy ends to teach us (like *Moſes*) to diſtinguiſh between an *Egyptian* whom

whom he flew and the *Israelites* whom he chid for wronging each other, since they were their Bre-thren; so that he is a poor Christian Goldsmith, that knows not to discern the Gold of Holiness, and the Copper of Hypocrisie; yea, and to give the best *Gold* in the World its due allowance, with which it will pass currant in Earth and Heaven with God, and such who truly know and love him. *G. Fox no true Goldsmith.*

But with *G. Fox.* in all this great Book, the most humble and able, godly and conscientious are with him but *Vipers, Serpents, Cains, Judasses, false Prophets, Pharisees, dumb Dogs, Sorcerers, Witches, Reprobates, Devils, &c.*

3. In this Book of *G. Fox* (all along) he denies the *Scripture* to be the Word of God : and he said, that every man in the world hath that Spirit that gave forth *Scriptures*, and that all Saints are [185 acted by the same Spirit immediately that moved the Prophets and Apostles and holy Pen-men of the holy *Scriptures*, all tending to *vilifie* and *nullifie* the *Holy Scriptures*.

Besides, his *Impiety* in these Assertions (which half an eye of *Mahumetans, & Jewes, & Papists, & Protestants* will see) I note his Simplicity (for a Fox though he be crafty is but a Beast still) For out of his *Piety* he grants the holy Scriptures through all his Book to be the *Words of God*, though not the *Word of God*: and for this his Grant he quotes *Exod.* 20. *God spake all these Words*, and the four Books of the *Revelations*, which I nor my Opposites could tell in publick what to make of : But if they are the *Words* of God, and some of them fearfully *Fox his subtilty and yet simplicity in granting the Script. to be the words of God.*

written,

written by the inconceivable Finger of God once and twice, then every particular *word* of thefe *words* muft needs be the *Word* or *Will* or mind *of God* every grain of gold is gold, and every drop in the Ocean is Water and Salt too, as I urged to them before concerning every word that proceedeth out of the mouth of God) elfe the *Words of God* when brought to particular examination, they are not the word of *God*, but of *Angels* or *Men* or *Devills*.

How fweet are (not Words but) right Words: every man fhall kifs his lips that gives a right Anfwer, how dirty then, how filthy and bloudy are thofe Lips that in fo many places, debating with fo many wife and learned and pious men, drop not *Honey* and *Milk*, but *Wormwood* and *Gall* the *Venome* and the *Poyfon* of Afps to them that lick up fuch deceitfull and deftroying *Doctrines*.

4.   In *G. Fox* his Book I obferve that all along he notorioufly nibbles ar *VVords* and quarrels at *VVords*, which he faith are not *Scripture*, as that wicked word [*Humane*] relating to the Perfon of the Son of God and man.

The word Humane abominable above all words to the Quakers Alfo the word *Trinity* and *Sacrament*. Oh how zealous is this *Fox* for the purity of *Language*? Why may not the word *Humane* be ufed as well as the word *Sabboth* and *Sabbaoth*, and *Bethlebem* and *Ierufalem* which are Hebrew words, and as well as the words *Baptifme* and *Jefus Chrift* which are Greek words, *Scribes* and *Scriptures* and *Pretorium* which are Latine words. That word *Humane* is odious *&c.* for *Chrift Jefus* fake, and therefore the more I love and honour it, as expreffing the appearance

pearance of God in Flefh, in that perfonal, Individual Flefh of *Chrift Jefus* the [186] *Mediator* pe-
tween God and Man, the Man *Chrift Jefus.*

5. I obferve the loofe and wild Spirit of *G.Fox*
in dealing with fo many heavenly *Champions,* the
Leaps and Skips like a wild *Satyre* or *Indian,* catching and fnapping at here and there a Sentence, like
Children fkipping ore hard places and Chapters,
picking and culling out what is common and eafie
with them to be paid of and anfwered.

6. Any fober Soul may read in moft of their *The fimple*
Books, and in *G.Fox* his Book fuch *Tautologies* and *tautologyes
of the*
needlefs *Repetitions* that may even *Turn* his Stom- *Quakers.*
ach, and make him abhor to touch a *Quakers* Book
more. How many hundred times have you, *Chrift
is within you except you be Reprobates* : Flefh of his
Flefh and Bone of his Bone *&c.* and I prefume
neer a thoufand times if not a full thoufand times
repeated [That lightens every man that comes into
the World, that lightens every man that comes into
the world] &c. *G.Fox* had many *Bullets* flying about
his eares, and therefore at every turn (like a man
fighting for his life) he is forced to hold out a *Pretence* a *Buckler* a *Breaft-plate,* fimply called *Light,*
and at every turn to cry *Oh the Light, the Light that
enlightens every man that comes into the World.*

7 Through all his Book like fome great *Com-
manders* or *Generals* by Land or Sea, yea like the *The infult-*
Emperors or *Dictators* among the *Romanes,* fo doth *ing &*
this wild devouring Soul give forth his high and *wild im-
perioufnefs*
haughty *Sentences* : this proud Bladder is big with *of G.Fox.*
Simon Magus his thoughts of being Some Body.

I fhall prefent one Inftance,   *Pag.*

Hen.
Haggar.

Pag. 253. His Oppofite *Henry Haggar* faith, you call ⌊*all men Dead and Carnall, in the Serpents nature in what form foever they differ from you*⌋ this proud Soul Anfwers, [*All that be not in the Light that enlightens every man that comes into the World, which is the way to the Father, differeth from us, fuch be dead, fuch be carnal in the nature: for none comes to the life but who comes to the Light, in what form foever they be, and fuch as differ from us differ from Chrift, for none comes from under the Satanical nature but who comes to the Light*⌋ what *Julian* the Apof-

Bloudy and devillifh Pride of the Foxians. tate, what Duke *D'Alva*, what *Wolfey* could have fpoken more imperioufly, infultingly & bloudily then this *wild Fox* hath done againft all the true *Servants & Witneffes* of the *Moft High* that ever have been or fhall be to the end of this world? they differ from *Fox* & therefore are *Devils &c.*

187] 8. I obferve that *G.Fox* all along his Book powres forth a flood of *Fire & Brimftone* againft all his Oppfites and tells us that it is not *Railing &c.* for (his chief *Adverfary*) the holy Scripture gives In-ftance of Chrift Jefus himfelf giving fuch Lan-guage; and alfo it is no other then the Oppofites to the *Quakers* give unto them: but Godly and Sober Souls will confider,

Fox his horrible railing. 1. That *Mofes* and the *Prophets,* and *Chrift Jefus* and his *Apoftles* do not univerfally abfolutely and promifcuoufly fling out *Fire-brands,* and fhoot *Arrowes* and *Death* into the Sides and Souls of all that differ from them, as here *G.Fox* doth.

We may obferve in the holy *Scripture,* that gen-erally they were *high handed hypocritical* and *hardned*
Sinners

Sinners againſt whome the holy Spirit thundred
out ſuch *Titles*, threatnings and Judgments : But
Fox in this place makes no Diſtinction, but as boldly as *Blind Bayard* ſaith all that differ from us *&c.*

2. This is no rare buſineſs, but *Fox* and his *Fox-*
ians common *Language* and *Barkings* : Thou *Cain*,
thou *Serpent*, thou *Devil*, (*Devil, Devil, Devil*, as
one of their *She-Apoſtles* have ſaid amongſt us.

3. It is *G.Fox* his bruitiſh and ridiculous Song
in the cloſe of his *Anſwers* (and ſometimes in the
beginning) without any *Truth, Humanity or Mod-*
eſty, to cry out ſaying [*And as for the reſt of thy*
Lyes and Slanders, they are not worth the mentioning] Fox *his*
when he hath pickt out a few *Sentences* or pieces of *bruitiſh*
and ridicu-
Sentences (eaſie for himſelf to carpe at &c.) his con- *lous Song.*
cluſion and Burthen of his bruitiſh ridiculous Song
is [*As for the reſt of thy Lyes and Slanders*] inſtead
of holy Scripture, or ſolid *Arguments* with *Anſ-*
wers to his Oppoſites *Reaſons* and *Replyes* and *Re-*
jonders that an humble ſoul may ſee ſome footing
to reſt on.

4. As we ſay in the death of the *Martyrs* or
Witneſſes of *Jeſus*, it is not the *Suffering*, but the *What*
Caufe & Spirit & Cariage is to be conſidered : So *Railing is*
in bitter Language, it is not lawfull to call every
Prince or *King, Fox*, as Chriſt called *Herod* : nor
every Oppoſite *Viper & Serpent, Fool* and *Blind* and
whited painted Wall and *Sepulchre* &c. They ſeemed
to ſpeak *Reaſon* to Chriſt upon his Croſs [*Thou that*
faveſt others, thou that deſtroyeſt the Temple &c. *come*
down now ſave thy ſelf] &c. and yet Gods Spirit
calls this *Reviling* and *Railing* at him.

9. All

9. All may see what a simple *Craking* Sound of vapouring and [188] boasting runs through all this *Foxes* Book: Doubtless *Sysera* and his *Mideanites*, *Goliah* and his *Philistines*, *Rabshekah* and his *Assirians* were types of of these Children of Pride, whose *Vapours* whose *Prophesies* (so me notoriously false, already proved) whose promised *Victoryes*, *Spoils*, *Threatnings* lye like black foul Blots of ink or grease over all his *Papers* and the *Papers* of most of them, far from that Closet *Content* and *Sincerity* of the true Saints who are content with the eye of God alone in secret.

Instances out of G. F. his Book

10.   For a more full proof of the *Lameness* and *Stark nakedness* of their Writings, I shall select and mention some *Particulars* out of this *Grand Alcoran* of *G. Fox*   1.   His Opposites Words, then his Answer. And, 3.   My Replyes *&c.*

Page 1. He brings in *Sam. Eaton* saying, [*He doth not believe that there is Substantial, Essential or Personal Union between the Eternal Spirit and Believers.*]

Sam. Eaton.

G. Fox Answers [*Though the Scripture saith the Spirit dwells in the Saints,* 1 Cor.6. *And he that is joyned to the Lord is one Spirit,* 1 Joh. 1. *As though the Saints had not Union with God which the Scripture say they have.*]

I Reply: concerning the *Essence* or *Being* of the Immortal, Invisible, Infinite, Eternal, Omnipotent, and Omniscient, and only Wise: we know no more then a Fly knows what a King is, and therefore 1 *Tim.*9.[1] *He dwells in the Light that no man can approach*

proach

1 " 1. Tim. 6."   *R. W. Ms. Ann.*

proach to: how fully doth the Holy Spirit in the Book of *Job*, and eſpecially in that dreadful Word or Voice of God in a *Whirlwind* knock out the brains of all theſe proud Fancies? let this proud *Fox*, or any of the ſtouteſt *Lions or Lioneſſes* amongſt them, look but a few minutes upon the glorious Sun in the Heavens, and then tell us how their eyes do: and yet thus like proud and pratling Children do they make a noiſe about their *Bibs*, and *Aprons*, and *Muckingers*: and how they are one with God his *Being* and *Eſſence*, &c.

Is it not enough for Sun, Moon and Stars, and *Gods being* Men to be enlightned by his Infinity, but they *out of our* muſt be God himſelf, and Light it ſelf, in the high- *reach* eſt ſence, becauſe God is Light, &c.

What impudence would it be in a Wife, becauſe ſhe is one with her Husband in Relation, to ſay, She is the Husband himſelf, and not to keep her juſt diſtinction and diſtance? or in a Subject (be- cauſe the Subjects and the *King* are Relatives, and in a ſence one) [189] therefore to ſay, that they are the *King himſelf*.

Again, we know that the word *Spirit* is taken in *Holy Scripture* for a *Spiritual Nature*. Hence it is ſaid that God is a Spirit, not that God is properly a Spirit, no more then he is Light (though my Oppoſites in our Diſpute affirmed he was) but of *The nature* ſuch a Heavenly and Spiritual Nature: For the *of Spirits* Devils alſo are Spirits, though defiled with ſin and wickedneſs: thus *Joh.* 3. *That which is born of the Spirit is Spirit*, not that Spirits beget Spirits, and

that

that a new Creature is a young holy Spirit or God himſelf, as I told one of the chief of the *Quakers* at *Newport*,

And that 1. *Cor*.6. ſhews us in what reſpect he that is joyned to the Lord is one Spirit : For know you not (ſaith *Paul*) *that your Bodies are the Temples of the Holy Spirit :* and *Epheſ.* 2. For an Habitation of God through the Spirit.

How God and Chriſt is in us.

Thus God dwelt in his Temple of old, as a Man in his Houſe and a King in his Palace : not that a Mans House, or the Kings Palace is of his Subſtance or Eſſence no more then an houſe is of the Suns Eſſence, &c. and no more was Gods Temple of old, nor his Temples his Saints now, after the blockiſh and blaſphemous nonſence of the *Quaker.*

Sam.Eaton

In Page 2. He brings in *Sam Eaton* ſaying [*The Scripture is to be judge of Doctrines and Manners.*]

G. Fox Anſwers [*The Jews had not the infallible Judgement, that had Scripture but ſtood againſt Chriſt the Light, and judged him to be a Devil, that judgement was not infallible, and that Doctrine and Manners of theirs was not right which goes againſt Chriſt the Light.*]

The Scripture the Rule.

I Reply, as the Sun in the Heavens is the Epitomy or Center of all Natural Light, though ſome eyes are ſore, look a ſquint, or are ſtark blinde.

And as the Rule or Canon (though *Fox* ſimply bogles at that as not a Scripture word) is the ſame, for it is in the Greek, though millions know it not, and millions (as the *Phariſes*) pervert and miſapply it.

The Holy Scripture is granted by *G. Fox* to be Gods

Gods Words (though in a ſubtle fancie, not his *The Holy*
Word,) but if it be every word of their Gods, then *Scripture a*
is every Word as *Dovid* ſaith *a Light to our feet, and* *Lanthorn*
a Lanthorn to our Paths, though we deſpiſe it and
wilfully refuſe it (as ſome ſometimes do Lanthorns)
and wilfully ſtumble [190] into the Ditch Eternal,
and other poor Souls after us : Thus the Heavenly
Sun-Dial is one and conſtant in its guidance and
direction to us poor Travellers, though we neglect
to look on it, or be ignorant of the figures and *Try all*
lines of it, and be willingly ignorant, &c. *things*

    We are not only commanded to read and medi-
tate in the Holy Scriptures, and to ſearch them as
the *Bereans* did, but we are commanded to try all
things, to try the very Spirits. The *Papiſts* ſlap us
in the mouth with the infallible Spirit of the *Pope*,
and that he is not to be judged : the *Quakers* ſay the
ſame of themſelves, which is no more then as I
ſaid in the Diſpute (when *W, Edmund.* interrupted
me, crying out *Blaſphemy*) for a Man to go for
Counſel to an arrant Cheater and Jugler (then
cheating moſt when he calls all others Cheaters.)

    In Page 3. He brings in the ſame Author ſaying *Sam Eaton*
[*That God did not intend immediate Teaching, nor to*
give out an immediate voice in after ages, which ſhould
direct and guid men in the way of Salvation.

    He Anſwers, which is contrary to the Scripture,
which ſaith, All the people of the Lord ſhall be
taught of the Lord, and he that is of God heareth
Gods word, and that is immediate and living, and
doth endure for ever, there is no fallibility nor deluſion in the Revelation of God, but all fallibility
and deluſion is out of it.   I Reply,

*Gods medi-
ate teach-
ings, his
word &
voice mani-
fold and
specified.*

I Reply, it is granted that God speaks mediately unto us by the light of Nature within us;
doth not nature teach you that it is a shame for a
man to have long hair, &c.

2. By his works of Creation.

3. His Providence without us in his mercies and
judgements, so that every drop of Rain and crumb
of Bread, and grain of Corn is Gods word and
witness:

And 4. The pains of the Body, and Dreams in
the night have much of Gods word and voice in
them, *Job* 33. God speaks once and twice but man
hears it not and is not Gods speaking his Word?

And 5, All grant that the words of Scripture are
the words of God.

And 6. The teachings of men, *Ephes.*4. are grant-
ed to be means, &c. both for the gathering of the
Church, as *Apostles*, and for the Governing of the
Flocks, as *Pastors and Shepherds*, &c.

191] 7. The Water, the Bread, the Wine, &c. are
appointed by Christ Jesus to be means while profession of Christ Jesus is made on earth to hold
forth a remembrance of him until his second
coming.

8. The private *Prayers* and *Fastings* and *Meditations* of the Saints day and night, are holy *Meanes*
in and by which the Eternal God speaks Peace, In-
struction, Reproof and Comfort to to them that fear
him.

9. Sometimes it pleaseth God by the Ministration
of his *Ministring Spirits* (the invisible Angels) to
work by unknown and unseen wayes to us: thus in
Pauls

Pauls Light and *Voice* and *Blindnefs*, and the *Jail-* *Pauls won-*
ors *Earthquake*, but afterward in *Ananias* his fend- *derful*
mediate
ing to *Paul* (as *Peter* to *Cornelius*) and *Paul* to the *and imme-*
Jailor, it pleafed God to ufe his holy means and *diate con-*
verfion.
inftruments of Men to men (Gods fweet and familiar way to men : the immediate Teachings of
God by *Dreams*, by *Vifion*, by *Voices*, *by* Motion, the
Holy Scripture mentions many before and fince the
coming of the Lord Jefus, the Queftion is not
whether it may not pleafe the moft Holy and in- *Immediate*
teachings
finite *Prerogative* of the moft High, fo to teach
where, and when, and whom he pleafe.

But whether it be Chriftian obedience, or Diabolical lazinefs to fling off all means (as *Fox* all
along teacheth) to fit ftill and liften to immediate
Teachings (that is fay I to the Devils whifperings)
I believe the *Papifts* and *Quakers* would give much
to be rid of the Scriptures : I know alfo, that notwithftanding their pretence of Spirit, yet both of
them are forced to ufe means, Praying, Preaching,
Congregating, and (in ftead of the holy means
by Gods Spirit) have appointed many Inventions
and Superftitions from a Satanical Spirit.

G. Fox faith, there is no Fallacy in the *Revela-*
tion of God?

Anf. True, but will he fay thefe feven things :

1. That all the pretended *Revelations* are the
Revelations of God. *Revelati-*
ons con-
2. That *Revelations* may not pretend *Angelical* *fidered in*
Light, and yet be *Diabolical Darknefs.* *7 particu-*
3. That we may receive any *Revelations* and *lars*
Teachings

Teachings (as Children and Mad Folks do) without chewing, and rational weighing & confideration.

4. That God hath not appointed his old Scripture and Writing [192] new fince Chrifts coming as a *Standard, Rule* or *Touchftone* to try all our own and others Infpirations by?

5. That *Mahomets Infpirations* are not one of the moft prevailing Snares, Traps, and Engines, whereby he hath catcht whole Nations and Kingdomes, and the greateft part of this poor world at this day.

6. That when God reveals his word or will in writing (which *G. Fox* grants to be the words of God, and they are flighted) it is not common and moft righteous with God to deliver up proud lazy Souls to ftrong Delufions to believe Lyes (as at this day it is moft wonderfull)

The great business of Revelations 7. Whether there be any way in this world to efcape the fnares of *Sathans Whifperings* but by humble attending to the fearch and Meditation of the heavenly *Records*, by humble cryes to the Father of *Spirits* for his holy *Spirit* and help in all the *Meanes* by himfelf appointed, in Love and Pitty to the Souls of men.

Sam Eaton A 4th. Inftance of *G, Fox* his lame ftuff is in *Pag.* 4. where he brings in the fame Author *Sam Eaton* faying, [*The Gofpel is the Letter, &c.*] He Anfwers, [*And the Apoftle faith, it is the power of God &c. and the Letter kills, and many may have the Form but deny the Power, and fo ftand againft the Gofpel which is the Power of God.*

I reply, we all know that the word *Gfopel* from the

the old *Saxon* is as ftrange to us *Englifh,* as the word
Evangelium or *Euangelion* (the Latine and Greek)
are: but we all agree that it may be turned (according to its meaning) *Glad Newes.* This wife cunning
man tels us the *Glad Newes* is not the *Glad Newes·*
Why fo? Becaufe it is the *Power* of *God.*who fees not
here the fimple fubtelty of this *Deceiver?* The *Gofpel*
or *Glad Newes* preached is the power of God unto
Salvation to every one that believeth &c. *Rom.* 1.
Therefore this *Glad Newes told, written, printed,
preached,* is not the *Glad Newes*: would he now
perfwade himfelf and us that *Mofes* and the *Prophets* that wrote of this *Glad Newes,* and thofe four
heavenly *Pen-men* (or *Pens*) which by the finger of
God, (his immediate *Spirit*) wrote the Hiftory of
the *Life* and *Death* of the Lord Jefus, &c. wrote
nothing of the Gofpel or glad news, for the glad
news is the power of God.

2. I know the trick of thefe old Cheaters and
Juglers to hide [193] themfelves, and their cheating in the *Bufhes* and *Thickets* of *words* of diverfe *Significations,* or figurative Speeches, which all
honeft Reason teacheth carefully to diftinguifh. I
know it is *Fox* his trick, and all their tricks in his
and their Writing, to make *God* and *Chrift* and
Spirit & Gofpel & Covenant & Juftification, (as before I proved) to be all that one cheating Fancy
called *Light* in them and in every one that cometh
into the World. Thefe bewitched fouls will not
owne a *figurative fpeech* when it makes not for their
Idols. 3.Is it not that the Lord calls the preaching
of the *Glad Newes* the *Power of God,* becaufe of
the

the wonderfull effect of it to him that believeth this *Glad Newes,* which few or none believe, as being a foolifh thing to believe (as the *Jews* and thoufands others fay, to believe in a beggars brat, laid in a *Manger* and a *Gallowes-Bird* &c. 4. *Paul* calls this *Glad news,* his *Gofpel* or *Glad news,* Rom. 2. Will the *Foxians* therefore fay that either *Paul* lyed, or elfe it is not Gods Gofpel nor Chrifts, but *Pauls* although it is moft true that as *Paul* had charge of it (as a *Shepheard* of another mans *Flock,* or a *Mariner* of an other mans *Ship*) it may [1]be common Phrafe of Speech (though not *literal* but *figurative*) be called *Pauls* (or any other Meffengers of *Chrift*) *Glad news* or *Gofpel.* 5. There is a wild beaft called a *Fox,* a fubtle and pernicious creature : there was a famous heavenly Man, a famous writer of the Book of *Martyrs, John Fox,* and there is this poor deluded & deluding Soul *G.Fox,* to whome I am now replying, ought not thefe to be *diftinguifhed?* Is there not fuch a mifchievous fubtle Beaft called the *Fox* becaufe *G.Fox* bears (and that moft juftly and by a finger of Gods *providence* bears it) the *wild Beafts* name : or was not fuch a *learned & heavenly & wonderfully deligent & zealous* man as *J. Fox,* becaufe *G.Fox* bears that name alfo *?* 6. But further, If the Glad news may not be called the *Glad news* when tis *Scripture* (that is *written*) or *preached,* then not *Glad news* when *fpoken.* 7. The Law denounceth Sentence of Death againft a Traitor &c. this Sentence is written, & in a Sence may be called a *Killing Letter:* the King pardons this

Traitor,

How it is called Pauls Gofpel.

Three Foxes.

The Scripture the word or glad news from Heaven written.

[1] "by" *R. W. Ms. Ann.*

Traitor, and this Sentence of *Pardon* is written :
this gracious word of a King is not leſs his *Word*
becauſe it is *Written* then it was when firſt ſpoken
by him; and this word or pleaſure of the King
written may be called Goſpel or *Glad news,* the
Glad news or *Goſpel* of his Temporal *Salvation* :
will any ſober man ſay as *G. Fox* impiouſly and
frantickly, that the writing of the Pardon and
the *Broad-Seal* is a *Dead letter* & a *Killing letter &c.*
becauſe Paper Parchment *&c.* If *G. Fox* from hunting after Souls by Sea and Land, arrive at ⌈194⌉ any
Port in *England* and ſend a Letter Poſt to his *Wife
& Friends,* containing his many *Deliverances,* many
Experiences, his ſafe *Arrivail* and his Purpoſe and *Counter-*
Hope ſhortly to ſee them : ſhall now this *Glad news* *feits de-*
(or *Goſpel*) though but a few raggs made (*Paper*) *ſtroy not*
be ſtiled a *Dead letter* yea a *Killing letter* though it *true heirs*
contain nothing (as the Chriſtian *Goſpel* or *Glad* *and owners*
news doth not) but *glad news* or *Tidings.* 8. Hence *for ever.*
it is that we read ſo often of *Preaching the Goſpel,*
of *Believing the Goſpel,* and that as before *Paul* calls
it his *Glad news,* or *Goſpel* becauſe it was his work
to tell it.

Yea but ſaith this Deceiver throughout his Book
*A man may have the Letter and Form, without the
Power and Life. &c.* I Anſwer Who knows not
that ? and that a *Form & picture* is not the man
himſelf ? who knows not that *Judas* notwithſtanding his pretended Love and *Kiſſing of Chriſt Jeſus*
that yet he had not the *Life & power* of true *Love*
and *heavenly affection* : but doth it follow that living and moving Bodyes have not Souls & Spirits
within

within them, becaufe that *pictures* have not ? That
none preach *Chrift Jefus* truly becaufe that *G. Fox*
preacheth an immaginary and *Allegorical Chrift*,
in order to eftablifh himfelf the only true Chrift,
and the *Eternal Son of God* as many bewitched
Souls call him.   9. What is this but to cheat poor
Birds with the *Chaff* & *Falacy* of dividing the
Body from the Soul, the *Letter* from the *Meaning*,
the *Inftrument* or *Tool* from the *Workman* or *Huf-*
A word to *bandman* ufing it, the *Gofpel* or *glad news* from *Be-*
all Fox- *lieving* of it.   Ah poor cheated Souls (called *Qua-*
ians. *kers* all of you) why do you willingly (out of pretended *Enlightnings* & *Experiences*) fhut your eye of
common *Senfe* and *Reafon*, not daring to call *good*
news, good news, becaufe fome, or the moft will not
Believe it ? was it not fo with the women preaching
or telling the *good news* or *gofpel*, although few or
none were found to believe that *Chrift* was rifen ?
10.   The truth is (fearch your cheating *Familiars*
narrowly &) you will find that *your felves* and the
Papifts would make an *Holy Day* of that Day, in
which all the *Bibles* in the world were burnt, that
you may eftablifh your infallible *fpirits* & *Tra-*
ditions.

I know I wronge you not, I have too much
proof of it, which you would fe if the heart were
Gods won- not the arranteft *Cheater* in the World, and your
derful pre- felves not willing to be cheated.   Tis true *Anti-*
fervation *ochus* attempted the burning of *Mofes* and the *Pro-*
of his *phets* out of the world : fome of the bloudy *Empe-*
word or *rours* followed on in *Antiochus* his bloudy Steps
wil to poor raging againft the Scriptures alfo, the *Romane Popes*
mankind

iii

in theirs, and common reaſon may tell all men, and
the *Quakers* themſelves, [195] that if the ſame
power come into their hands as *Antiochus* & the
Romane Emperours had the holy Scriptures ſhall not
if they can effect it trouble them or others one day
in the world longer. *But of this more in the next
and laſt Poſition.*

A *5th* Inſtance is *pag* 10 where *G. Fox* brings in
John Bunian ſaying, *It is not Faith and works that* John
juſtifie in the ſight of God, but it is Faith and good Bunian.
works which juſtifie in the ſight of men only. &c.
He anſwers, *Abraham* was not juſtified to men only
by his *Obedience,* but to *God,* and where is *Faith*
there is *Juſtification,* which works by *Love :* and The great
the Saints *Faith &* works were not only to *juſtifie* Poſition of
them in the *ſight of men ?* for the *Work of God* is to tion.
doe what he ſaith & his Will which who doth not
are not juſtified in ſo doing, but to be beaten with
Stripes *:* who ſeek to be *juſtified* by their Faith and
Works in the ſight of men, are Dead *Faith &
Works* both.

I Reply, In this great buſineſs of *juſtification &
Pardon* of Sin (which *Luther* called the great Wall
of Seperation between us and the *Papiſts*) I humbly
hope to ſhew how lame this Fox is, and that he
& his *Foxians* agree with the *Papiſts, Arminians,
Socinians* againſt the true *Proteſtants* in this funda-
mental buſineſs. For what is *Juſtification* but a
Pardon written and ſealed and declared from the
King of Heaven to poor condemned *Traitors.* Juſtifica-
That this *Pardon* may be merited by any *Price* that it is
we or all the World can offer, is denied by true
Proteſtants,

Proteſtants, but affirmed (in effeƈt) by the proud
unbroken Souls of *Papiſts, Arminians, Socinians*, and
theſe *Foxians* called *Quakers*. It is true after a condemned Soul hath received a *Pardon* or *Juſtification*
from his King freely without Deſert (upon the
Princes *Mediation*) he declares his loyal and thankfull Obedience &c. but is this his *Pardon & Juſtification* as our ſubtle *Simpletons* imagine ?

Again that *Abraham* was *pardoned* (or *juſtified*, it
is all one) for his Work ſake as this blind Soul
ſaith, how doth *Rom.* 3,4. and the *Epiſtle* to the *Ga-
lathians* cry out, and the experience of every true
broken Heart cry out *Lyar* againſt ſuch proud and
Popiſh Blaſphemies. Further, If all the *Righteouſneſs*
of the beſt of men, that is their good *Thoughts*, good
Words, good *Aƈtions Aims: Prayers, Preachings,
Sufferings*, be but as *Womens Menſtruous & filthy
Clouts*, (as the *Moſt High* calls them) what *Popiſh*
and frantick *Madneſs* is it in *Fox* to talk of *Juſtification before God by works or by Obedience ?*

A *6th*. Inſtance is Pag 16. where he brings in
Henoch Howet ſaying, *It is an Expreſſion of a dark deluded Mind to ſay that God is not diſtinguiſhed from
the Saints.* G.*Fox* Anſw. But God and Chriſt is in
196] the Saints, and walks in them, and he is is a
Reprobate and out of the *Apoſtles Doƈtrine*. I reply to this *Canting Gypſie*, in Pag. 74. He denyes
the Poſition of *Ralph Farmer*, viz. *That God the
Creator is eternally diſtinƈt from all Creatures, and
that Chriſt being God only in one Perſon, remains a
diſtinƈt perſon from all Men and Angels.* Alſo in the
ſame Page, *that God is diſtinƈt in his Being and Bleſſedneſs*

The proud Quakers affirm no diſtinƈtion between God & themſelves

sedness from all Creatures. I Anſwer, is it not Sufficient that poor *Duſt* and *Aſhes,* poor *Chaff and
Stubble* may be admitted to a Parly with the *Heavenly Majeſty,* and receive *Smiles* of his *Countenance,*
in the Face of the only begotten *Prince & Mediator?* to be cloathed with the *Virgins diverſe Colours,* and heavenly *Affections,* but with the Devil
and our firſt Parents, we muſt aſpire to the throne
of the *Incomprehenſible Majeſty* and *Godhead* also?
Beſides, Let mans *Common Sence* be *Umpire,* is there
no *Diſtinction* between *Infinite* and *Finite?* between
the *Infinite Ocean* of *Majeſty power, goodneſs, Wiſdome* &c., and the poor *Droſs*[1] of which Men &
Angels are Partakers? The King dwells in *White-
Hall* and in other of his *Royal Palaces;* is therefore
no Diſtinction between the King and his Houſes,
though ſome may be braver then others : And yet
Fox ſaith his *Oppoſite* is a *Reprobate.* I ask why?
The only Reaſon *Fox* gives is, becauſe he licks not
up the filthy and helliſh *poyſon* of *Foxes childiſh* and
helliſh *Blaſphemy againſt the Eternal Godhead.*

A *7th.* Inſtance is Pag. 22. where he brings in
Joſeph Kellet ſaying, [*They be all alienated from God,
and Enemies until Faith*] G. *Fox* Anſwers, [*So they
have denied their School-Maſter, which is until faith
which will keep them out of the Alienation which is the
Law.* *Joſeph Kellet*

I Reply with *Joſeph Kellet,* (and the reſt of thoſe
excellent men whom *Fox* uſeth as *Diſhclouts* that *Our natu-*
by nature our *Alienation* from God is ſo great, that *ral Aliena-*
the fineſt and ſweeteſt nature in the World is ſo *tion from*
God
alienated

---

[1] "Drops." *R. W. Ms. Ann.*

alienated and *oppofite unto God*, that it refolves like
fome Ships(againft a *Turk or other Enemy*) we refolve to kill or be killd, yea and to fink by his fide
before we will yield to be taken by him : therefore doth the Holy Spirit fo often fpeak of mans
hating of God and Gods hating of him, yea of
mans abhorring of God, and Gods abhorring of
him, and *Rom.*8. that not only mans wifdome is at
enmity but enmity it felf againft God. Hence it
is, few *Kings*, few *Counfellours*, few *Nobles*, few
Schollars, few *Merchants*, &c. (who ufe to be the

*Few ex-
cellent men
faved* wifeft of men) relifh the Doctrine of the *Manger*
and the *Gallowes* for the more natural Wifdome the
more averfation from the foolifhnefs of the glad
news to poor, loft, drown'd and damn'd Mankind.

197] 2. Again, I fay as *Solomon, the legs of the
lame are not equal,* &c. for how doth it follow that
we deny the Law to be a School-mafter, pointing
unto Chrift, becaufe we deny the Law can bring us
to Chrift, which is fo indeed in the *Englifh, Gal.* 3.
but is not fo in the *Greek*, yea, how could the Law
of Ceremonies, pointing out the *Lamb of God*, or
the Law of *Do this and live*, keep out of the *Alienation*, do they (more then the Law of Creation)
leave any converting Impreffion from the Soul, until Gods hand open a door of Believing?

The *Dyal* points to the Sun, &c. but who receives benefit by it but he that skills it, and looks
upon it, &c. and yet the Dyal is not the Sun, &c.
but points as all the *Proyhecies, Ceremonies, Commandments*, (before his coming unto that God Man,
the Sun of Righteoufnefs) Chrift Jefus. As to
the

the reft of his Anfwer, *viz.* [*Which will keep them out of the Alienation which is the Law*] it is a piece of bruitifh *Nonfence* (as are not a few more in his Book) and it may be taken (like the Anfwer of the Devil at *Delphos*) many wayes : for it may be taken, that Faith will keep them out *Alienation :* or, the *School-Mafter* will keep them out of the *Alienation* : or whether the *Alienation* is the Law, or Faith is the Law, is doubtful, and if his mean- *Our alien-* ing fhould be that thy[1] Law either of Ceremonies, *ation from* &c. fhould keep them from being Alienated from *God* God; and fo being acttually to God, how not only will all the Holy Scriptures but all Mankinde, *Jews* and *Gentiles* call him a fimple ane deftroying Lyar?

An eighth Inftance of *Foxes* poor, lame Anfwer is in *Page* 27. where he brings in *Richard Baxter*, *Richard Baxter* faying [*To fay that any is perfect and without fin is the Devil fpeaking in man* :] G. *Fox* Anfwers, con- trary to the language of the Apoftles and Chrift, who bid them be perfect, and the Apoftle fpake Wifdome, among them that be perfect : and faid they were made free from fin, and it is the Devil fpeaking in man that fpeaks for fin while Men are upon the Earth, for the Devil holds him up that makes men not perfect which Truth makes men free again from the Devil, & fpeaks in Man, and fays be perfect.

I Reply, (*whether this willingly ignorant Soul knows* *The mat-* *or no*) *I know that the Devil knows that there is a* *ters of per-* *Fallacie in this word Perfection.* 1. Sometime in *fection* Scripture, it fignifies no more then *Sincerity & Up-*
rightnefs,

[1] " Ye." *R. W. Ms. Ann.*

rightnefs, (and fo is tranflated) fometimes *Compleat-ness & Fulnefs* in its kinde, though but in a fmall Veffel ; fometimes *Fortified, Strong & Armed* ; and fometimes the *Fulnefs of the Godhead,* to whofe incomprehenfible *Ocean* not one Drop can be given, nor one Drop taken from him. In *Mat.* 5. *Be ye Perfect,* &c We are not exhorted [198] to be equal with God in Holinefs, for that is to be God our felves, and being fet down in the throne of the Godhead, to thruft the Eternal God out, for there can be but one in the Throne of the Godhead : But we are commanded to labour to be like unto God who not only is kinde to his Friends but his Enemies alfo : As when we are bid to be like the *Sun* to fhine upon the Bad as well as the Good : will a fober Soul imagine that we are bid to be as *Pure,* as *Glorious,* as *Vaft,* as *Swift* as the Sun is : but the Spirit tells us of a Generation *that are pure in their own eyes, and yet are not cleanfed from their filthinefs.*

Phil. 3. about perfection

Yea, but faith *Fox, Paul* fpake Wifdome amongft them that were perfect, *Phil* 3. I anfwer, what if the *Tranflators* had turned that word among them that be ftrong intelligent, capacious as the word often, and there fignifies, why doth *Paul* alfo fpeaking of fuch a ftrength or capacity as the Saints may attain to in this life profefs that he was yet (as it were but clambring up the Hill) this is the vote of all the higheft Saints in Scripture lamenting their Brethren and[1] Inabilities, and the Battle between the old Man and the new : Of which Battle *G. Fox* and his *Foxians* know not : for Sathan having Poffeffion

[1] Erafe "Brethren and." *R. W. Ms. Ann.*

seffion all is in peace. It hath been ever known that all Gods Children are like high and glorious *Queens & Empreffes* who wittingly endure, not as the Holy Scripture fpeaks) that fuch an ugly Fiend as the Devil fhould touch them, no not in an evil thought. 3. They are like *Fields & Gardens* in which the Husbandman and Gardiner allows not, nor endures not a Weed but with grief and endeavour of their extirpation. 4. And this is far from being Proctors and Advocates for fin (as *G. Fox* moft fimply and impudently urgeth) for the known truth is, that *Fox* and his *Foxians* fall moft foolifhly and fiercely upon fuch as profefs moft holinefs, moft fincerity, and moft Mortification, moft love to God, and his only begotten the Spirit of Holinefs, & the Holy Scriptures or written Will of God.

The eftate of Gods Children upon Earth

A ninth Inftance is in page 28. where G. Fox. tells how the fame Author preached an external word |*Which the Scripture fpeaks not of, but of the word that lives, abides and endures for ever, and of the Scriptures of Truth that cannot be broken: and of Gods words and Chrifts words, and that is not external: this is not agreeable to found words that cannot be condemned: but that is like his Doctrine that knows not the Eternal: but the Minifters of Chrift did not tell of an external word, but you being made by the will of man fpeaks to the People of an external word.*]

Richard Baxter

I Reply, The word (whether external, internal, or eternal) is a [199] fimilitude, for we know God hath no Mouth, nor Tongue, nor Words as we have: but as Kings, and Generals of Armies or Navies, or any Commanders in chief fignifie their minds

minds by Speech, by Writing, yea by fign (at a dif-
tance) this Word or will, which was before in the
Kings breaft, and internal is now outward or external. Hence Chrift Jefus above all other wayes
of Gods manifefting himfelf externally or outwardly is called the Word of God, and the Word
which was God. Hence in common fpeech we
call our Thoughts our felves [*So I think, &c. this is
my Word, my Vote, or Mind.*]

The great
confequence
of a word
And as it is the Field : If a General himfelf who
firft gave the external Word from his own internal
Thoughts : if he forget the word in the night a
common Sentinel will make him ftand, or fire upon him : and fhall men be fo careful in thefe tran-
fitory bufineffes, and fhall we fuffer open Enemies
to the true Lord Jefus prefumptuoufly to pafs without the external word or mind of God, and auda-
cioufly to deny fuch a word at all to be ? When
Chrift Jefus *Luke* 4 fpake out of the *Prophet Ifaiah* :
and when *Paul* difputed three Sabbath dayes out of
the Scriptures, and when *Apollos* mightily convinced
the *Jews* from the Scriptures that Jefus was the
Chrift, did they not ufe external, audible Expound-
ings and Applyings of that written word or mind
of God as the external and outward manifeftation
of his internal and eternal holy Pleafure.

Ellis
Bradfhaw
A tenth Inftance is in page 32. where *G. Fox*
brings in *Ellis Bradfhaw* faying [*The Quakers Spirit*
doth teach them to honour no Man.] He Anfwers,
[*That is a Lye : for it teacheth them to have all Men in*
efteem, and to honour all men in the Lord ; yet they
are convinced by the Law to be Tranfgreffors if they
refpect Mens perfons as you doe]   I Reply,

I Reply, I have fpoken of their proud and lofty behaviour toward all men, the *Higheft*, the *Eldeft*, the *Holyeft*, upon the 10*th. Pofition*, of their Pride &c. and therefore briefly fay, 1. That all men may fee how truely they honour and efteem all men in the Lord, and what Lord and honour it is that they mean: when G.F. his firft word to his Oppofite is in that moft provoking Term, *viz.* [*That is a Lye*] in his very pleading and the very firft words of it. It is true Chrift Jefus and his Servants the Prophets and Apoftles ufed fharp and bitter *Reproofs, Similitudes* &c. but thus fuddenly at the firft dash to give fire *Thou Lyeft, That is a Lye* &c. It fhews neither *Religion* nor *Civility* but a *Barbarous Spirit*, for they that know the *Barbarians* know how common that word is in all their mouths. Tis true of late divers of *Fox* his followers have followed him in courtefie [200] looking toward you, taking you by the hand, bowing and half uncovering the head more or lefs *&c.* But this is but a *Revolt* and *Apoftacy* from their firft *Rigid Spirit* and *Cariage* as *Humphrey Norton* rightly maintains againft them. Yea. 2. it is againft all *Foxes* and their firft Writings, and this very place of *James* here urged, *viz.* they are convinced by the Law if they refpect mens Perfons.

The honor which the Quakers give to others

Again, tis true in Chrift Jefus there is neither Bond nor Free, Male nor Female, and confequently no Mafter no Man, no Father no Child no King no Subject, but all are one in Chrift Jefus, and the fecond Birth: as all are of one kinde in the *firft Adam*, and the *firft Birth*.

1. Yet

*Civil
refpeft*

1. Yet firft how full is the Holy Scripture of
Commands and Examples of Gods Children, giving refpective Words and Titles, aud Bowings, even
to perfons that knew not God ?   2. *Fox* grants difference of gifts, and faith that fome (in comparifon of others of them not fo grown, &c. are Elders,
& fure this is fome refpect of perfons, according to
that of the 1 *Cor.* 12. Are all *Apoftles*, are all *Prophets*, are all *Teachers*, &c.   Therefore how ever
they Hypocritically lye, and pretend to honour all
men in the Lord : yet the moft Holy and only
Wife knows how proudly, and fimply, and barba-
roufly they have run into uncivil and inhumane
Behaviours towards all their Superiours, the eldeft
and higheft, how that they have declared by principle and practice, that there are no Men to be
refpected in the World but themfelves as being
Gods and Chrifts.   Tis true our *Englifh Bibles* and
Grammar (as *Fox* his great Learning often objects)
makes thou to a fingle perfon, and Thou in Holy
Scripture is ufed in a grave and refpective way unto
Superiours, unto Kings, and Parents, and God him-
felf: But 1. (As I have faid) the *Hebrew* and the
Greek fignifie no more Thou then You, and fo may

*Thou &
Thee*

be truely turned.   2.   Every Nation, every *Shire*,
every *Calling* have their particular *Properties* or
Idioms of Speech, which are improper and ridiculous with others : Hence thefe fimple Reformeis
are extreamly ridiculous in giving Thou and Thee
to every body, which our Nation commonly gives
to *Familiars* only ; and they are extreamly and in-
fufferably proud and contemptuous unto all their *Superiours*

periours in ufing Thou to every body which our
Englifh Ideom or propriety of fpeech ufeth in way
of familiarity or of Anger, Scorn and Contempt. *Incivilities*
I have therefore publickly declared my felf, that a *ought to be moderately*
due and moderate reftraint and punifhing of thefe *punifht*
incivilities (though pretending Confcience) is as far
from Perfecution (properly fo called) as that it is a
Duty and Command of God unto all mankinde,
firft in Families, and thence into all mankinde
Societies.

201] Having thus through Gods mercifull help
gone through the 13*th Pofition* in publick and this
private fupply of fome few Inftances of their *Lame
writings* of out *G.F*, referving the liberty (if God
pleafe) of prefenting the *Reader* with a further
Apendix or *Addition* of fome few further *Inftances*
out of *G. Fox* his *Writings*. I haften to the 14
Propofition, the laft of the feven at *Providence*,
They read it publickly, viz. *the fpirit of the Quakers tends mainly to the reducing of Perfons from* Civility *to* Barbarifme, *to an* Arbitrary Goverment, *and* *The* 14.
the Dictates *and* Decrees *of that* fudden Spirit *that* *Pofition debated.*
acts them. 3. *To a fudden cutting off of People yea
of Kings and Princes that oppofe them.* and 4. *To as
fierce and fiery* Perfecution *in matters of Confcience as
hath been, or can be practifed by any* Hunters *or* Perfecutors *in the World.*

I told them I could adde more Branches to this
Head, as unto the peace and civil Societyes of Mankind in the world : but I remembred my promife
of *Brevity*, and *W. E.* was often remembring me
fayinge *Is this thy Quarter of an hour ?* for I believe
they

they ſtood here upon *Coals* and were not willing
that I ſhould inſiſt upon it my full *Quarter*; and
they haſted me on to prove that their *ſpirit* tended

W E. &c
ſtanding
upon coals.
to *Barbariſme* : they ſaid (one and an other) that
their *ſpirit* was an *Holy Spirit*, the *Spirit* of God,
and the Grace of God had appeared to all men and
had taught them to deny all *ungodlineſs* and wordly
luſts, and to live *ſoberly, righteouſly & godly* in this
preſent world.

I told them that in our *Native Countrey*, and in
all *civilized Countreys*, the civility, Courteous Speech
Courteous Salutation, and reſpective Behaviour was
generally practiſed, oppoſite to the cariage of *Bar-*

Civility
and
Courteſie.
barous & Unciviliz'd People. This I ſaid was according to the command of the holy Spirit in *Paul Eph*
4. and in *Peter*, 1. *Pet* 3. Be pitifull, be Courteous,
&c. Such a Spirit was Chriſt Jeſus of, even to his
greateſt *Oppoſites*, and to the greateſt *Sinners*, inſo-
much that for his *Courteſie & Gentleneſs & Sociable-
neſs* with open *Sinners*, the dogged proud and ſullen
Phariſes counted him a *Drunkard* and *Glutton*, a
friend and *Companion* of *Publicans* and ſinners. We
Engliſh were our ſelves at firſt wild and ſavage *Bri-
tains* : Gods mercy had civilized us, and we were
now come into a wild and ſavage Countrey, without *Manners*, without *Courteſie*, ſo that generally
except you begin with a *What Chear* or ſome other

N.Eng.
one work to
civilize a
Barbarous
People.
Salutation, you had as good meet an *Horſe* or a *Cow*,
&c. And hath not the *Quaker ſpirit* been ſuch a
Spirit amongſt us? have we not known perſons
formerly loving, courteous &c. and as ſoon as this
Spirit hath come upon them have not our eyes ſeen
them

them paſs by their *Familiars,* their *Kindred,* [202 their *Elders* and *Superiours,* and though kindly ſpoken to, not give a *Word* or a *Look* toward them? as if they were not worthy of a *word* or a *look* from *The Quakers monſtrous Incivility.* ſuch *High Saints* &c. How like indeed have they been to the Popiſh Saints in a *Proceſſion,* they *See not, Hear not, Speak not* &c.? or like theſe very *Barbarians,* and therefore I ſaid, 2. *G.Fox* in his book affirms that the *Converſation* of theſe very *Barbarians,* in many things were better then his *Oppoſites* &c. I muſed in my ſelf (being much acquainted with the *Natives*) what *G. Fox* ſhould mean, he not having been in *N.England* when he wrote that paſſage; but ſince I have heard that the *Quakers* have commended the ſpirit of the *Indians,* for they have ſeen them come into *Engliſh Houſes* and ſit down by the fire, not ſpeaking a word to any body: But *The Indians and Quakers of one Spirit.* this cariage of the *Indians* proceeds from a *bruitiſh ſpirit,* for generally they have boldly come in without *Knocking* or asking of leave, and ſit down without any reſpect in word or geſture to the Governour or chief of the Family whoſoever (juſt the *Quakers* general faſhion and Spirit)

Further I told them, that in ſome reſpect the ſpirit and cariage of the *Quakers* was worſe then that of the *Indians,* for if they were ſaluted by the *Engliſh* in the *high-way* or coming into an *Houſe,* they are very ready to receive your *Salutation* kindly, and return you another: But commonly we know that it is not ſo with the *Quakers bruitiſh ſpirit.* 2. The *Indians* morning and evening, and upon all meetings, they give a reſpective and

proper

proper *Salutation* to their own *Superiours*, and sometimes in gesture as well as speech.   3. Although
the *Indians* are *bruits* in their *Nakedness* both men
and women, yet they never appear (no not in private houses) *stark naked* as the *Quaker men* and
women doe: yea they so abhor such a *bruitishness*,
(except it be in their mad *Drunkenness*, for then
they will be *stark naked*) that as to their *Female
kind*, they will carefully from their birth keep on
some modest covering before them.   *W.E.* rose up
and said they did abhor *Uncleaness* as well as our
selves or any, their women were sober, holy and
Modest, and would not endure (some of them) to
have a Toe to be seen naked :   but he said if the
Lord God did stir up any of his *Daughters* to be a Sign

*The Qua-
kers again
maintain
their
womens
Nakedness.* of the *nakedness* of others he believed it to be a
great Cross to a Modest womans Spirit, but the
Lord must be obeyed.   *John Stubs* immediately
seconded him, and quoted again the Command to
Isaiah, Chap. 20. to go naked, & he added, whereas
I said at *Newport* that it was in the time of *Signs,
Types, Figures &c.* He would now prove that all
Signs were not abolished by the coming of Christ;
for *Agabus Act.* 20. took *Pauls* [203] *girdle* and
bound himself.   I replyed that was indeed one of
my Replyes at *Newport*, and I was yet far from
binding the *sweet Influences* of the holy One by
*Dreams, Visions, immediate Impulses Revelations,
Signs* &c. but withall I said that before the coming
of the *Lord Jesus* and at his coming was the time

*Signs and
Figures
discussed.* and season of such *Appearances* from God : now he
hath fully declared his mind to us by the *Personal*

and

and most wonderfull coming of his *Son* out of his
Bosome : who had commanded his Pen-men to
write his *Birth,* his *Life,* his *Life* his *Doctrine* his
Miracles, his *Death, Resurrection, Ascension* and
promise of *Return* to us : he had also preserved
these holy *Writings* & *Records* most wonderfully
that (*Joh* 20) we might believe in him, follow him
and live with him. But   2. I said what did this
concern the *monstrous* stripping their *women naked,*
of which we never heard a tittle either at coming
of the Lord Jesus, or in those proper seasons of
such *Administrations* before his *Appearance.* *John* The Qua-
Stubs said he had been a *Quaker* 19 years and yet *kers spirit
had never seen a woman *Naked,* and some of the *enraged.*
Quakers said to me aloud, *when didst thou see any of
our women Naked?* and another of them said, *We
did not think that thou wouldest have been such a wicked
man.*   These two (though of the *Quakers spirit*) yet
of long time had been Loving and respective to
me, but now they were enraged, so that I said unto
my *Antagonists,* seeing some *Heat* is risen about
these matters, I will if you please go on to the second *Branch* of this 14*th Position.*   I told them the *The Qua-
2d. Branch* was,   *kers spirit
                                                              tending to
That the Spirit of the Quakers tendeth to bring in *Arbetrary*
an Arbetrary Government. I said we all knew how *Govern-
it had cost the blood of *thousands* & *ten Thousands* *ment.*
this matter of *Goverment* & *Lawes* : that the Most
High & only Wise choosing one *People* and *Nation
of Israel* to be his own, he wrote them Laws (some
with his own inconceivable *finger* written) and some
by *Moses* his inspired *Pen-man,* it pleased him not
                                                              to

to leave their *Wifeſt* and *Holyeſt Kings & Gover-*
nours without written known Lawes, with *Rewards*
and *Penaltyes* annexed. But I argued if that were
true that all the *Quakers* were guided in all they
ſaid and did by the immediate Spirit of God (as I
proved *Fox* maintained) then if they obtain higher
or lower Governours of their Spirits, Surely it
ſhines cleer that there is no need of Laws for them
to rule & act by, for they had no need of Scripture, and ſeing the *Immediate Inſpirations* of God
would not ſuffer them to erre in Judgment, for as
they ſaid of the holy Scripture, they had no need
of it, for they had the holy Scripture within them,
their Teacher within them, and all that they ſpake
was Scripture, and the voice of God, *&c.* So I ſaid
much more [204] might it be ſaid of Mens *Laws &*
Writings; that ſurely they had no need of them : for
what could be more juſt and equal, more pure &
holy in all Caſes Controverſies & Buſineſſes, then
the immediate *Voice of God?* *W. E.* ſaid, what doſt
thou fill peoples ears with ſtrange *Notions*, as if the
People of God called *Quakers* were a lawleſs people
and would bring all Goverment and all Laws to
nothing ? We are for righteous *Goverment*, and
righteous *Lawes*, we are not for any to rule by
Force, and more he ſpake to this purprſe.

I Replyed, that he miſtook me, by an *Arbetrary*
Goverment I did not intend a Goverment ruling by
Force (for there could be no Goverment in the
world without the *Sword*) but *Arbitrary* I ſaid came
from *Arbitrium* which ſignified *Will* or pleaſure :
and ſo my *Argument* was, that Perſons immediately
ſpeaking

The Qua-
kers have
no need of
Scripture
much leſs
of the
written
Laws of
men

The Qua-
kers &
none elſe
in the
World fit
forGovnrn-
ment as
they judge

speaking from God, it was impertinent and profane
to clog and cumber them with *Lawes*, for the
Voice of God (the *Law* of all *Laws*) proceeded
out of their mouth, then which there could be
none more Juft, more Wife, more Holy.

Here ftood up an *Aged man* (and as able as moft
in the company, *T. A.*) though much of late adhering to the *Quakers* and faid, Methinks there is
Weight in Mr. *VVilliams* his *Argument*. He being
a noted man, and his voice very audible (and fo
heard by all) *VV. E.* was forced to take notice of
his fpeech, and faid, wherein is there any weight in
it ? *T. A.* Anfwered, why if a *Magiftrate* be *im-*
mediately infpired by God, and fpeaks *Gods Laws &* T A his
Sentence, fure there feems to be no need of any other Teftimony
Laws. They faw they were in a *Pound*, and I perceived it, and yet (not being willing to *grate* upon
them but) watching my time (as I was glad all
along) to pafs handfomly from one *Point* unto
another, I faid unto them : if they pleafed I would
pafs on to the *Third Branch, viz.* *That the Qua-* The 3d.
kers Spirit tending to the fudden cutting off of People, Branch
yea, Kings and Princes that oppofe them. I here told
them that I muft crave their patience whiles I muft
profefs my fears, leaft that Spirit by which they
were guided, might run them upon their own and
others temporal Deftruction. I told them I thought
they had no fuch thing in their Thoughts or Eye
at prefent : but if power of the Sword come into
their hand, it was eafie to imagine that whom
their Spirit (infallible) decreed to death, *Peafant*
or *Prince*, if it were poffible, he muft be executed,
&c.

&c. *W. Edm.* said, *Thou here makeſt a falſe and ly-ing charge againſt the People of God, who are peacea-ble and quiet and yielding to Magiſtrates,* &c. I Replied, I charge them with no matter of Facts: but I charge them and their Spirit with a tendency, &c. For why [205] might they not ſay, that *Abra-ham,* with an impulſe was killing *Iſaak, Moſes* the *Egyptian, Ehud* killing *Eglon* the King of *Moab, Samuel* hewing *Agag* the King of *Amelech* in pieces, and *Paul, Ananias* and *Saphira,* &c. and why not Sathan ſtir up. his Inſtruments to pretend the like Spirit, as we know he hath done both in former & latter days?

My Antagoniſts joyntly bid me ſhew when any *Immediate* of the *Quakers* had done ſo: I *Anſw.* They ſpake *impulſes* not to the point, &c. for I did not charge them to have done ſo, but that their Spirit tended to it: I was ſaying that *Faubord* at *Grindleton* was killing his Son in imitation of *Abraham,* if his Sons cry-ing out, and the breaking open of the Houſe had not prevented: and that *James Parnel* moved by this Spirit to Faſt forty dayes, &c. periſhed the eleventh day, &c. but perceiving more than ordi-nary heats, and that *W. Edm.* charged me that I had a falſe heart of mine own, and would meaſure others by my buſhel: I told them of the wonder-ful actings of *Tho. Munſter,* and *J. Becold,* and *Fifer & Knipperdoling,* &c. in *Germany,* and of their Pre-tences, Murthers, Poligamies, and all by the Spirit, *The Kings* &c. I told them that our *Royal Sovereign* his *Grandfa-* *Grandfather Henry* 4*th* of *France* (that famous and *ther* H. 4. *of* France wonderful Man) he was ſtab'd to death by a Frier pretending

pretending a Vision of Angels on Christmas night, *murthered upon pretence of a vision of Angels*
who commanded him from God to dispatch and
kill the King, which he most desperately effected.
W. Edm. interrupted me, and spake (to this effect)
why should we suffer this man thus to wrong the
innocent people of God? we will measure him
with his own Bushel: For thy Book declares thy
approving of the killing of the Kings Father, and
said where is the Book? At which word W. Harris (a Fire-brand of *Town*, and *Colony & Country*)
rose up, and carried a Book (which they said was
mine) to W. Edmundson: I perceived that W. Edm. *W Edm.*
& W.H. who was for any Religion, and a malici- *& W. Harris*
ous mortal enemy to all good, had been a plotting: *their mal-*
and I said openly I knew what malicious bloody *lice*
counsel had been between W. Har. and themselves: *towards me*
but they would finde themselves befooled, for there
was nothing in the matter but ridiculous malice:
for all of us knew that W.H. loved the *Quakers*
(whom now he fawn'd upon) no more then he did
the *Baptists* (whom he till now fawn'd on) but
would love any, as a Dog for his Bone, for Land,
which he had a long Suit for as was known to all
the Country and their cost. Hereupon Capt.
Green of *Warwick* (Magistrate) desired that such
matters might be forborn, and others spake to the
same purpose: and *J, Stubs* and others are said to
speak to W. Edm. to forbear, so that the Book was
laid aside and delivered again to that [206] malicious bloody Soul W. Harris. I challenged them
again and again to read and improve what possibly
they could, which I knew was no more then some
words

words applauding the *Parliaments Juſtice* and *Mer-cy*: which theſe *Bloody Sophiſters* would (like *Wolves & Foxes* conſtrue as my approving the Kings Death, which God knows I never approved to this day. Upon this *Occaſion* I may now inform the *Reader*, how eaſily the malicious Spirit of *W. Edm. & W. Har.* met in one: formerly no man amongſt us had ſpoken more ſcornfully of the *Quakers* then *W Harris,* now he extreamly, privately and publickly fawns upon them, ſeeing them my Enemies, who had ever been his Friend, and never his Enemy but in his outragious practiſes againſt *Town, & Colony & Country.* He was a Pretender in *Old England,* but in *New* my experience hath told me, that he can be one with the *Quakers,* yea *Jeſuits* or *Mahume-tans* for his own worldly ends and advantage. He is long known to have put *Scorn*s *& Jeer*s upon the eminent Inhabitants of Town and Country. He hath been notorious for quarrelling, and challeng-ing, and fighting, even when he pretended with the *Quakers* againſt *Carnal Weapons*; ſo that there ſtands upon Record in the Town-book of *Provi-dence* an Act of *Disfranchiſement* upon him, for fight-ing and ſhedding Blood in the ſtreet, and for main-taining and allowing it (for ought I know) to this day. Then he turns *Generalliſt,* and writes againſt all *Magiſt-ates, Laws, Courts, Charters, Priſons, Rates,* &c. pretending himſelf and his Saints to be the *Higher Powers* (as now the *Quakers do*) and in publick writings he ſtir'd up the People (moſt ſe-ditiouſly and deſperately threatning to begin with the *Maſſachuſets*) and to cry out *no Lords,* no *Maſ-ters,*

W Harris his charac-ter and practiſe

W H & the Q the higher powers as they ſimply affirm

ters, as is yet to be feen in his Writing : this coft my felf and the Colony much trouble. Then (as the Wind favoured his ends) no man more cries up Magiftrates : then not finding that pretence, nor the People called *Baptifts* (in whom he confided) ferving his ends. He flies to *Connecticut Colony* (then and ftill in great Conteft with us) in hopes to attain his gaping about Land from them, if they prevail over us : to this end he in publick Speech and Writing applauds *Connecticut Charter* and damns ours, and his Royal Majefties favour alfo for grant- ing us favour (as to our Confciences) which he largely endeavours by writing to prove the *K. Ma- jefty* by Laws could not do. My felf (being in place) by Speech & Writing oppofed him, & Mr. *B. Ar- nold* then *Governour*, and Mr. *Jo. Clark Deputy Governour*, Capt. *Cranftone* and all the Magiftrates, he was Committed for fpeaking & writing againft his Majefties *Honour, Prerogative, & Authority* : He 207] lay fome time in Prifon until the *General Af- fembly*, where the *Quaker* (by his wicked, ungodly, and difloyal plots) prevailing, he by their means gets loofe, and leaves open a door for any man to challenge the Kings Majefty for being too Godly or Chriftian, in being too favourable to the Souls of his Subjects againft his Laws, &c.

I had thought to have declared thus much pub- lickly, and how feafonably the Kings *Declaration* came over againft him : alfo how that one *General Affembly*, and another, and another had been troubled with him, &c. and fined him, &c. but now my *Lord Edmundfon* grew hot, and told me that I

W Edm. his igno- rant and impudent zeal and upbraid- ings

had

had charged the People of the Lord with many great and grievous Charges, which he said I could not prove, yea, he said he would speak it before the Lord, I had not proved one of them, and therefore he warned me, being an old Man, that I should not carry such a *Burden* on my back to my Grave, and (among other angry insultings) he said he heard I had been a Magistrate, and said I was a fit man to be a Magistrate that would so wrongfully charge the Innocent. *Jo. Stubs* spake to the same effect, and how I had hindred them from going about the work of the Lord: he said also, that it was only the Light which they had spoke for, and that some had interrupted them, but he confest that *Roger Williams* himself had not done it: I saw God in their *Confession*.

The point of persecution

And for the last point and Branch of the 14 *Position*, viz. [*Their Persecuting Spirit*) having spoken to it before, and finding them unwilling to mention it, I urged it not, having (at *Newport*) shewed from *Page* 170 of *G.Fox* his Book, [*That the Magistrate (that is the Magistrate in their Light) ought to Subject the Nation to his Light, else he is not a faithful Magistrate.*] In *page* 90.&96. *G. Fox.* sets up his

So many Quak. so many Popes

Saints (as formerly *W. Harris* his Antagonists) to be the higher Powers, as knowing who Worship God aright, and who not, and only able to judge of *Powers, Magistrates, Kingdomes and Churches.* Herein *W.H.* and the *Quakers are one*, &c. It is

The pretended meekness of the Quakers.

true that *W. Edm.* declared that the People of God were not to meddle with *Carnal Weapons*: as also that before time, many of the People of God called

Quakers,

Quakers, had been Souldiers, *Captains and Colonels*, yet now coming to the *Light*, they had laid down their *Carnal Weapons:* but if *Fox* fay true in his Book, either they *Mope* or *Equivocate*: for *Fox* fpeaks of the Magiftrates for Chrift in the aforefaid Page 170. he difcerns who be I*dolaters*, who not, which true Churches, which not, and are to praife the *VVell Doers*, and terrifie the *Evill Doers* with the Carnal and Material *Sword*, or elfe they talk nothing.

208] But 2. If this *Confeffion* & *Profeffion* of theirs were not; yet if Chrft Jefus fay true, *viz. The Tongue tells to all the World what the Heart is :* was there ever People profeffing the Name of Chrift Jefus (except the *Papifts*) fo Reproaching the *Proteftants*, and amongft the *Proteftants* was there any ever fo *Reproaching* & *Reviling* the Profeffing and Confcientious People as *Quakers do* : was there ever any known (profeffing the fear of God in fo high a meafure) fo fharp and cutting in their Tongues even to eminently, knowing and Confcientious perfons, [*Thou Lyar, thou* Serpent, *thou* Cain, *thou* Judas *thou* Hipocrite, *thou* Devil] &c. Shall we rational*ly* queftion whether their hands (like *Simeons* and *Levyes*) will not be as fierce and cruel, if the moft holy and only Wife permits *Whips &* *Halters, Swords & Fagots* to fall into their Hands ? and what did *Sam. Fifher, & Ed. Burrowes* write lefs to the Souldiers at *Dunkirk*, that if they received the light they fhould on to *Rome*.

3. Have we not known the deceitfulnefs of mens hearts fly out into greater matters then *Perfecution ?*

The tongue of the Quakers is the Vipers what will their hand be

The Quakers common language

The cheat-
ing of
mans
*heart*secution? *Hazael* earneftly afked whether the Prophet thought him a *Dog* that he fhould doe fuch
matters &c. *Pendleton* vow'd his Collops fhould
fry ere he would to *Mafs* in Q *Maryes* dayes, and
yet to *Mafs* he went and perfecuted others alfo that
would not bow to the Image as he had done.

Juft here Capt *Green* of *Warwick* defired leave
to fpeak to two things,

1. To immediate *Revelations*, fuch as *Abraham*
and *Mofes* and *Ehud* had.

Capt
Green
his 2 points
with my
*Antagonift*2. As to the Soul being a part of God : I was
weary and withdrew, but afterward Capt. *Green*
told me that none of them were willing to fpeak
punctualy to either of thefe two, but rather defired to wave them as a bftrufe and high *matters*
and *Myfteryes.*

Then *Pardon Tillinghaft* (a leading man among
the People called *Baptifts* at *Providence*) he preft
againft them the continuation of *Chrifts Ordinances*
Pardon
Tillinghaft
his dif-
courfe with
my
*Oppofite*untill he came. The *Quakers* faid Chrift was come
again to his *Difciples.* He replyed, that after *Chrifts*
Afcention he fpake of another *Coming,* his fecond
Coming, Heb 9. *W. E.* fel to Prayer, (as with me
he ftl to *Preaching*) *Pardon Tillinghaft* (as himfelf
told me) declared to them, that he was free to difcourfe with them, but he was not free to joyn with
them in *Worfhip:* fo he departed, and after *W E.*
his *Prayer,* the whole Affemby.

The Con-
clufion was
ordered by
*the Father*And thus it pleafed the *God* and *Father of Lights*
and *Mercye*s to bring us to the end of this 4*th*
dayes Conteft, and the end of the whole matter,
in

in much *Peace* and *Quietneſs*, and the Conſideration *of Mercies with much peace and*
of matters left to every mans *Soul*, and *Conſcience*, *quietneſs*
and ſo doe I this *Narrative*, which God knows is *which had*
the *Sum* and Subſtance of all our *Tranſactions:* *not been if*

 Unto his *Eternal Majeſty* therefore I humbly *I had in-*
offer *Eternal Praiſe*, by and in the *Eternal Son of* *inſulted &*
God, the true *Lord Jeſus Chriſt:* whome I deſire *upbraided as W Edm.*
joyfully to expect to return from *Heaven*, as liter- *did.*
ally and perſonally as all true *Chriſtians* hold (*Act.*
1.) he is *aſcended.*

AN   APEN-

A N

APENDIX

O R

Addition of Proofs unto my thirteenth Po-sition,   Viz.

That the Quakers Writings are Poor, Lame and Naked (not able to defend themselves, nor comfort the Souls of others with any solidity.)

More Proofs of the Quakers lame writings   I could produce moſt of their chief extant, but I have been occaſioned to deal with *G. Fox*, their great *Goliah*, in ſome Scores of Paſſages of his Book in Folio, in the *Narrative* aforeſaid.

Unto which I judge fit to adde the Scores following, faithfully preſenting his Oppoſites, Words (as he quotes them) his *Anſwers* and then my *Reply*: let him that Readeth underſtand.

I Have

I Have chofen out the fhort Affertions of *G. Fox* his *Oppofites* as he quotes them, and his fhort Anfwer for brevity fake, &c.

1. The firft of this Addition I name, is in *pag.* 6. of *G. Fox* his Folio Book, where he brings in *Samuel Eaton* faying [The *Apoftle* faying to the Saints, *You know all things,* it is [2] an excef-five fpeech] *G. Fox* Anfwer [contrary to *John,* and would make him a *Lyar,* the *Minifter* of God : fo he is in the falfe fpirit gone out into the World, contrary to 1. *Ioh.*2. Who know all things]

1 John 2. You know all things.

I Reply, 1. I cannot learn that they litterally hold, that they know all things knowable as God (though G. *Fox* writes that they know all things as God (yet I can not think them fo grofs as to imagine that they know all things, paft, prefent, and to come, (as the Devil pretends he doth, and offers to reveal fo much to fome Conjurers) but I judge they muft come to fome figurative meaning, as their oppofite writeth.

For 2. What hinders (as before) but if the *Quakers* be *Omnifcient,* and know all things, but they fhould be alfo *Omnipotent* and do all things, for fo *Paul* writes, *Phil.* 4. *I can do all things* : I know they fay, they are one with God and Chrift, and they know all things, and can do all things ; and yet this fenfe which litterally is fo Proud and Blaf-phemous, muft be made out by a meaning and by a figure (which they cry out againft in others.)

3. Therefore doth not the Spirit of God in *Prov.* 28. open this to us, faying, *Evil men underftand not Iudgement, but they that feek the Lord underftand all things* :

About knowing all things.

things : that is, God anfwers their Prayers, and inables them to know and do, all that he calls them to, when the *proud* and *fcornful* are rejected.

4. Therefore I believe it is that the moft Holy and moft juft and wife Lord leaves thefe poor proud and fcornful Souls to feek *wifdome* and not to find it, to be ignorant, *knowing nothing*, (as *Gods Spirit* fpeaketh,) and to difcover their *Ignorance* in fo many *Fundamentals* of *Chriftianity*, and in fo many *practices immodeft, irrational, and more then favage*, as I have proved againft them.

2. In *pag.* 11. G. *Fox* brings in John *Bunyan*, &c. faying, [The *Scripture* plainly denies that *Confcience* can *juftifie* though it may *condemn*. [He Anfw. [which is contrary to Scripture, where the Apoftle faith Rom. 2. *their Confciences either accufing or excufing*.] And again, *herein do I exercife my felf to have a Confcience void of offence toward God and toward Men*, and the *Light* condemns, which you call *Confcience*, &c.

I Reply, *Confcience* (in *greek Latine* and *Englifh*, &c. fignifies a *Knowing together* : a *Reflexion*, or looking back of a mans mind or *Spirit* upon it *felf*, in point of *Juftification* or *pardon of fin* [3] *Confcience* looks upon a curfed rotten Nature, then upon millions of fins of *Omiffion* and *Commiffion*, which how to fatisfie an infinite Juftice for, and to attain a new heart and nature is the high bufinefs and out of the reach or thought of that poor *Confcience*, which every man *Iew* or *Gentile* Civilized, or *Pagan* comes into the World with. In the great Tryal of the three greateft finners that ever were

in

The Quakers proud of knowledge yet knowing nothing.

Pag.11. Joh Bunyan.

Confcience condemning not Juftifying.

The Quakers confeft their light to be Confcience.

The great Tryal of the 3 greateft actual Sinners that ever were in this World, the Devil, and the firſt Man, and firſt Woman: two of them their Conſciences condemned them, and they confeſt the Faɗ (though with extenuation and Excuſes) could this their condemning Conſcience (eſpecially with mincing of ſin as all mens natural Conſciences do) I ſay, could this Conſcience or Confeſſion pardon their ſin, reniew their hearts and be their Juſtification (or clearing) and Salvation?

Tis true *Abimelechs* Conſcience juſtified him from the Faɗ of lying with *Abrahams* Wife, as well as *Ioſephs* Conſcience juſtified him from the falſly imputed guilt of lying with his *Miſtreſs*, or attempting of it: But was this the Pardon of *Abimelechs* ſin, his Juſtification and Salvation after the *Canting Language* of this poor *Fox*, and all the *Foxians* that I have ſeen (and *I* have read all I could come at &c.) The excuſing of Conſcience

Oh how little do theſe poor *Beaſts* ſeek what infinite Juſtice, infinite Puniſhment, infinite Payment is! what Conſcience truly pacified is, upon the Pardon of Sin, and true peace of Conſcience Sprinkled with the Blood of that only Lambe of God Chriſt Jeſus.

Amongſt the *Indians* I have known ſome falſely accuſed of ſtealing *Engliſh* Mens goods, of killing *Engliſh* Mens Cattle, yea, of *Murther*; and *I* have heard them ſay that *Manit*: that is God and their own Souls know they are Innocent. This *Innocency* who queſtions but that it is their plea and excuſe and diſcharge from that guilt falſly charged on them: If this be all that G. *Fox* ſaith! *he beats the*

the Air and hath no Enemy: No, no, It is a *Conſcience* Juſtification within, a *Chriſt* ſhedding his
blood within; (in a ſubtle fly oppoſition to the pardon without us from the K. of *Heaven* for the ſake
of his Son wi thout us) this is the buſineſs which
theſe Traitors to the K. of *Heaven* aim at : Now
they will be perfect and never more admit a ſinful
thought ; and this their *preſent Honeſty* ſhall pay
the old ſcore of a Curſed Na- [4] ture, and millions
of Treaſons, and Rebellions in Commiſſions and
Omiſſion againſt the God of Heaven.

A fit Simi-
litude uſed
before Q.
Eliz beth
concern-
ing pardon
of ſin or
Juſtifica-
tion,
which I
had from
one
that heard
it being
near the
Queen

It was a pertinent Similitude uſed before *Q Elizabeth*.   A King ſent for his Lord Deputy of a Pro-
vince to come home and give account *&c.*   The
guilty *Deputy* goes to a great friend deſires his Company, *&c.* he ſaid, He was ſent for alſo himſelf,
and feard his own *Iſſue*: He goes to others deſires
their Company, *&c.*   They make excuſe and promiſe to have him or the way, *&c.*   Then goes the
Deputy to an old *friend*, who promiſed to go with
him, and what he could ſpeak for him : only, if
the *K.* aſked, he muſt ſpeak the Truth, and that will
be (ſaid he) your Deſtruction, and therefore adviz'd
him to make the young *Prince* his Friend and *Mediator* for whoſe ſake the King would deny no Favour, no pardon, no Honour, *&c.*

Con-
ſcience the
greateſt
Friend or
Foe.

The Application may be large and uſeful: but
in ſhort, A Soul Summond to Death and Judgement, looks to Relations, *&c.* they all Anſwer ,they
are in the ſame *Caſe*, &c.   It looks to *Wordly Eſtate*, &c: they tell us they will go with us as far as
the *Grave* and *provide* a *Coffin*, and a *Sheet*, and a
Burial, &c.   3. The

3. The old *friend is Conscience*, who will go with us, but can be a *thousand witnesses* against us, &c. It follows then clearly that the *young Prince* is the true *Lord Jesus Christ*, not vanished away into a *Light* in every *dark dungeon* in the World, but Conscience faith he is litterally ascended *up* into *Heaven*, and will as literally *make his speedy Return* again to Iudgement.

The third Instance, G. *Fox pag.* 12. brings in the same Author, faying, [the Light doth not *shine* in the *Consciences* of them that be *lost*.] The Answer, [But *Iohn* faith, *he Light shines in darkness but the darkness cannot comprehend it*, and there is *that of God* in the *Children of Disobedience* and *Reprobates*, as in *Rom.* 1. and 2. Chapters.] I Reply, G. *Fox* is here in his *Burrough*, and takes not the word *Light* in the fame Senfe his *Opposite* doth, (the Common trick of *Cheators*): His *Opposite* takes it not for the *heavenly Lights Sun, Moon,* nor *Earthly Light* of *Fire, Candles, precious Stones,* nor the *Metaphorical Light* of mens minds differing them from *Beasts, Birds, Fishes* : Nor the *Light* of *peace joy* and *Prosperity,* call'd in Scripture Light, &c. Nor the *Light* and Evidence of *witness* or *Reason* in Cafes depending : Nor the *Light* of the *holy Scriptures,* and the *preaching* and offering of a [5] *Saviour* to poor loft Sinners : But, for that *awakening, saving Light,* convincing all mens Condition to be miferable and damnable : of *Grace* and *mercy* offered and applied to a Soul by the *good News* of a *Saviour* fomeway heard of, and the *holy Spirit* the *finger* or power of God.

Pag. 2. Jo.
Bunyan,
&c.

The va-
rious
meanings
of the
word
Light

G. *Fox*

G. *Fox* faith, this faving Light is in mankind: only perfons don't mind it, and fo *Chriſt Ieſus* is *Crucified*, and ſlain in them, and God, and Chriſt, and Spirit, and Light, &c. are all captived, hindred from working, yea, altogether killd & ſlain in them becauſe a Soul doth not mind them, and hearken to Chriſt in them.

Ah poor ſimple bruitiſh Imagination that ever it ſhould enter into the thoughts of Men profeſſing to be Chriſtians, *&c.* or of men profeſſing to know more than the *Wolves* and *Foxes* in the wilderneſs: I have ſpoke to this before, therefore a word only to G. *Fox* his proof, *Rom.* 1. and 2. *Chapt.* From theſe two Chapters he proves that there is that of God in the Children of *Diſobedience*, and *Reprobates*, who denies it. For there is ſomething of God, that is from the power and wiſdome of God in the Fallen Spirits the Devils themſelves. But I know by that of God, G. *Fox* means God himſelf (*preſt down as a Cart with ſheaves*) the holy Seed *Chriſt Ieſus*, (under the *Clods*,) the holy *Spirit* in *priſon*, for the Soul is a part of the *Eſſence* or Being of God himſelf.

Marginal note: Rom. 1. & 2? Nor favouring Chriſt in all mankind

But that there is here a word or title of Colour to any of this dirt and filth flung in the face of the *Majeſtie* of *Heaven?*

This Scripture ſpeaks of the *work* (or working) *of the Law written in their hearts*: but what is this to a fecond *writing* of the holy *Scriptures*, or *writing inſpired* into the heart by the moſt holy *Spirit?* yea, what is this to a third *writing* of their *Names* written in *Heaven* in the *Lambs Book of Life?* yea, what

Marginal note: Four writings conſidered

what is this to a fourth *writing*, the *writing* of the
new Covenant Confifting of Sin and a *new heart, a
heart of flefh*, in which his Law is written as formerly *in Tables of Stone*, and yet we poor men of
I*abefh Gilead* muft leave the Teftimony (as *Gilead*
imports) and fuffer *Nahufh* (the *Serpent*) to put out
our *right eyes*, and believe that every man hath the
new *Covenant Chrift Iefus* and the *Kingdom* of God,
&c. with the *Pharifees* in every *mans heart and yet
he never knows of it* ?

4. Inftance : In the fame pag. 12 he brings in
the fame Author, faying, [It is a *Counterfeiting* of
the *new Birth* for men to [6] follow the *Light*
wherewith men coming into the world are inlightned : G. *Fox* Anfw. [which none comes to the
new Birth but who come to the *Light*, which every
man, *&c.* in which believing is a *Child* of the
Light, &c.

I Reply: G. *Fox* runs round agren and again,
like the *windmil Sails* : It is faith he, no *Counterfeiting* of a *new Birth*, why, becaufe it is no *Counterfeiting :* [none comes to the *new Birth* but who
comes to the *Light*, &c.]

As to the words in *Iohn* 1. [1]*Hitchcock* at *Newport*
alleadged, that it was not in his Bible [*enlightneeth
every man*, but lighteth every man, *&c.*] John *Stubs*
lockt in his *greek Teftament*, and confeft it was Pho-
tizes which is not *inlightneth* but *Lighteth*.

2. As to the *Light*, We know there are two
Opinions how *Chrift lighteth every man*, &c. Firft,
as God in the *Creation*. 2. As God man and *Mediatour,*

Several Expofitions of the Light in Jhon 1.

[1] Infert "W." *R. W. Ms. Ann.*

tour, and that the Greeks word *Erchomenon* doth not relate to the word [*anthropon*] the man or every man that cometh into the world, but [*phoce*] Light, and that it muſt be read in this Senſe, *viz* that *Chriſt Ieſus* the true *Light* cometh into the world lighteth every man that is in the world free-ly that will receive him : Even as many (whom-ſoever) look up to him, (as *Iohn* 3.) the ſtung Iſrael-ites to the *brazen Serpent* : and that *Chriſt Ieſus is*
The World all men and every man *the Light of the world*, John 8. and 12. to as many as receive him according to 1 *Iohn* 12. and that the meer phraſe imports no more then a *Light* held forth to all in the world, as the Sun in the *Heavens*, and *Chriſts Followers, Math.* 5. are called by *Chriſt Ieſus the Light of the World.* Thus the word *all* and *every man* (as I hinted before) is uſed not abſo-lutely, but *Comparatively*, and is *figuratively* taken in many places, and four[1] times in that one *ver.* 1 Col. 28. *viz. warning every man and teaching every man in all wiſdome that we may preſent every man per-feft in Chriſt Ieſus*, which literally cannot be true.

Chriſt as Mediator enlightens none but the Eleft. Now G. *Fox* runs into his *Burrough* of the many *ſignifications* of the word *Light*, and the word *all*, and the word *inlightneth*, willingly ignorant that *Chriſt Ieſus* as *Mediator* of the *new Covenant inlight-ens* none but thoſe whom his Father *gives* him : unto whom he gives *Repentance*, to whom he opens the *door* of *Faith*, and gives them to believe and ſuffer, *&c.*

So that G. *Fox* Confounds the *Eleft* and the *World* together and brings in a Counterfeit new
Birth,

[1] " 3 times." *R. W. Ms. Ann.*

Birth, a Counterfeit Chrift, and at laft a Counterfeit Salvation.

7] 5. Inftacne: G. *Fox pag.* 20. brings in *Henock* of Henoch Howet.
Howet, faying, [It is a fancy to fay the *Covenant* of
God is to all men in the world, and the grace of God
hath appeared to all men, *&c.* He *Anfw.* [contrary
to the *Apoftle,* who faith, *the grace of God which
brings Salvation hath appeared to all men:* & contrary
to the *Prophet,* who faith, *I will give him for a Light
unto the* Gentiles, *a Light to the people, Salvation to
the ends of the Earth,* and a *new Covenant* to the houfe
of *Ifrael* and *Iudah,* and they that do not believe
this are Condemned :]

I Reply in thefe Confiderations prefented to the
Confcientious :

1. All mankind being fallen from God : He gracioufly gave the Word or call to *Abraham,* and made
Promifes both to his *Natural* and *Spiritual Seed,* Jews & Gentiles
hence came the diftinction of Jews, (or the Child-
ren of *Abraham*) and the Gentiles [as we Englifh it.]

2. It pleafed God to make *two Covenants* or *Bar-
gains* with mankind. 1. that of Juftice and due The two great Bargains of God with mankind.
debt, to any man that yielded obedience in all
things, *&c. Rewards* according too, yea, above de-
fert. This *Bargain* was made with our *firft Parents:*
and with all mankind to this day, yea, even with
the moft favage and barbarous. The fecond is of
mercy and pity, *&c.* The *Labans* of the world
change *Covenants* and *Bargains* ten times, and ftill
for the worfe, *&c.* but the *Father* of *mercies* pity-
ing *Mans Mifery* and *Inability* offers a *New,* and
Infinitely eafier and *fweeter Bargain* upon the Terms
of only *Mercy* and *free grace* and pity.   3. It

3. It is one thing for God to offer this Covenant or *Bargain*, [wherever the found of this Gofpel or glad News comes] and another thing to embrace and receive it as all the Elect of God do, and another thing to work *freely* and give *freely* the *Means* and Power to fulfil this *Covenant*: as God doth by the *Merits* of his S n, and his own *powerful working* of *Repentance* and belief in the hearts of all his Chofen.

Scripture language

4. It is Common with the *holy Spirit* to fpeak *Figuratively* in the *holy Scripture*. To call the Sign the thing *fignified*, and the *Inftrument* or *Means*, the *work done*. Thus the *Lamb* is the *Paffover*, the *Bread* is *Chrifts body*, the *Cup* is his *Blood*: God and *Chrift* is called the *Hope* of his *people*, and *Chrift Iefus* the *Mediator* of the *Covenant*, called the Covenant it felf. The King pardons Rebels for his Sons fake, his Son may in a Senfe be faid [8] [though not *literally*] to be the *pardon* it felf: A man drives a *Bargain* between two Chapmen that are abfent and diftant drives on a *marriage* between a Man and a Woman abfent each from other, and may in a Figurative Senfe be called the *Bargain* or *Covenant*, and yet not *literally* and *properly* as the poor *Quakers* would their *Chrift* to be.

God offers the Gofpel divers wayes

5 The grace and mercy of God, the Gofpel or glad News is many wayes offered: fome are invited gently to come to the heavenly Wedding and Supper: other Meffengers (more vehement) even force perfons in, and the Kingdome of Heaven is taken by force; many feek to enter, many run; *It is not in him that willeth, nor runneth but in God that fheweth*

eth mercy, and the reſt he juſtly hardeneth that God may be *All in All.*

For as God walketh in the midſt of his (moſt wonderful) *Creation*, with his two feet of Mercy and Juſtice; ſo he hath his two fingers; and with one he wrote the Covenant of Juſtice in the Tables of Stone, and with thc fingers of his Mercy and Grace he freely writes his Mind and Will in the Tables of Fleſh and Hearts of his Choſen: Many offers of Bargains and Marriages are made which never are embraced &c. but in the new-Covenant God gives a new heart to his Choſen, and gives not, and is not the Covenant to any but his Choſen all the World over, even to the ends of the Earth.

Two Feet and 2 Fingers of God

6. For is it not a monſtrous Dream of the *Qua-kers*, to ſay, that God and Chriſt, Spirit and Cove-nant is in all Mankinde, and that in a Goſpel ſence? tis true as I ſaid, if G. *Fox* mean that the Knowl-edge of God in a ſence is offered to each mans Conſcience in the World, though more expreſly and glorioully where he ſends his Meſſengers, *Wiſ-domes Virgins*, &c. G. *Fox* beats the Fire,[1] I oppoſe him not, but to ſay the Covenant or Bargain & the Mediatour of the new Bargain, and the Applyer of it the Holy Spirit, is in every of Mankinde, and if they will turn to it, &c: and yet perſons know no ſuch thing, nor never heard of it, and none ever had it ſo as to be ſaved by it but theſe *Foxians*; is as wiſe as for a Man to have Fits of the Stone or Gout, or a Woman have Pangs of Child-bearing, and yet neither of them know any ſuch matter,

The Qua-kers mon-ſtrous Marriages

[1] "Air," not "Fire."   *R. W. Ms. Ann.*

matter, no nor how fhe had any fuch Marriage Covenant or Husband nor ever any Word or Thought of it.

7. The Bottome is this, G. *Fox* cares not for the *Jews* nor [9] *Gentiles*, no more then the *Fox* cares for *Lambs* and *Chickins* but to make a Prey of them, he pretends Love to all Man-kinde and tells them they have Chrift and the New Covenant and the Spirit within them ; yea, he tells them, he means not the Covenant of works, but the Covenant of Grace, he means that Chrift that dyed at *Ierufalem*, but when it comes too, they mean no other Chrift but a Spirit (as *Humphrey Norton* more plainly then *Fox* confeffeth) and this Spirit will be found to be an *Evil Spirit* by Gods moft wonderful, wife and righteous hand (as one faith) upon them.

A 7th Inftance. G. *Fox* brings in *pag.* 24. *Iofeph Kellet*, &c. faying, [*The Scriptures are the means of Faith,*] He *Anfwers*, and have thrown out Chrift the Authour of it, and God the Giver, and the Scripture is but a Declaration of the Saints Faith : and men had Faith before the Scripture was, as Inftance *Abraham* and *Enoch.*

I Reply, G. *Fox* Anfwers three things;

Firft, That his Oppofites throw out God, if they make the Scripture the means of Faith.

Secondly, He flights the Scripture with a *But, it is but a Declaration of the Saints Faith.*

Thirdly, He flights the Novelty of it, faying, *There was Faith before there was Scripture.*

I reply, I have had many Occafions to fpeak of the Scriptures already, I fhall therefore briefly fay,

it

G. Fox
and the
Quakers
pretences
of Soul
kindnefs
are Soul
cruelties

Pag. 24.
Jofeph
Kellet

it is wonderful what an aking Tooth againſt the Holy Writings of God : The old Serpent and all the *Wolves* and *Foxes* of this World have had, who hath more or leſs damned and curſed it, and longed to have it out of the World.

The *Jews*, the *Turks*, the *Papiſts*, the *Common Proteſtants*, the *Quakers*, &c make uſe of it for their ends ; but none can rightly uſe it, but as a bleſſed *Candle, Lanthorn* or *Torch* ſent down from Heaven into this dark *Dungeon* of the *World*, to guid us out unto the Saving Knowledge of God, and Eternal Bleſſedneſs with him.

For how doth this follow, that if God hath ap-pointed the Holy Writings as means that God and Chriſt are thrown out ; can there not be an Har-mony between the firſt and all ſubordinate Cauſes ? Did *Moſes* throw out God becauſe he took the Rod in his hand, when he wrought all thoſe Wonders ? Did *Solomon* [10] throw out God becauſe he uſed (as *Moſes* about the *Tabernacle*) ſo many means in rearing that Wondrous and Glorious *Temple*? Or did *Samſon* throw out God when he made uſe of the Jaw-bone of an Aſſe, &c. Or *Chriſt Jeſus* throw out his Father, when he made uſe of Clay and Spittle ? O what a throwing Spirit is this wild *Fox*, and his wild *Foxians* of; who toſs and throw the Eternal, Immortal and Inviſible God, and his only begotten Son in their wild Fancies, as if they were the Wool and Feathers of Lambs and Chick-ens which theſe *Foxians* have devoured.

Secondly, How is it that G. *Fox* here ſaith, *That the Scripture is but a Declaration of the* Saints *Faith* ?

For

[marginal notes:]
God is glorious in the means appointeth.

The Quakers ſimple and wild boldneſs with the eterna power & Godhead

For, is it not a Writing or Record of Heaven :

1. Of the Being and Names of the Eternal Power and Godhead .

The wonderful-Revelations of & in the Script.
2. Of his Glorious and Incomprehenſible Works, Creating and Forming the Heavens and all that is in them ; the Earth, and all that is therein, the Sea, and all that is therein out of nothing ; which Myſtery the Quakers have only from the Scripture.

3 Of the ſpecial and more particular framing of Men and Women above all his viſible Creatures :

4. Of the Fall of Mankinde from their glorious and firſt Making and Creation, which ſome talk idly to be every day.

5. Of the gracious Promiſe of the Father of Mercies, of a Redeemer and Reſtorer of undone mankinde.

1. By his Threatning to the Devil, and promiſe to the Woman of a Saviour, to be born in time of a Woman.

2 By Erecting ſuch a ſtate of *Iſrael* (*prevailers with God*) with all their Typical *Lands, Governours, Worſhips, Wars, Captivities, Deliverances, &c.*

3. Fulfilling of that Promiſe in the Wonderful Birth, Life Doctrine, Miracles, Death, Burial, Reſurrection and Aſſention of the Son of God, the Man Chriſt Jeſus, &c.

4. The Eſtate of the Believers in him after his Aſſention, called the *Primitive Church.*

6 Of the great change ſince his coming, in the riſing of his many Enemies, or Antichriſts eſpecially, of one with ſeven heads and ten Horns, and of another with two horns, &c.

7 Of

7 Of the Proteftant rifing and witneffing againft thefe Devilifh *Heads* and *Horns* of which the *Reve-lations* fpeak, and of [11] the burning up of the Whore and of all Chrifts Enemies and Antichrifts.

8. Of the never-ending Joyes of the Righteous after this life, and the everlafting Worm and Fire of the ungodly, which fhall never dye nor be quenched until the Eternal Power and Godhead (revealed in the Holy Scriptures) come to a Period and Diffolution.

It may be *G. Fox.* will fay, we *Quakers grant all this?*

I *Anfwer,* I queftion whether you fpeak *bona fide,* and in Truth without *Ifuitical* or *Foxian* Equivo-cations.

For 1. What means this *But* [*The Scripture is* Wonder-*But a Declaration of the Saints Faith*] O blinde ful Guids Guids that undertake (as in *Lincolnfhire, &c.*) to guide men through the Wafhes upon Life and Death, where *K.* I*ohn* of *Englands* Treafure and Supply perifhed ; to guid Souls through Hells Eter-nal *Wafhes*! what is your *But,* but the *Iews,* and *Papifts,* and *Quakers* cry Crucifie him, Hang up Chrift Jefus, burn up the Scriptures, and all Bibles, Old and New-Tements, &c?

2. What is this *Saints Faith?* You acknowledge none but the Faith of the wild Souls called *Qua-kers* or *Foxians*! we poor *Iews,* and *Papifts,* and *Proteftants,* though we own the Scriptures, fome a part, and the reft all, yet we are all but Infidels, Devils, &c.

3. What is this *Faith,* this *Saints Faith,* this *Foxes* Wonder-ful faith of and

the Qua-
kers

and the *Quakers Faith?* is it any thing elfe but (as before I have faid) but a meer *Babel* or *Confufion of God* and *Faith, Chrift and Faith, Spirit and Faith, Light and Faith, Iuftification and Faith, Sanctification and Faith, Salvation and Faith,* &c. and this in every one of Mankinde in the World, if they will believe it, &c.

The third Branch of G. *Fox* his Anfwer is, [*Men had Faith before the Scriptures were.*]

Gods feve-
ral wayes
of reveal-
ing him-
felf

I *Anfwer*, Neither *Abraham* nor ever any Man had Faith before it pleafed the Eternal and Invifible Deity to difclofe himfelf by Word, or Sight, or Dream, or Motion, or Writing, as *Heb.* 1. at feveral times and wayes *it pleafed him to fpeak,* and laft of all by the beft and cleareft of all, his only Begotten Chrift Jefus.

The mad
fancies of
the Qua-
kers as to
the Holy
Scriptures

2. When it hath pleafed the *incomprehenfible Majefty* to Command his *Appearances* by *Words, Vifions, Dreams,* &c. [12] to be written to ftand upon *File* and *Record,* (for all Generations) fhall we be fuch *Fools* and *Franticks* as to fay it was his Word when God fpake it to, and in his Prophets: but now it is written, it is but *pen, ink* and *paper,* it is but a dead Letter, it is not Gods word, God hath but One *Word, Chrift.* The Scripture is his *Words,* &c. Oh the *audacious brockifhnefs* of the *foul Spirit* in thefe wild *Foxians*: They dare not (though what dares not their *hellifh Spirit* againft the K. of Hea-

The word
of a King
and the
word of
God

ven yet) they dare not (they do not deny but predicate) that the *Kings Letters* from *Breda* are the *Kings Word,* that the *Kings Speeches* and *Declarations* are his *royal Word*: fhall a *Bargain,* a *Covenant,*

a *mar-*

a *marriage*, a *Laſt Will*, be our mind, our will, our
Word, when it is ſpoken! But when it is *written,
fairly drawn*, and *engroſſed, ſubſcribed* and *ſealed*
unto before many *Witneſſes attesting,* then it is not
our word, mind, or will, but words, &c, The bottom and Truth is : The Spirit by which the Quakers are acted would be glad that there were not
ſuch a perſon called the *Word of God,* nor ſuch a
writing declaring ſo *ſweetly, ſo plainly, ſo fully, and
ſo heavenly of him* :

    8. Inſtance : In the 25. *pag.* G. *Fox* brings in Pag. 25.
the ſame Author, ſaying, [that the Power which Joſeph
juſtles out the Form is an Error:] He Anſw. which Kellet &c.
was the Apoſtles work to bring of the Form into
the Power, the ſubſtance Chriſt which was not an
Error, but you bring in the Error, keep people in
the Form out of the Power, and not in the Apoftles work :]

    I Reply: G. *Fox* is in his *Burrough* of the vari-
ous Senſe of the word Form: It hath reſpect to The
Nature, to *Art,* to *Civil, Natural,* and *Divine mat-* Form de-
ters : Shall I now (like a Fool and a mad man) bated
Cry down all *Natural, Civil,* and *Divine Beings?*
Are not all the *internal* and *external Forms,* ſhapes,
or Beings of the Creatures in *Heaven, Earth,* and
Sea, of *Angels, Sun, Moon,* &c. *Men, Birds, Beaſts,
Fiſhes,,* admirably glorious and *ſtupendious?* G. *Fox*
runs to the Picture, or Forms of theſe Forms, and
ſaith childiſhly, that the Form or picture without
the Life is nothing: who knows not that, that as to
Life it is good as nothing.

    1. But to come to worſhip, was there not a Form,

or

or manner of *Circumſion*, the *Paſsover*, the *Tabernacle*, the *Temple*, &c.

2. Did ever the Servants of God when they inveighed againſt the *Cuſtomarineſs*, the Careleſsneſs, the pictures, and the meer [13] Formality of the Worſhippers (Jews or Chriſtians) inveigh againſt the worſhip it ſelf, and the Appointments of God and of his Son Chriſt Jeſus.

Gods Ordianees and Inſtitutions

3. Did the Servants of God ever labour to bring and hale off Gods people from the worſhip it ſelf, but only from the dead and meerly formal uſing of them, until the time appointed by God himſelf for their withdrawings, diſappearing and abrogation. What a ſhameleſs falſhood is it that any of Gods Meſſengers brought Gods people off from thoſe *heavenly Fabricks* which God erected by their Miniſtry or Service all the World over ?

4. May not *Gods Meſſengers* now Cry out againſt the *apiſh* Imitations & *Formalitie*s of the *Papiſts* (ſo horribly and bloodily) abuſing *Prayer, preaching, Baptiſme*, the *Lords Supper, Excommunication*, &c. but (like the *Aſſyrians* or *Babilonians*, Pſal. 74. All theſe *Chriſtian Appointments* muſt be broken and tumbled down with *Axes* and *Hammers*. &c.

The Quakers groſs Hypocriſie

5. This is Treaſon and Rebellion in any Atheiſts or whomſoever, but more abominable Hipocritical in theſe *Phariſaical Foxians*, who Cry out againſt the *apiſh Imitators*, and yet themſelves practice, *preaching, praying, Congregations*, or *Churches, ſingings, Conventings*, and (implicite though real) Addings to *Caſtings out*, &c   Full well (as the Lord
                                                                        Ieſus

Iefus fpeaks) abrogating the word and Appointments of God, that they may fet up and eftablifh
their own Traditions, &c.

6. Tis true, the Proteftants have made feparation
from the Church of *Rome*, as *whorifh* and *Bloody* :
in order to the Return to the firft Primitive purity,
from which the whore of *Rome* hath departed.

7. G. *Fox* Cries out againft all Scripture and
Common Senfe, againft all Forms, that is, wayes and
manners of Gods Worfhip : Cries up a Chrift within, *Scripture within, Church within, Minifters within,
Baptifme and Supper within*, yet practice they moft
of thefe [fo many as their Idol requires] and will
ferve his turn) as outwardly and vifibly as any in
the world.

8. I know it is the obfervation of one of G. *Fox* A paffage
his Oppofites ⌊a man of excellent knowledge, piety of Mr.
& induftry, M *Baxter*⌋ *viz.* that the Churches of ⌜Baxters
the *Independents*, & *Baptifts* have been the fource weighed
and Spring whence have flown the Generation of
the Quakers. For my felf I have obferved the
contrary in thefe parts, [14] and that [although fome
rotten Profeffors, or weak Souls though true] have
been bewitched by thofe Soul-witches yet generally
⌊where they have any Liberty] the *National Church*
fills up their nurbers : My Reafon I gave them Whence
in publick, when W. *Edm. Boafted* of their Num- the Qua-
bers, *viz.* their Religion is fo eafie, never coming kers Prof-
near the *Roots* of *rotten Nature*, but fo wonderfully elites do
agreeing with it, and changing one Devil for arife
another, as I have before inftanced, fo that I told them
I adored the *Infinite Power, wifdome* and *goodnefs* of
God,

God, that they were not *ten thousand* fold more, and
I say Millions more, then they are : For, I can demonstrate that if G: *Fox* (for all their *hypocritical
prating* against *Carnal Weapons*) get a Sword (as
Mahomet did) most of the Popish, and Protestant
and pagan World, will easily be brought to dance
after him.

9. As to the point of Separation : I pray Mr.
Baxter and others of G. *Foxes* learned and godly
opposites who are yet (in their Judgement and
Conscience perswaded to the *National Worships|*
to hear me patiently four words.

1. I pray them to remember what the word
Nazarite is in *English*. The word *Nazareth* and the
word [*Jesus of Nazareth|* and in plain English.[1]

2. Was there ever Child of God in this world
but he was a *Nazarate, separate* from worldly persons, worldly practice and worldly worships, as he
comes to see them, &c. *and endureth not that the evil
one should touch him* ¿

3. Is not *Gods* name *Iealous* in this end of the
World, not the west-world, as well as since he first
proclaimed it in the East.

Considera-
tion touch-
ing sepa-
rate
Churches

4. Hath not his Jealousie raged against the *Iew-
ish whoremongers*, who defiled his *first Bed*, and will
he wink at the *Christian Adulterers* and *Adulteresses*
either in Worship or Conversation ?

5. With what good Conscience can I (a national
Protestant) *separate* from my *Father* the *Pope* and
my *mother* the *Church of Rome*, and my Brethren
and Sisters the *Papists*, and yet it must not be

Christian

---

[1] Add " ye saviour of ye separate." *R. W. Ms. Ann.*

Chriſtian for other Souls to ſee further degrees of that *Separation* neceſſary, and I muſt bring up the foot of every mans Light, and *Sight*, and *Conſcience* to my *Laſte*.

6. This is the main ground of my Controverſy with the proud Quakers, they ſtir up in their Illuminations in themſelves, and [15] Condemnations againſt others, but they magnify (with the *Papiſts* and *Arminians*) Curſed, rotten Nature: their *Converts* and *Proſelites* have but a painted, formal Repentance, Faith, *&c.* Only if they can come to their Church, *&c.* and Thou and thee, and diſreſpᶜᵗ all Superiours then are they high Saints, cannot Sin, *&c.*

The Quakers Converts

7. This (as before I hinted) was the heavenly Principle of thoſe many precious and gallant *Worthies*, the *Leaders* and *Corner Stones* of theſe *New-England Colonies*, viz. they deſired to worſhip God in purity according to thoſe perſwaſions in their Conſciences, which they believed God had lighted up.

N. E. glory the very top bough of it

8. They deſired ſuch for their *Fellow Worſhippers* as they (upon a Chriſtian account) could have evidence that to be true and real *Worſhippers* of God in *Spirit* and *Truth* alſo.

But I forget this is but an Appendix, and therefore I return to another Inſtance of G. *Fox* his poor. and lame, and naked Anſwers, *&c.*

A 9th. Inſtance, is *pag.* 32. where G. *Fox* brings in *Ellis Bradſhaw*, ſaying, [*The Spirit of God doth not teach to judge before the time*] and he adds that others of them ſay [*The Saints ſhall not Iudge while*

Ellis Bradſhaw

they

they be upon the Earth.] To which he Anſwers,
[*But the Spirit did teach the Apoſtle to judge, and his
Time was come* ; And he tells ſome *that they were of
old ordained for Condemnation,* and *their Damnation
ſlumbred not,* and they went on to Eternal Judgement, *and it is high Time not to judge.*]

I Reply, Some of this his Anſwer, is ſome of his
wonted *Nonſence,* or the Printers overſight, *&c.*
But to the point the great Jugler hath taught G.
Fox and his *Foxians* a trick to outface *Death* and
Indgement. They now keep the great Seſſions and
call all the world to their *Bar* and Judgement.
Thus did the poor cheated *Souls in London* lately
Reeves and *Mugleton* thunder out their eternal Sentence of Damnation upon the Souls and bodies of
their *Oppoſites,* & that with ſuch Seriouſneſs, Confidence & Majeſty, that I have known ſollid Chriſtians put into a fright by them.

It is true there is a lawful judging not according
to raſhneſs or pride (as the Quakers is) but according to righteous Judgement.

It is true, *the ſpiriturl man judgeth and diſcerneth
all things,* that is, looks into the Cauſes and Natures
of things, Times and perſons : But what is this to
the Natural *Death* of all mankind. [16] *Heb.* 9?
I know the *Foxians* would turn this Scripture, and
that *golden Chain,* Heb. 6. the firſt *Chriſtian Principles* and the Eternal Judgement into *Myſteries,* and
that they now Judge the Secrets of Men, *Rom.* 2.
by *Pauls Goſpel* : (therefore by looking on a man
they can diſcern the inward parts, and what each
perſon is :) For the Lord is now come ſaith *Enoch*
and

The two
pretended
laſt wit-
neſſes
Reves and
Muggle-
ton

The
Jugling of
the Qua-
kers to
make
themſelves
eternal
Judgs

and I*ude* in *ten thoufands of his Saints, and now is the Day appointed in which God judgeth the World by that man Chrift Iefus* [which man they are] of which the word of God hath approved, in that they are raifed from the Dead in Souls and Bodies to keep the *Eternal Iudgement* : This Myftery many of their young Scholars and many that are truely fearing God amongft them will not believe. But they fpare not to owne their *high Court* of *Iuftice* [when they were put to it] by Speech and writing, and were it not for fome obftacles (efpecially two) this were a fine Colour for their Courts, like a Company of drunken Sots that kept a Court in *Hart-ford-Shire*, and feigned themfelves Judges, and Juftices, and Officers,& had almoft brought themfelves all to the Gallows,*&c.* by hanging up one man until he began to look black, and fome of them began to fear their own Necks, and to repent of their rafh madnefs. *A dangerous counterfeit Court.*

The firft Obftacle againft this their pretended high Court of Juftice, is their own Confeffion, *viz. Chrift Iefus was real a Man as any of us, and fo continues*, except they can give an account of what is become of him, which at *Newport* they could not do. *Two great Bars to the Quakers high Court of eternal Judgm.*

The fecond is, their own Spirit and Practifes, which I have proved to be fo far from *Iude* and *Enochs* 10000 Saints, that their Pride and Scornfulnefs, their Rafh, Revilings and Railings, their Rafh Curfings and Judgings, their Superftitious and New Inventions, their Blafphemies and Hypocrifies, their Inhumanities and Impudencies, fuch as render them fo far from being the high Saints and Judges of the World,

World, that they fall under the Judgement of all sober end modest persons.

The 10. Iustance, is in *pag.* 38. where he brings in *Tho. Collier*, saying, ⌊*All that hath been, are, or shall be Converted since the Gospel Ministration are* *Converted by the Apostles words*⌋ He Answers : So he hath thrown out the Spirit which doth regenerate, and Christ the way to the Father, the Word that Sanctifi- [17] eth, and Christ the power of God to Salvation : who said that they would not come to him that they might be converted, so if they get all the Apostles Words and come not to Christ they are not Converted, and none are Converted by the Apostles Words, but who comes to the Life that the Words come from.

P.38. T. Collier

I reply, and ask G. *Fox* what colour of Truth or Modesty is in his Inference, *viz. That if God please to appoint the Words his first Apostles used, to be still the means of Conversion to he end of the World, that then he hath thrown out himself,* &c.

For 1. Is not this Gods Covenant with Christ and all Christians, that his Word and Spirit should be in their Mouths to all Generations : wo be then to these wild frantick *Inferences* which disjoyn and separate what the most powerful, most wise and holy hath joyned together.

2. For, may there not be as before many Agents Imployed by one glorious Efficient : as in *Moses* building the Tabernacle, *Solomon* the Temple : Kings in their *Royal Navies* and *Armies, Fights* and *Battels* ; is *Moses* here thrown out, *Solomon* thrown out, and *Kings* thrown out &c? when *Abraham* sent his

G. Fox his throwing God overboard and his own Reason and

his Servants or *Kings* their Embaſſadours to Eſpouſe
Brides to their Sons and Heirs, muſt *Abraham* and
all wiſe *Princes* be thrown out, &c. Doth not
rather this mad Soul throw out *Moſes* and *Solomon*,
and *Abraham*, and all *Kings* and great *Efficients* or
firſt Cauſes, yea, and his own *Brains* (in a mad,
proud Frolick) all overboard together?

3. For, doth not *Paul* tell the *Corinthians, that
they were Gods Husbandry and Gods Buildings* ; in-
ferring that under God (not throwing him out) he
was a prime Husbandman, yea, (as himſelf ſaith
further) a Maſter Builder; yea, doth not *Paul* tell the
ſame *Corinthians*, that they were the Meſſengers,
were co workers or Labourers together with God.
Hence *Paul* Preaching, the Lord opened the Heart
of *Lydia* and *Philip* Preaching, the Lord opened
the heart of the *Eunuch*, and *Panl ſo ſpeaking*,
Joh,[1] 14. and *Barrabas*, that a great Multitude
both of *Jews and Greeks* believed.

4. It is true that without God and Chriſt, *Pauls*
Planting, and *Apollos Watering* is nothing, who denies this? but therefore ſhall not *Paul Plant* and
Apollo Water, though much in vain, as it was with
the Lord Jeſus, his own heavenly Preaching and
amazing Miracles.

18] 5. Do theſe *Foxians* themſelves throw out
God and Chriſt when (as they ſay) they uſe the
Apoſtles words, to gather Stones, and build up the
Church of God ; do they not ſay as much for their
new freſh *Foxian* as ever was ſpoken of the Apoſ-
tles,

---

[1] "Aɛts," not "Joh. 14." *R. W. Ms. Ann.*

tles, or any pretending to fucceed them ? I could
give many Inftances.

6. There have been many Converfions to the
Chriftian Name in thefe parts of the World called
Chriftendome.

Thefe the Papifts brag to have effected in all the
four parts of the World, both in the *Eaft* and *Weft-*
Indies, *Afia* and *America*, as alfo in *Africa* and efpecially in *Europe*, where their Man of fin chiefly
refideth : thefe Converfions have been wrought
fometimes in parts and by degrees, and fometimes
of the whole Nations, and this fometimes by the
Sword, fometimes by the Marriages of Princes, all
which are eafily effected ; becaufe (as in t*he Sheche-*
mites and *Samaritains* cafe) whole Peoples, Nations,
Tongues and Multitudes will eafily turn to the
Beaft with feven Heads and ten Horns; and that
very formidable Beaft alfo for Fear, and Gain, and
Hope, &c. will eafily fuffer the Whore of *Rome* to
ride him.

7. From thefe Peoples, Tongues, and Nations,
&c. it hath pleafed the moft Holy and only Wife,
to gather out a Peaple to Himfelf by his Heavenly
Witneffes ; the *Waldenfes* in *France*, the *Wickcle-*
vifts in *England*, the *Huffites* in *Bohemia*, the *Luther-*
ans in *Germany*, the *Calvanifts* in *France* &c. out of
the bloody *Romifh Whores* Dominions (144000.
Virgin Proteftants thirfting after the Blood of
Chrift Jefus only for Salvation)

8. The Father of Spirits hath ftirred up fome
Witneffes in all Proteftant Nations, to preach againft
a Formal, National or Parochial Converfion, to
witnefs

The Pa-
pifts brag
of their
Conver-
fions.

The Pro-
teftant
Conver-
fions

witneſs againſt the Formality and Prophaneſs of theCommon Proteſtants, (all one in Life and ſometimes worſe then the Papiſts,) and to bring thouſands and ten thouſands (even the *one hundred, forty four thouſand Virgins*) to endeavour after purity of heart and Life, purity of Doctrine, purity of worſhip, purity of Churches, &c. Theſe the Jeſuits call Puritans, and Confeſs that they only among the Proteſtants, (as themſelves among the Papiſts) are fit to be thought on as to pretence of the Chriſtian Name and Religion. The Jeſ-
uits and
Puritans
the two
great
Corrivals

9. At the coming of the Lord Jeſus there were two great Com- [19] petitours for preaching, *Firſt*, the *Phariſees* who by Laud and Sea ſent abroad their *Emiſſaries* to make Converts to the God of the Jews and their own Traditions, *Secondly*, The Apoſtles or Meſſengers of Chriſt Jeſus ſent abroad with the glad news of a new Bargain or Covenant of God with the Sons of men, *viz.* this ſecond ſort; It pleaſed the God of Heaven [not to be thrown out as this *Fox* frantickly barks] but to go out wonderfully miraculouſly, yea, alſo with the private labours and preachings of private Chriſtians ſcattered by Perſecution, as the holy Scripture recordeth. The two
great
Corrivals
in Chriſts
time.

10. For the ſlighting of this ineſtimable Pearl of this glad News, or Goſpel publiſhed by God to the World by writing, preaching, profeſſing, Suffering, &c. It hath pleaſed his Infinite Juſtice to plough[1] the World with Popery, a Religion [a baſtard Chriſtianity,] ſuited [as the Quakers is] to The Jeſ-
uits and
the Qua-
kers the
two great
Corrivals
abroad.
rotten

---

[1] " plague," not " plough." *R. W. Ms. Ann.*

rotten nature, and fit to carry the world after them as *Mahomet* and the *Pope* have done.

11. In this day the two greateſt wonders in the world [pretending to be Chriſts Meſſengers or Apoſtles to the Nations] are the Jeſuits and the Quakers: Their Faces look divers, but they both carry Firebrands in their Tails to burn up the holy Scripture, all truly holy Chriſtians, yet[1] all the world before them. Gods Infinite wiſdome hath Falſe Apoſtles figured by Abſolom. ſuffered them to be like *Abſolom* beautiful, and plauſible, and fit to play Soul Thieves and ſteal away the hearts of thouſands and ten thouſands from the true *David* the Lord Jeſus Chriſt.

Beſide, they are ſo fortified with the Faces of Men and hair of Women like the Locuſts, *Rev.* 9. The holy Scriptures the great Box both to Jeſuits and Quakers. ſuch pretences, ſuch Illuminations and Appearances, ſuch Aſſurances and Confidences, ſuch feelings of Experiences, that it is Gods Infinite Power and wiſdome, and goodneſs, to preſerve the holy Scripture a ſtanding Record of what the firſt Meſſengers and firſt Churches and firſt Doctrine and Chriſtians were: or elſe, the world would fall down and adore the Images which the Lord hath ſuffered the Devil in them to ſet up.

12. I know the Counſels *of the Father of Lights* are very deep, yea the Revelation needs a Revela- Great Converſion of Jews and Gentiles yet expected. tion, the *Prophecies* and *Canticles*, and *Daniel* need Heavenly Meſſengers, and the moſt holy Spirit or finger of God to untie ſuch knots: Sure it is that Millions [20] of Jews and Gentiles muſt yet enquire with tears of blood after the Blood of a

Saviour:

---

[1] "yea," not "yet." *R. W. Ms. Ann.*

Saviour: Sure they ſhall not awake out of their pits of Rottenneſs, without ſome means & Meſſengers ſent from Heaven to rouze and wak n them : Sure their ſhall be no other words in their Mouths then what were in the mouths of the firſt Meſſengers according to the Prayer of the Lord Jeſus on his Death bed to his Father, through whoſe Word all that have believed the report ever ſince have believed, *Ioh.* 17 and with which bleſſed word the Spirit of God will be in the mouths of all true Chriſtians, *Iſai.* 59. 20. &c. Surely the true Meſſengers of Jeſus will ſay no other word then what *Moſes* and the *Prophets* foretold and wrought, *Act.* 26. therefore *Fox* and his *Foxians* that tells us they have all by the Spirit and need no Record, are Thieves and Robbers, whom, *Moſes,* and the *Prophets,* and *Paul,* and the *Apoſtles* abhor'd to think of.

The true Apoſtles and Fox and his lying ones Compared

A 11. *Inſtance,* is in *Pag.* 40. where G. *Fox* brings in *I. Deacon,* ſaying [*The enjoyment of Immortulity is not till they have put off the Body.*]

I. Deacon.

He Anſwers, [Contrary to the Apoſtles Doctrine, who ſaith, *Immortality was brought to light through the Goſpel*: this was when they were upon the Earth, and the Word of God was in them which was Immortal.]

1. I Reply Firſt, G. *Fox* affirms an Immortality (that is a not dying of the Soul and Body) As for the Soul, all true Proteſtants affirm that the Soul once raiſed up to Spiritual Life never dyes, no more than Chriſt Jeſus, *Rom.* 6. as for the Body Papiſts and Proteſtants, and the Quakers and all the World grants, that *all Fleſh is as graſs,* &c. and the

The Quakers dream about not dying or Immortality.

Sentence

Sentence of Death, by ficknefs, Age or Cafualty is impartially executed upon the *Foxians* as well as other C ttel: As to the Soul, who of fober Papifts or Proteftants queftions the Immortality of it: and of the Body alfo, in joy or Sorrow to Eternity.

As for the Body the Quakers fay when the Soul is gone into God, yea, the Soul of *Iudas* as well as the Soul of *Peter* as fome of them fay, and all of them by Argument will be forced to fay, the Body returns to Earth and Rottennefs, never more to be raifed, and no more then Bodies of the Beafts, Birds and *Fi*fhes, (though we know who holds the Bodies of Beafts, Birds and Fifhes fhall live again as the Soul mortalifts do) what is it then [21] that G. *Fox* fputters out for Immortality, or a not dying in this Life? If he fpeak of the Soul who denies it? If of the Body he fpeaks a Beaftly Contradiction to the doleful Senfe of all mankind, and their own alfo, who die and rot as well as them.

2. It is true, 1 *Tim.* 6. *God only hath Immortality dwelling in the Light which no man can approach unto,* what ever thefe *Foxians* bruitifhly fancy of no dif- tinction between God and themfelves their Light and his. It is true, yet alfo that *Iefus Chrift,* 2 *Tim.* 1. *hath brought Life and Immortality to Light through the Gofpel.* But what is this but the joyful Condition of the Souls & Bodies of the godly? their Souls and Bodies raifed up with Jefus to a Spiritual holy Life in this World, their Souls going to Jefus, and their Bodies *fleeping in Iefus,* and the rifing of their Bodies and uniting to their Spirits in a Life Eternal?

The Doc-trine of Immortal-ity.

3. As

3. As to this *Immortality* of G. *Fox*: all that can be kuown of his mind is old H.*Nichols* and the *Ni-* A Charitable hope *colaitans* mad fictions and fancies of their becoming of fome God and Chrift. I hope charitably of many of Quakers. them, that run in their Simplicity, Ignorance and weaknefs with a true Love to the true Lord Jefus as fome did with *Abfalom*[1] who truly loved *David* but as for *Abfolom* himfelf the Polititians, the fubtle Plotters, and *Ahitophels* who love not the true Lord Jefus in fincerity, I fear inftead of their fancied Immortality before the Grave they will meet with a dreadful Mortality, or dearh of Soul and Body to Eternity.

A 12. Inftance is, *pag.* 47. where he brings in *Jofeph Miller*, faying, [*The wife heathen Philofophers* Jofeph *had a greater Meafure of Light in them* (which is Miller, the firft *Adam*) *then I can think any man hath now*]

G. *Fox* Anfw. which fhews, that he knows nothing of Chrift the *fecond Adam*, the quickning Spirit. He knows no New Creature, for who are *in Chrift are new Creatures*, nor none of Chrift the Covenant of God, of Light, of Life, of Peace, who was *glorified with the Father before the World began*, which is beyond the *firft Adam*, and hath fhut himfelf forth, not to be as high as his heathen Philofophers. And many witnefs Chrift in them in this Age, as in the dayes of the Apoftles, which is above the heathen Philofophers.]

I Reply, 1. I know it pleafed God (in all Ages) The Anto ftir up the Spirits of fome Men (as the Philofo- cient Phiphers amongft the Greeks [22] *Socrates, Plato,* lofophers *Ariftotle,* Confidered.

[1] Put " as fome did with Abfolom," in parenthefis. *R. W. Ms. Ann.*

Ariſtotle) to improve that excellent Light of Reaſon which he had given them as Men, and in ſo
great a meaſure above other men.

2. This wily Fo*x* he runs to his hole and Confounds this Common Light of Reaſon, with Chriſt
and God himſelf, who alſo are called Light by Simi-
lies from the Creature.

3. The Queſtion then follows : If this Light of
Knowledge were Chriſt, as God, and King, and
Mediatour : why is it that none of theſe excellent
Men knew nothing of God, nor Chriſt, nor Spirit,

The mad
neſs of
George
Fox his
Fancy
about
them. (Name nor Thing) but only of the firſt Creation :
Can ſuch a Court be kept, a Palace furniſhed, and
ſuch Royal and heavenly Gueſts be entertaind, and
no Body know any thing of it, nor themſelves neither;
when Chriſt Jeſus came into *Jeruſalem* (though but
in a poor Contemptible way) all I*oruſalem* was moved
at his coming : and ſhall this moſt glorious King (now
Infininitely more glorious) make his Ingreſs into the
Souls of ſuch wiſe and Excellent Men, and neither
they, nor others hear of it until juſt now, (twenty
years ſince) Some cheated Souls dream of it.

4. The utmoſt of Reaſon in theſe Excellent
Men, it is known I ſay, that the Activity of the
higheſt Reaſon in this World falls ſhort in two

The fail-
ing of the
higheſt
Reaſon in
this world
in many,
eſpecially
in two
particulars grand particulars.

1. As to the Creatures : For ſome of them muſt
needs fall ſhort, when *Plato* granted a Creation,
and a kind of *Father, Son* and *Holy Spirit* in the
Creation of it, *Ariſtotle* pretends to ſee further then
his Mr. *Plato* and all his Arguments. and aſſerts the
World to have no Beginning, nor Ending, *&c.*

Some

Some of them maintaind the Soul of man to be procreated by the Parents : others (as the Quakers) that it was part of the *Divine Essence*, others that it is created and infused by God, *&c*. Some that the *Center* of the World is the Terreftrial Globe, and that the Sun and heavenly Bodies move about it, others, that the Ceuter of the world is the *Sun*, and that this *Terreftrial Globe* moves about the Sun, and many other such, natural Myfteries. The drep knowledge of fome.

2. However that *Paul* tells us *Rom*, 1. That by the *Creation* fome come to know there is an *Eternal Power and Godhead*, yet 1 *Cor*. 1. he tells us *that the World by wifdome knew not God*, which muft be expounded (or elfe fwallow a Contradiction as the Quakers guife is) *viz*. that by the highth of their wifdome [23] they could not fee God fo as to make him alone their *Summum bonum* and *Bleffednefs*, fo *as to glorify him as God*: So, as the holy Scriptures and the moft holy Son of God from his Bofome hath revealed him, fo that in the highth of Reafons Reafonings the Spirit of God concludes, that the *natural man* can not reach or *perceive the things of God*, (and yet this foolifh Man makes every mans heart in the World the Court of Heaven) a thing which every Kingdom and all men may abhor to think of, but men are vain in all their Reafonings, and *their foolifh heart is darkned*, yea, *their wifdome is Enmity, hating God himfelf*, as the Scripture concludes, *&c*. The greater depth of the Creator himfelf, the Trinity, the Fall, Redemption Incarnation, Refurrection, &c.

It is true: We re read of *Noah Ark*, of *Mofes* his Tabernacle, *Solomon* his Temple, and we fee many *glorious Fabricks* and Works of the Sons of

men

The Ex-
cellent
Gifts of
Nature
reach not
heavenly
and Spi-
ritual
things Spi-
ritually. men in this world, which argue excellent Gifts of
God to them, both of *wifdome*, *Prudence*, *Fortitude*,
Patience, *Temperance*, &c. but do they all amount
in the Total to more then *Natural parts*, *good Education*, and *Induftrious diligence* can reach too? What
are all thefe to the enlightning of my Soul, with
my natural undone and damned Condition? to a
fight of Sin as Sin? to a fight of my utter Inability
to pay (or all the whole Creation for me) one farthing to Gods Juftice, or to work my defire to have
any thing to do with him? What are thefe to the
changing of, and a total turning of my whole Soul
unto God? to an humble fight of my Infinite neceffity of the alone Sufficiciency and Excellency of
the Lcrd Jefus the great and only Mediatour, and
of my becoming one with him in *Loves Eternal*?

Befide, what a fingle[1] Confequence doth this
high *Illuminiated Doctor* give to his Oppofite, viz.
that becaufe I magnify the Gifts of God to many
(yea, thoufands of Excellent Men whom *I*, nor *G.
Fox* are worthy to hold the Candle to) therefore I
fhut my felf out from Chrift and thofe wife men
too: It may be his Oppofite had fomewhat more
in his Affertion, but this is all this high wife man
in his own eyes prints and Anwfers to:

Who knows not how full the World is of admirable Men and Women that are not Chriftians? And
yet what a bafe efteem hath this proud Spirit of
all men, yea of all Chriftians too that dance not
after his foolifh pipe, &c.

A 13th. *Inftance*, I mention (though Inftances
are

---

[1] "Simple" not "fingle."   *R. W. Ms. Ann.*

are as Leprofie fpread over his whole Book) is in
pag. 48. where he brings in the [24] fame *Jofeph* Jofeph
Miller faying, [*The Prophets are more certain then any* Miller
other Revelation.] He Anfwers, [*was not the Son of*
God revealed, the end of the Prophets? Did not God re-
veal him which came in the Volume of the Book to
do the will of God? *And fo the Prophets, and the*
Law, and Types, and fhadows, which they that had the
Law, and Types, and fhadows, knew not the Son of
God that was revealed, that was their End fpoken of
in the Prophets, end Epiftles, who is now revealed.

I Reply, G. *Fox* (to pafs by his un-Englifh Nonfence obvious to any that underftand publick writings) I fay G. *Fox* either ignorantly or willingly The Pro-
knows not that the Queftion is not here, whether phets wit-
Chrift be the End of the Law and the Prophets, in nefs of
a true fenfe: or whether Chrift was not more re- Chrift
vealed at his coming in the Flefh, then before in ftronger
the Prophecies, &c. But, whether the written then the
word of the Prophets, of which *Peter* fpeaks and I Apoftles,
have fpoke before be not a more fure word of Com- Speeches:
mand and Comfort to us then any now to be ex- were
pected, yea, then that Revelation which we have
upon that holy Teftimony of *Peter* and *Iohn* themfelves?

As it is with an Anchor ftrong enough to ride a
Ship in moft weathers, yet fome are as the Seamen
fpake *fecond* and *third Bowers*, and one the beft and Bebaiote-
Sheet Anchor: and as it is in Witneffes fome fpeak ron Iogon
the Truth and Subftance of the matter: and yet a more
others fpeak more plainly and fully, &c. So Word.
speaks Gods Spirit in *Peter* of the Infinite Fulnefs
of

of the Prophecies of Scriptures, or the written foretellings and utterings concerning Jesus Christ.

The Word of God Confidered.

Thus the God of Heaven most holy and only wise stoops to our weakness, and calls his mind his word, his works his word, his Providences of mercy or Judgement, his Word, the Lord Jesus his only begotten his word, his writings his Word; and this in a way of Condescention to our Capacity, seeing that all the World over Kings and Rulers, Fathers, Masters of Families, of Ships, &c. give the word, that is the manifestation of their mind and

The Sripture or written Testimonie.

will, and this as the Spring in Clocks and watches turn about all other wheels and motions. Hence it is, that if ancient Records and Deeds with Hands and Seals be produced at the *Bar* of *Trial*, all mouths are stopt at such Evidences. Thus the

Much more their feigned Spirit of Prophecy the Quakers prate of

Word of God in the mouths of the Prophets written for after Generations, is (Comparatively) beyond the Report of *Peter* |25| and *John* themselves is in all Religions.[1] The *Iews* have their *Talmud*, the *Turks* their *Alcheron*, the *Pope* his *Decretans*, and the *Protestants* the *Written Word*, or *Scriptures*.

The Quakers Sandy Quicksauds

When therefore a *Pardon* is written and Sealed with the Broad Seal of a King or State, what a fancy is it for a condemned Wretch to hearken first to a Pardon revealed within : to a voice within, to a King within, to a Writing within, a Seal within, and so slighting the true pardon in the Kings way to be conveyed from without to the Mind and Spirit within, to lose his Pardon and Deliverance as thousands of such poor cheated Souls must do.

A 14.

[1] Erase " is in all Religions." *R. W. Ms. Ann.*

A 14 *Inftance* G *Fox* brings in *Pag.* 49. his Op- P. 47.
pofite *Ralph Hall* faying [*It is againft the Light of* ^{Preaching} of Wo-
Nature for Women to Preach: &c. ^{men Ralph} Hall

G. *Fox Anfwers* Contrary to the Apoftles Doctrine and the mind of God and the Prophets, who
faid, *God would pour out of his Spirit upon all Flefh,*
and his Sons and Daughters fhould Prophefie : So that
he is a limiter of the Holy one, a quencher of the
Spirit, and in the Darknefs, and this is above the
Light of Nature.

I Reply, Firft, What is the Light of Nature, but
that Light in which every man comes into the The light
World with (as the *Foxians* fpeak) a Light differing of Nature
from that Light which Beafts, wilde and tame, and difcuffed
Birds, and Fifhes have *:* And[1] a Second Light differing from what is [2]Supernatural, as that Light revealed from Heaven in the Holy Scriptures, and
infufed into the Souls of Men by the Holy Spirit
or Power of God.

2. What is the Light of Nature in Man, but
that Order which the moft Glorious Former of all
things hath fet (like Wheeles in Clocks or Watches)
a going in all his Creatures?

Some have obferved that in the Infenfible Crea-
tures to which the moft High hath only giving Male and
Beings, that there may be obferved a Male and Female
Female amongft them.

This is more obfervable in Vegetables or growing Creatures, as in Plants, Trees, Herbs, Flowers, &c.

More

[1] Infert " there is." *R. W. Ms. Ann.*
[2] Erafe " Super.*' *R. W. Ms. Ann.*

More yet in Senſitives, as Birds, Beaſts, Fiſhes.

Moſt of all in Rationals: Men and Women, whom the moſt High hath ſo wonderfully diſtinguiſhed.

It is true, that in Religious and Chriſtian Matters, there is no [26] reſpect of perſons with God, as of Man before the Woman: otherwiſe than to order Natural and Civil.

Men and Women compared

The Woman is Predeſtinated, is Called, is Juſtified, is Glorified, and wears that Golden Chain as well as the Wiſeſt and Strongeſt of Mankinde.

And it is true, the Wiſdome of God perfers ſome Women before thouſands of Men, in their being born of Nobles, in excellent parts (as is obſervable in the Lady *Iane*, and Queen *Elizabeth*, &c.) in ſome ſpecial favour, as Chriſt Jeſus firſt appearing to *Mary Magdalen* and other Women, and ſending them to carry the firſt Tydings or Goſpel of his Reſurrection to his Apoſtles: yea, in effuſions or powrings forth of an extraordinary meaſure of his Spirit before Chriſts coming, as on *Miriam, Deborah, Anna, Huldah,* &c. and at his coming (according to *Ioels* Prophesie) on his Daughters as well as his Sons (ſo that as my oppoſites alledged to me in publick: *Philip* the *Evangeliſt* had four Daughters thus extraordinarily endcwed) yet this favour of God toward Women deſtroys not the order which the God of Order or Nature hath ſet in thoſe Bounds, and Limits, and Diſtinctions between the Male and Female, the Man and Woman: though the Holy Scripture were ſilent, yet Reaſon and Experience tell us, that the Woman is the weaker Veſſel,

The kindneſs of God to women

Veſſel, that ſhe is more fitted to keep and order the House and Children, &c. that the Lord hath given a covering of longer Hair to Women as a ſign or teacher of covering Modeſty and Baſhfulneſs, Silence and Retiredneſs : and therefore not ſo fitted for Manly Actions and Employments. ^{Womens unfitneſs for manly employments}

Therefore becauſe of *Ioels* Propheſie, or becauſe we muſt not limit or quench the Spirit, as G. *Fox* ſaith, there is no ground in Gods ordinary courſe of Nature to permit Women to pretend to be Apoſtles or Meſſengers to the Nation, or Preachers and Teachers in the Publick Aſſemblies.

1. Becauſe we finde no ſuch Commiſſion given by Chriſt Jeſus or any ſuch Practice amongſt the firſt Believers.

2. The Lord hath ſet (as Seamen ſpeak) a preventer to ſuch an unnatural boldneſs by expreſs Prohibitions, with the Reaſons and Grounds to the *Corinthians* and to *Timothy* : and to anſwer thoſe Scriptures with a flam, *viz.* that *Eve* the Tranſgreſſor, and Women that be Tatlers are forbidden, and the Woman *Jezebel*, [27] &c. is all one to tell us, that *Paul* was not a Man, nor *Timothy* a Man, nor the Teachers Men, nor *Corinth* a City, but all ſignifie Metaphorical and Myſtical Buſineſſes. ^{And for being Preachers and poſtles eſpecially.}

3. Why may not Women much more be *Lord Majors*, and *Bailiffs*, and *Sherriffs*, and *Iuſtices*, and *Conſtables*, *Captains*, *Colonels*, *Generals* and *Commanders* by Sea and Land.[1]

4. That Reaſon the Spirit gives to the *Corinthians*, for the vailing of Women in publick Aſſemblies,

[1] Change the period to " ?." *R. W. Ms. Ann.*

blies, makes much more for their vailing and filence in matters of *Prophefying*, *Preaching* and *Praying*, viz. Becaufe of the Angels : I know not any fair and fober Expofition of this Scripture (except as the blind *Quakers* who fwallow down a fly & Camel too) but that of the Heavenly Angels and Spirits attending on and guarding the Affemblies of true Chriftians, and rejoycing in the comlinefs, order and beauty of their publick Adminiftrations.

Some few years fince there came to my Houfe two *Maries*, it is faid they came from *London* : they bid me Repent and Hearken to the Light within me, I prayd them o fit down, that we might quietly reafon together, they would not ; then ftanding, I askt them the ground of their fuch Travel and Employment, they alledged *Ioels Prophefie* ; I anfwered, that was fulfilled, that was not every dayes work ; befides their bufinefs was not Prophetical but Apoftolical, &c. they regarded not my Anfwers nor Admonitions, but powred the Curfes and Judgements of God againft me, and hurried away ; to *Barbadoes* they went, and (being War time, the Ship bound for *England*) they were fet upon by the *Dutch*, and though thefe Women animated the Seamen to fight, and Prophefied *that not an hair of their head fhould perifh*, yet they two were both flain, as afterward came certain Tydings of the whole matter.

I own that it may pleafe the Father of Spirits in cafes extraordinary, he may pleafe to alter his common courfe of Na u e (as in *Abrahams* cafe with *Ifaak*) but we muft not tempt God ; but if God

hath

Marginal notes:

A memorable and doleful ftory

What teaching the Lord requirs of Women

hath powred forth the gifts of Knowledge and Utterance npon fome Women more then other, they
have three large fields to walk in mentioned by the
Holy Scripture, *viz.* of their inftructing their Children, &c. 2. As occafion juftly calls them from
home, of inftructing other women efpecially the
younger. 3. Of confeffing boldly the Name and
Truth of Chrift Jefus, [28] when he fuffers Tyrants to bring Perfecution on them, &c.

 A 15*th. Inftance is in pag.* 56. where *George Fox* Tho. Hig-
brings in *Thomas Higinfon,* faying, [*The fight of the* ginfon
*Godhead without Faith in Chrift is the Foundation of
all falfe worfhips.*]

He *Anfwers,* Can any fee the Godhead? have a
fiht of the Godhead and uot fee Chrift, and have
Faith in Chrift? And who hath Faith in Chrift,
do they not fee *the Fulnefs of the Godhead dwels in
him, Chrift*? And was not their mind turneh from
that of God in them (which declared *the Invifible
things of him from the Creation of his Eternal Power
and Godhead*) which the Apoftle found fault withal
Let all Examine and Judge, and read the Scripture, *Rom.* 1. and try.]

 I Reply, In former years I have Converfed The
with all the *Indians* of this *New-England* by Land knowledge
and Seas, and I have read the 1. of the *Romans* of God by
often, and now once again at G: *Fox* his motion, nature
and I find that Firft, there is generally in all mankind in the World a Conviction of an *Invifible,
Omnipotent, and Eternal Power and Godhead.*

 2. That this Conviction doth arife from the Creation, (though fome of the wifeft of the World as
         Ariftotle,

Ariſtotle, &c. though Confeſſing a Godhead yet)
hold the world an Eternal Deity it ſelf, and never
to have been created.

3. I find not that ever any man or men (by all
their natural Light or wit, or Chriſt within,) could
find out how the World or himſelf, Man or Woman were created : Though *Iames Nailour* told us
in print, that if never a Letter of Scriptnre had
been written, yet their Spirit could tell them all
things.

The con-
victions of
nature
which the
4 Quakers
ſo fooliſh-
ly talk of

4. I find all men confeſs, that the will or Word,
or mind of God is pure, and as they could come to
know, it is to be adored, kept, and obſerved : and
that it was ever, and is wickedneſs to Sin againſt it.

5. All mankind having the Law or without it
are perſwaded that ſome actions are naught, and
againſt Gods will, as to ſteal, to Murther, &c.

6. None (for all the Light and Spirit in every
one) could ever find out how Sin how Sorrow and
Death came into the World: Nor how ſuch Incli-
nations and Diſpoſitions to Sin came into themſelves, &c.

7. I find in all mankind a Conviction that God
is juſt and [29] powerful, and doth bring plagues
and puniſhments upon perſons, and Nations for
thoſe groſs Sins of Adultery, Murther, &c.

8. I could never lea n (for all that Chriſt in every
man *Fox* ſings of) that ever any man living, or all
the Counſels of men could ever know or learn four
things, but as revealed by God, by *extraordinary*
wayes, of *Dreams*, *Viſions*, &c. or the ordinary of
his *holy Records*, and the *Doctrine* of them opened,
preached,

The loſs
of all men
as to God
& hraven-
ly things *preached*, &c. 1. How to pacifie Gods Juſtice? 2. How to reſiſt the *Devils Tyranny*: 3. How to wor-ſhip God? 4. How to get *true Bleſſedneſs* here, and in the World to come?

9. Hence (according to *Foxes Oppoſite*) all man-kind have invented ſo many falſe Gods, falſe worſhips, &c. all the world over, yet out of no moreLove to God then the Lamb bears to a Lyon: but out of Fear, as the old ſaying is, *primos in Orbe Deos*, &c. Fear made the firſt Gods. Hence the *Philiſtins* ſends the God of *Iſrael* a preſent and offering with Ark or Cheſt: Hence the *Samaritans* (with the *Sechemites*) for fear of Lyons or hope of gain will be of any worſhip or Religion, as moſt this day in the world will be, yea, all and every Soul except to whom (in and from the holy Scriptures) the holy Spirit reveals that Incomprehenſible Myſtery of a Mediatour.

Men natu-rally frame a God as the Devils do but cannot love him.

A 16*th. Inſtance* of *Foxes* lame writings, is *pag.* 56. where he brings in the ſame Author ſaying, [*The Iuſtification and Redemption by obeying the Light within, is the Myſtery of Iniquity*]

He Anſwers, [*He that believeth is juſtified from all things, and comes not into Condemnation: and he hath the wietnſs in himſelf: and that lets him ſee the Re-deemer, the Saviour, the Light which walking in it he is cleanſed from all Sin, and ſo no Myſtery of Iniquity For the Myſtery of Iniquity is out of the Light. None ſees Iuſtification and Redemption, but with the Light within which comes from Chriſt who hath enlightened him.*]

I Reply,

I Reply, This is fubtle, but being examined it will be a myftery of *hellifh Iniquity*, and lighter then vanity it felf.

Babilonian Jugling, & Egyptian canting

For 1. He ufually, and here (as before I have opened) confounds Juftification and Light, and Chrift, and Faith, and obedience, (after his *Babylonifh wont*) all in a Juglers box within together: So that the Englifh of Faith is Chrift, Obedience is Chrift, Juftification is Chrift, Light is Chrift, &c. It is true, fometimes it pleafed Gods Spirit to fpeak figuratively, and to [30] call Chrift fometimes our Juftification, and fometimes a Curfe for

Chrifts Name horribly prophaned

us: Sometimes Sanctification, and fometimes Sin for us: But it is a myftery or fubtle trick of Hell to call Faith Obedience, and Obedience to the Light Juftification and Redemption, and yet mean Chrift. So that *Fox* his words may be in plain Englifh thus rendred, [*None fees Chrift and Chrift but with the Chrift within, which comes from Chrift who hath Chrifted him.*]

The true Senfe, (as Mony) Anfwers all things, but it is a *Myftery of Iniquity* to darken any, much more heavenly matters with Confounding and not diftingu fhing aright when matters are in Examination.

2. It is another Gofpel (or glad News) yet not another, but is a dream and dead picture of an Image or Idol to put in our Obedience and working, though I know they Father this Baftard upon the moft holy God himfelf, faying, it is his Obedience, his Righteoufnefs,& his working,in the Room of the Death and blood fhedding, the Sufferings and merits of the Lord Jefus. 3. It

3. It is a *Myſtery of Iniquity*. (ſubtly and yet churliſhly and ſelfiſhly with *Laban*) to change wages and the Covenant or Bargain ſo often : to pretend (with the Papiſts) great abhorring of the *Jewiſh worſhip* and *Jewiſh Covenant*, the Bargain of, *Do this and live*, the Bargain of ſaving our ſelves, *&c.* and the Bargain of flying out of our ſelves and only to Gods mercy in the Mediation of Chriſt Jeſus : And then again to render our ſelves to be ſo holy, ſo righteous, ſo obedient, ſo loving, ſo Chaſt, ſo meek, ſo patient, ſo Temperate, that in thought word or deed we Sin not, and this our Holineſs is Chriſt, and God, and Spirit, and Juſtification, *&c.*

The Old and new Bargain to Love.

The great Deluſion of Quakers as to pardon of Sin and Righteouſneſs.

I know the writers of the Quakers make this high Obedience to be the Crown of ſome high Saints amongſt them as the Papiſts do, and that others come not ſo high, are taken by the fleſhly Spirit, and repent, and Confeſs, and be more watchful as they ſay, in a Contradiction of *I. Naylor*, but this is Contradiction to their general grant, *viz* that every Saint, every one, even the leaſt *that is born again, he can not Sin*: and I know alſo that they have a fooliſh Salve or plaiſter for this ſore too, and Contradict their denying of meanings given to the Scripture, and come to the meanings of the Proteſtants ſaying, they cannot Sin willingly, and ſo, and ſo; And yet again, (in a horrible Myſtery of 31] Iniquity) they exclaim againſt the Proteſtants for ſaying, a Child of God can not fall from true grace Finally or Totally.

The Quakers bewildred as to Perfection.

4. Here is a *Myſtery of hellyſh Iniquity*, in that

they

The Quakerr devilish Chimiftry

they Confefs fuch a man Chrift to have been, and his blood fhedding[1] the Types and real predictions and figures of him, a real Death, Refurrection and Affention, and yet upon the point (by a *Devilifh Chymiftry*) evaporate all thefe, and leave nothing but a Chrift within, as God and as Man, whofe Name is now Light, and our Obedience to the motions of this Light within this is Juftification, Righteoufnefs, Salvation, God, Chrift, Perfection, *perfect holinefs*, &c.

The feined hardnefs, but the real eafinefs of the Quakers Spirit.

The wonderful Harpficon

The vain dreams of the Quakers and their fools Paradice.

5. It is a *Hellifh Myftery* of the *Devil* to Cozen poor Souls with a Notion of the Difficulty and height of their Profeffion, and of worfhipping God in Spirit and Truth, which they fay no Body in the World do but they, *&c.* and yet the Truth is as I told them in publick, there is an Image in the Bed, but *David* was gone, yea, and that their Religion was one of the eafieft Religions in the world. For, as I have feen pluck but forth a fmall pin or peg in a *Harpfycon*, and that wonderful Inftrument will delight your Ear and mind with curious and various Tunes of Mufick: So if once a poor Soul gives way an Inch, and fets in one thought ot yielding to the voice of a Spirit within them, they are filled and ravifhed with curious Notions ot Juftification, Holinefs, God and Chrift, and Spirit within them, they can now *Thou* the King himfelf, they need no Scriptures, nor Teachers: and thus as in a dream their great Debts of Thoufands and Millions are paid and difcharged. The Cage door flies open, and they are delivered as a Bird, *&c.*

from

[1] Infert "according to." *R. W. Ms. Ann.*

from Sin and Devil, and Hell, &c. yea, Rapt up into
Paradice, and fee, and hear, and fpeak *unutterable
Ioyes*, &c. I Confefs as I faid in the Cafe of the
two hundred following *Abfolom*, I hope there is many
a precious Soul fincerely aiming at God, and as
precious Diamonds and Jewels fallen in the dirt,
&c. As I hope in the Parifhes of Proteftants and
Papifts alfo, who being only ignorant as the Difciples were of main points of Chriftianity, yet aim
uprightly at God, truly love him, and labour to *increafe in the knowledge and grace of Chrift Iefus.*

A 17th. *Inft.* is in *ag.* 63. where *G. Fox* brings in
his Adverfary *Ieremiah Ives* faying, [*There may be a
Light to Convince of Sin, and yet not within man.*] He
Anfwers, there is no people [32] Convinced of Sin,
but they are Convinced within themfelves and with
the Light within them : It is the Light which
makes manifeft to a man when he is Convinced :
It Anfwers to fomething, and reacheth to fomething in their particulars, though the words be
fpoken without them from the Light.

Jeremiah Ives

I Reply, *Firft*, it is a doleful Bufinefs to read and
hear how *Satan* (in his *Chains of Darknefs*) yet hath
Liberty to appear abroad as *an Angel of Light* from
Heaven, thus vapouring and fwaggering under the
Cloak and Colours of Light, the Light which is
Chrift, *the Light by which all things were made, the
Light that was glorified with the Father before the
World was, the Light that enlightens every man that
comes into the World: the Light within you*, &c. the
Light which will *guide* you up to *God*, up to *Chrift*,
up to *Salvation* and *Eternal Life*, and yet all this

The Devil
in Samu-
els Mantle

An Angel
of Light
but a Dra-
gon and
Devil of
darknefs.

vapourings

vapourings and Crakings are but Cheatings from *the God of this World* whofe eyes being beat out by Gods moft righteous Sentence, he labours to keep all in *blindnefs*, or to beat out the eyes of thofe whom God hath truly enlightned.

2. As I have faid before, and I faid truly, the word *Light* is a *Similitude* from *Light* and *darknefs* though my Oppofites in the difpute affirmed, that God was Light in a *proper* and not *figurative Senfe*, and it fignifies and intends Truth of all Sorts, whe-ther *Natural*, *Moral* or *Heavenly*: The natural Truth or Light is received within by a natural Light or underftandings: The Civil and moral Light or Truth fuits and agrees with thofe moral and Civil Convictions of the natural Light and underftanding? Hither to Natures Light will reach. But when we mount up to Divine and *Supernatural Truth*, here thefe very *Foxians* Confefs that *the Natural Man perceiveth not the things of God*: Only they fay, that befide Natural Light, Natural Reafon, *&c.* there is the holy Seed God and Chrift, *&c.* within every Son, and to this Spirit and Seed in Prifon they preach, and *Fox* in our difcourfes al-leadgeth and affirmeth God (in every man) to be a *Cart loaden with fheaves*, preft under, and as it were in Prifon, *&c.* blafphemous wretches if they keep not, but go beyond *Similitudes* and *Comparative Expreffions*[1] to make ns poor worms creep up to Heaven.

3. All *Light*, or *Truth Natural*, *Civil*, or *Divine* it comes from without, and is received by the *Internal*

Truth and Light the fame thing.

ternal

---

[1] Infert "ufed by yᵉ Lord." *R. W. Ms. Ann.*

ternal Faculty according [33] to the *Capacity, Na-* The way of Truth *ture* and *meafure* of it. All Truth or falfhood, or Lights Light or darknefs is firft efpied by the *watch* or goings. *Sentinel, Fancy* or *Comprehenfion,* &c. From thence it is conveyed to the *Court* of *Guard,* where Captain Reafon or his Lieutenant, common Senfe and Experience taketh Examination, and Memory keeps a Record of proceedings which go on by degreen to Actions, &c.

4. When I fay it comes from *without,* I intend not that Truth or Light comes any other way from Where no *without,* as by force and ravifhment, &c. I fay any[1] Receiver no Thief. other way then there is a door & Room and Receptive Faculty within willing to receive, and to make it welcome : This G. *Fox* urgeth there muft be a receiver, and fomething that Anfwers. I *Anfwer,* Natural Truth, or morals, Civil matters are foon received by all Natural and Moral Under- Natural ftandings, yea, in natural Commands and Threat- Understanding in nings, Beafts and Birds are admirably capacious and ftanding in obfervant. But when we fpeak of *Supernatural* Men and Beafts. *Heavenly* and *Eternal matters,* of *Spiritual things* to be difcerned *Spiritually* : What a difference is there as between *Heaven* and *Earth,* and Infinitely greater?

When the *Lord Jefus* asked his Difciples *how many loavs they had,* their *Natural Faculty* or *Reafon* An Infance of a could give an Anfwer : When he asked them *whom* ftance of a *do Men fay that I the Son of man am ?* This was a meerly Rational *Divine* and *Supernatural Queftion,* and for the outfide and an and Truth of the Fact, the Devils could Anfwer as heavenly well as the Difciples, not ouly that fame faid he, Power and Faculty. *was*

[1] Change " any " to " no." *R. W. Ms. Ann.*

was Elias, John Baptift, &c. but that he was the
Son of God : All this exceeds not Natural firft
Birth Powers or Faculties : But to give a believing
and an affectionate Anfwer as *Peter* did, this re-
quires a *Faculty* and *Power* which *Flefh* and *Blood*
could not reach too,[1] but the Spirit or fecret working
Power of God in the means wrought *Peters heart*
and the *Difciples hearts*, and to this day all *Believers
Hearts* to receive and welcome all truly Divine and
Heavenly Doctrines.

Whereas therefote G. *Fox* talks of fomething
within which is preached to : I may Anfwer as they
do, *viz.* that the natural man perceivs no fpiritual
matter, but when he is born again then he acts and
works, and it is moft certain, that as an Houfe re-
ceivs his Mafter, as Candle kiffeth Candle, the
Clafp the Hook, the mortife the Tenant, fo do
Natural or Spiritual Faculties receive *Natural* [34
or *Spiritual Faculties* receive *Natural* or *Supernatural Motions* and *Impreffions*.

The Proteftants fay, that before it pleafeth God
by fome word read, preached, &c. to fet up a Candle of wifdome in the Souls, and to work a fpiritual
favour in the Soul, all heavenly matters are nau-
feous and odious, though as pleafant, profitable and
honourable, to felf Ends they are welcome all the
word over, yet as fpiritual and heavenly abominable?

G. *Fox* faith there is a fomething, a Seed, though
but as *a Grain of muftard Seed*, a *Seed of God*, of
Chrift, of the *Spirit*, to which Chrift the Word is
preached, and which maketh Anfwer : Hence (horribly

A clofe Compan-ion be-tween all Faculties and Objects.

Nothing truly Spi-ritual in Nature as now de-generate.

[1] Change "too" to "to."   *R. W. Ms. Ann.*

ribly abufing *Scripture phrazes*) they fo often fay God is all (within and without:) Hence they maintain, *&c.* though men be dark and dead, yet Chrift within is Light and alive in them, and them only.

Hence appears *G. Fox* his lying Cheats of a *Sufficient Light* withiu to lead to God and to Salvation, a Teacher within all Sufficient, for then no need, yea, it is a fimple Superfluity, *&c.* to hold a Candle of outword words to awaken and enlighten fuch a glorious all-Sufficient Sun within.

5. I ask where this fomething, this fomething of God, (yea, God and Chrift and Spirit [1]) If he Anf- About the wer, in the underftanding he grants it, that[2] is dark, light fhin- and perceives no heavenly matters, *&c.* If in the ing in darknefs. Heart and Affections he Confeffeth, all there, is hard and dead : only he faith, *the Light fhineth in the darknefs*, &c. Implying that in the dark underftanding there is fome heavenly Light: in the hearts hardnefs there is fome foftnefs, and *the Light fhineth in darknefs*, &c.

I Anfwer, *Chrift Jefus tke Sun of Righteoufnefs* arofe with *faving Rayes* or *wings* of *Salvation*, but the *blind Jews* could not own him for the *Expected Meffiah*, what is this G. *Fox* his fomething? a Light of Chrift *inlightning every man that comes into the World*, though the man fee it not.

2. What is this to all the Generations of the World about *four thoufand* years before Chrift came, and was in that *vifible perfon* as *John* faith of him, *that lightens every man that comes*, &c. what is this

to

[1] Add " is " after " Spirit." *R. W. Ms. Ann.*
[2] Infert " it." *R. W. Ms. Ann.*

to a mixture of Light and darkneſs in the ſame
faculty, the eye blind and yet ſeeing, the man dead
and yet alive ? It is trne the *Lambs wife* confeſſeth
that *her Hear t was awae* [35] *while ſhe ſlept.* But
what is this to the heart being dead and no Life
at all and yet waking ?

6. The Concluſion is (as before I hinted) and
they Confeſs, when God in his own Means ordinarily works the will to hear, to turn, to believe, to
pray, he then gracioully works the work for us,
and being thus turned with *Ephraim,* we mourn and
lament, and ſay, *what have we done* ? when he turns
our wilderneſs (wholly a wilderneſs) into a Garden,
then we bring forth his ſweet Fruits, Flowers and
Spices : when he turns the Wolf into a Lamb, then
we are meek and Innocent, and patient : but to
talk of preaching to the Spirits in Priſon, yea, of
the Seed of God and the Spirit of God in priſon,
when the Lord ſpeaks of his warning and moving
men by *Noahs* preaching in the *old World,* as may
be evidently evinced,) is like the prophane teaching of *Parrots* to prate of Grace and Heaven, like
that *admirable Parrot* in *France,* who could ſay her
Pater noſter, her *Creed,* and *Ten Commandments,*
and yet knew as much of grace and the workings
of God in the Soul, as her *Popiſh Teachers,* &c.

An 1*8th. Inſtance* of *G. Fox,* his lame and cheating Anſwers is in *pag.* 64. where he brings in the
ſame Author *Jeremiah Jves* ſaying, [*It is a known
Error to ſay, that a man was in Hell and in Heaven.*]
He Anſwers, who in this ſhews his Ignorance of
Scripture, for it gives Teſtimony of men that did
witneſs

Gods grr-
cious
workings
with and
in the
Souls of
men.

A wonder-
ful Par-
rots
Religion.

Jeremiah
Ives

witnefs that they had been in Hell, in the *Nether-most Hell*, and witneffed again they were in *Heaven*, and *fate in heavenly places in Chrift Jefus*, and fuch were in *Heaven*, as is fpoken of in the Revelations.

I Reply, G. *Fox* and millions more talk of *Heaven* and *Hell* as the *Notable Parrot* (above faid)[1] our *Fore-Fathers*, & fome from the Scrip-ture, and fome out of *Reafons Light* talkt of places of *Ioy Eternal* for the *Righteous*, and of *mifery Eternal* for the *bad* and *wicked*. But the new Light from Chrift Jefus and his pen-men is the cleareft that ever fhined in this world, efpecially, that fa-mous Parable or Word proceeding out of the mouth of Chrift Jefus, *Luke* 16. that of *Dives* and *Lazarus* declaring (in fubftance) the ftate of the Life, to Come, and of the two great Parties of the poor afflicted Righteous, and the wicked living in pleafures, &c. *Heaven and Hel to come.*

G. *Fox* is in his *Burrough* of the various fignifica-tion of the words *Heaven* and *Hell*: He knows that a ftate of Sorrow and [36] Bitternefs is called *Hell*. That a ftate of *Death* and the *grave* is fet out by the word *Hell* in the fame *Hebrew phrafe*: And to either of thefe he wickedly applies the *thirft*[2] State, of which the Lord Jefus 1. fo clearly fpeaks : *viz.* The State of the ungodly after this Life, in the Life and World to come. *Fox his Hell and Heaven.*

2, Again, he knows the vifible State of the true Profeffion of Chrift Jefus is called *Heaven*.

3. Such as have Intereft in Chrift Jefus have fit-ten

[1] Infert " fo did." *R. W. Ms. Ann.*
[2] Erafe " thirft." *R. W. Ms. Ann.*

ten down with him in thofe *Heavenly Manfions* and *glories* into which he is entred bodily and gone to prepare for their Reception and coming.

4. The *third Heaven* (the place of *Pauls Rapture* and *Vifion*) the place of Joy, and Bleffednefs and Glory, when thefe *Heavens* and *Earth* are burnt up and confumed.

It is like G. *Fox* hath been occafioned to thefe thoughts by the *Papifts Fables* about *Heaven* and *Hell,* and *Purgatory,* and their curious Queftions as whether the Torment of Hell be as real and terrible as this *Elementary* and *Kitching Fire* : Whether the pain of Hell tranfcend not all pains of *Childbirth, Stone, gout, Collick, Burning* ? &c. Whether it be poffible for a Creature to Continue in fuch Torments perpetually without Intermiffiion ? Whether there fhall not be fome end after fome millions of years as well as of the pains of *Purgatory* : G. *Fox* knows how the *Papifts* get a world of Mony by thefe Notions of *Heaven* and *Hell* which the *Atheiftical Foxes* amongft them count but *Fables,* (as the *Pope* fpeaks of Chrift) The *Devils* have a more real Faith or Belief of thefe things and *tremble* : They cried out to the Lord Jefus, *why art thou come to torment us before the Time* ? &c. But G. *Fox* not believing (as they think) thefe Fables, he fancies that *Hell* is fome apprehenfions in the mind of wrath to come, and that is *Hell* and wrath it felf, and having had flafhes of *Pride* and *Peace* in their minds, thefe are the Joyes of *Heaven,* whereas the Lord Jefus tells us, that befide the hundred fold

The Papifts Queries about Hell

TheScripture, Hell and Heaven but Fables with G. Fox and other Popifh Foxes

fold of *Spiritual Ioyes* (*viz a hundred Fathers, Mo-thers*, &c.) there remains for his Followers in the World to come *Eternal Life*.
The Hea-ven and Hell to come.

They are but fhort Flafhes of *Hell* and *Heaven* which fome of thefe poor Cheated Souls dream of: I know they allow time more or lefs before they come into the perfect and heavenly State of Ne-ceffity.[1] Death prevents fome from coming to it, and makes the reign of the reft whom Satan has ticed into thefe [37] *proud Vanities* but fhort, as Experience hath declared: only they have a mad Fancy of their Souls going into *God*, and becom-ing more *God*, and yet this fome of them grant to the Souls of all men, to *Iudas* as well as *Peter*.
The Foxes mad Fancy of the Soul and next Life.

The true Proteftant believes thefe three things, *Firft*, that there is a State Eternal of Joy to the Righteous bodies and Souls after this Life: and a State of Eternal Mifery of Soul and Body to the ungodly: Although the exact knowledge of par-ticulars exceed the prefent fight of our *mortal eyes*, the hearing of our *Ears*, and the *Capacity* of our *Hearts*, &c.
The Pro-teftants Faith as to the Life to come.

2. The *firft Fruits* and a *Taft* both of the *hea-venly Ioyes* and the *Torments of the damned* are given by God in this Life, to the firft, in that *Solid Peace* and *Ioy* which they have in God: To the other in that *Horror* and *Defpair*, and *Enmity againft God*, &c.

3. Three Sorts of men efpecially will feek[2] there is an Hell to come, above other Sinners. *Firft*, The *Voluptuous*
Three Sorts will find Hell

---

[1] Erafe "of neceffity." *R. W. Ms. Ann.*
[2] Erafe " k " in " feek." *R. W. Ms. Ann.*

above
others.

Volnptuous and *Luxurious, whofe God is theii Belly,* and their *Sences,*&c. *Ars. potenter.*[1]

2. The *Devourers of the Poor and helplefs*, potenter,[2] &c.

3. The *proud* puft up with *foolifh Confidences*, boldly Crying, *Lord open to us, for we,* &c. alfo the Contrary to thefe three I might inlarge on, *and not Impertinently, but let him that readeth underftand,* is

Jeremiah
Ives.

in[3] *pag.* 64. where[4] G. *Fox* brings in *Ieremiah Ives* faying, ⌊*The Pharifeel were far enough from having the Kingdom of Heaven within them*⌋ He Anfwers contrary to Chrifts words, who faid it was within them.

I Reply, G. *Fox* his *Tutor* and *Teacher* within him knows, that the *Kingdom of God* and the *Kingdom of Huaven* fignifie but one, and not divers things : and yet alfo he knows that both of them

The King-
dom of
God figni-
fying
divers
things.

fignifie (in a Chriftian Senfe) *Firft*, the *Kingdome of Government* of God and Chrift in the Soul. *Secondly,* The Government of God in his holy Providence in the World. 3. His Government in the *Congregation* or *Churches* of his *Saints* called out of the World. *Fourthly,* the *glorious State* to come aft r this Life : He knowes that his I*ourney man* G. *Fox* is 5(fit Inftrument to deftroy all thefe, and to erect (in their ftead) a *dull, proud, dogged Confufion,* or *Babel within,* under the Name of *God, Chrift, Spirit, Light, Faith, Righteoufnefs, Refurrection.* The

---

[1] Erafe " *Ars. potenter.*" *R. W. Ms. Ann.*
[2] Erafe " potenter." *R. W. Ms. Ann.*
[3] Change " is in " to " yn." *R. W. Ms. Ann.*
[4] Erafe " where." *R. W. Ms. Ann.*
[5] Erafe the parenthefis, and infert "a." *R. W. Ms. Ann.*

The Lord Jefus knowing that not the *Phar*fees alone &c. but the *Iews* generally alfo, and his own *Chriftan Followers* were leavened [38] with a worldly notion, *viz.* thar their *Mefiah* fhould be a *glorious temporal King*, that he fhould make his *Entrance*, and *Exalt* his *Throne* with *great Pompe*, *Solemnity*, &c. The Lord Jefus tells them their miftake and faith, that his *Kingdome* was not fuch a *Kingdome*, but that it was within them: Of which words I find three Expofitions. *Firft*, that the *Kingdome of Heaven* is a *Spiritual, inward* and *Soul Kingdome*, concerning God and the Soul, and Spiritual matters, according to the faying of Chrift Jefus, *my Kingdome is not of this World*, &c. *(margin: The falfe and true Mefiah. The Kingdome of God within you. Three Expofitions.)*

2. From the word *Entos* within you, or amongft you, as certainly it was then amongft the *Iews*, and in the midft of them in their *Temple Streets* and *Houfes*, *Hearts* and *mouths* by the moft *wonderful fpeakings* of the Lord Jefus, as never man fpake amongft them, and the *wonderful power* and *gracious works* which never man wrought amongft them, nor in the whole World befide

3. The Kingdome of God, that is God and Chrift, and the Spirit were literally in the *Pharifees*, and fo Confequently in every hypocrite in the World, and every wicked and prophane Sinner, though they know it not, yea in all Creatures.

But this is againft a former, fair Expofition from the Greek word *Entos*, which cannot be refufed (fince fo agreeing with the Truth) except Reafons more prevalent, &c. *(margin: The Quakers Expofition.)*

2. The Spirit of God asks, *what agreement between*

*tween Chriſt and Belial, Light and Darkneſs, Righte-
ouſneſs & unrighteouſneſs?* &c.

And whereas it is moſt Improperly and Impiouſly Objected, that *the Light ſhines in darkneſs,* &c.   I

The Light
ſhining in
darkneſs.

have ſaid, that it can not be in the ſame Subject or
part predominate, the mind, or will, or Affections :
but the Light is at the window, and the Eye, and the
knock at the door, (by all the wayes and means by
which God viſits poor men) but the Eye, the door
is ſhut, *&c.* and the man within is not only aſleep,
but dead and rotten in *Natures filthineſs,* and *actual
Tranſgreſſions* and *Abominations.*

3. It is againſt all Colour of Reaſon to Imagine
that the Lord Jeſus ſhould tell the *Iews,* the *Phariſees,* and the reſt of his *bloody Enemies,* who ſome
weakly, ſome maliciouſly oppoſed his Kingdome,
and coming to Rule by his Grace over them, *viz.*
that his *grace* was *King* within them, what ever
their Heart or Tongues ſaid, or Hands hid, *&c.*

4. It is notoriouſly contrary to what G. *Fox,* and
his ſo often [39] Clamour that the *Kingdome of God
conſiſts in,* or its Nature is in *Righteouſneſs, and Peace
and Joy in the holy Spirit* : as oppoſite to the Kingdome in the *Phariſees,* and all *Hipocrites* and *prophane,* &c. as Hell to Heaven.

5. The thing is ſo notoriouſly childiſh and ri-

The grace
of God is
offered to
all, but em-
braced by
few that
are freely
choſen

diculous, *&c.* that a King ſhould affirm he was an
actual King in his *Enemies Country,* where the
whole is up in Arms againſt him : Or for a Lamb
to ſay, he was amongſt the Wolves and held his
Government in them : Or that a man pretending
Love to a Woman in way of marriage ſhould

boldly

boldly affirm, (though fhe abhord to hear of the motion yet) that he was in her *Heart* and *Affections*, as an *Husband, Lord*, &c. It is true, the motions of *War* and *Love* are made and offerd from the *King warring*, and the man *fuing*, but that their motions and Commands (that is Government and Kingdome) fhould be in them is nothing but impious and impudent, and childifh prating. The frantick fancy of Chrifts Kingdome in his Enemies hearts.

The 20*th Inftance*, is in *pag.* 75. where G. *Fox* brings in *Thomas Weld*, &c. faying, [*How clear the Scripture is, that Faith comes by hearing, and not by minding the Light within*] He *Anfwers*, Doth any man know Chrift but by the Light within? And is not Chrift the Word? And can any fee without Chrift the Word? Doth it not make manifeft? Nay, doth it not *give the Light of the knowledge of God in the face of Iefus Chrift*? read 2 *Cor.* 4. 1. from whence Faith comes, and fo Feith comes by minding the Light within, Chrift the Author of it, and brings to look at him, and hear him. Thomas Weld. Faith how wrought.

I Reply, mine eyes have feen a poor diftracted aged woman walking in State, boafting of her *Majefty, Iewels*, and *Crown*, with a Straw in her hand for her Scepter, *&c.* and thus doth this poor mad Soul walk even like *Nebuchadnezzar* upon his *Babel*. All is Chrift, and he is Chrift, Chrift is Faith and all, *&c* & therefore A diftracted old woman a picture of the Quakers.

1. He flights this fo known and unqueftionable Record, *Faith comes by hearing*, and that *heavenly Chain of Diamonds*, Rom. 10. concerning true Salvation, true worfhipping, true praying, true believing, true preaching, true fending, which holy writing or Record *Fox* dares not ferioufly and impartially, Rom. 10. The admirable Chain of Diamonds.

impartially, and in the fear of the moſt High conſider, as to the various means and wayes of Gods
ſending unto man.

2. For all G. *Fox* his Scepter of Straw, his mad
fancy of a [40] Light that works Faith, *&c.* I ask
what Faith is, and if it be not *Firſt,* a believing the
Goſpel, or Glad News to be true. *Secondly,* a receivi-
ving of it and believing in it mine own particular.

True Faith what

As *Firſt,* that a pardon is certainly come, *Secondly,*
that my *Name* is in it, my *deliverance* and *Salvation*
is wrapt up in it The great *King of Heaven* (like
Ahaſhueroſh) his *Angel* is ever : now he hath
thoughts of *marriage Loves* and *Joyes,* and *Secondly,* I (though a *poor Captive Jew, poor Eſther*)
I am ſhe his Eye hath fixt on, and his Soul delights in :

3*dly,* I askt what preaching is, but the publiſhing
or divulging, telling or declaring what the Word
or mind, or will of the *King Eternal* is, which he
hath revealed or declared to the *Patriarchs Moſes*
and the reſt of his *Prophets,* or *Meſſengers* from the
beginning of the World : And what ſaid the *Apoſtles* or *Meſſengers* of Chriſt Jeſus declare, but what
Moſes and the *Prophets* did ſay ſhould come to paſs?
Act. 26. which all was Scripture ? Was not this
Proclamation of *Good News,* or a pardon to be made
over all the World, and the firſt proclaiming of it
to be at *Jeruſalem,* Luke 24. And was there not
to be four ſorts of Hearers of this *glad News.*

Heb. 1.
Act. 26.

The four
ſort of
Hearers.

4. That receive and believe with a falſe and
overly, and looſe, and ſandy Belief: A *fourth,* only
with a deep and rockie Belief, cloſing and uniting
to

to God? Thus the men of *Samaria* told the woman *that they did not believe becaufe of her word,* (that muft be taken *Comparatively,* for the Hearing from her this *glad News,* was .he firft means of their believing) but becaufe they had heard Chrift themfelves,

5. I know thefe poor *Foxians* do hear a kind of *Motion within* them, but it is but as poor women that go with *falfe Conceptions* with *Tympanies* of *wind* and *water,* or with the *mola* that will refemble the *Motion* of a *true Child* : but after all their thoughts and fancies by day and night after all their *feeming feellings perfwafions, Experiences,* and *preparations,* this *falfe Conception, falfe Faith, falfe Chrift, falfe Light* fhall vanifh in fhame and grief, as did *Queen Maries* after the *Thanksgivings* and *Ringings* for her deliverance. The Quakers how cheated by Sathan as Queen Mary was of her Conception.

6. For my felf I dare thefe *felf Confidents* to *particularize* any one Scripture where the Spirit of God directs any poor Soul to liften and hearken to a *Light* and voice within him, affirming that ⌊41 this is the Hearing by which Faith is wrought? I dare them to clear Candidly and folidly, this, 10. to the *Rom.* wherein(as in the *8th* is the *Golden Chain of Election,* &c.) fo in this 10*th Chap.* the *Golden Chain* of the means of *praying, preaching,* &c. Challenges to the Foxians.

3. I ask for some *follid Inftances* where *Souls* have been truly Converted (the whole Soul unto God) by any fuch *Notion,* and not by fome *External means* and outward hearing of this *glad News* and Gofpel?

4. I ask if it be not a *ridiculous Contradiction*

in

in them to fill the World with the found of their new and only preachers *He Apoftles* and *fhe Apoftles*, &c.

5. I ask if this *Light within* (without and oppofite to the hearing without which is the queftion) be the means of Faith, how is it poffible, that fo many ferious Enquiring men in all Ages fhould not perceive a breath of this wind, no not in their own bofomes? and that *famous Paul* fhould be Confcientioufly and fully perfwaded that he ought to do many things againft Chrift Jefus, &c.

Pauls famous Cafe

If it be faid, *Paul* had not only the *Light within* him, but he had heard of the Doctrine of Chrift and of his *Followers*: he heard *Stephens Sermon*, and yet he believed not: and therefore it is *Grace* doth all. I *Anfwer*, this is fomething, but reacheth not home, for, if all the men in the world have this *Light* (which is infficient without hearing) why fhould not fome, (efpecially the wife and Enquirours, &c.) perceive it or fomething of it, as *Paul* did not, until he had heard fomething, (and becaufe God had a purpofe to make Extraordinary ufe of him, an Extraordinary hand from Heaven humbling and preparing him to publifh or preach unto the Nations.

80 Tko. Pollard.

The 21 *Inftance*, is in *pag.* 80. where G. *Fox* brings in *Tho. Pollard*, faying, [*To fay the Officers of the Church are Invifible, It is plain of their Father the Devil*] He Anfwers, The Holy Ghoft made the Officers of the Church Overfeers, and that made the Officers the Overfeers to be Invifible, for they faw with an Invifible Eye, and fo they was in the

the Spirit which is Invifible, and not in the Flefh:
elfe they could not be Overfeers in the Church of
God, and you are the vifible apoftatiz'd from them. *The Fox like and dog like Impudency of G. Fox &c.*

I Reply, This is one of the moft *impudent Foole-
ries* that either *Fox*, or (as the Proverb is) *any Dog
could be impudent in*: For Firft,

42] 1. He acknowledgeth a *publick Affembly* of
Chriftians; as well as of other pretending Worfh p-
pers, *Turks, Jews,* &c. Alfo he acknowledgeth the
Minifters, Officers, and Overfeers of their Affemblies.

2. His Reafon is notorioufly filly and impudent,
viz. becaufe the Church is in God, and the Overfeers are made by the holy Spirit: For are the fe-
cret works of God alwayes fecret, and never revealed? *The vifibility of Chrifts Church and her Officers.*
The *Child* in the *Wombe*, the *precious Stones*, and
Minerals when brought forth, are no more *Invifible* then the *Sun* in the *Firmament.*

3. The Chriftian profeffion and profeffours, however they were wrought and prepared, and by divers means by Gods Spirits: yet the Lord Jefus
compares them to the moft vifible Confpicuous and
glorious things and perfons. To the *Sun* and *Moon*
in the *Heavens,* and the *Heavens* and *Stars* alfo, to
Mountains, and *Cities* on thofe *Hills* or *Mountains*:
To *Kings,* To their *houfes* and *Palaces,* yea, to
Armes with *Banners,* &c.

4. Although the *Lord Major* of *London,* and the
feveral Officers of theCity are not made and ordained in the public Streets, nor *Generals* and other
Officers appointed by his *Majefty,* &c. are they not
therefore

therefore vifible, because their making and appoint-
ing was not Solemnized and performed in *Cheap-
fide*, &c.

5. It is moſt true and moſt ſweet, that the Church
is in God, *&c.* and is it not alſo true, that in one
Senſe, we *live in God* and *move in God, have our Being in God*, and yet the *whole Creation* is *glorioufly
vifible* in another Sence, the *Saints*, their *Affemblies*
and *Officers* are in God *vifible* to the world abundantly, though in an heavenly and ſpiritual Sence,
tranſcending the Being of the *firſt Creation*.

The
Church in
God.

6. G. *Fox* denies not, but that although the *firſt
Churches* were in God, and the *Officers* of the
Church, and ſome of them were appointed immediately, yet they were *vifible* and *audible* by thoſe
with whom they Converſed :

7. Yea, G. *Fox* and his *Foxians*, for all their being in God, and ſome of their proud and ſilly Anſ-
werings in Courts, that they live in God, and dwell
in God, yet they diſowne not their own *vifible
Congregatings* and *Affemblings*, their *vifible Teachers*,
Overfeers, or *Biſhops*, their *vifible* and *audible performances* and *Worſhips, praying, preaching, finging,*
&c. and wny then doth this [43] poor notoriouſly
vifible Cheatour thus prate of *Invifibilities eſpecially
in times of peace and not in* Elias *Caſe* ?

G Fox
a moſt viſi-
ble and
idle prater
of Inviſi-
bilities.

The 22 *Inſtance* is in *pag* 84. where G. *Fox* brings
in his oppoſite *Magnus Byne*; ſaying, [*The Scriptures
may be underſtood by the help of Tongues.*] He Anſwers, [*All Scripture was given forth by Inſpiration,
and ſo without the ſame Inſpiration, it is not underſtood again,* Pilate *had the Tongues, yet did not underſtand*

Magnus
Byne.

*ftand the Scripture, nor Chrift the Subftance of it:
And this you have fet up fince the Apoftacy, your
Tongues, you Raveners from the Spirit.*|

I Reply, Firft, I make ufe of G. *Fox* his *Confeffion,* viz. that *all Scripture is infpired,* &c. therefore
fay I, he Confeffeth that every *word, Syllable* and
Tittle in that *Scripture* or *writing,* is the *Word,* or
immediate revealed will of God: againft his and his
Foxians common Song: hath God any more wòrds
but one? God hath many words.

2. As to the Scriptures, the underftanding of
them is threefold. The understanding of the Scripture threefold.

Firft, Literal: who underftands not, *Thou fhalt
not kill, Thou fhalt not Steal?* &c.

The fecond is *Metaphorical,* as *I am the Dore, I
am the Bread,* &c.

The third is faving and Spiritual, when it pleafeth God to fet home the *heavenly Commands Promifes,* &c. in particular, *Soul Application.*

3. I obferve the End of G. *Fox* (and efpecially of
the *old Serpent* and *Fox* that acts him.) It is to deftroy the coming of *Gods holy Records* and *writings*
to poor loft men to their *Salvation,* that he may
foift and whifp in what his *hellifh malice* pleafeth
to their Damnation: For if no knowledge of the
Tongues in which the moft wife and moft holy
Lord *pend his Letters* or *writing* to us, then no
preaching of the Doctrine in them to the world
witout fome *new miraculous way,* then no tranflating
and reading of them, which is, that the Devil in
all Ages and at this day aims at with all his might. The Devils End in Cavilling againft the Scripture Tongues, yet J. Stnbs vapourd that he underftood as many Tongues as I, and may be more.

4. I therefore charge upon this *proud Ignoramus,*
and

The horrible Ingratitude of the Foxians.

The Tranſltion of the Scripture.

and all his *blind Diſciples* and *Followers* the horrible Crime of *Unthankfulneſs*, and *Ingratitude* : for were it not for *Tindal*, burnt to aſhes, and other *heavenly* Spirits ſet on work from Heaven to dig out the knowledge of the *Hebrew* and the *Greek*, and to turn it into *French, Dutch, Engliſh*, and now praiſed be God into the very [44] *Indian Language* of this Country, how would theſe S*eraphical Doctors* know whether there were ſuch a *Creation* of *Heavens* and *Earth*, or of man and his wife, which we now ſo talk of?

The Quakers Spirit for all pretences a lazie Spirit

I put this queſtion once to a Soul in this Country, who told me although they had no *Engliſh Scripture*, Gods Spirit would teach them *Greek* and *Hebrew* : but I can declare to any that ask me the dreadful End of that party.

5. I Charge upon this *Foxian party* the horrible Crime of a *proud Lazineſs* for not ſtudying the *Original Languages* themſelves ; It is a ſhameful Trade and deceitful, when perſons have mony in their hands, to take up all on truſt ! I have known very *Eminent Men* and *Women Independants* and *Baptiſts* , give themſelves up to ſerious ſtudy of the *Hebrew Language* : I never knew any of the *Foxian* S*pirits* ſo inclind, but according to the *Lazie fool* under the *Fig-Tree* which I have ſeen in an *Embleme* almoſt threeſcore year ſince, they lie down and cry.

> *Sweet Figs drop down in yielding w ſe*
> *For Lazie will not let me riſe.*

6. I Judge that G. *Fox* and his *wild Spirit* can
not

not prove that *Pilate* had the *Hebrew Greek* and *Latin*, for though he caufed by an *heavenly fin-* ger of God fuch a Title to be fet up in the three then moft known Languages *Hebrew*, *Greek*, and *Latin*, yet he himfelf might have no knowledge of any more then the *Latin*, which was his *Mother Romane Tongue* : As a *Book feller* may deal in Books of *Hebrew*, *Greek*, *Latin*, *French*, *Dutch*, *Italian*, *Spanifh*, &c. and yet underftand no more then his *Mother Englifh*. The three Languages upon the Crofs of Chrift.

7. I know the Devil abounds with Tongues, and can fpeak all Languages, and I know, and have feen his *Infpirations*, and three thoufands verfes in fh w very heavenly, infpir'd by him, in an Englifh wo- man of this Country, who had no fuch skill, *ex tempore*. They were taken and written from her mouth, and I have read them : and do believe from many Reafons which I have to fhew they were from Satan, yet I know alfo that Ignorance is fhame- ful, and that it pleafed God miraculoufly to infufe the knowledge of Tongues to his firft Apoftles, or Meffengers, to the Nations, and what he will fur- ther do in this kind, [45] before this *Worlds glass* is out who can tell? only I am fure thefe *Foxians* talk (like little Children in their grave Confulta- tions) without the leaft knowledge at all (genrally) of any thing, but their *mother Englifh*, and yet as proudly and imperioufly vapouring and triumphing, &c. like *Theora John* proclaming to the *World* his mad *Quaking Revelations*, *Infpirations*, writing of *Languages*, many which he Confeft, he underftood not, but *Myfteries*, *Myfteries*. The Dev- ils skill in Languages and Sub- tlety in Revela- tions. Theora John

8 G.

The Lord raiſeth his Witneſſes againſt Babel by his Spirit and bleſſing upon Tongues and *Tranſ-*lations.

8. G. Fox is no wiſer in affirming that *Tongues* came in place of the Spirit ſince the *Apoſtacy.* For before the *Apoſtacy* the Lord furniſhed his Servants with underſtanding of ſeveral Languages *miraculouſly:* with the *Apoſtaſie,* thoſe *heavenly miraculous gifts* ceaſed: In the *Apoſtacy the Father of Spirits* gave to his two witneſſes power, Authority & Ability to propheſy, preach, declare & witneſs to the Truths of Jeſus againſt the *Popiſh Inventions:* with the riſing of *Luther, Calvin,* &c. The Lord raiſed up the ſtudy of the *Hebrew* and *Greek Tongues* in many *heavenly Witneſſes,* who brought to Light the truth of the *firſt Copies* in Oppoſition to the Corrupt *Latin Tranſlation* (bruitiſhly ſettled under a Curſe by the *Counſel at Trent*): This mighty work of the Lord in his *Proteſtant Witn ſſes* drove the *Popiſh Foxes* into their *holes,* and hath driven (for ſhame) the *Jeſuits* to ſtudy the *Hebrew* and *Greek,* and by a *new Stratagem* partly made up of the pretence of their *Spirit* and partly of the pretence of *Corruptions* and *Variations* in the Copies) to aſſault the Camp of the *Proteſtant Witneſſes.*

The Papiſts former Ignorance & now their abuſe of knowledge

9. I deſpiſe not, yea, I praiſe God for, and honour the helps and helpers we have in Engliſh: yea, I would not diſcourage the weakeſt *Engliſh man* or *woman* (in Chriſtian humility) to ſound forth the praiſes of God in *writing, ſpeaking* and *printing* in *Engliſh* what they have Experimented of the *Son of God,* No, though they ſhould not *write* or *print,* or ſpeak true Engliſh, as G *Fox* hath not done: But when they lift up their *Horns* on high (or their *bruitiſh Ears* as *Foxes* do, in ſtead of *Horns*) then I

Engliſh helps a great mercy.

muſt

muſt tell G. *Fox*, that although he prat le amongſt
the *Engliſh*, and they be cheated with his *dying*
Spirit : yet if he go to other Nations, (as they ſimply pretend to do to *Turks* and *Pope*) they muſt
either be furniſhed with the Gift of Tongues miraculouſly, or they muſt fling of their *lazie Devil*,
and ſtudy the *Tongues* of thoſe Nations to whom
they carry their (*pretended*) *glad News* or *Goſpel*.

46] The 23. *Inſtance*: G. *Fox* in pag.86. brings in
the ſame Author, ſaying, [*Notwithſtanding thy paſſing through the firſt and ſecond Reſurrection* (as thou
ſaith) *there remains a Torment ſo thee at the laſt day
and Woe.*]

He *Anſwers*, They are bleſſed that have part in
the firſt Reſurrection : The ſecond Death have no
power over them, but are made free from Wrath
that is to come, and are paſſed from Death to Life,
and are tranſlated into the Kingdome of the Son
of God, and are in union with the Son of God and
the Father both; and ſo thou uttereſt forth Lies.

I Reply, G. *Fox* here Arrogates to himſelf and
his *Foxians*.

1. A Paſſing through the firſt and ſecond Reſurrection.

2. He triumpheth in their Bleſſedneſs pronounced
to their firſt Reſurrection, *viz.* of Communion with
God and Freedome from Wrath to come:

1. The Truth is G. *Fox* is in his Burrough of
Words of divers ſignifications: He wreſts and
winds what is for his wicked ends, but you ſhall
never take him in *Diſtinguiſhing* and *Defineing* what
the *firſt* and *ſecond Death* is, and what is the *firſt*
and *ſecond Reſurrection*. 2. The

2. The Truth is, as foon as they hearken to this *familiar Spirit*, they are fo Elevated, that they be in the *heavenly glory*, the *Refurrection* is paft, and (with K. *Agags dream*) the *Bitternefs* of *Death* and *Wrath* is paft for ever with them.

The great Expecta-tion of all the four great Re-ligions. 3. But no fuch *grapes* will be gathered of thefe *Thorns*, nor *Figs* of thefe *Thiftles* : For if we talk of efcaping wrath to come, and of enjoying *Blef-fednefs* : we muft prove to others, as well as to our felves, that the *Expectation* of the *Jews*, and *Mahu-metans* expecting a *Carnal Bleffednefs* to come, is falfe : We mnft prove the *Papifts* and *Common Pro-teftants* (for all their Prayers and Alms, *&c.*) are under that Sentence, *Depart from me ye workers of Iniquity.*

4. The Lord Jefus being queftioned about the great point of Salvation : he feems to Anfwer two things.

The great point of Salvation. 1. That the moft will hang their Souls upon the *Hedge*, and venture like the *high ways* and *hedges*.

2. Others will *fear* and look after *Redemption, Deliverance,* S*alvation,* &c. and of thefe two forts.

Two great Sorts of minders Eternal Life. Firft. Some that will endeavour and feek to en-ter I Judge both ⌊47⌋ of *Pagans* and *Mahumetans*, and *Jews*, and *Papifts* and *Proteftants*, and fhall not be able.

The fecond is of fuch as fenfible of the *Nar-rownefs* of the way, *ftraightnefs* of the dore, and the *Infinite neceffity incumbing*, and the *Infinite Ex-cellency inviting*, fling away *Preferments, Profits*, and *Pleafures*, and choofe to enjoy the *Mediator*, as loft and damned in our felves, and follow him from his
Cradle

Cradle and *Manger* to his *Crofs* and *Gallows*, and labouring to draw other poor drowning Souls out of the pit of *Eternal Rottennefs*,& *howling* with us.

5. The Spirit of God tells us of three forts of perifht Souls.

Firft, Thofe without Law, of which are *Millions* of *Millions innumerable*.

Secondly, Such as had the *Law* or *Word*, or will of God revealed to them in the Covenant of works, *Obedience* or *Juftice*, of which fort were[1] *Millions of Millions* alfo.

A third is of fuch to whom *Infinite pity* hath vouchfafed the *joyful Tidings* of the Son of God, his *Mediation, Interpofition, and Interceffion*.[2]

Amongft thefe the *Papifts*, and the Protefters againft the Papifts are chief : of the Papifts the *Jefuits* : of the Proteftant (therefo called) *Puritans* run for it: of thefe the Quakers pretend the higheft, but no otherwife then, *O thou* Capernaum, *which art Exalted, & Exalteft thy felf unto Heaven, thou fhalt be brought down to Hell*, &c. For *Tyre and* Sidon, Sodom, *and* Gomorrah,*&c.* the *poor Jews* and *Mahumetans*, yea, the Papifts and common Proteftants fhall have an eafier Cup to drink off then the *Foxians*, &c, that are fo high, & pure, and lofty, and yet abound with *Luciferian filthinefs*.

The 24. *Inftance*, is in *pag.* 89. where G. *Fox* brings in the fame Author, faying, [*The Saints are neither in the Fulnefs of the Godhead, nor in part : Away with this Blafphemy that faith this is*] He Anfwers,

[1] Infert "and are." *R. W. Ms. Ann.*
[2] Add " loft in themfelves but faved by grace." *R. W. Ms. Ann.*

The Quakers in the Fulnefs of the Godhead of their hellifh mouths and pens ay bebelieved

Anfwers, [*The work of the Miniftry was to bring people to the knowledge of the Son of God, to a perfect man, to the Unity of the Faith, to the meafure and ftature of the Fulnefs of Chrift and Chrift will dwell in the Saints; and God will dwell in them ;*] And thou faith, They have no part of the Fulnefs of the Godhead, and *John* faith, *of his Fulnefs have we all received, in whom dwells the Goahead bodily,* and ye be all in the Blafphemy that be out of this part of the Fulnefs.

I Reply, It was doubtlefs an *horrible Crime* which the Jews though malicioufly and falfly Objected. 48| 1. Againft the Lord Jefus, *viz.* that he being a man fhould make himfelf God. What fhall we fay to thefe *bruitifh* and *blafphemou*s *Foxian*s, vile worms of the Earth, yefterday creeping out of their holes, flaves and Hellhounds, as we all b Nature are, fo horribly to fet their faces as *David* fpeaks again the Heavens, vapouring themfelves to be in the Godhead, yea, in the Fulnefs of the Godhead, and that alfo *bodily,* fo that what was applicable and proper to the *Body* of the Son of God, is proper and applicable unto them, his *Body in whom the Fulnefs of the Godhead dwells bodily.*

2. See the *horrible Egyptian Darknefs* the Lord hath juftly poured upon thefe *feigned Gofhenites.*

The Quakers grutch Chrift the Title of God-man

They exclaim againft us for ufing that Title *Godman,* and ask where we find fuch a phraze in Scripture : And yet they reft not in that Title *Emanuel God with us* : nor the Fulnefs of the Godhead *bodily in Chrift,* but Sacrilegious Robbers (in Effect)

arrogate

arrogate the Title, and thing to themſelves to be God-men and God-women, the Godhead dwelling in them *bodily*.

3. Whereas G. *Fox* here ſaith, the work of the Miniſtry was to bring men to a *perfect man*, &c.

I Anſwer, He groſsly abuſeth that heavenly *Ephef.* 4. which concerneth the Fulneſs and per-fection of all the Elect of God, *the whole Body, the Church of the firſt-Born*, applying it unto every par-ticular deluded Convert of theirs, as being as per-fect, as holy, as much God as Chriſt Jeſus, *God bleſſed for ever* himſelf.

Ephef. 4. The work of Chriſts Miniſters.

4. I may uſe the Exprobations of *Moſes* againſt *Korah, Dathan* and *Abiram. Is it not enough for you*, &c. but will you ſeek the *Prieſthood* alſo. Is it not enough that the moſt *High Potter* made us Men and Women and not Serpents and Toads, *&c.* not *Pagans, Turks, Iews, Papiſts*, &c. but *Engliſh Proteſ-tants*, &c. but we will be alſo *Infinites, & Eternals, Omnipotents & Omniſcients?* Will not the Infinite favour of *Leave* to drink of ſome heavenly drops of the *Infinite & Inconceivable Ocean* of his Goodneſs, ſatiſfie and content us, but we will be Gods, with the Devil and our firſt Parents : We will be the *Inconceivable Ocean* it ſelf. Is it not enough for a *Proud Rebel* to be fetcht from the Gallows by a ſmile of his Prince, but he muſt be the *Prince* and *King* himſelf.

The hor-rible pride and Haughti-neſs of the Quakers.

5. The *Pagans* of the World as they are *wild* to all *Civility*, ſo to all *Divinity* and *heavenly matters :* They apprehend a *Doity*, [49] as a *Lyon, Whale, Dragon, Giant, Tyrant*; they feignedly will ſtrive to

The In-dians baſe eſteem of the God-head.

pacifie

pacifie him, to make ufe of his help in Sickneſs, in
Wars, in Plagues and Droughts : but they will call
Men and Women Gods too, yea Dogs and Geeſe,
yea any Creature *Manittoo*, God, that is, or doth
any thing ſtrange unto them : And thus the *Meli-
tans* preſently cried out of *Paul*, that he was a God,
And the God*s are come down to us in the likeneſs of
Men, &c.*

God and
the great
Adverſary
to all
Proud
ſpirits.

6. Therefore doth it pleaſe the moſt High and
only Wiſe to meet often with the *Pharaoh*'s the
Abſolom's the *Nebuchadnezzar*s, the *Haman*s the
*Herod*s of this World, yea, with whole Nations,
Cities Armies and Navies for their Pride, as he did
with S*odom*, in ſignal and remarkable ſtrokes and
Judgements : yea, with his *Iob*s, and *Hezechiah*'s,
and *Paul*'s in danger to be puffed up, in voices and
queſtions out of the Whirlwind, till we more and
more come to ſee how perfect we are in Dirt, and
Stink, and Filth of Death and Hell crawling like
Monſters of Pride and ſelf-conceitedneſs upon this
Earth his Glorious Footſtool.

*T*he *Soul*
of men
horribly
abuſed

The 25. Inſtance is in *Pag.* 90. He brings in the
ſame Author ſaying, [*There is a kinde of Infinite-
ne*ſs *in the Soul, and it cannot be Infinite*ne*ſs it ſelf.*]
He Anſwers : Is not the Soul without beginning
coming from God, and returning into God again,
who hath it in his hand, which Hand goes againſt
him that doth Evil, which throws down that which
wars againſt it : and Chriſt the power of God the
beſt[1] of the Soul, which brings it up into God,
which

---

[1] Change "beſt" to "reſt." *R. W. Ms. Ann.*

which came out from him; hath this a beginning or ending? and is not this Infinite in it felf, and more than all the World?

I Reply, More briefly, (having fpoken of the Soul before) That the Soul or Spirit of a Man fhould be boundlefs or without limits, without beginning or ending, is a *Blafphemous Monfter* begotten of *Hellifh Pride* the Father, and *Hellifh Ignorance* the Mother: for Infinity and Infinitenefs in that fence can be no other but the Infinite and Eternal Power and Godhead tranfcending the Capacity or Men or Angels to receive it or conceive the nature of it.

2. It is true in a fecondary way (*a pofteriori*) as they fay the Spirits of Angels and men are as a Lamp lighted by the moft high and In- [50] finite Majefty never to go out or be extinguifhed in joy or forrow, This Notion dazles the moft fober and fteady Eye and Braine; but who can finde a Centre or Clod of ftanding from whence to entertain a thought of no Beginning; no created finite power can reach to what Infinity is.

3. We fee the mighty Kings and Emperours, their mighty Armies and Navies have Bounds as the roaring Waves of the Ocean have: the moft Glorious Sun and Heavenly Bodies have their limited Motions: the Dayes and Nights, the Summer and Winter, the Light and Darknefs know their periods of beginning and ending &c. All have their hitherto and no further fet by the Infinite, *Eternal* Arm, & no further. But all the ftars of heaven, the drops of the Ocean, the Sand on the Sea fhore, the

The changes of all things created and their Periods

Leaves

4. Contrary to the Experience of the World in their daily obferving of the *Quakers Bodies* and *Worfhips.* (befide the Char- [53] ges againft them for their wild Doctrines and Difciplines) what known Divifions and Paffions about *I Nailors* and others Cafes? what Envyings Curfings, Apoftacies, and moral Idolatry, as that of Covetoufnefs in this *Colony* known notorioufly?

But fince G. *Fox* fpeaks fo Rationally to his Oppofite, Do you diftinguifh things in the Ground? I fhall remember them of the fairnefs of my *fourteenth Pofition* againft them, *viz.* that according to the Principles, Roots and grounds of things I have fairly Collected, that the Spirit of the *Quakers* tends to *Incivility* and *Barbarifme*, and to *fudden Affacinations, murther*s and *Perfecutions.* &c.

The *Eternal Father* of mercies (I believe that I have, and can further make it good:) ftops millions of mifchiefs in the world daily, which the Natures, grounds and Principles of men (and the Quakers Spirit alfo) now[1] to overrun and overwhelm the World withal.

A 27*th. Inftance* of G. *Fox* his lame Anfwer is in *pag.* 103. where he brings in *Jonathan Clapham*, faying, [*Men may be called of Men Mafters, and it is but a Cavil to deny it, and they may deny to be called Fathers as well as Mafters*] He Anfwers, Thou haft in this denied that Doctrine of Chrift, and flights it, who faith, *Be not ye of Men called Mafters, for you have all one Mafter which is Chrift, and you all are*

[1] Change "now" to "tend." *R. W. Ms. Ann.*

are Brethren, and thou haſt ſhow'd thy ſelf out of
the *Brother-hood*.   And there is a Birth to be born
which can call no man *Father* upon Earth which
thou art ignorant of.

I Reply, 1.   Amongſt other *fooliſh paſſions* and
Affections haunting all men, and the *Quakers* eſpecially, theſe two are notorious, *viz.* pride and a
lazie Ignorance : Thoſe two are the *Sire* and *Dam*
of moſt of theſe *wild monſters*.

2. For doth not this proud man know how many
of his excellent Oppoſites have laid open their
Foxians ſcornful pride in robbing all mankind of
many due reſpects and favorable glaunces of Gods
care, of order, and prudent diſtinctions and differences amongſt the Sons of men in Families, Cities,
Nations, Armies, Navies, &c.

3. Sure he can not but remember, and his own
and all the Light in the *Quakers* (if ſeriouſly minded) will tell them, that [54] in robbing all the
world of their ſeveral due moderate, and ſober Titles and Reſpects, they do but by a *jugling Hocas
pocas*; a *back dore*, &c. rob all others of their *points*, The Pope
Ribbons, and *Laces*, wherewithal only to adorn and and Qua-
trim, and trick their fooliſh ſelves : Juſt as the kers com-
Popiſh party practice to cry up their *Pope, ſervus
ſervorum Dei*, and yet be *Domine fac totum* your holineſs, *&c.* and yet the *Pope* and *Papiſts* herein out
ſhoot the *Quakers*, for the *Papiſts* give all men their
Civil and Courteous different Reſpects, and Ac-
knowledgements, which the *dogged* and *ſcornful
Quakers*, are far from their Spirit being prouder
then the *Papiſts*,

4. G.

4. G. *Fox* knows how others of his *Adverſaries* have in print told him that the Engliſh word [*Maſter*] Anſwers to many words in the *Greek* [*Kathegereſe Didarkalos*, &c.] and that theſe words *Rabbi* and *Pateer*, all ſhew that the Lord Jeſus only Condemned the *Phariſaical, Popiſh*, and *Foxian Itch* of being called *Maſters, Fathers, Leaders, Teachers* in Religion, undervaluing and ſlighting others, *&c.* Thus amongſt the *Papiſts* their *Magiſter noſter*, their *Patres*, &c. their *Irrefragable, Seraphical* and *Angelical Doctors*: thus among the *Foxians, James Naylor, Hoſanna*, &c. and G. *Fox* (at this Town of *Providence*) called the *Eternal* Son *of God*. *Chriſt Jeſus*.

Of Fathers and Maſters.

The Popiſh priority an6 the Foxian is of and in their Doctors.

5. Half a *Humane* and *ſober Eye* may ſee that in all his *Declamations* againſt the *Phariſaical*, or *Popiſh*, or *Foxian Rabbies*, the Lord Jeſus I ſay, comes not near in a Title, the Civil and Natural Reſpects of *Inferiours*, to *Heads* of *Families, Cities, Kingdomes*, &c. all of which, the very nature of man being *von politikon*[1] a ſociable Creature, and the holy Scripture is all over (from end to end) full of moſt frequent Examples, yea, Commands, and practices.

Meer Civil Reſpects

6. How Childiſhly doth *Fox* Anſwer his *Oppoſite*, *viz* that although it be unlawful to call *Maſter*, yet it is not unlawful to call *Father*, for there is a *Birth* which his *Oppoſite* is ignorant of, *&c.* I ask if G. *Fox* mean not their *Immediate Birth* of *Light* (which for a Cover) they call *Spirit* and *Chriſt*, &c. in Oppoſition to that true *Chriſtian Regeneration* and

The Quakers Maſters and Fathers.

Change,

[1] Change "*von politikon*" to "*animal politicon*." *R. W. Ms. Ann.*

Change, which it pleafeth God ordinarily to Effect ^{True Re-} by means, as *Paul* faid, though you have ten thouf-^{generatio1} and Teachers, yet I have begotten you, *&c,* Sure it is, their Immediate denies the mediate.

55] 7. Where there no *Ordinary means* appointed by God for *Natural* or *Spiritual procreation*: yet how fimple is that Confequence, that becaufe God is an *Extraordina y Father,* therefore I may call men *Fathers* but not *Mafters*! when God is both *Father* and *Mafter,* and both Titles are forbidden in a true Senfe, by one and the fame *heavenly Breath,* at the fame time.

A 28 *h. Inflance,* is *pag.* 106. where G. *Fox* brings ^{106. Wil-} in *W. Thomas,* faying, [*Men are faved, but not by* ^{liam} *Chrift within us.*] ^{Thomas.}

He Anfwers, [*How is mans Salva ion wrought out but by Chrift within? How is the Juftification fels but by Chrift wit in? And the Seeds we manifeft that fuffered without is made manifeft within, there is Redemption and Life: He that hath the Son of God hath Life, Redemption to God out of the firft Adam, and who feels Chrift within, feels Salvation, and who doth not, are Reprobates, though they may talk of him.*]

I Reply, This fubtle *Fox* is in his *Burrough* Confounding (under the Terms Chrift) the perfon of Chrift, and the *Love,* and *Spirit,* and *Grace* or *Fa-* ^{The per-} *vour* of Chrift, as if they were all one: As if ^{fon of} ^{Chrift and} where the Name and Authority, and writing of G. ^{the Grace} *Fox* comes, there of neceffity muft G. *Fox* in perfon ^{of Chrift} ^{diftingu-} be: Or, to rife higher, wherever the Name and ^{ifhed.} Authority, of a *King, General,* or *Admiral* is, there muft their perfons alfo be.   This

Chrifts
perfou.
This *Popifh Ubiquitary Fancy* all *fober Reafons*
have long fince laught at, and juftly, as being moft
Fancyfull and *Frantick*: what,

Not Ubi-
quirary.
2. What is this, but to make the *Kings* of men,
yea, the *King of Kings poor Mechanicks*, yea, lower,
that can do nothing by any *Means, Servants, Minifters, Legates, Embaffadours,* &c. except they be per-
fonaly prefent?

3. The Spirit of God refolves the Quefton, *Ephef*
3. *He dwels in the Heart by Faith*, or believing in
Faith not
Chrift
himfelf.
him, and *Gal.* 2. I *live by believing, or Faith in the
Son of God*: This *Faith* is given of God to fome
and not to others: This Faith or Belief is wrought
by Chrift Jefus, and fin fhed by him, and may with
as good Senfe be called Chrift himfelf, as a fhoo
which G. *Fox* hath begun and finifhed be called G
Fox himfelf.

4. With what Colour of Reafon or Senfe is it
K. Charles
King yer
not per-
fonally
prefent in
all his Do-
minions
that if I believe King *Charles* the fecond to be the
King of *Englifh Men* and my *King*, I muft of neceffity (becaufe of my belief which He by gra- [56
cious means hath wrought in me) I believe that K.
Charles is *perfonally prefent*, & *Ubiquitarily prefent*
in perfon in all his *Dominions* and all the world
over where ever his Loving *Subjects* have their
Refidence?

Humph.
Norton
yields
Chrift
ubiquitary
5. I grant if we as fome Quakers and *Humphry
Norton* by Name refolve Chrift only into a Spirit,
and God only he is *Ubiquitary:* But as man, why
may not the *General* of an *Army* fay, to his whole
Army, and every *Individual Souldier*, as *Paul* to the
*Corinthians, though I am abfent in Body yet am I prefent
in*

in S*pirit*, Chriſt Jeſus is in his Command, and Courage and Example in every *Regiment*, every *Squadron*, every *Band* and *Troop*, and every Souldier of the m ny Millions that have, and ſhall believe in him, and that in a Senſe,[1] both as God and man.

6. The *Hinge* and *pinch* of the *Difference* lies in the *Oppoſition*, which the *Quakers* make againſt the *Manhood* of Chriſt Jeſus to be yet Extant, many of them alleadging : *why ſtand you gazing*, Acts 1, *&c.* as if it were but gazing after a *Manhood* and all now were Spirit and Light within.

Which
word &
the word
humane
they
ſtartle ar

7. Who ever queſtiond, but that the Spirit or power of Chriſt Jeſus worketh in the Souls of his Elect the great ſaving change or regeneration, gives Repentance, opens the heart to Believe, and makes the heart of this Believer a Palace for three Kings, yet but one, the Father, the Son and the Spirit, in Holineſs, Love, Meckneſs, Patience, &c. and all theſe[2] Royal Attendants.

Chriſt Je-
ſus in the
Soul
makes it a
palace for
3 Kings
&c.

8. Who queſtions but Chriſt Jeſus (as the Sun in theſe Heavens) influenceth all parts of the World in ſeveral reſpects, and nothing is hid from his heat, He is felt in the bruiſed Reed and ſmoaking Flax ; in the poor in Spirit, in the hungry and thirſty after Righteouſneſs : ſometimes in the hope of Glory to come, yea, in preſent joy unutterable and glorious ; Sometimes the Lambs Wife is viſibly aſleep though her heart wakes, ſometimes ſhe is Alarmed by his knocking and is ſluggiſhly unwilling

The varie-
ty of
Chriſts
workings
& appear-
ances

ling

---

[1] Add " by faith." *R. W. Ms. Ann.*
[2] Change " theſe " to " their." *R. W. Ms. Ann.*

but opened his *Fathers Law* in the *purity* and *Spirituality* of it againſt the *rotten Expoſitions, Traditions* and practices of the *Phariſees.*

6. In particular, let all the Reaſons be expended and carefully weighed, which the Lord Jeſus ſo *wonderfully, exactly give*s why they ſhould not ſwear by *Jeruſalem,* nor the *Temple,* nor their *Head,* nor any *Oath,* to wit of ſuch a Nature, and half a ſober eye may ſee that the Lord Jeſus intends only to reduce them to an holy Swearing, only by God, in Gods way, *&c.* and in their *Common Converſe,* to uſe *yea, and nay,* &c.

The Quakers plainly Confeſs Swearing in Caſes lawful

7. I have read a *ſober* and *man like Anſwer* of *F. H.* called a Quaker againſt *A. S.* called a Doctour, concerning *Oaths,* not like *G. Fox* his *bruitiſh barkings* againſt all his Oppoſites and any that prate[1] may ſee *F. H.* yields to *A. S.* that himſelf, (and I preſume he ſpeaks the mind of all the Quakers) could yield to give a Teſtimony in weighty Caſes, by the Name and in the Name of God, as in the preſence of God, and atteſt or call God to witneſs, *&c.* And he ſaith, that they had offered ſo to give a Teſtimony, and that his Oppoſite Doctour *Snalwood,* and I think Biſhop *Gauden* ſo called, aſſented that this was Subſtantial and *Formal Swearing* : only the *Ceremonies* were enjoyned by Law, to which the Quaker could not yield, but ſuffer as indeed they have done upon this Account moſt lamentably in *London* and *Briſtol,* and all *England* over.

Caſes of Swearing

8. I have much to add both as to that *Fancy* of Chriſts end- [60] ing *Oaths* as *Ceremonies,* and of

Caſes

---

[1] Change " prate" to "pleaſe." *R. W. Ms. Ann.*

Cafes that have befallen my felf in the *Chancery* in *England*, &c. and of the lofs of great Sums which I chofe to bear through the Lords help, then yield to the *Formality* (then and ftill in ufe) in Gods worfhip, though I offered to Swear as *F. H.* mentions they have done, and the Judges told me they would reft in my Teftimony and way of Swearing, but they could not difpence with me without an Act of Parliament.

I believe this highly concerns the high Affembly of Parliament and all Law makers, to fearch well and to appoint a Committee of Searchers to Examine, if the Laws upon new appearances from Heaven have not need of rectifying and fome of cancelling for fin againft God or the Souls of men eftablifhed by Law, is like *Jereboams* making *Ifrael* to fin, and moft commonly after much patience of God brings double punifhment in the end.

Sin eftablifhed by Law, is Sin multiplied and multiplied, Judgement here and for ever.

The 30*th. Inftance* where G. *Fox* brings in *Tho Moor* faying [*It is not properly nor in a full fenfe that God is manifeft in the Flefh of his Saints.*]

30. Thomas Moor.

He Anfwers, The Saints are the Temple of God, and God dwells in them, and they come to witnefs the Flefh of Chrift. And they glorifie him in their Souls and bodies : And the Lord is glorified in their bringing forth much fruit. And the witnefs is the Seed, the one offering for fin to be manifeft within, and fuch are not Reprobates, yet witnefs the one offering Chrift Jefus, and them that have not Him within, they are Reprobates.

I Reply, a great Defigne of the Devil in all Ages hath

The Devils great work in all Ages. hath been to Cavil at, and hinder Gods love to mankind : Hence he plotted and effected *Mans Fall* from God : God Infinite in wifdome and mercy, out-fhoots and out-plots him, and defignes a Reconciliation and a Marriage between the Son of God the Prince of Life, and loft mankind : He promifed his coming in our Flefh ; prefigured Him, prophefied of Him, *and in the Fulnefs of Time fent Him,* &c.

Sathans Emiffaries to deftroy Chrift Jefus. Againft this Lord Jefus, this old Serpent hiffeth and rageth before his Birth, at his Birth, after his Birth, and in all Ages ever fince, as fearing the crufhing of his Brains, and the downfall of his Throne, if the Kingdome of the Lord Jefus ftand : Hence not long after Chrifts Affention, he ftirred up many *Anti Chrifts,* [61] *Simon Magus* and his *Followers,* the *Arrians,* the *Gnofticks, Cerdonians, Manicheans,* &c. the great *Anti-Chrift* of *Rome,* and fince the *Reformation,* the new *Manicheans,* thofe in *Luthers* and *Calvins* time called the *Spirituals* and *Libertines,* and in our times the *Adamites,* the

The perfon of Chrift Jefus the Devils great Eye fore. *Ranters,* the *Quakers,* and all in order to his *Dragons war* againft the perfon of the *Arch-Angel, Michael* the word of God, the *Individual perfon,* the Man Chrift Jefus, and after him all that fhould dare to follow him.

Some (as the *Arians,* &c.) have denied him to be fo, but Man, and not God ; fome (as the *Manicheans,* &c.) deny his *Manhood,* affirming him to be God, and a Spirit, but, with *Chrifts manhood* and the *Scriptures,* the *Devil* and the *Papifts,* and the *Quakers,* (for moft of them) could with all their hearts make

an

an *Everlafting parting* : The Devils and[1] is to deftroy this Saviour and Salvation to poor loft man :
The *Quakers* pretend their end to be the Exalring
and glorifying of God in the Flefh of his Saints,
therefore fome of thefe *Manicheans* render his Birth,
Life and Death to be only *Imaginary*, and *Allegori-*
cal : a *Figure* of what fhould be done in, and by
Chriftians : others of them fay it is real, but he
only lived and died for an *Example*, others, that he
was really fo born, he fo lived and died, but he is
now only within, *&c.* and after his Flefh no
Inquiry.

The Manicheans the great Oppofers of Chrifts Manhood.

G. *Fox* here plays upon the various meaning of
the word *Flefh*. Alfo he plays upon thofe holy
Scriptures, *viz. God is glorified in the Souls and Bo-*
dies of his Saints, &c.

This *fubtle Jonadab* he knows alfo, that the *Pro-*
teftants maintain that the *Godhead* and the Spirit
of God fo dwels not in the Souls and Bodies of his
Servants as in that Soul and Body of the Lord
Jefus. It is true he was not[2] born of a *Woman*,
but againft their wills they are forc't to Confefs
that he was not born of a *Wife*, but a *Virgin*,
though many Fancies are Coyned about that: They
Confefs that no man was *Father* of his flefhly Nature: He knows alfo that the *Proteftants* hold that
the *Godhead dwels in him*, and dwels in him as the
great *Mediator* and *Propitiation furety* and *Under-*
taker, fo as not in any of the Bodies, or all the
Bodies

That Individual Man Chrift Jefus muft have the prehemi-nence of the only Meffiah and Medi-ator.

The God-head of Chrifts Body after a Tranf-cendent way.

[1] Change "and" to "end." *R. W. Ms. Ann.*
[2] Erafe "not." *R. W. Ms. Ann.*

I *Reply*, 1. And ask of G. *Fox* and all his *Fox-*

About true bearing. *ians* : Have the *Papifts* the *Iews* or any Idolaters the Holy Spirit of God amongft them, whom we may go to hear God fpeaking in his own holy Promife, Ordinance and Appointment unto us ?

2. May I hear a *Papift*, or *Iew*, or any other Falfe Worfhippers or Idolaters to try them when I am convinced and fatisfied already that they fpeak not by the Holy *S*pirit, &c.

3. May I go to Worfhip God with them who either (as I believe) Worfhip a Falfe God, or Worfhip the true and living God, in Wayes and Worfhips of Mens Inventions and Appointments ?

4. May I hear a falfe Prophet, or be prefent at any falfe worfhip, but with actual reproving of them, and labouring to reduce them to the true God and his moft holy Inftitutions and Appointments ?

Upon this Reafon I went to the *General Aff mbly* of the *Quaker*s at *Newport* the laft year, I queried with them about the true Chrift, and the true Spirit : but I was ftopt by a fudden Spirit of Prayer in a Woman, and the unfeafonable Spirit of Prayer in a man, which forced me to ftop, and occafioned me to take this [65] way of offering an appointed and folemn difcourfe and difputation with them.

5. I ask, may any Soul out of Curiofity go to hear a ftrange Preacher, in whom I have not Faith, that he is fent from God, *&c.* efpecially, if there be not a free liberty for my Queries and Objections, and fearchings as the *Bereans* did?

6. Are there not two great Cautions given, us by

the

the Spirit of God! *Take heed whom you hear* : *Take heed how you hear*, and both of thefe in reference to Gods worfhip and mine own Salvation?

7. What do thefe *Foxians* mean by the *Spirits* quenching? Can the Spirit of God be *really quenched*, or put out, any more then the Sun in the Heavens by all the water in the Ocean? Is the Spirit of God *Metaphorically quenched* any other ways then by withdrawing the means or fuel which were to keep the Fire burning that came down from Heaven upon the *Altar*? why then do thefe *proud, lazie Souls* fo horribly flight *reading, ftudying* Books, yea, *Gods Book*, as one of their chief faid to me, (laying his hand upon the Bible of *Junius*, &c. art not thou paft thefe yet? And why do they worfhip a *dumb Devil* in their *dumb meetings*, and ftand ftill and liften, and lie upon their beds of *lazinefs* for *Revelations* and *Notions*, &c.

What the quenching of the Spirit is.

8. As for G. *Fox* his *fcornful fling* againft *old Authors*, what is it but *pride* and *Ingratitude* : *pride* to undervalne, much more to *fcorn* my *Progenitors* and *Anceftors* : *Ingratitude* to God for fo many helps, *&c.* and to them who have laboured and broke the Ice, and left their Labours behind them for the benefit of *after Commers* : yea, what Injuftice, when I difregard and flight their writings, and reproach them, calling them *Old Authors*, compared with their *new Fancies*, as *W. Edmundfon* did me frequently at *Newport, Old Man, Old Man*, &c.

Old Authors.

The 33 *Inftance* is in *Pag*, 206, where he brings in *John Burton*, fading, [*It is a Scripture of the Devils making, to apprehend Chrift within.*]   He

John Burton.

He Anſwers, If there be any other Chriſt but he, who was *Crucified within*, he is the *falſe Chriſt*, and the Scriptures hold forth this, and the Devil never made it, but he and his Meſſengers are againſt it. And he that hath not this Chriſt that was riſen and [66] Crucified within is a *Reprobate*, though *Devils* and *Reprobaes* may talk of him without.

I Reply, This is the great diſpute between the *Chriſtians* and the *Pagans*, the *Chriſtians* and the *Iews*, the *Chriſtians* and the *Mahumetans*, and the *Chriſtians* among themſelves ſo called, *viz*. Who is the great Prophet?

The great diſpute about the true Chriſt.

2. To what purpoſe ſhould I alleadge the whole hiſtory of the *Birth, Life, Death*, &c. of the Lord Jeſus, ſince the *Quakers* acknowledge all true, &c.?

3. Why ſhould I alleadge the *Sermons* and *Preachings*, and *Writings* of the *Apoſtles* or *Meſſengers* of *Chriſt Ieſus* after his *Aſcention*, all *harmonizing* with the *four Evangeliſts*, writing his *Life* and *Death*, &c.

Chriſt without and within

4. Certain it is, that he that ſhall turn over all the former Relations and Hiſtories, and all the writings and Sermons of the *Apoſtles* ſince, and predicate *a* Chriſt that was *riſen within, Crucified within*, (in *Oppoſition* to that *Ieſus of Nazareth without*) he muſt have the *Forehead* of a *Reprobate and Devil*, (as G. *Fox* phrazeth it)

The Proteſtants belief of Chriſt.

5. G. *Fox* knows the *Proteſtants* predicate (in Life and Death) the believing in Chriſt Jeſus ſo born, ſo living and dying: And the applying of the *price* of his *Death* and *merits* unto God for *Propitiation*:

tion: And the Applying of the *Promiſe* and *new Covenant* and *Bargain* in that Blood for a *new Heart*, a *new Spirit*, &c.

6. What ſhall then become of G. *Fox*, his believing in a Chriſt that was *Riſen* and *Crucified within*, in *Oppoſition* to this Lord Jeſus ſo *Promiſed*, ſo *Propheſied* of, ſo *prefigured*, ſo *brought forth*, ſo *living* and *dying*, ſo *preached*, ſo *believed* on, and what a *Forehead* of *Hell* muſt he have that calls all thoſe *Reprobates* and *Devils* that talk of *Chriſt without* ?

The 34*th Inſtance* is in *pag.* 214. where G, *Fox* brings in the *Elders* and *Meſſengers* of ſeveral Churches of *Ilſton*, *Abergevenny*, &c. ſaying, [*We are Conceived in Sin and brought forth in Iniquity*, &c.] ^{Churches in Wales.}

He Anſwers, [*David doth not ſay, you who were Conceived in Sin, but* I, *and* W. *ſaith, Iohn was ſanctified from the Wombe, and the Scriptures ſpeaks of ſuch as were ſanctified from the Wombe, and Children that were clean. And ſo you do not ſpeak as Elders and* [67] *Meſſengers of true Churches, or Men dividing the Word aright, but you are one againſt another, though you are all againſt them you call Quakers, that be in the Truth.*]

I Reply, 1. In the[1] paſſage G. *Fox* diſcovers to any *Intelligent* and *Savoury Spirit*, not only a weak and deluded Soul, but a *Popiſh* and *Arminian poyſon* about the Eſtate of all mankinde in their *firſt Birth*, a ſtrong preſumption that he never felt what the woful Eſtate of all mankinde by Nature is, and ^{The firſt Cry of every Child of God.}

what

---

[1] Change "the" to "this" *R. W. Ms. Ann.*

what to Cry out in his own particular, with *David,*
I was Conceived in Sin and brought forth in Iniquity,
which Cry is one of the *firſt* Soul Cries of every
Child of God.

Whence
Devils and
wicked
men come.

2. About 120 years ſince *the Father of Spirits*
ſtird up the Spirit of his *Famous Servant Calvin* to
batter down the *Babel* of a *Franciſcan Frantick,*
who maintained, that God from the firſt Created
both *Devils* and *wicked men* in the ſame Condition
of wickedneſs wherein we now find them : Contrary to the holy Scriptures Teſtimony (as that *Excellent Soul* proved) declaring their *pure Creation,*
their *Fall,* and their *reſpective future Eſtate* and condition to *Eternity.*

The low
Countries
hazard by
the Pela-
gians.

3. In the Reign of our late *Royal Sovereign* K.
Iames it pleaſed God to let looſe this *Devil* of *Pela-
gius,* who rowzed up the wits of *Arminius* and his
Followers in the *low Countries,* (during their twelve
years Truce with *Spain*) ſo that the Civil Diſcord
about this point and other *Pelagian* and *Semi-pelagian
Doctrines* had almoſt ruined *Holland,* &c. but that
the Lord mightily aſſiſted them. *Firſt,* By the
perſonal preſence and Forces of the *Prince* of
Orange, and *Secondly,* By the *Famous Aſſembly* and
Diſputes of the *Synod* at *Dort.*

Davids
Concep-
tions vin-
dicated
from
G. Foxes
Aſperſions

4. To follow the *Fox* into his *Burrough,* what if
David ſay not you but I *?* why ſhould the *Papiſts*
and *Arminians,* or *Foxians* have a more *holy Birth*
then *David* ? Wherein could *holy* D*avid, Father Jeſſe*
and his mother be charged ? Is not the Engliſh of
the word *Devil Accuſer, Reproacher, Slanderer,* Is
not Nature that *Law* and *Order* which the moſt
Infinite

Infinite Creator hath fet, in the propagation of all his Creatures, though the choiceſt of them Man be degenerated into the *foure Vine*, at firſt a *fweet Vine*, Nature or Gods Order goes on, though man- *What Na-ture is* kinde be Corrupted from the Womb, *and the Imagination of the Thoughts of mans Heart be only evil and that continually*, Gen. 6. and millions of [68] Experiences all the world over Confirm it what the Trade of all mankinde is from the *Birth*. The *Spots* of the *Leopard*, and the *Blackneſs* of the *Neger* comes not by Accident, *&c*.

6. The perverfneſs and Crookedneſs of the motions of Nature may continue, though Nature and the Courfe of it run on, as we fee in *Rivers* turn'd out of their *Chanels*, in *Clocks* and *Watches*, and *D al* , and *Lutes*, and *Harps* when out of Tune they give their *Natural* and *Artificial* (though diftempered) Sounds and operations.

7. Befide the holy Teſtimony of *Mofes*, Gen. 6, and *David*, Pfal. 51. and the Lord Jefus declaring what the heart of man is, *Mark* 7. How doth *Paul*, Rom. 5 and 7. declare the Entrance of Sin by the *firſt Man*, until by the *fecond Man* Sin and Death, and Hell be Conquered, and at laſt Sin in Gods Children fully diffolved, and abolifhed?

8. I end this paffage with *Appellation* to all that kn w what Children are all the world over, the *fweeteſt* and the *faireſt born* of the *holieſt* and *fweet- eſt Parents*, how *froward*, how *proud*, how *Revengeful* againſt their *Fathers*, *Mothers*, and moſt *tender Nurfes*. The pureneſs of the fweeteſt Infants.

1. Thefe rotten and crooked Difpofitions in every
Childe

Childe bring forth wilde Affes fruits in Youth, of
Rebellion againft Superiours, and of wicked defires
of Wine and Women, and fighting and pleafures
in perfons of greater growth, this rotten Nature
appears in their rooting (like Swine) for earthly
profits, or preferments, or fighting like Lions & Ty-
gers in Wars and Law-conttntions, and oppreffing
of Inferionrs, efpecially if they dare to reprove or
witnefs their Idolatries, Superftitions and Abominations.

The rot-
tennefs of
nature

2. The experience of all the Saints of God in
the Holy Scripture, who maintained a Battel between the Flefh and Spirit all their dayes, accord-
to *Gal.* 5. A Battel within them, fometimes the
Spirit (or new Man, the new Creature, or the Grace
of Chrift) prevailing, fometimes the Corruption or
Rottennefs of Nature (like the two Houfes of
Saul and *David*) the old Man getting the victory,
as we fee generally in *Abraham, Ifaak, Jacob, Mofes, Aaron, Eli, Samuel, David, Solomon,* &c. till we
come down to the higheft Saints *Paul* and *Peter* :
the one fhamefully again and again vanquifhed,
and the other (*Paul*) crying [69] out, that *the good
he would do he did not,* and yet when he did evil he
had two men within him, the Law of his Spirit
Heavenly, and the Law of fin which dwelt within
him, &c. they that know not and feel not this, they
are either dead or rotten, and fo feel nothing, or if
there be any life of God in them, and yet fay in the
litteral fenfe they fin not, their weaknefs is fuch,
that like very low and far gone weak bodies their
Filth

The ex-
periences
of Gods
Saints in
Scripture

Filth and Excrements come from them, but they know nothing of it, nor will believe or acknowledge any such matter.

The 35. *Instance* is in *Pag.* 217. where *G. Fox* brings in *John Jackson* saying, [*False Prophets and Chrifts, and Deceivers, many fhould come (if it were poffible) to deceive the very Elect.*]

He *Anfwers*, [Yes, Chrift faid they fhould come to the Apoftles, which before their Deceafe they did come, and went forth from them, which Chrift faid fhould inwardly Ravin , and get the fheeps cloathing: which fince the dayes of the Apoftles all the World went after them, as thou maieft read in the *Revelation*s: and now are People but coming from them to the Rock, and now fhall the Everlafting Gofpel be preached to them that dwell upon the Earth, over the heads of the Beaft and their falfe Prophet, and they fhall be taken, and the Lambe, and the Saints fhall have the victory.

I *Reply*, 1. As that great *Fox*, the *Pope of Rome* and his *Foxians* (the Worfh ppers of that Beaft) maintain that Antichrift is not yet come, that fo he may fcape a fcouring, or rather a burning or dafhing in pieces, fo doth our little *Fox*, G. *Fox* and his *Foxians* cry out another Lurry, [*Antichrift why he is come and gone long ago*, &c.] As if falfe Chrifts might not be then and now too: as if there were no more greedy Wolves to be found then in *Act.* 20 and no more Sheep-skins for them in *Matthew*, 7. &c.

The Spirit of God proclaims, 1 *Cor.* 11. that
there

217 Iohu Iackfon

The great and little Foxes.

there muſt be Hereſies,, and *Peter* tells us 2 *Pet.* 2. that *there muſt be falſe Teachers, falſe Prophets, and Damnable Hereſies, for the trial of the ſincere,* &c. And were all the *Foxes* hunted out and deſtroyed in the Apoſtles dayes, and none left ſince *Johns* time to our times to be hunted after and digd out of their Burroughs.

70| Are there none found, ſincere, and chaſte to be tried at this day to the Lord Jeſus the Heavenly *Bridegroom,* and to his Eternal King and Father, God bleſſed to Eternity.[1]

2. The Proteſtants maintain that the *Pope* or *Papacy* is the great Antichriſt, the Man of Sin, *with ſeven heads and ten horns,* &c. why ſhould not the Devil be able to raiſe beſides the *Pope,* the *Ceredonians, Valentinnians* and the *Arians, Manicheans, Gnoſticks,* &c. and ſince, or at the beginning of the Reformation, the *Quintinians,* and *Munſterian* Mouſters? why ſhould he not be able to raiſe in our time the *Nicholaitans* and *Foxians.*

The Hereſies of several Ages.

3. It is true that in the times of warm peace, &c. many Vermine breed, whom the cold winter of Perſecution utterly deſtroyes. I know alſo that in the late times of Freedome to mens Opinions in *England,* Many Opinions and promoters of them aroſe : Sharp times God hath to make diſcovery, I know ſome ſay that *Judas,* and *Theudas,* and *Barchochas,* and *Rabbi-Iudah,* &c. were the falſe Chriſts the Lord Jeſus ſpake of : I know alſo that amongſt the Profeſſours of the Chriſtian Name, falſe Chriſts and

Concerning falſe Chriſts &c.

---

[1] Ends with a "?" not a "period." *R. W. Ms. Ann.*

and falſe Prophets, Apoſtles, Preachers, &c. muſt pretend to the Chriſtian Name, alſo.

4. I know ſome affirm that though the Pope be Antichriſt, yet that he that letted was not the Roman Emperour until he was taken out of the way, but that he that letted was the Holy Spirit to which the Quakers now pretend, which Spirit being taken away the *Popes* aroſe : But in the dayes of *Iohn* when thoſe gifts did moſt flouriſh, yet then there were many Antichriſts, and the gift of the Holy Spirit did not hinder their riſing ; ſo that all ages are full of falſe Teachers. *Concerning him who letted Antichriſts riſing*

5. What Ignorance doth this little *Fox,* yet great *Boaſter* diſcover in ſaying [*Now are People coming forth from them,* &c.] doth he proudly look over all thoſe Glorious Proteſtant Witneſſes of Jeſus, before and ſince *Luther,* whoſe Names many of them, God commanded that Heavenly *I. Fox* to make Record of.

6. Do the *Foxians* juſt now about *twenty years* preach the everlaſting Goſpel : Now ſaith *W. Edm.* in our diſcourſe we preach the everlaſting Goſpel to you, that you ſhall be free from ſin, &c. But Gods Spirit tells us in *Peter* and *Iude* of pretenders to liberty, while themſelves are the Servants of Corruption or Rottenneſs. *The everlaſting Goſpel*

71] 7. Both Jews and Gentiles have done by the Name of Chriſt as the Jews and Romans with Chriſt Jeſus before they murthered him : they mockd him, &c. and then Murthered him ; that ſo they might be the *Heir* and *Meſſiah* themſelves : Juſt as the great *Fox* the *pope* and theſe little

Foxians

Foxians pretend to be the fole great *Heir* apparent to the Crown of Heaven, and all other Rebels and Reprobates againft and from their Heavenly Majefties.

John Jackfon

The 36. *Inftance*, is in page 218. Where G, *Fox* brings in the fame Author faying, ⌊*I hope you will not condemn the Generation of the Righteous becaufe they are vot perfeEt.*⌋

He Anfwers, That which condemneth is Righteous ; it condemns that which is not perfeEt, and the Generation is Righteous and not to be condemned.

I Reply, He Anfwers four things : Firft, that which Condemns is righteous. Secondly, That which is Righteous Condemns that which is not

The horrible pride of the Foxians

perfeEt. Thirdly, That which is righteous is perfeEt. Fourthly, The Generation is Righteous (that is them felves being perfeEt) and not to be Condemned, the Summe of his Anfwer is, *Himfelf* and his *Foxian*s are *Gods*, as *pure*, & *holy*, as God is, and therefore now keep the *Eternal Seffion*s and *Affizes* at the *Tribunal* of their *high Court*, muft all the Generations of the World receive their *Eternal Doom* and *Sentence*, I know they know this is the bottom.

1. But ftay, this *Fox* is in his *Burrough* of *Equivocation* : for *Judgement* is twofold : Firft, *Judgement Righteous* : Secondly, According to *Appearance*, as

Falfe appearances

the Lord Jefus diftinguifheth : How many are declared by *Appearances* to their Eyes, *Clouded*[1]
pride

[1] Infert " with." *R. W. Ms. Ann.*

*pride, malice, Envy, Lafcivioufnefs, Covetoufnefs, Am-
bition*, &c. And therefore away with the Son of
God, hang him, and give us *Barrabas*, though a
Boutefeau and *Murtherer*, &c·

2. It is not true, that all that is not perfect (in
the *Foxians* Senfe) is not *Righteous*: For 1. (as hath
been before obferved) the words *Tam* and *Tomjin* in
Hebrew, and *Telos* and *Teleios*, and *Teleion* in the
Greek, have divers fignifications, and accordingly,
muft be, and are tranflated and expounded, Contrary to the *proud Ignorance* of thefe *Cheators*.

The word
perfect in
the greek
and
Heqrew

2. The Generation of all Gods Children (in all
the holy Scrip- [72] ture) have ever acknowledged
their weaknefs, folly, pride, and many Tranfgreffions, with *true Quaking* and *brokennefs*, and *bitter
weeping*, &c :

3. In a true Senfe, that which is *Righteous* is *perfect Iuftification* or *Remiffion* of Sin for Chrift Jefus
fake is perfect, it admits (as they fay of no *magis & mi-
nus*) more or lefs, the truely humble *Ethiopian* is as
truly and *perfectly pardoned* and *Iuftified* as *David*
himfelf, and the *bleffed Mother* of the Lord Jefus,
the *Virgin Mary*.

The Saints
pardon of
Sin and
Juftifica-
tion
perfect.

4. We maintain, though pardon of Sin and Juftification, and Acceptation with God before Angels, Men and Devils be perfect, and though a poor
Child of God be born of God, be paft from *Death*
to *Life*, can not Sin in a Senfe, nor fuffer the Devil
to touch him : yet there remains till Death a Combate to be fought between the Law of the Spirit,
and Law of the members, the *old Man* and the *new
Man*, the *Flefh* and the *Spirit*, &c.

The
Saints bat-
tel and
daily
Combate

5. Hence

5. Hence (in an holy Senfe) *Paul* faith, *it is not I, but Sin that dwels in me, that is in my Flefh wherein dwels no good thing,* So that David might fay in one Senfe, It was not I that committed *Adultery,* and *Murther,* and *Peter* fay, It was not I that *denied my Mafter with Swearing and Curfing,* &c. *but the rotten old man and Sin dwelling in me.*

Devilfh
Tenents
of the Spi-
rituals in
Calvins
time.

He that knows not to untie thefe Knots, and yet prates of Righteoufnefs and perfection: He is proud and foolifh, and ignorant, and he will proudly and foolifhly fooner or later commit thefe five great evils.

1. He will not difcern what the *Generation* of the *Righteous is.*

2. He will fay Sin is nothing but *Imagination.*

3. He will caft wickednefs upon God, and fay God doth all, and what God doth that is good, therefore no Sin.

4. He muft call David and Peter fools for Confeffing their *Guilt* and *weeping bitterly,* &c.

5. That it is in vain to watch againft Sin, and to cry *Lord lead us not into Temptation,* &c.

In the laft place I Affirm (and have made it good) that the *Generation* of the *Papifts* and *Quakers:* though fo pure in their own eyes, *yet they are not cleanfed from their filthinefs:* The *Papifts* are juftly charged with *Superflition* and *Idolatry* & with drinking the Blood of Saints. And have not the *Generation* of the *Quakers:* [73] their Images and Idols alfo, (as I have manifefted) their pride and Ignorance & Idlenefs in not ufing means, and their paffionate Railings and Curfings? and I believe if

their

their *Spirit* get a *Sword* (what ere they ignorantly prate) they will drink the *Blood* of all their *Enemies* as *Hereticks, Idolaters, Reprobates*, and *Devils*.

The 37*th. Inftance* is in *Pag.* 220. wherein G. *Fox* brings in the *Author* of *Hofanna* to the Son of *David*, faying, [*Man is not able to difcern the things of God till he be born again.*]

margin: 220 Hofanna to the Son of David

He Anfwers, the Scripture fpeaks of difcerning *the Eternal Power and Godhead*, and that was a thing of the *Spirit* of God: and the *Apoftle* faith not that they were born again: And yet I fay *that none knows the things of God but the Spirit of God*, and that which may be known of God is manifeft in them, for God hath fhewd it to them: For that of God in them was of the Spirit, *who is the God of the Spirits of all Flefh*, which brings them to difcern the *Eternal Power and Godhead*.

I Reply, 1. With Amazement at the dreadful Juftice of God hardening this daring Soul for playing away his own Light and the Name of God, and the Light which the Lord hath fent him from fo many *Excellent pens* out of which he hath raked nothing but handfuls of Reproaches to fling in the Faces of his beft Friends, and turned Truth into Lyes, and poyfon to murther himfelf and others.

margin: G Fox his Judgment from God

2. It is clear, that (as in all Anfwers to the *Quotations* of his *Oppofites* which he picks out) that he holds the Contrary to his *Oppofite*, fo here *viz.* That a man may be able to difcern the things of God before he be born again.

3. He proves his point from two Scriptures,
Rom.

Rom. 1. *Cor.*2. As to the firſt, I will not repeat what I have before written as to the Nature of the *holy* Spirit, his *Godhead*, his *Operations, ſeven Eyes,* & *ſeven Horns, and ſeven Lamps,* his *Common workings* in all men! his *ſpecial working* in the Elect, *Regenerating, Juſtifying, Sanctifying, quickning, Comforting,:* &c. Nor will I repeat matters concerning the power of Nature in the *Philoſophers,* and all mankinde: Only from this *Rom.* 1. I obſerve,

1. That *the Eternal Power and Godhead* cannot be ſeen by *mortal Eyes.*

2. We may reach ſome *mental Light* of this *Eternal Power* [74] *and Godhead,* by a ſerious pondering of his works.

3. All mankinde are bound by the Law of their Nature to put forth their utmoſt in ſearching after God.

Kom. 1. Diſcuſſed as to the Eternal Power and Godhead.

4. We may gain a great ſight of the Godhead, and yet not ſee him nor glorifie him, that is love him as *Paul,* 1 *Cor.* 8.

5. Natural men until changed and born again of Gods power and Spirit, doe but prate (*as the Devils do and tremble*) *their imaginations are vain, and their fooliſh hearts are darkened.*

The natural power of men and Devils.

6. Yet this ſight of God which men and Devils may get of God by their own Remainders of natural Abilities will leave them without excuſe whatever *Papiſts, Arminians* and *Quakers* talk of Gods requiring no more then he gives, for in Juſtice God is not bound to give *Sampſon* his Locks or his Eyes when he hath willingly ſuffered *Dalilah* and by her the *Philiſtims* to cut them off, and pluck them out.   2. Beſide

2. Befide our wils and wifdome are now become *Enmity againft God*, and no man fpends equal Care and pains for God, until Gods Spirit in free grace ch nge and quicken him with what he does for thefe *temporary Dreams* and *Shadows*.

The fecond Scripture is 1 *Cor.* 2. *viz* But God hath revealed them unto us by his Spirit: *For `the Spirit fearcheth all things, yea, the deep things of God: For what man knows the things of a man fave the Spirit of a man*, &c. now we have not received the Spirit of the world, but the Spirit which is of God, that we may know *the things which are freely given to us of God.* 1 Cor. 2. as to Gods Spirit difcuffed.

In *ver.* 6. the Spirit of God fpeaks of a twofold wifdome, firft, the wifdome of this world, and the Principles[1] of this world which come to nought. Secondly, the wifdome of God in a Myftery, even the *hidden wifdome which God ordained before the world unto our glory.* : Again, *ver.* 12. God tells us of two Spirits: The Spirit of the world, Secondly, The Spirit of God. Now this *woful Cheator* finding the word Spirit, Confounds as his Courfe is all together, and becaufe Gods Spirit regenerates the *Corint ians*, and opens to them a glimpfe of the Godheads power and wifdom, and Goodnefs by *Pauls preaching*, and opens their hearts to it therefore he muft alfo enlighten the world with the fame Light, *whereas that which is born of the Spirit is Spirit, and that of Flefh is Flefh*; This Change and renewing of the Spirit by the Holy Spirit, I fear G. *Fox* and moft of his *Fox-ians* never Experimened, [74] though they enjoy in common Wifdome. The Cafe of G Fox and moft of his Foxians.

---

[1] Chauge " Principles " to " Princes." *R. W. Ms. Ann.*

common a Light of Nature, though God hath endowed him and many of them with excellent Natural Part*s* : yea, with a Light from the *holy Scripture* : yea, with a Light of *Experience* and *common Motions* from Gods holy Spirit, and have been lifted
up by their own thoughts and others (as *Capernaum*)
up to the Heaven ! and therefore my Soul fears (as to
moſt of them) *that God will bring them down to Hell
with the greater Condemnation.*

222. Ho-
ſanna to
the Son of
David

The 38*th Inſtance* is in *Pag.* 222. where he brings
in the ſame Author ſaying, [*Salvation and Faith are
the gifts of God diſtinct from Chriſt*]

He Anſwers, *They are all of him, and from him,
and with him,* And how is he *the Author of Faith in
whom it ends, and from whence it comes.*]

Chriſts
Name
hotribly
abuſed

I Reply, as *Potiphars wife* cries out againſt *Jo-
ſeph* : and pretends *Chaſtity,* ſo doth this *ſubtle
Whoremonger,* pretending that all is *pure Chriſt* : the
Light is *Chriſt,* their *Hope* is *Chriſt,* their *Faith,* their
Spirit is *Chriſt* himſelf, yea, the *Saints are Chriſt* :
No diſtinction between Chriſt and them, *for they
are all of him, from him, and with him* ?

Coloſſians
1. Con-
ſidered.

The Na-
ture and
admirable
Miſtery
and Excel-
len- of
Chriſt
Jeſus

In ſhort, I pray the Reader to mind with me the
firſt Chapter to the *Coloſſian*s, where *ver.* 1. The Spirit of God declares how Gods Children (poor ſlaves
at firſt in S*athan*s *Clutches) are Tranſlated from the
Kingdome of Darkneſs into the Kingdome of his dear
Son: In whom we have Redemption through his Blood,
even the Forgiveneſs of Sins.* I know the *Foxians*
turn Chriſt, yea, his Blood alſo into a *Spirit,* a God.
How admirably doth the holy Spirit of God declare

clare the *Godhead,* or *Divinity* of Chrift Jefus and his *Manhood* or *Humanity*, unto *ver.* 21? out of both which I fhall felect two or three Attributes of the Lord Jefus.

1. The State of Chriftianity, amongft many other high Expreffions in the Scripture, is here called *the Kingdome of Gods dear Son*, which argues a diftinction from all other Kingdomes, and a diftinction from his *Saints*, as a *King* is not his *Subjects*, nor their *Gifts* and *Honours*, and *Eftates*, and *peace*, and *Joy* though given by him to them,, and procured by his *great wifdome* and *love* for them.

Oh *poor Ungrateful Monfters*, not content to be taken from [76] the *Kingdome*, from the *Dungeon*, of *Darknefs* and *Hell*, and that by the *Ranfome* and *price* paid and *Blood* and *Death* of his *only Beloved the Prince of Life*, but we muft be the King *of Heaven* and *Prince of Life* our felves.

2. I obferve, The *Inftrumental* and *purchafing Caufe* or *price*, is faid to be his *Blood*, which argues the *Infinite value* of his Sufferings, in which Ref- pect only it is called *the Blood of God*: I know the flight efteem that fome of thefe *Foxians* have of the *Blood* of the *Lord Jefus* faying, that *wicked men* the *Souldiers* fhed it; that it was fpilt upon the *ground*, that there was no difference between that *Blood* and the *Blood* of another *Saint*: That by *Gods blood* is only meant *godly* and *heavenly power*, and *Spirit* by which God applies Mercy and *pardon, Juftification, Righteoufnefs,* &c.

I have read the Blafphemous Difcanting of the *Jefuit* concerning *Maries* white Milk, and Chrifts

The Blood of Chi .
The Blood of God.

The Blood of Chrift def- pifed by

Crimfon

Papifts and
Quakers. Crimfon Blood, & in the clofe, his preferring the
Milk of the Mother before the Sons Blood.

I have heard alfo the foolifh Blafphemy of one
of my own Neighbours, faying, That the Blood of
the Quakers, and by name of *W. B.* was Saving
and Salvation to the World.

Chrift the
picture of
God. 3. But I pafs on, The Lord Jefus is here called
the Image of the invifible God: If this fhould refpect the Godhead only, which is invifible, how
could Chrift be a vifible Picture of Invifibility? If
the Manhood only? is God a Man, and Man his
Image or Picture, as the old Heretick, and late in
London, Reeves and *Mugleton fancied.*

Chrift
God and
Man. The Truth is, as Chrifts Blood is but figuratively
for an Antitipe and fulfilling of all the Figures
foregoing him, and for all his Sufferings, and many
Blood-fheddings both of Minde and Body, fo this
Image or Picture, this Bleffed Lamb of God, confifting of the Godhead, wonderfully affuming fuch
a *none fuch Manhood*, both which the *Papifts* and
Quakers are forced to confefs, I fay, it is clear he
was the brighteft Image or Picture of God to the
World that ever God appeared in, and therefore
called the Word of God the fulleft and loudeft of
all the Words of God in which ever he fpake, &c.

Chrift
Fulnefs
filling all. 4. Many more I might infift on, but I muft ab-
breviate, and only mention *ver.* 18. where the Lord
Jefus is made the Pallace of [77] the Godhead,
that in him as the Head of the Body, his Church,
fhould all fulnefs dwell, reconciling and making peace,
through the Blood of his Croffe, &c. *Iohn* tells us,
that of this fulnefs in him, we receive: all the
World

World receives the Mercy and Patience of God by him ; all his Followers receive his Grace and Spirit, Converting, Sanctifying, Comforting, &c. so that his most holy and glorious Manhood, visible amongst us, &c. was as a fair and spacious, beauti- *A wonderful Conduit,* into which the eternal and inconceivable Counsels of the eternal Power and Godhead *duit.* flowed, and from whom by all those blessed means and Ordinances, as by so many Cocks turned and let loose, flow and run into poor empty Souls as Pails and Tankards all sorts of mercies to the whole World, and especially to the Elect, and Chosen, his Church and Body that believe in him : what *The proud phrenzie of the* poor Children and Frantick Souls are we then that *Quakers.* cry out (poor Pots, and Pails, and Tankards) that we are the Conduit it self ; yea, we the Well-head, Fountain and Spring, and (as this frantick *Fox* in his Book once and again affirms) no distinction between God & Christ & his Saints, yea, though he often acknowledge that Christ is the *Author and Finisher of Faith* ; So that the Gift of God, the words of God, which are his *Tokens, Love Tokens,* and *Love Letters,* they are God and Christ, themselves the *heavenly Father,* and his Son the *heavenly Bridegroom.*

John the *Baptist* cried out to all such *proud Souls, I am not He, I am not worthy to untie his Shoe Latchet : He it is that Baptizeth with Fire : He is the Lamb of God, &c. He, even that man upon whom he The Papists and saw the Spirit descending like a Dove, &c. and blessed Quakers Paul with Iob, abhors himself, and counts his Holy Christ Life, his Prayers, his Fastings, his Righteousness Dung*

Dung and Dirt compared with that of Chrift Iefus, in Oppofition to that of the Law, &c. In which *mud* ftill the moft zealous *Papifts* and *Quakers* ftick, and talk idly of their fulfilling of the Law now, by Chrifts Righteoufnefs, Grace and Spirit in them, which they will at laft find to be no more but the *firft Bargain* or *Covenant,* let them pride themfelves never fo much in their filthy *menftrous Clouts* and *Rags of Holinefs,* that is their *Chrift within* them.

The 39*th. Inftance* is in *Pag.* 223. where he
223 Ho-
fanna to
the Son of
David
brings in the fame Author faying, [*The Light which difcovers Sin and Iniquity* [77] *in Mans Heart is not Chrift the dore*] He *Anfwers,* [*The firft* Adam *was the Dore wh reon all Sin and Tranfgreffion entred: Chrift the Light, the fecond* Adam *which doth inlighten every man,* &c. *faith, I am the Dore, the Way, and the Life, which finifh Sin and Tranfgreffion, and brings in Everlafting Righteoufnefs, and the way of Dife[1] out of Death, which Light difcovers Sin*]

I Reply, *Edmund Burroughs* in his *large Epiftle* to G. *Fox* thi h s Book, he tells us that this Light (which they thus boaft of) fhews mans threefold
The
Eftate of
mankinde
Eftate, before Tranfgreffion: in Tranfgreffion and what he is by being faved out of Tranfgreffion: It is true, Chrift Jefus doth this by many gracious means, but not Immediately, nor to every man that comes into the world: For *the World lies in wickednefs and Darknefs.* We are not only bleeding in our wounds, but we are loft in the *Wildernefs:* We are ftark dead in Sin, and know no more that we are

dead

---

[1] Change " *Dife* " to " *Life.*" *R. W. Ms. Ann.*

dead then a dead man knows of his Condition : what do then thefe poor deluded Souls tell us of a Light and Chrift within every man in the world discovering his pure Eftate, his foul Eftate, and his raifed Eftate, which no man or woman in this world that I have read or heard of by Nature had any Spark or fhine of fuch a Light : no nor thefe proud Ignorants neither, but they have read or heard of thefe things (more or lefs) from the holy Scriptures and Records.

2. It is granted, that *Natures Light* difcovers a God, fome fins a Judgement, as we fee in *Indians* : Education and preaching difcovers more, as in *Saul,* *Achitophel, Judas* : The Word and Afflictions makes *Pharoah* cry out *I have finned* : Miracles make *Nebu-chadnezzar* and *Darius* cry out *There is no God fo great as* Daniels, and to make dreadful Laws againft blafphemers of him, though themfelves continue in their *old* I*dolatries :* yea, doubtlefs *Natures Light* is able (in felf deceitfulnefs) wonderfully to Counter-fiet *true heavenly Light,* and the *Devil* feem an *Angel* or *Meffenger of Light* from Heaven ! *[margin: Convictions of Nature one thing, Converfion another]*

3. What is this to a *faving Conviction* which Gods Spirit worketh in thofe that fhall be faved, when they cry out as the *wounded Jews, what fhall we do to be faved* ? and as the *Gaolour, what fhall I do to be faved* ? : until this faving Senfe of my Condition, and Gods Juftice, what is Chrift, a Phyfitian, a Sa-viour, a Redeemer, *Bread, Water, Wine* and *oil* to me ? All is needlefs, yea, loathfome, (though an *bony Comb*) to a full Soul : what talk [78] you of a pardon to an honeft man ? or if a *Rope* or *Barr* to fave a fecure *Epicure* in his *downe Bed* ? 4. Again *[margin: Saving Convictions]*

The State of Adam in his Fall 4. Again, how poor a plea is this, *Adam* was the dore to fin, therefore Chrift is the dore to the difcovery of fin? For, look upon *Adam* in his *Fall*. 1. He faw his fin? 2. He had horrour of Confcience: 3. He run from God. 4. He hides himfelf. 5. He He fals to mincing end excufing his fin. All this is revealed to us, and not a word yet heard of, Chrift the *promifed See*d, or a *Light*, Chrift Jefus to Convince him of fin: That was another work, a faving work, which we may hope the Spirit of God wrought in him upon the preaching of Chrift Jefus, the *promifed* Seed nd *Mediatour* to come.

Sathans Cunning with the Quakers 5. I know the Song of the great deluder is: Turn to the *Light*, hearken to the *Light*; thou feeft it chides thee for thy Stealing, for thy lying, *&c*. Is not this the Chrift, *&c*. liften to him, be ftill, fink down, obey him, he will teach thee & fave thee, *&c*. But the Bottom is, the Englifh and meaning is, hearken to Sathan, *the God of this world*, be ruled and taught, and guided by him, : The Scripture is but a *dead Letter*, the true Chrift is within thee, he will turn thee from thefe fins, and make thee perfe& as God is perfeft, *&c*. Chrift is come now in Chrifts coming us the *fecond Time without fin to Salvation*. He is come in us (*Ten thoufand of his Saints*) to Judgement: He within thee is the word of God, the Chrift of God, the Light of God, the Spirit of God, God himfelf, and He feeks *Worfhippers in Spirit and Truth*, for the vifible things are temporal, *&c*

6. But what is there in all this, but the noife of
Fenny

Fenny bitter in *hollow Canes,* &c? What is here but Two common that common Bufineffes may reach to? Traps and

1. The Confcience of good and evil which every Engines *favage Indian* in the world hath. of Sathan

2. The *whifperings,* the *bl ndings* and *cheatings* of in cheat-the *Devil,* in Samuels *mantle,* pretending *vowing* and Foxians Swearing to be the word of the Lord to be Chrift Jefus, yea, & that to your feeling &c.

7. But what are thefe to Chrift Jefus, *a dore of Hope* to *poor, wounded,* and *damned finners*? God by his Law and Juftice, by outward hearing or reading, and inward Convictions of *Natural Confcience* hath When paffed Sentence of *Eternal Death* and *Hell* on them : Chrift is They feel it they cry out now the Gofpel or *glad* welcome *news* of a Saviour, a Jefus is *Hony* in the mouth, &c. Now *Luke* 4. he [80] *heals the broken heart, he fets free the Prifoners, ho gives Light to them that fee themfelves blind,* and Cry to him as the blind man did, Chrift medles not with found perfons who have no need of his *Bloud, Righteoufnefs, and Mer-its,* &c.

The 40 *Inftance* is in *Pag.* 224. where G. *Fox* Ellis brings in *Ellis Bradfhaw,* faying, [*There is more words* Bradfhaw *then one*]

He *Anfwers,* God is the word, and the Scrip-tures are the words which Chrift fulfil,.

I Reply, 1. As the defigne of the *bloudy Pope* and *Jefuits* are to kindle wars between the *Proteftants,* that the *Proteftant*s may do the *Papifts work* and fave labour and Charges, and fo the *Pope* and his *bloudy Whore* of *Rome* may march away fecurely by the

the Light of the *Proteftants fires.* So deals the Devil *the old* Serpent with Chrift Jefus, and the holy Scripture or Records which are but One, in a Senfe, as the Sun and the Sun-dial: His end is to tear down the Sun dial the Scriptures, under pretence that the Sun is within them, and they need no Dials and Clocks, no vifible thing that are temporal, *&c.* and fo to deftroy the perfon and Commands of the Lord Jefus, as vifible and flefhly pretending all to be Light and Spirit.

Two great defigns of Sathan

2. The words in the *Hebrew Aamar* and *Dabar,* as alfo the *Greek, Logos* and *Rema* fignifie a word, and divers other matters, as I told my *Antagonifts* in the difpute.

The Word and Words of God

1. In both thefe Languages, and divers other Languages it fignifies the will and pleafure of the Mind given forth by *Command,* or *Decres,* or *Proclamation* made by word, or writing from Kings and States, and *Commanders of Armies, Navies,* &c.

2. In a *Metaphor* or *Figure* it is attributed to God, though he have no word properly, having no mouth, no Tongue, no Braine, *&c.* but as Nurfes he deals with us *poor Infants* and fucklings, *&c.*

3. It is another *Metaphor* or *Figure* to fay God is the word for God is no more a word, then he is a Man or a Spirit, or a Sun, or Shield, or a Houfe, or a Fountain, or a Shepard litterally *&c.* For as a word or Expreffion proceeds from the mind & thoughts within: fo are the Thoughts and mind of God declared many wayes, but chiefly by that man Chrift Jefus called the Word.

3. The *Inconceivable Godhead* being pleafed to
vouch

vouch-fafe in Infinite Goodnefs fome back parts
and glimpfes of his *Infinite glori-* [81] *rious Majef-*
ty in the Framing of this world, and in the reftor-
ing of this world, by making a *Marriage* between
his Son and mankind! all his words and Expreffions tend mightily to advance this *marriage* and
great manifeftation, or Word of God.

Whether
God have
any more
wordsthen
one.

4. I was once asked by a *poor Foxian,* whether
God had any more words but one?

I *Anfwered,* (and do now) that God hath a great
many words or Expreffions of his mind and Coun-
fels unto *Men* and *Angels*: and fo G. *Fox,* and all
the *Foxians* Confefs the Scriptures to be the Words
of God, and therein Confefs that all, and every word
of Scripture is a word of God.

The Truth is, when God gives forth a word or
Command by *Angels,* by *Men,* and by other of his
Armies, (wherein his *Infinite Power* and *Providence*
daily appeareth) his word runneth very fwiftly, as
we fee when the word is given in a Kingdome,
Navy or *Army,* (as in *Ahafhueros* his one hundred
and twenty feven Provinces: *&c.*) He fends out his
word, that is, his mind or pleafure, and melteth
them, *Pfal.* 147.

Infinite
millions of
millions of
Gods
word.

5. So that I Affirm, that the *two great Lights*
of *Heaven,* the *Sun* and *Moon,* and all the *leffer Lights*
the *Stars* are *Words* and *Preachings,* and *preachers of*
God to us: Every wind and Cloud, and drop of
Rain and Hail, every Flake of Snow, every Leaf,
every Grafs, every drop of water in the Ocean, and
Rivers, yea, every Grain of Corn, and Sand on the
Shore, is a Voice or word and witnefs of God
unto us.   6. Hence

6. Hence (as in that *Admirable* 107 *Pſalm*, &c. Every Turn of the *holy hand* of God in *Ruling* and *Over-ruling* all things in the world upon the *two great Hinges* of *Mercy* and *Judgement*, Pſal, 110. are but ſo many Voices or words of God, *God ſpeaks once and twice*, Job. 33. *but man hears it not, in Viſions, in Dreams, in Health, and Sickneſs, in Eaſe, and pain, in wants, in plenty, in dangers and Deliverances, Croſſes, Loſſes,* &c.

The Voice of Gods works and Providences

7. That the *Hebrew* is moſt full, *viz.* that God ſpake by his Prophets (or Preachers, or declarers of his will) divers wayes and divers times, *but now he hath ſpoken by his Son: From the beginning of the world,* Luke 1. he hath ſpoken of the coming of this Son *by the mouths of all his Prophets even from the beginning of the World.* Therefore though God have many Sons, yet Chriſt Jeſus (that man Chriſt Jeſus) among the many millions of [82] Sons is ſtiled the only Begotten Son of God, the Head of all the Elect, purchaſed to God out of every Nation by his Blood, &c. ſo by the ſame excellency and eminency (above all the manifeſtations and appearances of God to the World) no word or appearance of God is comparable to that appearance of God in Chriſt Jeſus, and therefore called *the Word of God* as the greateſt appearance of the eternal Power and Godhead.

Gods Spirit in his word

Chriſt the word of God

8. Hence it follows, that theſe poor *Foxians* are ſo much the more ſhameleſs and monſtrous, not only in robbing the Scriptures of their moſt Heavenly and common Title of the Word of God, common to all Gods appearances, but alſo in turning

The ſhameleſs wickedneſs of the Quakers againſt the

ing

ing this Word of God Chrift Jefus into a Spirit Scriptures & Chrift himfelf without any body : but what is gone for ever from us, and by their parting him (his God-head from his Man-hood) into a Fancie, a Dream, a meer Whimfie, and Devellifh Imagination.

9 When we deal with *Indians* about *Religion,* The way of dealing with Indians our work is to prove unto them by Reafon, that the *Bible* is *Gods Word,* for by Nature they are much affeǒted with a kind of Deity to be in Writing : That all their Revelations, and Vifions, and Dreams (in which the Devil wonderfully abufeth them) are Falfe and Cheating.

That this Scripture or Writing we pretend to, is They fee infinite Reafon in the holy Scriptures from God by their own experience, becaufe it agrees with their own Confciences, reproving them for thofe fins their Souls fay they are guilty of : That the terrible Majefty of Gods Juftice in pun- ifhing Sinners fo fhines in it, and alfo his infinite goodnefs and mercy in finding out fuch a way of Mediation, and fuch a Mediator that their Souls cannot but adore Infinite Juftice and Mercy in it. That the Holy power of God fo appears in it in working upon the Souls of Millions, turning them from Dogs, and *Swine,* and Wolves, and Lions, and Sheep, and Lambs, and Doves, &c. in Love, Meeknefs, Patience, &c.

That it could be none but an Omnipotent Arm The pre- fervation of the Scripture that hath preferved the *Holy Scripture* fo many thoufand years (fome part of it) through fo many wonderful changes, through fo many *Bloody Hunt-* *ings* of *Kings, Emperours, Popes* ; and this more fub-
tile

tile Hunting of thefe *Foxians*, to run it out of this World. and by feeming to embrace it to deftroy and kill it.

Tho. Weld

83] The 41. *Inftance* is in *Page* 228. Where G. *Fox* brings in *Thomas Weld*, faying, [*There lies a Myftery of Iniquity, for to fay the World calls them fo, by fuch and fuch Names or gives them their Chrif-tian Nam*e.]

He Anfwers, [There are Names given by the Hea-then, the Heathen outward which men are called : There is a new Name which the World knows not written in the Book of Life: Here is the new Man known after God in Righteoufnefs and true Holinefs ; Now who is the New Man, and this new Name ? the World may call him by the old, fo it is not a myf-tery of iniquity to fay the World calls him fo.]

As to Chriften Names, & Names to Children

I *Reply*, 1. As to Chriftian or Chriften Names or Things bearing or pretending to bear the Name, Authority or an Uniting of Chrift Jefus (as we know the word Chriftian fignifies) it is incumbent on every Chriftian Soul to fearch into the Root, and Rife, and Practife, and Warrant of them with holy fear and trembling in the prefence of God.

The Foxians fcornful pride

2. But to the myftery of Iniquity here infinua-ted againft them, Is it not a proud trick of a *Phari-fee* thus to fcorn the poor *Heathens* and *Publicans*, as not worthy to know the *Foxians* high Names, or take up fuch facred Names and Myfteries upon their Lips ? yea, is it not a ridiculous Fancie thus to prate, and (like *Pharifees* to fcold about wafhing of Hands, and Pots, and Cups, therein placing in-vented Holinefs, &c.   For,

For, 1. VVhat are the Heathen, this Heathenifh Who are G. Fox his Heathen Soul here ftrikes at? doth he mean the wilde *Sav-ages*, who give Names to their Children, and oft times full of Reafon and Significance, &c. Or doth he account all Nations *Savages* and *Barbarians* that give Names to their Children, and confequently themfelves *Savages* and *Barbarians* alfo, for they give Names unto their Children alfo.

2. It is true that by the word *Heathen* (the *Goj* The Words Heathen in the *Hebrew* and *Ethne* in the *Greek*) the Nations or Gentiles were fignified as diftinct from the Holy Nation or Church of God the *Jews*, but fo it is not common in our Englifh Phraze, to call all the Nations *Heathen* that are not of the *Jewifh Nation*.

3. Did not the Saints before the coming of Chrift give Names to their Children? did not *Leah* and *Rachael* (by *Jacobs* leave) give all thofe fignificant Names unto the *twelve Patriarchs*? and [84] have not the Saints of God (as well as all Nations) ftill fo practifed?

4. Doth *Chriftian Regeneration* or *New Birth* deftroy *Natural Births* or *Marriages*, or *Procreations*, or *Name*s, and *Educations*? (Only as *Diamonds* in *Gold-Rings*, and *Aples of gold in pictures of filver*) Chriftianity beautifies and adorns all thefe, *Natural* and *Civil Action*s, with an heavenly Spirit,[1] Carriage in *Earthly matters*.

5 Can there be any Inftances given of any Ser- Chrift deftroys not but beautifies Civility vants of God before or fince the coming of Chrift Jefus, difowning or flighting the Names which their Parents had given them: yea, though there were

---

[1] Infert "&." *R. W. Ms. Ann.*

were fome feeming honour to falfe Gods in them, *Fortunatus*, *Apollo*, *Phebe*, &c.

6. Why may we not (though we are for[1] his Heathens) call the *Foxians* by the fame Names by which they call themfelves? for, in this great Book we find G. *Fox* and *Edmund Burrough* fubfcribed? It is a Query why they fo plainly fubfcribe and yet defend them that do not, Have they a Priviledge? Or do they thus quarrel with us, (poor Heathens) about ftraws or things Indifferent? and yet fo weighty as the *new Name, and new man created in holinefs*, &c?

The new Man and new Name

7. But what is this *new Creature* and *new Name* they fpeak of? How fhall the world call them by it if they know it not? Such are their *Nonfenfical Fancies* of giving no Refpect to any in word or geftures: Such are their *Fantaftical Conceited Anfwers*, when being asked where they dwell, they Anfwer, they dwell in God, and where they live, they Anfwer, They live in God, &c,

The Popes flingiug to the world their old Names.

8. Are not thefe *Foxians* a kin to the *Popes* in this Fancy alfo, when raifed to the *Devils Pinacle*, to the *Popedome*, they throw down their old Names to the world, and though they be as fubtle as *Foxes*, yet now they will be called *Leones* Lions, though they be as fierce and Cruel as Lyons, they will now be called *Clement* and though they be as Impious as fwine, even as *Os pores*, they muft be called *pius*.

In the laft place, as the *Pope* caft away his net which he ufed as the Remembrance of the Fifherman *Peter* when he had catcht the *Popedome*, fo

G.

---

[1] Change "for" to "but." *R. W. Ms. Ann.*

G. *Fox* having made his Fortune as it is prophane- G. Fox
ly called, having attaind a great Marriage : His his great change.
new Carriage and Courtefie, and Civility condemns
*Humphry Norton*s [85] and his own *former Rigidity*
as I am fure they will do moft of them[1] for worldly Advantages, For, as they abufe that *Scripture*, Ecclef. 11.
The World is in their Heart. I may truly ufe it and
affirme the world and the pride and Advantage of
it, though they deny it as the *Pope* and *Cardinals*
and *Jefuits* do[2] is in their Heart, and is the Body
and Soul, the Root and Branch of all their whole
Religion.

The 42 *Inftance* is in *pag.* 243. where G. *Fox* 243. Rich-
brings in *Richard Sherlock* faying [*We muft not look* and
for an Immediate Extraordinary and miraculous Teach- Sherlock.
ing from the Lord.]
He *Anfwers*, Yet he faith, *all men are taught of
God,* what Confufion is here? *The grace of God
which bringeth Salvation hath appeared unto all men*
and this he calls an outward Teaching by the Lord
Jefus Chrift. Is that *which brings Salvation* outward : All in the Truth may judge this and try thy
Spirit : And the Teachings of the Lord is not mediate, but *Extraordinary* above all yours, which are
men got up fince the dayes of the Apoftles.
I Reply, 1. Although I have fpoken before of
their *Immediate Infpirations* : yet feeing how greed-
ily and boaftingly this deluded Soul with fcorn and
Contempt

---

[1] Place " moft of them " in parenthesis. *R. W. Ms. Ann.*

[2] Place " as the *Pope* and *Cardinals* and *Jefuits* do" in parenthefis. *R. W. Ms. Ann.*

Contempt of all his *Oppofites*, fucks in the poyfon
of *Devilfh Infpirations* in ftead of the *pure wine*
and *milk* of *Chriftian Truth*, and milks out this poyfon into the mouths of his *poor bewitched Followers*,
I fhall add a few words.

The
Teachings
of God.
G. *Fox* here affirmeth that the Teachings of the
Lord are not *mediate*, but *Immediate, Extraordinary*
and *miraculous*, Contrary to the whole ftream of
Scripture and Experience.

1. Contrary to the *Ordinary* and *daily*, and *mighty
preaching* of the *whole Creation:* Pfal. 9. *The
Heavens*, &c.

2. Contrary to the Teachings of God in every
mans Nature, and making, being taug*ht* of God,
above Gods Teaching, the *Fowls* of the *Air* and
Beafts of the *Field:* Doth not Nature teach you, 1
Cor. 11. as to long hair.

3. Contrary to *Abrahams Teaching* of his Children, and the Command of God to all Parents.

4. Contrary to *Ordinary Teachings* of the *Priefts*
and *Levites* Commanded by God, in fo much that
Chrift Jefus Commanded the *Scribes* and *Pharifees
fitting in* Mofes *Chair* to be heard and attended.

5. Contrary to the *Ordinary* and *Conftant feeding*
by *Sheep-* [89] *herds* and *Teachers* in the Chriftian
Flocks and Affemblies.

6. Contrary to the Teachings of the *holy writings*
or *Scripture* written by *Immediate breathing* of God,
for our Inftruction and Confolation, *&c.*

Ob. Yea, but faith this great wrefter of *holy
writing*s : *They fhall be all taught of God.*

I *Anfwer*, 1. Who, or how *fhall they be all taught
of*

of God? that teaching in the *Hebrew* applied from the new[1] *Prophets,* Iſaiah and *Jeremiah* is the teaching of the *new Covenant,* and that is the promiſe of Grace and *Mercy* to ſo many as are *predeſtinate* and *called,* &c.

2. That is no *Immediate, Extraordinary,* and *miraculous buſineſs,* for this is common to all that repent or turn to God.

3. Many had, and may have the *ſpeaking with Tongues,* and *working with Miracles,* and yet not know what the teaching of the Spirit in a *new Birth* is.

4. In the *Ordinary Teaching* to Converſion, the Lord owns his Servants as *Fellow Labourers, Workers, Builders, Huſbandmen, Fathers,* &c. wherein he is pleaſed to open the hearts of *one[2] Thouſand* and *Ten Thouſand* as he did in the *firſt preachings* of that *glad News,* and I hope will do ſo again.

5. The great Promiſe to Chriſt Jeſus and his Seed is, that there ſhall be a *gracious Continuance* in *Chriſts mouth,* & the *mouth* of his *Seed,* of both the word, (that is preached) and the holy *Spirit* more or leſs) *accompanying* and *Teaching,* Iſa. 59.

Outward means.

6. What is there in G. *Fox* his wild Notion, [*Can that which brings Salvation be outward?*] Againſt all the Proofs before I mentioned, and ſo many others concerning the *Fooliſhneſs of Preaching,* &c.

Object. He ſaith, *The grace of God teacheth every man to deny ungodly Luſts,* &c. And I ask,

1. If every man in the world hath this *Immediate*

---

[1] Eraſe "new." *R. W. Ms. Ann.*

[2] Change "one" to "many." *R. W. Ms. Ann.*

mediate work on them? what's the Reaſon we find
none in the world (no not the wiſeſt) until they
have the Scripture, or the Doctrine thereof ſome
way opened to them, that have been able to give
us the leaſt Tidings of any ſuch buſineſs.

2. What's the Reaſon that ſo few in the world
have any ſhew of Repentance, *&c.* much leſs a
ſound and and ſaving turning of the whole Soul
unto God?

87] Why do the *Quakers* make ſuch adoe about
their *Apoſtles* Men and Women as if that *glorious
Light* the *Father*, *Son* and *Spirit* in every man were
not able to teach *Effectually* (by his *Extraordinary*
and *miraculous power*) without their outward ſpeaking to the *Seed*, that is to *God within* them?

Miracles. 4. If they themſelves teach by ſuch an *Extraordinary* and *miraculous power* as the Prophets of old,
and the Apoſtles of Chriſt Jeſus did, what ſhould
be the Cauſe why we ſee no ſuch *miraculous deeds*
done by any of them? The Truth is, God is pleaſed
to chain up *Sathan*: otherwiſe, the *Foxians* would
have their longing (which it may be ſome ſhall
after them) But if they ſhall be permitted by God
and aſſiſted by the *Devil* to do as the *Magicians*
did: yet if their *Doctrine* be other then what is
written (as I have abundantly proved it to be) while
they cry out *Light, Light*, there is none as *Iſaiah*
ſpeaketh, not a Spark of *Light* within them.

247.
Chriſto-
pher Wade The 43. *Inſtance* is in *Pag.* 247. where G. *Fox*
brings in *Chriſtopher Wade* ſaying, [*The written
Word*

Word is the Sword of the Spirit :] And he makes another Rule befide the Scripture[1] falfe.

He *Anfwers*, which we fay is the Spirit which gave them forth, whereby Peace is known upon the *Ifrael* of God : And the *Pharifees* had the Scripture but had not th*e* S*word of the* S*pirit*, the Scriptures teftifies of *the Sword of the Spirit*.

I Reply, 1. With all *humble Reverence* to the moft holy Spirit of God, who is God himfelf. I affirme, the Spirit or God can not here be the *Sword* intended.

For 1. This S*piritual Furniture* being a *Similitude* taken from *warlike* and *Military Provifion* and *Artillery* from *Head* to *Foot*, the *Helmet, Breaftplate*, the *Shield*, the *girdle*, the S*hoes*, and every one applied to gifts and means flowing from Gods Spirit, as *Faith, Hope,* S*incerity*, &c. it were moft improper then to bring in God or the Spirit to be the *Sword*, or any of the other pieces. The Sword of the Spirit

2. For there is no more Reafon to make the Spirit or God to be the *Sword*, then the S*hield* or any other piece.

3. It feems too low to the holy Spirit and God to be here in this *Similitude*, refembled to a *Sword* or *Inftrument* in the hands of men to be drawn and brandifhed and fought withal for *Offence* and *Defence* at mens pleafure, though in fome Sence[2] God.

88] 4. This was the Sword, the only Sword, is called a Sword with which the Lord Jefus fought and vanquifhed the Devil, *Gegraptas, Gegraptai* :

It

---

[1] Place " befide the Scripture." in parenthefis.   *R. W. Ms. Ann.*
[2] Infert " from."   *R. W. Ms. Ann.*

It is written, it is written, and we may well fay of it as *David* of the Sword of *Goliah,* by which *David* cnt off his head, *there is none to that,* &c.

The holy Spirit, Chrift and God are Authors of all thefe *heavenly Gifts* and *Graces, the Beginner and Finifher of Faith,* and therefore not *Faith* nor *Hope,* nor any other piece of the *Artillery* themfelves, no more then the *Armorer* is the *Helmet,* or the *Cutler* the *Sword,* &c.

6. In *Revel.* 1. Chrift and the Sword with two Edges (which cometh forth of his mouth) are diftinct, and can not be the fame, as G. *Fox* ufually Confounds and mixeth all together. Hence the the Word of Chrift, *Col.* 3. can not be Chrift himfelf, but that which cometh from him and tendeth to him.

7. Thefe great Interpreters are Confounded in themfelves, for here in *Ephef.* 4. the Spirit muft be the *Sword* and Word of God, But in *Heb.* 4. Chrift muft be the *Sword,* with *two Edges,* being the Word of God, and not the Spirit : So like *Juglers* do they fhift from one hand to another, to Confound and beguile the Beholders.

Object. But the Spirit faith G. *Fox* was before the Scripture, and gave forth the Scripture.

I *Anfwer,* what then, G. Fox is before his Book, and gave it forth, is it not therefore G. *Fox* his word & writing but G. *Fox* himfelf? Or is it not the *Kings Majefty* before his *Declaration,* or *Proclamation* to the world? Is it not therefore the Kings word, or is it the King himfelf? This *Immediate Infpiration* of the holy Scripture from the Spirit makes

makes it a Word fo powerful, a *Magazine* & *Store-houfe* fo full of Treafury, fo rich a Standard, *Touch-ftone* or *Weight*s fo perfect, for the trial of all Spirits, all writings, all Doctrines, all Religions, Worfhips, Actions, *&c.*

Object. But the *Pharifees* faith G. *Fox* had the Scripture, but they had not the Sword of Gods Spirit :

I *Anfwer,* The *Jews* had, and have, and fo the *Turks* have had much of it, the *Papifts* and the Quakers, and other Blafphemors, yea, and the *Dev-ils* themfelves may have the Scripture, the word of God in their Hands and mouths: for may not a true Sword, a choice Sword be in a mad mans hand, whereby he may [89] mifchief and wound, and kill himfelf and others : Hence men make merchandize of it, *fophifticate* and *Adulterate*, and turn it into a *Lie*, &c.

The Scripture horribly abufed

On the other hand, the Spirit of God is promifed to God⁵ Children : Gods Spirit and Word are promifed to go together in the mouths of all true Chriftians, *Ifa.* 55. this holy Spirit is to be praid for, *Luke* 11. and is therefore *powerfully prefent* with Gods true Meffengers, while they *Tranflate, Expound, Preach* as *Paul* did, *Acts* 26. No other things but what *Mofes* and the *Prophets* wrote of.

The 44*th. Inftance* is in *Pag.* 253. where he quotes *Henry Haggar,* faying, [*You call all men dead and Carnal in the Serpents Nature, in what Form foever if they differ from you*] G. *Fox* Anfwers, [*All that be not in the Light that inlightneth every man that*

253. Henry Haggar

that cometh into the world which is the way to the
Father, differeth from us: such be dead, such be Car-
nal in the Seepents Nature; For none comes to the
Life, but who comes to the Light, in what Form so
ever they be: And such as differ from us differ from
Christ: For none come from under the Serpents head
and Nature, but who comes to the Light.

I *Reply,* 1. As *David* said of some whose *Teeth*
were as *Swords*, and *Solomon* saith, *there is a Genera-*
tion &c. *of such whose Teeth are as Swords*, and if
ever there were a Generation of such in the world
the *Papists* and these *Foxians* are the *Generations*
here intended: For it is in vain to tell them of
Christ *the Foundation*, and of building *Wood, Hay,*
Stubble, &c. If you come not roundly to the *Pope*
with the *Papists*: Or to the *Light within*, &c. nothing remains but *Fire and Brimstone, Damnation*, &c.

2. It is true, in some of their writings, and in
Edmund Burroughs himself there seems to be some
charitable hopes of some having something of *Sin-*
cerity in them, and of breathing after the Lord,
but I observe they fall in with *G. Fox* again, *viz.*
except that those persons owne their Idols[1] called
Light within them.

3. The *Protestants* overcome the *Papists* not only
by Scripture and Argument, but in *Charity* also,
for they profess to have *Hope* of many among the
Papists, as they do also of many amongst the *Qua-*
kers, But the *Papist* and *Quaker* like *Fire-ships* burn
and blow up all, that bow not down to theis
Image, &c.

The Pa-
pists and
Quakers
of a dam-
ning and
damne
Spirit.

The true
Protestants
Charity.

4. How

---

[1] Erase " s " in "Idols." *R. W. Ms. Ann.*

90] 4. How far are thefe from the Spirit of The Quakers far from the Spirit of Chrift Jefus. Chrift Jefus toward the *poor Woman*, the *Syrophenician*, who by her *worſhip* was a *dog*, (and he told her ſo) yet believing in him and content to gather up *Crumbs* (as a *Dog*) under his *Table*, he grants her *Suit*, and magnifies her *perſonal Excellency*! Thus dealt he with the *Centurion* and *Cornelius*, and with every *poor Reed* if truly bruiſed for Sin, and every Lock of *ſmoaking Flax* reaking in truth of Love to God, and the Lord Jeſus.

He proclaims the Kingdome of Heaven to the *poor* in *Spirit*, who ſee themſelves *dead* and *loſt*, and *damned*, and ſeeing no help, no Grace, (not a penny nor a patch of any good in them but) waiting as Beggars at the *gate*, the *beautiful* and *glorious gate* of *mercy*. The meek and merciful Spirit of Jeſus.

He proclaims *Bleſſedneſs* and *Promiſes* to the *bleating Lambs* as the *fruitful Sheep* to the *Infants* and *new born Babes, that hunger and thirſt for the milk of Righteouſneſs*, that by the Patience and Comfort held forth in the writings or Records they may have hope, although yet they cannot be Confident of any work of God in them, and are not ſo bold to Confeſs Chriſt Jeſus openly, and kiſs him in the Streets, but ſteal to him by night as *Nicodemus*, and *Joſeph*, until they ſaw him bleeding on the *Gallows*. The different ſtate of Gods Children.

He bare with his *Diſciples though fooliſh and ſlow of Heart, hard-hearted*, ignorant of his *Death* and *Reſurrection*, and loath to hear of ſuch metters.

The 45th. *Inſtance* is in *Pag.* 259. where he quotes *John Brown* ſaying, [*And them that bring people* 259. John Brown *people to look at the Light within them, are as* Korah, Dathan *and* Abriam.]

G. *Fox* Anſwers, [*All that go from the Light within them, are as* Korah, Dathan, *and* Abiram *amongſt the Lords Prophets, Exalting themſelves and Perſecuting.*]

1. I Reply, and Examine unto whom this Famous Hiſtory may moſt properly be *Applicable*, for ſure it was a *Type* and word of God

1. Then, that which the Spirit of God chargeth upon *Korah*, is a riſing up, a *Revolt* ʋud *Rebellion* againſt the Lord, his Appointments and Miniſters or Officers, *Moſes* and *Aaron*, &c.

I know G. *Fox* chargeth this upon all that pretend to any *Miniſtry* and *Miniſtration*, and have not the *Immediate Spirit* of |91| God as the *Apoſtles* had but as (he ſpeaks ſimply) are *Ravened* from it, and are ſtill *Apoſtates*, &c.

But I *Anſwer*, the *Proteſtant Religion* is a Religion proteſting againſt the abominations of that *bloody man* of Sin the *Pope* both in his *Doctrines* and *Worſhips* and Converſations: Theſe Proteſters have been ſince the *Waldenſes*, in *France* and *Germany*, and *low Countries*, and *England*, *Scotland*, *Denmark*, *Swedland*, *Polonia*, *Tranſylvania*, *Norway*, *Ireland*, &c. Conflicting, Contending with their *Tongues*, their *pens*, and their *Blood* againſt the *Bloody Whore* and *Church of Rome*, according to many paſſages in the *Revelations*, moſt *wonderfully* and *miraculouſly fulfilled* upon them.

From theſe all their holy Doctrines and Endeavours after Gods pure worſhip are the *Quakers* Revolted

Number 16. Korah, Dathan and Abirams Revolt applied to the pretended Quakers.

The Proteſtant Religion Revolted from by the Quakers

Revolted and fet up a *Flag* of *Defiance* againft all
but pretended *Immediately Infpired perfons, Invifibl*e
Worfhips, and *Minifters*, and a *fullen, proud,* and
dogged Converfation, (for the general of them.)

2. As *Abfoloms* and *Shebahs Confpiracies* were
notable and Signal againft *King David*, the *Pro-*
phetical and *Kingly Type* of the Lord Jefus, fo was
Korahs and his *Confpirators* very Confiderable and
Eminent againft *Mofes* and *Aaron* Types of the
Prophetical, Prieftly, and *Kingly Office* of the *bleffed*
Lord Jefus Chrift : It is faid, *Numb.* 16. that *Korah*
the Levite, and *Dathan* and *Abiram the Sons of* Reu-
ben, and *two hundred and fifty Princes* and *Notable*
Men of Fame in the *Affembly* thus kindled the *Coals*
of this *proud Confpiracy*, which had broke forth
into *devouring Flames*, except that the *Sheepherd of*
Ifrael (who never flumbers nor fleeps) had moft gracioufly and wonderfully watcht for the *timeous* and
early Extinguifhing of it.

As to the *pretending Quakers*, it is known that
they are not *Sons of Obfcurity*, (as *Bull* and *Far-*
minton, Reeves and *Mugleton*) but for *Eftate* and
parts, for Education and Learning, fome of them[1] for
pretences of Piety, *Confcience, patience, Zeal and*
Mortification, yea, and alfo for their Numbers, all
which they predicate in their Books, and in my
difpute with them with *loud Trumpets*) they are
known to bè *Confiderable*, and as like to fpread as
did the *Arrians Papifts* or *Mahometans*.

3. *Korah* and *Dathan*, &c. they were by Gods
righteous Judgement fo fixed, and fetled, and hardned

Side notes:

Confpira-
tors agaiuft
the Prieft-
ly, Pro-
phetical,
and Kingly
Office
and Power
of Chrift
Jefus

The con-
fpiracy of
the Qua-
kers

Againft
Chrift
Jefus.

---

[1] Place " fome of them," in parenthefis. *R. W. Ms. Ann.*

ned in their Perſwaſion [92] and Confidence, that
they Contemned all *Moſes meekneſs*, and *Anſwered
ſtoutly*, *We will not come up*, when he Cited them
before the Lord : yea, ſay they, *wilt thou pluck out
the Eyes of theſe men*, and they daringly and deſperately brought their *Cenſers* to offer *Incenſe* and
Worſhip to God : as may be applied to theſe *proud*
and *Confident*, and *deſperate Foxians*.

Korah and the Quakers Confidence & fierceneſs.

4. Their Charge was notoriouſly falſe againſt
Moſes, as the Charge of the *Quakers* againſt ſuch
bleſſed Inſtruments which God hath uſed like *Moſes* to bring the *Proteſtants* out of the *Egypt* of *Popery* :) *viz.* a Charge of Pride and Ambition, *wilt
thou make thy ſelf a Prince over us*? a Charge of
which the *Foxians* are notoriouſly guilty.

And lying Charges.

5. I obſerve their *horrible* Ingratitude both unto
the moſt holy God himſelf, and unto *Moſes* and
Aaron, Gods Servants, by whom he had wrought ſo
many wonders for this people in ſo many *wonderful* and *miraculous Directions*, *Preſervations* and *Deliverances*.

Ingratitude.

6. Their *Impatiencci* and *Unbelief*, &c. *Thou haſt
not yet brought us unto a Land flowing with milk and
hony*, as if God and *Moſes* had only fed them with
Sugred and *honied Words*, and no Effects and performances.

Impatience.

7. I obſerve their ſubtle and falſe pretences and
Suggeſtions *:* Is not all the *Lords people* holy every
one of them, and the Lord is amongſt them, juſt
the *Quakers Language*, who ſo advance every one
of the people of the Lord : (as they call their
Proſelites) *viz.* that they are juſt now *born of God*,
and

and Literally, *can not Sin*, are *Immediately Inspired*,
need no Teachers, no Scriptures, &c.

8. I obferve, and I humbly beg of *the Father of
mercies* to caufe thefe *poor Foxians* to obferve the
Confpiracy of the two Elements, *Earth*, and *Fire* to
Confume and devour thefe *Famous- proud Confpirators*: I fpare *Applications*, begging mercy from *the
Father of Lights* and *mercies*, for their *Humiliations*
and *Salvation*: Only I Remember, *that every Plant
the Heavenly Father hath not planted*, flourifheth it
*never fo green, fo high, fo long, fhall be plucked up,
and caft into the Fire*, &c.

The Wonderful Judgements of God upon the Korathites in this world

The 46*th*. *Inftance* is in *pag*. 262. Where he
brings in *George Johnfon* f ying, [*The Americans
were never ordained for Grace and Salvation, and the
Grace of* God *never appeared to the Americans*.]
93] G. *Fox* Anfwers, which is contrary to the
Scriptures, which faith, *the grace of* God *which
brings Salvation hath appeared to all men, &c. and I
will give him for a Light, and for a Covenant to the
Gentiles, a new Covenant to the Houfe of Ifrael and
Judah, and that he may be my Salvation to the ends of
the Earth*; *and many in America have received Truth
and Salvation*.

62 George Johnfon.

I Reply, 1. To the Covenant or Bargain of God
with Man, firft and fecondly I have fpoke, as alfo
to the figurative calling of Chrift Jefus the Covenant to *Jews and Gentiles*, and that this blind Soul
taking it litterally, he runs upon the Rocks of the
Arminian general Redemption, and the *Univerfal-
ifts* general Salvation, and that with a known Contradiction

Thoughts about America

tradiction againſt their own Foundation of none having any benefit of Chriſt, that own not their Light, &c. as alſo with a known Contradiction to all Expeiience, which ſaith, the whole World lies in Wickedneſs, and this *America* in *Barbariſme*, and *Barbarous Wickedneſs* of all ſorts.

Now Chriſt a Light & Covenant.

2. I have ſaid Chriſt is the Light, the Covenant, the Brazen Serpent, the Bridegroom held forth as the Sun in the Heavens to all the World : So Chriſtians are the Salt, the Light of the World, and the Church the Pillar and Firmament of Truth, holding it out to all the World ; is therefore all the World ſeaſoned, enlightened, converted, ſaved. yea, doth he not only deny the *Americans*, but the *Europeans*, *Aſians*, and *Africans* alſo any Salvation (though never ſo holy Profeſſour of Chriſt) except they bow down to their new black Image of Light within them?

N Englands Plantaaion

3. It was a large effuſion of the *Holy Spirit* of *God* upon ſo many precious Leaders and Followers, who ventured their All to *New-England* upon many Heavenly Grounds, three eſpecially.

Firſt, The enjoyment of God according to their Conſciences.

Secondly, Of holding out Light to *Americans*.

Thirdly, The advancing of the *Engliſh Name* and *Plantations*.

Theſe three ends the moſt High and Holy God hath graciouſly helpt his poor *Proteſtants* in a Wilderneſs to Endeavour to promote, &c.

The Indians of N. England

And as to theſe *Barbarians*, the Holy God knows ſome pains I took uprightly in the Main Land and

Iſlands

Iſlands of *New-England* to dig into their Barbarous, Rockie Speech, and to ſpeak ſome- [94] thing of God unto their Souls; and ſurely God hath ſtirred up the Spirit of my ancient dear Friend *Mr. Eliot* to gain their Language, to Tranſlate them the *Bible*, and many other wayes to bring the ſound of a Saviour amongſt them, which I humbly beg of God to perfect and finiſh for the Glory of his Great Name, &c.

The Indians of New England

4. What G. *Fox* means by ſaying ſome in *America* have received Truth and Salvation I can but gueſs at; It is known he owns nothing of God in *Indians* or *Engliſh*, until they bow down to their Idol, and that he intends none but ſuch *Engliſh* in *America* as he and others have Poyſoned and Bewitched with Heliſh Sorceries.

5. This laſt Year a Paper was ſent me from the Quakers, deſiring me to turn it into *Indian*, that ſo it might be Printed in *England*, and ſo diſperſed amongſt them: it contained two things:

The Quakers deſire of perverting the Indians.

Firſt, *That they had a Light within them which told them that it was evil to Steal*, &c.

Secondly, *That if they did hearken to this Light, it would lead them to God*, &c.

I returned the Paper, and my refuſing in Writing, affirming it not to be Truth, &c. and I queſtioned the Quakers themſelves for a falſe Chriſt, falſe Light and Spirit, which they would infect the *Indians with*.

The 47*th Inſtance* is in *pag.* 263. Where he quotes

John Owen 263   quotes *John Owen*, faying, [*All Truth concerning God and our felves is to be learned from the Holy Scripture, the Word of God*]

    G. *Fox* Anfwers, There was Truth learned before the Scriptures were written, and the Scriptures of Truth are the Words of God, which ends in Chrift the Word, and there is no Truths learned but as the Spirit doth lead into all Truth : And many has the Scriptures but know not Chrift and the Truth, &c. fo he hath thrown out Chrift and the Spirit.

    I *Reply*, 1. I have more then once before Anfwered this *Childish Anfwer*. There was Truth, (and the Spirit, and Chrift, and Light,) before Scripture, as alfo that which no *true Proteftant* denies, *viz.* that the Scriptures, nor preaching, nor Baptifme, nor the Supper, nor Afflictions avail except the Spirit (the *Fin-* [85] *ger* or *Power* of God) fet *t*hem home upon us : As alfo that many have the Scriptures yet know not Chrift, which who queftions? So that his Anfwers are fo loofe and Childifh that none but *Fools* and *Children*, and *Frantick perfons* can find any Savour and taft in them.

Owens writings about the Scripture Excellently learned and Spiritual and Invincible   2. I therefore further Anfwer to this Quotation, pray the Reader to read fome former paffages, but efpecially, thofe publick difcourfes of this excellently learned and pious Author, wherein he hath admirably (both in *Latin* and *Englifh*) maintained the *Authority* and *perfection* of this *Ineftimable Jewel*, the holy Scripture : both againft *Atheifts* and *Papifts*, and *Jews*, and *Quakers*, &c. and proved (as clear as at Noon-day) the holy Scriptures, and

        every

every Tittle of them to be the *holy Word*, or *Will*, or *Declaration* of the holy mind of God.

The 48*th Inftance* is in *Pag.* 264. where he brings in *Samuel Palmer*, faying, [*The State of the Soul in this Life is threefold Creation, Corruption and Regeneration.*] 264 Samuel Palmer

G. *Fox* Anfwers, [*In Regeneration the Life is changed from the Life which is in the Fall, So Regeneration and Corruption is not one in the new Life*]

I Reply, who faith they be? who faith that Regeneration and Corruption are one in the new Life? what a foul Trick is this of a falfe man to impute that to his Oppofite which he abhorreth? I guefs, or he means that in Regeneration, there is perfection and no Sin, or Corruption left, &c. Hence the plea of fome of their Spirits for *Adams nakednefs* being come to the State of *Innocency*: Hence the poor frantick Souls cry out that the *Proteftants* preach for Sin, for Tearme of Life, &c, Mans threefold Condition in this Life

I *Anfwer*, queftionlefs the Devil deals with the *Foxians* as the Pirat doth with Ships, he makes no Oppofition againft fuch he hath taken, and is poffeffed of: So that no queftion but the *Quakers* may be freed from many Tranfgreffions and Temptations to them, which others are affaulted with. The Devil too Crafty for the Foxians

2. Thefe poor Souls foolifhly and extream fimply Anfwer *Pauls* Complaints and Cryes and bewailing himfelf, *Rom.* 7. with *Pauls* giving thanks for his fudden victory in the laft words, as if juft then the Battel had turn d, and *Paul* had not fpoke of the Conftant Battel and Warfare, which all the Saints of God (in about four thoufand years together
ther

ther throughout the holy Scripture) [96] Experimented : *Noah*, *Abraham*, *David*, *Peter*, *John*, *Barnabas*, &c.

A great
miſtery.

3. It is a miſtery which neither *Jews* nor *Turks*,
Atheiſts or *Papiſts*, or *Quakers* know, *viz.* how the
Seed of all grace may be in the *new born*, and yet
the Seed alſo of all ſin (except the ſin againſt the
holy Spirit) remaining in them : Therefore when
they hear of the Falls of the Saints in Scripture,
and ſo great? Some queſtion the Truth of the

The Qua-
kers devil-
iſh pride.

Scripture : others make a ſport of them, and pretend a Cloak for their ſins, ſaying, none are perfect,
why may we not as well as they? Others, (as the
Foxians ſay,) We are come to a more perfect and
pure Eſtate then *Paul* at firſt was in : or *John*, who
ſaith, *If we Confeſs our Sin :* or *Iames*, who ſaith, *In
many things we offend all :* or the Father that cried,
help my Unbelief, &c. But the *Papiſts* and *Qnakers*
are ſo *perfect* and *Superperfect*, that though they be
full of *pride*, *Ambition*, *Unbelief*, *Unthankfulneſs*,
Intemperancy, *Covetouſneſs*, full of *raſh Anger*, *bitter
Railings*, and *dreadful Blaſphemies* againſt *Heaven*,
yet they can with the *Whore* wipe their mouths,
and ſay they are pure from all uncleanneſs.

275. Rich-
ard Meyo.

The 49*th*. *Inſtance* of G. *Fox* his lame writings
is in *Pag.* 275. where he quotes *Richard Meyo*, ſaying, [*To ſay the Goſpel is the Power of God is but a
Metaphorical Speech.*]

G. *Fox* Anſwers, [*The Apoſtle doth not ſay ſo, for
the Apoſtle ſaith, the Goſpel is the Power of God
unto Salvation to every one that believes, in plain words*,
Rom. 1.   I Reply,

I Reply, 1. (As before, and as thoufands know) that the word *Gofpel* is in all *Languages glad News,* the fame which the *Angel* brought to the *Sheep-herds* of a *Saviour born, and laid in a manger at* Bethlehem, this is the *News,* the *placid good News,* though fet forth and beautified in the holy Scripture with variety of Figures and *Metaphors.*

2. The *great Fox* the Devil who thirfts after the Blood of the *Quakers,* and of all mens Souls, he whifpers, *viz.* the Gofpel is Chrift, it is the Spirit, the Light, and God himfelf, why talk you of a written Gofpel? of a preached Gofpel the Scriptures are within you, the Gofpel is within you, *Tranflations* & *Interpretations* within you: why gaze you upon pen and Ink, and after a man. *&c.* _{The Devils bloody Craft.}

The Devils bloody Craft.

3. As if the glad Tidings or Gofpel to a dying man of a par- [97] don, & of Life, *&c.* founding to his Ear, were not by the *External Dore* of his Ear conveyed (by that Dore) to the *inward dore* and *Clofet* of his mind? who but *Frantick Souls in Bed-lam* will fay, what need you mind the *Kings Decla-rations* or *Proclamations* of *pardon* or *Liberty?* The King himfelf is the *Gofpel,* the *Declaration,* and the *Librty,* the King is within you, the Gofpel or glad News is within you?

The Kings Declaration of mercy and Liberty.

4. The Devil hates the *glad News* of Chrift Jefus as much as Darknefs hateth Light, therefore he hath two forts of Souldiers.

The Devils two forts of Souldiers Anti-Chriftianifme.

1. Some that fay, what tell you us of Reading and praying, and preaching, mind the *Kernel with-in,* while the fecond fort are all for the outfide, which without the In-fide are but *Shels,* and *Husks,* and *Shadows.* 5. How

The Fig-
ures in
Scripture. 5. How commonly doth the holy Spirit in the
Scriptures fpeak *Ridles* and *Figures*, that they that
fee not may fee, and they that fay they fee (*Papifts*,
Quakers, &c. may be blinded) why is the *Lamb*
called the Pafsover, Chrift the *Temple*, the *Cup* his
Blood, the *Bread* his *Body*, &c.

There were many *hundreds* brought before *King
Henry* and *Queen Mary*, after him, *&c.* for Infur-
rections with Haltars about their Necks : Thefe
Princes (and others) pronounced their inward mind
by *word External*, the *Heralds* and *Proclamations*,
and *Trumpets* were in a *Figurative Senfe* all glad
News and Gofpel, and yet the fubftance of the glad
News or Gofpel was the pardon offered and vouchfafed to them?

6. Mine Eyes have feen a Condemned Soul
turned off at the Gallows : a Poft comes galloping
all drive, waving his hat, which being efpied, Exe-
A lively
picture of
the Gof-
pel. cution is ftaid : the people cried a pardon, the
Poft cried a *Reprieve* : The *Sheriff* cried neither no
Reprieve, &c. until he faw the *Kings hand* or *Authority* from him, the Poft delivers to the *Sheriff* a
bit of paper, which the *Sheriff* reading He Commanded the *Halter* to be taken off, and the Prifoner
to be delivered to the Poft : the Prifoner with joyful lips bid *Death* and his *Fellow Sufferers Farewel*,
and with joyful Legs leaps up behind the *welcome
Meffenger* of his *Deliverance*, for, afterward he had
his *pardon* under the *broad Seal of England*. I ask
here how many paffages and particulars may *Figuratively* be ftiled *Glad News*, or the Gofpel to this
dying man.

7. I

7. I ask whether the glad News or Gospel which this Post, [98] *Messenger* or *Preacher* brought, might not *Figuratively* be called his Gospel or glad News, as *Paul* Rom. 2. calls it his Gospel, and 2. *Cor*. 4. *our Gospel if hid, it is hid to them that be lost?* It is hid two wayes. Why it is called Pauls Gospel.

1. When not by writing or preaching it is preached or declared (as it is not as yet discovered to innumerable millions in the world.) How it is hid.

2. When the Power or Spirit of God opens not (as he did *Lidiahs*) the Ears and Hearts and Spirits of men to embrace the Gospel, or glad News of a Saviour to them : and this outward and inward hearing of this glad News, it is the Devils and the *Jews*, and all *Atheists*, and (these *refined Atheists*) the *Quakers* work to hinder.

The 50*th Instance* of G. *Fox* his lame Answer is in *Pag*. 282. where he brings in *Daniel Cawdry* saying, [*The Saints were come to the Spirits of just men made perfect, but not on the Earth.* 282. Daniel Gawdry.

G. *Fox* Answers, [*The just mens Spirits that led them to give forth the Scripture was the Spirit of God, and that was perfect, and was while they were upon the Earth: The Saints were come to, (which was Christ the End of all words) and so to God the Judge of all the world.*]

I *Reply*, I have spoke before, that Spirits are *Invisible Beings*, both good and bad, Contrary to the *Sadduces*, who held neither.

First, That, of good Spirits there are three sorts. The Variety of Spirits.

1. The *Increated* God himself : 2. The Spirit of

God

God called (becaufe of his manifold operations) the feven Spirits of God, &c

2. Thofe *Invifible, holy Meffengers*, or *Angels*, called *Miniftring Spirits*, and *Flaming Attendants* upon Chrift and his, *Heb*: Oppofite to thefe are the *unclean* Spirits fpirits of Devils, &c.

3. The Spirits of men, firft, faints, as *Mary* fings, *my* Spirit *hath rejoyced in* God *my* Saviour, &c. and oppofite to thefe are the Spirits of the wicked as *Peter* tels us of the Spirits of the wicked, of the old world now in prifon, &c.

Why it is faid the Spirits made per-fect.

2. I obferve that in this *Heb*. 12. the Spirit of God fpeaks not of the Bodies of the Saints neither Conjoynd, nor a-part. Nor fecondly of the Righte-ous, made perfect, but the Spirits of Firft, the Righteous: Therefore it feems to hold forth not a perfect State of the Saints in this Life, Confifting of Spirits and Bodies, [99] which our proud Boaft-ers fay of themfelves, nor that they are perfect: Nor fecondly, of the Eftate of the Saints in the world to come, where all *true Proteftants* hold, that the Bodies and Souls of the Saints fhall be perfected, and *Everlaftingly* (and as to us now) *Inconceivably glorified.*

But the Eftate of the Souls or Spirits of the Elect, who are (as fome Tranflate) perfected, fome *Confummated* or *finifhed*, fome grounded, or now (*Everlaftngly Eftablifhed,* while their vifible part, *the Body fleeps in Jefus* until the *joyful Refurrection.*

2. Thus it appears the rather to be, becaufe we find in all the *holy Records* the Spirits, Souls, and Bodies of the higheft Saints in this world defective and fubject to great failings, &c.   3. It

3. It is faid, 1 *Pet.* 3. the Spirits in prifon, not the Bodies nor the wicked, but thofe Spirits of the wicked which believed not *Noahs preaching*, &c.

4. Doth the Scripture fpeak of the Spirit of God here at all? but of the Spirits of men; or of thofe Penmen of the holy Scriptures, or of any prefent ftate of perfection in this Life at all, which might occafion his Anfwer?

The Devil would be rid of Scripture and all Learning.

5. What Truth or pertinency is in thofe words, *Chrift the end of all words*: Doth he mean that now there ought to be no more words or writings? or that Chrift ends all Scripture Words, and there is no further ufe of them? fo they hold out, and yet they fay and practice the Contrary. The Truth is, their horrible unclean and *foul Spirit* would fain be rid of all *Scripture Words*, and all Learning alfo, &c. that he may bring the more of miferable man-kinde (under the cheating found of Light] into his *Eternal Darknefs.*

The 51th. *Inftance* is in *Pag.* 325. where he quotes *Timothy Trevis*, faying, *God hath ordained to Eternal Life all that fhall be faved, before they had a Being in this World: But none comes to poffeffion of this Salvation, but through Obedience of the Spirit.*

325 Timothy Trevis.

G. *Fox* Anfwers, [*The ground of mans belief and obedience is Chrift, who doth inlighten him to the intent that he might believe and obey the Truth, and who knows the Seed, knows the Election before the World was made.*]

I *Reply*, 1. If he means that Chrift is the Ground or Author, the Giver of Repentance and Faith to all

all the Elect whom God [100] the Father hath given him, we fay fo, &c. But if he put in their *Invented Light* in the Room of *Gods Election* and *Predeftination,* as the *Efficient* and *firft Caufe,* and of Chrift as the *Mediator* and *Meritorious Caufe* according to the *golden Chain,* Rom. 8. and *Ephef.* 1. and the *fifth Chap.* He fpeaks blafphemoufly of God, and of the Son of God, and of the glorious work of their *Redemption,* and *poor mankinds Salvation.*

G. Fox deftroys the working of the Father and the Son.

2 He is now in the *Burrough* of the *Arminians,* who deftroy *Gods Election* before the world was, and fay, that when a man believes he is Elected, when he is predeftinate, or (being obedient) is Inconftant, he is then *Reprobated.*

G. Fox and the Arminians one as to predeftination.

1 Contrary to all the *precious beds* of *Flowers* and *Spices* in the *Garden* of the *Scripture,* which thefe *rooting Swine* getting in, they root and tear up all the ways and methods of *Gods Councels* and *Salvations.*

2 Contrary to the wit and skill of men, who framing a *Book,* an *Houfe,* a *Ship,* a *Navie,* an *Army,* or any *Sublunary matters,* have all in their *Thoughts, Minds,* and *Councels* before they begin their *Enterprize,* they provide their *Materials,* their *Agents,* their means they fit all to their Ends, though all may faile, all mens Affairs being but *Vanity* and *Vexations.* But to whom fhall we liken the *Eternal* and *Infinite Maj fty,* to whom all his works and Events are known (in a moft *Inconceivable way* as to us) even from Eternity to Eternity, his *Juftice,* his *Goodnefs,* his *Power,* all being *Infinite.*

Mans wifdome about his Earthly bufinefs

3. As to the Seed and Election : We know they make

make themselves, the feed and the Election : fecondly, They make Christ the feed, that is, (in the End) themselves. And thirdly, They make God and the Spirit of God the feed, the feed in every man which is preached to, by them the *Imprifoned Seed*, and when one turns *Quaker*, then God comes out of *Prifon*: The Truth is, they make no diftinction between God and Chrift, and *Spirit*, and themfelves, as *Fox* in this Book as before plainly tels us, but when this pretended feed of God, or God himfelf is hearkened to, then the foul fo heark ning, is become Goddified, and God with God, whofe *Infinite Being* and Effence thefe *poor, proud Bruits,* have not fo much fight of as the Devils have, who cried out to Jefus, *I know thee whom thou art the holy One of God,* knowing that God and the *Son* of God were *Infinitely diftinct* in them- [101] felves, and all *Created Beings* : Yet fuch is the *Inconceivable wrath* and *Juftice* of the Eternal God u pon thefe fallen Spirits who kept not their *firft Habitation* (as the *pretended Quakers* many of them have not done) that (as *Pharaoh*) they can not but *lye and flander, and kill till the time of their Torment come.*

The Miftery of the Quakers Seed.

The Foxians grofs Ignorance of the Godhead

The 52d. *Inftance* of G. *Fox* his flight dealing is in *Pag.* 326. where he brings in the fame Author, faying, [*The manifeftation of the Spirit is given to every man in the Church to profit withal, and not to every man in the World.*]

326 Timothy Trevis.

G. *Fox* Anfwers, [*The manifeftation is given to every man to profit withal without diftinction, I will*

pour

pour out of my Spirit upon all Flesh : For the Spirit of Truth shall lead the Saints into all Truth : And he shall reprove the World, and that which doth reprove the World is manifest to the World.]

I Reply, I spake to this Text before, in Answer to the Letter of my Neighbour I. *T.* (as is to be seen in the Letters before our Disputes) who declared himself satisfied with my Answers, but G. *Fox* (like a *Cow* with a Kettle on her head, giving every one warning to stand clear) he boldly slanders[1] on, and tumbles *Heaven, Earth* and *Hell* together, *&c.*

1. This 1 *Cor.* 12. expresly declares three things.

1. That it pleased God to appoint in his Christian Church and Worship the Ministry of *Apostles, Prophets, Teachers,* &c. according to *Rom.* 12 *Ephes.* 4, *&c.*

2. He bestoweth several Gifts and Endowments on such persons whom he pleaseth to call unto such Ministrations.

3. He vouchsafeth to give a gracious *Concurrent Operation* of his *Spirit* unto these his Gifts & Ministrations, what now is this gracious promise of *the Father of Lights* to the Garden of his Church & *Saints,* the *howling Desart* of the whole world, from whence the Garden is taken in, inclosed and separate? Because a *Queen* is a Woman, must therefore all the *Honours* and *kindnesses* of a *glorious Prince* due to his *Royal Consort* be dispensed in Common to all the Women in his Kingdome or Dominions? The Garment in which the Queen is brought, is a

Garment

The manifestation of the Spirit discussed.

The Garden of Chrifts Church and the Wilderness, &c. of the World differ as Heaven and Earth

[1] Change "flanders" to "blunders." *R.W. Ms. Ann.*

Garment of *Needle work*, richly and moſt curiouſly
embroydered with the *graces* and *Operations* of the
holy Spirit, doth it therefore follow, that thoſe
Heavenly Embroyderies, &c. belong to every *nnclean*
and *Louſie Begger* ?

102] Yea, but this prophane Mouth hath ſomething to ſay for it ſelf, three things he ſaith full of
Prophaneneſs and *Simplicity*.

1. *I will pour out my Spirit upon all Fleſh*.

But, 1. Was this (as he ſpeaks) without all diſtinction done actually? was it, *Univerſally* ſo with
all the *Individuals* of mankind in the world at
that time ?

2. Was not there a *wonderful Wall of ſeparation* The par-
between the *Jews* and all other Nations, which the tition Wall
Lord promiſed by the *Prophets* to break down, and between
at the coming of the Lord Jeſus, and ever ſince Jews and
hath more and more broke down and aboliſhed ? Gentiles.
Is not *Gideons Floor* which was dry (the *poor Gen-*
tiles and *we Engliſh* among them) now wet with the
Dews of Heaven, while the *poor Jews* (which were
only wet at firſt) are dry and barren ?

3. What is that *Extraordinary Promiſe* of *Gods*
Extraordinary pouring out of his Spirit, in Fiery
Tongues and Propheſyings, fitting ſome to go unto
all Nations to carry the glad News or Goſpel, had
others and all Believers thoſe Gifts [leaſt of all
with any ſhew of Reaſon] belong they to all the
Men and Women in the world, who have never
ſeen and heard of any Glimpſe of the Sun of
Righteouſneſs.

4. Again, I obſerve how vainly and wickedly
this

G. Fox his not cleaving the Hoof though full of Scripture.

this deluded and deluding Soul cheats himfelf, and others with this Tearme, *All Flefh, Every man, All the World*, and fo with the Terms *Light, Chrift, Spirit*, his *proud Fancy* playeth, &c. not dividing the *Hoof* by juft and holy diftinguifhing a Crime that he often upbraids his Oppofites moft odioufly with in his Book, not dividing, &c. but is moft notorioufly guilty as ever was filthy Camel in this world, or any of the *unclean Beafts*, &c.

G. Fox his wonderful Confufion.

G. *Fox* his fecond Anfwer here is, [*The Spirit of God fhall lead the Saints into all Truth.*] I obferve here how like a Skittifh Jade this wild Soul runs in and out, and cannot keep to one *fteady Affirmation* : Before he brings in the Spirit of God poured out upon the Common of the World, now he brings in the fpirits leading the faints, *Gods Garden and Paradice* : Yet again, in his next words he concludes every man in the World to have the fpirit becaufe faith he, [*The fpirit reproves the World, and that which doth Reprove the World is manifeft to the World.*].

The Spirit of God and the world are extream Contraries

I *Anfwer*, The holy fpirit teftifies that he is the Comforter of the faints, but a Reprover of the World, that he Comforts the [103] Saints in the Promifes, & Affurances, &c. that he Reproves the world in his Threatenings and Judgments. That the world knows not, fees not the Spirit, but mocks at, receives it not, but banifheth, imprifoneth, murthereth fuch in whom the true Spirit of God appeareth : Hence it is, that becaufe of this Spirit of God in any foul, three are againft two, & two muft be againft three in the fame houfe, the Parents againft
the

the Children, and the Children betray their Parents unto Death : yea, two in a Bed, and two in a Belly, and yet he whom Gods Spirit choofeth, fhall be mockt and murthered by the other' and yet this lying *Peor* tells us that all the world (without dif-tinction) have the manifeftation of the Spirit of God to profit withal.

Prophners of the holy Spirit.

5. There have been perfons profeffing the Order of the holy Ghoft, yet far from the favour of the holy Spirit, there hath been a great Ship in the world full of Sailors and Souldiers, called the *holy Ghoft*, and yet fcarce one man in it known to have any Acquaintance with Gods Spirit : Alas, what are the *Babilonifh Orders* of thefe pretenders to the Holy Ghoft or Spirit ? what are they but a poor Ship full of Refifters of Gods Spirit, and Enemies to the greateft Enjoyers of him in the World, the true *Proteftant Witneffes*, whom they profeffedly oppofe under the Name of Profeffors, I hope as I have often faid, that many of them are of the *two hundred* that followed *Abfolom* in honefty and fimplicity.

G. Fox, &c. refift-ing and fighting againft the holy Spirit.

6. But, Oh what Reproofs of Gods Spirit hath G. *Fox* and others of their Leaders had in, and by fo many excellent Oppofites and Scriptures, and Arguments, which G. *Fox* here proudly tramples under his prophane feet, without any favour of the holy Spirit of God !

The ftriv-ing of Gods Spirit.

It is true, it pleafeth God as I faid, to ftrive with men by preachings, by writings, by their own Readings, by *publick Judgments* and *private*, and alfo by *publick mercies* and *private*, for *Acts* 14.

every

every *Drop* of *Rain* is Gods *voice, word* or *witnefs,* &c, but what is this *Common grace* to that *Regenerating* and *changing Spirit,* John 3. to the opening of *Lidiahs,* and fo of all faints hearts by his free and holy fpirit or Finger? what is this to the fame Power that raifed Chrift Jefus from the Dead, *Ephef.* 1. that raifeth any poor finner unto a new and holy, and fpiritual Cond tion?

The free and powerful working of Gods fpirit.

104] 7. Excellent and moft heavenly is that fimilitude, *Cant.* 1. *Becaufe of the favour of thy good Ointments therefore do the Virgins love thee* : Oh how many prate of this fpirit or Ointment, and yet hate the true Lord Jefus, hate his *Love Letters,* the holy fcriptures, and would be glad to fee them in a *Bone fire,* hate his poor true Quakers that defire to fear before him, and tremble at his Word, and to mourn that having received fuch manifeftations of the holy fpirit of God they have profited others fo little, and glorified God in their Generations?

8. I might Infift upon the End which G, *Fox* infifteth on, *viz.* to profit withal, and ask why *David,* Pfal. 53. Complains that all the Children of men not one excepted, are *unprofitable,* good for nothing, yea, *abominable,* that is, to fpiritual matters, heavenly things, the world to come : All even the *fweeteft Natures,* the *faireft,* the *wittieft,* the *wifeft,* the *learnedft,* the *devouteft,* untill the fpirit of God come and truly change the heart and whole Frame of Nature. Till then, we as profitable as *Hogs,* as *Moles* in a Garden, as *Water* or *Fire* breaking into a fhip, and as *devouring Foxes amongft the true Lambs and Chickens of Chrift Jefus.*

The whole world unprofitable.

The

The 53*d Inſtance* of G. *Fox* his lame Anſwer is
in *pag.* 328: where he quotes *Hugh Archbal,* ſaying, 328 Hugh Archbal
[*Chriſt doth enlighten none but them that do receive
him.*]

He Anſwers, Contrary to John 3. which ſpeaketh of them that hate the Light, and are enlightened, and will not come to it, becauſe the Light
will reprove them : ſo he that hates the Light is
enlightned, and will not receive Chriſt.

I *Reply,* though I have ſpoken much of the
Light and of receiving Chriſt Jeſus, &c, yet ſince
this *proud Boaſter* drags his *Oppoſites* out of *Scotland* alſo : I pray the Readers patience while I tell
him of a manifold Light which the Holy ſpirit
mentions under a *Metaphor* or *Figure of Light.*

1. The Natural perceiving of Natural things, as
Chriſt Jeſus ſaith : *The Light of the Body is the Eye.* The manifold Light

2. The Light of *peace* and *joy,* whether Corpo- mentioned
ral or ſpiritual, Temporal, or Eternal : The *Iews* in in the
Holy
Hamans down-Fall, and their own Deliverance had Scripture
Light and Joy, *&c. and Light is ſown for the Right-
eous,* &c.

105] 3. The common offers of the Goſpel as
Light, whence ſome have obſerved that the word
(ſo cried up in *John* 1.) is not *inlightneth* but *lighteth* : but the word *Photizei* may ſignifie both, and
yet be no more then the Common offer, preaching
and ſound of the *glad News,* or Goſpel : The people that ſate in *Darkneſs* ſaw *great Light,* &c, As
the Light of a candle coming in *lightens* or *enlightens* the *Walls* and *Room* but being taken away
again leaves no Impreſſion or change upon the *Wall,*

or

or as the *Sun* shining or guilding the Earth being

The Common offers of mercy.

clouded leaves no *Impreſſion* of shining on the Earth behind it : So is it with the Common offers of *Trading* or marriages in the world, and ſo of the *heavenly Offers* of *Merchandize* and *Heavenly Marriage*, &c.

4. There is yet a *higher Light* which ſome are *affected, Tinctur'd* and *enlightened,* and yet not the *true* and *ſaving Light* : that in *Heb.* 6. where ſome perſons (as the *pretended Quakers* and G. *Fox* eſpecially) have ſeen much of the *Nature of God,* his *holineſs,* his *Juſtice,* &c. and had a *Taſt* of the *Joyes* of the *next world,* but proudly turned from the *holy Scripture,* from the true Lord Jeſus, and the *true, holy, enlightning, humbling and ſaving Spirit* of God.

The true Illumination.

5. The *true Lighting* or *Enlightning* of which the *holy Scripture* ſpeaketh, is that of 2 *Cor.* 4 (a place fouly and ſimply abuſed by G. *Fox* to prove the Light in every man) where *Paul* ſhews, how by the preaching of the *glad News* or *Goſpel* God had ſhined in their hearts, (not in the hearts of all the men in the world, nor in the hearts of all the *Corinthians*) and had given them a ſight *of the glory of God in the Face,* or from the *Reflexion* or means of the face of the *Mediator,* the man Chriſt Jeſus.

As the firſt Chriſtians were called.

Hence all thoſe *Heavenly Appellations* or *phrazes,* or *Names,* Children of the Day : *Illuminated,* or *Inlightned Ones, You were Darkneſs, but now you are* (not only *Inlightened,* but) *Light in the Lord,* that is, become, (not as *Fox* pretends Chriſts and Gods and no diſtinction) but of a *bright Spiritual Nature,* longing *humbly* and *mournfully* in the uſe of the holy

holy Scripture, and all other means) more to come out of Darkneſs into the Light of holineſs and likeneſs unto God.

Object. G *Fox* alleadgeth *John* 3. They which hated the Light were inlightned :

I *Anſwer*, No queſtion, but with the *general Offer* of mercy, [106] as of the *Candle* or *Sun* to the Eyes of a blind man, which is yet their Condemnation, becauſe if they had power, yet their *wills* and *Luſts*, and *Reſolutions* refuſe and abhor it, and abhor their eyes ſhould be opened to ſee it. The two-
fold ſuc-
ceſs of the
Goſpel.

Whereas the *Goſpel* or *glad News* is publiſhed or preached, there is a twofold Effect of it: as *Acts* 13. and *Acts* 17. and *Acts* 28. and through all Experience in all Ages and in all parts of the world ſome *mock*, ſome *demur*, ſome *perſecute* others, the Spirit or Power of God opens their hearts to fear, to believe, to ſubmit, and in Gods time to rejoyce for ever in a Saviour.

The 54*th Inſtance* is in *Pag.* 330. where G. *Fox* brings in *James Dorram*, ſaying | *The Believer is not in ſin as the Unbeliever is, he ſins not as the Unbeliever doth: and in another place he ſaith, the Law is the ſame to the Believer that it is to the Unbeliever.* 330. James
Dorram.

G. *Fox* Anſwers, Here any may read thy Confuſion, but I ſay unto thee He that believeth doth not commit Sin, but the unbelief is Sin, *Rom.* 11. 20. *And Chriſt is the End of the Law to every one that believes for Righteonſneſs ſake,* Roms 10. 4. and yet thou puts both Believers and unbelievers under the power of the Law.

I Reply,

The light of sin as Sin.

I *Reply*, The Devils (no queſtion) know Sin, they ſee Sin, but not in the true glaſs of the holy Scripture : They ſee ſin as *Saul* and *Judas*, &c. in the fire of the Coal, as dreadful in the puniſhment, but not in the blackneſs of the Coale, as againſt their new Life and Nature, and the purity of the *Eternal*, who hath begotten them unto holineſs. The *Robber* and *Murtherer* bewails his offence at the *Gallows*, though yet his heart is not changed, but, (could he) he would murther the Judge, and all that had a hand in his Condemnation and Execution. The Drunkard hates his Sin as a Tyrant over him, only as it brings Diſcredit to him, ſo is it with the unclean perſon, and every other ſinner.

The Sins of the Regenerate.

But it is not ſo with the *Regenerate* or *new Born*, who can no more (unleſs deceived and Circumvented) touch Sin, then the Devil the Father of it, nor then Fire can delight in Water, nor Light in Darkneſs.

3. It is true, that 7 of the *Romans* is contended for by the *Papiſts* and *Arminians*, and in a great meaſure by the *Quakers*, [107] to Contain not the Combate of the Saints, but of the unregenerate within themſelves : But the true Proteſtants have proved from the Scripture, and the Experience of all true Saints that ſin and grace, Fleſh and Spirit,

Whit the Combate between the Fleſh and Spirit in Rom. 7.

the Law of the Spirit, and the Law of ſin may, and do continue Combating in the Regenerate, or New born, Contrary to that *proud perfection* of *Papiſts* and *Foxians* in this Life, is more clear then *Pauls Argumentation*, and upon that his Concluſion, *viz.* That with his mind, that is, his Spirit, will,

Affections,

Affections, (renewed by Gods Spirit) *he ferved the Law of God*: *But with his Flefh*, which muft be his *finful Defires* and *Difpofitions* yet remaining in him, *he ferved the Law of Sin?* This was the Reafon of his Cry, *O wretched man*, &c. and G. *Fox* his filly fhifts faying, that in the End of the Chapter, *Paul* was perfect, and gave thanks for victory, it is like that *Fantaftical faying*, of the *Generalifts*, being forced to Confefs Repentance neceffary to Salvation, *viz.* [*In a moment in the Twinkling of an Eye*] wofully abufing that holy Scripture about the *Refurrection*.

4. The fame 7 of the *Romans*, and other holy Scriptures, and Experience prove that the Sin of the Regenerate, whether of Ignorance, as the *Fathers*, many wives, &c. or of *unwatchfulnefs* as *David* and *Peter's* &c. It is as an honeft man taken prifoner, or as *Souldiers* and Seamen wounded and carried Captive, or as a *Virgin* by force *deflowred*, and crying out, whom therefore both Law and Reafon, and the holy Scripture in a holy Figure declare to be clear and Innocent. *The Sin of the Regenerate as a wound and Captivity.*

5. Hence *Paul* fhews the Sincerity of the *Chaft Will* and *Affections* unto the *Heavenly Bridegroom*, faying, *I delight in the Law of God, in the inner man*: Delight we know is the *Top* and *Flowre*, and *Cream* of all the *Affections*, and the *fierceft hatred* flies in the Face of that which takes away our delight from us. The wicked may defire, and may act heavenly things for his own felf Ends, for his Credit, his profit, his Salvation, but he can not make God to be himfelf, and delight in God. *The Souls delight in God, and Hatred to Sin*

What

6. What Confusion is it to affirm that the Saints
of God though they see Christ fulfilling the Law
of works for them, which none in the world could
ever do but He, yet they ought to strive after perfect holiness and Righteousness, *to love the Lord
with all their Heart, soul, might, strength,* &c. as a
Child going after his Father, the Scholar or maiden following their Copies and Samplers, [108
though they never come near the full Exactness
and perfection of them.

The 55*th Instance* of G. *Fox* his simple and soul
Answer is in *Pag.* 338. where he brings in *Iohn
Nasmith* from *Scotland,* saying, [*Tha the Evil Spir-
its are both sinful and Reasonable.*]

He *Answers,* This is a lye, for Reasonable is not
sinful, and unreasonable is sinful? 1 *Thes.* 3. *they
have not the Faith.* And if the Evil Spirit be Reasonable and the Good Reasonable, they are both
one: who is then unreasonable, thou puts no difference between the precious and the vile? Thou
hast the mark of a *blinde guide* and of a *false Prophet* in thy *Forehead.*

1. I *Reply* and observe *First,* the *filthy rash Fury*
of his mind and Pen: Beginning with that's a lye,
and after a silly Line and Answer: Thou hast the
Marck of a *Blind guide* and of a *false Prophet* in thy
Forehead.

2. This *proud Pharisee* will appear to be a *Sad-
ducee* also, and to hold no *Angels* nor *Spirits:* It is
true, as they pretend to owne Scripture and a Christ,
and *Resurrection,* They with *Jesuitical Equivocations*
name *Angels* and *Spirits,* but the bottom as some
of

of them, and that in print difcover is, they hold The Fox-ians are both Pharifees and Sadduces. there is but one Spirit, which is in *All*, and into which *All Return*, and the Soul of *Iudas* is as happy as the Soul of *Peter*.

3. G. *Fox* runs into his *Burrough* of the *various fignifications* of the word *Reafonable*. A man is a *Reafonable Creature* as Oppofite to *Wolves* and *Foxes*, &c. and yet he may be unreafonable in in his Actings, as Wolves and Foxes, who though unreafona- An Item to G. Fox. ble in their Natures, yet are not finful, though a plague to man fince his Fall. Oh happy were it for G. *Fox* that he had been of the wild *Foxes* in the Woods, and had not been fo finful, by fo *horribly abufing* fo great a *Talent* of *Wit* and Reafon which *the Father of Lights* hath given him.

4. We know the Admirable Wit and Reafon as well as the Power of thofe unclean Spirits, the Lord Jefus caft out, they did believe and Confefs The Nature of the Devils the Lord Jefus, and made their Requeft unto him : This their knowledge and Ability is from God, though their *finful hardnefs* by Gods juft Sentence, runs them upon fuch mad and defperate Courfes, as it is with the Sons of men, when the moft holy and Righteous Judge delivers them up to the *Councels* 109| and *Projects* of their *proud and deceitful Hearts and Spirits* :

The *56th. Inftance* is in *Pag.* 345. where he 345 Hen-Forefide. brings in *Henry Forefide* (from Scotland,) faying, [*Concerning thofe words of* Ezekiel 18. 28. *If the Righteous turn away from his Righteoufnefs, his former Righteoufnefs fhall be no more remembred,* and he
said

ſaid *the meaning of that Scripture was* : *They thought they had been Righteous, but were not, but ſuppoſed it had been ſo.*]

Ezek. 18
Conſider-
ed

He Anſwers, [*Herein thou art a Miniſter of un-righteouſneſs thou goeſt about to make God a Lyar, and the Prophets, and perverts the Scripture* : *For if he forſakes his Righteouſneſs and commits Sin and Iniquity, and Treſpaſſes he ſhall dye and not live in the Right-eouſneſs* : *But if he ſo ſakes his Sins, Treſpaſſes and Tranſgreſſions, in the Righteouſneſs that he hath done and doth, he ſhall live* : *So Gods wayes are equal,* Ezek. 18.] And thou ſayes, they thought they had been Righteous, but it was not ſo: And the Lord by the Prophet ſaith it was ſo, *that they ſhould live in their Righteouſneſs* and die if they did depart from it and Tranſgreſſed: Here thou art a diminiſher from the *Prophets* and *Apoſtles* words, whoſe Name is *di-miniſhed out of the Book of Life,* read *Rev.* 22. 19

The
Spirit of
Falling
from
Grace.

I Reply, The Queſtion is about *Falling away* from *ſaving grace* and Righteouſneſs, wherein it is no-torious, (as I have formerly proved) that the *Qua-kers* joyn their Forces to the *Standards* of the *Papiſts* and *Arminians,* though herein the *Armini-ans* (though highly abuſing an high wit as the *Papiſts* and *Quakers* do) yet are they not ſo guilty and Inſufferable as the *Papiſts* and *Foxians* are, be-cauſe they pretend not to ſuch an *Infallible Chair*

The Pa-
piſts, Ar-
minians
and Fox
ians one
in this
point.

as the *Papiſts* and *Quakers* do, which is the more *wonderful* and *monſtrous,* becauſe the *Papiſts* are forced to grant that the Head of their Church the *Pope* may Himſelf fall away and be a Reprobate, and the *Foxians* are forced to Confeſs as much, even

of

of divers of their Heads and Teachers, fome getting *Saving Grace* again, as they fay, and fome
never. The *Quakers* yet are more grofs in this
point, becaufe they maintain that the leaft that
hearken to the Light are born again. That they
which are born again cannot Sin, that they which
can not Sin are pure as God is pure, and therefore
they Falling away from them, they muft neceffarily
hold that which is blafphemous of all to be abhorred, that God himfelf may fall from Grace alfo,
and is kept down as the ⌊110⌋ as this barking *Fox*
fpeaks, as a *Cart laden with fheaves* (perverting the
Scripture) by wickednefs & wicked fpirits which
are too hard for God and Chrift, and Spirit in all
the Men and Women in the world, that do not
hearken to their *feigned Light,* and let loofe the
Imprifoned Cart and *Seed,* &c.

Wee may make a ftand here and obferve three
things.

1. The *horrible abufe of Gods Excellent Gifts* of
Reafon and Acutenefs, which thefe men fo grofsly
defile in handling the Mifteries and Parables of
the holy Scripture.

2. *Gods Infinite Patience* in bearing with fuch a
rotten ftinking thing as man is.

3. What kind of Grace it is that fo eafily perfons Fall away away from, and part withal.

2. As to *Ezek.* 18. How doth it follow, that becaufe the word Righteoufnefs in which *Fox* in his
wonted Burrough, fignifies divers things, that therefore in this firft place it muft fignify the Imputed
Righteoufnefs of God in Chrift, from which a

man

[marginal notes]
Whab Grace it is that Pa-pifts Ar-minians and Fox-ians Fall from.

Neceffary Obferva-tions.

The Word Righteouf-nefs of many fig-nifications

man really Invested with it may really, Totally and Finally depart. And Secondly the *Sanctifying Righteousness* of Christ Jesus adorning a poor sinner Justified and pardoned, and of that true Righteousness, a truly sanctified Soul and member of Christ Jesus may make shipwrack. But is there not beside these a very thirdly, I*ndian Righteousness*, when a *Barbarian* is Innocent and free from Crimes falsly charged on him ?

4. Is there not a *C*ivil Righteousness when men are free from *Gross* and *Barbarous Courses*, and live Civilly, soberly and justly among their Neighbors ?

5 Yea, is there not a Pharisaical Righteousness which *Paul* prided himself in, *viz* that *concerning the Law he was blameless*, and yet saith the Lord Jesus, *Except your Righteousness go beyond this Righteousness, you shall not enter into the Kingdome of Heaven*

6. Again, Is there not a Righteousness of the *foolish Virgins*, who hath a *shew* and *Lamp* of *Profession*, and make as brave a shew in building as the house upon the Rock, it may be fairer) and yet no true work of Conversion of the Soul to God, nor the Oyle of Gods Spirit in the heart for all their boasting of it. The most High and holy will be clear when he is Judged. *Adam* shall live if he keep his *Bargain* : and so shall all his Posterity if they keep the *first Covenant*.

111| If any shall say God knows the *Bargain* is too hard for us : Our *first Father* did not, how shall we ? *&c.*

I *Answer*, what will become then of the *Papists* and

God's Covenant with the first man.

and *Quakers,* who fay, they can, and the *Papifts* more alfo then God commandeth?

2. Chrift did not mock, but meekly and favingly teach the young man, when he Anfwered, *If thou wilt enter into Life keep the Commandments* : nor doth he mock the *Jews,* dealing with them upon the Terms of *Juftice* : *Obey and live, Tranfgrefs and die.*

It is a pertinent queftion, why was the holy Law of God written and given fo many hundreds of years after man was Fallen and not able to keep his *Bargain* : The Spirit of God *Gal.* 3, tels us that *four hundred* and *Thirty Years* after the Promife to *Abraham,* the Law was written by Gods own *Immediate Finger* to fhew unto man his Sin, and Judgements, and need of a *Mediator promifed.* The Law given fo many hundreth of years after mans Fall.

3. As to G. *Fox* Curfing his Adverfary as a Diminifher from the holy Scripture.

I *Anfwer,* Doth this Face of Brafs, who hath fo horribly flighted the holy Scripture : now adore them? Is he now zealous for them, and againft the violation of them? Doth he regard the adding to, or Detracting from them, or the Plagues and Curfes therein denounced againft the Adders to, or Detracters from them? Doth he not throughout all his Book, and all of them in word and writing deny the holy Scripture to be the word of God, and only that *Frantick Light* or *Chrift,* (imagined by them to be in all mankinde) to be the only Word of God? yea, is it of any ufe or more availe to them that have the Scripture in their heart, as they faythen a *dead Letter,* and an *Old Almanack,* &c. *O hear O Heavens and give Ear O Earth,* did

G. Fox making ufe of the Scripture to Curfe his Oppofites.

Their horrible Contempt of Scripture.

ever

all that *Heavenly Artillery*, Ephef. 6. 1. And Commands his Servants (even *Timothy*) *to flie youthful Lufts*, if he were paft wounding by them?

4. And to ftand upon the Guard and watch againft *Gluttonly* and *Drunkennefs*, and *worldly Cares*, which would lull the Souls of the *Difciples* afleep, except they kept the better watch &c. Luke 21.

Scriptural dangers and fpiritual Watch.

5. And why then doth the Lord Jefus Command us to pray daily againft Temptations, yea, and to pray daily for the pardon of fin, if his *Followers* be for ever efcaped out of the reach of Sinful thoughts, words and actions, and many *thoufand finful Omiffions?*

Chrifts Difcipline with his Saints and Churches.

6. What was the Reafon of the Cemmand of Chrift Jefus to the *Churches* to *watch*, to *Overcome*, to *repent*, threatning them with *difcharging*, and *Excommunication* which we fee dolefully Effected upon the *Afian Profeffors*, and which was followed with a rich blefling upon that Ordinance, Executed upon the *Inceftuous Corinthian*, which brought forth thofe *feven Heavenly Fruits*, both in him and that Church alfo, 2 *Cor.* 7.

G. *Fox* his *third Anfwer* is, [*The Saints are come to the Kingdome of God witneffing Sin and Iniquity blotted out, and the Everlafting Covenant of Peace and Life with God.*]

But 1. Take thefe words in his Senfe, *viz.* that all that are in their *Fancied Kingdome* are thus free from Sin, and come to this Peace and Joy: why then do themfelves ftill Confefs themfelves to be fubject to *quaking* and *trembling*, as if they were at the *black* and *burning Foot* of *Mount Sinai*, where indeed they are, and not upon the *bright* and *fhining Hill* of *Zion*. 2. Is

2. Is not this Contrary to the Covenant of God The Qua-
kers dole-
ful miſtake with *David*, concerning *Solomon*, and (in the *Anti Type*) with all Chriſtians, *viz.* that if they Sin he will Chaſtiſe them with *the Rods of men, but not take away his mercy,* as he took it from *Saul*, &c.

3. Is there not a *falſe Peace,* a *falſe Joy* as well as a *falſe quaking, a falſe Repentance, a falſe morti-fication,* and *Sanctificatio* , and in Concluſion, a *falſe Salvation* : and therefore the Lord Jeſus tels us of the *high pretenders,* Math. 7. yet by him *Ever-laſtingly rejected.*

114] The 59*th Inſtance* is in *Pag.* 365. where G. 365. Rob-ert Tu-chin, &c. Fox brings in *Robert Tuchin,* &c. ſaying, [*The moſt Faithful Meſſengers of Chriſt have acknowledged that they have come ſhort of their duty.*]

G. *Fox* Anſwers, [*They that are Faithful Meſſen-gers of Chriſt have the Anſwer well done thou good and Faithful Servant : where did* John, *or* Paul, *or* Peter *acknowledge that they came ſhort of their duty : Hath not thou ſlandred the Servants of the Lord, thinking them to be like yourſelves, and falſly accuſing them that you may ſeem Juſtified, who are falſe Meſſengers and come in his Name, when you have no Commiſſion from him : and you come ſhort of every good work : But thus it is not with Chriſts true Meſſengers, for they fulfil his Will that ſent them. It is the Lord that worketh in them, whoſe th y are, and whoſe duty they perform by his Spirit*]

I *Reply,* this *deluded Soul* (as it is written) muſt G Fox prouder and prouder, wo ſe and grow worſe and worſe (except the Lord *wonderfully awaken* him) to all Eternity : Inſtead of ſeeing any failing againſt God and Chriſt, the Spirit and Ser-

vants

worſe to
the End of
his Book. vants of God, &c. he claps his wings upon his Dunghil, and vapours, that in all theſe Tranſactions he hath not faild, no not in a *ſinful word or Thought*.

1. But he muſt remember that ſuch was the *Infinite, Incomprehenſible Purity* and *Juſtice*, and *wiſdome* of God, *that the Heavens were not pure in his ſight, and he laid Folly to the Charge of his Angels*, and I am ſure, their *Natures*, their *Endowments*, their *Employments*, G. *Fox* comes ſhort of, and yet they came ſhort of their duty, and are now faſt in *Chains of Darkneſs*, expecting *Judgement* and *Torment* to come,

The Fall
of Angels.

2. I preſume G. *Fox* will grant that our *firſt Parent*s were *Innocent* and *perfect*, as *highly Gifted* and as *highly Employed* as ever G. *Fox* is like to be, and yet they came ſhort, and We all by them fallen ſhort of the Glory and love of God into the *Dunghill* of *Helliſh Darkneſs*.

Fall of
Man.

3. After the *Promiſed Reſtoration* by the Son of God what *Excellent Gifts* had *Noah, Abraham, Lot, Iſaac, Jacob, Joſeph, Moſes, Aaron, Sampſon, Iepthe, Gideon, Eli, Samuel, Nathan, Solomon, Aſa, Iehoſhaphat, Hezekiah, Ioſiah*, and many other glorious Saints, what *wonderful Aſſiſtance* and *Extraordinary Appearances of* God had they in their high Services for God, and yet how grea ly: (ſome of them wonderfully fouly) did they come ſhort of their 115] duty? I remember I was once asked by one of theſe high Boaſters whether I would deny the Scripture: *viz* that ſaid, *David* did not ſin but in the Caſe of *Uriah*: unto which I know many full Anſwers may be given. Here only I obſerve how

Davids
ſin.

ready

ready thefe (willingly Ignorant) Souls are to Catch Sacrifice for Sins of Ignorance
at any Word that may Fortifie their *proud Fancy*,
though againft many other Scriptures and unqueftionable Examples, &c.

4. Until the coming of Chrift Jefus we know
the Command of the moft holy God to private
perfons, to the Princes, to the Priefts, to the whole
Affembly to offer up Sacrifice and Expiation for all
forts of failings, yea, for Sins of Ignorance, yea, and
for their coming fhort in their holy offerings:
Hence *David* cries out, *Pfal.* 143. *Enter not into
Iudgement or Reckoning with thy Servant,* &c. and
Pfal. 19. *Cleanfe thou me from fecret fins, for who
knows how oft he offendeth?*

5. I know G. *Fox* ufeth to fay all thefe were
Types and Chrift is the body, &c.

I *Anfwer*, There are more *Anti-Types* then the
perfon of Chrift, for the *Quakers* themfelves, they
make themfelves Kings and Priefts, and the Temple as well as Chrift, &c.

But come to the time of the Lord Jefus, and Great failing of Chrifts Difciples
look upon the *Famous firft Apoftles*, who had freely
left all to follow him, who enjoyed his *perfonal*
preaching and *praying*, his *wonderful Miracles*, his
Heavenly Converfe, his *holy* and *Powerful Spirit* in
their own preaching, healing all Difeafes, raifing
the dead, cafting out Devils, &c. and yet how doth
the Lord Jefus frequently and fharply chide them
for their coming fhort of their duty, for their Ignorance, negligence, unbelief, forgetfulnefs, Inhumanity, Ambition, &c.

6. Yea, as to thofe three whom G. *Fox* boafts of,
Iohn,

Iohn, Paul and *Peter* : Doth not *Iohn* cry out, 1
Iohn 2. *If we Confefs our fins, he is Faithful and juft
to forgive us, and to cleanfe us from all unrighteoufnefs?*
Doth not *Paul* Confefs and bewail his coming fhort,
when he cries out, *that the good he would do he did
not, but did the Evil he would not, and with his flefh
did ferve the Law of fin,* though it was not *Paul*
that finned, *but fin that dwelled in him?* A Miftery
which I more then fear the moft High hath hidden from this *poor Foxes Eye.*

And as to *Peter,* to fay nothing of his ftupendi-
ous failing of his [116] Mafter, *&c.* even after his
awakening, after the *Lords rifing,* and *Peters feeing*
and *talking* with him, his bold profeffion and preaching of him to the Converfion of *hundreds* and
thoufands : yet how is he charged by *Paul* for coming fhort of his Duty, for Grofs Weaknefs and (in
a kind) *Hipocrify* and *Diffimulation?* So that fuch a
cloud of witneffes o'rewhelming thefe new Gods,
(*Papifts* and *Quakers*) how Righteous is it with God
to make their Faces afhamed with the filth of their
own nakednefs, in the highth of the *pride of their
conceited Deities.*

The 60 *Inftance* of G. *Fox* his lame Anfwer is
in *pag.* 372. where he brings in *Thomas Hodges,*
faying, [*The Scripture fpeaks of God after the manner of men.*]

He Anfwers, The Scripture fpeaks of God after
the manner of the Spirit and to the Spirit, whereby men may receive him, and know him by the
Spirit which natural men can not.

1. I

1. I *Reply,* This bewitched and bewitching Soul hath all along his Book been picking out fweet Flowers out of his Oppofites Gardens, from whence he hath fuckt, turned the fweet juice of Heavenly Truths into the poyfon and Venome of his proud Conceits. So here he denies this *Heavenly Myftery* of Gods revealing himfelf to us after the way and manner of men, having Head, and Hair, and Eyes, and mouth, *&c.* wherein his Incomprehenfible Goodnefs is pleafed to ftoop to us (even the higheft and proudeft Souls) as Nurfes do to Children, or as Phyfitians to weak and Crazy and diftempered perfons. *G Fox hath affirmed the Contrary to all the Heavenly Affertions of his Oppofites which I have produced.*

2. But what fhall we fay to all thofe holy Scriptures, which not only liken God to a man, a man of war, a Sheepherd, a *Warfaring man,* an *Hufband man,* &c. but alfo to a Shield, and other Infenfibles, Natural or Artificial, as a Sun, a Tree, a Rock, an Houfe, a Fort, a High Tower, *&c.* When God revealed himfelf to *Abraham,* Gen. 15. *I am thy Shield,* &c. will this foul mouth fay that this fimilitude of a Shield was not a *Familiar Metaphor,* or *Figure,* wherein God fpeaks to *Abrahams weak Capacity?* Or will he fay, that God fpeaking fo to *Abraham,* fpake not alfo in the way the Spirit, Or that God is Litcrally a Shield? *God fets forth to us in Scripture by Natural and Artificial things.*

3. It was a late Speech of one of the beft Philofophers, and of the beft Chriftians that *Old England* or *New* ever had: Then fhall we know (to wit in the next life, in the *Heavenly State* to Come) how to anfwer that great Queftion, *What is God?* But this *poor wild Affes Colt,* G. *Fox* he can [117 *The great Queftion what God is.*

refolve

refolve the Queftion : He can gather up the *Ocean* in the *hollow* of his *hand*, he can weigh the *Everlafting Mountains* and *Winds* in *Scales*, and Inclofe not only the *Sun*, &c. but alfo the *Incomprehenfible Sun of Glory and Purity within his Juglers Box*, &c.

The Devil Gods Ape in Infpirations.

4. For, what would this *little Thief* and *Fox*, or the *great Thief* and *Fox* the *Devil* have, but blow out the *Candle* and *Torch*, and *Sun* of the *holy Books* and *Records*, that fo *the Father of Lies* and *Murthers* may be heard, (as he hath been heard in the *Grecian Oracles* in *Mahomet*, and the *Mahumetans*, in the *Pope* and the *Papifts*) fo by his whifperings in the *Foxians*, as if he were the moft holy Spirit of the *Eternal God himfelf, Immortal, Invifible, and only Wife*.

The Subtlety of the Devil and his Agents in Catching of men.

5. For, is it not the *Devils Trade* to play the *fubtle Hunter*, (as do alfo his *Journey-men* who ly in wait to catch men) and to trim his *Pits* and *Gins*, and *Snares*, with *green leaves* and *Boughs*, and *Twigs*, viz : *fair pretences* of the Spirit, the Spirit, the *Immediate Spirit*, the *Infallible Spirit*, the Teachings of the Spirit, the manner of the Spirit, fpeaking to the Spirit, and Chrift within you, *Chrift within you except you be Reprobates, Chrift within you the hope of Glory*, &c. Thefe are *fair Leaves*, and *fweet, heavenly green Boughs*, on which the *Old Serpent* twineth, and from whence he uttereth even Scripture it felf, and the *fweet Names* God and Chrift, and Spirit, in a *frantick purpofe* to ftab (for he knows he can not) the holy Scriptures, and *God*, and *Chrift*, and *Spirit* alfo :

6. More particularly, what doth he mean, that
God

God fpeaks not to us after the manner of men, but by the way of the Spirit, after the manner of the Spirit? He grants that the holy Scriptures were given forth from the *Immediate Infpration* of the Spirit: He knows that we maintain from *Ifai.* 59. the great Promife of the Word and Spirit together, to the mouth of Chrift Jefus and his Seed, and his *Seeds Seed.* And alfo that we affirme that no Reading, no Hearing, no Meditation, no Afflictions, *&c.* can do a Soul any good, until God by the Power or Finger of his own felf, or Spirit, makes the means *Powerful* and *Effectual.* What G. Fox means by the manner of the Spirit.

All this ferves not, but that which Sathan drives at, and which alone muft ferve his Ends is, *Immediate, Immediate Infpiration* with a *damning,* or changing the means by the *moft Holy, and only Wife God Appointed.*

118] 7. It is one of the *Proverbs* of the *Ancients Sus Minervam docet.* The Sow teacheth the Goddefs of *Wifdome.* It is moft *Infallibly true* here, this *filthy Sow* (that feems to be wafht from Common vices and yet wallows in the *mud & Dunghils* of *Myftical Filthinefs*) He muft teach wifdome it felf how to fpeak, and appoint him his way, and (by wrefting and racing out what he can the *Holy Records*) how to reveal himfelf unto the Sons of men. G. Fox his proud Simplicity

8. It is pertinent to Confider the ground of this his only owning the manner of the Spirit, *viz.* [*This Immediate Spirit fpeaks to the Spirit within.*] What is the Englifh of this *Ridle* [*The Immediate Spirit within fpeaks to the Spirit within,*] But their Spirit will tell us that God and Chrift, and Spirit, The Monftrous Ridle of the Foxians Spirit.

and

and Light, and New Covenant, and Faith, and Holinefs, &c. are all in prifon within, in every man,
until the *Immediate Spirit* without means perfwade
a perfon to hearken within to him as to *Chrift*,
Light and *Spirit*, which will bring him to God and
Chrift, (round in a *Conjuriug Circle Chrift* brings to
Chrift, the *Spirit* brings to the *Spirit*,) which though
it be true, after Converfion and *in growth* and *Increafe* of the Grace and Knowledge of Chrift by
the ufe of means appointed by Chrift Jefus, yet I
deny it ever to be done in the *firft turning* of the
Heart and *working* of *Faith*, that is by any fuch
Immediate Spirit, and *Chrift* and *God* in every of
mankind before, or fince the coming of Chrift
Jefus, efpecially, for they fay, that he is the *true
Light* (of which *John* fpake, then Come, to *Inlighten the World, &c.*

9. I Conclude this *Inftance* and the whole with
a *Reflection* upon Gods wonderful dealing with *Job*:
In the 1. *Chap.* the Lord boafts of his fervant *Iob*
to the *Devil* to be a *perfect man*, (as the *Foxians*
often urge this place) But God Schoold him for
his *pride* and *Impatience*, &c. by *Elihu*, and by his
own *Voice* out of a *Whirlwind*: and now *Iob* Confeffeth his *Pride* and *Ignorance*, and profeffeth his
Rifolution to prate no more, &c. but to *abhor himfelf* (that is, as fome *loathfome Thing*) *in Duft and
Afhes*, G. *Fox* in this his Book abhors the Term of
Duft and Afhes, as being Elevatedabove *Abraham
& Iob* (*punies* to him) with high Fancies of his
Immortality, though we fee they dy, & ftink & Rot
as well as others.

Job a per-
fect man
yet abhors
himfelf
for his
filthinefs.

But

But if God pleafe to fhew him, and me, truly what Sin is, What Gods Juftice is, what an *Infinite price* muft pay for the leaft *Evil Thought* and *Natu-**ral Difpofition*, on the Old Score: [119] If God pleafe by any of thofe many gracious means he ufeth to Imprint thefe & other fuch *Heavenly Confidertions* upon our Souls! We fhall then for all our pretences cry out with *Peter, depart from me for I am a finful man O Lord:* and with *Iob, Once have I fpoken, yea, twice,* &c. but no more, &c. I *abhor myfelf* as a *loathfome, Rotten, ftinking Carrion in Duft and Afhes.* But alas I fear G. *Fox* is fo taken up with his *fitting with Chrift in Heavenly Places*, with *Immediate Dictates* of his fuppofed holy Spirit: That Gods fpeaking thus to his *poor Worms* after the way of Men, and by thefe outward means ftinks in his *Noftrils*; which if fo, and fo Irrecoverably, I defire, and defire all that love God and their own Salvations, to flee from him as from *Korahs Pride* and *Korahs Plagues*, for his *Viol* is pouring on him in *fpiritual Indgements*, and fhall be pouring on him in *fpiritual* and *Corporal Tor-**ments to all Eternity.*

The Authors humble defire for himfelf and G. Fox

The Authors fear as to G. Fox his cafe

F I N I S